STUDENT ATLAS

WORLD

LONDON, NEW YORK, MELBOURNE, MUNICH AND DELHI
www.dk.com

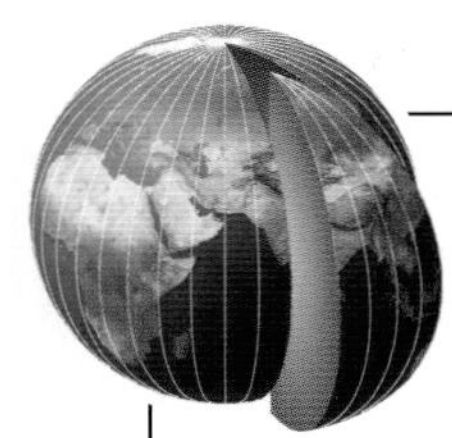

LONDON, NEW YORK, MELBOURNE, MUNICH AND DELHI

FOR THE SEVENTH EDITION

Senior Cartographic Editor Simon Mumford
Jacket Designer Mark Cavanagh **Production Controller** Charlotte Cade **Producer** Rebekah Parsons-King
Publisher Jonathan Metcalf **Art Director** Philip Ormerod **Associate Publisher** Liz Wheeler

DORLING KINDERSLEY CARTOGRAPHY

MANAGING EDITOR
Lisa Thomas

MANAGING ART EDITOR
Philip Lord

PROJECT EDITORS
Debra Clapson, Wim Jenkins, Jill Hamilton (US)

PROJECT DESIGNERS
Rhonda Fisher, Karen Gregory

EDITORIAL CONTRIBUTORS
Thomas Heath, Kevin McRae, Constance Novis, Iris Rossoff (US), Siobhan Ryan

DESIGNERS
Carol Ann Davis, David Douglas, Nicola Liddiard

MANAGING CARTOGRAPHER
David Roberts

SENIOR CARTOGRAPHIC EDITOR
Roger Bullen

CARTOGRAPHERS
Pamela Alford, James Anderson, Chris Atkinson, Dale Buckton, Tony Chambers, Jan Clark, Martin Darlison, Damien Demaj, Paul Eames, Sally Gable, Jeremy Hepworth, Michael Martin, Ed Merritt, Simon Mumford, John Plumer, Gail Townsley, Julie Turner, Sarah Vaughan, Jane Voss, Peter Winfield

DATABASE MANAGER
Simon Lewis

DIGITAL MAPS CREATED IN DK CARTOPIA BY
Phil Rowles, Rob Stokes

PLACENAMES DATABASE TEAM
Natalie Clarkson, Julia Lynch,

EDITORIAL DIRECTION
Andrew Heritage

PICTURE RESEARCH
Louise Thomas

EDUCATIONAL CONSULTANTS
Dr. David Lambert, Institute of Education, University of London, David R Wright, BA MA

TEACHER REVIEWERS
US: Ramani DeAlwis; UK: Kevin Ball, Pat Barber, Stewart Marson

First published in Great Britain in 1998 by
Dorling Kindersley Limited,
80 Strand, London WC2R ORL
Penguin Group (UK)

2 4 6 8 10 9 7 5 3 1
001 – 188127 – November 2013

Second Edition 2002, Reprinted 2003, Third Edition 2004, Fourth Edition 2006, Fifth Edition 2008, Sixth Edition 2011, Reprinted with revisions 2012, Seventh Edition 2013

A CIP catalogue record for this book is available from the British Library.

ISBN: 978-1-4093-3450-7

Printed and bound by Hung Hing, Hong Kong.

Discover more at **www.dk.com**

ACKNOWLEDGMENTS

The publishers are grateful for permission to reproduce the following photographs:

t=top, b=bottom, a=above, l=left, r=right, c=centre

Axiom: Jiri Rezac 64br; J Spaull 92br. **Bridgeman Art Library**: Hereford Cathedral, Trustees of the Hereford Mappa Mundi 8tr. **J Allan Cash**: 120cr. **Bruce Coleman Ltd:** C Ott 28cr (below); Dr E Pott 4bc; H Reinhard 19cr; J Murray 130bl; Peter Terry 19crr. **Colourific**: Black Star/R Rogers 113br; Frank Herrmann 119bc. **Comstock**: 17tc. **Corbis**: Bob Daemmrich 30bl. **James Davis Travel Photography**: 44tr, 119tr. **Robert Harding Picture Library**: 6tr (below), 21c, 21cr, 22br, 92cr (above), 28bl, 30cr, 30br, 31bl, 38tr, 118bl; A Tovy 120br; Adam Woolfitt 62br; C Bowman 112tr; Charcrit Boonson 90cr (below); David Lomax 20tr; Franz Joseph Land 19tr; G Boutin 120cl (below); G Renner 17c, 118cr(above); Gavin Hellier 31tr; Geoff Renner 39cr (above); H P Merten 23tl; Jane Sweeney 23bl; Louise Murray 93tr; Peter Scholey 91tr; Robert Francis 23cr; Schuster/Keine 62cr (above); Simon Westcott 90br. **Hutchison Library:** A Zvoznikov 19cl; J Nowell 93bl; R Ian Lloyd 10cl. **Image Bank:** Carlos Navajas 17bl; M Isy-Schwart 17bc; P Grumann 64cr (below); Steve Proehl 30cr (below); Terje Rakke 17br. **Images Colour Library**: 19c, 62cr (below), 118br. **Impact:** Jeremy Nicholl 121cl (below); Mark Henley 20bl; Paul O'Driscoll 63cr; Robin Lubbock 118br. **Frank Lane Picture Agency:** D Smith 19bc; W Wisniewsli 17cr. **Magnum:** Chris Steele Perking 120tr (below); Jean Gaumy 65cl. **N.A.S.A**: 9tc. **N.H.P.A**: M Wendler 4cl, 110bl. **Oxford Scientific Films:** Konrad Wothe 19tc; L Gould 4tr; Nobert Rosing 28cl. **Panos Pictures**: Alain le Garsheur 92cr; Alain le Garsmeur 31cl (below); Alberto Arzoz 63tr; Bruce Paton 121bl; Jeremy Hartley 120bl; Maria Luiza M Cavalho 112cl (below); Paul Smith 111cr; Rhodri Jones 113bl; Ron Gilling 119cr; Trygve Bolstad 22bl. **Edward Parker:** 17cr (above). **Pictor International**: 4tc, 10bc, 18tr, 20br, 36bc, 38br. **Planet Earth Pictures**: J Waters 113bc. **South American Pictures**: Robert Francis 29br; Tony Morrison 110cr, 111cl. **Spectrum Colour Library:** 29br. **Frank Spooner Pictures**: Gamma/E Baitel 91cl. **Still Pictures**: J Frebet 113cr; R Seitre 90cr (above). **Tony Stone Images:** 17tr, 112cl; A Sacks 28cr; Alan Levenson 92cr; Charles Thatcher 39tr; D Austen 131cr; D Hanson 17cl; Donald Johnson 62bc; Earth Imaging 6tr (above); G Johnson 90bl; H Strand 113tr; Hans Schlapfer 38bc; J Jangoux 19bcr; J Warden 110bc; John Garrett 121br; L Resnick 121tr; Larry Ulrich 37br; P Chesley 130tr; Paul Chesley 36br; Randy Wells 19br; Robert Frerck 65tr; Tom Walker 36bl; Tony Craddock 65cr. **Telegraph Colour Library**: 29tr. **Travel Ink**: Colin Marshall 22bc. **Trip**: A Kuznetsov 92bc; H Rogers 90cr; M Barlow 112bl; N Ray 10tr; Robert Belbin 92bl; V Kolpakov 93cr (below); V Sidoropolev 64cr; W Jacobs 130c. **World Pictures:** 131tr. **ZEFA Picture Library**: 19bcl, 19cll, 63bc; Damm 119cl; Heilman 110cr (below); K Siewert 110cl; Kitchen 19bll; Sunak 91cr; Surpress 111tr. **JACKET IMAGES:** Front: **Corbis:** Richard Berenholtz br; Bob Krist tc, bl; JamesRandklev tr, bl; Keren Su tl.; **Science Photo Library/NOAA**. Back: **Corbis:** Robert Y. Ono bc; James Randklevbl; Paul A. Souders br; Royalty Free Images: Cobis tc; Corbis tr. Spine: **Corbis:** Robert Y. Ono

CONTENTS

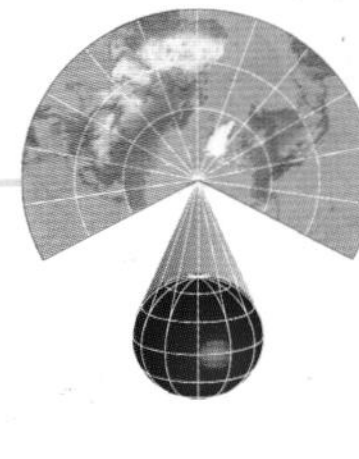

LEARNING MAP SKILLS

AMAZING EARTH 4
MAPPING THE WORLD 6
HOW MAPS ARE MADE 8
READING MAPS 10
USING THE ATLAS 12

THE WORLD ABOUT US

THE PHYSICAL WORLD 14
THE EARTH'S STRUCTURE 16
Dynamic Earth, Plate Boundaries, Shaping the Landscape, The World's Oceans
CLIMATE AND LIFE ZONES 18
Winds, Ocean Currents, Life Zones
WORLD POPULATION 20
Population Structures, Population Density, Urban Growth, Population Growth
THE WORLD ECONOMY 22
Measuring Wealth, Types of Industry, Patterns of Trade, Developing Economies, Tourism
BORDERS AND BOUNDARIES 24

THE WORLD ATLAS

THE NATIONS OF THE WORLD 26

NORTH AMERICA

CONTINENTAL NORTH AMERICA 28
NORTH AMERICAN GEOGRAPHY 30
WESTERN CANADA 32
Alberta, British Columbia, Manitoba, Northwest Territories, Nunavut, Saskatchewan, Yukon Territory
EASTERN CANADA 34
New Brunswick, Newfoundland and Labrador, Nova Scotia, Ontario, Prince Edward Island, Québec
USA: THE NORTHEASTERN STATES 36
Connecticut, Delaware, Maine, Massachusetts, New Hampshire, New Jersey, New York, Pennsylvania, Rhode Island, Vermont
USA: THE SOUTHERN STATES 38
Alabama, Arkansas, District of Colombia, Florida, Georgia, Kentucky, Louisiana, Maryland, Mississippi, North Carolina, South Carolina, Tennessee, Virginia, West Virginia
USA: THE GREAT LAKES STATES 40
Illinois, Indiana, Michigan, Ohio, Wisconsin
USA: THE CENTRAL STATES 42
Iowa, Kansas, Minnesota, Missouri, Nebraska, North Dakota, Oklahoma, South Dakota
USA: THE SOUTHWESTERN STATES 44
Arizona, New Mexico, Texas
USA: THE MOUNTAIN STATES 46
Colorado, Idaho, Montana, Nevada, Utah, Wyoming,

HE ARCTIC
p 143
GERMANY &
THE ALPINE STATES
pp 100-101
THE LOW
COUNTRIES
pp 84-85
ORTHERN EUROPE
pp 82-83
RUSSIA & KAZAKHSTAN
pp 118-119
EUROPEAN RUSSIA
pp 110-111
E BRITISH
ISLES
pp 86-95
CENTRAL
EUROPE
pp 104-105
EUROPE
pp 78-111
ASIA
pp 114-133
FRANCE
pp 96-97
EASTERN
EUROPE
pp 108-109
ITALY
pp 102-103
SOUTHEAST
EUROPE
pp 106-107
TURKEY &
THE CAUCASUS
pp 120-121
CENTRAL
ASIA
pp 124-125
EAST
ASIA
pp 128-129
JAPAN &
KOREA
pp 132-133
SPAIN &
RTUGAL
pp 98-99
Malta
p 112
Cyprus
p 112
THE
MEDITERRANEAN
pp 112-113
Israel
p 123
NORTH AFRICA
pp 70-71
SOUTHWEST
ASIA
pp 122-123
SOUTH
ASIA
pp 126-127
Ryukyu
Islands
p 133
PACIFIC
OCEAN
EST AFRICA
pp 72-73
EAST
AFRICA
pp 74-75
Andaman
& Nicobar
Islands
p 127
SOUTHEAST
ASIA
pp 130-131
AFRICA
pp 68-77
SOUTHWEST
PACIFIC
pp 140-141
AUSTRALASIA
& OCEANIA
pp 134-141
Samoa
p 140
SOUTHERN
AFRICA
pp 76-77
INDIAN
OCEAN
AUSTRALIA
pp 136-137
NEW ZEALAND
pp 138-139
ANTARCTICA
p 142

JSA: THE PACIFIC STATES 48
alifornia, Oregon, Washington

LASKA, HAWAII, US OVERSEAS TERRITORIES 50

MEXICO 52

ENTRAL AMERICA 54
elize, Costa Rica, El Salvador, Guatemala, Honduras, Nicaragua, Panama

HE CARIBBEAN 56

SOUTH AMERICA

ONTINENTAL SOUTH AMERICA 58

OUTH AMERICAN GEOGRAPHY 60

NORTHERN SOUTH AMERICA 62
razil, Colombia, Ecuador, Guyana, Peru, Surinam, Venezuela

OUTHERN SOUTH AMERICA 64
rgentina, Bolivia, Chile, Paraguay, Uruguay

AFRICA

ONTINENTAL AFRICA 66

AFRICAN GEOGRAPHY 68

NORTH AFRICA 70
lgeria, Egypt, Libya, Morocco, Tunisia

WEST AFRICA 72
enin, Burkina, Cameroon, Central African Republic, Chad, quatorial Guinea, Gambia, Ghana, Guinea, Guinea-Bissau, Ivory Coast, iberia, Mali, Mauritania, Niger, Nigeria, Sao Tome & Principe, Senegal, ierra Leone, Togo

EAST AFRICA 74
urundi, Djibouti, Eritrea, Ethiopia, Kenya, Rwanda, Somalia, Sudan, outh Sudan, Tanzania, Uganda

OUTHERN AFRICA 76
ngola, Botswana, Comoros, Congo, Dem. Rep. Congo, Gabon, esotho, Madagascar, Malawi, Mozambique, Namibia, South Africa, waziland, Zambia, Zimbabwe

EUROPE

ONTINENTAL EUROPE 78

UROPEAN GEOGRAPHY 80

NORTHERN EUROPE 82
enmark, Estonia, Finland, Iceland, Latvia, Lithuania, Norway, Sweden

THE LOW COUNTRIES 84
elgium, Luxembourg, Netherlands

THE BRITISH ISLES 86
reland, United Kingdom

RELAND 88

SCOTLAND 90

NORTHERN ENGLAND & WALES 92

SOUTHERN ENGLAND 94

FRANCE 96
rance, Monaco

SPAIN AND PORTUGAL 98
ndorra, Portugal, Spain

GERMANY AND THE ALPINE STATES 100
ustria, Germany, Liechtenstein, Slovenia, Switzerland

ITALY 102
Italy, San Marino, Vatican City

CENTRAL EUROPE 104
Czech Republic, Hungary, Poland, Slovakia

SOUTHEAST EUROPE 106
Albania, Bosnia and Herzegovina, Bulgaria, Croatia, Greece, Kosovo, Macedonia, Montenegro, Serbia

EASTERN EUROPE 108
Belarus, Moldova, Romania, Ukraine

EUROPEAN RUSSIA 110

THE MEDITERRANEAN 112

ASIA

CONTINENTAL ASIA 114

ASIAN GEOGRAPHY 116

RUSSIA AND KAZAKHSTAN 118

TURKEY AND THE CAUCASUS 120
Armenia, Azerbaijan, Georgia, Turkey

SOUTHWEST ASIA 122
Bahrain, Iran, Iraq, Israel, Jordan, Kuwait, Lebanon, Oman, Qatar, Saudi Arabia, Syria, United Arab Emirates, Yemen

CENTRAL ASIA 124
Afghanistan, Kyrgyzstan, Tajikistan, Turkmenistan, Uzbekistan

SOUTH ASIA 126
Bangladesh, Bhutan, India, Maldives, Nepal, Pakistan, Sri Lanka

EAST ASIA 128
China, Mongolia, Taiwan

SOUTHEAST ASIA 130
Brunei, Burma, Cambodia, East Timor, Indonesia, Laos, Malaysia, Philippines, Singapore, Thailand, Vietnam

JAPAN AND KOREA 132
Japan, North Korea, South Korea

AUSTRALASIA & OCEANIA

AUSTRALASIA & OCEANIA 134

AUSTRALIA 136

NEW ZEALAND 138

SOUTHWEST PACIFIC 140

POLAR REGIONS

ANTARCTICA, THE ARCTIC 142

TIMEZONES 144

GEOGRAPHICAL COMPARISIONS 145

WORLD FACTFILE 146

GLOSSARY AND INDEX 154

KEY TO MAP SYMBOLS ON FRONT ENDPAPER

FLAGS ON BACK ENDPAPER

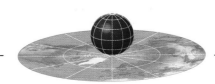

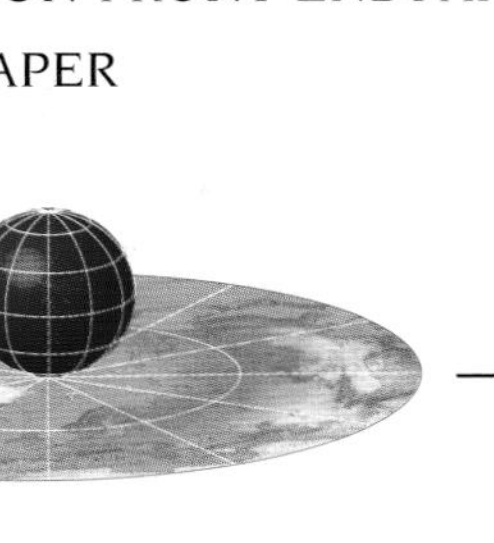

Amazing Earth

Earth is unique among the nine planets that circle the Sun. It is the only one that can support life, because it has enough oxygen in its atmosphere and plentiful water. In fact, seen from space, the Earth looks almost entirely blue. This is because about 70% of its surface is under water, submerged beneath four huge oceans: the Pacific, Atlantic, Indian and Arctic oceans. Land makes up about 30% of the Earth's surface. It is divided into seven landmasses of varying shapes and sizes called continents. These are, from largest to smallest: Asia, Africa, North America, South America, Antarctica, Europe and Australia.

WATERY WORLD

The Earth's oceans and seas cover more than 367 million sq km – that is twice the surface of Mars and nine times the surface of the moon.

Beneath the ocean waves lies the biggest and most unexplored landscape on Earth. Here are coral reefs, enormous, open plains, deep canyons and the longest mountain range on Earth – the Mid-Atlantic Ridge – which stretches almost from pole to pole.

THE SHAPE OF THE EARTH

Photographs taken from space by astronauts in the 1960s, and more recently from orbiting satellites, have proven beyond doubt what humans had already worked out long ago – that the Earth is shaped like a ball. But it is not perfectly round. The force of the Earth's rotation makes the world bulge very slightly at the Equator and go a little flat at the North and South poles. So the Earth is actually a flattened sphere, or a 'geoid'.

HEIGHTS AND DEPTHS

The Pacific Ocean contains the deepest places on the Earth's surface – the ocean trenches. The very deepest is Challenger Deep in the Mariana Trench which plunges 10,916 m into the Earth's crust. If Mount Everest, the highest point on land at 8,848 m, was dropped into the trench, its peak wouldn't even reach the surface of the Pacific.

WATER

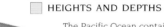

Over 97% of the Earth's water is salt water. The total amount of salt in the world's oceans and seas would cover the whole of Europe to a depth of five km. Less than 3% of the Earth's water is fresh. Of this, 2.06% is frozen in ice sheets and about 0.9% is stored underground as groundwater. The remainder is in lakes and rivers.

COASTS

The total length of the Earth's coastlines is more than 350,000 km – that is the equivalent of 8.75 times around the globe. A high percentage of the world's people live in coastal zones: of the ten most populated cities on Earth, seven are situated on estuaries or the coast.

BIODIVERSITY

Today, almost 7,000,000,000 humans, an estimated 7.7 million animal species and 300,000 known plant species depend on the air, water and land of planet Earth.

VANISHING FORESTS

10,000 years ago, thick forests covered about half of the Earth's land surface. Today, 33% of those forests no longer exist, and more than half of what remains has been dramatically altered. During the 20th century, more than 50% of the Earth's rainforests were felled.

WET EARTH

Tropical rainforests grow in areas close to the Equator, where it is wet and warm all year round. Although they cover just 7% of the Earth's land, these thick, damp forests form the richest ecosystems on the planet. More plant and animal species are found here than anywhere else on Earth.

DRY EARTH

Deserts are among the most inhospitable places on the planet. Some deserts are scorching hot, others are freezing cold, but they have one thing in common – they are all dry. Very few plant and animal species can survive in these harsh conditions. The world's coldest and driest continent, Antarctica (*left*), is a cold desert.

DIFFERENT WORLD VIEWS

Because the Earth is round, we can only see half of it at any one time. This half is called a hemisphere, which means 'half a sphere'. There are always two hemispheres – the half that you see and the other half that you don't see. Two hemispheres placed together will always make a complete sphere.

Equator 0°

NORTH AND SOUTH

The Equator is an imaginary line drawn around the middle of the Earth, where its circumference is greatest. If we cut along the Equator, the Earth separates into two hemispheres: the northern and southern hemispheres. Most of the Earth's land is the northern hemisphere. Europe and North America are the only continents which lie entirely in the northern hemisphere. Australia and Antarctica are the only continents that lie wholly in the southern hemisphere.

The southern hemisphere contains three of the Earth's four great oceans: the Pacific, Indian and Atlantic oceans.

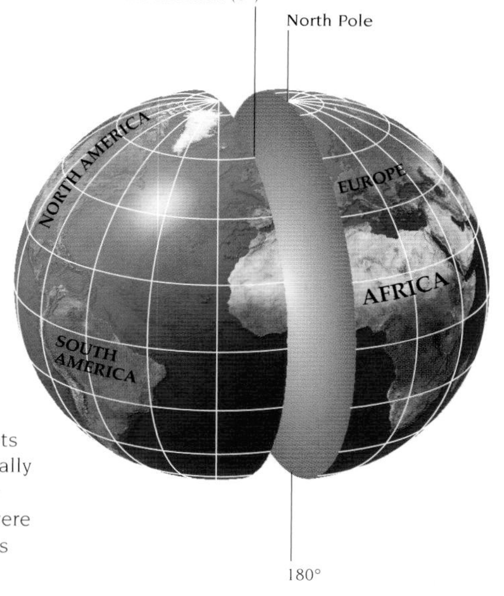
Prime Meridian (0°)
North Pole
NORTH AMERICA
EUROPE
AFRICA
SOUTH AMERICA
180°

EAST AND WEST

The Earth can also be divided along two other imaginary lines – the Prime Meridian (0°) and 180° – which run opposite each other between the North and South poles. This creates eastern and western hemispheres. The continents in the eastern hemisphere are traditionally called the Old World while those in the western hemisphere – the Americas – were named the New World by the Europeans who explored them in the 15th century.

PLANET WATER, PLANET LAND

The Earth can also be divided into land and water hemispheres. The land hemisphere shows most of the land on the Earth's surface. The water hemisphere is dominated by the vast Pacific Ocean – from this view, the Earth appears to be almost entirely covered by water.

LAND HEMISPHERE

Although this view of the globe is dominated by the continents of Asia, Africa and Europe, a large area is still taken up by the waters of the Pacific, Atlantic and Indian oceans.

ASIA
NORTH AMERICA
PACIFIC OCEAN
AUSTRALIA
ANTARCTICA

WATER HEMISPHERE

The Pacific Ocean is so enormous it stretches across a whole hemisphere, reaching halfway around the globe at its widest point. It is bigger than all the land put together and contains almost half of all the water on the planet.

THE SEASONS

As the Earth orbits the Sun, it is also spinning around an imaginary line called its axis, which joins the North and South poles. The Earth's axis is not quite at right angles to the Sun, but tilts over at an angle of 23.5°. As a result, each place gradually moves closer to the Sun and then further away from it again. Summer in the northern hemisphere is when the north is closest to the Sun. In winter, the northern hemisphere tilts away from the Sun, receiving far less heat and light. In the southern hemisphere the seasons are reversed, with summer in December and winter in June.

JUNE 21st

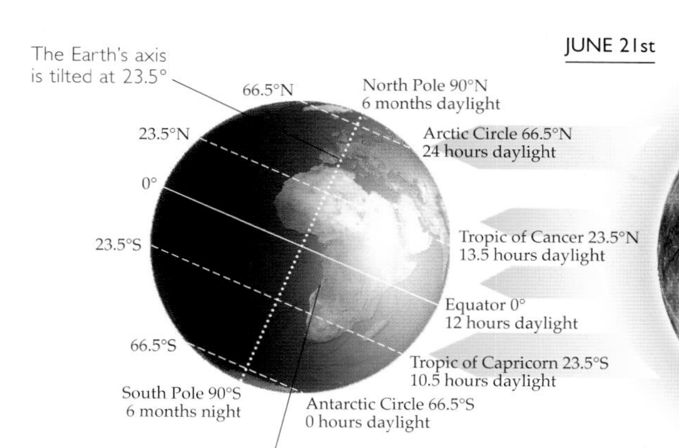
The Earth's axis is tilted at 23.5°
66.5°N
North Pole 90°N
6 months daylight
23.5°N
Arctic Circle 66.5°N
24 hours daylight
0°
23.5°S
Tropic of Cancer 23.5°N
13.5 hours daylight
Equator 0°
12 hours daylight
66.5°S
Tropic of Capricorn 23.5°S
10.5 hours daylight
South Pole 90°S
6 months night
Antarctic Circle 66.5°S
0 hours daylight

SUN
(not to scale)

DECEMBER 21st

Arctic Circle 66.5°N
0 hours daylight

North Pole 90°N
6 months night

Tropic of Cancer 23.5°N
10.5 hours daylight

66.5°N

Equator 0°
12 hours daylight

Tropic of Capricorn 23.5°S
13.5 hours daylight

23.5°N

0°N

Antarctic Circle 66.5°S
24 hours daylight

23.5°S

South Pole 90°S
6 months daylight

66.5°S

Places between the Tropics are hot all year round. This is because the Sun's rays strike the Equator almost vertically, heating the land more intensely.

On June 21st, the strongest and most direct light from the Sun is in the northern hemisphere. The Arctic Circle has 24 hours of daylight, and the northern hemisphere has its longest day.

On December 21st, the direct light and heat from the Sun strike south of the Equator. This is the longest day in the southern hemisphere. The northern hemisphere has its shortest day and longest night.

Places near the poles have the coldest climates because the Sun's rays hit them at an angle. The Sun's warmth is therefore spread out over a much wider area.

MAPPING THE WORLD

The main purpose of a map is to show, or locate, where things are. The only truly accurate map of the whole world is a globe – a round model of the Earth. But a globe is impractical to carry around, so map-makers (cartographers) produce flat paper maps instead. Changing the globe into a flat map is not simple. Imagine cutting a globe in half and trying to flatten the two hemispheres. They would be stretched in some places, and squashed in others. In fact, it is impossible to make a map of the round Earth on flat paper without some distortion of area, distance or direction.

MODELS OF THE WORLD

Satellite images can show the whole world as it appears from space. However, this image shows only one half of the world, and is distorted at the edges.

A globe (*right*) is the only way to illustrate the shape of the Earth accurately. A globe also shows the correct positions of the continents and oceans and how large they are in relation to one another.

LATITUDE

We can find out exactly how far north or south, east or west any place is on Earth by drawing two sets of imaginary lines around the world to make a grid. The horizontal lines on the globe below are called lines of latitude. They run from east to west. The most important is the Equator, which is given the value 0°. All other lines of latitude run parallel to the Equator. and are numbered in degrees either north or south of the Equator.

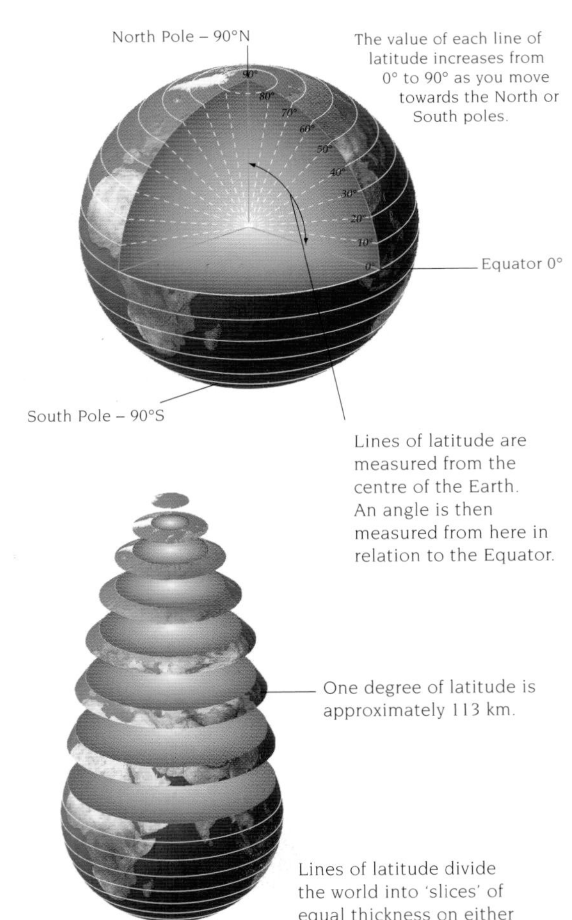
North Pole – 90°N
Equator 0°
South Pole – 90°S

The value of each line of latitude increases from 0° to 90° as you move towards the North or South poles.

Lines of latitude are measured from the centre of the Earth. An angle is then measured from here in relation to the Equator.

One degree of latitude is approximately 113 km.

Lines of latitude divide the world into 'slices' of equal thickness on either side of the Equator.

LONGITUDE

The vertical lines on the globe below run from north to south between the poles. They are called lines of longitude. The most important passes through Greenwich, London and is numbered 0°. It is called the Prime Meridian. All other lines of longitude are numbered in degrees either east or west of the Prime Meridian. The line directly opposite the Prime Meridian is numbered 180°.

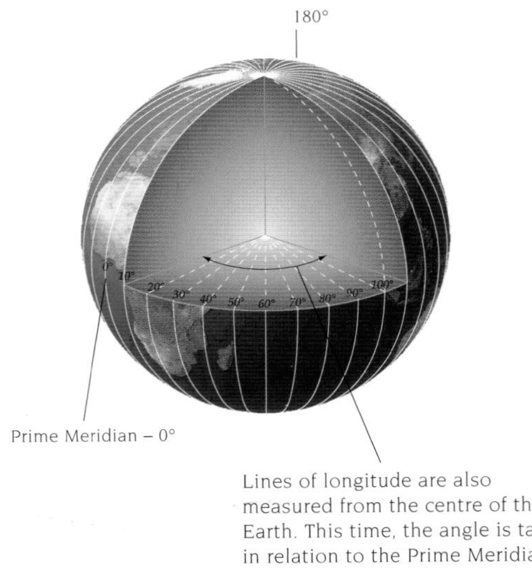
180°
Prime Meridian – 0°

Lines of longitude are also measured from the centre of the Earth. This time, the angle is taken in relation to the Prime Meridian.

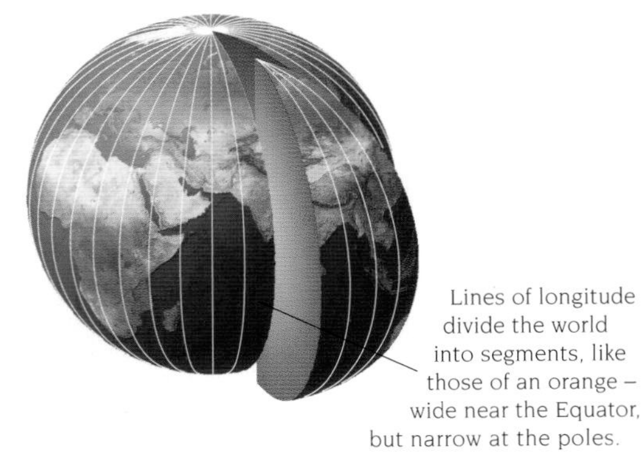

Lines of longitude divide the world into segments, like those of an orange – wide near the Equator, but narrow at the poles.

WHERE ON EARTH?

When lines of latitude and longitude are combined on a globe, or as here, on a flat map, they form a grid. Using this grid, we can locate any place on land, or at sea, by referring to the point where its line of latitude intersects with its line of longitude. Even when a place is not located exactly where the lines cross, you can still find its approximate position.

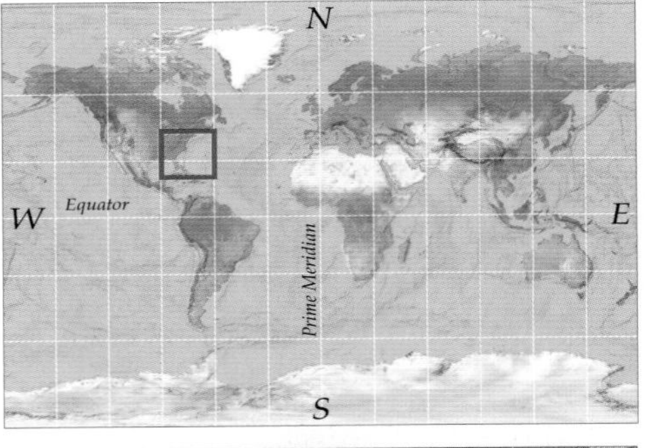
N
W
Equator
E
Prime Meridian
S

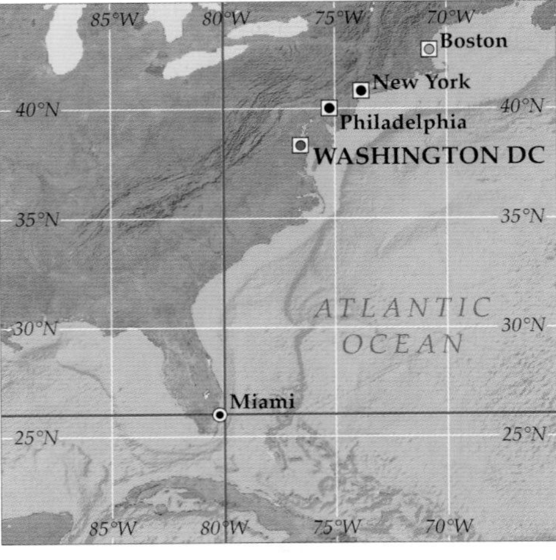
85°W
80°W
75°W
70°W
Boston
New York
Philadelphia
WASHINGTON DC
40°N
35°N
30°N
25°N
ATLANTIC OCEAN
Miami

The map above is of the eastern USA. It is too small to show all the lines of latitude and longitude, so they are given at intervals of 5°. Miami is located at about 26° north of the Equator and 80° west of the Prime Meridian. We write its location like this: 26°N 80°W.

MAKING A FLAT MAP FROM A GLOBE

Cartographers use a technique called projection to show the Earth's curved surface on a flat map. Many different map projections have been designed. The distortion of one feature – either area, distance, or direction – can be minimized, while other features become more distorted. Cartographers must choose which of these things it is most important to show correctly for each map that they make. Three major families of projections can be used to solve these questions.

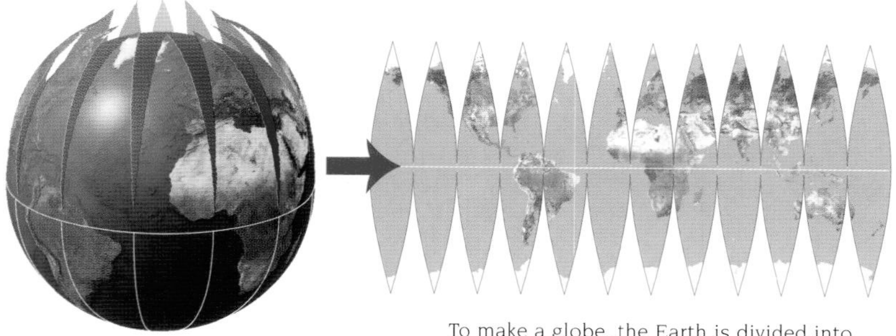

To make a globe, the Earth is divided into segments or 'gores' along lines of longitude.

1 CYLINDRICAL PROJECTIONS

These projections are 'cylindrical' because the surface of the globe is transferred onto a surrounding cylinder. This cylinder is then cut from top to bottom and 'rolled out' to give a flat map. These maps are very useful for showing the whole world.

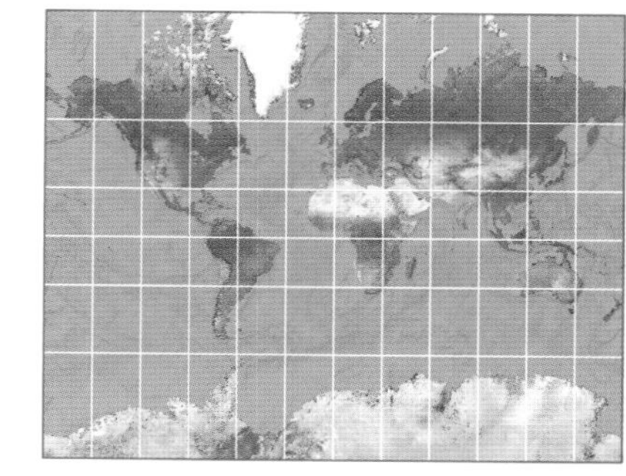

The cylinder touches the globe at the Equator. Here, the scale on the map will be exactly the same as it is on the globe. At the northern and southern edges of the cylinder, which are furthest away from the surface of the globe, the map is most distorted. The Mercator projection (*above*), created in the 16th century, is a good example of a cylindrical projection.

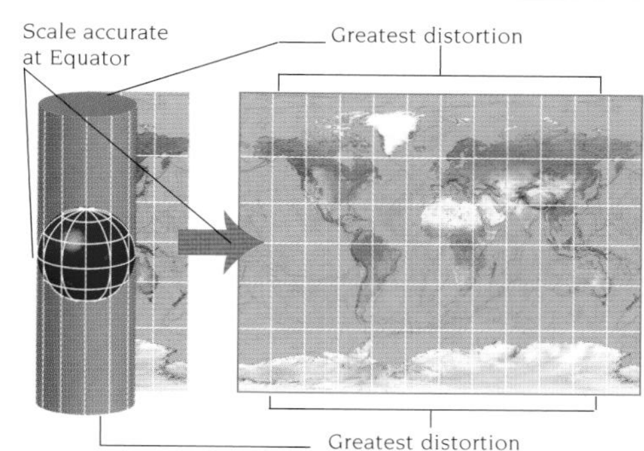
Scale accurate
at Equator
Greatest distortion
Greatest distortion

2 AZIMUTHAL PROJECTIONS

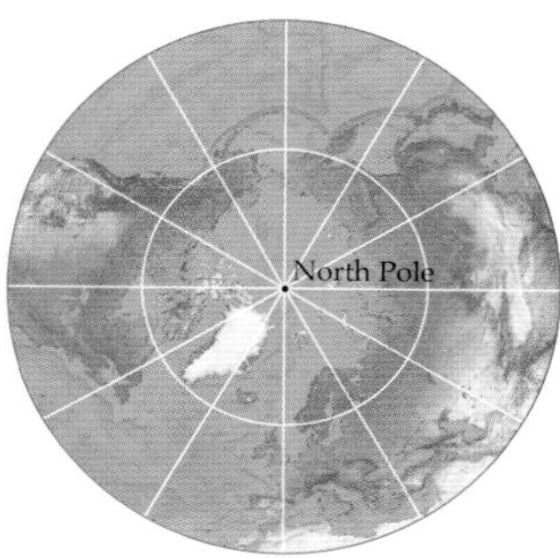
North Pole

Azimuthal projections put the surface of the globe onto a flat circle. 'Azimuthal' means that the direction or 'azimuth' of any line coming from the centre point of that circle is correct. Azimuthal maps are useful for viewing hemispheres, continents and the polar regions. Mapping any area larger than a hemisphere gives great distortion at the outer edges of the map.

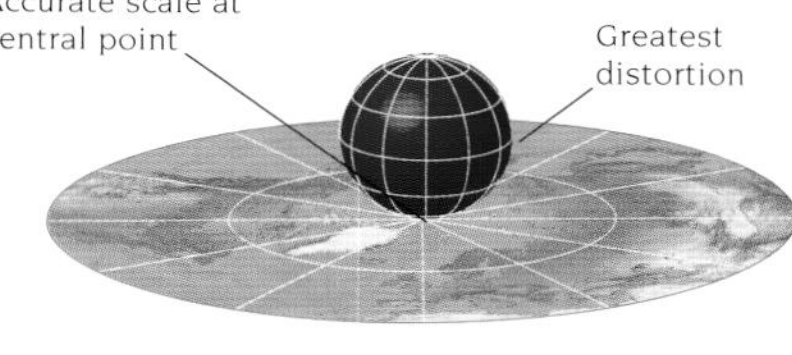
Accurate scale at
central point
Greatest
distortion

The circle only touches the globe's surface at one central point. The scale is only accurate at this point and becomes less and less accurate the further away the circle is from the globe. This kind of projection is good for maps centering on a major city or on one of the poles.

3 CONIC PROJECTIONS

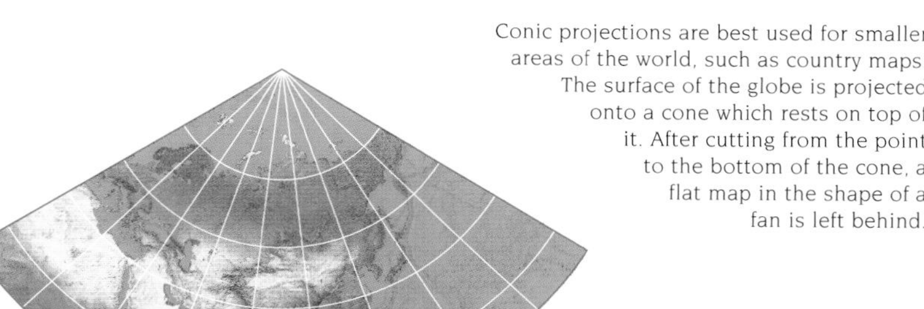

Conic projections are best used for smaller areas of the world, such as country maps. The surface of the globe is projected onto a cone which rests on top of it. After cutting from the point to the bottom of the cone, a flat map in the shape of a fan is left behind.

The conic projection touches the globe's surface at one latitude. This is where the scale of the map will be most accurate. The parts of the cone furthest from the globe will be the most distorted and are usually omitted from the map itself.

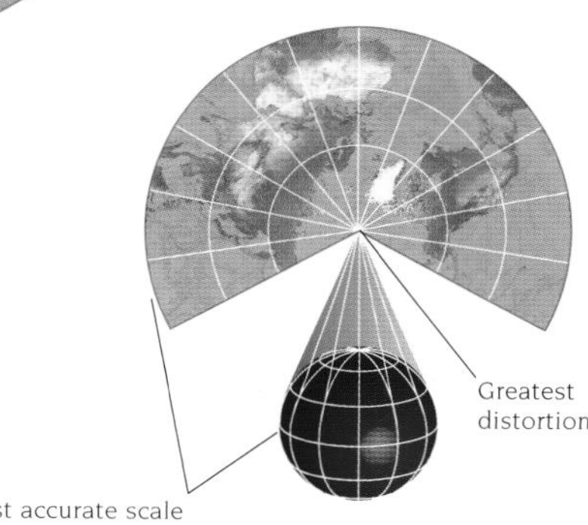
Greatest
distortion
Most accurate scale

PROJECTIONS USED IN THIS ATLAS

The projections which are appropriate for showing maps at a world, continental or country scale are quite different. The projections for this atlas have been carefully chosen. They are ones that show areas as familiar shapes and ensure that they are distorted as little as possible.

1 World Maps

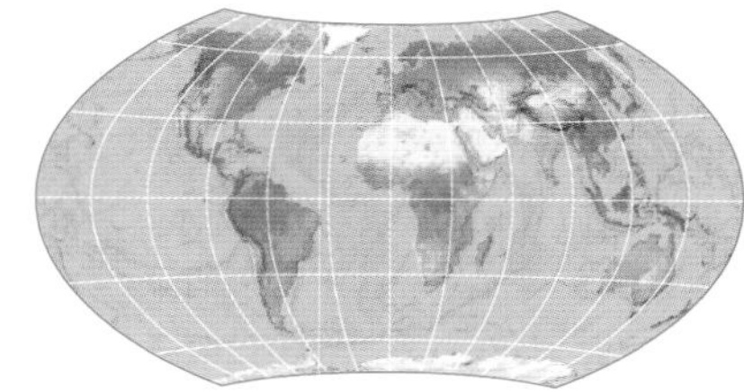

The Wagner VII projection is used for our world maps as it shows all the countries at their correct sizes relative to one another.

2 Continents

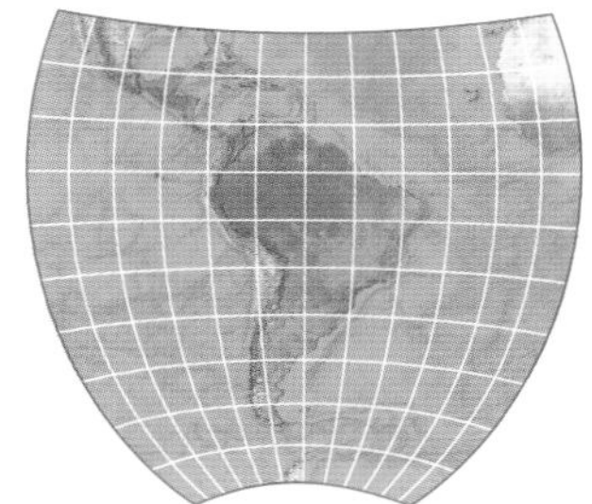

The Lambert Azimuthal Equal Area is used for continental maps. The shape distortion is relatively small and countries retain their correct sizes relative to one another.

3 Countries

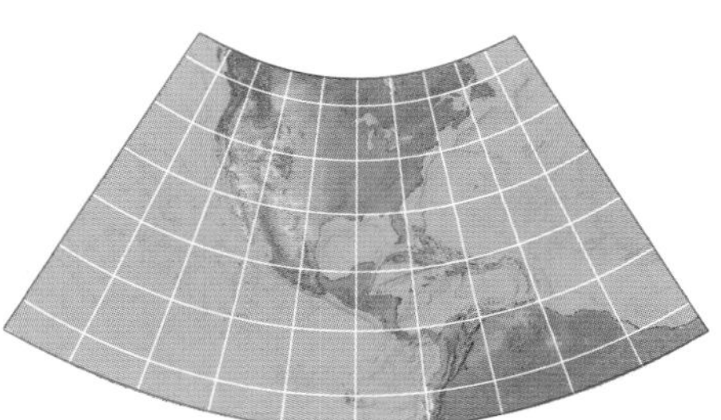

The Lambert Conformal Conic shows countries with as little distortion as possible. The angles from any point on the map are the same as they would be on the surface of the globe.

HOW MAPS ARE MADE

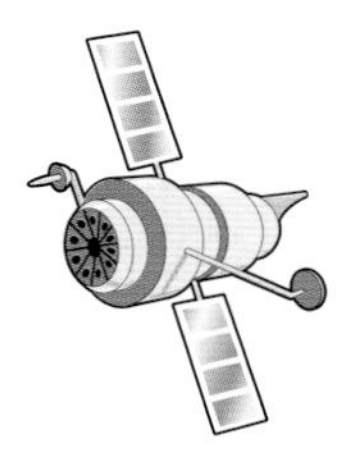

New technologies have revolutionized map making. Computers and information from satellites have replaced drawing boards and drafting pens, and the process of creating new maps is now far easier. But map making is still a skilled and often time-consuming process. Information about the World must be gathered, sorted and checked. The cartographer must make decisions about the function of the map and what information to select in order to make it as clear as possible.

THE MAPPA MUNDI

Maps have been made for thousands of years. The 13th century Mappa Mundi, meaning 'known world' shows the Mediterranean Sea and the Don and Nile rivers. Asia is at the top, with Europe on the left, and Africa to the right. The oceans are shown as a ring surrounding the land. The map reflects a number of biblical stories.

HISTORICAL MAP MAKING

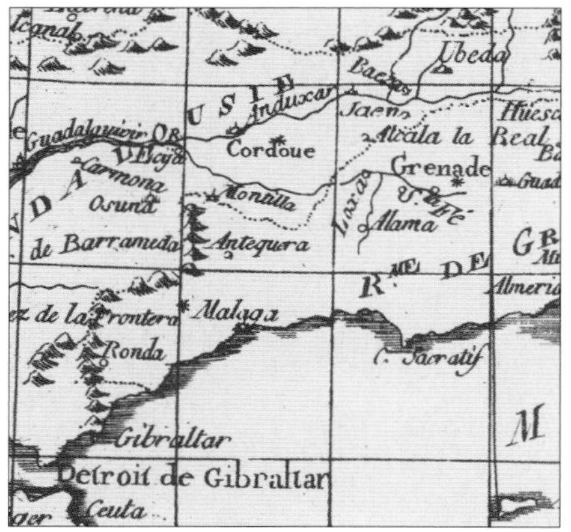
Ubeda
Cordoue
Grenade
Antequera
Malaga
Ronda
Gibraltar
Detroit de Gibraltar
Ceuta

This detailed hand-drawn map of the southern coast of Spain was made in about 1750. The mountains are illustrated as small hills and the labels have been hand lettered.

For centuries, maps were drawn by hand. Very early maps were no more than a pictorial representation of what the surface of the ground looked like. Where there were hills, pictures were drawn to represent them. Later maps were drawn using information gathered by survey teams. They would carefully mark out and calculate the height of the land, the positions of towns and other geographical features. As knowledge and techniques improved, maps became more accurate.

NEW TECHNIQUES

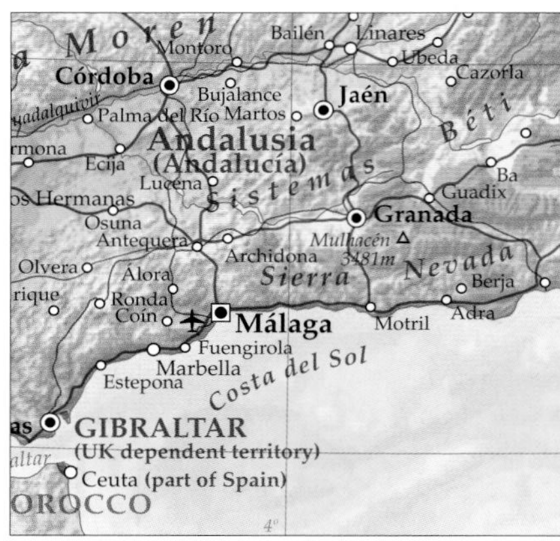
Córdoba
Bailén
Linares
Úbeda
Cazorla
Montoro
Bujalance
Palma del Río
Martos
Jaén
Andalusia
(Andalucía)
Écija
Lucena
Guadix
Osuna
Antequera
Granada
Archidona
Mulhacén
3481m
Sierra Nevada
Olvera
Álora
Ronda
Coín
Málaga
Motril
Adra
Berja
Fuengirola
Marbella
Estepona
Costa del Sol
GIBRALTAR
(UK dependent territory)
Ceuta (part of Spain)

Computers make it easier to change map information and styles quickly. This map of the southern coast of Spain, made in 1997 has been made using digital terrain modelling (see below) and traditional cartography.

Today, cartographers have access to far more data about the Earth than in the past. Satellites collect and process information about its surface. Further elements may then be added in the traditional way. Computers are now widely used to combine these different sorts of map information. More recently, the use of Global Positioning Systems (GPS) linked to satellites, and the increased availability of Internet based mapping, has revolutionised the way that maps are created and used.

MODERN MAP MAKING

1 Measuring the Earth's surface

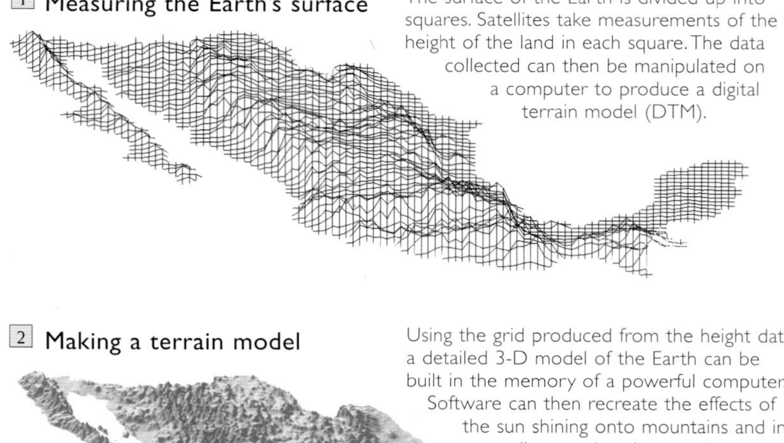

The surface of the Earth is divided up into squares. Satellites take measurements of the height of the land in each square. The data collected can then be manipulated on a computer to produce a digital terrain model (DTM).

2 Making a terrain model

Using the grid produced from the height data, a detailed 3-D model of the Earth can be built in the memory of a powerful computer. Software can then recreate the effects of the sun shining onto mountains and into valleys so that they can be seen much more clearly.

3 Adding detail to the land surface

The height of the land can be shown using bands of colour, or by contour lines, which are applied to the digitally-created surface of the Earth. Colour can also be used to show different kinds of vegetation, such as deserts, forests and grasslands.

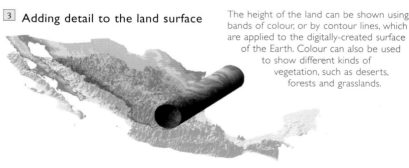

4 Adding map detail

Features such as roads, rivers, towns and cities can now be added to the map. They are selected, and compiled and scanned digitally into the computer. The information can then be 'draped' on top of the terrain model to create a map.

SHOWING INFORMATION ON A MAP

A map is a selective diagram of a place. It is the cartographer's job to decide what kind of information to show on a map. They can choose to highlight certain kinds of features – such as roads, rivers and land height. They can also show other features such as sea depth, place names, and borders which would be impossible to see either on the ground or from a photograph. The information that can be shown in a map is influenced by a number of factors, most notably by its scale.

This is a satellite photograph of the harbour area of Rio de Janeiro in Brazil. Although you can see the bay and where most of the housing is, it is impossible to see roads or get any sense of the position of places relative to one another.

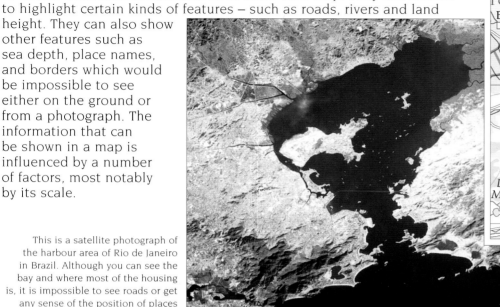

This is a map of the same area as you can see in the photograph. Much of the detail has been greatly simplified. Towns are named and marked; contours indicate the height of the land; and roads, railways and borders between districts have been added.

SCALE

To make a map of an area it needs to be greatly reduced in size. This is known as drawing to scale. The scale of the map shows us by how much the area has been reduced. The smaller the scale, the greater the area of land that can be shown on the map. There will be far less detail and the map will not be as accurate. The maps below show the different kinds of information that can be shown on maps of varying scales.

WAYS TO SHOW SCALE

When using a map to work out what areas or distances are in reality, we need to refer to the scale of that particular map. Map scales can be shown in several ways.

1 Representative fraction

One unit on the map would be equal to 1,000,000 units on the ground.

1:1,000,000

2 Linear scale

The line is marked off in units which represent the real distances of the map, given in both miles and kilometres.

SCALE BAR

0 km 10 20

0 miles 10 20

3 Statement of scale

It means that 1-mm on the map represents 1-km on the ground.

1 mm represents 1 km

LONDON 1:21,000,000

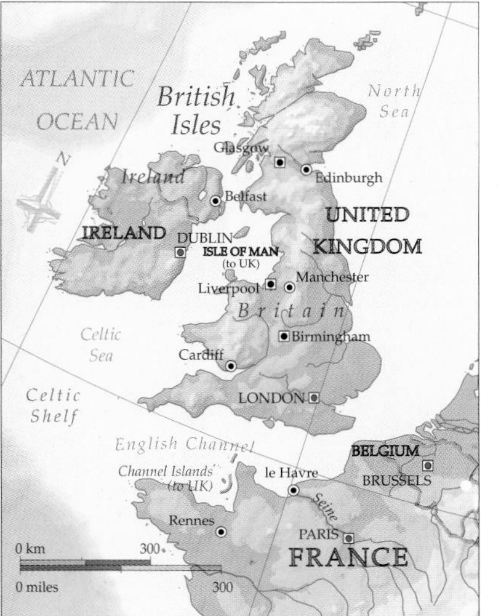
ATLANTIC OCEAN
British Isles
North Sea
Ireland
Glasgow
Edinburgh
Belfast
UNITED KINGDOM
IRELAND
DUBLIN
ISLE OF MAN (to UK)
Manchester
Liverpool
Britain
Celtic Sea
Birmingham
Cardiff
Celtic Shelf
LONDON
English Channel
BELGIUM
Channel Islands (to UK)
le Havre
BRUSSELS
Rennes
PARIS
Seine
FRANCE
0 km 300
0 miles 300

This small-scale map shows the position of London in relation to Europe. Very little detail can be seen at this scale – only the names of countries and the largest towns.

LONDON 1:5,500,000

Doncaster
Grimsby
Sheffield
Louth
Lincoln
Skegness
ENGLAND
Boston
The Wash
Nottingham
Derby
Great Yarmouth
Norwich
Leicester
Fens
King's Lynn
Birmingham
Peterborough
Lowestoft
Kettering
Newmarket
Coventry
Cambridge
Ipswich
Northampton
Bedford
Felixstowe
Milton Keynes
Harwich
Stevenage
Colchester
Luton
Oxford
Harlow
Southend-on-Sea
Swindon
St Albans
Watford
LONDON
Margate
Reading
Windsor
Croydon
Canterbury
Andover
Woking
Guildford
Maidstone
Dover
Winchester
Crawley
Folkestone
Channel Tunnel
Southampton
Brighton
Havant
Hastings
Newport
Portsmouth
Hove
Eastbourne
Isle of Wight
English Channel
Bournemouth
0 km 50
0 miles 50

At a scale of 1 to 5,500,000 you can see the major road network in the southeast of the UK. Many towns are named and you can see the difference in size and status.

LONDON 1:900,000

0 km 10
0 miles 10
M1
M25
M11
Watford
Enfield
Barnet
Edgware
Finchley
Wembley
Hampstead
Walthamstow
St Paul's Cathedral
Trafalgar Square
City
Buckingham Palace
Greenwich
Houses of Parliament
Richmond
Wandsworth
Bexley
Wimbledon
Bromley
Kingston upon Thames
Croydon
M3
A21
A3
Epsom
A23
M23
M25
Places of interest
Regions/suburbs

This map is at a much larger scale. You can see the major roads that lead out from London and the names of many suburbs, places of interest and airports.

LONDON 1:12,500

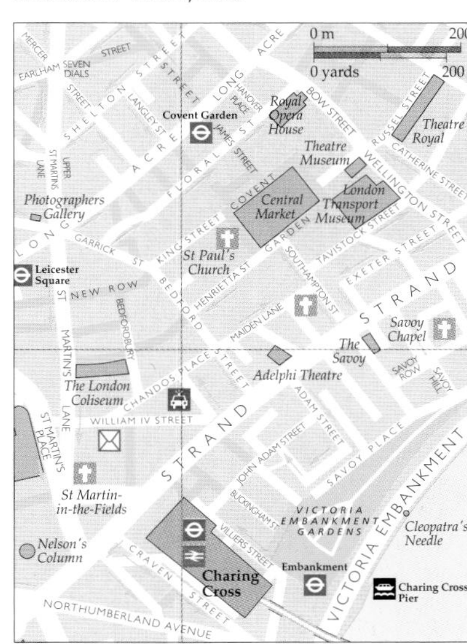
0 m 200
0 yards 200
Covent Garden
Royal Opera House
Theatre Royal
Theatre Museum
London Transport Museum
Photographers Gallery
Central Market
St Paul's Church
Leicester Square
STRAND
The Savoy
Savoy Chapel
Adelphi Theatre
The London Coliseum
WILLIAM IV STREET
St Martin-in-the-Fields
VICTORIA EMBANKMENT GARDENS
VICTORIA EMBANKMENT
Nelson's Column
Cleopatra's Needle
Charing Cross
Embankment
Charing Cross Pier
NORTHUMBERLAND AVENUE

This is a street map of central London. The streets are named, as are places of interest, train and underground stations. The scale is large enough to show plenty of detail.

Reading maps

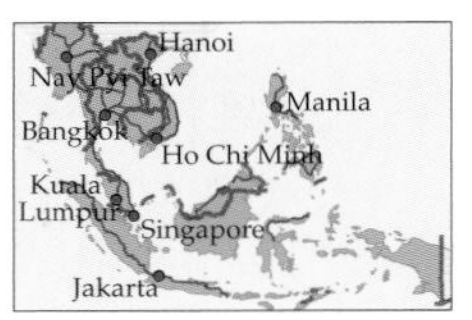
Hanoi
Nay Pyi Taw
Manila
Bangkok
Ho Chi Minh
Kuala Lumpur
Singapore
Jakarta

Maps use a unique visual language to convey a great deal of detailed information in a relatively simple form. Different features are marked out using special symbols and styles of print. These symbols are explained in the key to the map and you should always read a map alongside its key or legend. This page explains how to look for different features on the map and how to unravel the different layers of information that you can find on it.

Physical features

All the regional and country maps in this atlas are based on a model of the Earth's surface. The computer-generated relief gives an accurate picture of the surface of the land. Colours are used to show the relative heights of the land; green is for low-lying land, and yellows, browns and greys are for higher land. Water features like streams, rivers and lakes are also shown.

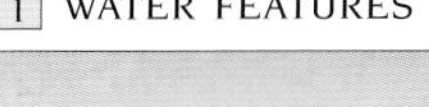
1 WATER FEATURES

On this map extract, the blue lines show a number of rivers, including the Salween and the Irrawaddy. The Irrawaddy forms a huge delta, splitting into many streams as it reaches the sea.

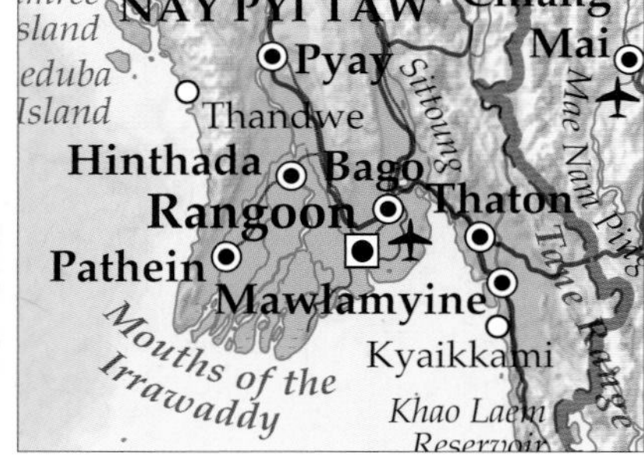
NAY PYI TAW
Pyay
Thandwe
Hinthada
Bago
Rangoon
Thaton
Pathein
Mawlamyine
Mouths of the Irrawaddy
Kyaikkami
Khao Laem Reservoir
Mai
Sittoung
Mae Nam Ping

2 RELIEF

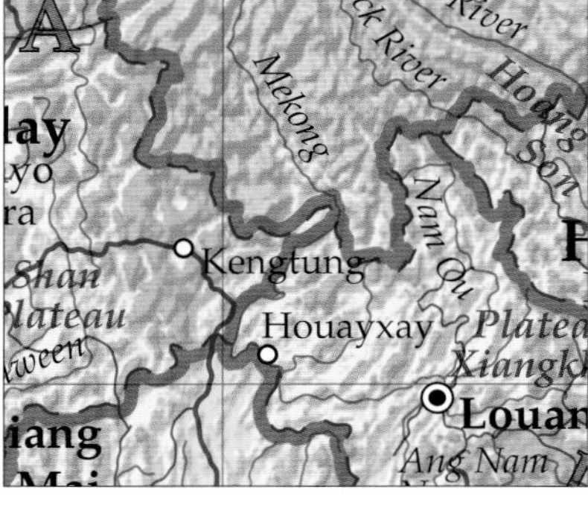
Mekong
Black River
Kengtung
Houayxay
Nam Ou
Shan Plateau
Louan

These mountains are in the north of Southeast Asia. The underlying relief on the map and the coloured bands help you to see the height of the land.

Human features

Maps also reveal a great deal about the human geography of an area. As well as showing where towns and roads are, different symbols can tell you more about the size of towns and the importance of a road. Borders between countries or regions can only be seen on a map.

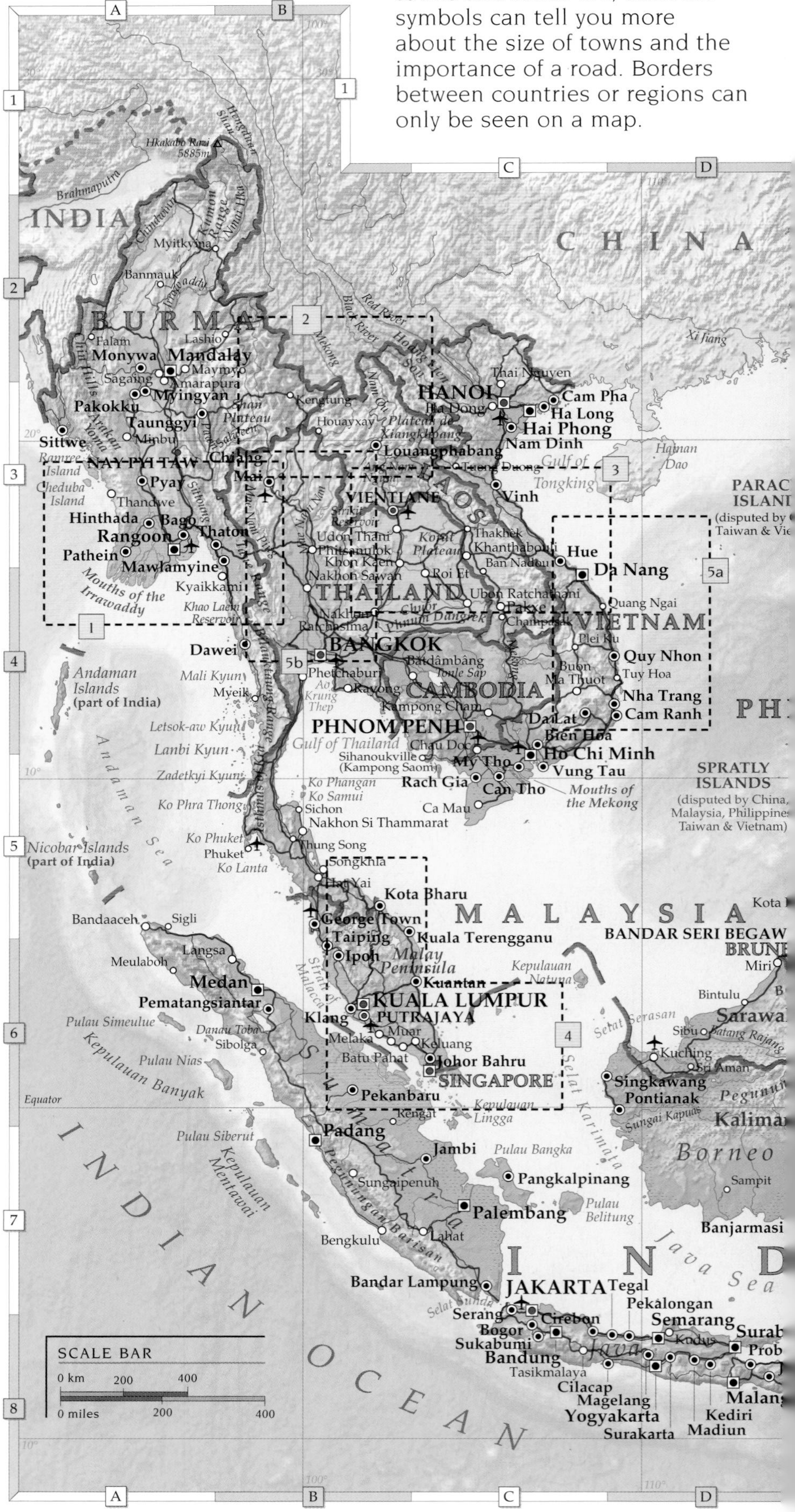

SCALE BAR
0 km 200 400
0 miles 200 400

3 BORDERS

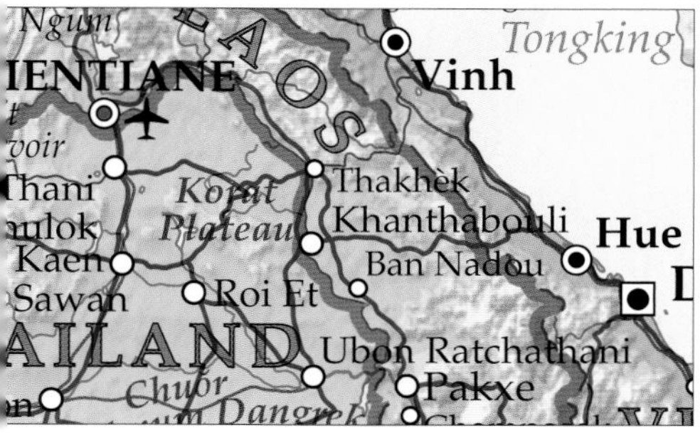

Borders on the map are marked by a thick purple line. The boundary between Laos and Vietnam is in sparsely populated mountainous terrain, with the border generally running along a mountain range.

KEY TO MAP SYMBOLS

BOUNDARIES
- Full international border
- Disputed border

COMMUNICATION FEATURES
- Major road
- Minor road
- Railway
- International airport

DRAINAGE FEATURES
- Major river
- Minor river
- Lake
- Wetland

LANDSCAPE FEATURES
- Mountain

POPULATED PLACES
- Capital city
- Greater than 500,000
- 100,000–500,000
- 50,000–100,000
- Less than 50,000

NAMES

BURMA	Country
PARACEL ISLANDS (disputed by China, Taiwan & Vietnam)	Dependent territory
JAKARTA	Capital city
Sarawak	Cultural region
Chin Hills	Landscape feature
Puncak Jaya 5040m	Mountain/pass
Red River	River/lake
Java Sea	Sea feature

LAND HEIGHT	SEA DEPTH
Above 4000 m	0–250 m
2000–4000 m	250–500 m
1000–2000 m	500–1000 m
500–1000 m	1000–2000 m
250–500 m	2000–3000 m
100–250 m	3000–4000 m
0–100 m	Below 4000 m

CITIES AND TOWNS
- Over 500,000 people
- 100,000–500,000
- 50,000–100,000
- Less than 50,000

MALAYSIA'S TWO CAPITALS
KUALA LUMPUR - capital
PUTRAJAYA - administrative capital

4 SETTLEMENTS

Songkhla
Kota
George Town
Taiping
Ipoh
Peninsula
Kuantan
KUALA LUMPUR
PUTRAJAYA
Muar
Melaka
Keluang
Batu Pahat
Johor Bahru
Pekanbaru

The symbol for a settlement can tell you its position, population and political status. Most towns are shown by a circle or a square. These represent the size of their population. Where a town is coloured red, this shows that it is a capital city such as Kuala Lumpur in Malaysia.

FINDING PLACES

Alphanumeric grid references

All the maps in this book are indexed using their alphanumeric grid reference – for example, G4. To find a place you must first look up its page number and then its grid reference. Read the letters and numbers off the bottom and side of the grid. Using rulers held at right angles to one another you will find the point where the lines meet. The place will be located within this square.

Latitude and longitude references

The lines of latitude and longitude are known as graticules. They are shown on the map as thin blue lines with the value of their latitude or longitude given as a blue number at the edge of the map.

5 ROADS AND RAILWAYS

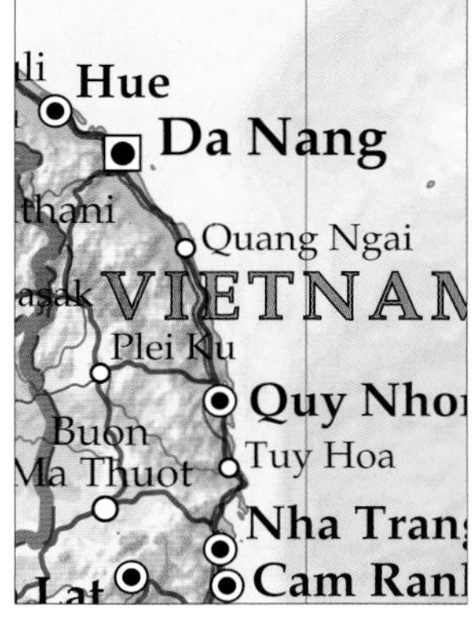
Hue
Da Nang
Quang Ngai
Plei Ku
Tuy Hoa

a The major road and railway links between Hue and Nha Trang hug the Vietnamese coast. A string of coastal towns is often connected by road and rail in this manner.

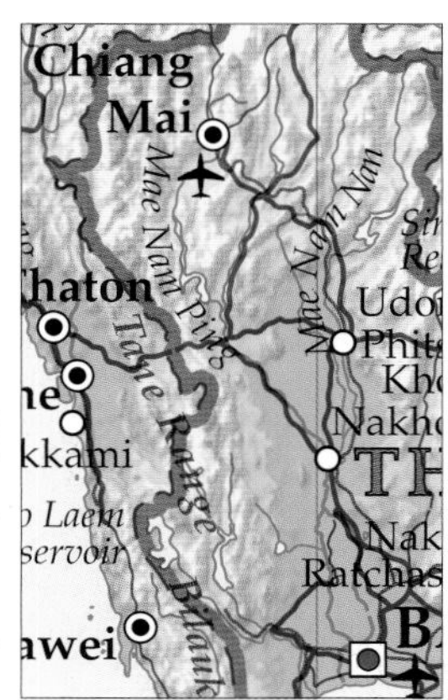
Chiang Mai

Chiang Mai, in northern Thailand, is linked to the capital Bangkok to the south by railway and road. At Chiang Mai, the mountains are too high for the railway to continue, and only roads go north into Burma. b

USING THE ATLAS

This Atlas has been designed to develop map-reading skills and to introduce readers to a wide range of different maps. It also provides a wealth of detailed geographic information about the world today. The Atlas is divided into four sections: **Learning Map Skills**; **The World About Us**, covering global geographic patterns; the **World Atlas**, dealing with the world's regions, and an **Index**.

THE WORLD ABOUT US

These pages contain a series of world maps which show important themes, such as physical features, climate, life zones, population and the world economy, at a global scale. They give a worldwide picture of concepts which are explored in more detail later in the book.

Text introduces themes and concepts in each spread.

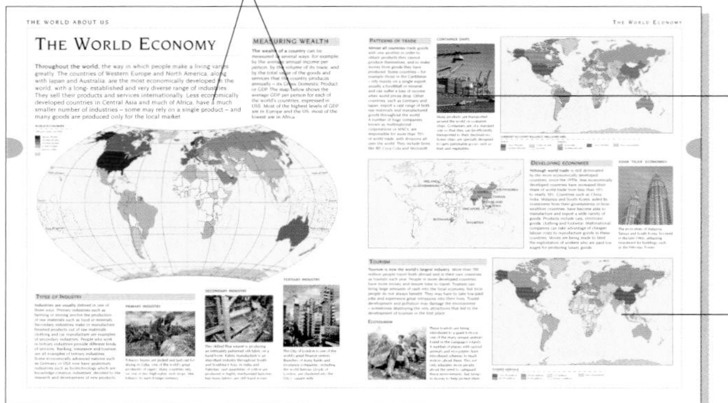
THE WORLD ECONOMY

Photographs illustrate examples of places or topics shown on the main map.

World maps show geographic patterns at a global scale.

LEARNING MAP SKILLS

Maps show the Earth – which is three-dimensional – in just two dimensions. This section shows how maps are made; how different kinds of information are shown on maps; how to choose what to put on a map and the best way to show it. It also explains how to read the maps in this Atlas.

Introduction to projections: different projections and how they work.

Choosing the best projections: the map projections used in this book.

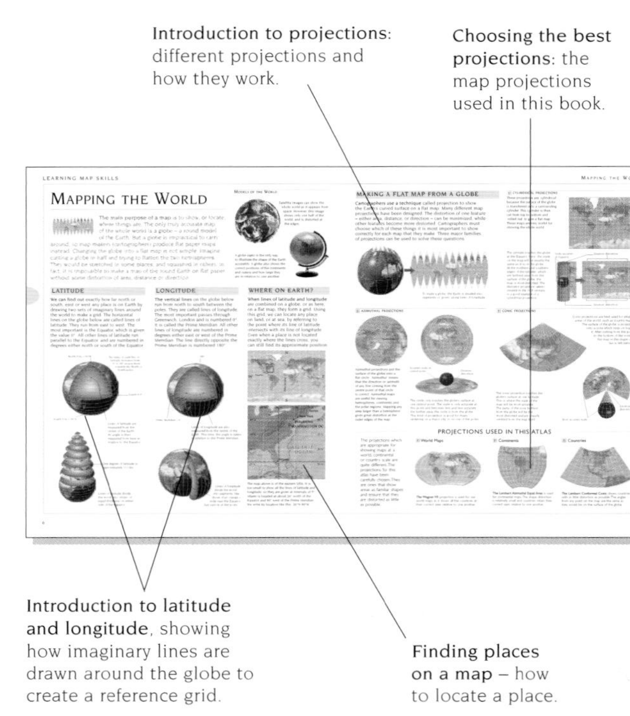
MAPPING THE WORLD

Introduction to latitude and longitude, showing how imaginary lines are drawn around the globe to create a reference grid.

Finding places on a map – how to locate a place.

CONTINENTAL MAPS

A cross-section through the continent shows the relative height of certain features.

A detailed physical map of the continent shows major natural geographic features, including mountains, lakes and rivers.

Photographs and locator maps illustrate the main geographic regions and show you where they are.

The industry map shows the main industrial towns and cities and the main industries in each continent. It also shows the wealth of each country relative to the rest of the world.

The political map of the continent shows country boundaries and country names.

CONTINENTAL PAGES

These pages show the physical shape of each continent and the impact that humans have made on the natural landscape – building towns and roads and creating borders between countries. They show where natural features such as mountain ranges and rivers have created physical boundaries, and where humans have created their own political boundaries between states.

CONTINENTAL GEOGRAPHY PAGES

Humans have colonized and changed all the continents except Antarctica. These pages show the factors which have affected this process: climate, the availability of resources such as coal, oil and minerals, and varying patterns of land use. Mineral resources are directly linked to many industries, and most agriculture is governed both by the quality of the land and the climate.

The climate map shows the main types of climates across the continent and where the hottest and coldest, wettest and driest places are.

The mineral resources map shows where the most important reserves of minerals, including coal and precious metals, are found.

The land use map shows different types of land and the main kinds of farming that take place in each area.

REGIONAL MAPS

The main part of the Atlas contains detailed maps of countries and regions. Each of these is accompanied by a series of small thematic maps, models and charts, which give information about the climate, where people live, how they use the land, the different kinds of industry, and important environmental issues.

TERRAIN MODEL

A computer-generated landscape model shows what the land really looks like. There are no roads or towns to mask the physical geography of the country or region. Mountain ranges, plains and river basins can be easily seen.

COLOURED THUMB TAGS

Each section has its own colour code.

- Learning Map Skills
- The World About Us
- North America
- South America
- Africa
- Europe
- Asia
- Australasia and Oceania
- Antarctica and the Arctic

CLIMATE MAPS

These maps show the temperature and rainfall patterns in January and July. Coloured bands indicate temperatures: blue for low temperatures, orange for high ones. Rainfall is represented by black lines with a number giving the average amount of rain. These are called isohyets.

Isohyets show the rainfall patterns in millimetres per year. The areas between the lines are either over or under the figures shown on the isohyets.

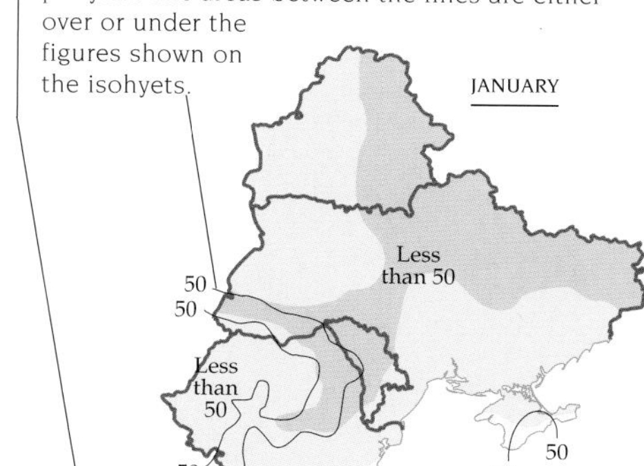

JANUARY
Less than 50
50
50
Less than 50
50
50
50
50

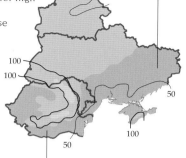

JULY

The hottest areas are coloured orange.

50
100
100
50
100
50

Here the rainfall is between 50 and 100 mm per year.

LOCATOR GLOBE

This shows the location of the country or region both within its continent, and in relation to the rest of the world.

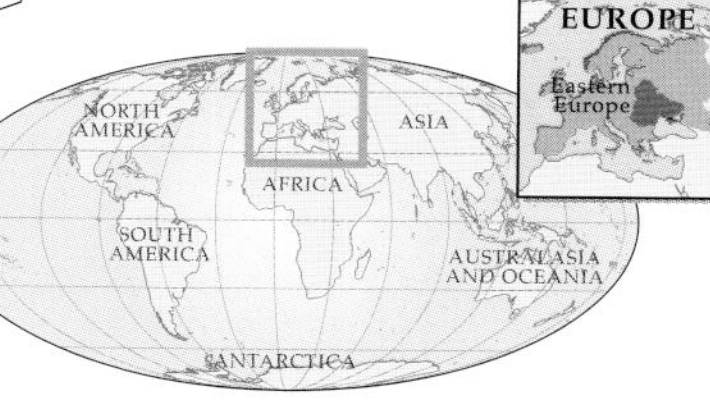

EUROPE
Eastern Europe
NORTH AMERICA
ASIA
AFRICA
SOUTH AMERICA
AUSTRALASIA AND OCEANIA
ANTARCTICA

EASTERN EUROPE

MAP GRID

Each main map has a grid. Using the grid will help you to find a place on the map. Grid references are expressed as letters (running from left to right across the frame), and numbers (running from the top to the bottom of the frame), for example, A-4, G-6. Everything on the map is referenced in the **Index** at the back of the book.

REGIONAL MAPS

The main map on each regional page shows the main topographical features of the area: the height of the land, the major roads, the rivers and lakes. It also shows the main cities and towns in the region – represented by different symbols.

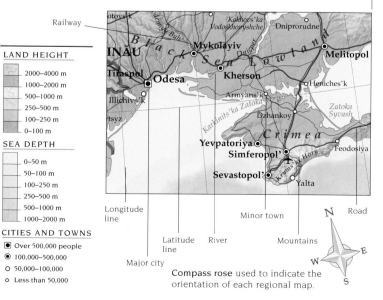

Railway

LAND HEIGHT
- 2000–4000 m
- 1000–2000 m
- 500–1000 m
- 250–500 m
- 100–250 m
- 0–100 m

SEA DEPTH
- 0–50 m
- 50–100 m
- 100–250 m
- 250–500 m
- 500–1000 m
- 1000–2000 m

CITIES AND TOWNS
- Over 500,000 people
- 100,000–500,000
- 50,000–100,000
- Less than 50,000

Longitude line

Latitude line

River

Major city

Minor town

Mountains

Road

Compass rose used to indicate the orientation of each regional map.

THEMATIC MAPS

These small maps show various aspects of the geography of the country or region. The environment maps cover topics such as the effects of pollution. Industry, land use and population maps locate the major industries, types of agriculture and the distribution of population.

Diagrams are used to show the geographic information on the map statistically.

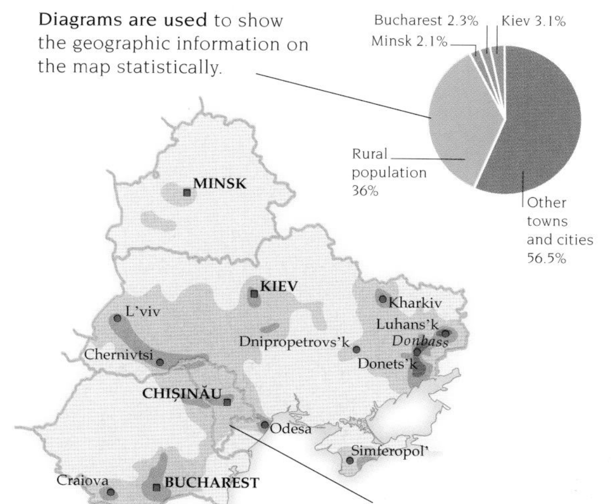

Bucharest 2.3%
Kiev 3.1%
Minsk 2.1%
Rural population 36%
Other towns and cities 56.5%
MINSK
KIEV
L'viv
Kharkiv
Luhans'k
Donbass
Dnipropetrovs'k
Donets'k
Chernivtsi
CHIŞINĂU
Odesa
Simferopol'
Craiova
BUCHAREST

POPULATION MAP

INDUSTRY MAP

LAND USE MAP

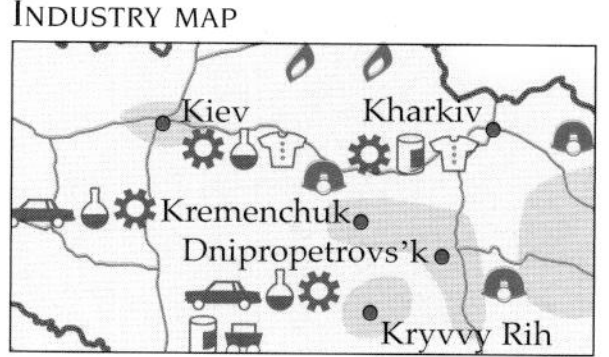

Kiev
Kharkiv
Dnipropetrovs'k
Donets'k

ENVIRONMENT MAP

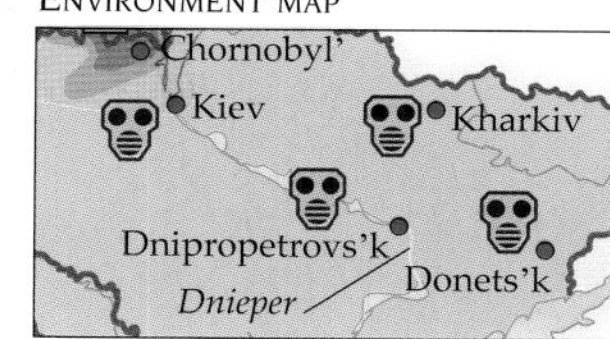

Chornobyl'
Kiev
Kharkiv
Dnipropetrovs'k
Donets'k
Dnieper

THE PHYSICAL WORLD

This map shows the main physical features of the world: the mountain ranges, the great rivers and lakes, deserts, grassland plains, seas and oceans. No human settlements are named on this map – only the physical or landscape features.

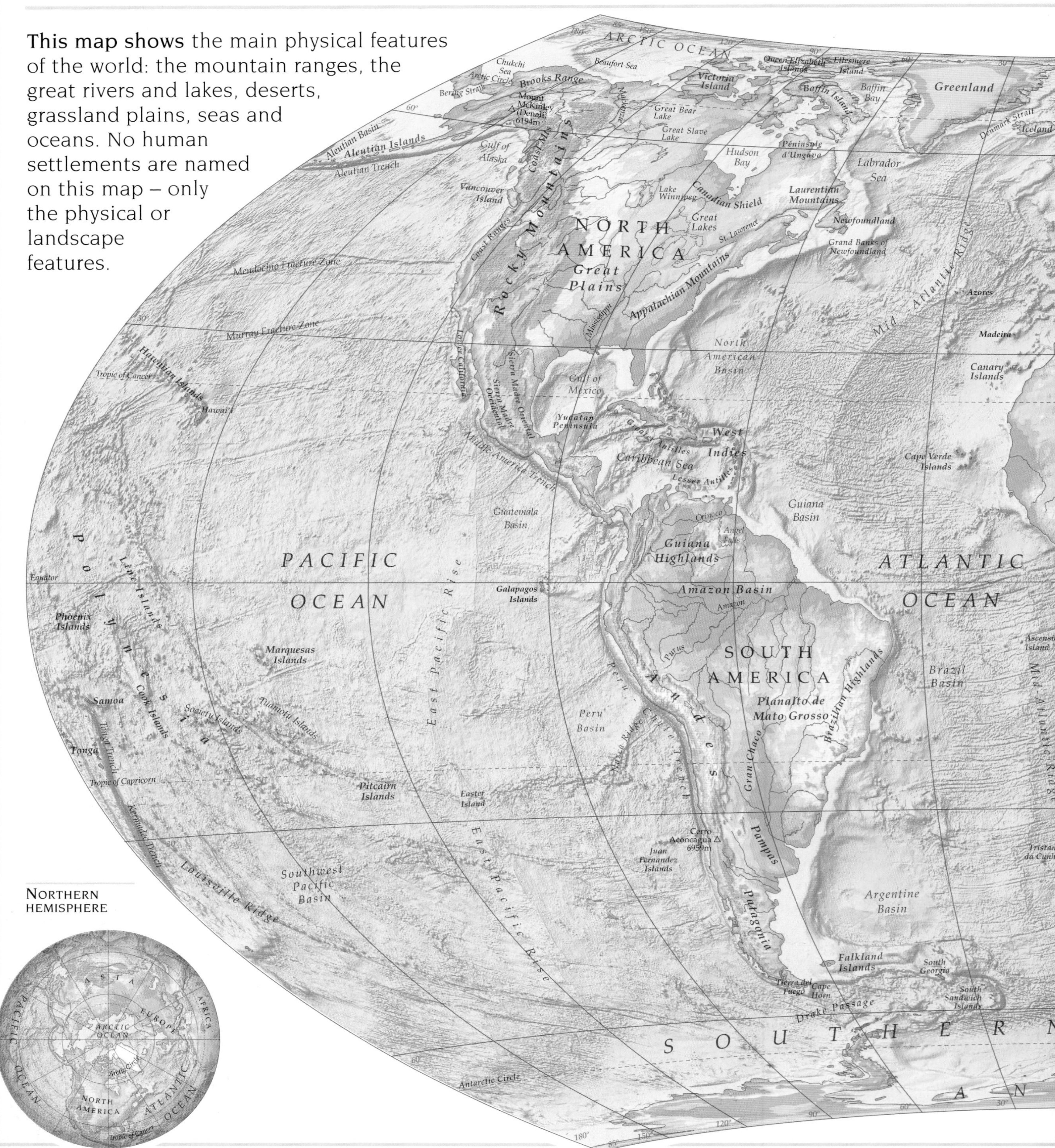
ARCTIC OCEAN
Beaufort Sea
Chukchi Sea
Arctic Circle
Brooks Range
Bering Strait
Mount McKinley (Denali) 6194m
Mackenzie
Victoria Island
Queen Elizabeth Islands
Ellesmere Island
Baffin Island
Baffin Bay
Greenland
Denmark Strait
Iceland
Great Bear Lake
Great Slave Lake
Péninsule d'Ungava
Hudson Bay
Labrador Sea
Aleutian Basin
Aleutian Islands
Aleutian Trench
Gulf of Alaska
Coast Mts
Rocky Mountains
Vancouver Island
Lake Winnipeg
Canadian Shield
Laurentian Mountains
Great Lakes
St. Lawrence
Newfoundland
Grand Banks of Newfoundland
NORTH AMERICA
Great Plains
Coast Ranges
Mendocino Fracture Zone
Appalachian Mountains
Mississippi
Mid Atlantic Ridge
Azores
Madeira
Murray Fracture Zone
Hawaiian Islands
Hawai'i
Tropic of Cancer
Lower California
Sierra Madre Occidental
Sierra Madre Oriental
Gulf of Mexico
North American Basin
Canary Islands
Yucatan Peninsula
Greater Antilles
West Indies
Caribbean Sea
Lesser Antilles
Middle America Trench
Cape Verde Islands
Guatemala Basin
Orinoco
Angel Falls
Guiana Highlands
Guiana Basin
PACIFIC OCEAN
ATLANTIC OCEAN
Equator
Polynesia
Line Islands
Galapagos Islands
Amazon Basin
Amazon
Phoenix Islands
Marquesas Islands
East Pacific Rise
Purus
SOUTH AMERICA
Brazilian Highlands
Brazil Basin
Ascension Island
Mid Atlantic Ridge
Samoa
Cook Islands
Society Islands
Tuamotu Islands
Peru Basin
Peru-Chile Trench
Nazca Ridge
Andes
Planalto de Mato Grosso
Gran Chaco
Tonga
Tonga Trench
Tropic of Capricorn
Pitcairn Islands
Easter Island
Kermadec Trench
Cerro Aconcagua 6959m
Juan Fernandez Islands
Pampas
Tristan da Cunha
Louisville Ridge
Southwest Pacific Basin
Patagonia
Argentine Basin
Falkland Islands
South Georgia
Tierra del Fuego
Cape Horn
South Sandwich Islands
Drake Passage
SOUTHERN
Antarctic Circle
NORTHERN HEMISPHERE
ASIA
EUROPE
AFRICA
ARCTIC OCEAN
PACIFIC OCEAN
Arctic Circle
NORTH AMERICA
ATLANTIC OCEAN
Tropic of Cancer

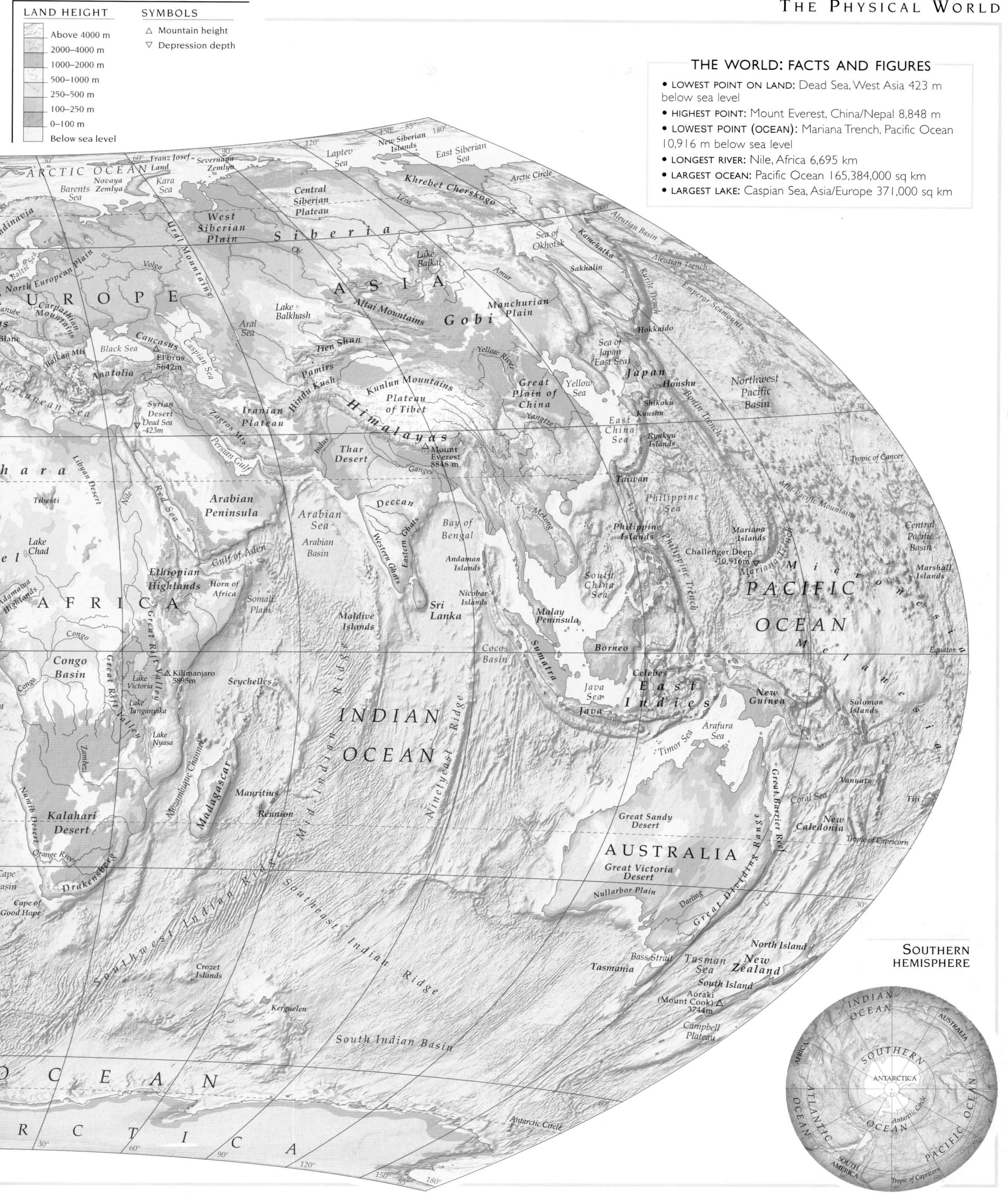
LAND HEIGHT
Above 4000 m
2000–4000 m
1000–2000 m
500–1000 m
250–500 m
100–250 m
0–100 m
Below sea level
SYMBOLS
△ Mountain height
▽ Depression depth
ARCTIC OCEAN
Franz Josef Land
Severnaya Zemlya
New Siberian Islands
Laptev Sea
East Siberian Sea
Barents Sea
Novaya Zemlya
Kara Sea
Central Siberian Plateau
Khrebet Cherskogo
Arctic Circle
West Siberian Plain
Siberia
Ural Mountains
Ob'
Lena
Lake Baikal
Sea of Okhotsk
Kamchatka
Aleutian Basin
Aleutian Trench
Sakhalin
Kurile Trench
Emperor Seamounts
Baltic Sea
North European Plain
Volga
EUROPE
ASIA
Amur
Manchurian Plain
Danube
Carpathian Mountains
Altai Mountains
Gobi
Lake Balkhash
Aral Sea
Caucasus
Black Sea
Caspian Sea
El'brus 5642m
Balkan Mts
Anatolia
Tien Shan
Pamirs
Hindu Kush
Kunlun Mountains
Plateau of Tibet
Himalayas
Yellow River
Great Plain of China
Yellow Sea
Sea of Japan (East Sea)
Hokkaido
Japan
Honshu
Shikoku
Kyushu
Bonin Trench
Northwest Pacific Basin
Syrian Desert
Dead Sea -423m
Zagros Mts
Iranian Plateau
Mediterranean Sea
Yangtze
East China Sea
Ryukyu Islands
Persian Gulf
Indus
Thar Desert
Mount Everest 8848 m
Ganges
Taiwan
Tropic of Cancer
Sahara
Libyan Desert
Tibesti
Nile
Red Sea
Arabian Peninsula
Arabian Sea
Deccan
Bay of Bengal
Mekong
Philippine Sea
Mid-Pacific Mountains
Arabian Basin
Western Ghats
Eastern Ghats
Andaman Islands
Philippine Islands
Philippine Trench
Mariana Islands
Central Pacific Basin
Lake Chad
Gulf of Aden
Challenger Deep -10,916m
Mariana Trench
Micronesia
Marshall Islands
Ethiopian Highlands
Horn of Africa
Nicobar Islands
South China Sea
PACIFIC OCEAN
AFRICA
Somali Plain
Sri Lanka
Malay Peninsula
Maldive Islands
Congo
Great Rift Valley
Borneo
Cocos Basin
Sumatra
Melanesia
Equator
Congo Basin
Kilimanjaro 5895m
Seychelles
Celebes
East Indies
Lake Victoria
Java Sea
Java
New Guinea
Solomon Islands
Lake Tanganyika
INDIAN OCEAN
Ninetyeast Ridge
Mid-Indian Ridge
Timor Sea
Arafura Sea
Lake Nyasa
Zambezi
Mozambique Channel
Madagascar
Mauritius
Réunion
Great Barrier Reef
Coral Sea
Vanuatu
Fiji
Namib Desert
Kalahari Desert
Great Sandy Desert
New Caledonia
Tropic of Capricorn
Orange River
AUSTRALIA
Great Dividing Range
Cape Basin
Drakensberg
Great Victoria Desert
Nullarbor Plain
Darling
Cape of Good Hope
Southwest Indian Ridge
Southeast Indian Ridge
North Island
New Zealand
Bass Strait
Tasman Sea
Tasmania
South Island
Crozet Islands
Aoraki (Mount Cook) 3744m
Kerguelen
Campbell Plateau
South Indian Basin
OCEAN
ANTARCTICA
Antarctic Circle
SOUTHERN HEMISPHERE
INDIAN OCEAN
AUSTRALIA
AFRICA
SOUTHERN OCEAN
ATLANTIC OCEAN
PACIFIC OCEAN
SOUTH AMERICA
Tropic of Capricorn

THE WORLD: FACTS AND FIGURES

- LOWEST POINT ON LAND: Dead Sea, West Asia 423 m below sea level
- HIGHEST POINT: Mount Everest, China/Nepal 8,848 m
- LOWEST POINT (OCEAN): Mariana Trench, Pacific Ocean 10,916 m below sea level
- LONGEST RIVER: Nile, Africa 6,695 km
- LARGEST OCEAN: Pacific Ocean 165,384,000 sq km
- LARGEST LAKE: Caspian Sea, Asia/Europe 371,000 sq km

THE EARTH'S STRUCTURE

The shape and position of the Earth's oceans and continents make a familiar pattern. This is just the latest in a series of forms which the Earth has taken in the hundreds of millions of years since its creation. Massive forces inside the Earth cause the continents and oceans to move apart and together again, forming larger landmasses and then breaking them apart – a process known as plate tectonics. The movement is very slow – but over millions of years, the changes can be enormous.

DYNAMIC EARTH

The heart of the Earth is a solid core of iron surrounded by several layers of very hot – sometimes liquid – rock. The crust is relatively thin and is made up of a series of 'plates' which fit closely together. Movement of the molten rock deep within the mantle of the Earth causes the plates to move, creating changes in the surface features of the Earth.

THE EARTH'S PLATES

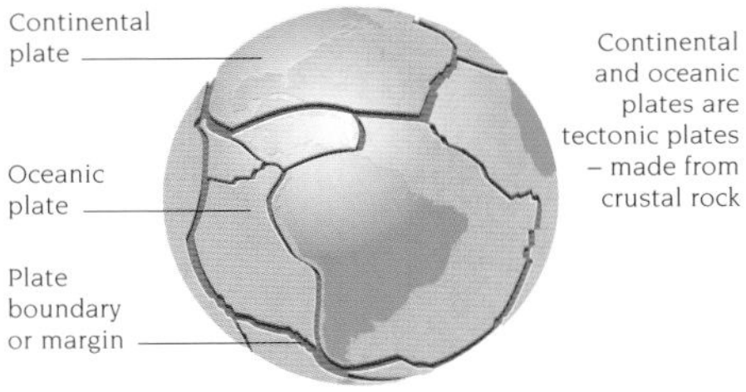

Continental plate

Oceanic plate

Plate boundary or margin

Continental and oceanic plates are tectonic plates – made from crustal rock

INSIDE THE EARTH

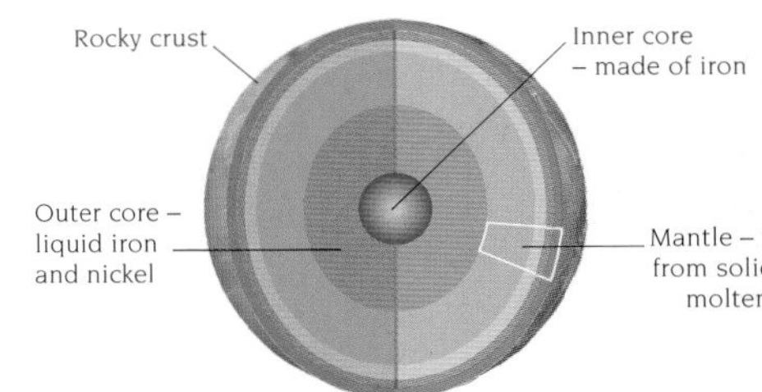
Rocky crust
Inner core – made of iron
Outer core – liquid iron and nickel
Mantle – r
from solid
molten

TECTONIC PLATES, VOLCANOES AND EARTHQUAKES

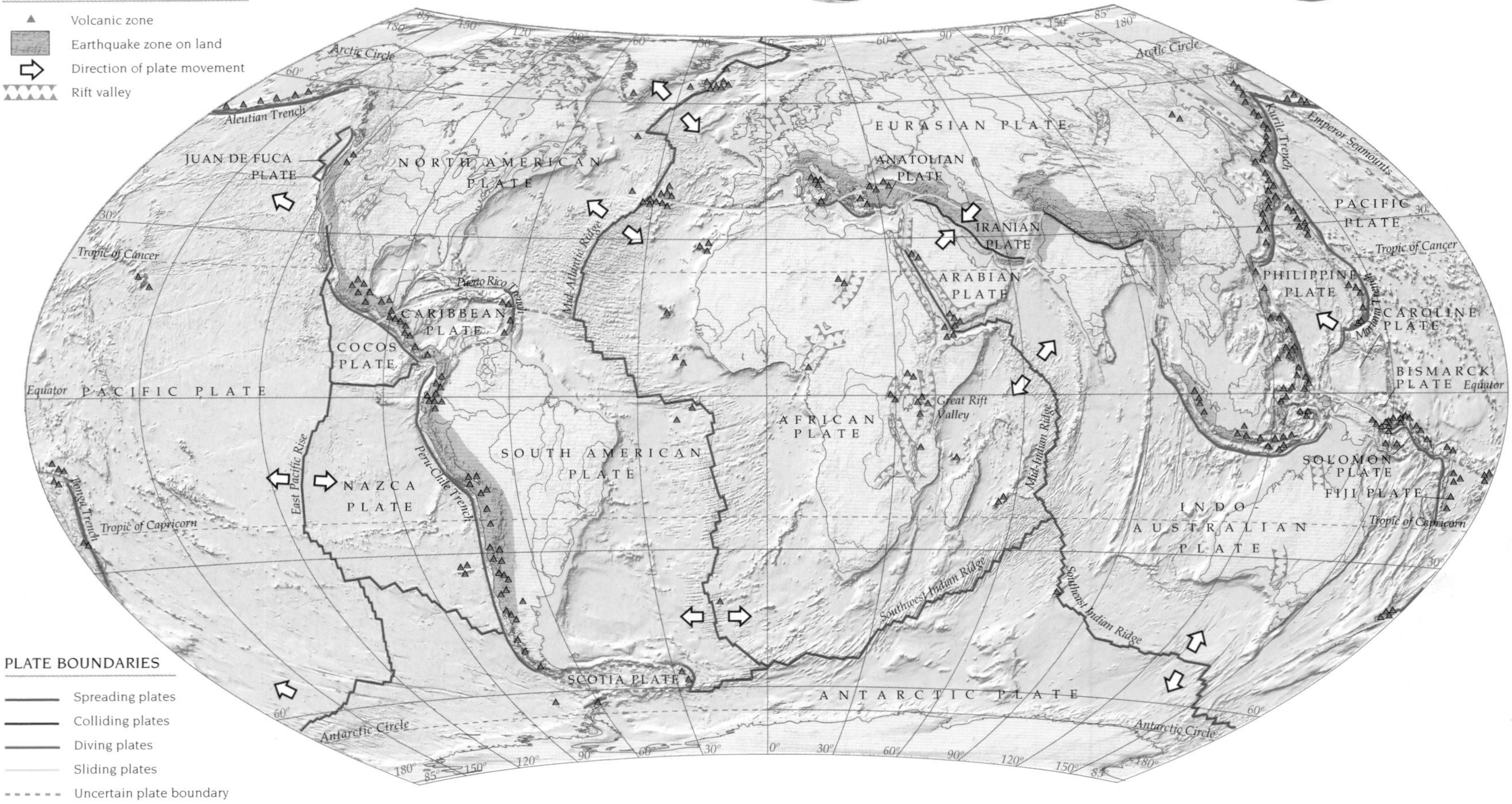

- Volcanic zone
- Earthquake zone on land
- Direction of plate movement
- Rift valley

PLATE BOUNDARIES

- Spreading plates
- Colliding plates
- Diving plates
- Sliding plates
- Uncertain plate boundary

PLATE BOUNDARIES

The point where two plates meet is known as a plate boundary. As the Earth's plates move together or apart or slide alongside one another, the great forces which result cause great changes in the landscape. Mountains can be created, earthquakes occur and there may be frequent volcanic eruptions.

SPREADING PLATES

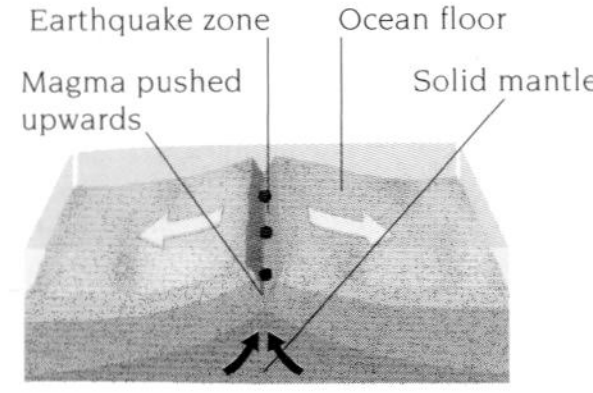
Earthquake zone
Ocean floor
Magma pushed upwards
Solid mantle

As plates move apart, magma rises through the outer mantle. When it cools, it forms new crust. The Mid-Atlantic Ridge is caused by spreading plates.

COLLIDING PLATES

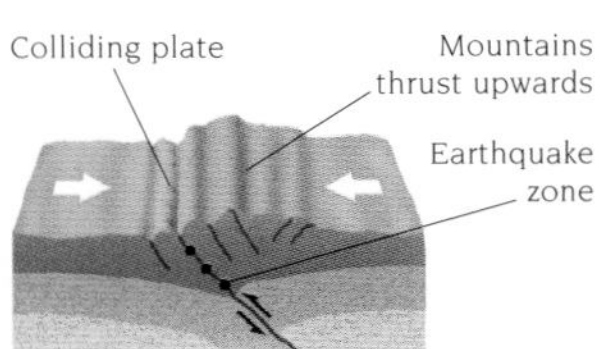
Colliding plate
Mountains thrust upwards
Earthquake zone

When two plates bearing landmasses collide with one another, the land is crumpled upwards into high mountain peaks such as the Alps, and the Himalayas.

DIVING PLATES

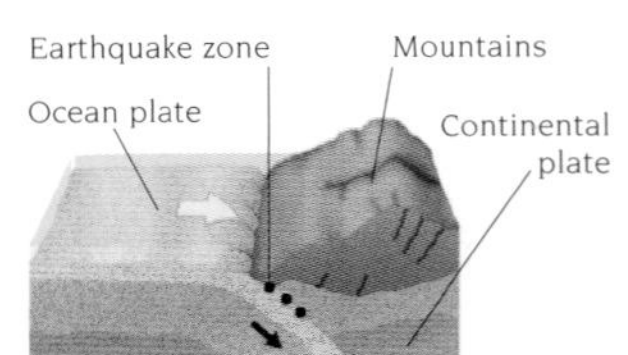
Earthquake zone
Mountains
Ocean plate
Continental plate

When an ocean-bearing plate collides with a continental plate it is forced downwards under the other plate and into the mantle. Volcanoes occur along these boundaries.

SLIDING PLATES

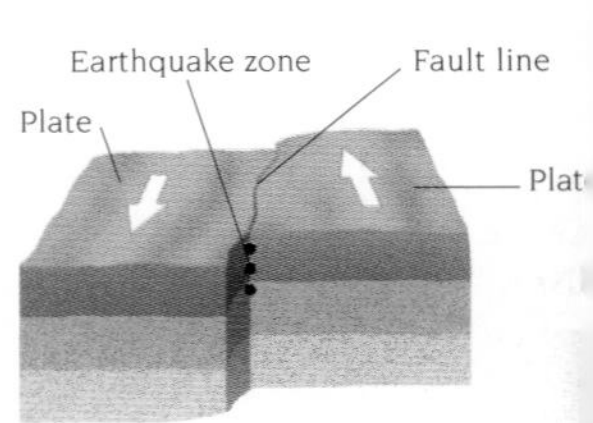
Earthquake zone
Fault line
Plate
Plat

As two plates slide past each other, great friction is set up along the fault line which lies between them. This can lead to powerful earthquakes.

SHAPING THE LANDSCAPE

The Earth's surface is made from solid rock or water. The land is constantly re-shaped by external forces. Water flowing as rivers or in the oceans erodes and deposits material to create valleys and lakes and to shape coastlines. When water is built up and compressed into solid sheets of ice, it can erode more deeply, creating deeper, wider valleys. Wind also has a powerful effect; stripping away vegetation and transporting rock particles vast distances.

RIVERS

Most rivers have their sources in mountain areas. They flow fast through the mountains, eroding deep V-shaped valleys. As they reach flatter areas they begin to meander in great loops, both eroding and then depositing rock particles as they slow down.

GLACIERS

In cold areas, close to the poles or on mountain tops, snow is built up into rivers of ice called glaciers. They move slowly, eroding deep U-shaped valleys. When the glacier melts, ridges of eroded rock called moraines are left at the sides and end of the glacier.

SEA ACTION

The oceans change the landscape in two major ways. They batter cliffs, causing rock to break away and the land to retreat, and they carry eroded material along the coast, to make beaches and sand bars.

WIND

Wind can erode and break down rock into smaller boulders and stones and eventually into sand. Desert sand dunes are shaped by the force of the wind and vary from ripples to hills 200 m high.

LANDSLIDES

Heavy rain can loosen soil and rock beneath the surface of slopes. As this moves, the top layers slip forward, to form heaps of rubble at the base of the slope.

THE WORLD'S OCEANS

Just over two-thirds of the Earth's surface is covered by water and more than 97% of this water is contained in the oceans. Movements within the Earth shape the ocean floor in the same way as they do the land surface, creating mountain ranges, trenches and plateaus, and changing the shape and size of the oceans. The difference between an ocean and a sea is simply its size; oceans are much bigger.

POLAR OCEANS

The Southern and Arctic Oceans contain large icebergs, that have broken away from the ice shelf.

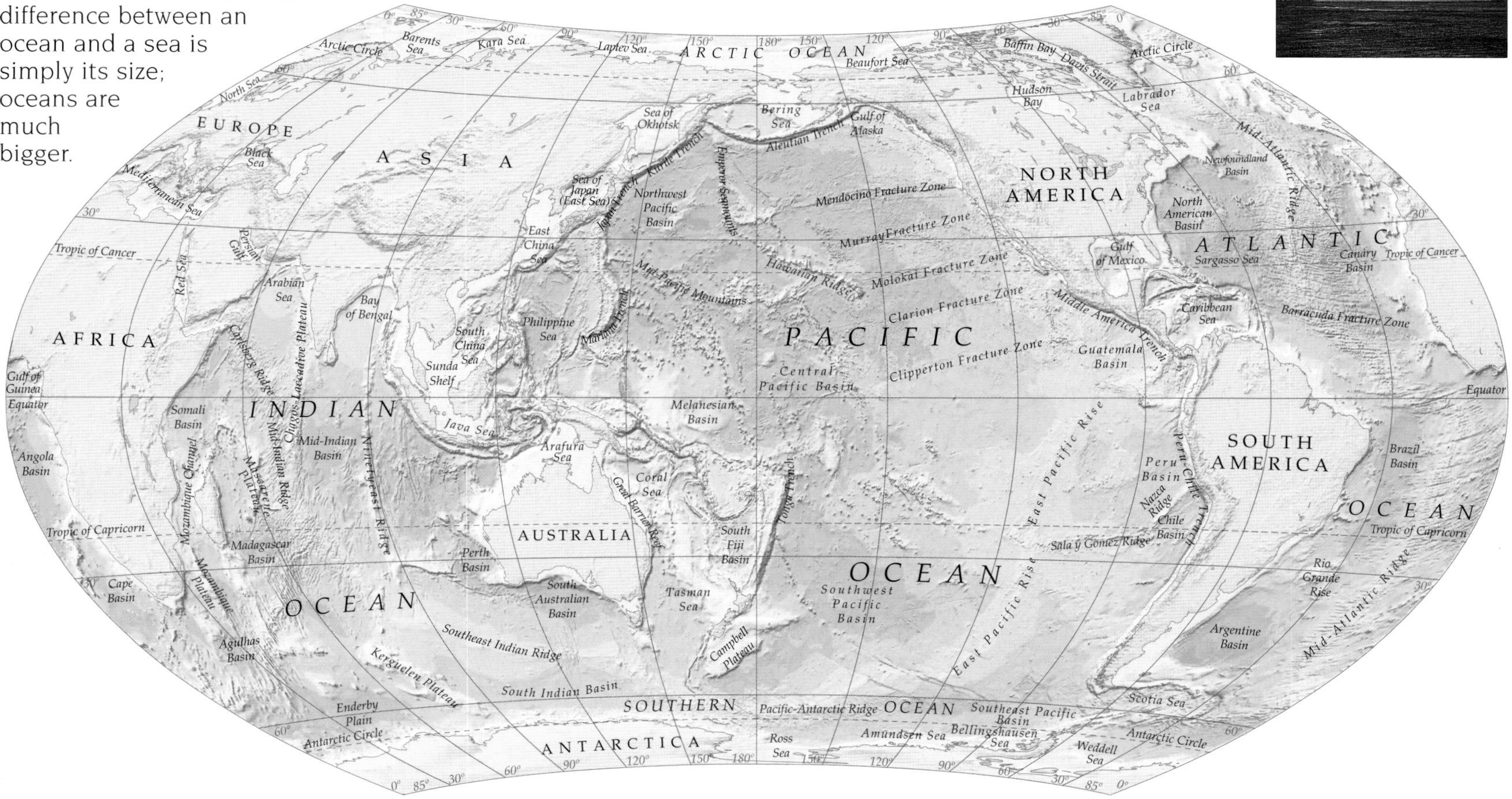

ARCTIC OCEAN
Arctic Circle
Barents Sea
Kara Sea
Laptev Sea
Beaufort Sea
Baffin Bay
Davis Strait
Hudson Bay
Labrador Sea
North Sea
EUROPE
ASIA
Black Sea
Mediterranean Sea
Sea of Okhotsk
Bering Sea
Gulf of Alaska
Aleutian Trench
Sea of Japan (East Sea)
Kuril Trench
Japan Trench
Emperor Seamounts
Northwest Pacific Basin
Mendocino Fracture Zone
Murray Fracture Zone
Hawaiian Ridge
Molokai Fracture Zone
Clarion Fracture Zone
Clipperton Fracture Zone
NORTH AMERICA
Newfoundland Basin
North American Basin
Mid-Atlantic Ridge
Gulf of Mexico
ATLANTIC
Sargasso Sea
Canary Basin
Tropic of Cancer
Caribbean Sea
Barracuda Fracture Zone
Middle America Trench
Guatemala Basin
East China Sea
Mid-Pacific Mountains
Mariana Trench
Philippine Sea
South China Sea
Sunda Shelf
Persian Gulf
Red Sea
Arabian Sea
Bay of Bengal
Carlsberg Ridge
Chagos-Laccadive Plateau
AFRICA
Gulf of Guinea
Equator
Somali Basin
INDIAN
Mid-Indian Basin
Mid-Indian Ridge
Ninetyeast Ridge
Java Sea
Arafura Sea
Coral Sea
Great Barrier Reef
Melanesian Basin
PACIFIC
Central Pacific Basin
Tonga Trench
East Pacific Rise
Peru Basin
Peru-Chile Trench
Nazca Ridge
Chile Basin
Sala y Gomez Ridge
SOUTH AMERICA
Brazil Basin
OCEAN
Tropic of Capricorn
Angola Basin
Mozambique Channel
Mascarene Plateau
Madagascar Basin
Mozambique Plateau
Cape Basin
Agulhas Basin
AUSTRALIA
Perth Basin
South Australian Basin
Tasman Sea
South Fiji Basin
Campbell Plateau
Southwest Pacific Basin
Rio Grande Rise
Argentine Basin
Southeast Indian Ridge
Kerguelen Plateau
South Indian Basin
Enderby Plain
Antarctic Circle
SOUTHERN OCEAN
Pacific-Antarctic Ridge
Southeast Pacific Basin
Bellingshausen Sea
Amundsen Sea
Ross Sea
ANTARCTICA
Scotia Sea
Weddell Sea

INDIAN OCEAN

The Indian Ocean covers about 20% of the world's surface. Ocean swells, starting deep in the Southern Ocean, often cause flooding in Sri Lanka and the Maldives.

PACIFIC OCEAN

The Pacific is the largest and deepest ocean in the world. It is surrounded an arc of volcanoes, including Japan, Indonesia and the Andes, known as the 'Ring of Fire'.

ATLANTIC OCEAN

The Atlantic Ocean was formed about 180 million years ago. The land which now forms Europe and Africa pulled apart from the Americas to create an ocean 3,000 km wide.

Climate and Life Zones

This map shows the different climates found around the world. Climates are particular combinations of temperature and humidity. Climates are affected by latitude, the height of the land, winds and ocean currents. Climates can change, but not overnight. Weather is local and consists of short-term events such as thunderstorms, hurricanes and blizzards.

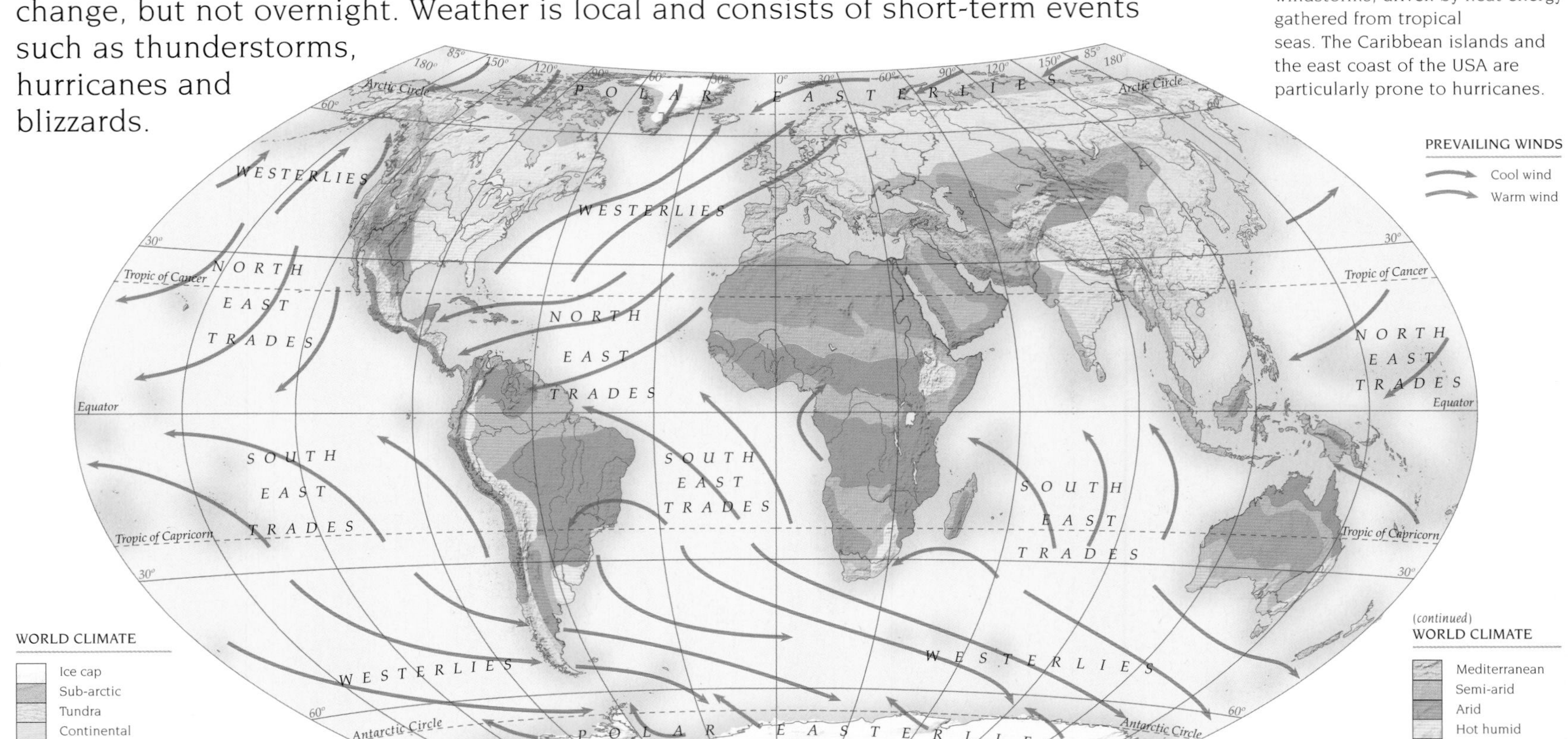
POLAR EASTERLIES
WESTERLIES
WESTERLIES
NORTH EAST TRADES
NORTH EAST TRADES
NORTH EAST TRADES
SOUTH EAST TRADES
SOUTH EAST TRADES
SOUTH EAST TRADES
WESTERLIES
WESTERLIES
POLAR EASTERLIES
Arctic Circle
Tropic of Cancer
Equator
Tropic of Capricorn
Antarctic Circle
30°
60°
180°
150°
120°
90°
60°
30°
0°

HURRICANES

Hurricanes are violent cyclonic windstorms, driven by heat energy gathered from tropical seas. The Caribbean islands and the east coast of the USA are particularly prone to hurricanes.

PREVAILING WINDS

- Cool wind
- Warm wind

WORLD CLIMATE

- Ice cap
- Sub-arctic
- Tundra
- Continental
- Temperate
- Warm temperate

(continued) WORLD CLIMATE

- Mediterranean
- Semi-arid
- Arid
- Hot humid
- Humid equatorial
- Tropical

Climate change

The Earth's climate is a constantly changing system resulting from a complex interaction of different geographical factors. Throughout history there have been several periods when the Earth's climate has been either hotter or colder than today. However, many scientists think that human activity is causing problems to this system by increasing levels of 'greenhouse gases' in the atmosphere. These gases, including carbon dioxide (CO_2), allow heat from the Sun to enter the atmosphere and then trap some of this heat like a greenhouse. Most scientists believe that unless action is taken to reduce greenhouse gases, temperatures will rise in a process known as global warming.

MAP KEY

Predicted change in average surface air temperature between 1960–1990 and 2070–2100

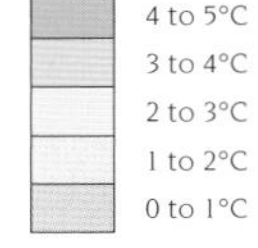

- 4 to 5°C
- 3 to 4°C
- 2 to 3°C
- 1 to 2°C
- 0 to 1°C

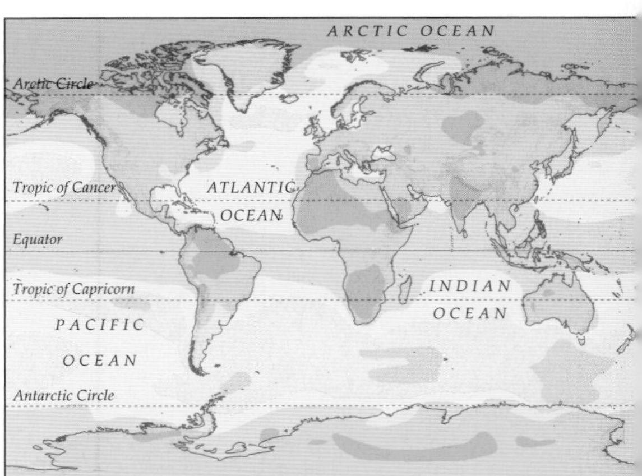
ARCTIC OCEAN
Arctic Circle
Tropic of Cancer
ATLANTIC OCEAN
Equator
Tropic of Capricorn
INDIAN OCEAN
PACIFIC OCEAN
Antarctic Circle

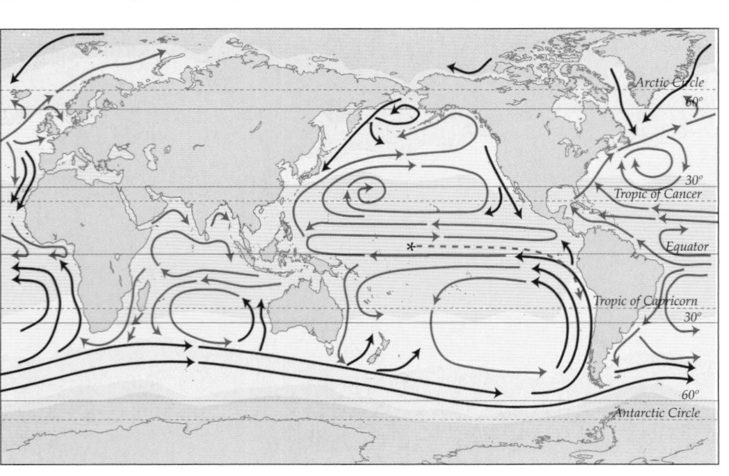
Arctic Circle
60°
30°
Tropic of Cancer
Equator
Tropic of Capricorn
30°
60°
Antarctic Circle

Ocean currents

Ocean currents help to distribute heat around the Earth and have a great influence on climate. Convection currents circulate massive amounts of warm and cold water around the oceans. Warm water is moved away from the tropics to higher latitudes and cold water is moved toward the tropics.

OCEAN CURRENTS AND SURFACE TEMPERATURES

- Cold currents
- Warm currents
- El Niño

- 20 to 30°C
- 10 to 20°C
- 0 to 10°C
- Sea-water –2° to 0°C
- Sea-ice (average) below –2°C

LIFE ZONES

The map below shows the Earth divided into different biomes – also called biogeographical regions. The combination of climate, the type of landscape, and the plants and animals that live there, are used to classify a region. Similar biomes are found in very different places around the world.

POLAR REGIONS

The North and South poles are permanently covered by ice. Only a few plants and animals can live here.

TUNDRA

Tundra is flat, cold and dry with few trees. Plants such as mosses and lichens grow close to the ground.

DESERTS

Very little rain falls in desert areas, whether they are hot deserts such as the Sahara or cold deserts like the Gobi.

NEEDLELEAF FORESTS

Tall coniferous trees such as pine and spruce, with spines or needles instead of leaves, grow in the far north of Scandinavia, Canada and the Russian Federation.

BROADLEAF FORESTS

Broadleaf or deciduous forests once covered temperate regions over most of the northern hemisphere. They contain trees of many varieties – all of which shed their leaves every year.

TEMPERATE RAINFORESTS

Evergreen, broadleaved trees need a warmer, wetter climate than deciduous trees. They are known as temperate rainforests.

MEDITERRANEAN

Close to the shores of the Mediterranean Sea, the vegetation consists mainly of herbs, shrubs and drought-resistant trees.

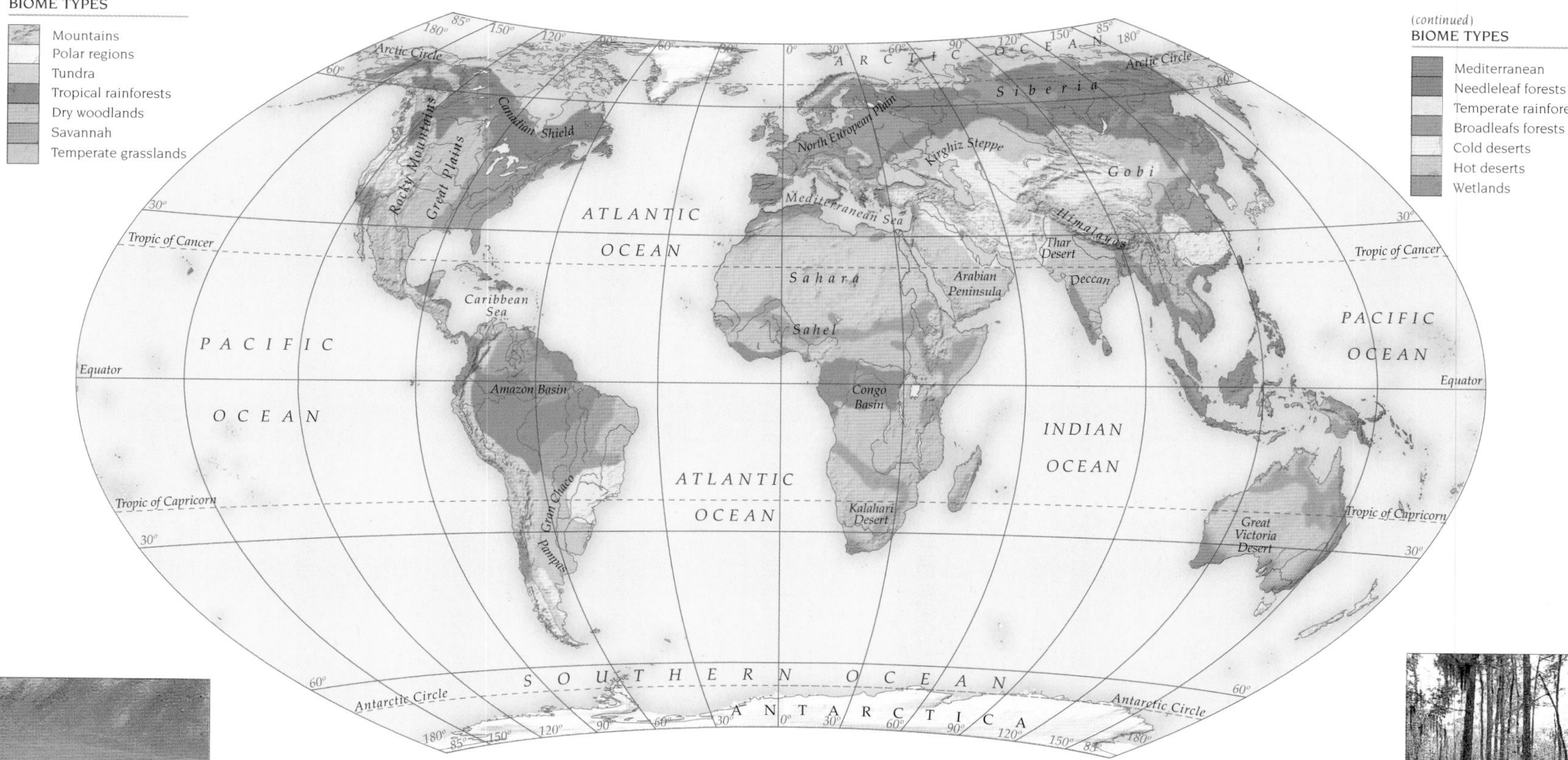
BIOME TYPES
Mountains
Polar regions
Tundra
Tropical rainforests
Dry woodlands
Savannah
Temperate grasslands
(continued) BIOME TYPES
Mediterranean
Needleleaf forests
Temperate rainforests
Broadleafs forests
Cold deserts
Hot deserts
Wetlands
ARCTIC OCEAN
Arctic Circle
Siberia
Canadian Shield
Rocky Mountains
Great Plains
North European Plain
Kirghiz Steppe
Gobi
Mediterranean Sea
Himalayas
Thar Desert
Deccan
ATLANTIC OCEAN
Tropic of Cancer
Sahara
Arabian Peninsula
Caribbean Sea
Sahel
PACIFIC OCEAN
Equator
Amazon Basin
Congo Basin
INDIAN OCEAN
Gran Chaco
Pampas
Kalahari Desert
Great Victoria Desert
Tropic of Capricorn
SOUTHERN OCEAN
Antarctic Circle
ANTARCTICA

TEMPERATE GRASSLANDS

Grasslands cover the central areas of the continents. They are known in the middle latitudes as prairies, steppe and pampas.

SAVANNAH

The savannah consists of woodland, interspersed with grassland. These regions lie between the tropical rainforest and hot desert regions.

DRY WOODLANDS

Dry woodlands are found at the edge of grasslands. They contain small trees and shrubs adapted to dry conditions.

TROPICAL RAINFORESTS

Around the Equator, where temperatures are high and there is plenty of rain, tropical rainforests can flourish. Trees grow continuously and are tall with huge, broad leaves.

WETLANDS

Low-lying swamps and marshes are known as wetlands. They are often home to a rich variety of animal, plant and bird species.

WORLD POPULATION

There are now just over 7 billion people on Earth. The population has increased nearly four times since 1900. Before that date, the number of people increased slowly as people were born and died at similar rates. With improved living conditions, better medical care and more efficient food production, more people survived to adulthood and the population began to grow much faster. If growth continues at the present rate, the world's population is likely to reach 7.5 billion by the year 2020.

OVERCROWDING

Favelas – or shanty towns – have grown up around many South American cities because of overcrowding.

POPULATION STRUCTURES

Measuring the numbers of old and young people gives the age structure of a country or continent. If there are large numbers of young people and a high birth rate, the population is said to be youthful – as is the case in many African, Asian and South American countries. If the birth-rate is low but many people survive into old age, the population distribution is said to be ageing – this is true of much of Europe, Japan, Canada and the USA. Extreme events like wars can distort the population, leading to a loss of population in certain age groups.

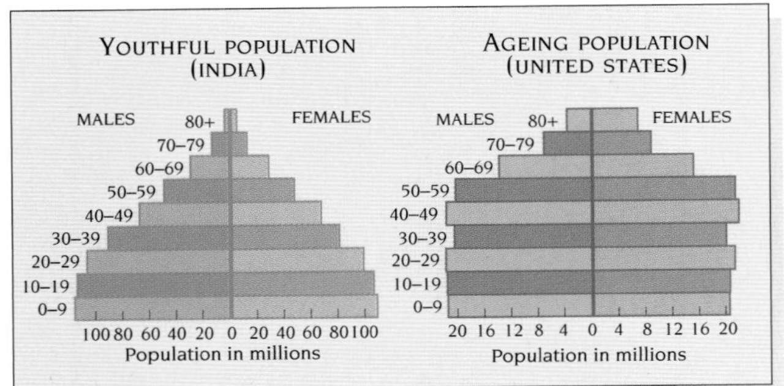
YOUTHFUL POPULATION (INDIA)
MALES
FEMALES
80+
70–79
60–69
50–59
40–49
30–39
20–29
10–19
0–9
100 80 60 40 20 0 20 40 60 80 100
Population in millions
AGEING POPULATION (UNITED STATES)
MALES
FEMALES
80+
70–79
60–69
50–59
40–49
30–39
20–29
10–19
0–9
20 16 12 8 4 0 4 8 12 16 20
Population in millions

POPULATION DENSITY

The main map (*centre*) and the map below both show population density – the number of people who live in a given area. The map below shows the average population density per country. You can see that European countries and parts of Asia are very densely populated. The large map shows where people actually live. While the average population density in Brazil and Egypt is quite low, the coasts of Brazil and the areas close to the River Nile in Egypt are very densely populated.

DENSE POPULATION

Huge crowds near the Haora Bridge in Kolkata (Calcutta), India – one of the world's most densely populated cities.

POPULATION DENSITY

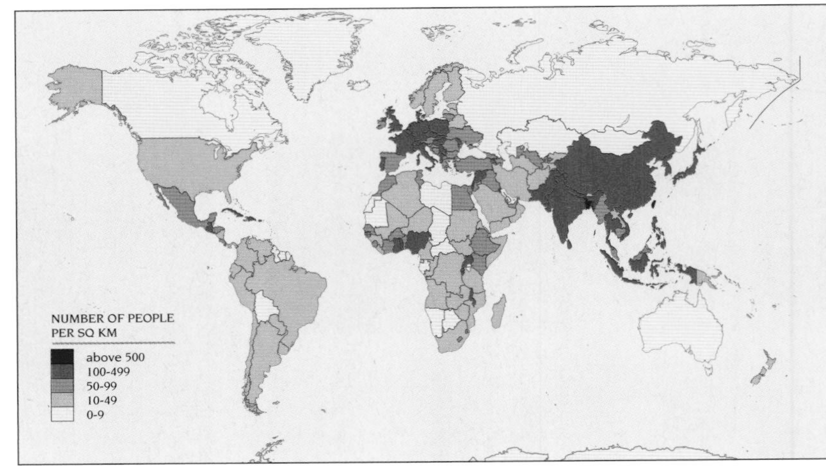
NUMBER OF PEOPLE PER SQ KM
above 500
100-499
50-99
10-49
0-9

SPARSE POPULATION

The cold north of Canada has one of the lowest population densities in the world. Some people live in extreme isolation, separated from others by lakes and forests.

URBAN GROWTH

The 20th century saw a huge increase in the number of people living in cities. This has led to more large cities and the development of some 'super cities' such as Mexico City and Tokyo, each with more than 20 million people. In 1900, only about 10% of the population lived in cities. Now it is closer to 50% and soon the figure may be nearer two in three people. Some continents are far more 'urbanized' than others: in South America nearly 80% of people live in cities, whereas in Africa the figure is only about 30%.

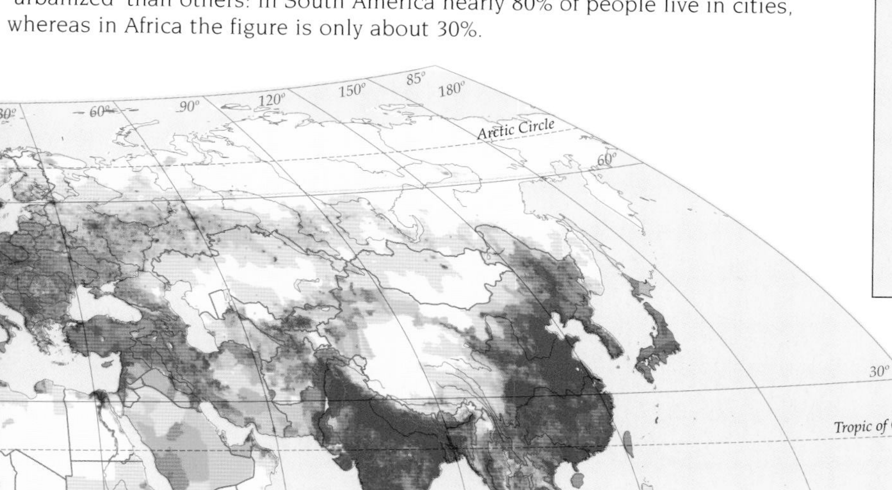

Arctic Circle
Tropic of Cancer
Equator
Tropic of Capricorn
Antarctic Circle
POPULATION DENSITY
(People per sq km)
Below 1
1–5
6–10
11–20
21–50
51–100
101–200
Above 200

LEVELS OF URBANIZATION

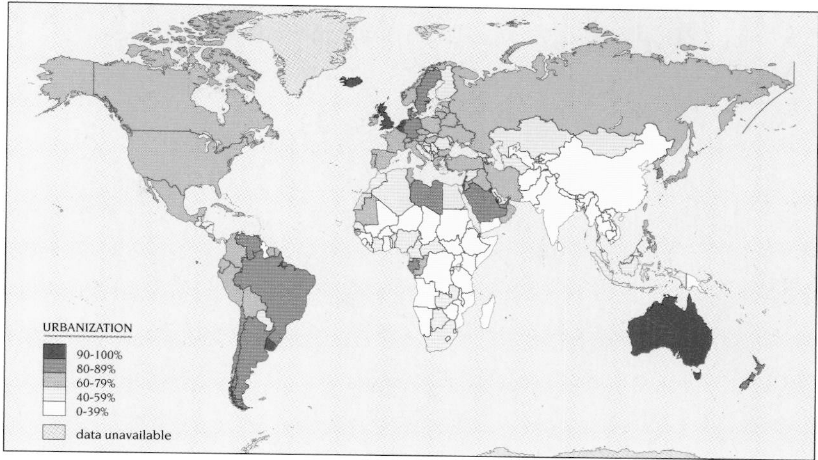

URBANIZATION
90-100%
80-89%
60-79%
40-59%
0-39%
data unavailable

POPULATION GROWTH

The rate of population growth varies dramatically between the continents. Europe has a large population but it is increasing slowly. Africa is still sparsely populated, but in some countries such as Kenya, the population is growing very rapidly, increasing pressure on the land. China and India have the world's largest populations. Both countries now have laws to try and curb the birth rate.

CONTROLLING GROWTH

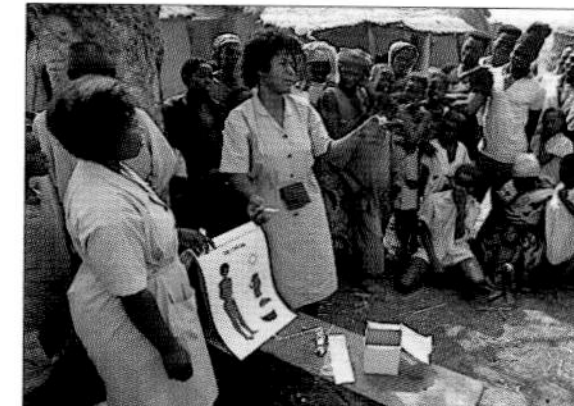

In 1980, fewer than 25% of women in less developed countries used birth control. Education programmes and more widely available contraceptives are thought to have doubled this figure. But many families still have no access to contraception.

AN AGEING POPULATION

In some countries, a low birth-rate, and an increasingly long-lived elderly population has greatly increased the ratio of old people to younger people, putting a strain on health and social services. For example, in Japan, most people can now expect to live to at least 80 years of age.

BIRTH RATE

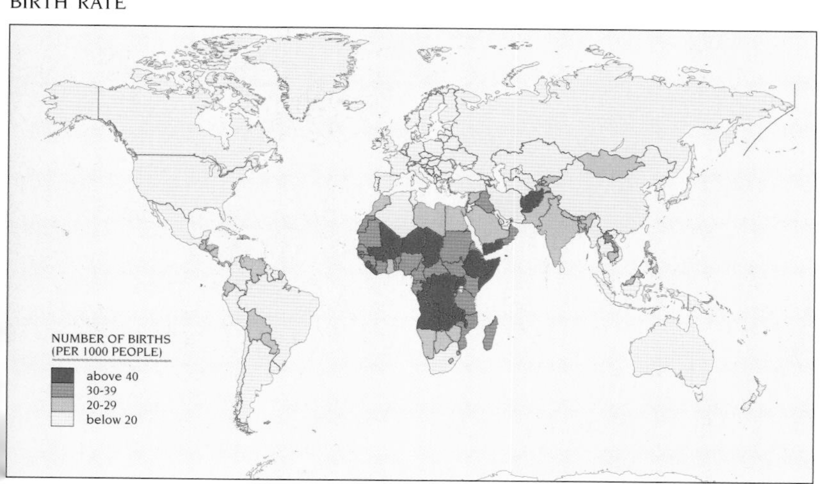

NUMBER OF BIRTHS
(PER 1000 PEOPLE)
above 40
30-39
20-29
below 20

LIFE EXPECTANCY

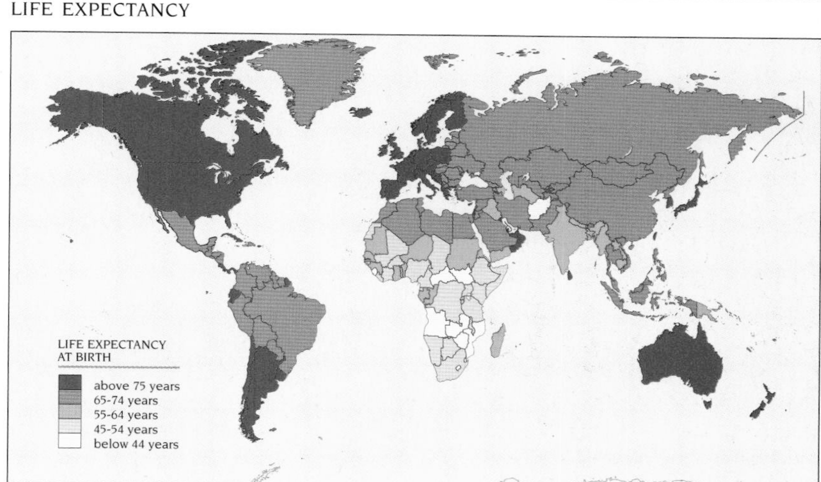

LIFE EXPECTANCY
AT BIRTH
above 75 years
65-74 years
55-64 years
45-54 years
below 44 years

THE WORLD ECONOMY

Throughout the world, the way in which people make a living varies greatly. The countries of Western Europe and North America, along with Japan and Australia, are the most economically developed in the world, with a long- established and very diverse range of industries. They sell their products and services internationally. Less economically developed countries in Central Asia and much of Africa, have a much smaller number of industries – some may rely on a single product – and many goods are produced only for the local market.

MEASURING WEALTH

The wealth of a country can be measured in several ways: for example, by the average annual income per person; by the volume of its trade; and by the total income from the goods and services that the country trades annually – its Gross National Income or GNI. The map below shows the average GNI per person for each of the world's countries, expressed in US$. Most of the highest levels of GNI are in Europe and the US; most of the lowest are in Africa.

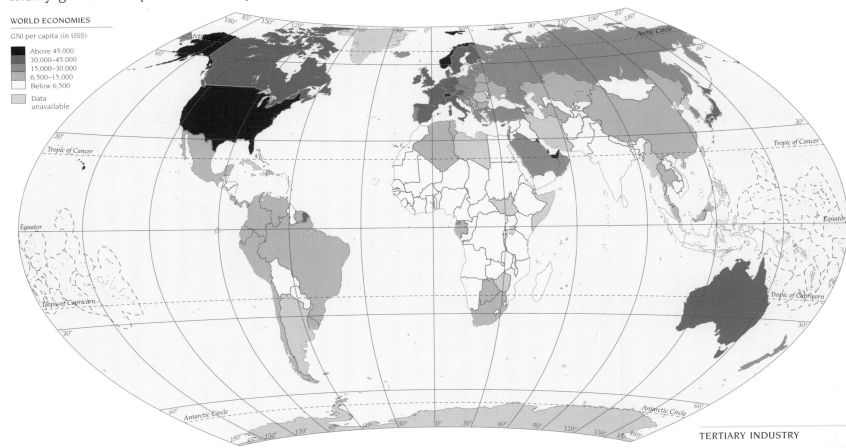

WORLD ECONOMIES

GNI per capita (in US$)

- Above 45,000
- 30,000–45,000
- 15,000–30,000
- 6,500–15,000
- Below 6,500
- Data unavailable

Arctic Circle · Tropic of Cancer · Equator · Tropic of Capricorn · Antarctic Circle

TYPES OF INDUSTRY

Industries are usually defined in one of three ways. Primary industries such as farming or mining involve the production of raw materials such as food or minerals. Secondary industries make or manufacture finished products out of raw materials: clothing and car manufacture are examples of secondary industries. People who work in tertiary industries provide different kinds of services. Banking, insurance and tourism are all examples of tertiary industries. Some economically advanced nations such as Germany or USA now have quaternary industries such as biotechnology which are knowledge-creation industries, devoted to the research and development of new products.

PRIMARY INDUSTRY

Tobacco leaves are picked and laid out for drying in Cuba, one of the world's great producers of cigars. Many countries rely on one or two high-value 'cash crops' like tobacco to earn foreign currency.

SECONDARY INDUSTRY

This skilled Thai weaver is producing an intricately patterned silk fabric on a hand loom. Fabric manufacture is an important industry throughout South and Southeast Asia. In India and Pakistan, vast quantities of cotton are produced in highly mechanized factories, but many fabrics are still hand woven.

TERTIARY INDUSTRY

The City of London is one of the world's great finance centres. Branches of many banks and insurance companies, including the world famous Lloyds of London, are clustered into the City's 'square mile'.

PATTERNS OF TRADE

Almost all countries trade goods with one another in order to obtain products they cannot produce themselves, and to make money from goods they have produced. Some countries – for example those in the Caribbean – rely mainly on a single export, usually a foodstuff or mineral, and can suffer a loss of income when world prices drop. Other countries, such as Germany and Japan, export a vast range of both raw materials and manufactured goods throughout the world. A number of huge companies, known as multinational corporations or MNCs, are responsible for more than 70% of world trade, with divisions all over the world. They include firms like BP, Coca Cola and Microsoft.

CONTAINER SHIPS

Many products are transported around the world on container ships. Containers are of a standard size so that they can be efficiently transported to their destinations. Some ships are specially designed to carry perishable goods such as fruit and vegetables.

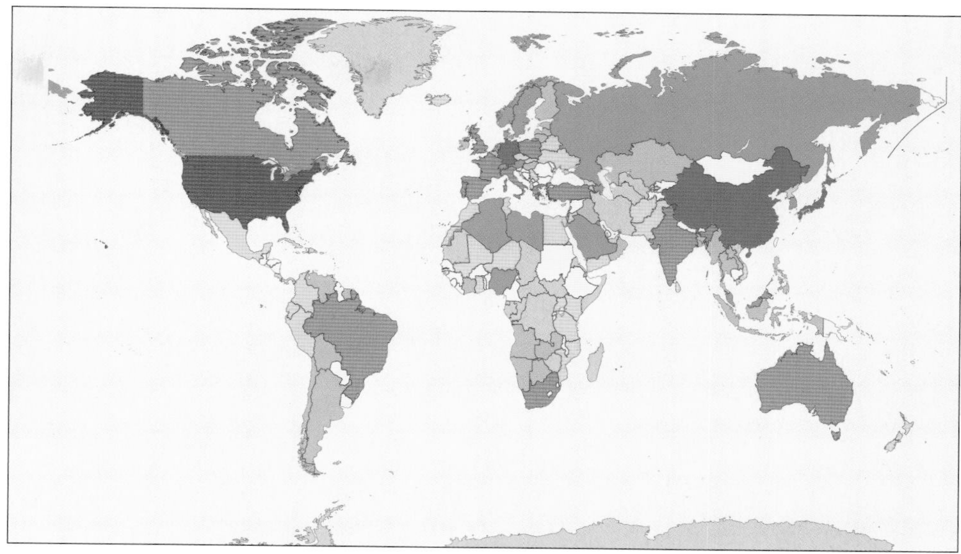

CURRENT ACCOUNT BALANCE (MILLIONS US$)

Deficit: Over 450,000; 10,000–450,000; 1,000–10,000; 0–1,000

Surplus: 0–10,000; 10,000–100,000; Over 100,000

Data unavailable

IRELAND
LUXEMBOURG
CYPRUS
CHINA
SOUTH KOREA
TAIWAN
INDIA
THAILAND
MALAYSIA
SINGAPORE
BOTSWANA
MAURITIUS

DEVELOPING ECONOMIES

Although world trade is still dominated by the more economically developed countries, since the 1970s, less economically developed countries have increased their share of world trade from less than 10% to nearly 30%. Countries such as China, India, Malaysia and South Korea, aided by investment from their governments or from wealthier countries, have become able to manufacture and export a wide variety of goods. Products include cars, electronic goods, clothing and footwear. Multinational companies can take advantage of cheaper labour costs to manufacture goods in these countries. Moves are being made to limit the exploitation of workers who are paid low wages for producing luxury goods.

ASIAN 'TIGER' ECONOMIES

The economies of Malaysia, Taiwan and South Korea, boomed in the late 1980s, attracting investment for buildings such as the Petronas Towers.

TOURISM

Tourism is now the world's largest industry. More than 700 million people travel both abroad and in their own countries as tourists each year. People in more developed countries have more money and leisure time to travel. Tourism can bring large amounts of cash into the local economy, but local people do not always benefit. They may have to take low-paid jobs and experience great intrusions into their lives. Tourist development and pollution may damage the environment – sometimes destroying the very attractions that led to the development of tourism in the first place.

ECOTOURISM

These tourists are being introduced to a giant tortoise, one of the many unique animals found in the Galapagos Islands. A number of places with special animals and ecosystems have introduced schemes to teach visitors about them. This not only educates more people about the need to safeguard these environments, but brings in money to help protect them.

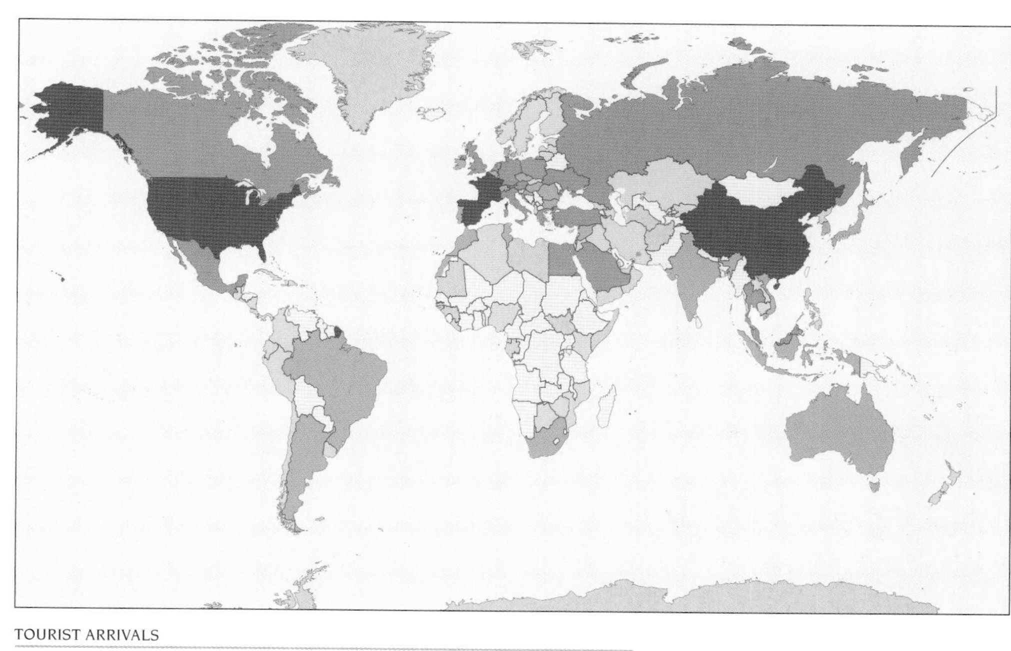

TOURIST ARRIVALS

Over 50 million; 20–50 million; 10–20 million; 5–10 million; 1–5 million; below 1 million; Data unavailable

BORDERS AND BOUNDARIES

There are more countries in the world today than ever before – almost 200 – whereas in 1950, there were only 82. Since then, many former European colonies and Soviet states have become independent. The establishment of borders for each of these countries has often been the subject of disagreement.

Military borders

At the end of wars, new borders are often drawn up between the countries – frequently along ceasefire lines. They may remain there for many years. At the end of the Korean War in 1953, North and South Korea were divided close to the 38° line of latitude. This border has remained heavily fortified.

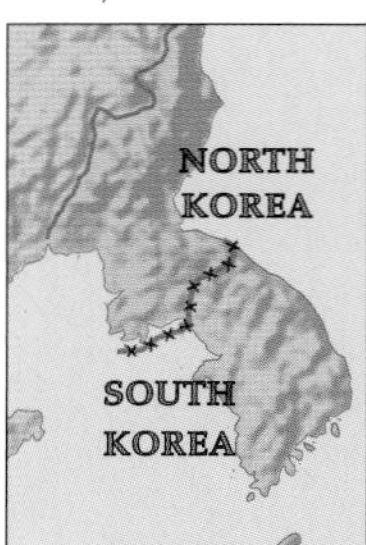
NORTH KOREA
SOUTH KOREA

Long borders

The border between the USA and Canada is the second longest continuous border in the world. It cuts through the centre of the Great Lakes. To the west of the Great Lakes, the border runs along the 49° line of latitude.

Enclaves

If part of a country's territory has become separated from the rest of the country, and is surrounded by foreign territory, it is called an enclave. Kaliningrad is part of the Russian Federation, but is cut off from it by Lithuania and Belarus.

LATVIA
RUSSIAN FEDERATION
LITHUANIA
KALININGRAD (part of Russ. Fed.)
POLAND
BELARUS

River borders

Over one-sixth of the world's national borders are formed by rivers. Long stretches of the Danube form natural borders in southeastern Europe.

GERMANY
SLOVAKIA
UKRAINE
Danube
AUSTRIA
MOLDOVA
HUNGARY
CROATIA
ROMANIA
SERBIA
Danube
BULGARIA

Mountain borders

Mountain ranges such as the Pyrenees, Alps and Himalayas form natural borders between many countries. In the Andes, border disputes between Chile and Argentina centred on finding the highest point in the mountain range which divided them.

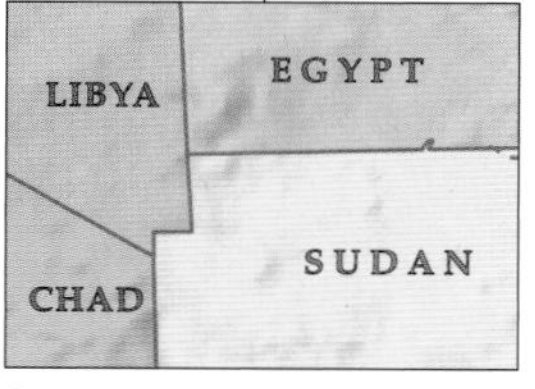
LIBYA
EGYPT
CHAD
SUDAN

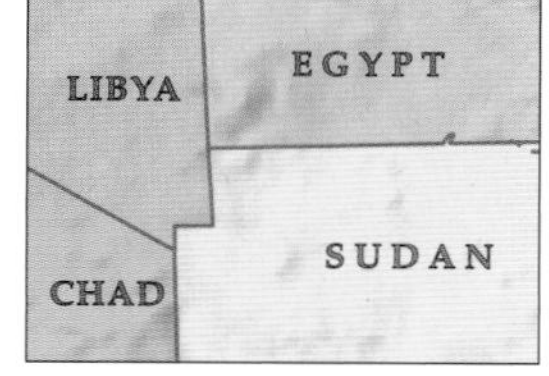

Straight line borders

The borders of many countries in Africa and other former colonial territories are straight lines. This was the simplest solution for colonial administrators, who often knew little of the country's geography or population.

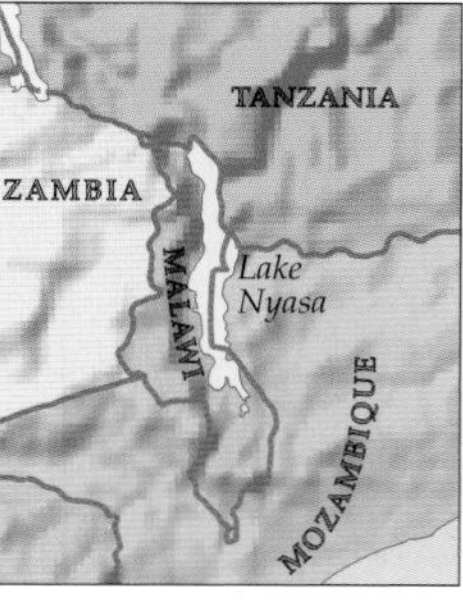
TANZANIA
ZAMBIA
MALAWI
Lake Nyasa
MOZAMBIQUE

Lake boundaries

Countries which lie next to lakes usually fix their borders in the middle of the lake. Complicated agreements between colonial powers led to the awkward division of Lake Nyasa in Africa.

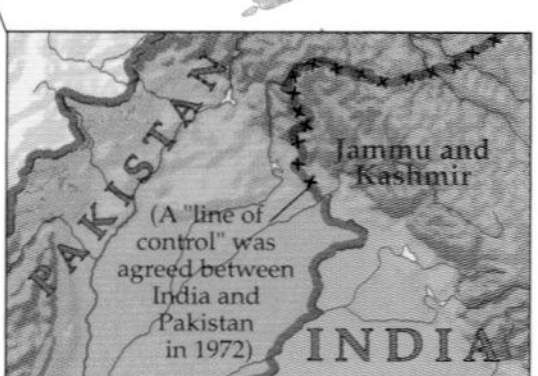
PAKISTAN
Jammu and Kashmir
(A "line of control" was agreed between India and Pakistan in 1972)
INDIA

Territorial disputes

There are still many disputed territories and borders. One of the most serious territorial disputes is between India and Pakistan over Jammu and Kashmir, which has led to three wars since 1947.

THE ATLAS OF THE WORLD

The Nations of the World

The world is divided into 196 independent countries, and about 60 overseas territories or dependencies. The largest country is the Russian Federation covering 17,075,200 sq km; the smallest is Vatican City in Rome, with an area of 0.44 sq km.

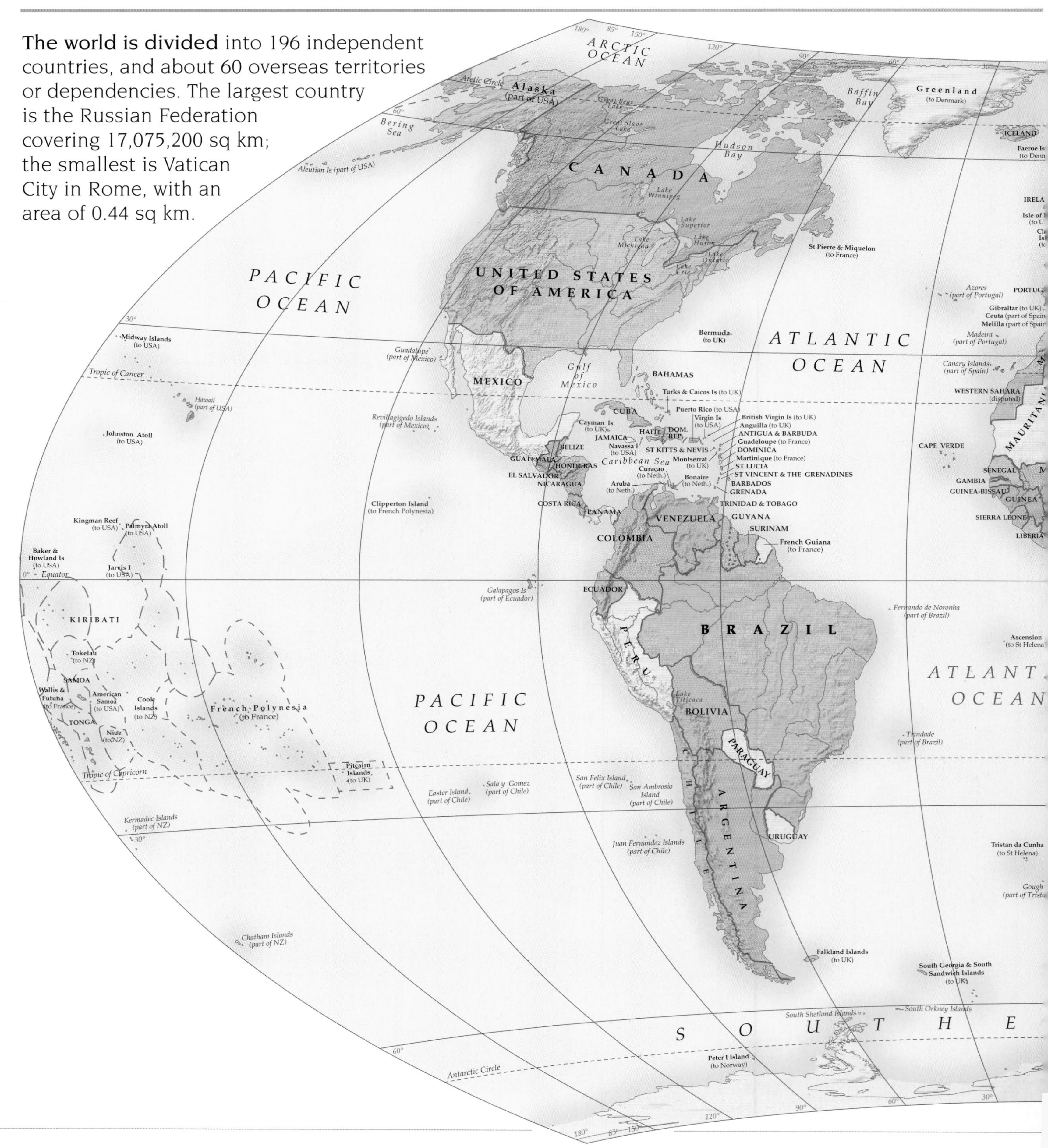

ARCTIC OCEAN
Arctic Circle
Alaska (part of USA)
Bering Sea
Aleutian Is (part of USA)
Great Bear Lake
Great Slave Lake
Baffin Bay
Greenland (to Denmark)
ICELAND
Faeroe Is (to Denm
Hudson Bay
CANADA
Lake Winnipeg
Lake Superior
Lake Michigan
Lake Huron
Lake Ontario
Lake Erie
St Pierre & Miquelon (to France)
UNITED STATES OF AMERICA
PACIFIC OCEAN
IRELA
Isle of (to U
Azores (part of Portugal)
PORTUG
Gibraltar (to UK)
Ceuta (part of Spain)
Melilla (part of Spain)
Madeira (part of Portugal)
Midway Islands (to USA)
Tropic of Cancer
Hawaii (part of USA)
Guadalupe (part of Mexico)
Bermuda (to UK)
ATLANTIC OCEAN
Canary Islands (part of Spain)
WESTERN SAHARA (disputed)
MAURITANIA
Gulf of Mexico
MEXICO
BAHAMAS
Turks & Caicos Is (to UK)
CUBA
Puerto Rico (to USA)
Virgin Is (to USA)
British Virgin Is (to UK)
Anguilla (to UK)
ANTIGUA & BARBUDA
Guadeloupe (to France)
DOMINICA
Martinique (to France)
ST LUCIA
ST VINCENT & THE GRENADINES
BARBADOS
GRENADA
Revillagigedo Islands (part of Mexico)
Johnston Atoll (to USA)
Cayman Is (to UK)
JAMAICA
HAITI
DOM. REP.
Navassa I (to USA)
ST KITTS & NEVIS
Montserrat (to UK)
Caribbean Sea
Curaçao (to Neth.)
Bonaire (to Neth.)
Aruba (to Neth.)
BELIZE
GUATEMALA
HONDURAS
EL SALVADOR
NICARAGUA
COSTA RICA
PANAMA
CAPE VERDE
SENEGAL
GAMBIA
GUINEA-BISSAU
GUINEA
SIERRA LEONE
LIBERIA
Clipperton Island (to French Polynesia)
TRINIDAD & TOBAGO
VENEZUELA
GUYANA
SURINAM
French Guiana (to France)
COLOMBIA
Kingman Reef (to USA)
Palmyra Atoll (to USA)
Baker & Howland Is (to USA)
Jarvis I (to USA)
Equator
Galapagos Is (part of Ecuador)
ECUADOR
Fernando de Noronha (part of Brazil)
KIRIBATI
BRAZIL
PERU
Ascension (to St Helena)
Tokelau (to NZ)
SAMOA
Wallis & Futuna (to France)
American Samoa (to USA)
Cook Islands (to NZ)
TONGA
Niue (to NZ)
French Polynesia (to France)
Lake Titicaca
BOLIVIA
Trindade (part of Brazil)
PARAGUAY
Tropic of Capricorn
Pitcairn Islands (to UK)
Easter Island (part of Chile)
Sala y Gomez (part of Chile)
San Felix Island (part of Chile)
San Ambrosio Island (part of Chile)
CHILE
ARGENTINA
URUGUAY
Kermadec Islands (part of NZ)
Juan Fernandez Islands (part of Chile)
Tristan da Cunha (to St Helena)
Gough (part of Trista
Chatham Islands (part of NZ)
Falkland Islands (to UK)
South Georgia & South Sandwich Islands (to UK)
South Shetland Islands
South Orkney Islands
SOUTHE
Peter I Island (to Norway)
Antarctic Circle

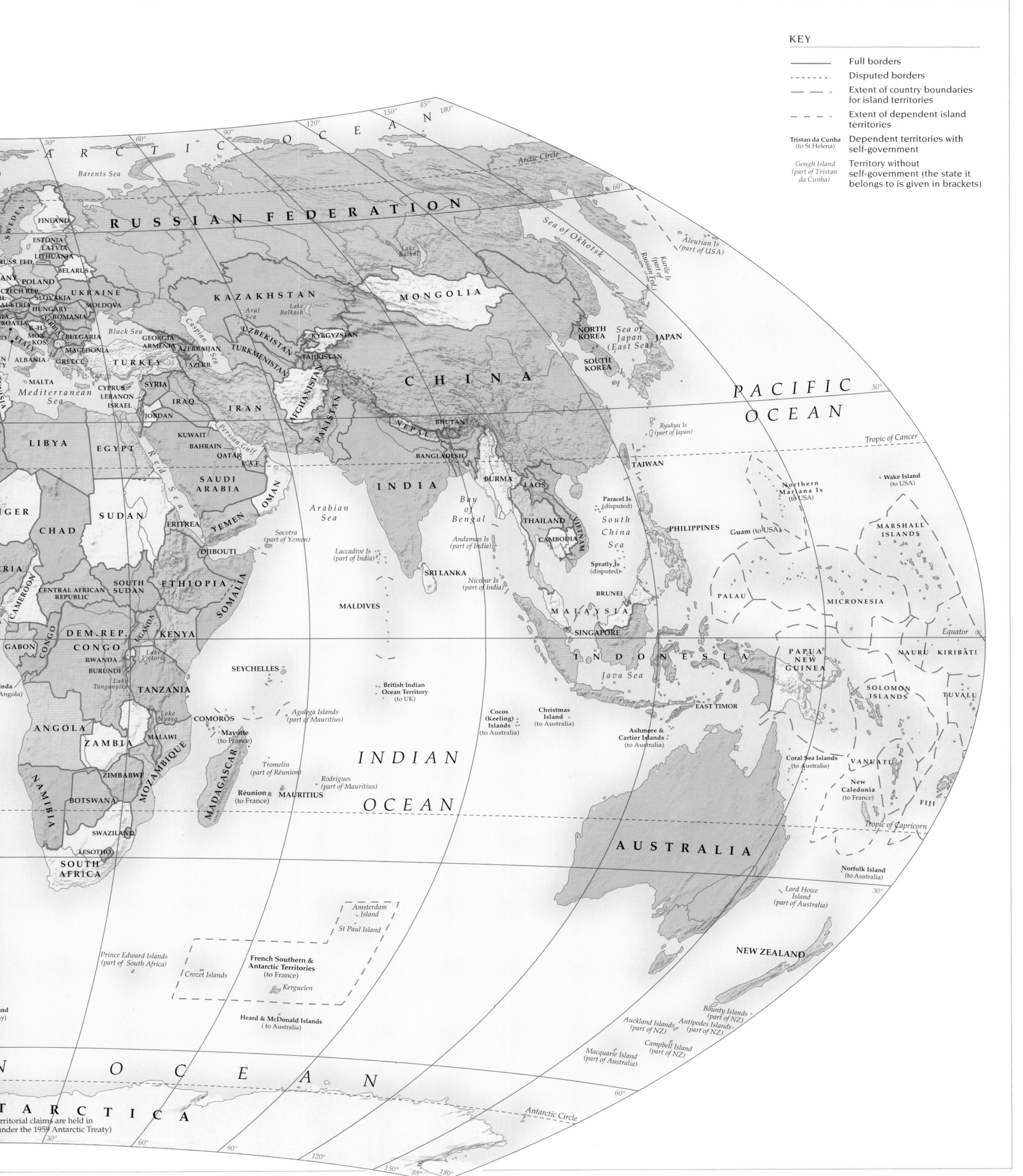
KEY
Full borders
Disputed borders
Extent of country boundaries for island territories
Extent of dependent island territories
Tristan da Cunha (to St Helena)
Dependent territories with self-government
Gough Island (part of Tristan da Cunha)
Territory without self-government (the state it belongs to is given in brackets)
ARCTIC OCEAN
Barents Sea
Arctic Circle
RUSSIAN FEDERATION
FINLAND
SWEDEN
ESTONIA
LATVIA
LITHUANIA
RUSS. FED.
BELARUS
POLAND
CZECH REP.
UKRAINE
SLOVAKIA
AUSTRIA
HUNGARY
MOLDOVA
ROMANIA
CROATIA
SERBIA
BULGARIA
MACEDONIA
ALBANIA
GREECE
ITALY
MALTA
Black Sea
GEORGIA
ARMENIA
AZERBAIJAN
AZERB.
TURKEY
Mediterranean Sea
CYPRUS
LEBANON
ISRAEL
SYRIA
IRAQ
JORDAN
KAZAKHSTAN
Aral Sea
Lake Balkash
Caspian Sea
UZBEKISTAN
TURKMENISTAN
KYRGYZSTAN
TAJIKISTAN
AFGHANISTAN
PAKISTAN
IRAN
KUWAIT
BAHRAIN
QATAR
U.A.E.
Persian Gulf
SAUDI ARABIA
OMAN
YEMEN
Red Sea
LIBYA
EGYPT
SUDAN
CHAD
ERITREA
DJIBOUTI
ETHIOPIA
SOMALIA
SOUTH SUDAN
CENTRAL AFRICAN REPUBLIC
CAMEROON
GABON
CONGO
DEM. REP. CONGO
UGANDA
KENYA
RWANDA
BURUNDI
Lake Victoria
Lake Tanganyika
TANZANIA
Lake Nyasa
ANGOLA
ZAMBIA
MALAWI
MOZAMBIQUE
ZIMBABWE
NAMIBIA
BOTSWANA
SWAZILAND
LESOTHO
SOUTH AFRICA
MADAGASCAR
COMOROS
Mayotte (to France)
SEYCHELLES
Agalega Islands (part of Mauritius)
Tromelin (part of Réunion)
Réunion (to France)
MAURITIUS
Rodrigues (part of Mauritius)
Socotra (part of Yemen)
Arabian Sea
Laccadive Is (part of India)
MALDIVES
British Indian Ocean Territory (to UK)
INDIA
NEPAL
BHUTAN
BANGLADESH
SRI LANKA
Bay of Bengal
Andaman Is (part of India)
Nicobar Is (part of India)
MONGOLIA
Lake Baikal
CHINA
Sea of Okhotsk
Kurile Is (part of Russian Fed.)
Aleutian Is (part of USA)
NORTH KOREA
SOUTH KOREA
Sea of Japan (East Sea)
JAPAN
Ryukyu Is (part of Japan)
TAIWAN
BURMA
LAOS
THAILAND
VIETNAM
CAMBODIA
Paracel Is (disputed)
South China Sea
Spratly Is (disputed)
PHILIPPINES
BRUNEI
MALAYSIA
SINGAPORE
INDONESIA
Java Sea
EAST TIMOR
PACIFIC OCEAN
Tropic of Cancer
Northern Mariana Is (to USA)
Wake Island (to USA)
Guam (to USA)
MARSHALL ISLANDS
PALAU
MICRONESIA
Equator
NAURU
KIRIBATI
PAPUA NEW GUINEA
SOLOMON ISLANDS
TUVALU
VANUATU
FIJI
New Caledonia (to France)
Coral Sea Islands (to Australia)
Tropic of Capricorn
Norfolk Island (to Australia)
Lord Howe Island (part of Australia)
Cocos (Keeling) Islands (to Australia)
Christmas Island (to Australia)
Ashmore & Cartier Islands (to Australia)
INDIAN OCEAN
AUSTRALIA
NEW ZEALAND
Amsterdam Island
St Paul Island
Prince Edward Islands (part of South Africa)
Crozet Islands
French Southern & Antarctic Territories (to France)
Kerguelen
Heard & McDonald Islands (to Australia)
Bounty Islands (part of NZ)
Antipodes Islands (part of NZ)
Auckland Islands (part of NZ)
Campbell Island (part of NZ)
Macquarie Island (part of Australia)
OCEAN
Antarctic Circle
ANTARCTICA
Territorial claims are held in abeyance under the 1959 Antarctic Treaty
30°
60°
90°
120°
150°
180°
85°

CONTINENTAL NORTH AMERICA

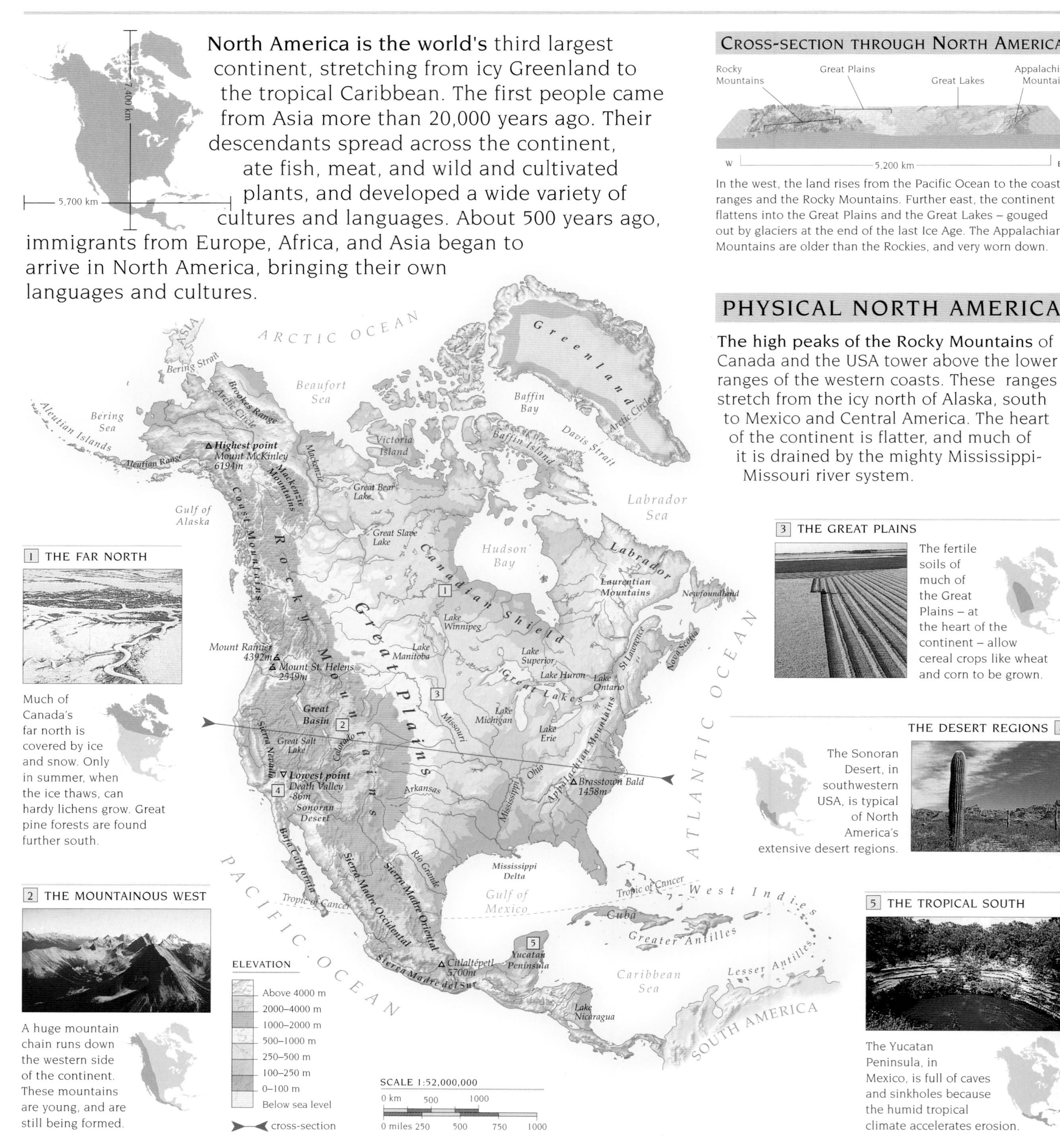
7,400 km
5,700 km
ARCTIC OCEAN
ASIA
Bering Strait
Beaufort Sea
Bering Sea
Aleutian Islands
Aleutian Range
Brookes Range
Arctic Circle
Highest point Mount McKinley 6194m
Mackenzie Mountains
Mackenzie
Victoria Island
Baffin Bay
Baffin Island
Greenland
Davis Strait
Arctic Circle
Great Bear Lake
Gulf of Alaska
Coast Mountains
Labrador Sea
Great Slave Lake
Hudson Bay
Labrador
Rocky Mountains
Canadian Shield
Laurentian Mountains
Newfoundland
Lake Winnipeg
Lake Manitoba
Great Plains
Lake Superior
Lake Huron
Lake Ontario
St Lawrence
Nova Scotia
Great Lakes
Mount Rainier 4392m
Mount St. Helens 2549m
Lake Michigan
Missouri
Lake Erie
Great Basin
Sierra Nevada
Great Salt Lake
Colorado
Appalachian Mountains
Lowest point Death Valley -86m
Sonoran Desert
Arkansas
Ohio
Mississippi
Brasstown Bald 1458m
ATLANTIC OCEAN
Baja California
Sierra Madre Occidental
Sierra Madre Oriental
Rio Grande
Mississippi Delta
PACIFIC OCEAN
Tropic of Cancer
Gulf of Mexico
Tropic of Cancer
West Indies
Cuba
Greater Antilles
Citlaltépetl 5700m
Yucatan Peninsula
Sierra Madre del Sur
Caribbean Sea
Lesser Antilles
Lake Nicaragua
SOUTH AMERICA
ELEVATION
Above 4000 m
2000–4000 m
1000–2000 m
500–1000 m
250–500 m
100–250 m
0–100 m
Below sea level
cross-section
SCALE 1:52,000,000
0 km 500 1000
0 miles 250 500 750 1000
Rocky Mountains
Great Plains
Great Lakes
Appalachian Mountains
W
5,200 km
E

North America is the world's third largest continent, stretching from icy Greenland to the tropical Caribbean. The first people came from Asia more than 20,000 years ago. Their descendants spread across the continent, ate fish, meat, and wild and cultivated plants, and developed a wide variety of cultures and languages. About 500 years ago, immigrants from Europe, Africa, and Asia began to arrive in North America, bringing their own languages and cultures.

CROSS-SECTION THROUGH NORTH AMERICA

In the west, the land rises from the Pacific Ocean to the coastal ranges and the Rocky Mountains. Further east, the continent flattens into the Great Plains and the Great Lakes – gouged out by glaciers at the end of the last Ice Age. The Appalachian Mountains are older than the Rockies, and very worn down.

PHYSICAL NORTH AMERICA

The high peaks of the Rocky Mountains of Canada and the USA tower above the lower ranges of the western coasts. These ranges stretch from the icy north of Alaska, south to Mexico and Central America. The heart of the continent is flatter, and much of it is drained by the mighty Mississippi-Missouri river system.

1 THE FAR NORTH

Much of Canada's far north is covered by ice and snow. Only in summer, when the ice thaws, can hardy lichens grow. Great pine forests are found further south.

2 THE MOUNTAINOUS WEST

A huge mountain chain runs down the western side of the continent. These mountains are young, and are still being formed.

3 THE GREAT PLAINS

The fertile soils of much of the Great Plains – at the heart of the continent – allow cereal crops like wheat and corn to be grown.

THE DESERT REGIONS 4

The Sonoran Desert, in southwestern USA, is typical of North America's extensive desert regions.

5 THE TROPICAL SOUTH

The Yucatan Peninsula, in Mexico, is full of caves and sinkholes because the humid tropical climate accelerates erosion.

POLITICAL NORTH AMERICA

The USA, Canada and Mexico are all federal countries. This means that political power is shared between the national government and the state or provincial governments. Canada and the USA are democracies with a long history of freedom and equal rights. Governments in the countries south of the USA have been less stable, often ruled by dictators or harsh regimes. Many people have suffered for their political beliefs. During the 1960's and 1970's many of the Caribbean islands gained independence from their European colonial rulers.

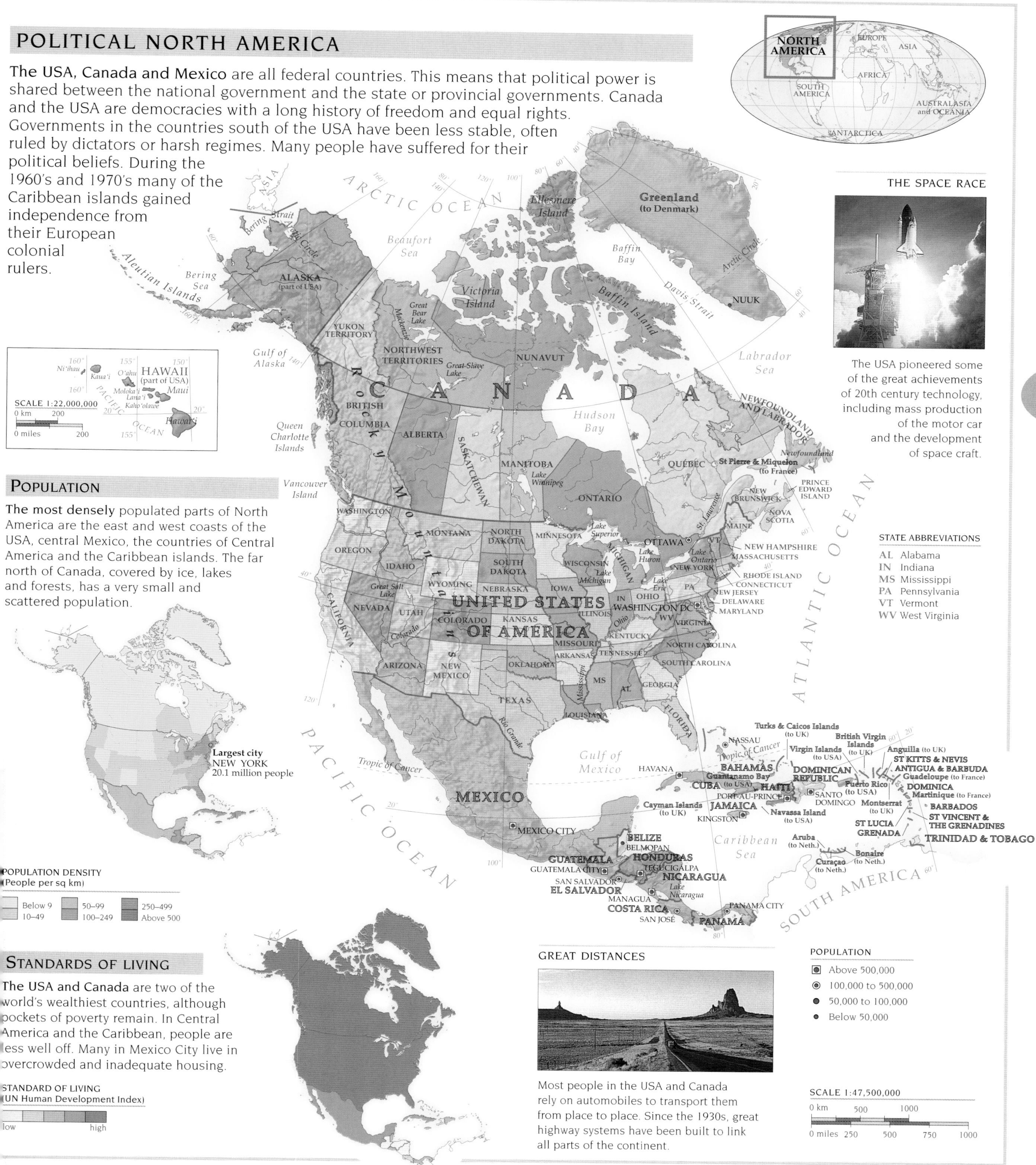
NORTH AMERICA
EUROPE
ASIA
AFRICA
SOUTH AMERICA
AUSTRALASIA and OCEANIA
ANTARCTICA
ARCTIC OCEAN
Greenland (to Denmark)
Ellesmere Island
Baffin Bay
Beaufort Sea
Bering Strait
Arctic Circle
ALASKA (part of USA)
Bering Sea
Aleutian Islands
Victoria Island
Baffin Island
Davis Strait
NUUK
YUKON TERRITORY
Great Bear Lake
NORTHWEST TERRITORIES
NUNAVUT
Great Slave Lake
Gulf of Alaska
Labrador Sea
CANADA
Hudson Bay
NEWFOUNDLAND AND LABRADOR
Newfoundland
BRITISH COLUMBIA
ALBERTA
SASKATCHEWAN
MANITOBA
Lake Winnipeg
ONTARIO
QUÉBEC
St Pierre & Miquelon (to France)
PRINCE EDWARD ISLAND
NEW BRUNSWICK
NOVA SCOTIA
Queen Charlotte Islands
Vancouver Island
Rocky Mountains
HAWAII (part of USA)
Ni'ihau
Kaua'i
O'ahu
Moloka'i
Lana'i
Maui
Kaho'olawe
Hawai'i
PACIFIC OCEAN
SCALE 1:22,000,000
WASHINGTON
OREGON
IDAHO
MONTANA
NORTH DAKOTA
SOUTH DAKOTA
MINNESOTA
WYOMING
NEBRASKA
IOWA
WISCONSIN
MICHIGAN
Lake Superior
Lake Huron
Lake Michigan
Lake Ontario
Lake Erie
OTTAWA
NEW YORK
VT
MAINE
NEW HAMPSHIRE
MASSACHUSETTS
RHODE ISLAND
CONNECTICUT
NEW JERSEY
DELAWARE
MARYLAND
PA
OHIO
IN
ILLINOIS
WASHINGTON DC
WV
VIRGINIA
KENTUCKY
CALIFORNIA
NEVADA
UTAH
Great Salt Lake
COLORADO
KANSAS
MISSOURI
UNITED STATES OF AMERICA
ARIZONA
NEW MEXICO
OKLAHOMA
ARKANSAS
TENNESSEE
NORTH CAROLINA
SOUTH CAROLINA
MS
AL
GEORGIA
TEXAS
LOUISIANA
FLORIDA
Rio Grande
Mississippi
Colorado
ATLANTIC OCEAN
STATE ABBREVIATIONS
AL Alabama
IN Indiana
MS Mississippi
PA Pennsylvania
VT Vermont
WV West Virginia
Gulf of Mexico
Tropic of Cancer
MEXICO
MEXICO CITY
HAVANA
CUBA
NASSAU
BAHAMAS
Turks & Caicos Islands (to UK)
British Virgin Islands (to UK)
Virgin Islands (to USA)
Anguilla (to UK)
ST KITTS & NEVIS
ANTIGUA & BARBUDA
Guadeloupe (to France)
DOMINICA
Martinique (to France)
BARBADOS
ST VINCENT & THE GRENADINES
ST LUCIA
GRENADA
TRINIDAD & TOBAGO
DOMINICAN REPUBLIC
SANTO DOMINGO
Puerto Rico (to USA)
Montserrat (to UK)
Guantanamo Bay (to USA)
HAITI
PORT-AU-PRINCE
Cayman Islands (to UK)
JAMAICA
KINGSTON
Navassa Island (to USA)
Caribbean Sea
Aruba (to Neth.)
Curaçao (to Neth.)
Bonaire (to Neth.)
BELIZE
BELMOPAN
GUATEMALA
GUATEMALA CITY
HONDURAS
TEGUCIGALPA
SAN SALVADOR
EL SALVADOR
NICARAGUA
Lake Nicaragua
MANAGUA
COSTA RICA
SAN JOSÉ
PANAMA
PANAMA CITY
SOUTH AMERICA
POPULATION
Above 500,000
100,000 to 500,000
50,000 to 100,000
Below 50,000
SCALE 1:47,500,000
0 km 500 1000
0 miles 250 500 750 1000

THE SPACE RACE

The USA pioneered some of the great achievements of 20th century technology, including mass production of the motor car and the development of space craft.

POPULATION

The most densely populated parts of North America are the east and west coasts of the USA, central Mexico, the countries of Central America and the Caribbean islands. The far north of Canada, covered by ice, lakes and forests, has a very small and scattered population.

Largest city NEW YORK 20.1 million people

POPULATION DENSITY (People per sq km)

Below 9 | 10–49 | 50–99 | 100–249 | 250–499 | Above 500

STANDARDS OF LIVING

The USA and Canada are two of the world's wealthiest countries, although pockets of poverty remain. In Central America and the Caribbean, people are less well off. Many in Mexico City live in overcrowded and inadequate housing.

STANDARD OF LIVING (UN Human Development Index)

low — high

GREAT DISTANCES

Most people in the USA and Canada rely on automobiles to transport them from place to place. Since the 1930s, great highway systems have been built to link all parts of the continent.

NORTH AMERICAN GEOGRAPHY

Canada and the USA are among the world's wealthiest countries. They have rich natural resources, good farmland and thriving, varied industries. The range of different industries in Mexico is growing, but other Central American countries and the Caribbean islands rely on one or two important cash crops and tourism for most of their incomes. They have a lower standard of living than Canada and the USA.

INDUSTRY

The USA and Canada have an extremely wide range of industries, from mining and the processing of farm produce, to heavy and light manufacturing and service industries like banking. A variety of goods are produced, including aeroplanes, cars and computers. Oil exports and machine assembly are Mexico's main industries. In Central America and the Caribbean nations, most industry is based on agricultural produce.

INDUSTRY

- Aerospace
- Brewing
- Car/vehicle manufacture
- Chemicals
- Coal
- Defence
- Engineering
- Film industry
- Finance
- Food processing
- Hi-tech industry
- Iron & steel
- Oil & gas
- Pharmaceuticals
- Printing & publishing
- Research & development
- Shipbuilding
- Textiles
- Timber processing

GNI per capita (US$)

- Below 2,500
- 2,500–9,999
- 10,000–14,999
- 15,000–34,999
- 35,000–49,999
- Above 50,000
- Industrial centre

MANUFACTURING

Mexico has many car part assembly plants. Labour costs in Mexico are low, making it cheap to assemble car parts here.

MINERAL RESOURCES

North America still has large amounts of minera resources. Canada has important nickel reserves Mexico is renowned for its silver, and bauxite – used to make aluminum – is found in Jamaica. Oil and gas are plentiful, particularly in the arcti northwest by the Beaufort Sea, and further south by the Gulf of Mexico.

MINERAL RESOURCES

- Bauxite
- Copper
- Iron
- Nickel
- Phosphates
- Silver
- Uranium
- Oil/gas field
- Coal field

TIMBER PROCESSING

Huge tracts of forest are found toward the north of the continent; nearly 30% of Canada is covere by forest. Timber is processed to make paper in cities such as Portland and Vancouver.

HI-TECH INDUSTRY

The Santa Clara Valley, jus south of San Francisco is also known as Silicon Valley, because of the number of firms producin computer hardware and software and micro-electronics which have set up in the area.

FOOD PROCESSING

Jamaica has been famous for its rum since the 16th century. Syrup is extract from sugar cane which is then fermented to make rum

CLIMATE

Much of northern Canada lies within the Arctic Circle and is permanently covered by ice or the sparse vegetation known as tundra. Southern Canada and much of central USA have a continental climate, with hot summers and cold winters. The southern parts of the USA, Central America and the Caribbean have a hot, humid tropical climate. The Caribbean and the eastern and central states of the USA often experience hurricane-force winds, waterspouts and tornadoes.

EXTREME WEATHER EVENTS

Symbols indicate climatic extremes

Coldest place
NORTHICE (Greenland)
Temperature -66°C

Wettest place
HENDERSON LAKE (BC, Canada)
Annual rainfall 6650mm

Hottest place
DEATH VALLEY (CA, USA)
Temperature 57°C

Driest place
BATAQUES (Mexico)
Annual rainfall 30mm

CLIMATE

- Ice cap
- Tundra
- Sub-arctic
- Cool continental
- Warm temperate
- Mediterranean
- Semi-arid
- Arid
- Humid equatorial
- Tropical
- Hot Humid

NORTH AMERICA'S HOTTEST PLACE

Death Valley in California is the hottest and driest place in the USA. Strong, dry winds sweep through the valley, constantly reshaping the sand and salt deposits which cover its floor.

LAND USE AND AGRICULTURE

On the Great Plains and Prairies of the USA and Canada, vast quantities of cereal crops, including corn and wheat, grow in the fertile soils. Cattle are also raised on great ranches throughout these regions and on the foothills of the Rocky Mountains. In California, vegetables and fruits are grown with the aid of irrigation. Bananas, coffee and sugar cane are grown for export in Central America and the Caribbean, while sorghum and maize are grown as subsistence crops.

BANANA PLANTATION

Banana plantations are common in the Caribbean and Central America. The fruit is grown for local consumption and for export to the USA and Europe, where they are valued for their flavour and nutritional qualities.

FISHING

The Grand Banks off the eastern coast of Canada were once home to almost limitless fish stocks. Overfishing has reduced the number of fish to very low levels. Quotas limiting the numbers of fish caught are helping numbers to rise.

LAND USE AND AGRICULTURE

- Cattle
- Poultry
- Pigs
- Reindeer
- Sheep
- Bananas
- Cereals
- Citrus fruits
- Coffee
- Corn (maize)
- Cotton
- Fishing
- Fruit
- Peanuts
- Rice
- Shellfish
- Soya beans
- Sugarcane
- Timber
- Tobacco
- Vineyards

- Cropland
- Desert
- Forest
- Ice cap
- Mountain region
- Pasture
- Tundra
- Wetland
- Major conurbation

Western Canada

ALBERTA, BRITISH COLUMBIA, MANITOBA, NORTHWEST TERRITORIES, NUNAVUT, SASKATCHEWAN, YUKON TERRITORY

The first inhabitants of Canada's western provinces were Native Americans. By the late 1800s, the Canadian Pacific Railroad was completed and European settlers moved west, turning most of the prairie into huge grain farms. North of the prairies lie the vast, empty territories that have significant Native American populations. In 1999, part of the Northwest Territories, known as Nunavut, became a self-governing Inuit homeland.

INDUSTRY

The major industries in the prairie provinces are related to agriculture, such as meat-processing in Manitoba. Alberta has huge reserves of fossil fuels, and the other provinces are rich in minerals, including zinc, nickel, silver and uranium. British Columbia's economy depends on manufacturing, especially automobiles, chemicals and machinery, along with paper and timber industries.

Resolute
Kitimat
Edmonton
Flin Flon
Vancouver
Calgary
Winnipeg
Regina

STRUCTURE OF INDUSTRY

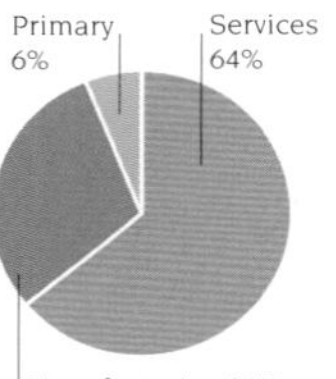
Primary 6%
Services 64%
Manufacturing 30%

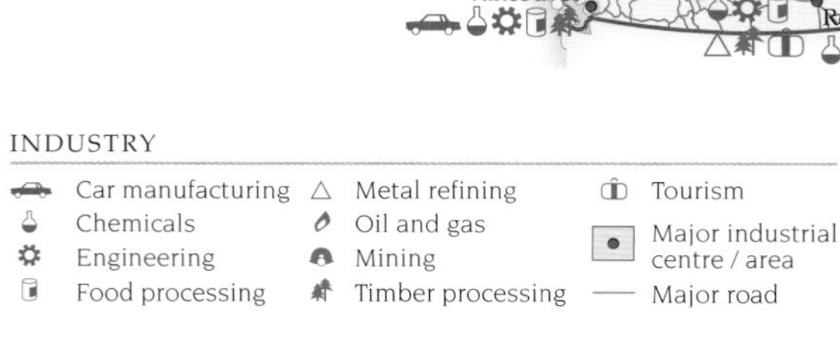
INDUSTRY
Car manufacturing
Chemicals
Engineering
Food processing
Metal refining
Oil and gas
Mining
Timber processing
Tourism
Major industrial centre / area
Major road

ENVIRONMENTAL ISSUES

For hundreds of years sailors have searched in vain for a route from Europe to Asia via the Northwest Passage, through the north of this region. In recent summers the sea ice has retreated further north, and in 2007 the route was completely navigable.

Many of the extensive forests in British Columbia are used for commercial lumbering. The province produces more than half of Canada's timber.

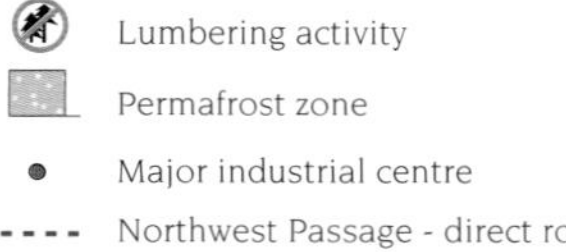
ENVIRONMENTAL ISSUES
Lumbering activity
Permafrost zone
Major industrial centre
Northwest Passage - direct route

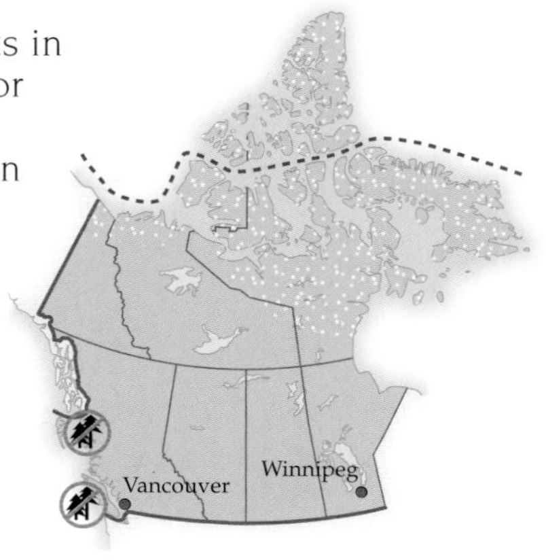
Vancouver
Winnipeg

FARMING AND LAND USE

More than 20% of the world's wheat is grown in Canada's prairie provinces: Manitoba, Alberta and Saskatchewan. Beef cattle graze on the ranches of Alberta and British Columbia. Fruits, especially apples, flourish in the sheltered southern valleys of British Columbia, and Pacific salmon and herring are caught off the west coast.

Edmonton
Vancouver
Calgary
Winnipeg

LAND USE

Pasture 5%
Cropland 4%
Forest 38%
Other (including mountains) 53%

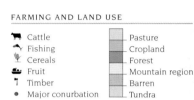

FARMING AND LAND USE

Cattle
Fishing
Cereals
Fruit
Timber
Major conurbation
Pasture
Cropland
Forest
Mountain region
Barren
Tundra

THE LANDSCAPE

The prairie provinces are mostly flat. Occasionally, the level plains are broken up by river valleys such as that of the Qu'Appelle in Saskatchewan. In the west, the jagged peaks and steep passes of the Rocky Mountains and the Coast Mountains are covered in snow for months on end. West of the Rockies, the land descends sharply towards the coast of British Columbia. The far north is covered by dense forests and many glacial lakes.

The Arctic
Most of Canada's northern islands are within the Arctic Circle. They are covered by ice year-round.

Mount Logan (B5)
Mount Logan is Canada's tallest peak. It rises 5,959 m.

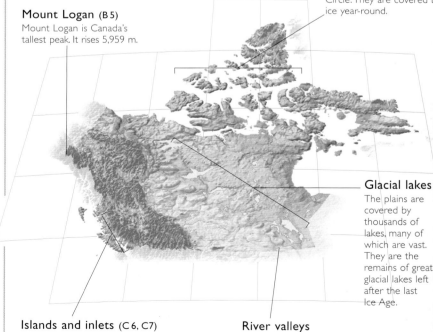

Glacial lakes
The plains are covered by thousands of lakes, many of which are vast. They are the remains of great glacial lakes left after the last Ice Age.

Islands and inlets (C6, C7)
The British Columbia coast is peppered with islands and fjord-like inlets, created by the force of the Pacific Ocean.

River valleys
Prairie river valleys such as the Qu'Appelle (F7) (French for 'who calls') were cut by glacial meltwater thousands of years ago.

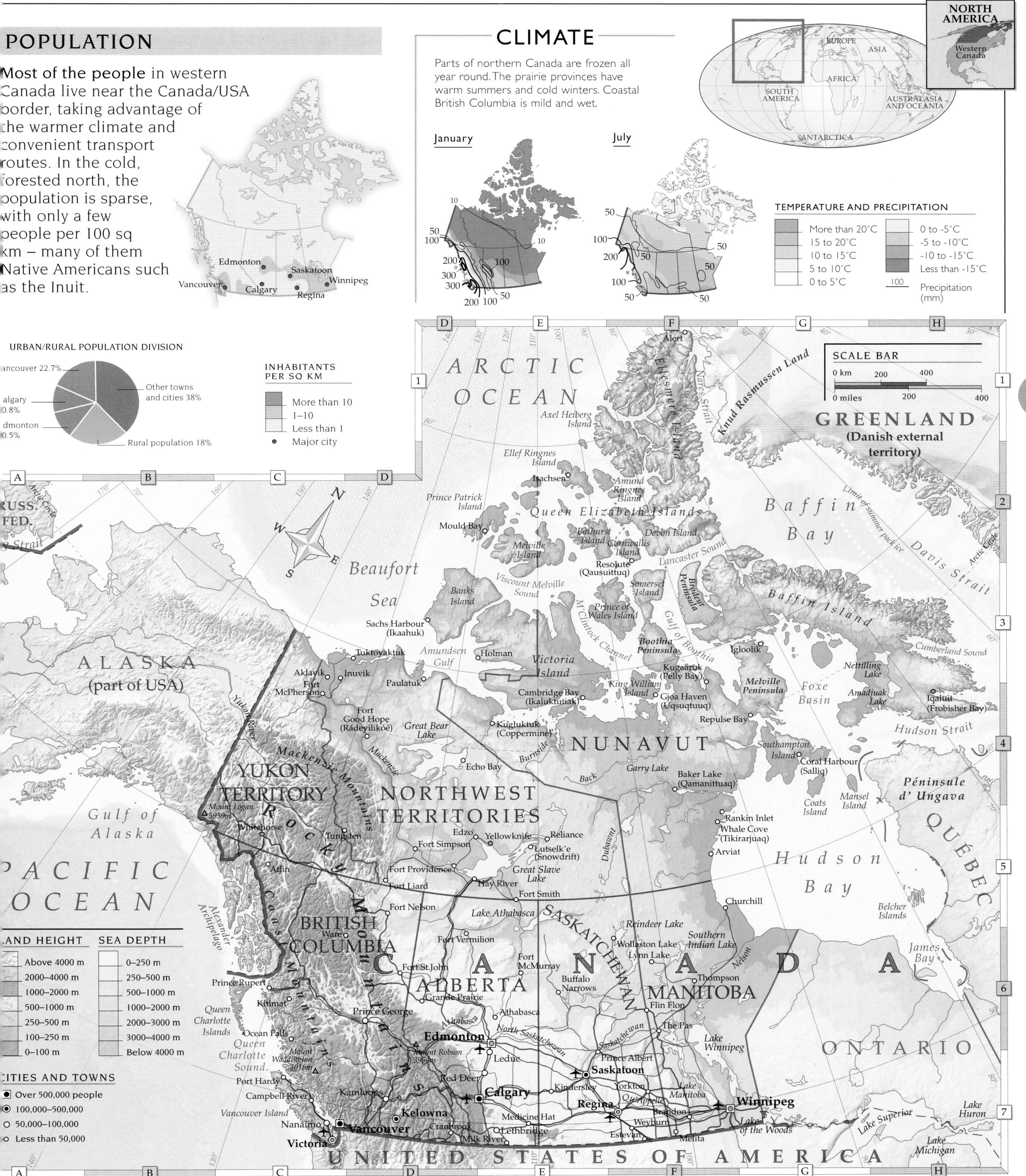
NORTH AMERICA
Western Canada
EUROPE
ASIA
AFRICA
SOUTH AMERICA
AUSTRALASIA AND OCEANIA
ANTARCTICA
POPULATION
Most of the people in western Canada live near the Canada/USA border, taking advantage of the warmer climate and convenient transport routes. In the cold, forested north, the population is sparse, with only a few people per 100 sq km – many of them Native Americans such as the Inuit.
Edmonton
Saskatoon
Winnipeg
Vancouver
Calgary
Regina
CLIMATE
Parts of northern Canada are frozen all year round. The prairie provinces have warm summers and cold winters. Coastal British Columbia is mild and wet.
January
July
TEMPERATURE AND PRECIPITATION
More than 20°C
15 to 20°C
10 to 15°C
5 to 10°C
0 to 5°C
0 to -5°C
-5 to -10°C
-10 to -15°C
Less than -15°C
Precipitation (mm)
URBAN/RURAL POPULATION DIVISION
ancouver 22.7%
algary 0.8%
dmonton 0.5%
Other towns and cities 38%
Rural population 18%
INHABITANTS PER SQ KM
More than 10
1–10
Less than 1
Major city
SCALE BAR
0 km 200 400
0 miles 200 400
ARCTIC OCEAN
GREENLAND (Danish external territory)
Knud Rasmussen Land
Ellesmere Island
Nares Strait
Alert
Axel Heiberg Island
Ellef Ringnes Island
Isachsen
Amund Ringnes Island
Prince Patrick Island
Mould Bay
Queen Elizabeth Islands
Bathurst Island
Cornwallis Island
Devon Island
Melville Island
Resolute (Qausuittuq)
Lancaster Sound
Baffin Bay
Davis Strait
Limit of summer pack ice
Beaufort Sea
Banks Island
Viscount Melville Sound
Somerset Island
Brodeur Peninsula
Prince of Wales Island
M'Clintock Channel
Gulf of Boothia
Baffin Island
Sachs Harbour (Ikaahuk)
Boothia Peninsula
Igloolik
Cumberland Sound
Nettilling Lake
Amadjuak Lake
Iqaluit (Frobisher Bay)
Hudson Strait
Tuktoyaktuk
Amundsen Gulf
Holman
Victoria Island
Kugaaruk (Pelly Bay)
Melville Peninsula
Foxe Basin
ALASKA (part of USA)
Aklavik
Inuvik
Fort McPherson
Paulatuk
Cambridge Bay (Ikaluktutiak)
King William Island
Gjoa Haven (Uqsuqtuuq)
Repulse Bay
Fort Good Hope (Rádeyilikóé)
Great Bear Lake
Kugluktuk (Coppermine)
NUNAVUT
Southampton Island
Coral Harbour (Salliq)
Burnside
Garry Lake
Baker Lake (Qamanittuaq)
Péninsule d' Ungava
Yukon River
Mackenzie Mountains
Mackenzie
Echo Bay
Back
Coats Island
Mansel Island
YUKON TERRITORY
NORTHWEST TERRITORIES
Mount Logan 5959m
Whitehorse
Tungsten
Gulf of Alaska
Edzo
Yellowknife
Reliance
Lutselk'e (Snowdrift)
Fort Simpson
Dubawnt
Rankin Inlet
Whale Cove (Tikirarjuaq)
Arviat
QUEBEC
PACIFIC OCEAN
Atlin
Fort Providence
Great Slave Lake
Hay River
Fort Liard
Fort Smith
Hudson Bay
Rocky Mountains
Coast Mountains
Alexander Archipelago
Fort Nelson
Lake Athabasca
SASKATCHEWAN
Churchill
Belcher Islands
BRITISH COLUMBIA
Ware
Fort Vermilion
Reindeer Lake
Wollaston Lake
Lynn Lake
Southern Indian Lake
Nelson
James Bay
CANADA
Fort St.John
Fort McMurray
Thompson
ALBERTA
Buffalo Narrows
MANITOBA
Prince Rupert
Grande Prairie
Flin Flon
Kitimat
Queen Charlotte Islands
Prince George
Athabasca
The Pas
Ocean Falls
Queen Charlotte Sound
Edmonton
North Saskatchewan
Lake Winnipeg
ONTARIO
Mount Waddington 4016m
Mount Robson 3954m
Leduc
Prince Albert
Saskatoon
Port Hardy
Red Deer
Kindersley
Yorkton
Qu'Appelle
Lake Manitoba
Campbell River
Kamloops
Calgary
Regina
Winnipeg
Vancouver Island
Kelowna
Medicine Hat
Brandon
Lake Superior
Lake Huron
Nanaimo
Vancouver
Cranbrook
Lethbridge
Weyburn
Estevan
Lake of the Woods
Victoria
Milk River
Melita
Lake Michigan
UNITED STATES OF AMERICA
RUSS. FED.
Arctic Circle
LAND HEIGHT
Above 4000 m
2000–4000 m
1000–2000 m
500–1000 m
250–500 m
100–250 m
0–100 m
SEA DEPTH
0–250 m
250–500 m
500–1000 m
1000–2000 m
2000–3000 m
3000–4000 m
Below 4000 m
CITIES AND TOWNS
Over 500,000 people
100,000–500,000
50,000–100,000
Less than 50,000

EASTERN CANADA

NEW BRUNSWICK, NEWFOUNDLAND AND LABRADOR, NOVA SCOTIA, ONTARIO, PRINCE EDWARD ISLAND, QUÉBEC

The first European settlements grew up in the Atlantic provinces, and along the St. Lawrence River, where Québec City and Montréal were founded. People gradually migrated further west along the St. Lawrence River and the Great Lakes, establishing other cities including Toronto. Although the majority of Canadians speak English, people in Québec speak mainly French, and both English and French are official languages in Canada.

FARMING AND LAND USE

The best farmland lies on the flat, fertile plains close to the St. Lawrence River and on the strip of land between Lake Erie and Lake Ontario. It is used to grow fruits such as grapes, cherries and peaches, and to raise cattle. Nova Scotia has fruit farms, and the rich red soils of Prince Edward Island produce a big potato crop. The vast forests that grow across the north are a major source of timber.

LAND USE

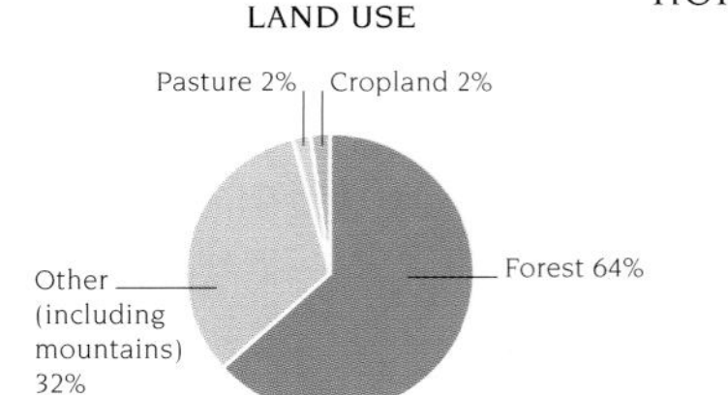

Pasture 2%
Cropland 2%
Forest 64%
Other (including mountains) 32%

FARMING AND LAND USE

- Cattle
- Fishing
- Fruit
- Potatoes
- Timber
- Pasture
- Cropland
- Forest
- Tundra
- Major conurbation

INDUSTRY

In the Atlantic provinces the traditional fishing industry has declined, causing unemployment. However, Newfoundland has a thriving food processing industry. Ontario and Québec have a wide range of industries, including the generation of hydro-electricity, mining, and chemicals, car manufacturing and fruit canning in the great cities. Large amounts of wood pulp and paper are also produced.

STRUCTURE OF INDUSTRY

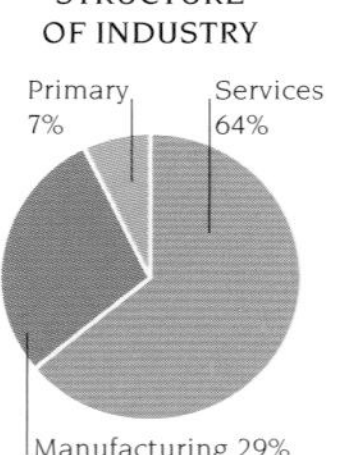

Primary 7%
Services 64%
Manufacturing 29%

INDUSTRY

- Car manufacture
- Chemicals
- Fish processing
- Food processing
- Hydro-electric power
- Metal refining
- Mining
- Timber processing
- Hi-tech industry
- Tourism
- Major industrial centre / area
- Major road

ENVIRONMENTAL ISSUES

Acid rain caused by emissions from factories in the USA and along the St. Lawrence River destroys forests and kills marine life. Massive hydro-electric power projects in James Bay on Hudson Bay have flooded huge areas of land, affecting the environment and the local Cree people. Overfishing in the Atlantic has led to limits being set on the number of fish that can be caught.

ENVIRONMENTAL ISSUES

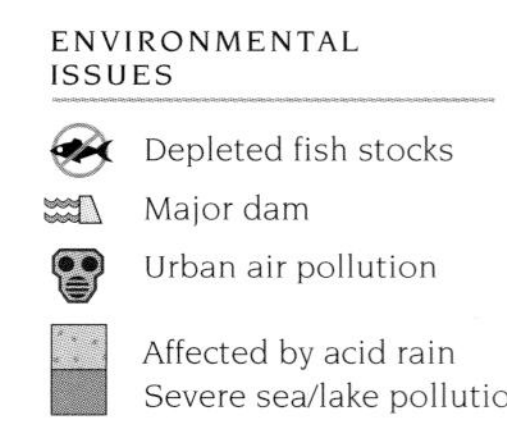

- Depleted fish stocks
- Major dam
- Urban air pollution
- Affected by acid rain
- Severe sea/lake pollution
- Major industrial centre

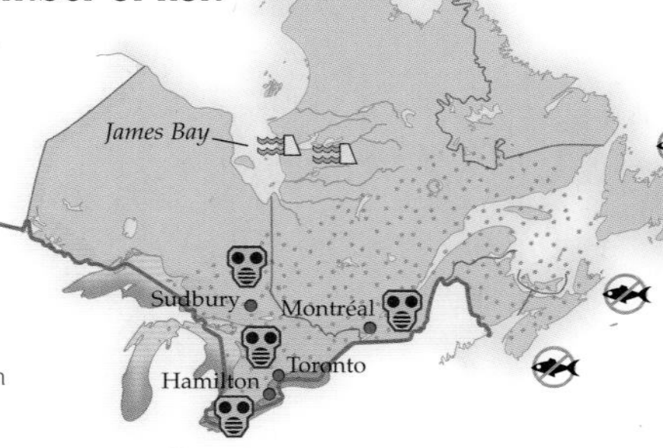

James Bay
Sudbury
Montréal
Toronto
Hamilton

THE LANDSCAPE

A huge, ancient mass of rock called the Canadian Shield lies beneath much of eastern Canada. It is covered by low hills, rocky outcrops, thousands of lakes, and huge areas of forest. Much of the Canadian Shield is permanently frozen. The St. Lawrence River flows out of Lake Ontario and into the Atlantic Ocean. It is surrounded by rolling hills and flat areas of very fertile farmland.

Scoured by ice
About 20,000 years ago, Labrador and northern Québec were completely covered by ice. The glaciers scraped hollows in the rock beneath. When the ice melted, lakes were left in the hollows that remained.

Lake Superior (B5)
Lake Superior is the largest freshwater lake in the world. It covers an area of 83,270 sq km and lies between Canada and the USA.

St. Lawrence River (E5)
The St. Lawrence River is 1,197 km long. Parts of it have become silted up, causing it to be braided into many different channels. Between December and mid-April the river freezes over.

Highlands
The highlands of New Brunswick, Nova Scotia and Newfoundland are the most northerly part of the Appalachian mountain chain.

The Bay of Fundy (F5)
This bay has the world's highest tides. It is shaped like a funnel, and as the Atlantic flows into it, the ever narrowing shores cause the water level to rise 6–15 m at every high tide.

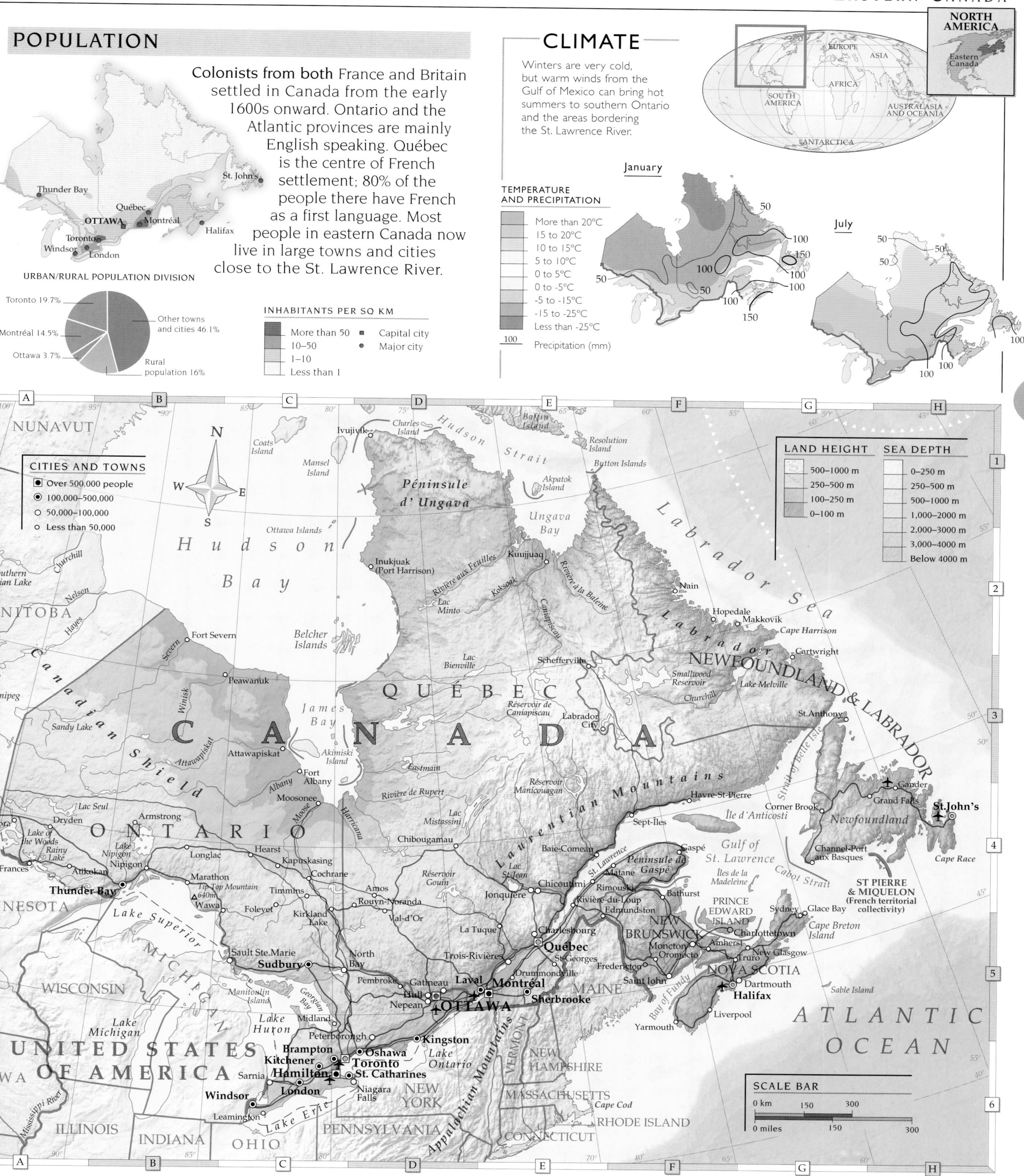
POPULATION
Colonists from both France and Britain settled in Canada from the early 1600s onward. Ontario and the Atlantic provinces are mainly English speaking. Québec is the centre of French settlement; 80% of the people there have French as a first language. Most people in eastern Canada now live in large towns and cities close to the St. Lawrence River.
Thunder Bay
Québec
OTTAWA
Montréal
St. John's
Halifax
Toronto
Windsor
London
URBAN/RURAL POPULATION DIVISION
Toronto 19.7%
Montréal 14.5%
Ottawa 3.7%
Other towns and cities 46.1%
Rural population 16%
INHABITANTS PER SQ KM
More than 50
10–50
1–10
Less than 1
Capital city
Major city
CLIMATE
Winters are very cold, but warm winds from the Gulf of Mexico can bring hot summers to southern Ontario and the areas bordering the St. Lawrence River.
NORTH AMERICA
Eastern Canada
EUROPE
ASIA
AFRICA
SOUTH AMERICA
AUSTRALASIA AND OCEANIA
ANTARCTICA
January
July
TEMPERATURE AND PRECIPITATION
More than 20°C
15 to 20°C
10 to 15°C
5 to 10°C
0 to 5°C
0 to -5°C
-5 to -15°C
-15 to -25°C
Less than -25°C
100 Precipitation (mm)
CITIES AND TOWNS
Over 500,000 people
100,000–500,000
50,000–100,000
Less than 50,000
LAND HEIGHT
500–1000 m
250–500 m
100–250 m
0–100 m
SEA DEPTH
0–250 m
250–500 m
500–1000 m
1,000–2000 m
2,000–3000 m
3,000–4000 m
Below 4000 m
SCALE BAR
0 km 150 300
0 miles 150 300
NUNAVUT
Hudson Bay
Hudson Strait
Labrador Sea
Péninsule d'Ungava
Ungava Bay
James Bay
QUÉBEC
CANADA
Canadian Shield
ONTARIO
NEWFOUNDLAND & LABRADOR
Labrador
Newfoundland
Laurentian Mountains
Gulf of St. Lawrence
Île d'Anticosti
Péninsule de Gaspé
NEW BRUNSWICK
PRINCE EDWARD ISLAND
NOVA SCOTIA
ST PIERRE & MIQUELON (French territorial collectivity)
ATLANTIC OCEAN
UNITED STATES OF AMERICA
WISCONSIN
MICHIGAN
ILLINOIS
INDIANA
OHIO
PENNSYLVANIA
NEW YORK
VERMONT
NEW HAMPSHIRE
MAINE
MASSACHUSETTS
CONNECTICUT
RHODE ISLAND
Lake Superior
Lake Michigan
Lake Huron
Lake Erie
Lake Ontario
Appalachian Mountains
OTTAWA
Montréal
Québec
Toronto
Hamilton
Kitchener
Brampton
Oshawa
St. Catharines
London
Windsor
Kingston
Laval
Sherbrooke
Sudbury
Thunder Bay
Halifax
St.John's
Charlottetown
Fredericton
Saint John
Moncton
Sydney
Corner Brook
Gander
Sept-Îles
Chicoutimi
Trois-Rivières
Gatineau
Nepean
Sault Ste.Marie
North Bay
Timmins
Moosonee
Schefferville
Kuujjuaq
Inukjuak (Port Harrison)
Nain
Hopedale
Cartwright
Fort Severn
Peawanuk
Attawapiskat
Fort Albany

USA: The Northeastern States

CONNECTICUT, DELAWARE, MAINE, MASSACHUSETTS, NEW-HAMPSHIRE, NEW JERSEY, NEW YORK, PENNSYLVANIA, RHODE ISLAND, VERMONT

The dynamic 200-year boom of the northeastern states has been the result of a combination of factors. Between 1855 and 1924, over 20 million people poured into the region from all over the world, hoping to build a new life. Natural resources, including coal and iron, fuelled new industries and fertile farmland provided food for the region's growing population. The 'gateway' cities of the Atlantic seaboard, New York and Boston, enabled manufacturers to export their goods worldwide.

INDUSTRY

Boston, New York and Philadelphia are international centres of industry and commerce. Electronics and communications are growing throughout the Northeast alongside traditional industries such as fishing and wood products. Tourism is vital for the northeastern states, particularly along the Atlantic coast.

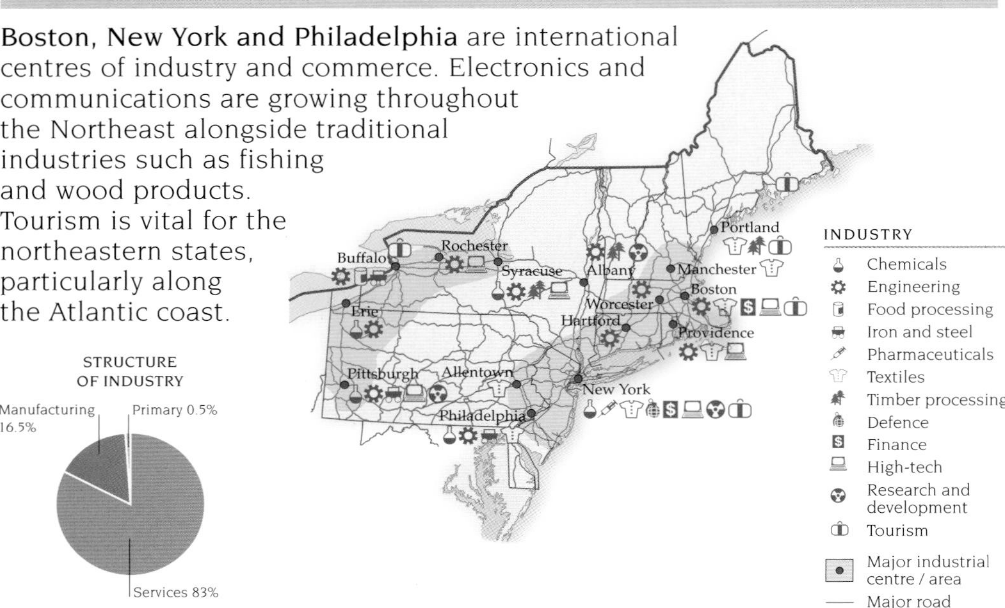

Buffalo
Rochester
Syracuse
Albany
Portland
Manchester
Boston
Worcester
Hartford
Providence
Erie
Pittsburgh
Allentown
New York
Philadelphia
INDUSTRY
Chemicals
Engineering
Food processing
Iron and steel
Pharmaceuticals
Textiles
Timber processing
Defence
Finance
High-tech
Research and development
Tourism
Major industrial centre / area
Major road
STRUCTURE OF INDUSTRY
Manufacturing 16.5%
Primary 0.5%
Services 83%

ENVIRONMENTAL ISSUES

The high level of industry and the large population puts great pressure on the environment. Air pollution from vehicles and industry led to poor air quality in many cities and caused acid rain. The problem is worse close to the Great Lakes, where severe lake pollution has occurred.

ENVIRONMENTAL ISSUES
- Urban air pollution
- Wind farm
- Affected by acid rain
- Severely affected by acid rain
- Polluted rivers
- Sea/lake pollution
- Severe sea/lake pollution
- Major industrial centre

Rochester, Buffalo, Erie, Pittsburgh, New York, Philadelphia, Boston, *Hudson River*, *Delaware River*

FARMING AND LAND USE

The varied landscape of the northeastern states supports a great range of farming. Livestock, including cattle, horses, poultry and pigs, are raised throughout the region. The main crops are fruits and vegetables. Fishing is important, especially off the Atlantic coast of Maine.

FARMING AND LAND USE
- Cattle
- Pigs
- Poultry
- Fishing
- Cereals
- Cranberries
- Fruit
- Maple syrup
- Timber
- Cropland
- Forest
- Pasture
- Major conurbation

Buffalo, Rochester, Albany, Boston, Pittsburgh, Allentown, New York, Philadelphia

LAND USE
Pasture 6%
Cropland 14%
Other 16 %
Forest 64%

THE LANDSCAPE

The Appalachian and Adirondack Mountains form a barrier between the marshy lowlands of the Atlantic coast and the lowlands further west. The interior consists of rolling hills, fertile valleys and thousands of lakes created by the movement of glaciers.

Appalachians (E3)
The Appalachian Mountains, which run through most of this region, are the eroded remnants of peaks that were once much higher.

Rocky coastline (G3)
The coast of Maine is made up of rocky bays, islands, and inlets. If the shoreline were stretched out, it would be 4,000 km long.

Adirondacks (E3)
The Adirondacks are a broad, wide mountain range, formed when older rocks were forced into a 'dome' shape by movements in the Earth's crust many millions of years ago.

Long Island Sound (F5)
Long Island Sound is a river valley that was drowned by rising sea levels.

Finger Lakes (D3)
The long, narrow Finger Lakes lie in upper New York state. They were cut by glaciers.

Delaware Bay (D6)
Deep bays such as Delaware Bay are often surrounded by salt marshes and barrier beaches that create ideal breeding conditions for a wide variety of birds and animals.

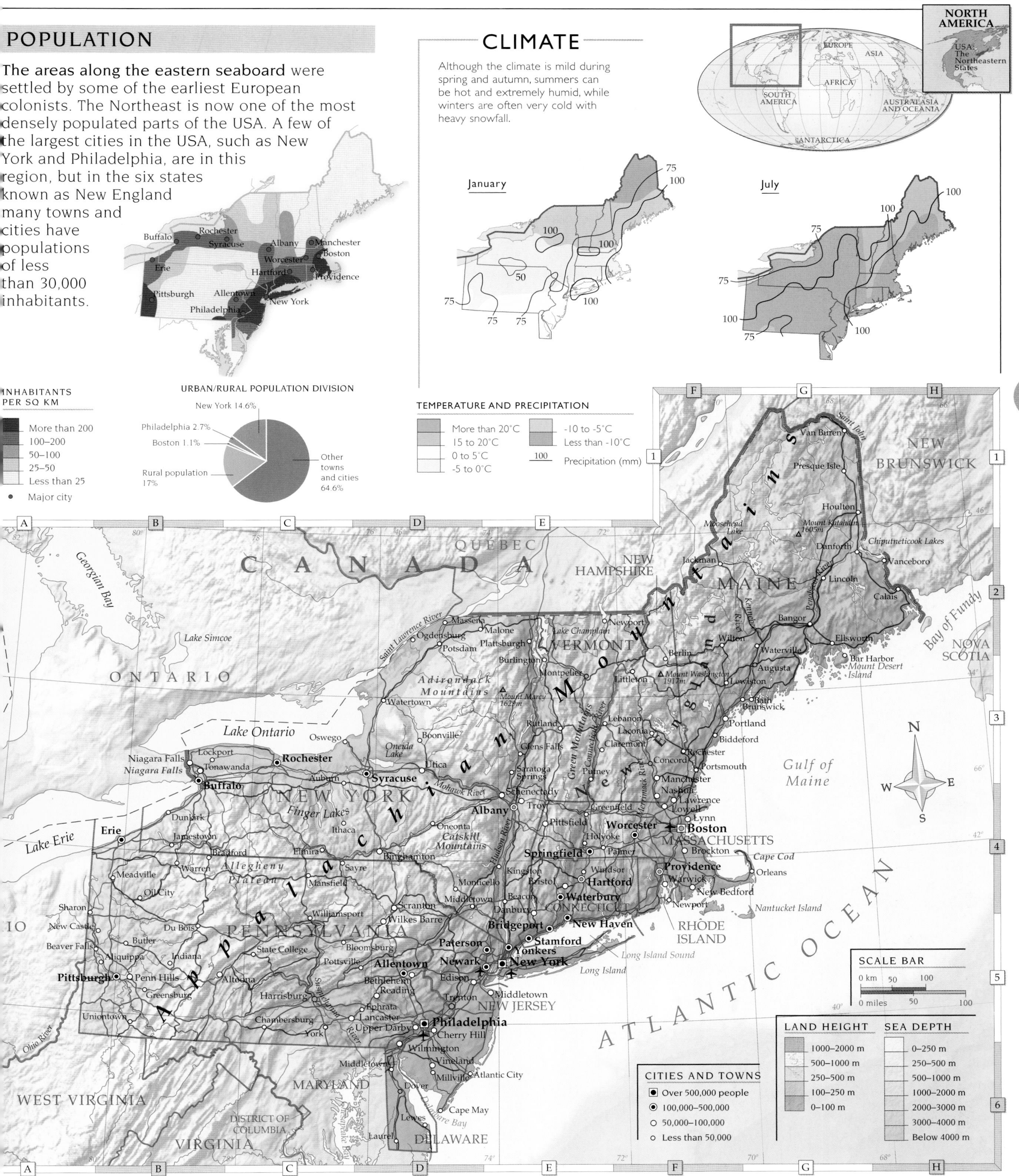
POPULATION
The areas along the eastern seaboard were settled by some of the earliest European colonists. The Northeast is now one of the most densely populated parts of the USA. A few of the largest cities in the USA, such as New York and Philadelphia, are in this region, but in the six states known as New England many towns and cities have populations of less than 30,000 inhabitants.
Buffalo
Rochester
Syracuse
Albany
Manchester
Boston
Erie
Worcester
Hartford
Providence
Pittsburgh
Allentown
New York
Philadelphia
INHABITANTS PER SQ KM
More than 200
100–200
50–100
25–50
Less than 25
Major city
URBAN/RURAL POPULATION DIVISION
New York 14.6%
Philadelphia 2.7%
Boston 1.1%
Rural population 17%
Other towns and cities 64.6%
CLIMATE
Although the climate is mild during spring and autumn, summers can be hot and extremely humid, while winters are often very cold with heavy snowfall.
January
July
TEMPERATURE AND PRECIPITATION
More than 20°C
15 to 20°C
0 to 5°C
-5 to 0°C
-10 to -5°C
Less than -10°C
100 Precipitation (mm)
NORTH AMERICA
USA: The Northeastern States
EUROPE
ASIA
AFRICA
SOUTH AMERICA
AUSTRALASIA AND OCEANIA
ANTARCTICA
CANADA
QUEBEC
ONTARIO
NEW BRUNSWICK
NOVA SCOTIA
Georgian Bay
Lake Simcoe
Lake Ontario
Lake Erie
Bay of Fundy
Gulf of Maine
ATLANTIC OCEAN
Appalachian Mountains
New England
MAINE
NEW HAMPSHIRE
VERMONT
MASSACHUSETTS
RHODE ISLAND
CONNECTICUT
NEW YORK
PENNSYLVANIA
NEW JERSEY
DELAWARE
MARYLAND
WEST VIRGINIA
VIRGINIA
DISTRICT OF COLUMBIA
Adirondack Mountains
Mount Marcy 1629m
Mount Washington 1917m
Mount Katahdin 1605m
Catskill Mountains
Allegheny Plateau
Finger Lakes
Green Mountains
Lake Champlain
Moosehead Lake
Chiputneticook Lakes
Mount Desert Island
Cape Cod
Nantucket Island
Long Island
Long Island Sound
Saint Lawrence River
Mohawk River
Hudson River
Connecticut River
Merrimack River
Kennebec River
Penobscot River
Saint John
Susquehanna River
Delaware Bay
Chesapeake Bay
Ohio River
Niagara Falls
Boston
New York
Philadelphia
Pittsburgh
Buffalo
Rochester
Syracuse
Albany
Erie
Worcester
Springfield
Providence
Hartford
Waterbury
Bridgeport
New Haven
Stamford
Yonkers
Paterson
Newark
Allentown
Portland
Bangor
Augusta
Montpelier
Burlington
Concord
Manchester
Atlantic City
Cape May
SCALE BAR
0 km 50 100
0 miles 50 100
LAND HEIGHT
1000–2000 m
500–1000 m
250–500 m
100–250 m
0–100 m
SEA DEPTH
0–250 m
250–500 m
500–1000 m
1000–2000 m
2000–3000 m
3000–4000 m
Below 4000 m
CITIES AND TOWNS
Over 500,000 people
100,000–500,000
50,000–100,000
Less than 50,000

USA: The Southern States

ALABAMA, ARKANSAS, DISTRICT OF COLUMBIA, FLORIDA, GEORGIA, KENTUCKY, LOUISIANA, MARYLAND, MISSISSIPPI, NORTH CAROLINA, SOUTH CAROLINA, TENNESSEE, VIRGINIA, WEST VIRGINIA

The southern states suffered great devastation and poverty as a result of the Civil War (1861–65). Recovery has come with the discovery and exploitation of resources and the development of major commercial and industrial centres. Yet these states retain the vibrant mix of cultures that reflect their French, Spanish, English and African heritage.

INDUSTRY

Tourism is a major industry in the 'sunbelt' states, especially Florida, and many people move to the area when they retire to enjoy the climate. Oil and gas are extracted along the coast of the Gulf of Mexico, and there are many related chemical industries. Textiles are still produced in North and South Carolina, but aerospace and other high-tech industries have been established as well.

STRUCTURE OF INDUSTRY

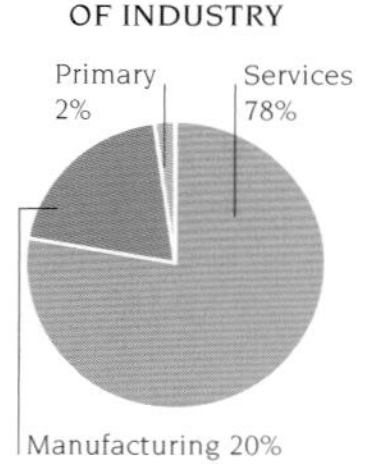

Primary 2%
Services 78%
Manufacturing 20%

Baltimore
Washington DC
Louisville
Lexington
Norfolk
Winston Salem
Greensboro
Raleigh
Knoxville
Charlotte
Little Rock
Memphis
Huntsville
Greenville
Birmingham
Atlanta
Baton Rouge
Mobile
New Orleans
Jacksonville
Orlando
Tampa
Miami

INDUSTRY
Aerospace
Chemicals
Engineering
Food processing
Iron and steel
Textiles
Coal
Oil and gas
High-tech
Research and development
Tourism
Major industrial centre / area
Major road

POPULATION

Creoles, descended from Spanish and French colonizers, and Cajuns, of French-Canadian ancestry, live in the south of this region. Florida has a large Hispanic population, increased by migration from the Caribbean. In the early 20th century, five million black people, the descendants of slaves, left the South for cities in the North.

WASHINGTON, DC; Baltimore; Louisville; Huntington; Richmond; Norfolk; Knoxville; Charlotte; Memphis; Greenville; Huntsville; Birmingham; Atlanta; Savannah; Mobile; Baton Rouge; Tallahassee; New Orleans; Jacksonville; Orlando; Tampa; Miami

INHABITANTS PER SQ KM

- More than 200
- 100–200
- 50–100
- 25–50
- Less than 25
- Capital city
- Major city

URBAN/RURAL POPULATION DIVISION

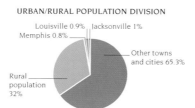

Louisville 0.9%, Jacksonville 1%, Memphis 0.8%, Other towns and cities 65.3%, Rural population 32%

FARMING AND LAND USE

Cotton is still the South's main crop, but many old cotton fields are now pastures where all types of livestock are raised. Florida is famous for citrus fruits, while Georgia is renowned for peanuts. Sugarcane, soya beans, tobacco, corn, fruits and rice are grown in other areas.

Baltimore; Washington, DC; Memphis; New Orleans; Jacksonville

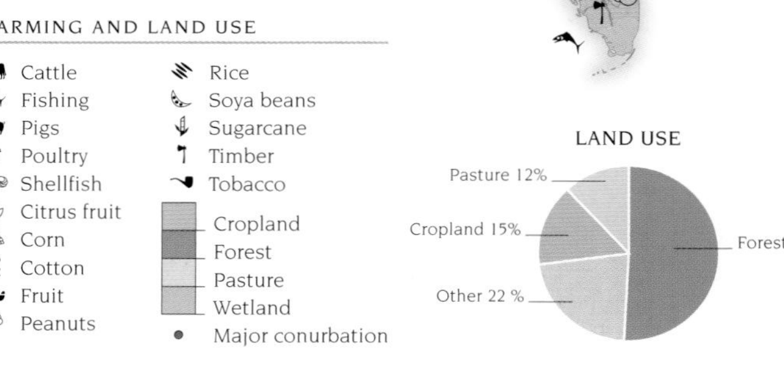

FARMING AND LAND USE
Cattle
Fishing
Pigs
Poultry
Shellfish
Citrus fruit
Corn
Cotton
Fruit
Peanuts
Rice
Soya beans
Sugarcane
Timber
Tobacco
Cropland
Forest
Pasture
Wetland
Major conurbation
LAND USE
Pasture 12%
Cropland 15%
Other 22 %
Forest 51%

THE LANDSCAPE

The South is a land of contrasts – the uplands of the Appalachians, the foothills of the Piedmont, and low-lying coastal regions are all featured. The interior lowlands are drained by the Mississippi. Florida is dotted with thousands of lakes and is home to the Everglades, a giant sawgrass swamp.

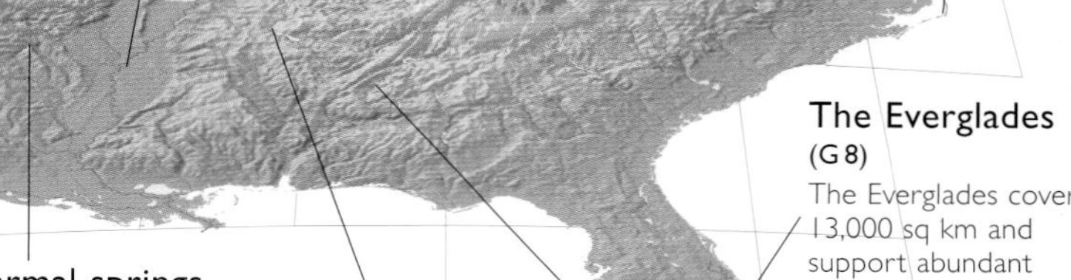

Mississippi River (C4)
A major transport artery, the Mississippi was an essential route in opening up the interior region. With its main tributary, the Missouri, it is nearly 6,115 km long, making it the world's fourth-longest river.

Kentucky Bluegrass (E2)
The gently rolling bluegrass landscape of northern Kentucky is ideal country for raising horses and livestock.

Barrier beaches (I 3)
Sandy barrier beaches and islands line the eastern and southern coasts, along with sheltered lagoons and salt marshes.

The Everglades (G8)
The Everglades cover 13,000 sq km and support abundant wild animals and plants, many unique to the area.

Thermal springs (B4)
Hot Springs National Park in Arkansas has 47 thermal springs and is a popular tourist and health resort. Visitors relax here in the hot water that trickles from the hillsides.

Tennessee River (D4)
The Tennessee River is 1,000 km long. Dams along the river generate hydro-electricity to provide most of the region's energy needs.

Limestone caves (E4)
Cathedral Caverns in Alabama is a collection of enormous limestone caves. The main entrance is more than 300 m high and 45 m wide.

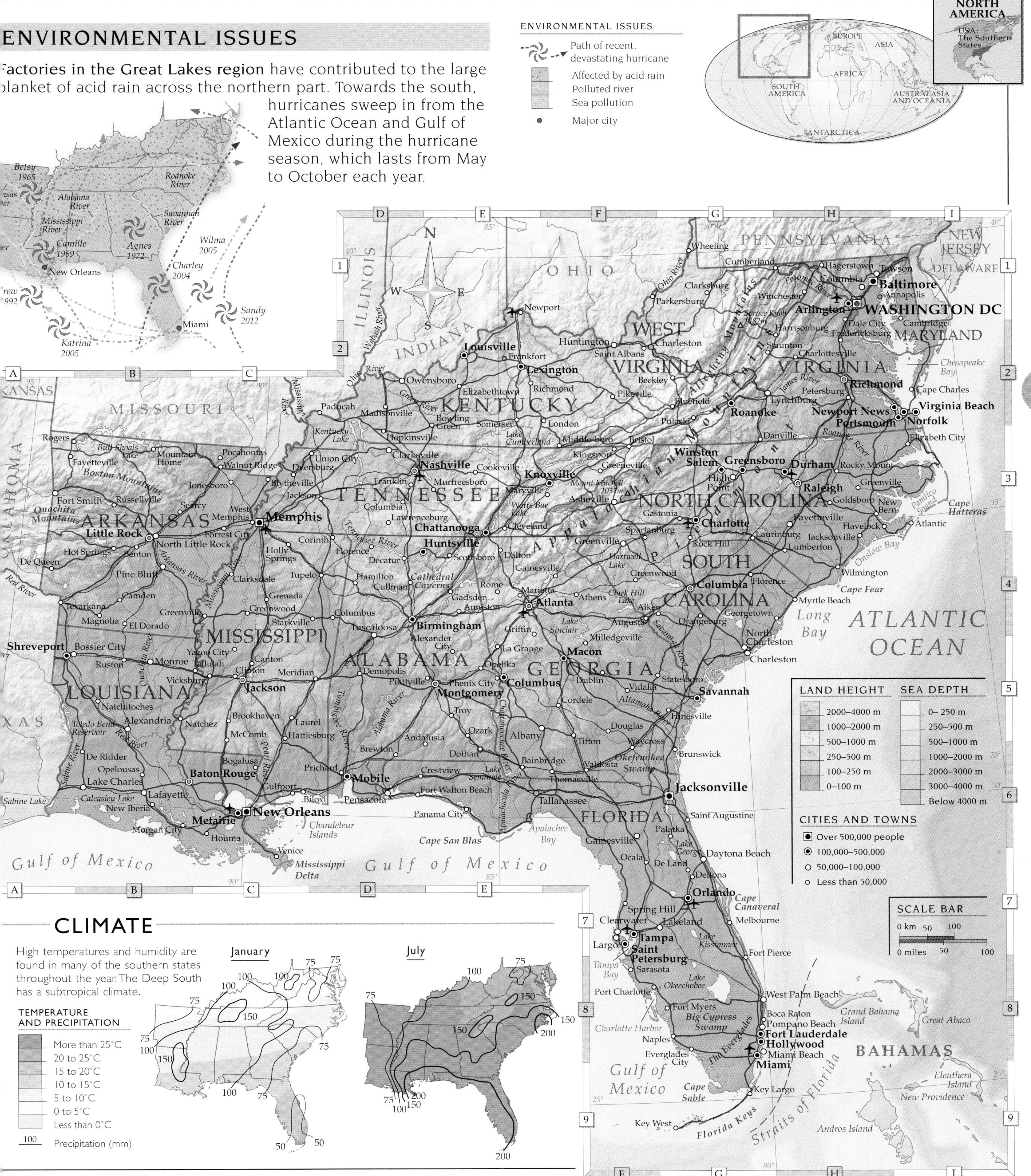

NORTH AMERICA
USA: The Southern States
EUROPE
ASIA
AFRICA
SOUTH AMERICA
AUSTRALASIA AND OCEANIA
ANTARCTICA
ENVIRONMENTAL ISSUES
Path of recent, devastating hurricane
Affected by acid rain
Polluted river
Sea pollution
Major city
Betsy 1965
Roanoke River
Alabama River
Savannah River
Mississippi River
Camille 1969
Agnes 1972
Wilma 2005
Charley 2004
New Orleans
Sandy 2012
Miami
Katrina 2005
PENNSYLVANIA
NEW JERSEY
DELAWARE
OHIO
ILLINOIS
INDIANA
WEST VIRGINIA
VIRGINIA
MARYLAND
WASHINGTON DC
Baltimore
KENTUCKY
MISSOURI
TENNESSEE
NORTH CAROLINA
SOUTH CAROLINA
ARKANSAS
MISSISSIPPI
ALABAMA
GEORGIA
LOUISIANA
FLORIDA
ATLANTIC OCEAN
Gulf of Mexico
BAHAMAS
Straits of Florida
Florida Keys
Nashville
Memphis
Atlanta
Charlotte
Jacksonville
New Orleans
Miami
LAND HEIGHT
2000–4000 m
1000–2000 m
500–1000 m
250–500 m
100–250 m
0–100 m
SEA DEPTH
0– 250 m
250–500 m
500–1000 m
1000–2000 m
2000–3000 m
3000–4000 m
Below 4000 m
CITIES AND TOWNS
Over 500,000 people
100,000–500,000
50,000–100,000
Less than 50,000
SCALE BAR
0 km 50 100
0 miles 50 100
January
July
TEMPERATURE AND PRECIPITATION
More than 25°C
20 to 25°C
15 to 20°C
10 to 15°C
5 to 10°C
0 to 5°C
Less than 0°C
100 Precipitation (mm)

ENVIRONMENTAL ISSUES

Factories in the Great Lakes region have contributed to the large blanket of acid rain across the northern part. Towards the south, hurricanes sweep in from the Atlantic Ocean and Gulf of Mexico during the hurricane season, which lasts from May to October each year.

CLIMATE

High temperatures and humidity are found in many of the southern states throughout the year. The Deep South has a subtropical climate.

USA: The Great Lakes States

ILLINOIS, INDIANA, MICHIGAN, OHIO, WISCONSIN

Good transport links, excellent farmland and a wealth of natural resources drew settlers from Europe and the south and east of the USA to the Great Lakes states during the late 19th century. By the 1930s, they had become one of the world's most prosperous industrial and agricultural regions. In recent years, the decline in traditional heavy industries has hit some cities hard, leading to unemployment and a rising crime rate.

POPULATION

The Great Lakes states are one of the most densely populated parts of the USA. Many of the largest cities in this region – Chicago, Detroit and Milwaukee – grew up on the banks of the lakes and are connected to each other and the rest of the USA by an impressive road and rail network.

INHABITANTS PER SQ KM

- More than 200
- 100–200
- 50–100
- 25–50
- Less than 25
- Major city

URBAN/RURAL POPULATION DIVISION

- Detroit 2%
- Chicago 6.3%
- Indianapolis 1.7%
- Other towns and cities 66%
- Rural population 24%

CLIMATE

Plentiful rainfall waters the agricultural lands. In winter, strong winds sweep across the lakes, and water close to the shore may freeze.

January

July

TEMPERATURE AND PRECIPITATION

- More than 25°C
- 20 to 25°C
- 15 to 20°C
- 0 to 5°C
- -5 to 0°C
- -10 to -5°C
- Less than -10°C
- 100 Precipitation (mm)

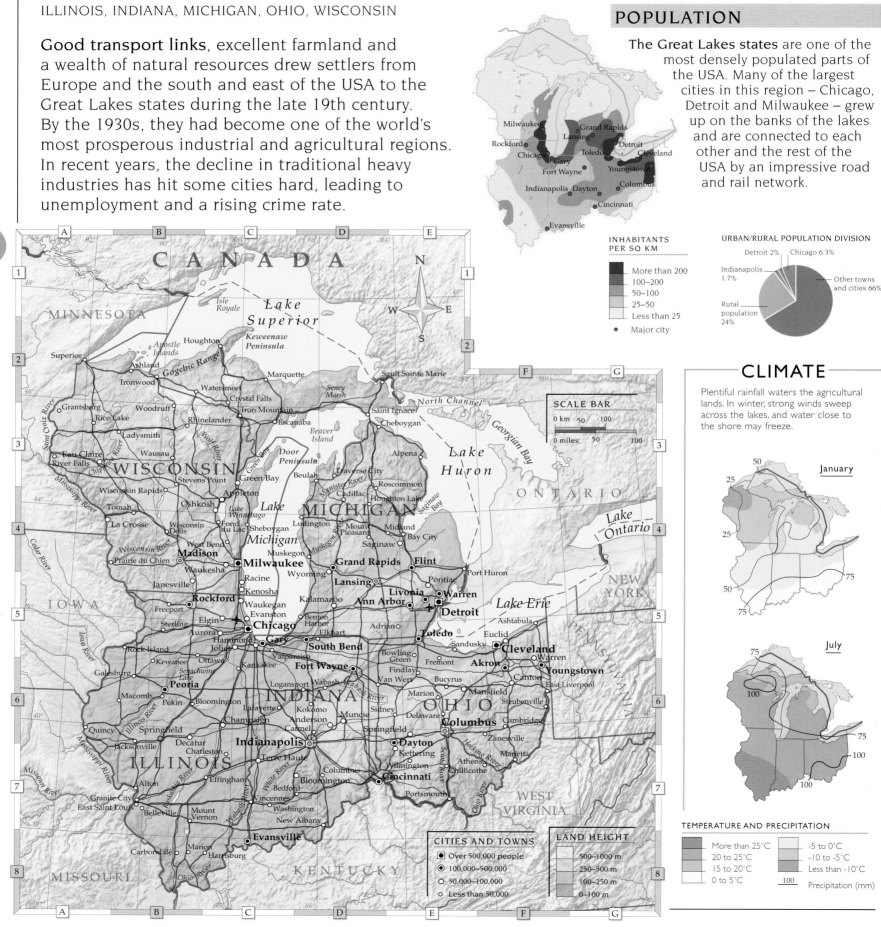

SCALE BAR

0 km 50 100

0 miles 50 100

CITIES AND TOWNS

- Over 500,000 people
- 100,000–500,000
- 50,000–100,000
- Less than 50,000

LAND HEIGHT

- 500–1000 m
- 250–500 m
- 100–250 m
- 0–100 m

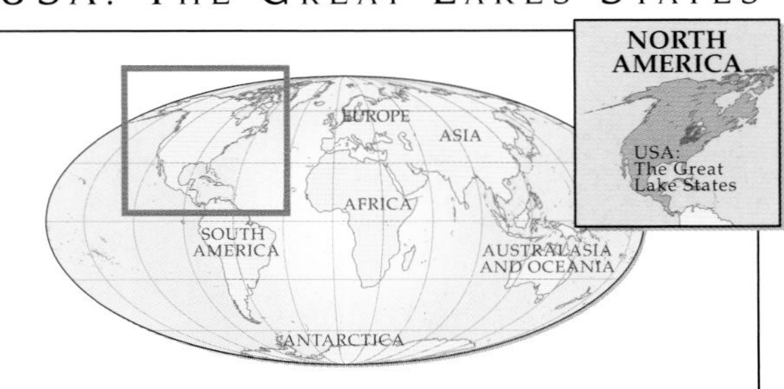
NORTH AMERICA
USA: The Great Lake States
EUROPE
ASIA
AFRICA
SOUTH AMERICA
AUSTRALASIA AND OCEANIA
ANTARCTICA

FARMING AND LAND USE

Michigan is renowned for its cherries and apples. Corn and soya beans are the main crops produced in the region's southern states. Livestock-rearing includes pig and poultry farms – many very large – in Illinois, Indiana and Ohio. Cattle rearing and dairy farming are common in Michigan and Wisconsin.

LAND USE
Pasture 8%
Other 16%
Cropland 47%
Forest 29%

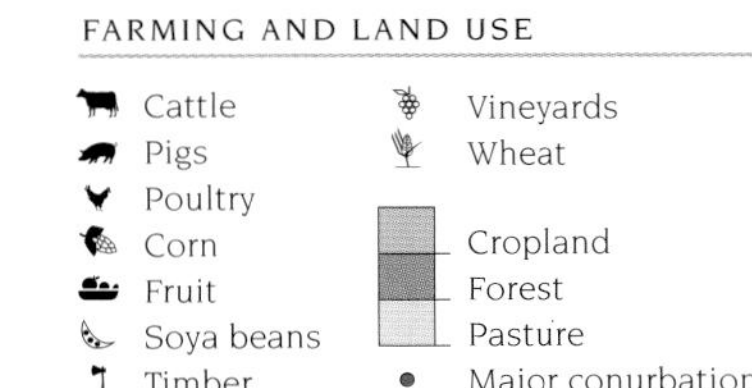
FARMING AND LAND USE
Cattle
Pigs
Poultry
Corn
Fruit
Soya beans
Timber
Tobacco
Vineyards
Wheat
Cropland
Forest
Pasture
Major conurbation

THE LANDSCAPE

Until about 10,000 years ago, much of this region was covered by great ice sheets that extended south to Illinois and Ohio. When the ice melted the Great Lakes were left in large hollows that the ice had scoured. The ice sheets changed the course of many rivers, so today most rivers flow south into the Mississippi/Missouri River system.

Lakes and marshes (B3)

Wisconsin is scattered with thousands of smaller lakes and many marshy areas. Like the Great Lakes, they were formed by erosion by the retreating ice at the end of the last Ice Age.

Underground water

In northern Illinois much of the water is pumped from underground reservoirs. In some places, the water table has dropped by 215 m over the last century, so many areas now face a water shortage.

Moraines

When the last ice age ended, the retreating ice sheets left long ridges and piles of rock to the south of Lake Michigan. Some of these ridges, known as moraines, can be up to 90 m high.

Limestone region

Limestone in the hills of southern Indiana has been dissolved by acid rainwater. This has produced features such as sinkholes and underground caves.

Lake Erie (F5)

Lake Erie is the shallowest of the Great Lakes. Its average depth is about 19 m. Storms that sweep across from Canada have eroded its shores and caused the silting of its harbours.

INDUSTRY

The US vehicle industry grew up on the banks of the Great Lakes, supported by the manufacture of iron and steel. Both industries have suffered in recent years from competition from cheap foreign imports. Meat packing has moved out from cities such as Chicago closer to the farms. New industries which have developed since the 1970s include electronics, service and finance industries.

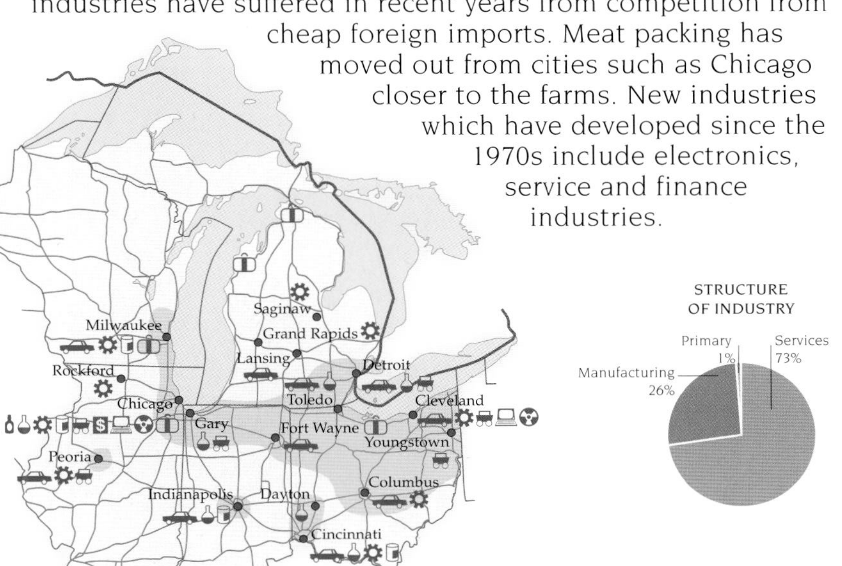
Milwaukee
Saginaw
Grand Rapids
Lansing
Rockford
Detroit
Chicago
Gary
Toledo
Cleveland
Fort Wayne
Youngstown
Peoria
Indianapolis
Dayton
Columbus
Cincinnati
Evansville
STRUCTURE OF INDUSTRY
Primary 1%
Services 73%
Manufacturing 26%

INDUSTRY

- Brewing
- Car manufacturing
- Chemicals
- Engineering
- Food processing
- Iron and steel
- Finance
- High-tech
- Research and development
- Tourism
- Major industrial centre / area
- Major road

ENVIRONMENTAL ISSUES

The heavy industries on the banks of the Great Lakes have caused terrible pollution over the last century. Industrial effluent has polluted the lakes themselves, and factory emissions have led to severely acidic rain, which affects forests and lakes both here and further away in Canada.

ENVIRONMENTAL ISSUES

- Urban air pollution
- Wind farm
- Affected by acid rain
- Severely affected by acid rain
- Polluted rivers
- Lake pollution
- Severe lake pollution
- Major industrial centre

Milwaukee
Detroit
Chicago
Gary
Cleveland
Mississippi River
Ohio River

USA: The Central States

IOWA, KANSAS, MINNESOTA, MISSOURI, NEBRASKA, NORTH DAKOTA, OKLAHOMA, SOUTH DAKOTA

The prairie states of the central USA became one of America's richest agricultural regions in the mid-19th century. Despite the 'Dustbowl' crisis of the 1930s, which led many farmers to leave their ruined lands, agriculture is still crucial to the economy, and one third of the people still live in rural areas rather than large cities.

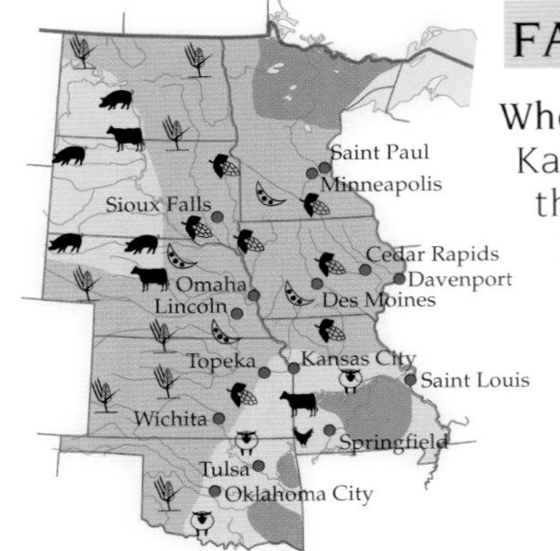

Saint Paul
Minneapolis
Sioux Falls
Cedar Rapids
Davenport
Omaha
Lincoln
Des Moines
Topeka
Kansas City
Saint Louis
Wichita
Springfield
Tulsa
Oklahoma City

FARMING AND LAND USE

Wheat and corn grow on the fertile plains. Kansas is the leading grower of wheat in the entire USA, while Iowa is one of the leaders in corn and livestock. Irrigation projects to combat drought are crucial in large areas. Livestock – including cattle in vast herds; pigs, particularly in Iowa, the Dakotas and Nebraska; sheep; and turkeys – are raised throughout these states.

LAND USE

Other 37%
Cropland 43%
Forest 11%
Pasture 9%

FARMING AND LAND USE

- Cattle
- Pigs
- Poultry
- Sheep
- Corn
- Soya beans
- Wheat
- Cropland
- Forest
- Pasture
- Major conurbation

INDUSTRY

Industries related to agriculture, such as food processing and the production of farm machinery, are traditional in these states but high-tech industries – such as aeronautical engineering – are increasing and large aerospace plants are found in Wichita and Saint Louis. Oil and gas are extracted in great quantities toward the south of the region, especially in Oklahoma and Kansas.

STRUCTURE OF INDUSTRY

Primary 4%
Services 76%
Manufacturing 20%

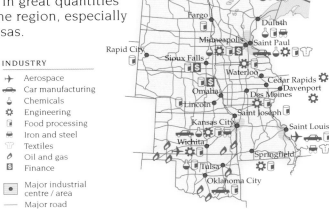

INDUSTRY

- Aerospace
- Car manufacturing
- Chemicals
- Engineering
- Food processing
- Iron and steel
- Textiles
- Oil and gas
- Finance
- Major industrial centre / area
- Major road

Fargo
Duluth
Minneapolis
Saint Paul
Rapid City
Sioux Falls
Waterloo
Cedar Rapids
Davenport
Omaha
Des Moines
Lincoln
Saint Joseph
Kansas City
Saint Louis
Wichita
Springfield
Tulsa
Oklahoma City

THE LANDSCAPE

Most of the eastern edge of this region is marked by the Mississippi River, while the Missouri bisects it, running from northwest to southeast. The Great Plains cover most of this area, gradually rising towards the Rocky Mountains at the far western edge of the Central States.

The Badlands (A 4)
The Badlands cover an area of about 5,200 sq km in South Dakota. Heavily eroded by wind and water, almost nothing grows there.

Minnesota
Minnesota is filled with lakes, hills strewn with boulders, and mineral-rich deposits that have been left behind by the scouring movement of glaciers.

Chimney Rock (A-5)
Chimney Rock stands 150 m above the plains. It is a remnant of an ancient land surface that was eroded by the North Platte River.

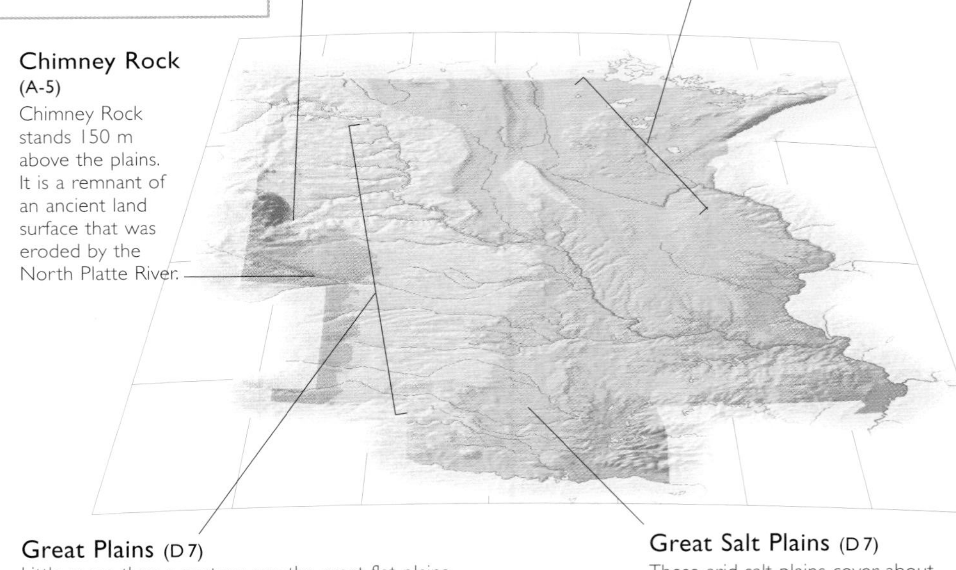

Great Plains (D 7)
Little more than a century ago the great flat plains that cover most of these states were home to wild grasses and massive herds of buffalo. In areas where lack of water has made farming impossible, large tracts of land are being allowed to return to grassland.

Great Salt Plains (D 7)
These arid salt plains cover about 120 sq km of northern Oklahoma. An ancient salt lake once occupied the area. When the salt evaporated, only the salt flats were left.

ENVIRONMENTAL ISSUES

Intensive agriculture requires large quantities of water to grow crops. Over-intensive use of the land has destroyed the balance of soil and water in the past, leading to fertile farmland being turned into useless areas of 'Dustbowl'. These states have a great underground store of water known as the Ogallala Aquifer, but over-extraction for irrigation is reducing the amount of available water.

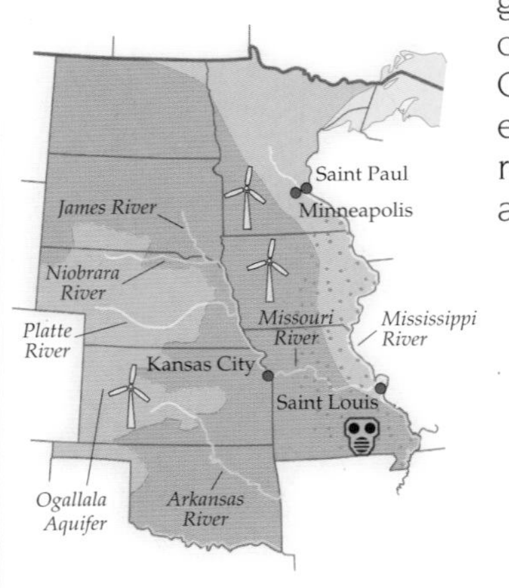

Saint Paul
Minneapolis
James River
Niobrara River
Platte River
Missouri River
Mississippi River
Kansas City
Saint Louis
Ogallala Aquifer
Arkansas River

ENVIRONMENTAL ISSUES

- Urban air pollution
- Wind farm
- Affected by acid rain
- Aquifer
- Polluted river
- Risk of desertification
- Major industrial centre

POPULATION

The inhabitants are largely the descendants of Europeans who came to the region in the late 1800s. The entire region is primarily rural, with enormous tracts of land devoted to growing crops. North Dakota has no city with a population greater than 100,000.

CLIMATE

The Central States have a continental climate, with hot, dry summers and long, cold winters. Unreliable rainfall can be a problem for farmers on the Great Plains.

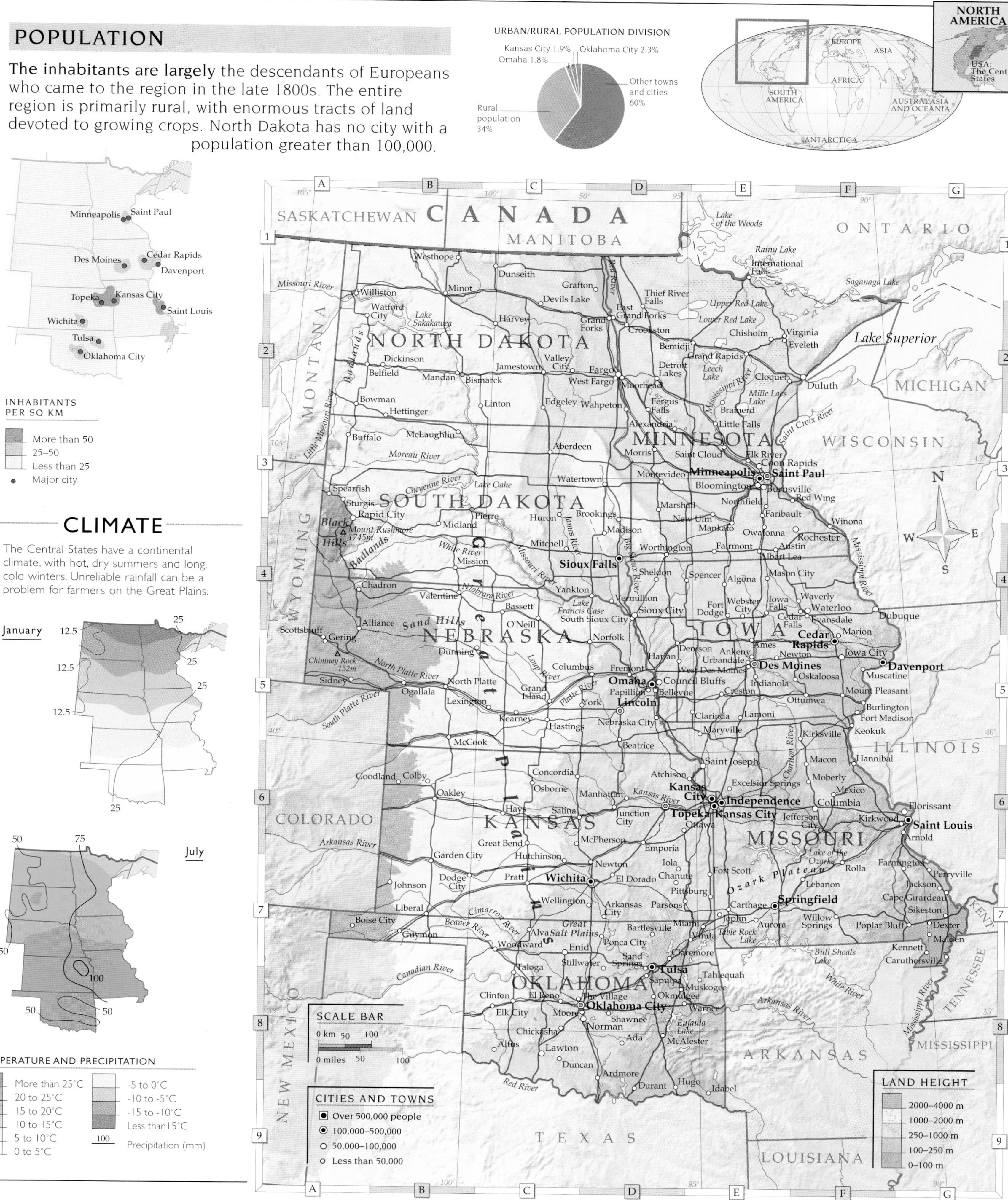

URBAN/RURAL POPULATION DIVISION
Kansas City 1.9%
Oklahoma City 2.3%
Omaha 1.8%
Other towns and cities 60%
Rural population 34%
NORTH AMERICA
EUROPE
ASIA
AFRICA
SOUTH AMERICA
AUSTRALASIA AND OCEANIA
ANTARCTICA
USA: The Central States
Minneapolis
Saint Paul
Des Moines
Cedar Rapids
Davenport
Topeka
Kansas City
Saint Louis
Wichita
Tulsa
Oklahoma City
INHABITANTS PER SQ KM
More than 50
25–50
Less than 25
Major city
January
July
TEMPERATURE AND PRECIPITATION
More than 25°C
20 to 25°C
15 to 20°C
10 to 15°C
5 to 10°C
0 to 5°C
-5 to 0°C
-10 to -5°C
-15 to -10°C
Less than 15°C
Precipitation (mm)
CANADA
SASKATCHEWAN
MANITOBA
ONTARIO
NORTH DAKOTA
SOUTH DAKOTA
NEBRASKA
KANSAS
OKLAHOMA
MINNESOTA
IOWA
MISSOURI
WISCONSIN
MICHIGAN
ILLINOIS
MONTANA
WYOMING
COLORADO
NEW MEXICO
TEXAS
ARKANSAS
LOUISIANA
MISSISSIPPI
TENNESSEE
KENT.
Lake Superior
Lake of the Woods
Great Plains
Ozark Plateau
Black Hills
Mount Rushmore 1745m
Badlands
Sand Hills
Chimney Rock 152m
Missouri River
Mississippi River
Red River
Arkansas River
Canadian River
Platte River
North Platte River
South Platte River
Niobrara River
Cheyenne River
White River
Kansas River
Cimarron River
Lake Sakakawea
Lake Oahe
Fargo
Bismarck
Sioux Falls
Omaha
Lincoln
Minneapolis
Saint Paul
Des Moines
Cedar Rapids
Davenport
Kansas City
Independence
Topeka
Saint Louis
Springfield
Wichita
Tulsa
Oklahoma City
Duluth
Rochester
SCALE BAR
0 km 50 100
0 miles 50 100
CITIES AND TOWNS
Over 500,000 people
100,000–500,000
50,000–100,000
Less than 50,000
LAND HEIGHT
2000–4000 m
1000–2000 m
250–1000 m
100–250 m
0–100 m
N
E
S
W

USA: The Southwestern States

ARIZONA, NEW MEXICO, TEXAS

Large parts of the southwestern states were purchased from Mexico in 1848. This land of expansive plateaus, spectacular canyons, prairies and deserts is home to several distinct peoples, whose customs and traditions are still practised. The Navaho and Hopi own one-third of the land in Arizona, and the ruins of thousand-year-old cliff dwellings built by the Anasazi people are still preserved there today.

ENVIRONMENTAL ISSUES

Desertification is a serious problem in the southwestern states. Lack of water combined with intensive farming has allowed soils to erode. Drought is held at bay by irrigation, but falling water table levels are a cause for concern. New Mexico was the site for many early nuclear weapons tests, and some places remain contaminated.

ENVIRONMENTAL ISSUES

- Urban air pollution
- Former nuclear test site
- Path of recent, devastating hurricane
- Wind farm
- Desert area
- Risk of desertification
- Polluted river
- Major industrial centre

Phoenix
Mesa
El Paso
Dallas
Red River
Rita 2005
Brazos River
Houston

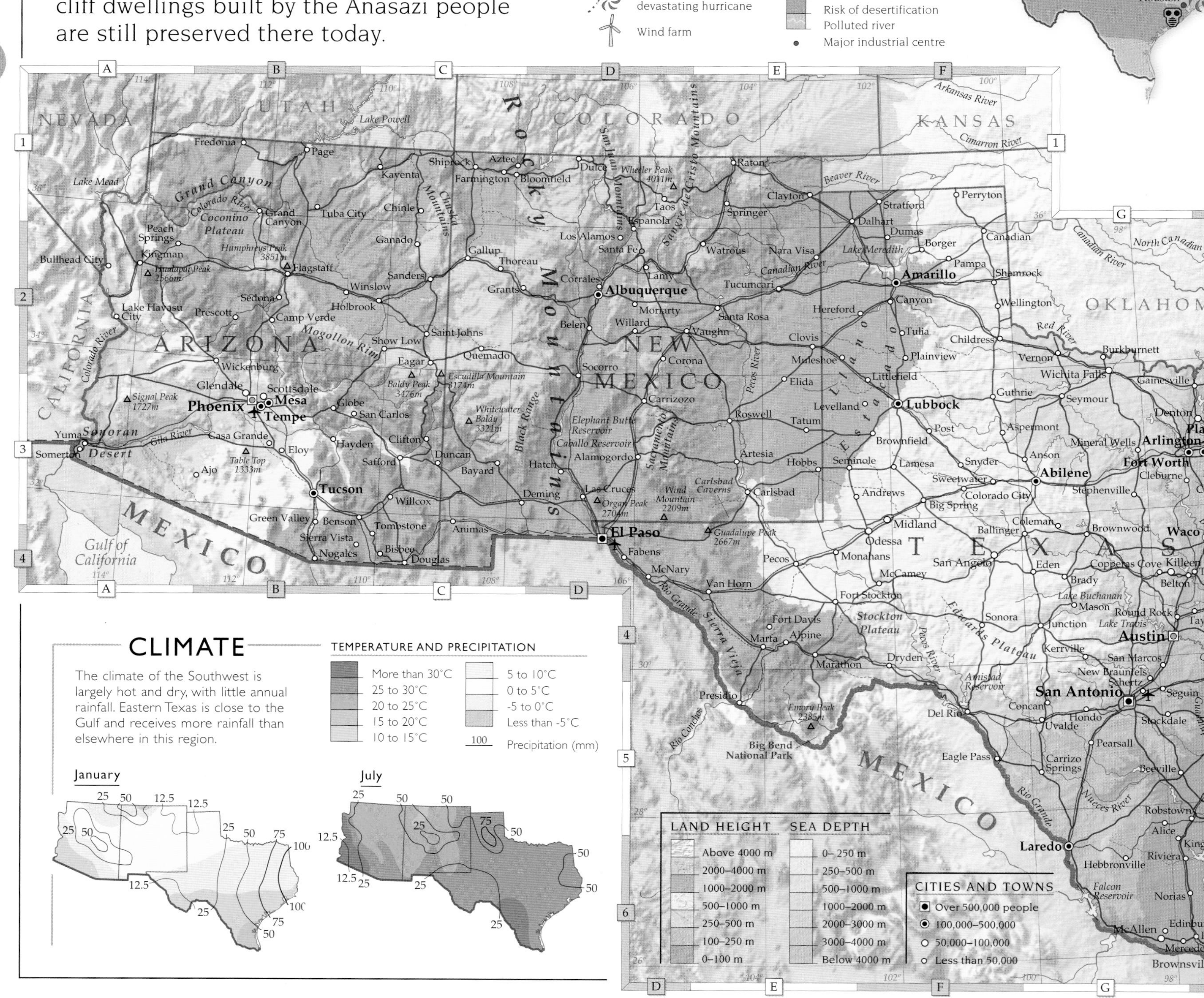
UTAH
COLORADO
KANSAS
NEVADA
CALIFORNIA
OKLAHOMA
ARIZONA
NEW MEXICO
TEXAS
MEXICO
Rocky Mountains
Grand Canyon
Lake Powell
Lake Mead
Coconino Plateau
Mogollon Rim
Sonoran Desert
Gulf of California
Colorado River
Gila River
Rio Grande
Pecos River
Canadian River
Red River
Arkansas River
Cimarron River
Beaver River
Llano Estacado
Edwards Plateau
Stockton Plateau
Sierra Vieja
Big Bend National Park
Phoenix
Tucson
Mesa
Tempe
Scottsdale
Glendale
Flagstaff
Albuquerque
Santa Fe
Los Alamos
Las Cruces
El Paso
Amarillo
Lubbock
Midland
Odessa
Abilene
San Angelo
Austin
San Antonio
Laredo
Arlington
Fort Worth
Waco
Wichita Falls
Roswell
Carlsbad
Humphreys Peak 3851m
Wheeler Peak 4011m
Guadalupe Peak 2667m
Emory Peak 2385m
CLIMATE
The climate of the Southwest is largely hot and dry, with little annual rainfall. Eastern Texas is close to the Gulf and receives more rainfall than elsewhere in this region.
TEMPERATURE AND PRECIPITATION
More than 30°C
25 to 30°C
20 to 25°C
15 to 20°C
10 to 15°C
5 to 10°C
0 to 5°C
-5 to 0°C
Less than -5°C
100 Precipitation (mm)
January
July
LAND HEIGHT
Above 4000 m
2000–4000 m
1000–2000 m
500–1000 m
250–500 m
100–250 m
0–100 m
SEA DEPTH
0–250 m
250–500 m
500–1000 m
1000–2000 m
2000–3000 m
3000–4000 m
Below 4000 m
CITIES AND TOWNS
Over 500,000 people
100,000–500,000
50,000–100,000
Less than 50,000

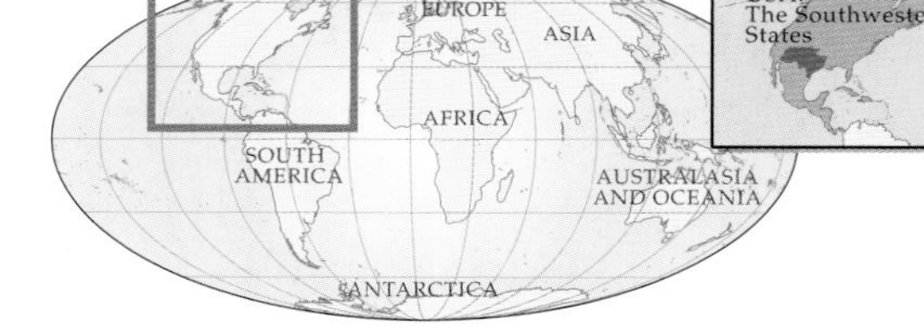
NORTH AMERICA
USA: The Southwestern States
EUROPE
ASIA
AFRICA
SOUTH AMERICA
AUSTRALASIA AND OCEANIA
ANTARCTICA

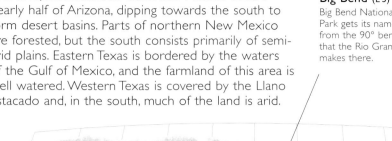

THE LANDSCAPE

The arid, mountainous Colorado Plateau covers nearly half of Arizona, dipping towards the south to form desert basins. Parts of northern New Mexico are forested, but the south consists primarily of semi-arid plains. Eastern Texas is bordered by the waters of the Gulf of Mexico, and the farmland of this area is well watered. Western Texas is covered by the Llano Estacado and, in the south, much of the land is arid.

Big Bend (E5)
Big Bend National Park gets its name from the 90° bend that the Rio Grande makes there.

Invading sea
The crust of southeastern Texas is warping, causing the land to subside and allowing the sea to invade. Hurricanes make the situation worse.

Grand Canyon (B1)
The Grand Canyon is a dramatic gorge cut in the rock by the Colorado River. It is about 450 km long, 675 km wide, and up to 1.6 km deep.

Carlsbad Caverns (B3)
Carlsbad Caverns are a series of underground caves, consisting of a three-level chain of limestone chambers studded with towering stalactites and stalagmites. They are millions of years old.

Rio Grande (G5)
The Rio Grande, or 'Great River' forms all of the border between Texas and Mexico. It flows from its source high up in the Rocky Mountains, to the Gulf of Mexico.

FARMING AND LAND USE

Many cattle and sheep ranches have been set up on the open plateaus. Fruit and vegetables, grown in hothouses and cotton, hay and wheat are among the major crops. Beef cattle and broiler chickens are raised on huge farms while sheep graze the drier parts of Texas. Extensive irrigation has made farming possible in even the most arid areas.

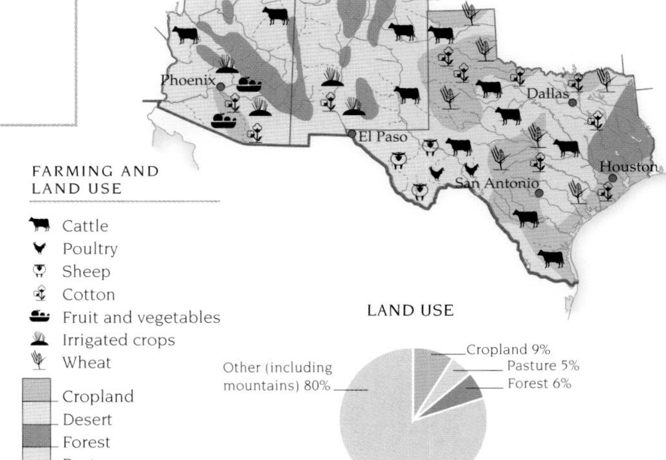
Phoenix
El Paso
Dallas
Houston
San Antonio
FARMING AND LAND USE
Cattle
Poultry
Sheep
Cotton
Fruit and vegetables
Irrigated crops
Wheat
Cropland
Desert
Forest
Pasture
Major conurbation
LAND USE
Other (including mountains) 80%
Cropland 9%
Pasture 5%
Forest 6%

INDUSTRY

Mining and related industries are one of the most important sources of income in the Southwest. Great deposits of oil lie under about 65% of Texas; copper and coal are mined in Arizona and New Mexico. Defence-related industries, including NASA have encouraged the development of many high-tech companies in Texas – and high-tech is also growing in larger cities such as Santa Fe and Phoenix.

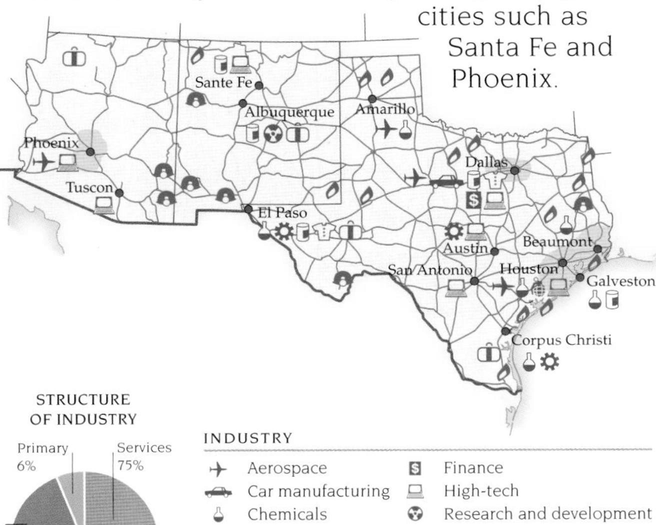
Sante Fe
Albuquerque
Amarillo
Phoenix
Tuscon
El Paso
Dallas
Austin
Beaumont
San Antonio
Houston
Galveston
Corpus Christi
STRUCTURE OF INDUSTRY
Primary 6%
Services 75%
Manufacturing 19%
INDUSTRY
Aerospace
Car manufacturing
Chemicals
Engineering
Food processing
Mining
Oil and gas
Defence
Finance
High-tech
Research and development
Tourism
Major industrial centre / area
Major road

POPULATION

The descendants of Mexican and Spanish settlers and numerous groups of Native Americans live in the southwestern states. The great cities of Texas grew up on income from cattle-ranching and the oil industry. Much of Arizona and New Mexico is sparsely populated, but today people are moving to these states to escape the cold winters elsewhere.

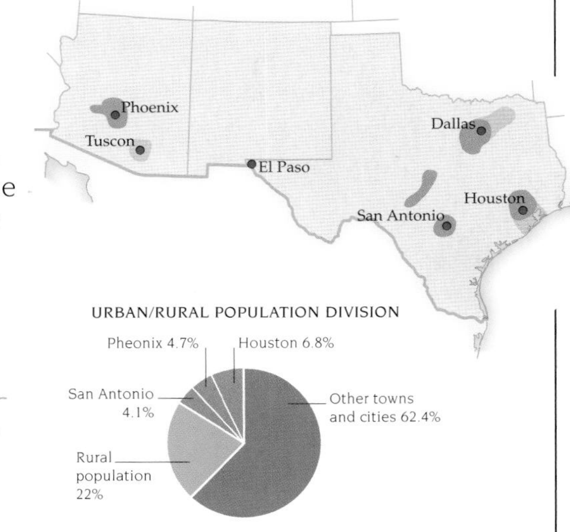
Phoenix
Tuscon
El Paso
Dallas
Houston
San Antonio
INHABITANTS PER SQ KM
More than 50
25–50
Less than 25
Major city
URBAN/RURAL POPULATION DIVISION
Pheonix 4.7%
Houston 6.8%
San Antonio 4.1%
Other towns and cities 62.4%
Rural population 22%

USA: The Mountain States

COLORADO, IDAHO, MONTANA, NEVADA, UTAH, WYOMING

These states are home to some of the nation's most fantastic landscapes: endless treeless plains, craggy peaks, incredible desert landforms, and the salt flats of Utah. Although this was one of the last regions of the USA to be settled, great mineral reserves have been exploited here in recent years, and new industries have grown up in some of the larger cities. Utah is the headquarters of the Mormon religion.

POPULATION

Colorado, with the growing city of Denver, is the most populous of the mountain states. In other states, people have settled close to sources of water such as Great Salt Lake in Utah. Many towns have less than 10,000 people and are far apart.

Salt Lake City
Denver
Colorado Springs
Pueblo
Las Vegas

INHABITANTS PER SQ KM

- More than 50
- 25–50
- Less than 25
- Major city

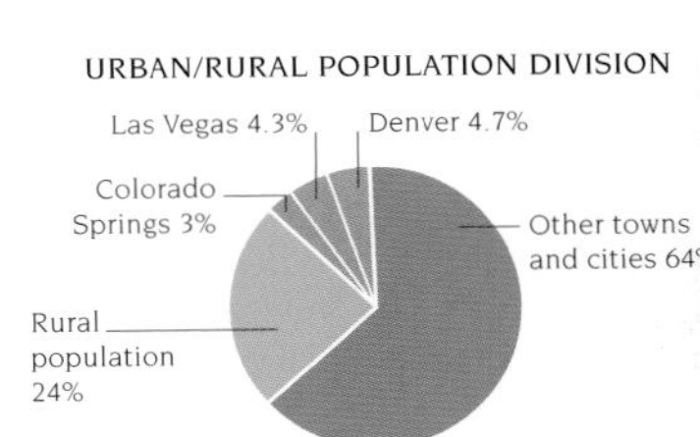
URBAN/RURAL POPULATION DIVISION
Las Vegas 4.3%
Denver 4.7%
Colorado Springs 3%
Other towns and cities 64%
Rural population 24%

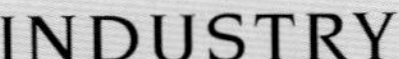

INDUSTRY

Rich mineral reserves, including coal, oil and gas, are mined throughout the region and forests are a source of good-quality timber. In the larger cities of Colorado and Utah, growing industries include high-tech computer firms. Many tourists are drawn to this region to ski in the resorts of Colorado and to explore the wilderness.

STRUCTURE OF INDUSTRY

Manufacturing 16%
Primary 4%
Services 80%

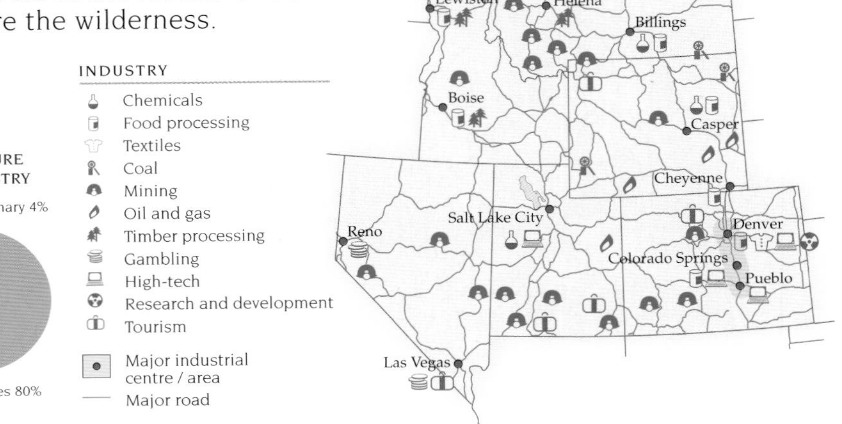
INDUSTRY
Chemicals
Food processing
Textiles
Coal
Mining
Oil and gas
Timber processing
Gambling
High-tech
Research and development
Tourism
Major industrial centre / area
Major road
Great Lakes
Lewiston
Helena
Billings
Boise
Casper
Cheyenne
Reno
Salt Lake City
Denver
Colorado Springs
Pueblo
Las Vegas

FARMING AND LAND USE

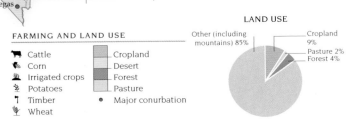

In the southern mountain states, cattle ranching is the main form of farming. Wheat and corn are grown in the eastern states, and the fertile soils of the Snake River valley in Idaho produce large crops of potatoes and many other vegetables. The northern states have many large commercial forests.

Boise
Reno
Salt Lake City
Denver
Colorado Springs
Pueblo
Las Vegas

FARMING AND LAND USE

- Cattle
- Corn
- Irrigated crops
- Potatoes
- Timber
- Wheat
- Cropland
- Desert
- Forest
- Pasture
- Major conurbation

LAND USE

Other (including mountains) 85%
Cropland 9%
Pasture 2%
Forest 4%

THE LANDSCAPE

The great Rocky Mountains and many smaller mountain ranges cover almost all of this region. Only eastern Montana is not mountainous. Here western parts of the Great Plains rise to meet the mountains. Parts of the southern mountain states are very arid with spectacular scenery, including block-like mesas, formed by erosion.

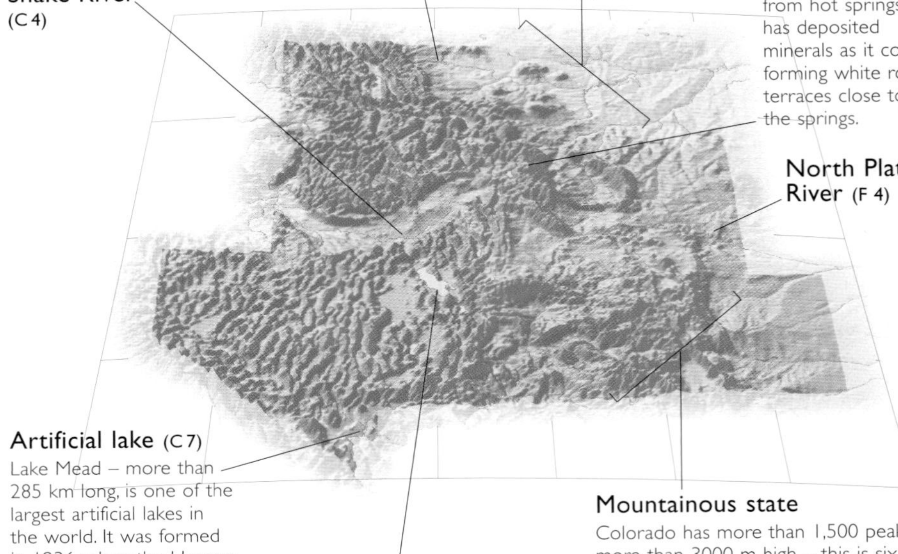
Snake River (C 4)
Great Plains (E 2)
North Platte River (F 4)
Great Salt Lake (C 5)

Continental Divide
From this watershed, crossing the Lewis Range, rivers flow in different directions across North America. Some flow east to Hudson Bay, some south to the Gulf of Mexico and others west to the Pacific Ocean.

Yellowstone National Park (D 3)
Yellowstone was set up in 1872 as the first national park in the USA. Water from hot springs has deposited minerals as it cools forming white rock terraces close to the springs.

Artificial lake (C 7)
Lake Mead – more than 285 km long, is one of the largest artificial lakes in the world. It was formed in 1936, when the Hoover Dam was built across the Colorado River.

Mountainous state
Colorado has more than 1,500 peaks more than 3000 m high – this is six times the number of high mountains found in the Swiss Alps.

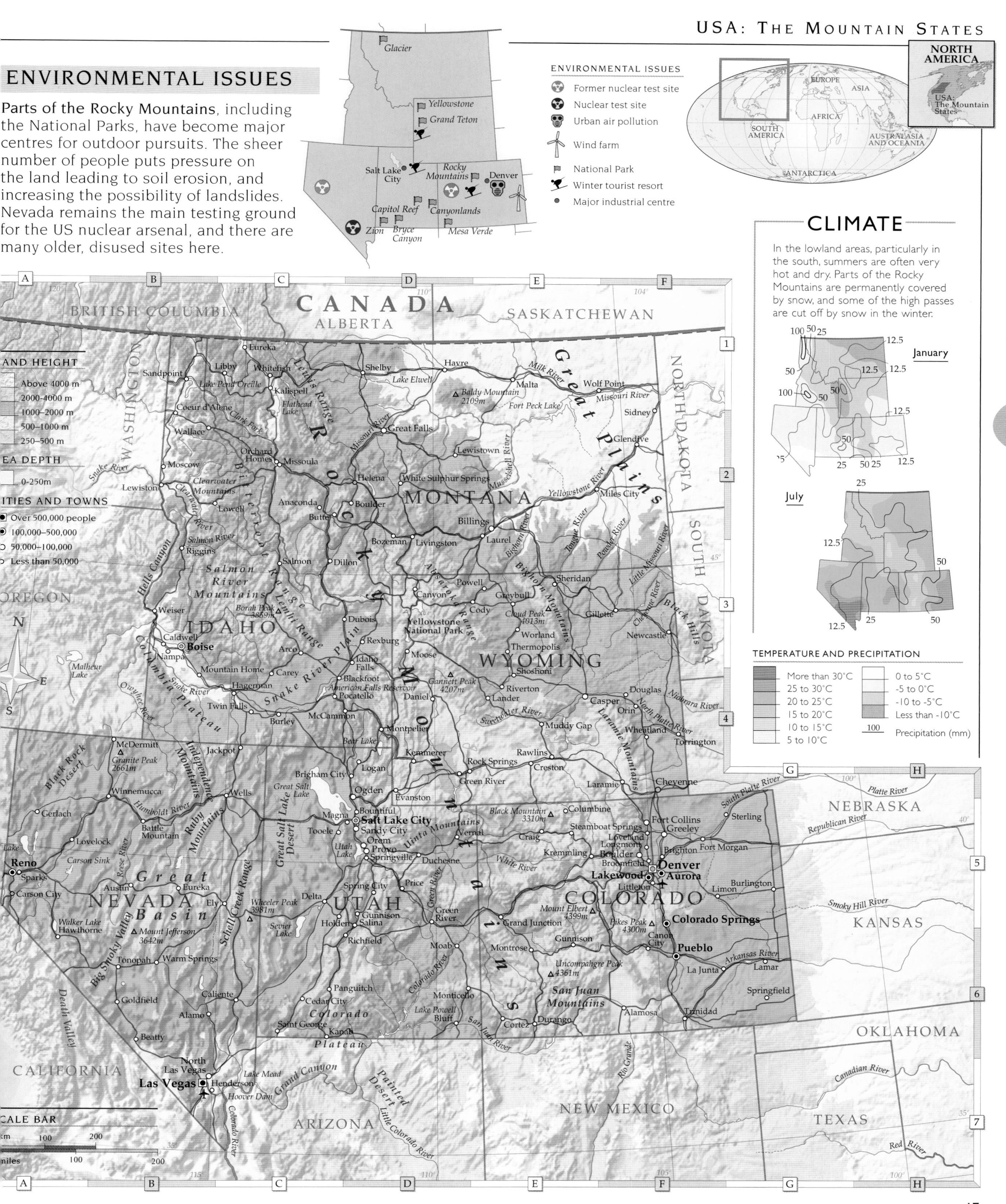
ENVIRONMENTAL ISSUES
Parts of the Rocky Mountains, including the National Parks, have become major centres for outdoor pursuits. The sheer number of people puts pressure on the land leading to soil erosion, and increasing the possibility of landslides. Nevada remains the main testing ground for the US nuclear arsenal, and there are many older, disused sites here.
Glacier
Yellowstone
Grand Teton
Salt Lake City
Rocky Mountains
Denver
Capitol Reef
Canyonlands
Zion
Bryce Canyon
Mesa Verde
ENVIRONMENTAL ISSUES
Former nuclear test site
Nuclear test site
Urban air pollution
Wind farm
National Park
Winter tourist resort
Major industrial centre
NORTH AMERICA
USA: The Mountain States
EUROPE
ASIA
AFRICA
SOUTH AMERICA
AUSTRALASIA AND OCEANIA
ANTARCTICA
CLIMATE
In the lowland areas, particularly in the south, summers are often very hot and dry. Parts of the Rocky Mountains are permanently covered by snow, and some of the high passes are cut off by snow in the winter.
January
July
TEMPERATURE AND PRECIPITATION
More than 30°C
25 to 30°C
20 to 25°C
15 to 20°C
10 to 15°C
5 to 10°C
0 to 5°C
-5 to 0°C
-10 to -5°C
Less than -10°C
100 Precipitation (mm)
AND HEIGHT
Above 4000 m
2000–4000 m
1000–2000 m
500–1000 m
250–500 m
EA DEPTH
0-250m
ITIES AND TOWNS
Over 500,000 people
100,000–500,000
50,000–100,000
Less than 50,000
CALE BAR
CANADA
BRITISH COLUMBIA
ALBERTA
SASKATCHEWAN
WASHINGTON
OREGON
IDAHO
MONTANA
WYOMING
NEVADA
UTAH
COLORADO
NORTH DAKOTA
SOUTH DAKOTA
NEBRASKA
KANSAS
OKLAHOMA
TEXAS
NEW MEXICO
ARIZONA
CALIFORNIA
Rocky Mountains
Great Plains
Great Basin
Colorado Plateau
Salt Lake City
Denver
Aurora
Lakewood
Colorado Springs
Pueblo
Boise
Reno
Las Vegas
Great Falls
Billings
Missoula
Helena
Casper
Cheyenne
Ogden
Provo
Fort Collins
Boulder

USA: THE PACIFIC STATES

CALIFORNIA, OREGON, WASHINGTON

The earliest European visitors to the West Coast were fur-trappers and miners, but the Gold Rush of 1849 brought in the first major wave of settlers. Drawn by tales of the beautiful scenery, pleasant climate, and fertile valleys, more people arrived on the newly built railways. People from all over the world are still moving into this region, seeking jobs in the dynamic economy and the famous laid-back lifestyle.

ENVIRONMENTAL ISSUES

Some of the great national parks of the USA, including Yosemite and Sequoia, are found here. The immense numbers of visitors put great pressure on the landscape. Water is in short supply in large parts of California, and desertification, caused by over-intense farming methods, is a problem. Wind farms have been set up on the hills above the San Joaquin valley to provide alternative energy.

ENVIRONMENTAL ISSUES

- National park
- Urban air pollution
- Wind farm
- Risk of wild fire
- Desert area
- Risk of desertification
- Severe risk of desertification
- Polluted rivers
- Major industrial centre

INDUSTRY

The Pacific States are the centre of the high-tech computer industry with Silicon Valley between San Francisco and San Jose, and electronics industries growing in Portland and Seattle. Other major industries include research and development for the defence industry, film making in Los Angeles, food processing and lumbering. Tourism is well developed throughout the Pacific States.

STRUCTURE OF INDUSTRY
Primary 2%
Services 81%
Manufacturing 17%
INDUSTRY
Aerospace
Chemicals
Engineering
Food processing
Iron and steel
Shipbuilding
Textiles
Timber processing
Film industry
High-tech
Research and development
Tourism
Major industrial centre / area
Major road

THE LANDSCAPE

The Coast and Cascade ranges run north–south through Oregon and Washington while further south, the high Sierra Nevada run along California's eastern fringes. Two broad valleys, the Sacramento and San Joaquin, are known as the Central Valley, and form a trough beneath the Sierra Nevada. The south is extremely dry – Death Valley is the hottest place in the entire USA.

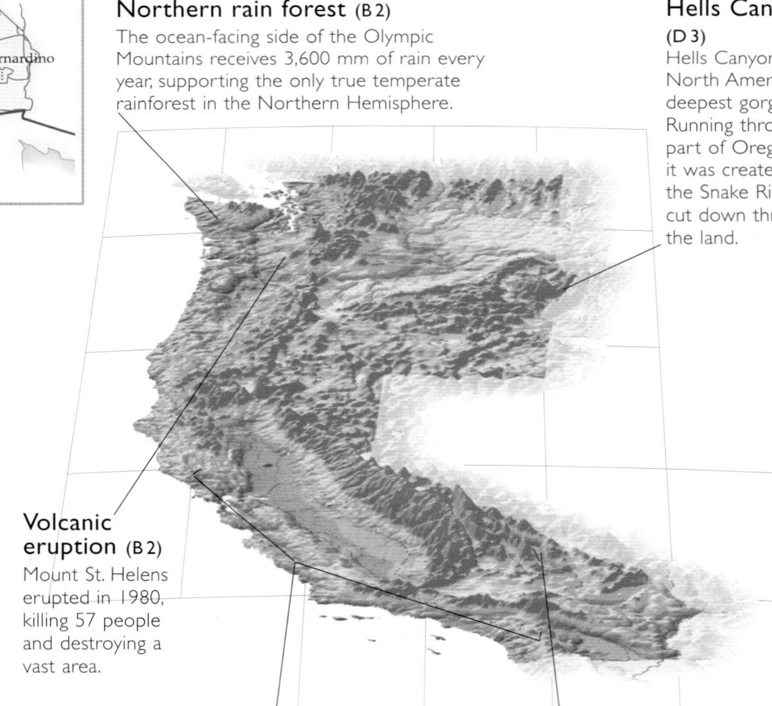

Northern rain forest (B 2)
The ocean-facing side of the Olympic Mountains receives 3,600 mm of rain every year, supporting the only true temperate rainforest in the Northern Hemisphere.

Hells Canyon (D 3)
Hells Canyon is North America's deepest gorge. Running through part of Oregon, it was created as the Snake River cut down through the land.

Volcanic eruption (B 2)
Mount St. Helens erupted in 1980, killing 57 people and destroying a vast area.

San Andreas Fault
The San Andreas Fault runs for 1,050 km underneath California. When both sides of the fault move at different rates, tremors and earthquakes result.

Hottest place (D 7)
In 1913, Death Valley set the record for the highest temperature ever recorded in the US, at 56.6°C.

FARMING AND LAND USE

California's Central Valley and the river valleys of Washington and Oregon provide ideal conditions for a wide range of fruit and vegetables, including citrus fruit and grapes. Poultry farming is widespread in the northwest and there are many large cattle ranches. Millions of hectares of commercial forest are located in this region.

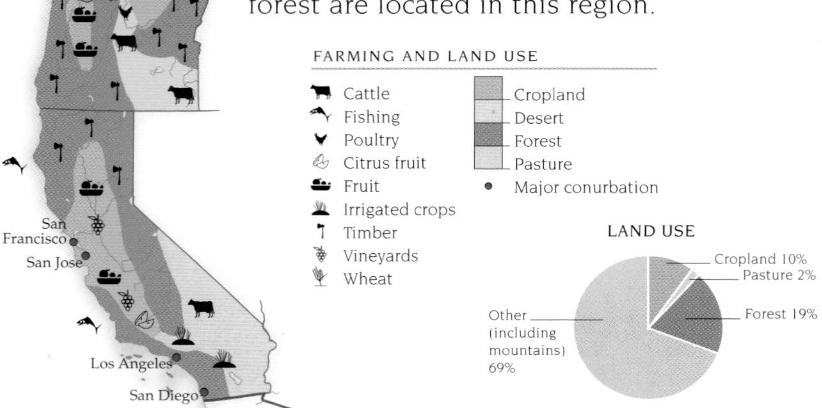
Seattle
San Francisco
San Jose
Los Angeles
San Diego
FARMING AND LAND USE
Cattle
Fishing
Poultry
Citrus fruit
Fruit
Irrigated crops
Timber
Vineyards
Wheat
Cropland
Desert
Forest
Pasture
Major conurbation
LAND USE
Cropland 10%
Pasture 2%
Forest 19%
Other (including mountains) 69%

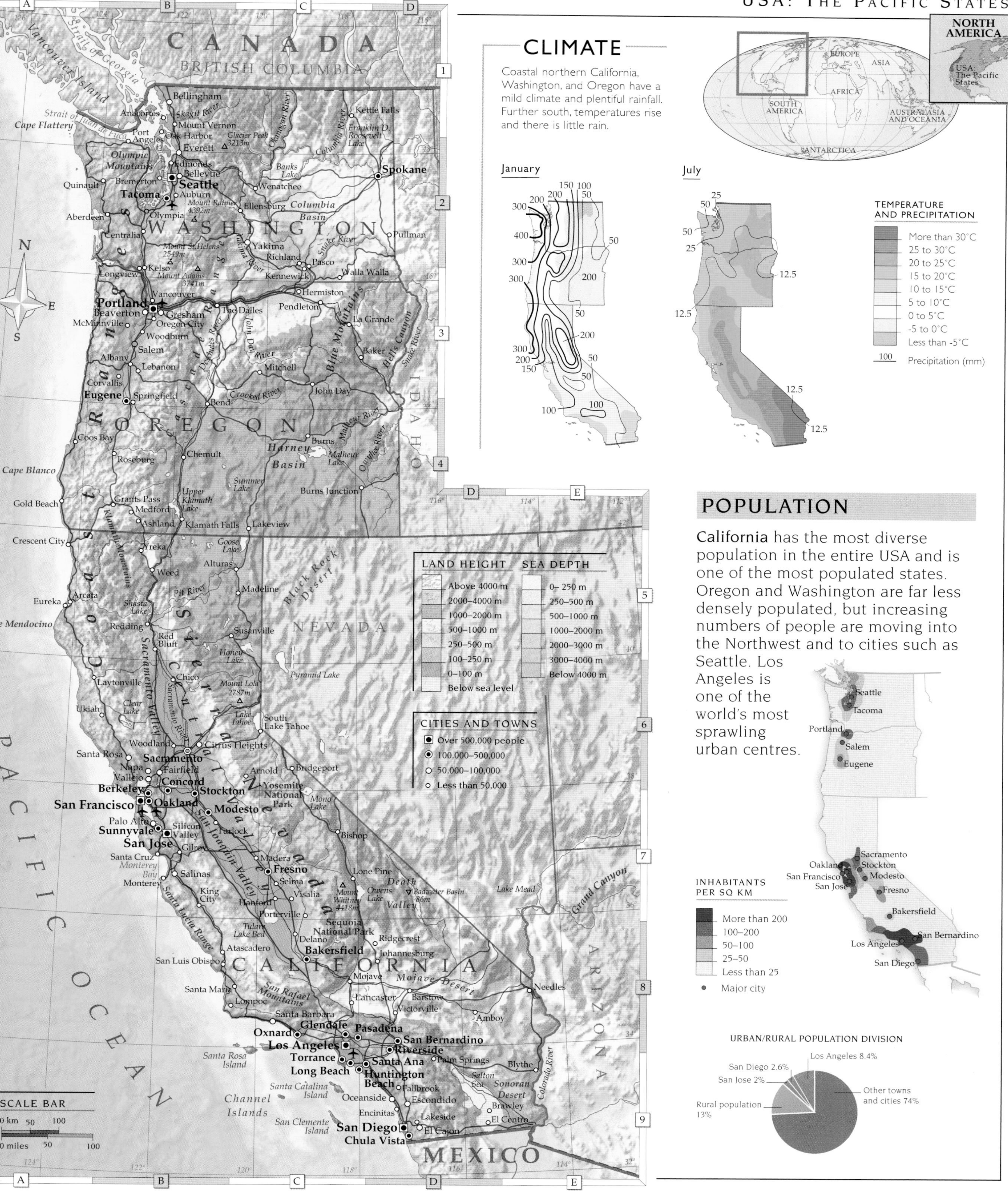
NORTH AMERICA
USA: The Pacific States
EUROPE
ASIA
AFRICA
SOUTH AMERICA
AUSTRALASIA AND OCEANIA
ANTARCTICA
CLIMATE
Coastal northern California, Washington, and Oregon have a mild climate and plentiful rainfall. Further south, temperatures rise and there is little rain.
January
July
TEMPERATURE AND PRECIPITATION
More than 30°C
25 to 30°C
20 to 25°C
15 to 20°C
10 to 15°C
5 to 10°C
0 to 5°C
-5 to 0°C
Less than -5°C
100 Precipitation (mm)
POPULATION
California has the most diverse population in the entire USA and is one of the most populated states. Oregon and Washington are far less densely populated, but increasing numbers of people are moving into the Northwest and to cities such as Seattle. Los Angeles is one of the world's most sprawling urban centres.
INHABITANTS PER SQ KM
More than 200
100–200
50–100
25–50
Less than 25
Major city
Seattle
Tacoma
Portland
Salem
Eugene
Sacramento
Stockton
Oakland
San Francisco
Modesto
San Jose
Fresno
Bakersfield
San Bernardino
Los Angeles
San Diego
URBAN/RURAL POPULATION DIVISION
Los Angeles 8.4%
San Diego 2.6%
San Jose 2%
Rural population 13%
Other towns and cities 74%
LAND HEIGHT
Above 4000 m
2000–4000 m
1000–2000 m
500–1000 m
250–500 m
100–250 m
0–100 m
Below sea level
SEA DEPTH
0– 250 m
250–500 m
500–1000 m
1000–2000 m
2000–3000 m
3000–4000 m
Below 4000 m
CITIES AND TOWNS
Over 500,000 people
100,000–500,000
50,000–100,000
Less than 50,000
SCALE BAR
0 km 50 100
0 miles 50 100
CANADA
BRITISH COLUMBIA
Vancouver Island
Strait of Georgia
Strait of Juan de Fuca
Cape Flattery
WASHINGTON
Bellingham
Anacortes
Mount Vernon
Oak Harbor
Everett
Port Angeles
Olympic Mountains
Glacier Peak 3213m
Kettle Falls
Franklin D. Roosevelt Lake
Spokane
Edmonds
Bellevue
Seattle
Bremerton
Quinault
Tacoma
Auburn
Mount Rainier 4392m
Olympia
Aberdeen
Centralia
Wenatchee
Ellensburg
Columbia Basin
Banks Lake
Pullman
Yakima
Richland
Mount St. Helens 2549m
Mount Adams 3741m
Kelso
Longview
Pasco
Kennewick
Walla Walla
Hermiston
Vancouver
Portland
Beaverton
Gresham
Oregon City
McMinnville
Woodburn
The Dalles
Pendleton
La Grande
Salem
Albany
Lebanon
Corvallis
Eugene
Springfield
Baker
Mitchell
Blue Mountains
Hells Canyon
John Day
Bend
Crooked River
OREGON
IDAHO
Coos Bay
Roseburg
Chemult
Burns
Harney Basin
Malheur Lake
Cape Blanco
Summer Lake
Upper Klamath Lake
Burns Junction
Gold Beach
Grants Pass
Medford
Ashland
Klamath Falls
Lakeview
Crescent City
Yreka
Goose Lake
Alturas
Weed
Madeline
Black Rock Desert
Arcata
Eureka
Shasta Lake
Cape Mendocino
Redding
Red Bluff
Susanville
NEVADA
Honey Lake
Chico
Pyramid Lake
Mount Lola 2787m
Laytonville
Ukiah
Clear Lake
Lake Tahoe
South Lake Tahoe
Woodland
Citrus Heights
Santa Rosa
Sacramento
Napa
Fairfield
Vallejo
Concord
Arnold
Bridgeport
Berkeley
Stockton
Yosemite National Park
Mono Lake
San Francisco
Oakland
Modesto
Palo Alto
Sunnyvale
Silicon Valley
San Jose
Turlock
Bishop
Santa Cruz
Monterey Bay
Gilroy
Madera
Salinas
Fresno
Lone Pine
Monterey
Selma
Death Valley
Visalia
Mount Whitney 4418m
Owens Lake
Badwater Basin -86m
Lake Mead
Grand Canyon
King City
Hanford
Porterville
Sequoia National Park
Tulare Lake Bed
Delano
Ridgecrest
Johannesburg
Atascadero
Bakersfield
San Luis Obispo
CALIFORNIA
Mojave
Mojave Desert
ARIZONA
Santa Maria
San Rafael Mountains
Lancaster
Barstow
Needles
Lompoc
Victorville
Santa Barbara
Amboy
Oxnard
Glendale
Pasadena
San Bernardino
Los Angeles
Riverside
Torrance
Santa Ana
Palm Springs
Blythe
Long Beach
Huntington Beach
Santa Rosa Island
Santa Catalina Island
Salton Sea
Sonoran Desert
Colorado River
Channel Islands
Oceanside
Fallbrook
Escondido
Brawley
Encinitas
Lakeside
El Centro
San Clemente Island
San Diego
El Cajon
Chula Vista
MEXICO
PACIFIC OCEAN

Alaska

A magnificent land of mountains, forests and snowfields, with rich oil and mineral reserves, Alaska was purchased from Russia for $1 million in 1867. Almost 650,000 people live here, many drawn by the oil industry. Some of Alaska's native peoples like the Aleuts and Inupiaq still live by hunting and fishing.

ENVIRONMENTAL ISSUES

Much of northern Alaska is covered by permafrost (permanently frozen ground). The Trans-Alaska Pipeline, which brings oil from Prudhoe Bay to Valdez, was built above ground to stop the permafrost melting. A number of major oil spills have threatened Alaska's unique envrionment.

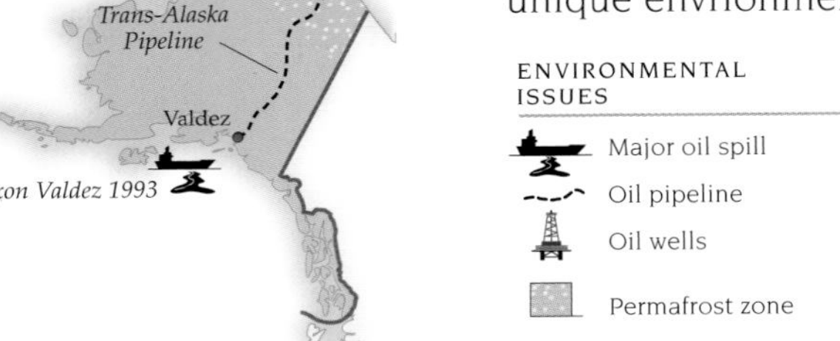

Prudhoe Bay
Trans-Alaska Pipeline
Valdez
Exxon Valdez 1993

ENVIRONMENTAL ISSUES
- Major oil spill
- Oil pipeline
- Oil wells
- Permafrost zone
- Major town

INDUSTRY

Prudhoe Bay
Anchorage
Valdez
Juneau

The Alaskan economy is dominated by the oil business. The oilfields of Alaska are of a similar size to those in the Persian Gulf. Minerals including gold are mined in the mountains, and paper products are exported to countries on the Pacific Rim.

INDUSTRY
- Chemicals
- Mining
- Oil and gas
- Timber processing
- Major industrial centre
- Major road

FARMING AND LAND USE

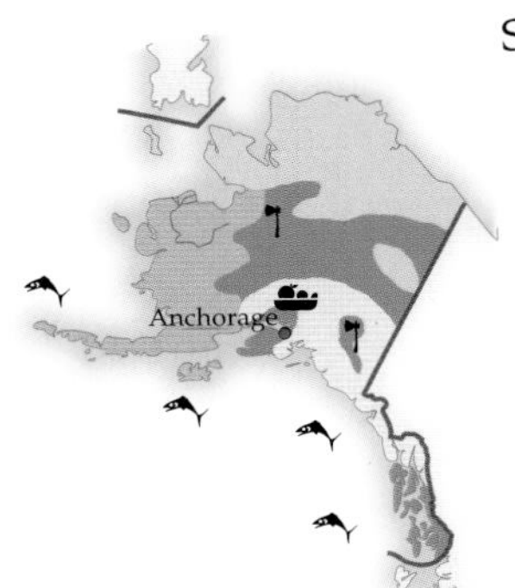

Anchorage

Salmon are caught in great numbers in the waters of the north Pacific. Much of the state – more than 9 million hectares – is covered by forest which is commercially lumbered. Most food must be imported, although fruit is grown in hothouses near the larger cities.

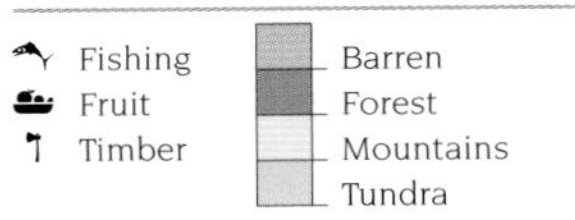

FARMING AND LAND USE
Fishing
Fruit
Timber
Barren
Forest
Mountains
Tundra
Major conurbation

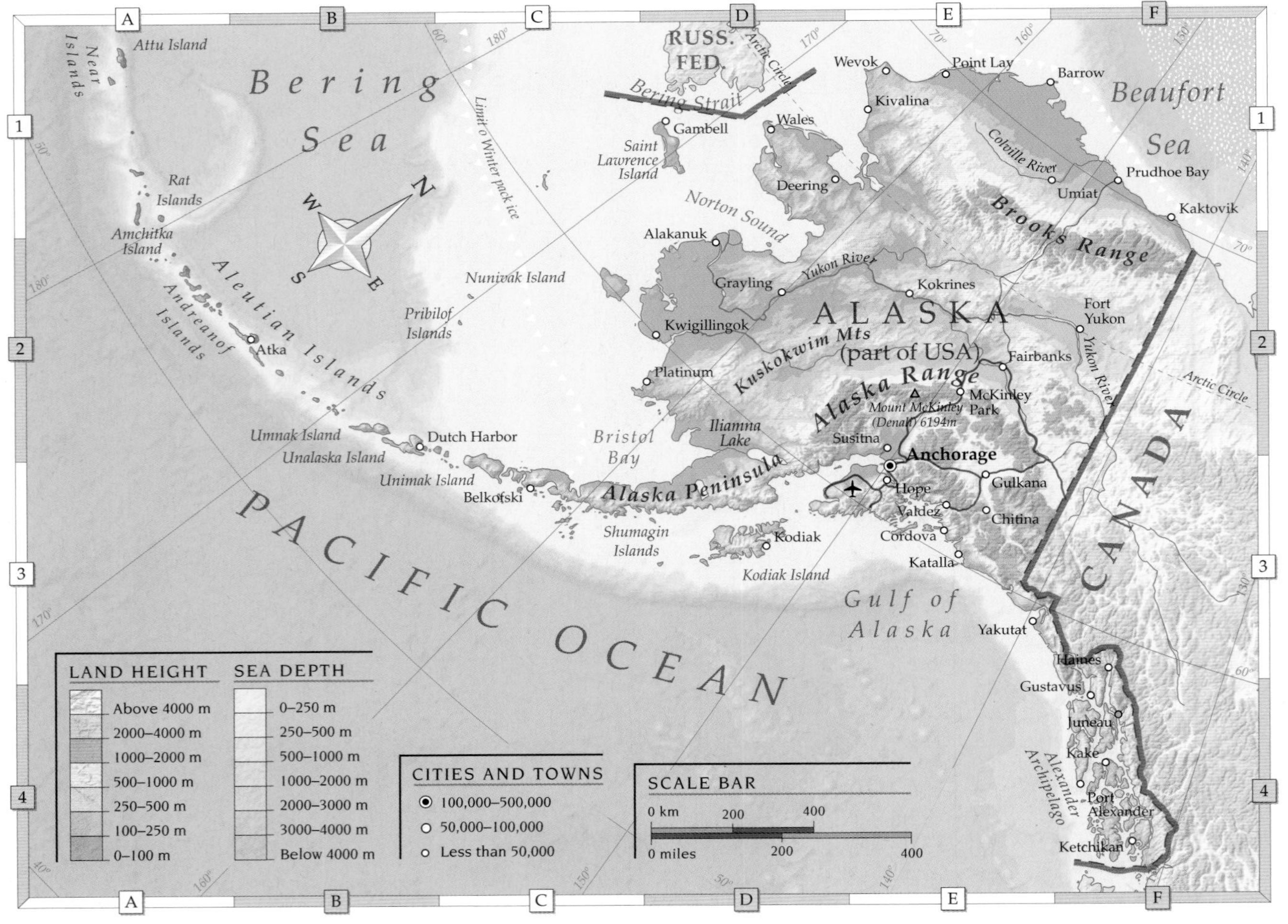

A
B
C
D
E
F
1
2
3
4
Attu Island
Near Islands
Bering Sea
RUSS. FED.
Arctic Circle
Bering Strait
Limit o Winter pack ice
Gambell
Saint Lawrence Island
Wales
Wevok
Kivalina
Point Lay
Barrow
Beaufort Sea
Colville River
Prudhoe Bay
Umiat
Kaktovik
Deering
Norton Sound
Brooks Range
Rat Islands
Amchitka Island
Alaknuk
Yukon River
Kokrines
Fort Yukon
Nunivak Island
Grayling
ALASKA (part of USA)
Aleutian Islands
Andreanof Islands
Atka
Pribilof Islands
Kwigillingok
Kuskokwim Mts
Fairbanks
Yukon River
Platinum
Alaska Range
Mount McKinley (Denali) 6194m
McKinley Park
Arctic Circle
Umnak Island
Unalaska Island
Dutch Harbor
Bristol Bay
Iliamna Lake
Susitna
Anchorage
CANADA
Unimak Island
Belkofski
Alaska Peninsula
Hope
Gulkana
Valdez
Chitina
Shumagin Islands
Kodiak
Cordova
Katalla
Kodiak Island
PACIFIC OCEAN
Gulf of Alaska
Yakutat
Haines
Gustavus
Juneau
Kake
Alexander Archipelago
Port Alexander
Ketchikan
LAND HEIGHT
Above 4000 m
2000–4000 m
1000–2000 m
500–1000 m
250–500 m
100–250 m
0–100 m
SEA DEPTH
0–250 m
250–500 m
500–1000 m
1000–2000 m
2000–3000 m
3000–4000 m
Below 4000 m
CITIES AND TOWNS
100,000–500,000
50,000–100,000
Less than 50,000
SCALE BAR
0 km
200
400
0 miles
200
400

CLIMATE

Parts of northern Alaska are frozen year-round and can be cut off entirely in the winter. Summers are milder – especially in the Aleutians.

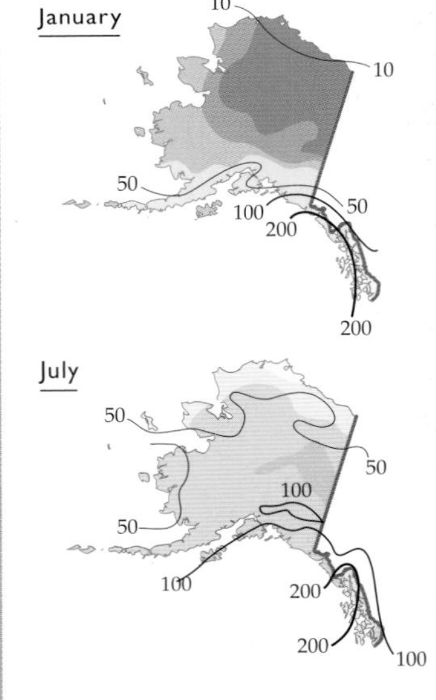

January
10
10
50
100
50
200
200
July
50
50
100
50
100
200
200
100

TEMPERATURE AND PRECIPITATION

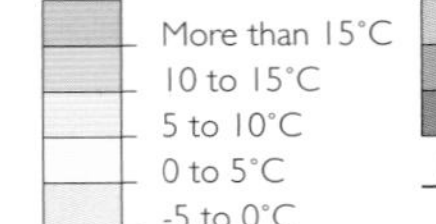

More than 15°C
10 to 15°C
5 to 10°C
0 to 5°C
-5 to 0°C

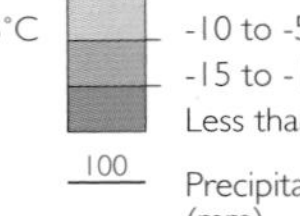

-10 to -5°C
-15 to -10°C
Less than -15°C
100
Precipitation (mm)

HAWAII

Hawaii is the 50th US state. It lies far from the mainland in the middle of the Pacific Ocean. The island chain was formed by volcanoes, only one of which, Mauna Loa, remains active today. The islands' indigenous peoples are Polynesians, but continued immigration means that they now make up only 9% of the population.

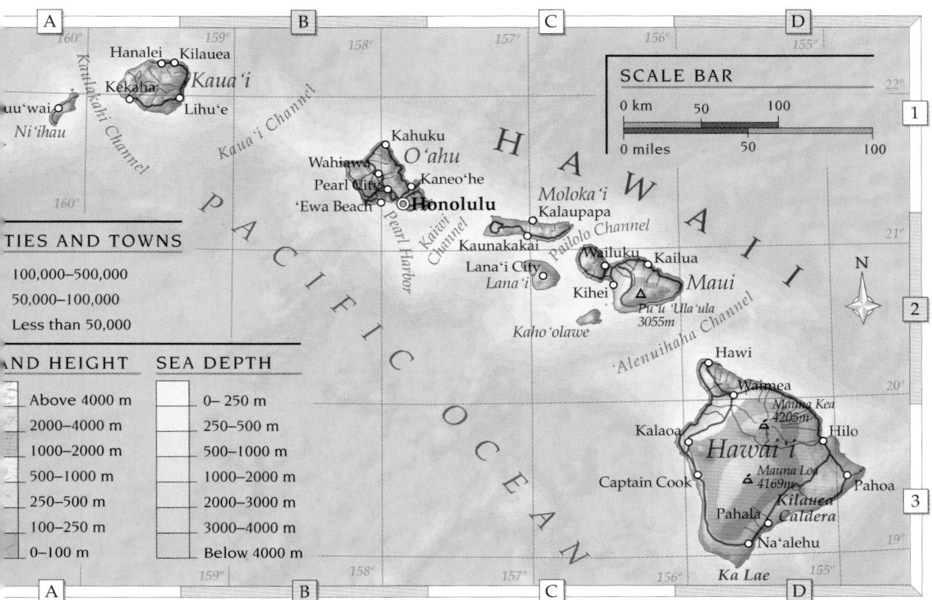

Hanalei
Kilauea
Kekaha
Kaua'i
Lihu'e
Ni'ihau
Kaulakahi Channel
Kaua'i Channel
Kahuku
O'ahu
Wahiawa
Pearl City
Kaneo'he
'Ewa Beach
Honolulu
Pearl Harbor
Kaiwi Channel
Moloka'i
Kalaupapa
Pailolo Channel
Kaunakakai
Lana'i City
Lana'i
Wailuku
Kailua
Kihei
Maui
Pu'u 'Ula'ula 3055m
Kaho'olawe
'Alenuihaha Channel
Hawi
Waimea
Mauna Kea 4205m
Kalaoa
Hilo
Hawai'i
Mauna Loa 4169m
Captain Cook
Kilauea Caldera
Pahoa
Pahala
Na'alehu
Ka Lae
HAWAII
PACIFIC OCEAN
SCALE BAR
0 km 50 100
0 miles 50 100
CITIES AND TOWNS
100,000–500,000
50,000–100,000
Less than 50,000
LAND HEIGHT
Above 4000 m
2000–4000 m
1000–2000 m
500–1000 m
250–500 m
100–250 m
0–100 m
SEA DEPTH
0– 250 m
250–500 m
500–1000 m
1000–2000 m
2000–3000 m
3000–4000 m
Below 4000 m

INDUSTRY AND LAND USE

Tourism is the most important industry in Hawaii, accounting for one in every three jobs. The naval base at Pearl Harbor also provides jobs for numerous people. The many large plantations grow sugarcane, bananas and tropical fruit for export.

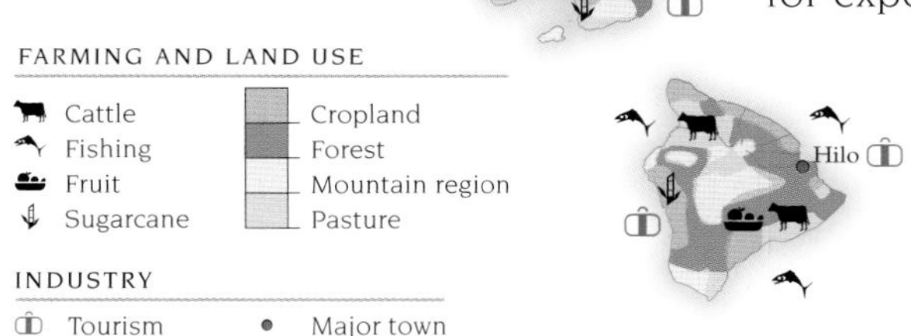

Honolulu
Kailua
Hilo
FARMING AND LAND USE
Cattle
Fishing
Fruit
Sugarcane
Cropland
Forest
Mountain region
Pasture
INDUSTRY
Tourism
Major town

ENVIRONMENTAL ISSUES

Climatic occurrences, combined with the growth of tourism, have an adverse effect on the indigenous flora and fauna. Eruptions from Mauna Loa are an accepted risk for the population.

Honolulu
Mauna Loa – 1984
Kilauea – 1983
ENVIRONMENTAL ISSUES
Tourist resort
Volcanic eruption
Major town

UNITED STATES OVERSEAS TERRITORIES

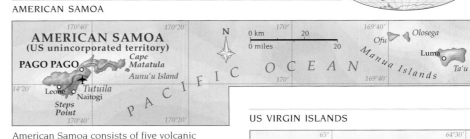

America's overseas territories have traditionally been seen as strategically or economically important. In most cases, the local population has been given a say in deciding whether it wants to govern itself. A US commonwealth territory has a greater level of independence than a US unincorporated or external territory. The US has 13 overseas territories: the four largest are shown here.

AMERICAN SAMOA

AMERICAN SAMOA (US unincorporated territory)

American Samoa consists of five volcanic islands and two coral atolls in the south Pacific. The people are among the last true Polynesians.

PUERTO RICO

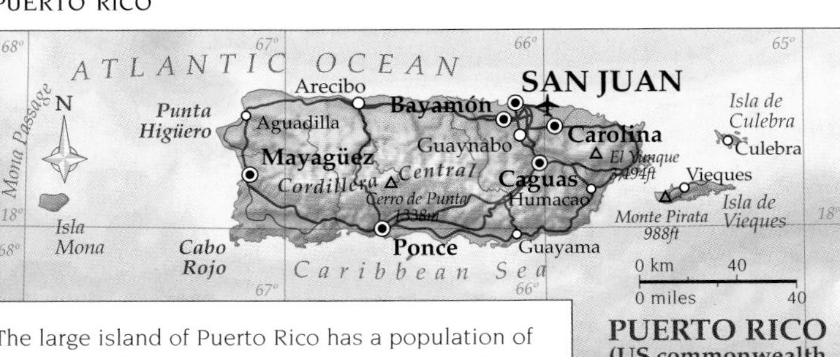

ATLANTIC OCEAN
SAN JUAN
Arecibo
Bayamón
Punta Higüero
Aguadilla
Guaynabo
Carolina
Isla de Culebra
Culebra
Mayagüez
Cordillera Central
Cerro de Punta 1338m
El Yunque 3494ft
Caguas
Humacao
Vieques
Isla de Vieques
Monte Pirata 988ft
Mona Passage
Isla Mona
Cabo Rojo
Ponce
Guayama
Caribbean Sea
0 km 40
0 miles 40
PUERTO RICO (US commonwealth territory)

The large island of Puerto Rico has a population of almost 4 million people. In recent years there have been campaigns to make it the 51st US state.

GUAM

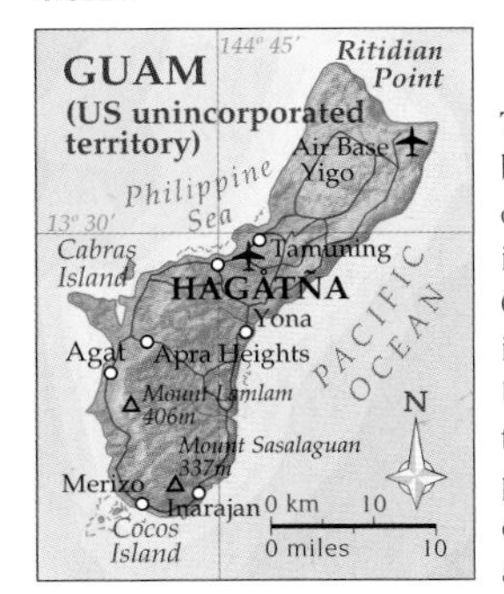

GUAM (US unincorporated territory)
Ritidian Point
Air Base
Yigo
Philippine Sea
Cabras Island
Tamuning
HAGÅTÑA
Yona
Agat
Apra Heights
PACIFIC OCEAN
Mount Lamlam 406m
Mount Sasalaguan 337m
Merizo
Inarajan
Cocos Island
0 km 10
0 miles 10

The US military base that covers one-third of the island makes Guam strategically important to the US. The Chamorro, the indigenous people, are in charge of political and social life.

US VIRGIN ISLANDS

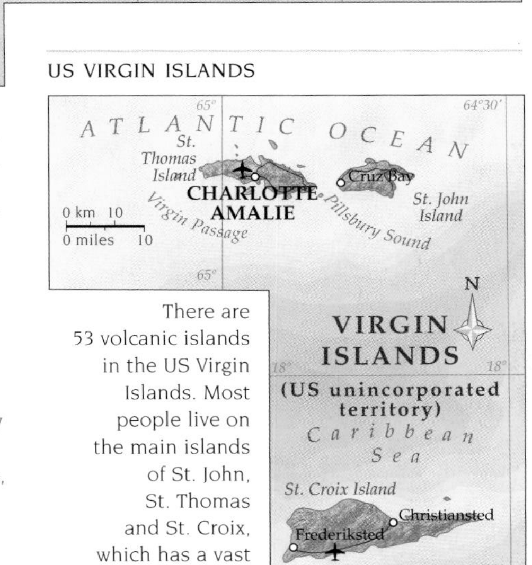

ATLANTIC OCEAN
St. Thomas Island
CHARLOTTE AMALIE
Cruz Bay
St. John Island
Virgin Passage
Pillsbury Sound
0 km 10
0 miles 10
VIRGIN ISLANDS (US unincorporated territory)
Caribbean Sea
St. Croix Island
Christiansted
Frederiksted

There are 53 volcanic islands in the US Virgin Islands. Most people live on the main islands of St. John, St. Thomas and St. Croix, which has a vast oil refinery.

MEXICO

Mexico is a large country with a rich mixture of traditions and cultures. The ancient civilization of the Aztecs which flourished here was crushed by Spanish invaders in the 16th century. Spain ruled Mexico until its independence in 1836 and today, the country has the world's largest Spanish-speaking population. Mexico is mostly dry and mountainous, and farm land is limited, so the country has to import most of the basic foods it needs to feed its people.

FARMING AND LAND USE

Most of the land suitable for farming is planted with corn – a big part of the Mexican diet. Along the Gulf coast coffee, sugarcane and cotton are grown on plantations for export. Parts of the dry north are irrigated to grow cotton, but most of the land is taken up by large cattle ranches. Fishing, especially for shellfish such as lobster and shrimp is important in coastal areas.

Ciudad Juárez
Chihuahua
Monterrey
Mérida
San Luis Potosí
Guadalajara
Puebla
Mexico City
Acapulco

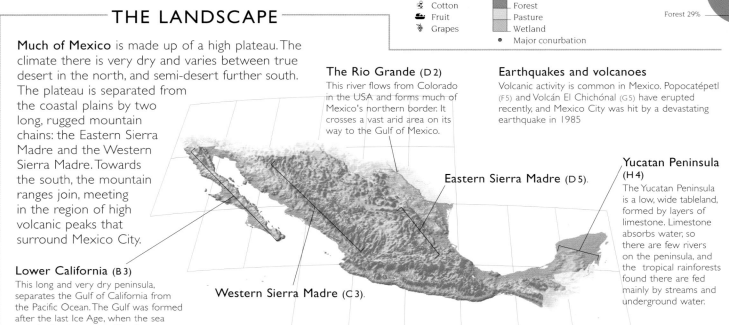

FARMING AND LAND USE

Cattle
Fishing
Sheep
Bananas
Coffee
Corn (maize)
Cotton
Fruit
Grapes
Shellfish
Sugarcane
Timber
Cropland
Desert
Forest
Pasture
Wetland
Major conurbation

LAND USE

Cropland 14%
Other 15%
Forest 29%
Pasture 42%

THE LANDSCAPE

Much of Mexico is made up of a high plateau. The climate there is very dry and varies between true desert in the north, and semi-desert further south. The plateau is separated from the coastal plains by two long, rugged mountain chains: the Eastern Sierra Madre and the Western Sierra Madre. Towards the south, the mountain ranges join, meeting in the region of high volcanic peaks that surround Mexico City.

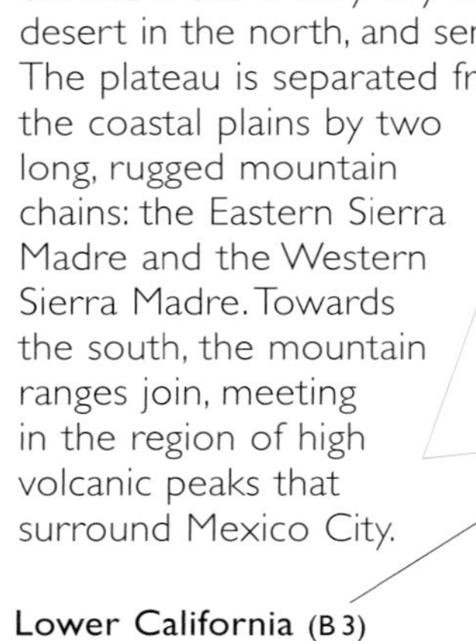

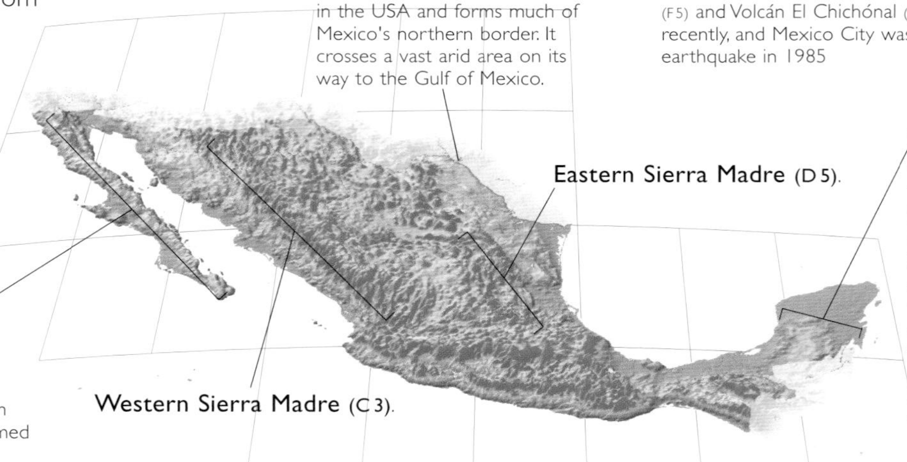
Eastern Sierra Madre (D 5).
Western Sierra Madre (C 3).

The Rio Grande (D 2)
This river flows from Colorado in the USA and forms much of Mexico's northern border. It crosses a vast arid area on its way to the Gulf of Mexico.

Earthquakes and volcanoes
Volcanic activity is common in Mexico. Popocatépetl (F5) and Volcán El Chichónal (G5) have erupted recently, and Mexico City was hit by a devastating earthquake in 1985

Yucatan Peninsula (H 4)
The Yucatan Peninsula is a low, wide tableland, formed by layers of limestone. Limestone absorbs water, so there are few rivers on the peninsula, and the tropical rainforests found there are fed mainly by streams and underground water.

Lower California (B 3)
This long and very dry peninsula, separates the Gulf of California from the Pacific Ocean. The Gulf was formed after the last Ice Age, when the sea rose to flood a major rift valley.

POPULATION

Most of the north is sparsely populated due to the hot, dry climate and lack of cultivable farm land. As people have migrated from the countryside in search of work, the cities have grown dramatically; almost 75% of Mexicans now live in urban areas. Mexico City is home to almost a fifth of the population and is one of the world's largest cities.

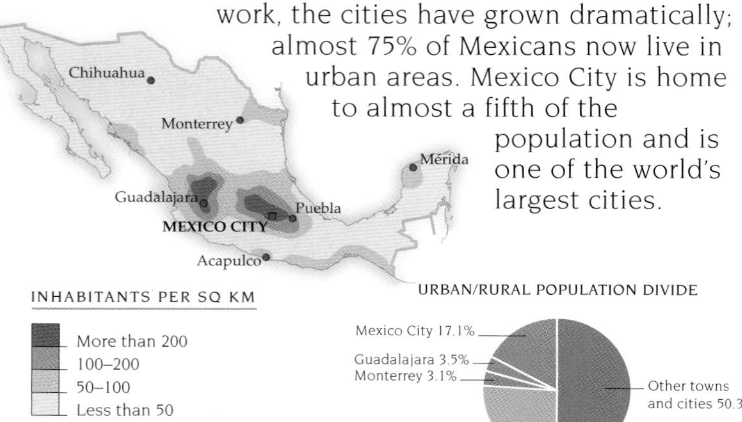
Chihuahua
Monterrey
Mérida
Guadalajara
Puebla
MEXICO CITY
Acapulco
INHABITANTS PER SQ KM
More than 200
100–200
50–100
Less than 50
Capital city
Major city
URBAN/RURAL POPULATION DIVIDE
Mexico City 17.1%
Guadalajara 3.5%
Monterrey 3.1%
Other towns and cities 50.3%
Rural population 26%

ENVIRONMENTAL ISSUES

Fast, unplanned growth has led to poor sanitation and water supplies in Mexico City, while the wall of mountains which surround the city traps pollution from cars and factories, giving it some of the world's worst air pollution. Much of Mexico's tropical rainforest has been felled, leading to increased soil erosion. Land clearance further north is also causing desertification.

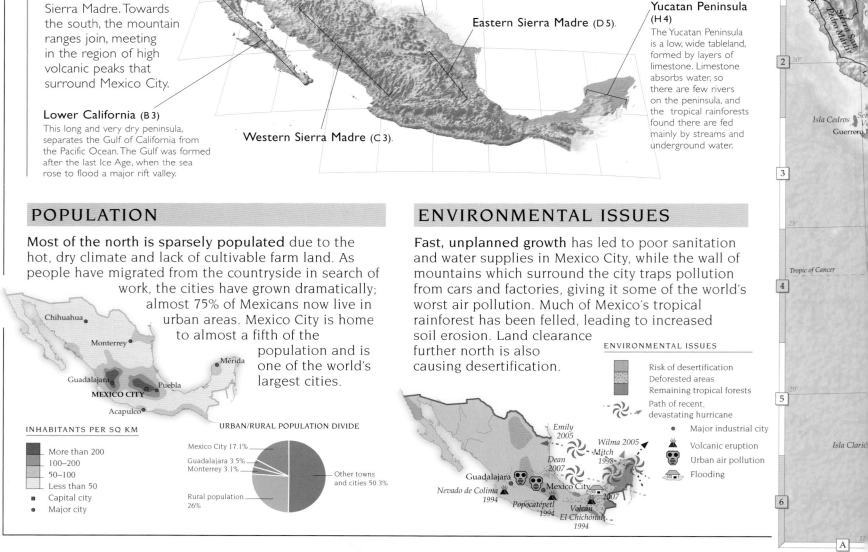

ENVIRONMENTAL ISSUES

Risk of desertification
Deforested areas
Remaining tropical forests
Path of recent, devastating hurricane
Major industrial city
Volcanic eruption
Urban air pollution
Flooding

Emily 2005
Wilma 2005
Mitch 1998
Dean 2007
Guadalajara
Mexico City
2007
Nevado de Colima 1994
Popocatépetl 1994
Volcán El Chichónal 1994

CALIFORNIA
Mexicali
Tijuana
Rosarito
Ensenada
Sierra San Pedro Mártir
Isla Cedros
Guerrero
Tropic of Cancer
Isla Clarión
A 1 2 3 4 5 6

NORTH AMERICA

INDUSTRY

Oil and gas on the Gulf coast are the biggest source of income. Mexico is also rich in other minerals; it is the world's top silver producer. Manufacturing is centred around Mexico City and along the US border, where mainly foreign owned factories assemble products for export. Tourism is also very important to Mexico.

STRUCTURE OF INDUSTRY

Primary 4%

Services 70%

Manufacturing 26%

INDUSTRY

- Car manufacture
- Electronics
- Engineering
- Food processing
- Iron & steel
- Oil refining
- Textiles
- Mining
- Oil and gas
- Tourism
- Major industrial centre / area
- Major road

CLIMATE

Northern Mexico and the peninsula of Lower California are dry, hot and largely desert. Towards the south, rainfall increases, especially in July. Moist, warm conditions allow rainforests to grow.

January

July

TEMPERATURE AND PRECIPITATION

- More than 30°C
- 25 to 30°C
- 20 to 25°C
- 15 to 20°C
- 10 to 15°C
- 5 to 10°C
- Less than 5°C
- 100 Precipitation (mm)

LAND HEIGHT	SEA DEPTH
Above 4000 m	0–250 m
2000–4000 m	250–500 m
1000–2000 m	500–1000 m
500–1000 m	1000–2000 m
250–500 m	2000–3000 m
100–250 m	3000–4000 m
0–100 m	Below 4000 m

CITIES AND TOWNS

- Over 500,000 people
- 100,000–500,000
- 50,000–100,000
- Less than 50,000

SCALE BAR

CENTRAL AMERICA

BELIZE, COSTA RICA, EL SALVADOR, GUATEMALA, HONDURAS, NICARAGUA, PANAMA

Central America lies on a narrow bridge of land which links North and South America. All the countries here, except Belize, were once governed by Spain. Today, most of their people are *mestizos* – a mix of the original Maya Indian inhabitants and Spanish settlers. The hot, steamy climate is ideal for growing tropical crops, such as coffee and bananas, which are exported worldwide.

FARMING AND LAND USE

About half of all the agricultural products grown here are exported. The Pacific coast has fertile, well-watered land suitable for growing cotton and sugarcane. In the central highlands are big coffee plantations, and ranches where beef cattle are raised. Bananas grow well along the humid Caribbean coastal plain, and shrimp and lobster are caught offshore.

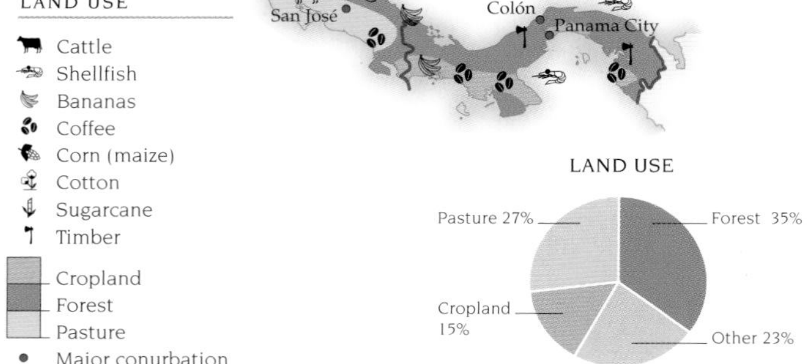
Guatemala City
San Salvador
Tegucigalpa
Managua
San José
Colón
Panama City
FARMING AND LAND USE
Cattle
Shellfish
Bananas
Coffee
Corn (maize)
Cotton
Sugarcane
Timber
Cropland
Forest
Pasture
Major conurbation
LAND USE
Pasture 27%
Forest 35%
Cropland 15%
Other 23%

ENVIRONMENTAL ISSUES

Central America's rainforests are rapidly being cut down for timber and to make way for farmland and land for building. Over half of Guatemala's forests have been felled, mostly in the last 30 years. The situation is also bleak in Honduras, Costa Rica and Nicaragua. Central America has a line of volcanoes running through the region which are still active.

Mitch 1998
Felix 2007
Volcán Tacaná 1986
Volcán de Fuego 1974
Volcán de Izalco 1958
Volcán San Cristobal 2000
Volcán Cerro Negro 1995
Volcán Masaya 2001
Volcán Concepcion 1986
Volcán Arenal 1998, 2000
Volcán Rincon de la Vieja 1998
ENVIRONMENTAL ISSUES
Volcanic eruption
Deforested areas
Remaining forests
Path of recent, devastating hurricane

POPULATION

Central America's people live mainly in the valleys of the central highlands or along the Pacific coastal plains. Despite the threat of volcanic eruptions and earthquakes, towns and cities developed in these areas because of the fertile volcanic soils found there. Around half the population still live in rural areas, mostly in small villages or remote settlements, but the cities have expanded rapidly and overcrowding has become a serious problem.

BELMOPAN
GUATEMALA CITY
SAN SALVADOR
TEGUCIGALPA
MANAGUA
SAN JOSÉ
PANAMA CITY
INHABITANTS PER SQ KM
More than 50
25–50
Less than 25
Capital city
URBAN/RURAL POPULATION DIVIDE
Managua 2.2%
Tegucigalpa 2%
Guatemala City 2.4%
Other towns and cities 43.4%
Rural population 50%
MEXICO
GUATEMALA
Sierra Madre
Volcán Tacaná 4093m
Champerico

THE LANDSCAPE

The Sierra Madre in the north and the Cordillera Central to the south form a mountainous ridge that stretches down most of Central America. Along the Pacific coast north of Panama is a belt of more than 40 active volcanoes. The mountains are broken by valleys and basins with large, fertile areas of rich, volcanic soil.

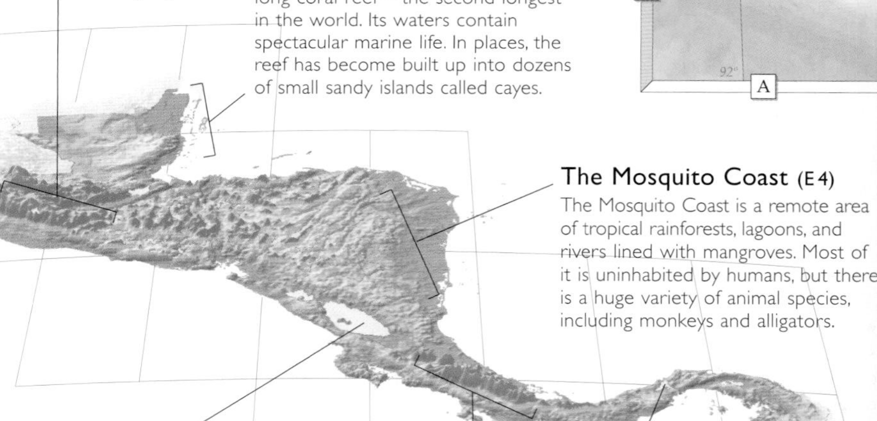

Sierra Madre (A 3)

Coral reef (C 2)
Off the coast of Belize is a 290 km long coral reef – the second longest in the world. Its waters contain spectacular marine life. In places, the reef has become built up into dozens of small sandy islands called cayes.

The Mosquito Coast (E 4)
The Mosquito Coast is a remote area of tropical rainforests, lagoons, and rivers lined with mangroves. Most of it is uninhabited by humans, but there is a huge variety of animal species, including monkeys and alligators.

Lake Nicaragua (E 5)
This large freshwater lake contains about 400 islands, some of which are active volancoes like Volcán Concepcion. The lake is also home to the world's only freshwater sharks.

Cordillera Central (G 6)

The Panama Canal (H 6)
The Panama Canal links the Atlantic and Pacific oceans along a distance of 82 km. Half of its route passes through Lake Gatún, a freshwater lake which acts as a reservoir for the canal, providing water to operate the locks.

CLIMATE

Temperatures are high all year round, although in January the Caribbean side of Central America is is cooler and wetter than the Pacific side. Summers are generally much wetter, especially in the Sierra Madre in Guatemala and on the Pacific coasts of Costa Rica and Panama.

INDUSTRY

Coffee, fish, and timber processing, fruit exporting and textile-weaving are typical of the small-scale industries found in Central America. Most industries are based in the capital cities and larger towns. In Panama, many people work at the Panama Canal, which is one of the world's busiest shipping routes. The country is also a major financial centre, with many banking and insurance companies.

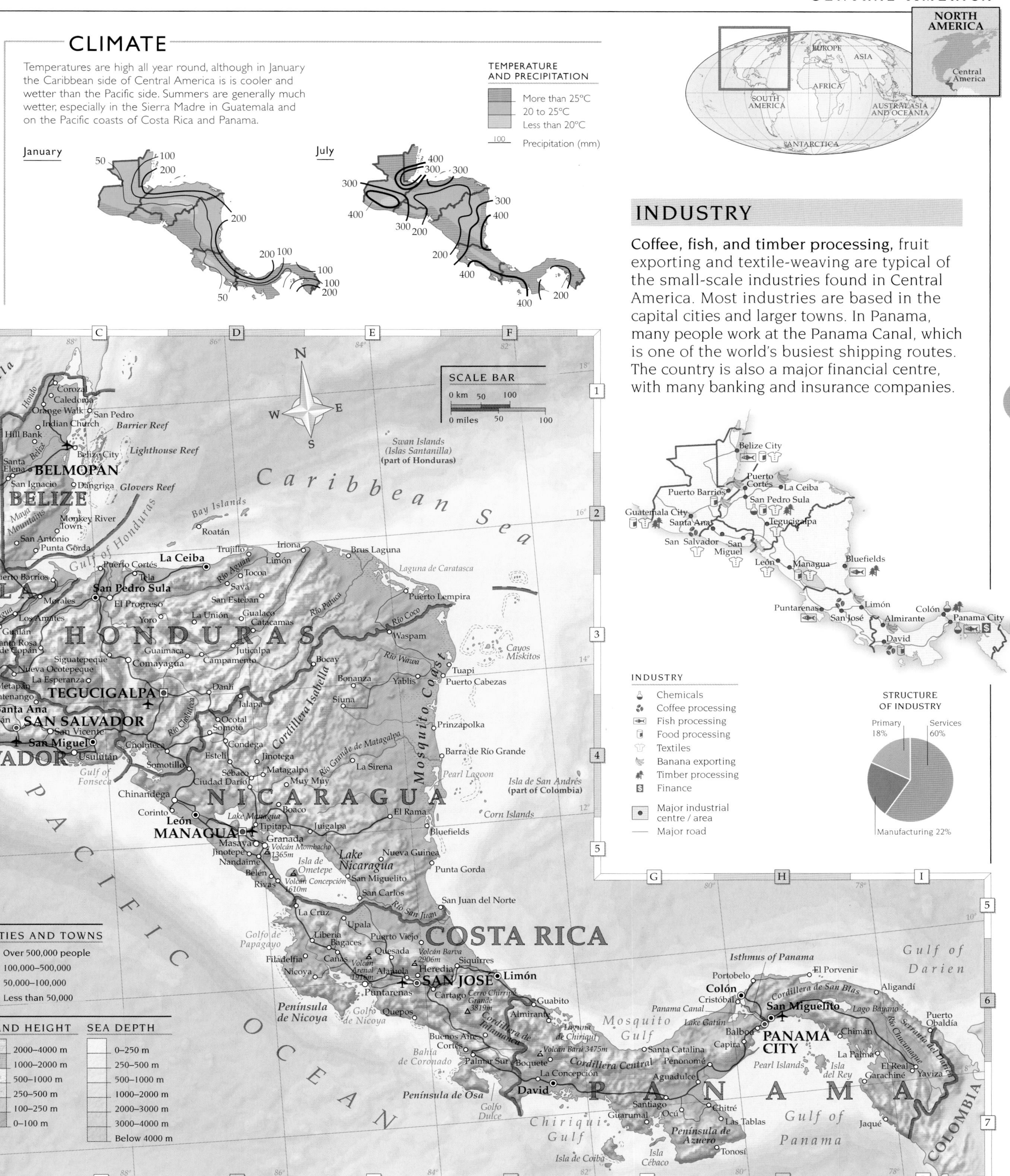

January
July
TEMPERATURE AND PRECIPITATION
More than 25°C
20 to 25°C
Less than 20°C
Precipitation (mm)
NORTH AMERICA
Central America
EUROPE
ASIA
AFRICA
SOUTH AMERICA
AUSTRALASIA AND OCEANIA
ANTARCTICA
INDUSTRY
Chemicals
Coffee processing
Fish processing
Food processing
Textiles
Banana exporting
Timber processing
Finance
Major industrial centre / area
Major road
STRUCTURE OF INDUSTRY
Primary 18%
Services 60%
Manufacturing 22%
SCALE BAR
0 km 50 100
0 miles 50 100
Caribbean Sea
PACIFIC OCEAN
BELIZE
BELMOPAN
HONDURAS
TEGUCIGALPA
SAN SALVADOR
NICARAGUA
MANAGUA
COSTA RICA
SAN JOSÉ
PANAMA
PANAMA CITY
Swan Islands (Islas Santanilla) (part of Honduras)
Isla de San Andrés (part of Colombia)
Gulf of Honduras
Gulf of Fonseca
Mosquito Coast
Lake Nicaragua
Isthmus of Panama
Panama Canal
Gulf of Darien
Gulf of Panama
Chiriqui Gulf
Mosquito Gulf
Península de Nicoya
Península de Osa
Península de Azuero
CITIES AND TOWNS
Over 500,000 people
100,000–500,000
50,000–100,000
Less than 50,000
LAND HEIGHT
2000–4000 m
1000–2000 m
500–1000 m
250–500 m
100–250 m
0–100 m
SEA DEPTH
0–250 m
250–500 m
500–1000 m
1000–2000 m
2000–3000 m
3000–4000 m
Below 4000 m

THE CARIBBEAN

The Caribbean Sea is enclosed by an arc of many hundreds of islands, islets and offshore reefs which reach from Florida in the USA round to Venezuela in South America. From 1492, Spain, France, Britain and the Netherlands claimed the islands as colonies. Most of the islands' original inhabitants were wiped out by disease and a wide mixture of peoples – of African, Asian and European descent – now make up the population. In 2010, a huge earthquake killed around 250,000 people in Haiti.

THE LANDSCAPE

The islands are formed from two main mountain chains: the Greater Antilles, which are part of a chain running from west to east, and the Lesser Antilles, which run from north to south. The mountains are now almost submerged under the Atlantic Ocean and Caribbean Sea. Only the higher peaks reach above sea level to form islands.

The Bahamas
The Bahamas are low-lying, islands formed from limestone rock. Their coastlines are fringed by coral reefs, lagoons and mangrove swamps. Some of the bigger islands are covered by forests.

Hispaniola (F 4)
Two countries, Haiti and the Dominican Republic occupy the island of Hispaniola. The land is mostly mountainous, broken by fertile valleys.

Cuba (C 3)
Cuba is the largest island in the Antilles. Its landscape is made up of wide, fertile plains with rugged hills and mountains in the southeast.

The Lesser Antilles
Most of these small volcanic islands have mountainous interiors. Barbados and Antigua & Barbuda are flatter, with some higher volcanic areas. Montserrat was evacuated in 1997, following volcanic eruptions on the island.

ENVIRONMENTAL ISSUES

The islands of the Caribbean are often under threat from hurricane storm systems which sweep in from the Atlantic Ocean between May and October. The winds can reach speeds of up to 300 km per hour, devastating everything that lies in their path and causing severe flooding. The storms themselves are enormous; a hurricane can extend outwards for 650 km from its calm centre, which is known as the 'eye'.

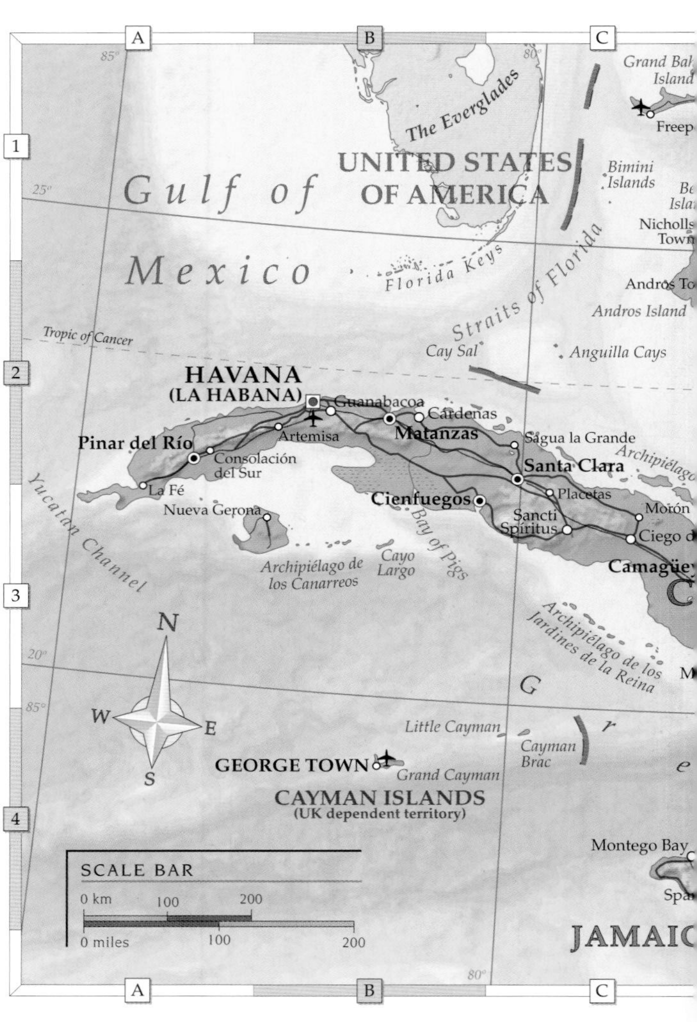

A
B
C
1
2
3
4
Gulf of Mexico
UNITED STATES OF AMERICA
The Everglades
Florida Keys
Straits of Florida
Tropic of Cancer
Grand Bahama Island
Bimini Islands
Nicholls Town
Andros Island
Cay Sal
Anguilla Cays
HAVANA (LA HABANA)
Guanabacoa
Cárdenas
Matanzas
Artemisa
Pinar del Río
Consolación del Sur
La Fé
Nueva Gerona
Sagua la Grande
Santa Clara
Placetas
Cienfuegos
Bay of Pigs
Sancti Spíritus
Morón
Archipiélago de los Canarreos
Cayo Largo
Yucatan Channel
Archipiélago de los Jardines de la Reina
Little Cayman
Cayman Brac
GEORGE TOWN
Grand Cayman
CAYMAN ISLANDS
(UK dependent territory)
Montego Bay
JAMAICA
N
S
E
W
SCALE BAR
0 km 100 200
0 miles 100 200

FARMING AND LAND USE

Agriculture is an important source of income, with over half of all produce exported. Many islands have fertile, well-watered land and large areas are set aside for commercial crops such as sugarcane, tobacco and coffee. Some islands rely heavily on a single crop; in Dominica, bananas provide over half the country's income. Cuba is one of the world's biggest sugar producers.

Havana
Kingston
Port-au-Prince
San Juan

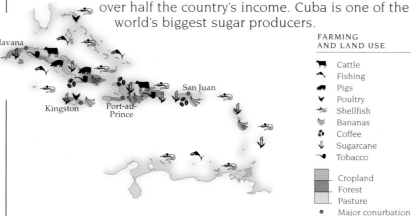

FARMING AND LAND USE
- Cattle
- Fishing
- Pigs
- Poultry
- Shellfish
- Bananas
- Coffee
- Sugarcane
- Tobacco
- Cropland
- Forest
- Pasture
- Major conurbation

TOURISM

Tourism is thriving in the Caribbean, often bringing more income to the region than other, traditional industries. Long sandy beaches, clear, warm waters and the climate are the main attractions. In Cuba and the Dominican Republic, tourism is expanding at some of the fastest rates in North America. As hotel complexes and new roads and airports are developed, the environment is often damaged. Local people who work in the industry often receive little of the extra cash brought in by the tourists.

TOURISM
Major tourist destinations

Bahamas, Cuba, Jamaica, Dominican Republic, Puerto Rico, Virgin Islands, Antigua & Barbuda, Guadeloupe, St Lucia, Barbados, Grenada, Aruba, Trinidad & Tobago

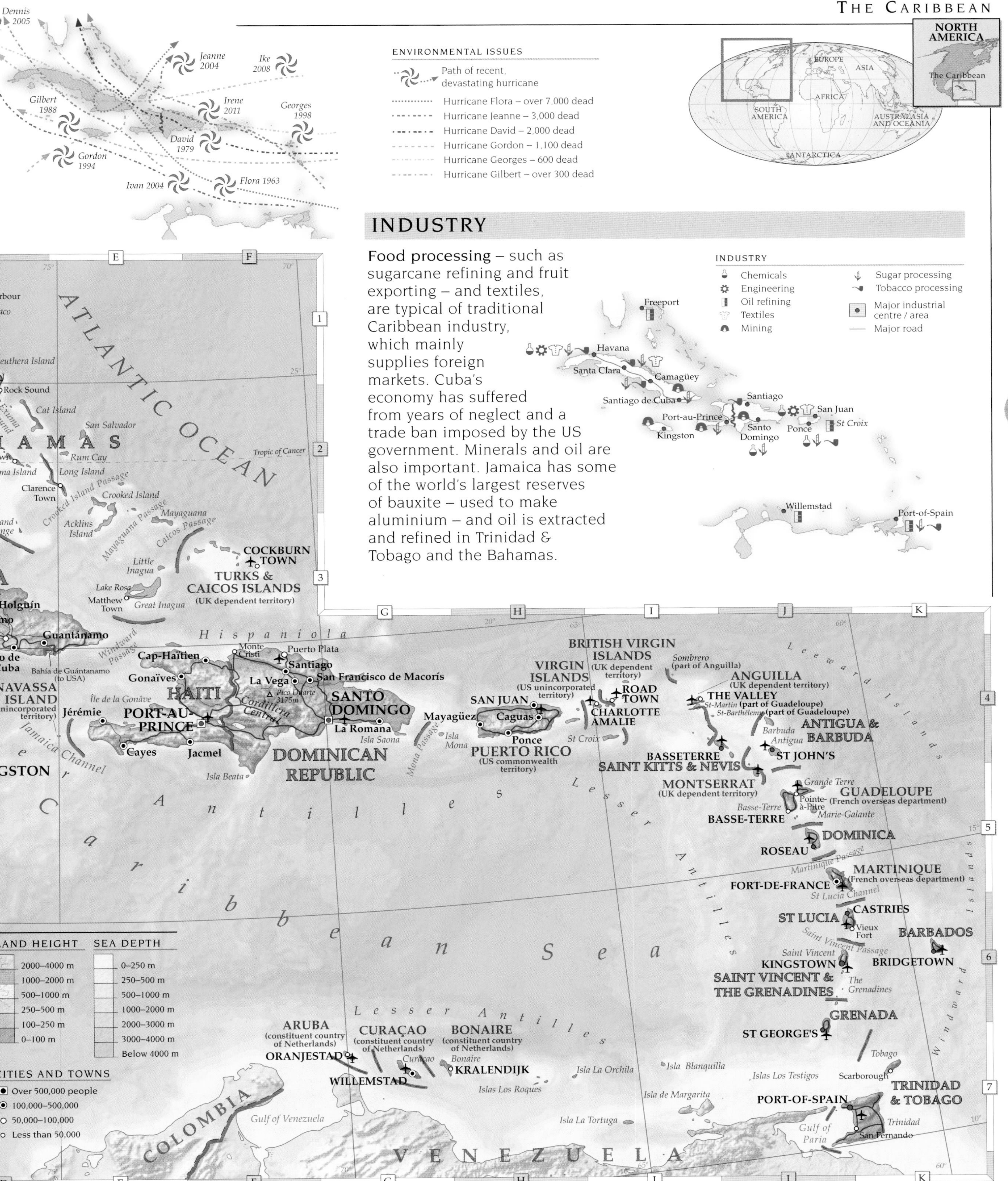

ENVIRONMENTAL ISSUES
Path of recent, devastating hurricane
Hurricane Flora – over 7,000 dead
Hurricane Jeanne – 3,000 dead
Hurricane David – 2,000 dead
Hurricane Gordon – 1,100 dead
Hurricane Georges – 600 dead
Hurricane Gilbert – over 300 dead
Dennis 2005
Jeanne 2004
Ike 2008
Gilbert 1988
Irene 2011
Georges 1998
David 1979
Gordon 1994
Ivan 2004
Flora 1963
NORTH AMERICA
The Caribbean
EUROPE
ASIA
AFRICA
SOUTH AMERICA
AUSTRALASIA AND OCEANIA
ANTARCTICA
INDUSTRY
Chemicals
Engineering
Oil refining
Textiles
Mining
Sugar processing
Tobacco processing
Major industrial centre / area
Major road
Freeport
Havana
Santa Clara
Camagüey
Santiago de Cuba
Santiago
San Juan
Port-au-Prince
Kingston
Santo Domingo
Ponce
St Croix
Willemstad
Port-of-Spain
ATLANTIC OCEAN
BAHAMAS
Rock Sound
Cat Island
San Salvador
Rum Cay
Long Island
Clarence Town
Crooked Island Passage
Crooked Island
Acklins Island
Mayaguana Passage
Mayaguana
Caicos Passage
Little Inagua
Lake Rosa
Matthew Town
Great Inagua
Tropic of Cancer
COCKBURN TOWN
TURKS & CAICOS ISLANDS
(UK dependent territory)
Holguín
Guantánamo
Bahía de Guantánamo (to USA)
Windward Passage
NAVASSA ISLAND
Hispaniola
Cap-Haïtien
Gonaïves
Île de la Gonâve
HAITI
Jérémie
PORT-AU-PRINCE
Cayes
Jacmel
Jamaica Channel
Monte Cristi
Puerto Plata
Santiago
La Vega
Pico Duarte 3175m
Cordillera Central
San Francisco de Macorís
SANTO DOMINGO
La Romana
Isla Saona
DOMINICAN REPUBLIC
Isla Beata
Mona Passage
Isla Mona
Mayagüez
SAN JUAN
Caguas
Ponce
PUERTO RICO
(US commonwealth territory)
VIRGIN ISLANDS
(US unincorporated territory)
CHARLOTTE AMALIE
St Croix
BRITISH VIRGIN ISLANDS
(UK dependent territory)
ROAD TOWN
Sombrero
(part of Anguilla)
ANGUILLA
(UK dependent territory)
THE VALLEY
St-Martin (part of Guadeloupe)
St-Barthélemy (part of Guadeloupe)
Barbuda
Antigua
ANTIGUA & BARBUDA
ST JOHN'S
BASSETERRE
SAINT KITTS & NEVIS
MONTSERRAT
(UK dependent territory)
Grande Terre
GUADELOUPE
(French overseas department)
Basse-Terre
Pointe-à-Pitre
Marie-Galante
BASSE-TERRE
DOMINICA
ROSEAU
Martinique Passage
MARTINIQUE
(French overseas department)
FORT-DE-FRANCE
St Lucia Channel
CASTRIES
ST LUCIA
Vieux Fort
BARBADOS
BRIDGETOWN
Saint Vincent Passage
Saint Vincent
KINGSTOWN
SAINT VINCENT & THE GRENADINES
The Grenadines
GRENADA
ST GEORGE'S
Tobago
Scarborough
TRINIDAD & TOBAGO
PORT-OF-SPAIN
Trinidad
San Fernando
Gulf of Paria
Leeward Islands
Windward Islands
Lesser Antilles
Antilles
Caribbean Sea
ARUBA
(constituent country of Netherlands)
ORANJESTAD
CURAÇAO
(constituent country of Netherlands)
Curaçao
WILLEMSTAD
BONAIRE
(constituent country of Netherlands)
Bonaire
KRALENDIJK
Islas Los Roques
Isla La Orchila
Isla Blanquilla
Islas Los Testigos
Isla de Margarita
Isla La Tortuga
Gulf of Venezuela
COLOMBIA
VENEZUELA
LAND HEIGHT
2000–4000 m
1000–2000 m
500–1000 m
250–500 m
100–250 m
0–100 m
SEA DEPTH
0–250 m
250–500 m
500–1000 m
1000–2000 m
2000–3000 m
3000–4000 m
Below 4000 m
CITIES AND TOWNS
Over 500,000 people
100,000–500,000
50,000–100,000
Less than 50,000

INDUSTRY

Food processing – such as sugarcane refining and fruit exporting – and textiles, are typical of traditional Caribbean industry, which mainly supplies foreign markets. Cuba's economy has suffered from years of neglect and a trade ban imposed by the US government. Minerals and oil are also important. Jamaica has some of the world's largest reserves of bauxite – used to make aluminium – and oil is extracted and refined in Trinidad & Tobago and the Bahamas.

Continental South America

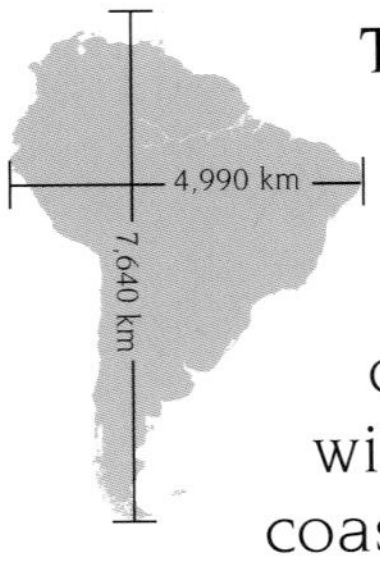

7,640 km
4,990 km

The towering peaks of the Andes stand high above the western side of South America. They act as a barrier to the sparsely inhabited interior of the continent which includes the dense rainforest of the Amazon Basin – one of the Earth's last great wildernesses. Most people live on South America's coastal fringes. Brazil is both the largest country, and the most populous. Over half the continent's land area and half its people are found there.

Cross-section across South America

Andes
Amazon River
Guiana Highlands
Mouths of the Amazon
Brazilian Highlands
W
5,400 km
E

The high peaks of the Andes rise up from a narrow strip of land bordering the Pacific Ocean. East of the Andes, the land flattens into a broad, shallow basin into which the Amazon River flows. To the north are the older Guiana Highlands where rock has been eroded to form flat-topped 'table' mountains.

Physical South America

Ancient masses of rocks, like the Guiana and Brazilian highlands, which are known as shields, form the core of South America. The Andes are the solid backbone of the continent. They are relatively young, formed by collisions between different plates of the Earth's crust. The major rivers; the Paraná and the mighty Amazon flow in deep depressions to the east of the mountains.

ELEVATION

- Above 4000 m
- 2000–4000 m
- 1000–2000 m
- 500–1000 m
- 250–500 m
- 100–250 m
- 0–100 m
- Below sea level

cross-section

SCALE 1:40,000,000

0 km 400 800

0 miles 400 800

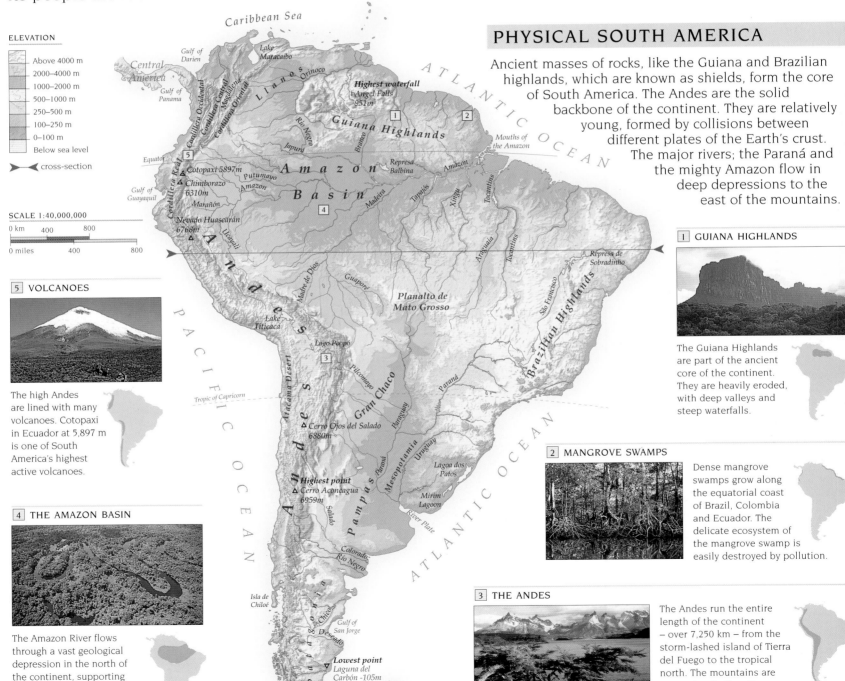

Caribbean Sea · Gulf of Darien · Central America · Gulf of Panama · Lake Maracaibo · Llanos · Orinoco · Highest waterfall Angel Falls 951m · Guiana Highlands · Río Negro · Japurá · Branco · Mouths of the Amazon · ATLANTIC OCEAN · Equator · Cordillera Occidental · Cordillera Central · Cordillera Oriental · Magdalena · Cordillera Real · Cotopaxi 5897m · Chimborazo 6310m · Putumayo · Amazon · Amazon Basin · Represa Balbina · Gulf of Guayaquil · Marañón · Madeira · Tapajós · Xingu · Tocantins · Nevado Huascarán 6768m · Ucayali · Araguaia · Represa de Sobradinho · Guaporé · Madre de Dios · Planalto de Mato Grosso · São Francisco · Brazilian Highlands · PACIFIC OCEAN · Andes · Lake Titicaca · Lago Poopó · Pilcomayo · Gran Chaco · Paraná · Tropic of Capricorn · Atacama Desert · Cerro Ojos del Salado 6880m · Paraguay · Uruguay · Mesopotamia · Highest point Cerro Aconcagua 6959m · Pampas · Salado · Lagoa dos Patos · Mirim Lagoon · River Plate · Colorado · Río Negro · Isla de Chiloé · Patagonia · Chico · Gulf of San Jorge · Deseado · Lowest point Laguna del Carbón -105m · Bahía Grande · Falkland Islands · Strait of Magellan · Tierra del Fuego · Cape Horn

5 VOLCANOES

The high Andes are lined with many volcanoes. Cotopaxi in Ecuador at 5,897 m is one of South America's highest active volcanoes.

4 THE AMAZON BASIN

The Amazon River flows through a vast geological depression in the north of the continent, supporting thousands of square kilometres of tropical rainforest.

1 GUIANA HIGHLANDS

The Guiana Highlands are part of the ancient core of the continent. They are heavily eroded, with deep valleys and steep waterfalls.

2 MANGROVE SWAMPS

Dense mangrove swamps grow along the equatorial coast of Brazil, Colombia and Ecuador. The delicate ecosystem of the mangrove swamp is easily destroyed by pollution.

3 THE ANDES

The Andes run the entire length of the continent – over 7,250 km – from the storm-lashed island of Tierra del Fuego to the tropical north. The mountains are on a volcanically active zone, and earthquakes are common.

POLITICAL SOUTH AMERICA

In the 17th century, explorers from Spain and Portugal claimed most of South America for their rulers in Europe. Their influences are still strong today: Brazilians speak Portuguese, while much of the rest of the continent is Spanish-speaking. The small nations of the north, Surinam and Guyana, were Dutch and British colonies and French Guiana is a French overseas department. The mix of peoples is mainly European, native American and African. Some native peoples still live in the dense Amazon rainforest.

SCALE 1:35,000,000

TRANSPORT LINKS

The Pan American Highway is a vital transport link, running from the far south of the continent, northwards along the Pacific coast. Its route takes it through sparsely populated areas like the Atacama Desert.

POPULATION

Many South American countries have a similar pattern of population distribution. The largest numbers of people are found near the coasts. Migration to the coastal cities has led to rocketing population figures, and growing social problems. São Paulo is now one of the world's largest cities; its outskirts are fringed with sprawling, shantytown suburbs – known as *favelas*.

Largest city
SÃO PAULO
19.6 million people

POPULATION DENSITY
(People per sq km)

Below 5
5–9
10–14
15–19
20–29
Above 29

POPULATION

Capital cities
Above 500,000
100,000 to 500,000
50,000 to 100,000
Below 50,000

Other cities
Above 500,000
50,000 to 100,000

BORDER DISPUTES

Many of South America's borders have been, or remain, disputed. Bolivia is landlocked as a result of a dispute with Chile in 1883, when it lost its lands bordering the Pacific Ocean.

URBAN GROWTH

Urban growth has transformed São Paulo into a major population and industrial centre. Its rapid growth has created many problems, like traffic congestion, overcrowding, and inadequate sewerage.

STANDARDS OF LIVING

There are many inequalities in living standards across South America. Argentina's economy has suffered during the regional recession but living standards are still above those of Guyana and Bolivia, which have weak economies, and are heavily reliant upon trade in raw materials. The booming black market drug trade increases crime and corruption.

STANDARD OF LIVING
(UN Human Development Index)

low
high
no data

SOUTH AMERICAN GEOGRAPHY

Agriculture is still the most common form of employment in South America. Cattle and cash crops of coffee, cocoa and, in some places, coca for cocaine, provide the main sources of income. Brazil has the greatest range of industries, followed by Argentina, Venezuela and Chile. The large coastal cities such as Rio de Janeiro, Lima and Buenos Aires are where most of the jobs are found. This encourages people to migrate from the country to the city, in search of employment.

INDUSTRY

Brazil is the continent's leading industrial producer and São Paulo the major industrial city. Manufactured products include iron and steel, automobiles, chemicals, textiles, and meat and leather products from the continent's vast cattle herds. In the mountains of Bolivia and Colombia, coca plants are grown to make cocaine, which has created a black market for this illegal drug.

OIL AND GAS

Under the waters of Lake Maracaibo, Venezuela, lie some of South America's biggest oil reserves. Oil exploitation has brought great wealth to Venezuela. The money has helped the country to build new roads and develop other industries.

INDUSTRIAL CENTRE

São Paulo, Brazil, is the largest city in South America and a leading industrial centre. A wide range of goods is manufactured here, including automobiles, chemicals, textiles and electronic products. São Paulo is also a leading financial centre Hundreds of people flock to the city daily in search of work.

TRADE AND EXPORTS

The Chilean port of Valparaíso ships many different products out of South America. Trade is growing with Japan and other countries around the Pacific Ocean.

CLIMATE

South America's mineral resources are highly localized. Few countries have both fossil fuels and metallic ores. The richest oilfields are in the north, especially in Venezuela. Coal, however, is scarce. When the Andes formed, heat helped create the many metallic minerals which are mined today.

MINERAL RESOURCES

- Bauxite
- Copper
- Iron
- Lead
- Silver
- Tin
- Oil/Gas field
- Coal field

COPPER MINES

Metallic mineral reserves are abundant in the Andes. Chuquicamata, northern Chile, is one of the world's largest copper mines.

ECONOMIC ACTIVITY

- Aerospace
- Brewing
- Car/vehicle manufacture
- Chemicals
- Coal
- Electronics
- Engineering
- Finance
- Fish processing
- Food processing
- Hi-tech industry
- Iron & steel
- Metal refining
- Narcotics
- Oil and gas
- Pharmaceuticals
- Printing & publishing
- Shipbuilding
- Textiles
- Timber processing
- Tobacco processing

GNI per capita (US$)

- Below 3,000
- 3,000-4,999
- 5,000-6,999
- 7,000-8,999
- 9,000-10,999
- Above 11,000
- Industrial centre

CLIMATE

South America has four main climatic regions; ropical, arid, temperate, and the cold climate of the ar south. The Amazon Basin, covered by massive ain forests, and the Guiana Highlands have a umid, tropical climate which allows vegetation o flourish. West of the Andes the climate tends o be very dry. Moist air flowing west from the tlantic Ocean is prevented from reaching the hores of the Pacific Ocean by the Andes and rain alls before it can pass over the mountains. This reates arid deserts like the Atacama.

EXTREME WEATHER EVENTS

Symbols indicate climatic extremes

Wettest place
QUIBDO (Colombia)
Annual rainfall 899cm
Equator
Driest place
ARICA (Chile)
Annual rainfall 0.08cm
Tropic of Capricorn
Hottest place
RIVADAVIA (Argentina)
Temperature 49°C
Coldest place
SARMIENTO (Argentina)
Temperature -33°C

CLIMATE

- Subarctic
- Cool continental
- Warm temperate
- Semi-arid
- Arid
- Temperate
- Tropical
- Humid equatorial

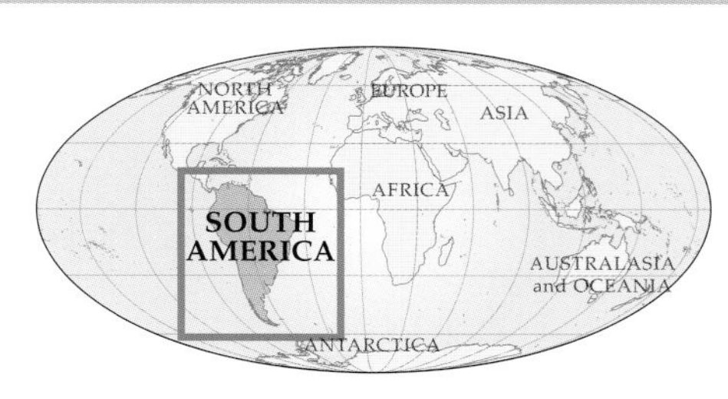
NORTH AMERICA
EUROPE
ASIA
AFRICA
SOUTH AMERICA
AUSTRALASIA and OCEANIA
ANTARCTICA

PATAGONIAN ICEFIELDS

Towards the south of the continent, the climate becomes very cold. Large expanses of ice, forming glaciers are found in southern Patagonia and on islands such as Tierra del Fuego at the tip of South America.

AND USE AND AGRICULTURE

- Cattle
- Pigs
- Sheep
- Bananas
- Corn (Maize)
- Citrus fruits
- Coca
- Cocoa
- Cotton
- Coffee
- Fishing
- Oil palms
- Peanuts
- Rubber
- Shellfish
- Soya beans
- Sugarcane
- Vineyards
- Wheat

- Barren land
- Cropland
- Desert
- Forest
- Mountain region
- Pasture
- Wetland
- Major conurbation

LAND USE AND AGRICULTURE

Many plants now found throughout the world originated in South America, like the tomato, potato and cassava. Today, coffee, cocoa, rubber, soya beans, corn (maize), and sugarcane are widely cultivated, and grapes are grown in sheltered valleys in the Andes. Much of the Amazon Basin is covered by dense rainforest and is unsuitable for cultivation, although some farmers practise 'slash and burn' techniques to make land for crops and cattle farming, which destroy ancient forest.

COFFEE

South America, and Brazil in particular, is a major producer of coffee. The plants thrive in the rich red soils of southern Brazil and are grown on huge plantations on the mountain slopes.

OCAL MARKETS

t traditional markets such as his one in Ecuador, high in the ndes, local people trade fruit, egetables and goods such as lothing, rugs and blankets. ome goods produced by cuadorean Indians are now xported world wide.

CATTLE

The vast plains of the Pampas, to the west of Buenos Aires, support large herds of cattle. Meat processing and canning is a major industry in Argentina, Paraguay and Uruguay.

NARCOTICS

Coca, grown in forest clearings in remote mountain areas, is used to make the drug cocaine. Government troops burn any coca plants they discover to discourage production.

NORTHERN SOUTH AMERICA

BRAZIL, COLOMBIA, ECUADOR, GUYANA, PERU, SURINAM, VENEZUELA

High mountains, steamy rain forests and hot, grassy plains cover much of northern South America. From the 16th century, after the conquest of the Incas, the western countries were ruled by Spain, while Brazil was governed by Portugal, Guyana by Britain, and Surinam by the Dutch. The more recent history of some of these countries has included periods of civil war and military rule. Most are still troubled by widespread poverty.

FARMING AND LAND USE

The variety of climates means a wide range of crops including sugarcane, cocoa and bananas can be grown for export. Coffee is the most important cash crop; Brazil is the world's leading coffee grower. Cattle are farmed on the plains of Colombia, Venezuela and southern Brazil. Much of the good farmland is owned by a few rich landowners, and many peasant farmers do not have enough land to make a living.

FARMING AND LAND USE

- Cattle
- Fishing
- Goats
- Sheep
- Bananas
- Cocoa
- Cotton
- Coffee
- Rubber
- Sugarcane
- Timber
- Cropland
- Forest
- Mountain region
- Pasture
- Wetland
- Major conurbation

LAND USE

Cropland 6%
Other (including mountains) 15%
Pasture 23%
Fores 56%

INDUSTRY

Important oil reserves are found in Venezuela and parts of the Amazon Basin; Venezuela is one of the world's top oil producers. Brazil's cities have a wide range of industries including chemicals, clothes and shoes, and textiles. Metallic minerals, particularly iron ore, are mined throughout the area and specially-built industrial centres like Ciudad Guayana have been developed to refine them.

STRUCTURE OF INDUSTRY

Primary 11%
Services 50%
Manufacturing 39%

INDUSTRY

- Aerospace
- Chemicals
- Food processing
- Iron & steel
- Metal refining
- Textiles
- Mining
- Oil
- Timber processing
- Tourism
- Major industrial centre / area
- Major road

POPULATION

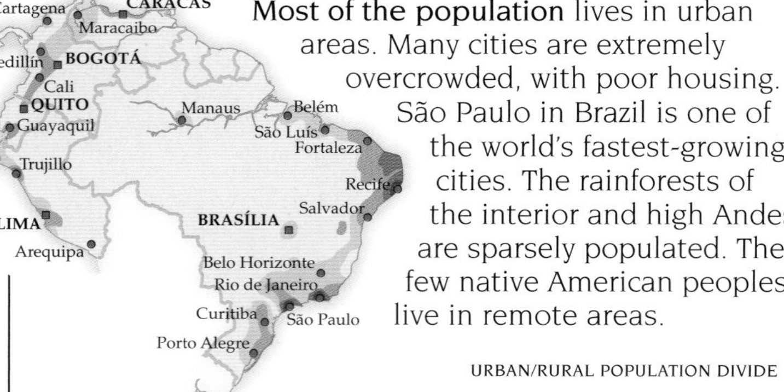
Cartagena
CARACAS
Maracaibo
Medellín
BOGOTÁ
Cali
QUITO
Guayaquil
Manaus
Belém
São Luís
Fortaleza
Trujillo
Recife
LIMA
BRASÍLIA
Salvador
Arequipa
Belo Horizonte
Rio de Janeiro
Curitiba
São Paulo
Porto Alegre

Most of the population lives in urban areas. Many cities are extremely overcrowded, with poor housing. São Paulo in Brazil is one of the world's fastest-growing cities. The rainforests of the interior and high Andes are sparsely populated. The few native American peoples live in remote areas.

INHABITANTS PER SQ KM

- More than 200
- 100–200
- 50–100
- 10–50
- Less than 10
- Capital city
- Major city

URBAN/RURAL POPULATION DIVIDE

Rio de Janeiro 4%
São Paulo 6.4%
Bogotá 2.6%
Rural population 21%
Other towns and cities 66%

THE LANDSCAPE

The Andes run down the western side of South America. There are many volcanoes among their peaks and earthquakes are common. The tropical rainforests surrounding the River Amazon take up most of wester Brazil. Huge, dry, flat grasslands called *llanos* cover central Venezuela and part of eastern Colombia.

Angel Falls (D 2)
Venezuela's Angel Falls is the world's highest waterfall. Twenty times as high as Niagara Falls, it drops 979 m from a spectacular plateau deep in the Guiana Highlands.

River Amazon (D 4)
The Amazon is the longe river in South America, an the second longest in the world. It flows over 6,516 km from the Peruv Andes to the coast of Br. One-fifth of the world's f water is carried by the ri

Andes (B 5)
The snow-capped Andes are the longest mountain range on Earth. They stretch 7,250 km down the whole length of South America.

Lake Titicaca (C 6)
South America's largest lake is the highest navigable lake in the world at 3,810 m above sea level. It lies across the border between Peru and Bolivia.

Pantanal (E 6)
This is the largest area of wetlands in the world. It spreads across 130,000 sq km of Brazil. Many hundreds of plant and animal species are found here.

Amazon rainforest (D 4)
The enormous rainfores surrounding the River Amazon and its tributar covers 6,500,000 sq km, an area almost as big as Australia. It is estimated that at least half of all known living species are found in the forest.

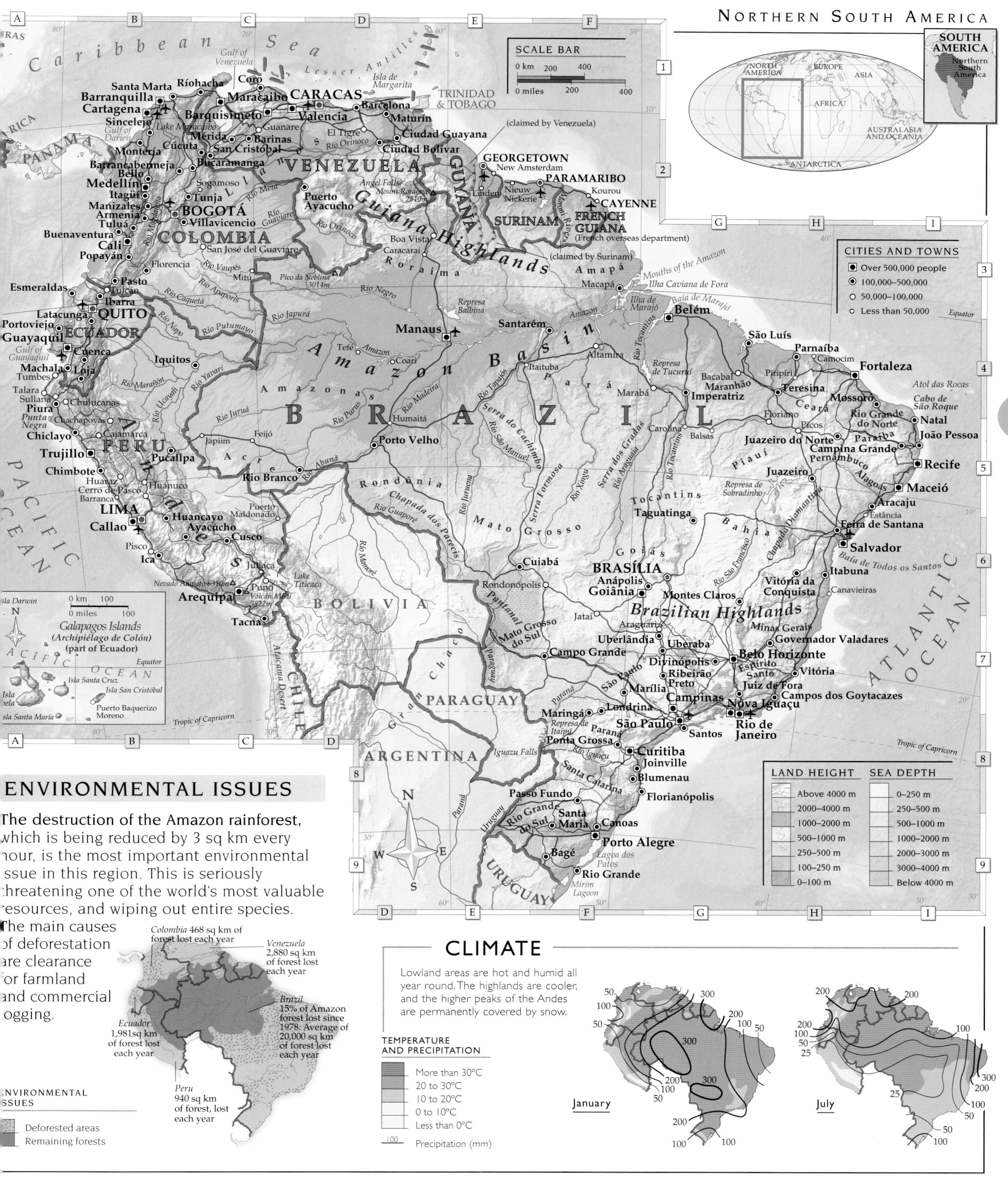
SCALE BAR
0 km 200 400
0 miles 200 400
SOUTH AMERICA
Northern South America
NORTH AMERICA
EUROPE
ASIA
AFRICA
AUSTRALASIA AND OCEANIA
ANTARCTICA
CITIES AND TOWNS
Over 500,000 people
100,000–500,000
50,000–100,000
Less than 50,000
LAND HEIGHT
Above 4000 m
2000–4000 m
1000–2000 m
500–1000 m
250–500 m
100–250 m
0–100 m
SEA DEPTH
0–250 m
250–500 m
500–1000 m
1000–2000 m
2000–3000 m
3000–4000 m
Below 4000 m
Caribbean Sea
Gulf of Venezuela
Lesser Antilles
Isla de Margarita
TRINIDAD & TOBAGO
PANAMA
VENEZUELA
COLOMBIA
ECUADOR
PERU
GUYANA
SURINAM
FRENCH GUIANA
(French overseas department)
(claimed by Venezuela)
(claimed by Surinam)
BRAZIL
BOLIVIA
PARAGUAY
CHILE
ARGENTINA
URUGUAY
CARACAS
BOGOTÁ
QUITO
LIMA
GEORGETOWN
PARAMARIBO
CAYENNE
BRASÍLIA
Guiana Highlands
Amazon Basin
Brazilian Highlands
Andes
Mato Grosso
Pantanal
Gran Chaco
Atacama Desert
Lake Titicaca
Mouths of the Amazon
Ilha de Marajó
Equator
Tropic of Capricorn
PACIFIC OCEAN
ATLANTIC OCEAN
Galapagos Islands
(Archipiélago de Colón)
(part of Ecuador)
0 km 100
0 miles 100
Isla Santa Cruz
Isla San Cristóbal
Puerto Baquerizo Moreno
Manaus
Belém
Fortaleza
Recife
Salvador
Belo Horizonte
Rio de Janeiro
São Paulo
Curitiba
Porto Alegre
Goiânia
Guayaquil
Medellín
Cali
Maracaibo
Valencia
Barranquilla
Cartagena
Arequipa
Trujillo
N
S
E
W

ENVIRONMENTAL ISSUES

The destruction of the Amazon rainforest, which is being reduced by 3 sq km every hour, is the most important environmental issue in this region. This is seriously threatening one of the world's most valuable resources, and wiping out entire species. The main causes of deforestation are clearance for farmland and commercial logging.

Colombia 468 sq km of forest lost each year
Venezuela 2,880 sq km of forest lost each year
Brazil 15% of Amazon forest lost since 1978. Average of 20,000 sq km of forest lost each year
Ecuador 1,981sq km of forest lost each year
Peru 940 sq km of forest, lost each year
ENVIRONMENTAL ISSUES
Deforested areas
Remaining forests

CLIMATE

Lowland areas are hot and humid all year round. The highlands are cooler, and the higher peaks of the Andes are permanently covered by snow.

TEMPERATURE AND PRECIPITATION
More than 30°C
20 to 30°C
10 to 20°C
0 to 10°C
Less than 0°C
100 Precipitation (mm)
January
July

SOUTHERN SOUTH AMERICA

ARGENTINA, BOLIVIA, CHILE, PARAGUAY, URUGUAY

The southern half of South America forms a long, narrow cone, with landscapes ranging from barren desert in the west, to frozen glaciers in the far south. The whole area was governed by Spain until the early 19th century, and Spanish is still the main language spoken, although the few remaining native American groups use their own languages. Most people now live in vast cities such as Buenos Aires and Santiago.

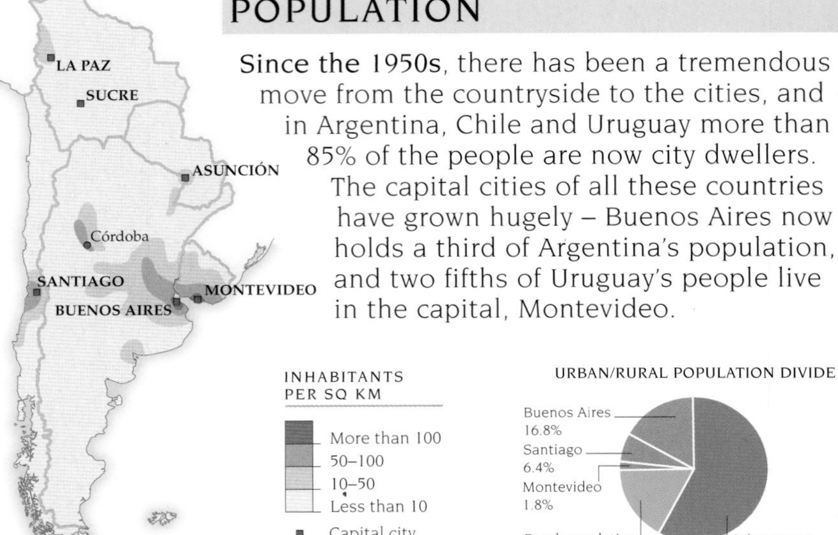

LA PAZ
SUCRE
ASUNCIÓN
Córdoba
SANTIAGO
BUENOS AIRES
MONTEVIDEO

POPULATION

Since the 1950s, there has been a tremendous move from the countryside to the cities, and in Argentina, Chile and Uruguay more than 85% of the people are now city dwellers. The capital cities of all these countries have grown hugely – Buenos Aires now holds a third of Argentina's population, and two fifths of Uruguay's people live in the capital, Montevideo.

INHABITANTS PER SQ KM
- More than 100
- 50–100
- 10–50
- Less than 10
- Capital city
- Major city

URBAN/RURAL POPULATION DIVIDE
- Buenos Aires 16.8%
- Santiago 6.4%
- Montevideo 1.8%
- Rural population 17%
- Other towns and cities 58%

INDUSTRY

Rich deposits of minerals – especially copper – in the Andes have led to the development of large metal refining industries in Chile. The capital cities, Buenos Aires and Santiago, are home to the widest range of industries and Argentina is an important producer of processed foods like canned beef. There are fewer industries in the south, although oil and gas are extracted in southern Argentina and Chile.

La Paz, Santa Cruz, Sucre, Chuquicamata, Antofagasta, San Salvador de Jujuy, Asunción, Resistencia, Córdoba, Valparaíso, Mendoza, Rosario, Santiago, Buenos Aires, Montevideo, Concepcíon, Valdivia, Neuquén, Bahía Blanca, Comodoro Rivadavia, Punta Arenas, Rio Grande

INDUSTRY
- Car manufacture
- Chemicals
- Food processing
- Metal refining
- Textiles
- Oil and gas
- Timber processing
- Major industrial centre / area
- Major road

STRUCTURE OF INDUSTRY
- Primary 10%
- Services 55%
- Manufacturing 35%

ENVIRONMENTAL ISSUES

Many of southern South America's rivers are polluted, particularly close to Buenos Aires. The Itaipú Dam on the Paraná River is the world's largest hydro-electric power project. Deforestation is a persistent problem in Bolivia, Paraguay and northern Argentina with 6,000 sq km cut down every year. Air quality in Buenos Aires and Santiago is poor, especially in Santiago which is surrounded by mountains, making it difficult for pollution to escape.

Río Loa
Itaipú Dam
Paraguay
Paraná
Río Salado
Río Carcaraña
Santiago
Buenos Aires
Río Bío Bío
Río Colorado

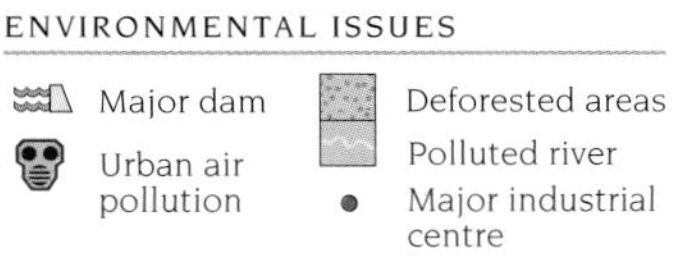

ENVIRONMENTAL ISSUES
Major dam
Urban air pollution
Deforested areas
Polluted river
Major industrial centre

THE LANDSCAPE

Southern South America's landscape varies from tropical forest and dry desert in the north, to sub-Antarctic conditions in the south. The towering Andes divide Chile from Argentina. East of the Andes lie forests and rolling grasslands. To the west is a thin coastal strip. The wet, windswept, freezing southern tip of the continent has volcanoes alongside glaciers and fjords.

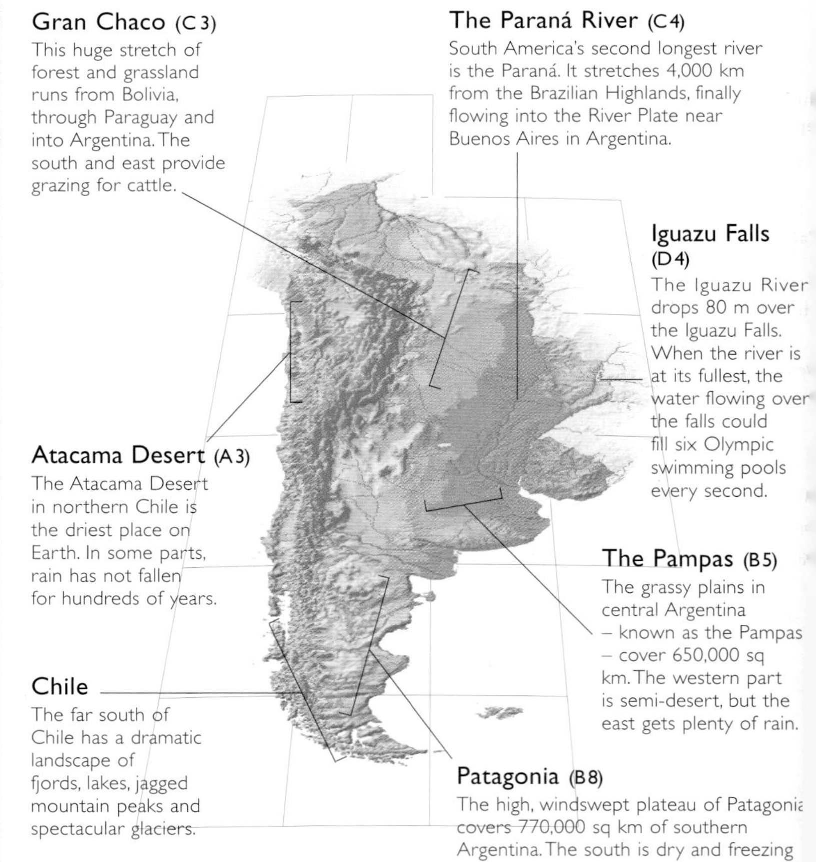

Gran Chaco (C3)
This huge stretch of forest and grassland runs from Bolivia, through Paraguay and into Argentina. The south and east provide grazing for cattle.

The Paraná River (C4)
South America's second longest river is the Paraná. It stretches 4,000 km from the Brazilian Highlands, finally flowing into the River Plate near Buenos Aires in Argentina.

Iguazu Falls (D4)
The Iguazu River drops 80 m over the Iguazu Falls. When the river is at its fullest, the water flowing over the falls could fill six Olympic swimming pools every second.

Atacama Desert (A3)
The Atacama Desert in northern Chile is the driest place on Earth. In some parts, rain has not fallen for hundreds of years.

The Pampas (B5)
The grassy plains in central Argentina – known as the Pampas – cover 650,000 sq km. The western part is semi-desert, but the east gets plenty of rain.

Chile
The far south of Chile has a dramatic landscape of fjords, lakes, jagged mountain peaks and spectacular glaciers.

Patagonia (B8)
The high, windswept plateau of Patagonia covers 770,000 sq km of southern Argentina. The south is dry and freezing cold, with very little vegetation.

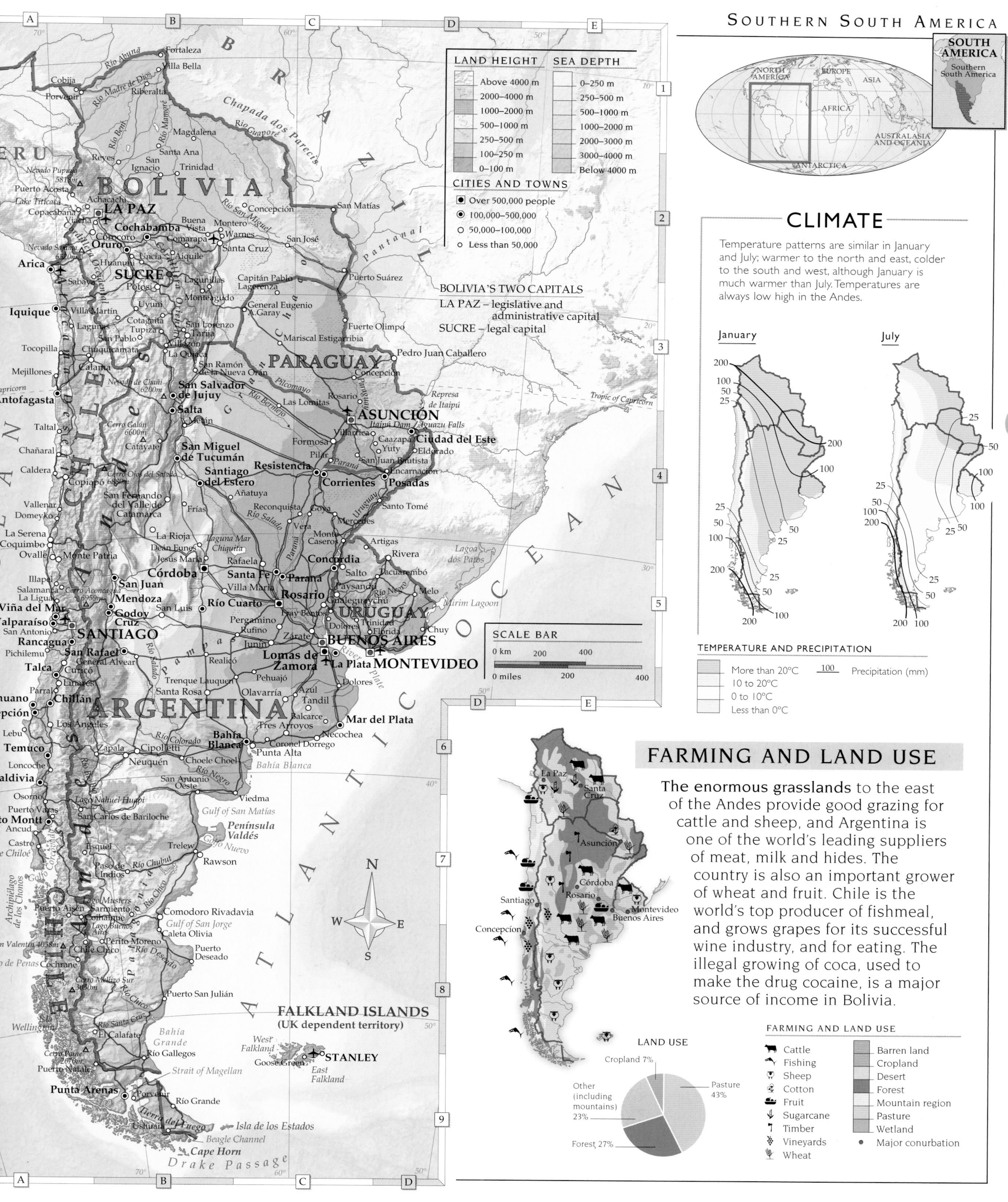

LAND HEIGHT
Above 4000 m
2000–4000 m
1000–2000 m
500–1000 m
250–500 m
100–250 m
0–100 m
SEA DEPTH
0–250 m
250–500 m
500–1000 m
1000–2000 m
2000–3000 m
3000–4000 m
Below 4000 m
CITIES AND TOWNS
Over 500,000 people
100,000–500,000
50,000–100,000
Less than 50,000
BOLIVIA'S TWO CAPITALS
LA PAZ – legislative and administrative capital
SUCRE – legal capital
BOLIVIA
PARAGUAY
URUGUAY
ARGENTINA
CHILE
BRAZIL
ATLANTIC OCEAN
FALKLAND ISLANDS
(UK dependent territory)
LA PAZ
SUCRE
ASUNCIÓN
SANTIAGO
BUENOS AIRES
MONTEVIDEO
STANLEY
SCALE BAR
0 km 200 400
0 miles 200 400
SOUTH AMERICA
Southern South America
NORTH AMERICA
EUROPE
ASIA
AFRICA
AUSTRALASIA AND OCEANIA
ANTARCTICA

CLIMATE

Temperature patterns are similar in January and July; warmer to the north and east, colder to the south and west, although January is much warmer than July. Temperatures are always low high in the Andes.

January
July
TEMPERATURE AND PRECIPITATION
More than 20°C
10 to 20°C
0 to 10°C
Less than 0°C
100 Precipitation (mm)

FARMING AND LAND USE

The enormous grasslands to the east of the Andes provide good grazing for cattle and sheep, and Argentina is one of the world's leading suppliers of meat, milk and hides. The country is also an important grower of wheat and fruit. Chile is the world's top producer of fishmeal, and grows grapes for its successful wine industry, and for eating. The illegal growing of coca, used to make the drug cocaine, is a major source of income in Bolivia.

LAND USE
Cropland 7%
Pasture 43%
Other (including mountains) 23%
Forest 27%
FARMING AND LAND USE
Cattle
Fishing
Sheep
Cotton
Fruit
Sugarcane
Timber
Vineyards
Wheat
Barren land
Cropland
Desert
Forest
Mountain region
Pasture
Wetland
Major conurbation

Continental Africa

Africa is the second largest continent in the world. Its dramatic landscapes include arid deserts, humid rainforests, and the valleys of the east African rift – the place where humans first evolved. Today, there are 54 separate countries in Africa, and its people speak a rich variety of languages. The world's highest temperatures have been recorded in Africa's deserts.

7,260 km

7,623 km

Cross-section through Africa

Niger Delta

Congo Basin

Lake Victoria

Great Rift Valley

Ethiopian Highla

Horn of Afr

W

5,200 km

In the west, the Niger River flows into the Atlantic Ocean through the swampy Niger Delta. Further east is the immense Congo Basin, where the Congo River winds its way through thick rainforests. In the east is the Great Rift Valley, and the Ethiopian Highlands. The Horn of Africa is Africa's most easterly point.

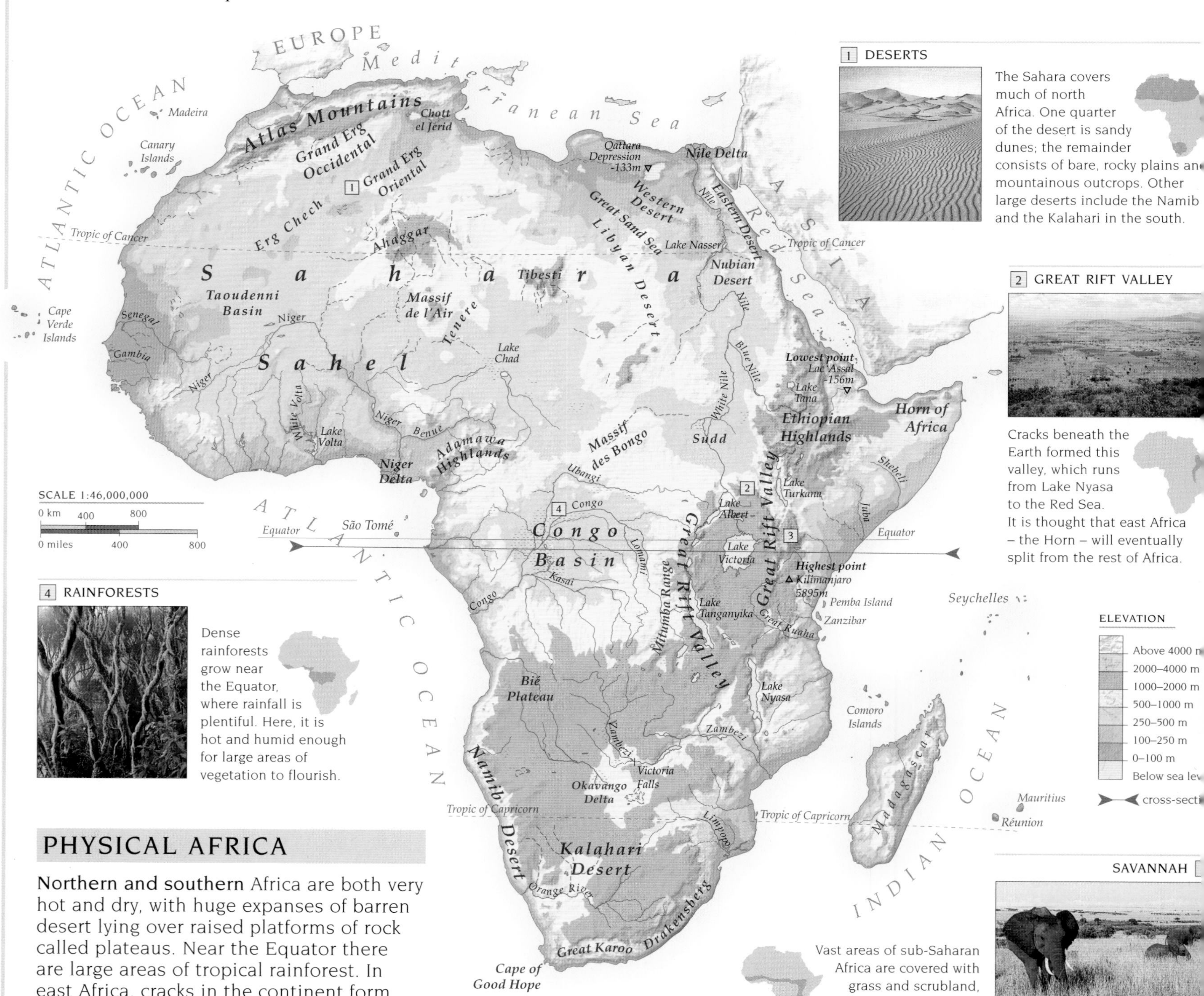

EUROPE
Mediterranean Sea
ATLANTIC OCEAN
Madeira
Canary Islands
Atlas Mountains
Chott el Jerid
Grand Erg Occidental
Grand Erg Oriental
Qattara Depression -133m
Nile Delta
Western Desert
Great Sand Sea
Libyan Desert
Eastern Desert
Nile
Red Sea
ASIA
Erg Chech
Ahaggar
Tropic of Cancer
Lake Nasser
Sahara
Tibesti
Nubian Desert
Cape Verde Islands
Taoudenni Basin
Senegal
Niger
Massif de l'Aïr
Tenere
Gambia
Lake Chad
Blue Nile
Sahel
Lowest point Lac Assal -156m
Lake Tana
White Volta
Lake Volta
Benue
White Nile
Ethiopian Highlands
Horn of Africa
Massif des Bongo
Sudd
Adamawa Highlands
Niger Delta
Ubangi
Shebeli
Lake Turkana
SCALE 1:46,000,000
0 km 400 800
0 miles 400 800
Congo
Lake Albert
Great Rift Valley
Juba
São Tomé
Equator
Congo Basin
Lake Victoria
Lomami
Kasai
Highest point Kilimanjaro 5895m
Pemba Island
Zanzibar
Seychelles
Mitumba Range
Lake Tanganyika
Great Ruaha
ELEVATION
Above 4000 m
2000–4000 m
1000–2000 m
500–1000 m
250–500 m
100–250 m
0–100 m
Below sea lev
cross-secti
Bié Plateau
Lake Nyasa
Comoro Islands
Zambezi
Namib Desert
Victoria Falls
Okavango Delta
Madagascar
Mauritius
Réunion
Tropic of Capricorn
Limpopo
Kalahari Desert
Orange River
Drakensberg
Great Karoo
Cape of Good Hope
INDIAN OCEAN

1 Deserts

The Sahara covers much of north Africa. One quarter of the desert is sandy dunes; the remainder consists of bare, rocky plains and mountainous outcrops. Other large deserts include the Namib and the Kalahari in the south.

2 Great Rift Valley

Cracks beneath the Earth formed this valley, which runs from Lake Nyasa to the Red Sea. It is thought that east Africa – the Horn – will eventually split from the rest of Africa.

4 Rainforests

Dense rainforests grow near the Equator, where rainfall is plentiful. Here, it is hot and humid enough for large areas of vegetation to flourish.

Savannah

Vast areas of sub-Saharan Africa are covered with grass and scrubland, known as savannah. Many of Africa's largest animals, such as elephants, live here.

Physical Africa

Northern and southern Africa are both very hot and dry, with huge expanses of barren desert lying over raised platforms of rock called plateaus. Near the Equator there are large areas of tropical rainforest. In east Africa, cracks in the continent form a string of flat-bottomed, steep-sided rift valleys, many of which contain vast lakes.

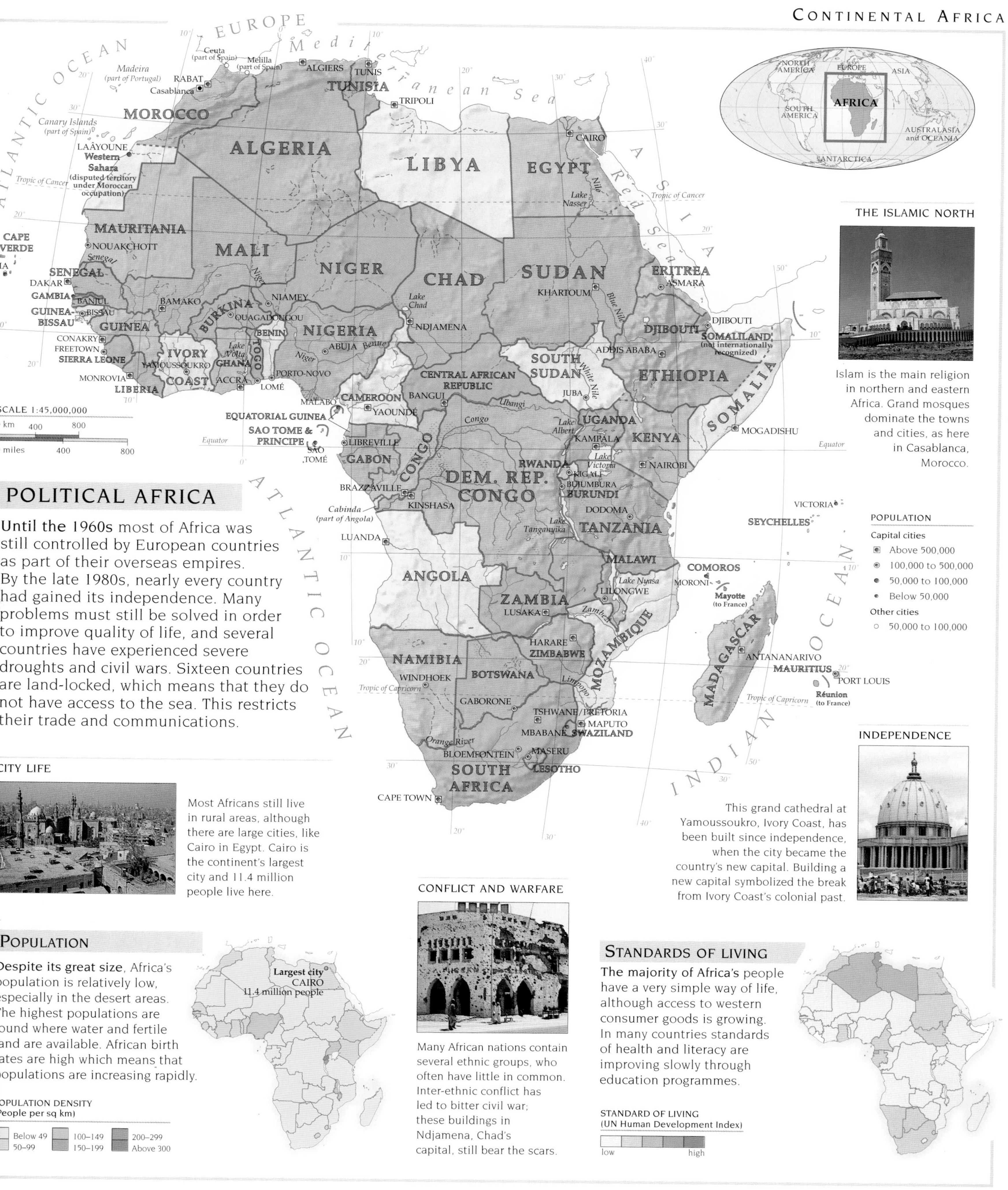
EUROPE
ATLANTIC OCEAN
Mediterranean Sea
Red Sea
ASIA
INDIAN OCEAN
Madeira (part of Portugal)
Canary Islands (part of Spain)
Ceuta (part of Spain)
Melilla (part of Spain)
RABAT
Casablanca
MOROCCO
ALGIERS
ALGERIA
TUNIS
TUNISIA
TRIPOLI
LIBYA
CAIRO
EGYPT
Lake Nasser
Nile
LAÂYOUNE
Western Sahara (disputed territory under Moroccan occupation)
Tropic of Cancer
MAURITANIA
NOUAKCHOTT
Senegal
CAPE VERDE
SENEGAL
DAKAR
GAMBIA
BANJUL
GUINEA-BISSAU
BISSAU
GUINEA
CONAKRY
FREETOWN
SIERRA LEONE
MONROVIA
LIBERIA
MALI
BAMAKO
Niger
NIAMEY
NIGER
BURKINA
OUAGADOUGOU
IVORY COAST
YAMOUSSOUKRO
Lake Volta
GHANA
ACCRA
TOGO
LOMÉ
BENIN
PORTO-NOVO
NIGERIA
ABUJA
Benue
CHAD
Lake Chad
NDJAMENA
SUDAN
KHARTOUM
Blue Nile
ERITREA
ASMARA
DJIBOUTI
SOMALILAND (not internationally recognized)
ADDIS ABABA
ETHIOPIA
SOMALIA
MOGADISHU
SOUTH SUDAN
White Nile
JUBA
CENTRAL AFRICAN REPUBLIC
BANGUI
Ubangi
MALABO
CAMEROON
YAOUNDÉ
EQUATORIAL GUINEA
SAO TOME & PRINCIPE
SÃO TOMÉ
LIBREVILLE
GABON
CONGO
Congo
BRAZZAVILLE
KINSHASA
DEM. REP. CONGO
Cabinda (part of Angola)
Lake Albert
UGANDA
KAMPALA
KENYA
NAIROBI
Lake Victoria
RWANDA
KIGALI
BUJUMBURA
BURUNDI
DODOMA
TANZANIA
Lake Tanganyika
Equator
LUANDA
ANGOLA
MALAWI
Lake Nyasa
LILONGWE
ZAMBIA
LUSAKA
Zambezi
HARARE
ZIMBABWE
MOZAMBIQUE
NAMIBIA
WINDHOEK
BOTSWANA
GABORONE
Limpopo
Tropic of Capricorn
TSHWANE/PRETORIA
MAPUTO
MBABANE
SWAZILAND
Orange River
BLOEMFONTEIN
MASERU
LESOTHO
SOUTH AFRICA
CAPE TOWN
VICTORIA
SEYCHELLES
COMOROS
MORONI
Mayotte (to France)
MADAGASCAR
ANTANANARIVO
MAURITIUS
PORT LOUIS
Réunion (to France)
SCALE 1:45,000,000
km 400 800
miles 400 800
NORTH AMERICA
EUROPE
ASIA
AFRICA
SOUTH AMERICA
AUSTRALASIA and OCEANIA
ANTARCTICA
POPULATION
Capital cities
Above 500,000
100,000 to 500,000
50,000 to 100,000
Below 50,000
Other cities
50,000 to 100,000
Largest city CAIRO
11.4 million people
POPULATION DENSITY
People per sq km)
Below 49
50–99
100–149
150–199
200–299
Above 300
STANDARD OF LIVING
(UN Human Development Index)
low
high

POLITICAL AFRICA

Until the 1960s most of Africa was still controlled by European countries as part of their overseas empires. By the late 1980s, nearly every country had gained its independence. Many problems must still be solved in order to improve quality of life, and several countries have experienced severe droughts and civil wars. Sixteen countries are land-locked, which means that they do not have access to the sea. This restricts their trade and communications.

THE ISLAMIC NORTH

Islam is the main religion in northern and eastern Africa. Grand mosques dominate the towns and cities, as here in Casablanca, Morocco.

CITY LIFE

Most Africans still live in rural areas, although there are large cities, like Cairo in Egypt. Cairo is the continent's largest city and 11.4 million people live here.

INDEPENDENCE

This grand cathedral at Yamoussoukro, Ivory Coast, has been built since independence, when the city became the country's new capital. Building a new capital symbolized the break from Ivory Coast's colonial past.

POPULATION

Despite its great size, Africa's population is relatively low, especially in the desert areas. The highest populations are found where water and fertile land are available. African birth rates are high which means that populations are increasing rapidly.

CONFLICT AND WARFARE

Many African nations contain several ethnic groups, who often have little in common. Inter-ethnic conflict has led to bitter civil war; these buildings in Ndjamena, Chad's capital, still bear the scars.

STANDARDS OF LIVING

The majority of Africa's people have a very simple way of life, although access to western consumer goods is growing. In many countries standards of health and literacy are improving slowly through education programmes.

African Geography

Africa's massive reserves of minerals, including oil, gold, copper and diamonds, are amongst the largest in the world. Mining is a very important industry for many countries, and has provided money for growth and development. Africa's wide range of environments means that many different types of crops can be grown. Rubber, bananas and oil palms are grown for export in the tropics, and east Africa is especially famous for its tea and coffee.

Industry

Most African industries are based on processing raw materials such as food crops or mineral ores. Some African countries depend on one product or crop for most of their income, but in many larger cities different industries are developing. Northern Africa, Nigeria, and South Africa have the widest range of industries.

INDUSTRY

- Brewing
- Car/vehicle manufacture
- Cement
- Chemicals
- Coal
- Engineering
- Fish processing
- Finance
- Food processing
- Iron & steel
- Mining
- Oil and gas
- Pharmaceuticals
- Shipbuilding
- Textiles
- Timber processing

GNP per capita (US$)

- Below 500
- 500-999
- 1,000-1,999
- 2,000-3,999
- 4,000-5,999
- Above 6,000
- Industrial centre

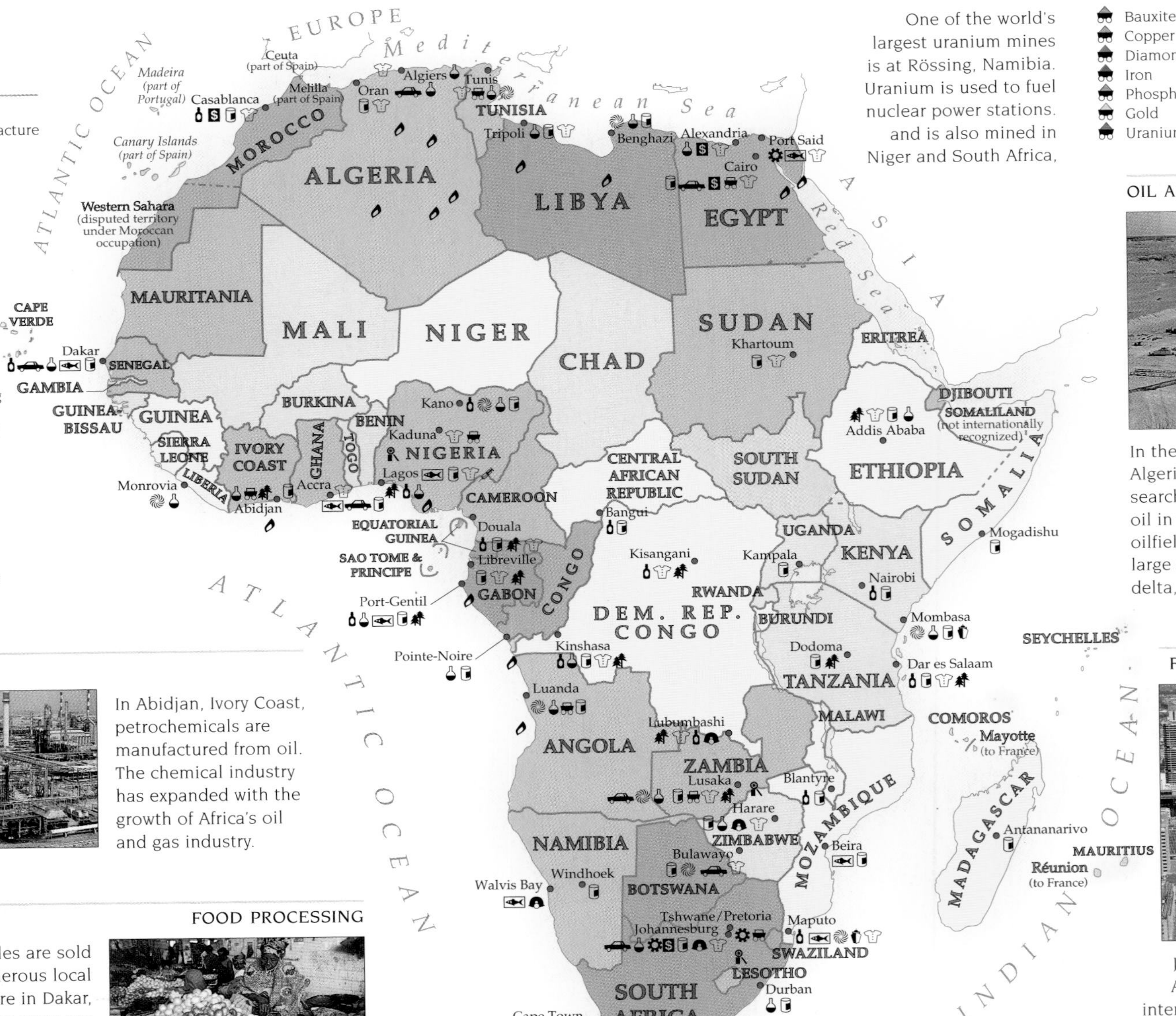

EUROPE
Mediterranean Sea
ATLANTIC OCEAN
ASIA
Red Sea
INDIAN OCEAN

Madeira (part of Portugal)
Canary Islands (part of Spain)
Ceuta (part of Spain)
Melilla (part of Spain)
Casablanca
Oran
Algiers
Tunis
TUNISIA
Tripoli
Benghazi
Alexandria
Port Said
Cairo
MOROCCO
ALGERIA
LIBYA
EGYPT
Western Sahara (disputed territory under Moroccan occupation)
MAURITANIA
MALI
NIGER
CHAD
SUDAN
Khartoum
ERITREA
CAPE VERDE
Dakar
SENEGAL
GAMBIA
GUINEA-BISSAU
GUINEA
SIERRA LEONE
LIBERIA
Monrovia
IVORY COAST
Abidjan
BURKINA
GHANA
Accra
TOGO
BENIN
Kano
Kaduna
NIGERIA
Lagos
CAMEROON
Douala
EQUATORIAL GUINEA
SAO TOME & PRINCIPE
Libreville
GABON
Port-Gentil
CONGO
Pointe-Noire
CENTRAL AFRICAN REPUBLIC
Bangui
SOUTH SUDAN
ETHIOPIA
Addis Ababa
DJIBOUTI
SOMALILAND (not internationally recognized)
SOMALIA
Mogadishu
UGANDA
Kampala
KENYA
Nairobi
Mombasa
Kisangani
RWANDA
BURUNDI
DEM. REP. CONGO
Kinshasa
TANZANIA
Dodoma
Dar es Salaam
SEYCHELLES
Luanda
ANGOLA
Lubumbashi
ZAMBIA
Lusaka
MALAWI
Blantyre
COMOROS
Mayotte (to France)
Harare
ZIMBABWE
Bulawayo
MOZAMBIQUE
Beira
MADAGASCAR
Antananarivo
MAURITIUS
Réunion (to France)
NAMIBIA
Windhoek
Walvis Bay
BOTSWANA
Tshwane/Pretoria
Johannesburg
Maputo
SWAZILAND
LESOTHO
Durban
SOUTH AFRICA
Cape Town
East London
Port Elizabeth

Mineral Resources

The southern countries, in particular South Africa, have large reserves of diamonds, gold, uranium and copper. The large copper deposits in Dem. Rep. Congo and Zambia are known as the 'copper belt'. Oil and gas are extracted in Algeria, Angola, Egypt, Libya, and Nigeria.

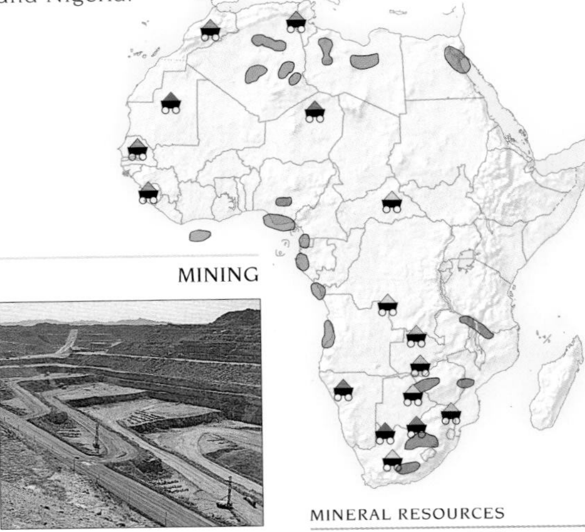

MINERAL RESOURCES

- Bauxite
- Copper
- Diamonds
- Iron
- Phosphates
- Gold
- Uranium
- Oil/gas field
- Coal field

MINING

One of the world's largest uranium mines is at Rössing, Namibia. Uranium is used to fuel nuclear power stations, and is also mined in Niger and South Africa.

OIL AND GAS

In the desert wastes of Algeria, a drilling rig searches for new sources of oil in the rich north African oilfields. There are several large oil fields in the Niger delta, and north Africa.

CHEMICALS

In Abidjan, Ivory Coast, petrochemicals are manufactured from oil. The chemical industry has expanded with the growth of Africa's oil and gas industry.

FOOD PROCESSING

Fruit and vegetables are sold in Africa's numerous local markets, as here in Dakar, Senegal. Many crops are grown specially for canning and export overseas and are known as 'cash crops.'

FINANCE AND TRADE

Johannesburg, in South Africa, is home to many international banks. Wealth has been generated from the country's large mineral resources, such as diamonds.

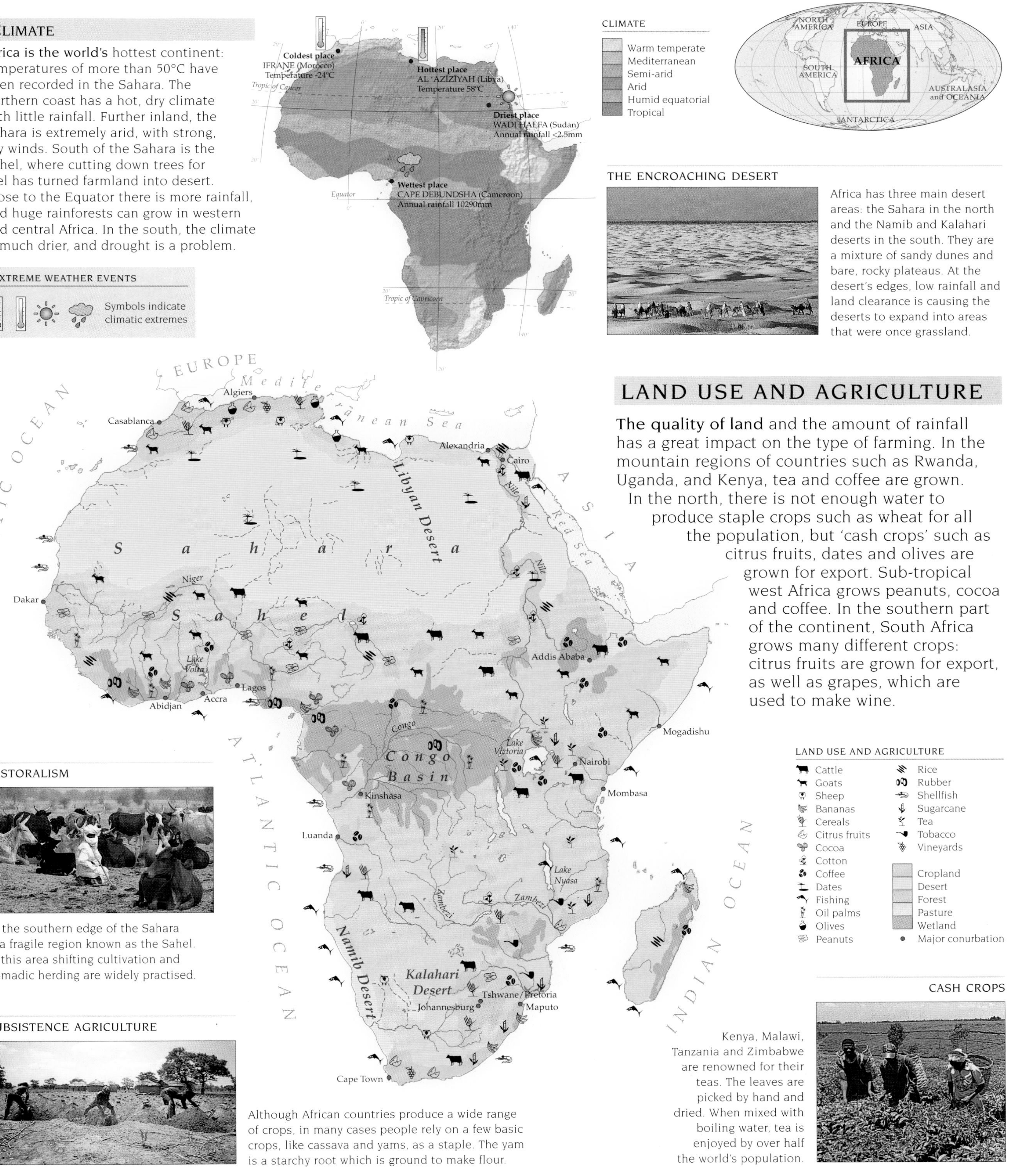
Coldest place
IFRANE (Morocco)
Temperature -24°C
Hottest place
AL 'AZIZIYAH (Libya)
Temperature 58°C
Driest place
WADI HALFA (Sudan)
Annual rainfall <2.5mm
Wettest place
CAPE DEBUNDSHA (Cameroon)
Annual rainfall 10290mm
Tropic of Cancer
Equator
Tropic of Capricorn
NORTH AMERICA
EUROPE
ASIA
AFRICA
SOUTH AMERICA
AUSTRALASIA and OCEANIA
ANTARCTICA
EUROPE
ASIA
Mediterranean Sea
ATLANTIC OCEAN
INDIAN OCEAN
Algiers
Casablanca
Alexandria
Cairo
Libyan Desert
Nile
Red Sea
Sahara
Niger
Sahel
Dakar
Lake Volta
Lagos
Accra
Abidjan
Addis Ababa
Mogadishu
Congo
Congo Basin
Lake Victoria
Nairobi
Mombasa
Kinshasa
Luanda
Lake Nyasa
Zambezi
Namib Desert
Kalahari Desert
Tshwane/Pretoria
Johannesburg
Maputo
Cape Town

CLIMATE

frica is the world's hottest continent: emperatures of more than 50°C have een recorded in the Sahara. The orthern coast has a hot, dry climate ith little rainfall. Further inland, the ahara is extremely arid, with strong, ry winds. South of the Sahara is the ahel, where cutting down trees for uel has turned farmland into desert. lose to the Equator there is more rainfall, nd huge rainforests can grow in western nd central Africa. In the south, the climate s much drier, and drought is a problem.

EXTREME WEATHER EVENTS

Symbols indicate climatic extremes

CLIMATE

- Warm temperate
- Mediterranean
- Semi-arid
- Arid
- Humid equatorial
- Tropical

THE ENCROACHING DESERT

Africa has three main desert areas: the Sahara in the north and the Namib and Kalahari deserts in the south. They are a mixture of sandy dunes and bare, rocky plateaus. At the desert's edges, low rainfall and land clearance is causing the deserts to expand into areas that were once grassland.

LAND USE AND AGRICULTURE

The quality of land and the amount of rainfall has a great impact on the type of farming. In the mountain regions of countries such as Rwanda, Uganda, and Kenya, tea and coffee are grown. In the north, there is not enough water to produce staple crops such as wheat for all the population, but 'cash crops' such as citrus fruits, dates and olives are grown for export. Sub-tropical west Africa grows peanuts, cocoa and coffee. In the southern part of the continent, South Africa grows many different crops: citrus fruits are grown for export, as well as grapes, which are used to make wine.

LAND USE AND AGRICULTURE

- Cattle
- Goats
- Sheep
- Bananas
- Cereals
- Citrus fruits
- Cocoa
- Cotton
- Coffee
- Dates
- Fishing
- Oil palms
- Olives
- Peanuts
- Rice
- Rubber
- Shellfish
- Sugarcane
- Tea
- Tobacco
- Vineyards
- Cropland
- Desert
- Forest
- Pasture
- Wetland
- Major conurbation

ASTORALISM

t the southern edge of the Sahara s a fragile region known as the Sahel. n this area shifting cultivation and omadic herding are widely practised.

UBSISTENCE AGRICULTURE

Although African countries produce a wide range of crops, in many cases people rely on a few basic crops, like cassava and yams, as a staple. The yam is a starchy root which is ground to make flour.

CASH CROPS

Kenya, Malawi, Tanzania and Zimbabwe are renowned for their teas. The leaves are picked by hand and dried. When mixed with boiling water, tea is enjoyed by over half the world's population.

North Africa

ALGERIA, EGYPT, LIBYA, MOROCCO, TUNISIA.

Sandwiched between the Mediterranean and the Sahara, North Africa has a history dating back to the dawn of civilization. 6,000 years ago, settlements were established along the banks of the River Nile, and since that time, waves of settlers, including Romans, Arabs and Turks have brought a mix of different cultures to the area. In the 19th century, Spain, France and Britain claimed colonies in the region, but today North Africa is independent, although Western Sahara is occupied by Morocco.

FARMING AND LAND USE

Most farming in North Africa is restricted to the fertile Mediterranean coastal strip, and the banks of the Nile where it relies heavily on irrigation. In spite of these seemingly inhospitable conditions, the region is a major producer of dates, which grow in desert oases, and of cork, made from the bark of the cork oak tree. A wide variety of other crops is also grown, including grapes, olives and cotton.

FARMING AND LAND USE

- Fishing
- Goats
- Sheep
- Citrus Fruits
- Cork
- Cotton
- Dates
- Olives
- Vineyards
- Cropland
- Desert
- Forest
- Pasture
- Major conurbation

CLIMATE

Most of north Africa is desert, and the climate is harsh. Rainfall is scarce, and drought is common. Temperatures are freezing at night, scorching by day and have been known to climb to over 50°C.

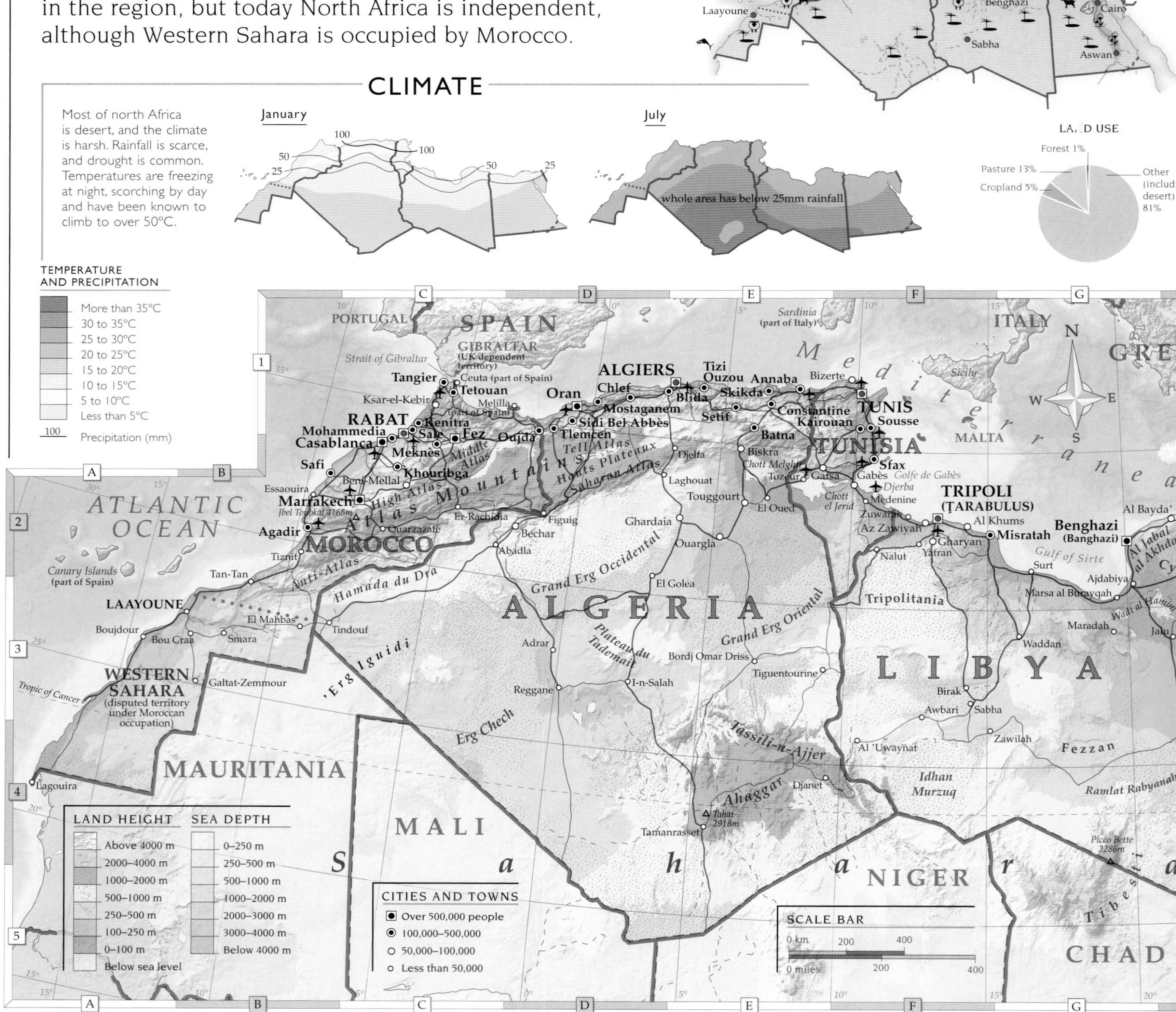

Casablanca
Rabat
Oran
Algiers
Tunis
Marrakech
Tripoli
Benghazi
Alexandria
Cairo
Laayoune
Sabha
Aswan
January
July
whole area has below 25mm rainfall
LAND USE
Forest 1%
Pasture 13%
Cropland 5%
Other (including desert) 81%
TEMPERATURE AND PRECIPITATION
More than 35°C
30 to 35°C
25 to 30°C
20 to 25°C
15 to 20°C
10 to 15°C
5 to 10°C
Less than 5°C
Precipitation (mm)
PORTUGAL
SPAIN
GIBRALTAR (UK dependent territory)
Strait of Gibraltar
Sardinia (part of Italy)
ITALY
Sicily
MALTA
Mediterranean
ATLANTIC OCEAN
Canary Islands (part of Spain)
ALGIERS
TUNIS
RABAT
TRIPOLI (TARABULUS)
LAAYOUNE
MOROCCO
ALGERIA
TUNISIA
LIBYA
WESTERN SAHARA (disputed territory under Moroccan occupation)
MAURITANIA
MALI
NIGER
CHAD
Atlas Mountains
High Atlas
Middle Atlas
Anti-Atlas
Tell Atlas
Hauts Plateaux
Saharan Atlas
Grand Erg Occidental
Grand Erg Oriental
Erg Iguidi
Erg Chech
Hamada du Dra
Plateau du Tademait
Tassili-n-Ajjer
Ahaggar
Tahat 2918m
Jbel Toubkal 4165m
Tripolitania
Fezzan
Idhan Murzuq
Ramlat Rabyanah
Gulf of Sirte
Golfe de Gabès
Chott Melghir
Chott el Jerid
Tropic of Cancer
Picco Bette 2286m
Tibesti
Tangier
Tetouan
Ceuta (part of Spain)
Melilla (part of Spain)
Ksar-el-Kebir
Kenitra
Mohammedia
Casablanca
Sale
Fez
Meknes
Oujda
Safi
Khouribga
Beni-Mellal
Essaouira
Marrakech
Agadir
Ouarzazate
Er-Rachidia
Tiznit
Tan-Tan
Boujdour
Bou Craa
Smara
El Mahbas
Tindouf
Galtat-Zemmour
Lagouira
Oran
Chlef
Mostaganem
Sidi Bel Abbès
Tlemcen
Blida
Tizi Ouzou
Annaba
Skikda
Setif
Constantine
Batna
Biskra
Djelfa
Laghouat
Touggourt
El Oued
Ghardaia
Ouargla
El Golea
Figuig
Bechar
Abadla
Adrar
Reggane
I-n-Salah
Bordj Omar Driss
Tiguentourine
Djanet
Tamanrasset
Bizerte
Sousse
Kairouan
Sfax
Gafsa
Tozeur
Gabès
Djerba
Medenine
Zuwarah
Az Zawiyah
Al Khums
Misratah
Gharyan
Yafran
Nalut
Benghazi (Banghazi)
Al Bayda'
Al Jabal al Akhdar
Ajdabiya
Surt
Marsa al Burayqah
Maradah
Jalu
Waddan
Birak
Awbari
Sabha
Zawilah
Al 'Uwaynat
LAND HEIGHT
Above 4000 m
2000–4000 m
1000–2000 m
500–1000 m
250–500 m
100–250 m
0–100 m
Below sea level
SEA DEPTH
0–250 m
250–500 m
500–1000 m
1000–2000 m
2000–3000 m
3000–4000 m
Below 4000 m
CITIES AND TOWNS
Over 500,000 people
100,000–500,000
50,000–100,000
Less than 50,000
SCALE BAR
0 km 200 400
0 miles 200 400
N
S
E
W

POPULATION

The majority of the population, and all of the big towns and cities, are found on the coastal plains, or along the banks of the Nile – about 99% of Egyptians live along the river. Egypt's capital, Cairo, is Africa's largest city, with over 11 million people. Western Sahara, and the southern portions of Egypt, Algeria and Libya are sparsely populated by Tuareg nomads who roam the Sahara.

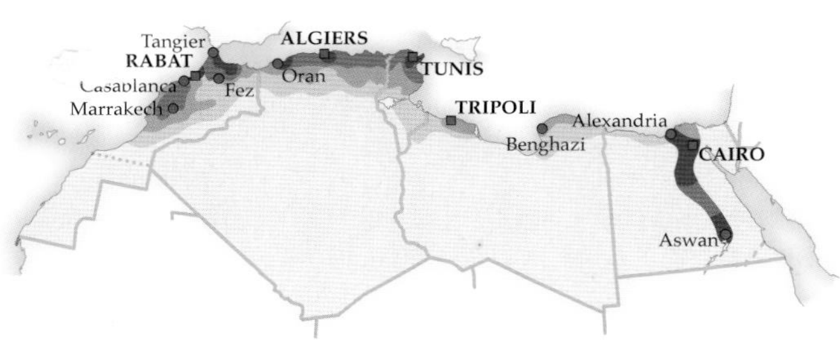

Tangier
RABAT
Casablanca
Marrakech
Fez
ALGIERS
Oran
TUNIS
TRIPOLI
Benghazi
Alexandria
CAIRO
Aswan

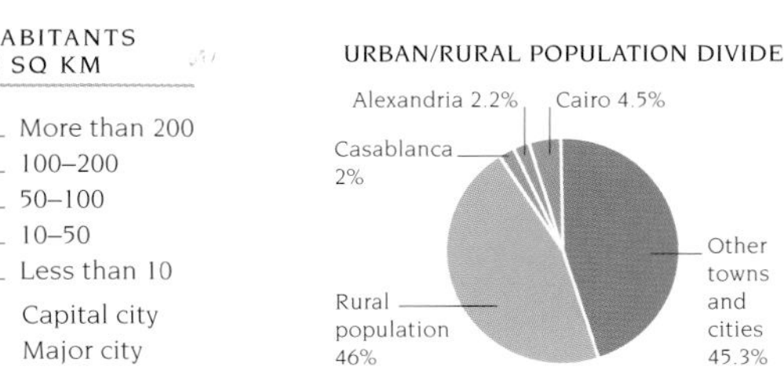

INHABITANTS PER SQ KM
More than 200
100–200
50–100
10–50
Less than 10
Capital city
Major city
URBAN/RURAL POPULATION DIVIDE
Alexandria 2.2%
Cairo 4.5%
Casablanca 2%
Rural population 46%
Other towns and cities 45.3%

THE LANDSCAPE

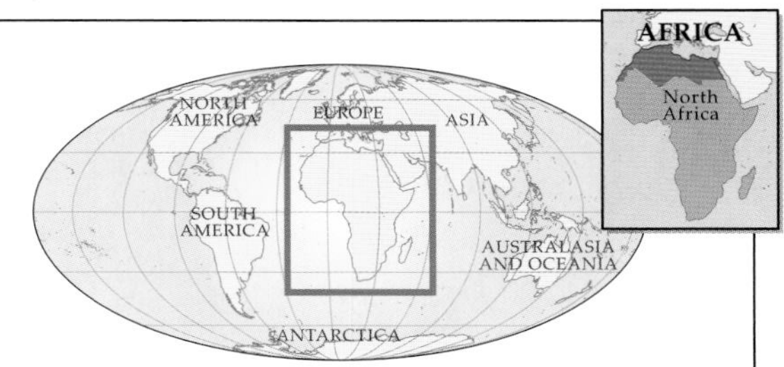

NORTH AMERICA
EUROPE
ASIA
SOUTH AMERICA
AUSTRALASIA AND OCEANIA
ANTARCTICA
AFRICA
North Africa

The parched rocks and endless sandy expanses of the Sahara occupy much of North Africa. The only major river here is the Nile, with a delta that extends into the Mediterranean Sea. The old, eroded Atlas Mountains are the highest mountain range.

Sand dunes
Winds blowing across the Sahara cause the sand to build up into dunes which can reach heights of up to 430 m.

Nile Delta (I 2)
As the River Nile nears the Mediterranean, it separates into many small streams, which flow over a fertile triangle of land. Mud and rock carried by the river and deposited in the delta have formed new land.

Red Sea (J 3)
The Red Sea may get its name from red algae that live on the sea floor and occasionally make the water appear red during algae blooms.

Atlas Mountains (C 2)
The Atlas Mountains are made up of a number of different ranges – the Anti-Atlas, High Atlas, Middle Atlas, Tell Atlas and Saharan Atlas. They stretch some 2,250 km from the north of Tunisia to the Atlantic coast of Morocco.

Qattara Depression (I 3)
In the northwest of Egypt is a huge desert depression 320 km long and 120 km wide. Its floor, part of which is 134 m below sea level, is covered with sand, brackish ponds and salt marshes.

The River Nile (I 3)
The world's longest river flows 6,695 km to the Mediterranean Sea. The system of rivers and lakes that flow into the Nile drain some 2,850,000 sq km – about 10% of the entire African continent.

INDUSTRY

Oil and natural gas have brought wealth to the area, particularly to Libya, which has enough oil reserves to last into the middle of this century. Textile manufacture is widespread – North Africa is famous for its exotic cloths and rugs. Several large chemical refineries and steel plants have been established along the coast, especially in the major industrial cities like Alexandria and Cairo in Egypt.

STRUCTURE OF INDUSTRY
Primary 16%
Services 44%
Manufacturing 40%

INDUSTRY
Chemicals
Food processing
Iron and steel
Textiles
Oil and gas
Tourism
Major industrial centre / area
Major road

ENVIRONMENTAL ISSUES

Droughts, overgrazing and the stripping of vegetation for fuelwood and animal fodder have caused the Sahara to expand northwards. This has reduced the already limited amount of land available for farming. The risk of desertification is acute in many coastal areas. North Africa is very dry, and there are severe droughts periodically. Many of the larger cities like Alexandria and Cairo have very poor air quality.

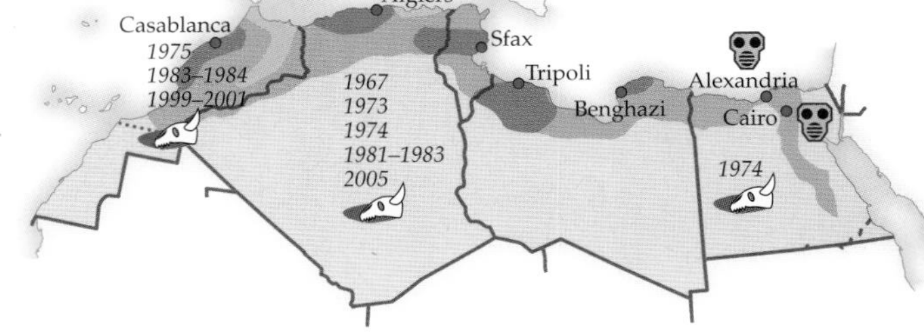

Casablanca
1975
1983–1984
1999–2001
Algiers
Sfax
Tripoli
Benghazi
Alexandria
Cairo
1967
1973
1974
1981–1983
2005
1974

ENVIRONMENTAL ISSUES
Drought
Urban air pollution
Existing desert
Risk of desertification
Severe risk of desertification
Non-affected area
Major industrial centre

West Africa

BENIN, BURKINA, CAMEROON, CENTRAL AFRICAN REPUBLIC, CHAD, EQUATORIAL GUINEA, GAMBIA, GHANA, GUINEA, GUINEA-BISSAU, IVORY COAST, LIBERIA, MALI, MAURITANIA, NIGER, NIGERIA, SAO TOME & PRINCIPE, SENEGAL, SIERRA LEONE, TOGO

West Africa's varied climate and agricultural and mineral wealth have provided the foundation for some of Africa's greatest civilizations, like those of the Malinke and Asante people. The area remains ethnically and culturally diverse today, as well as densely populated; Nigeria is by far the most populous country in Africa. Since independence from European colonial powers in the 1960s, political instability has been a feature of many countries here.

INDUSTRY

Agricultural products still form the basis of most economies in West Africa. Food processing is widespread – oil palms and peanuts are processed for their valuable vegetable oils. Oil and gas are found off the coast of Ivory Coast and around the Niger delta, where a large chemical industry has developed.

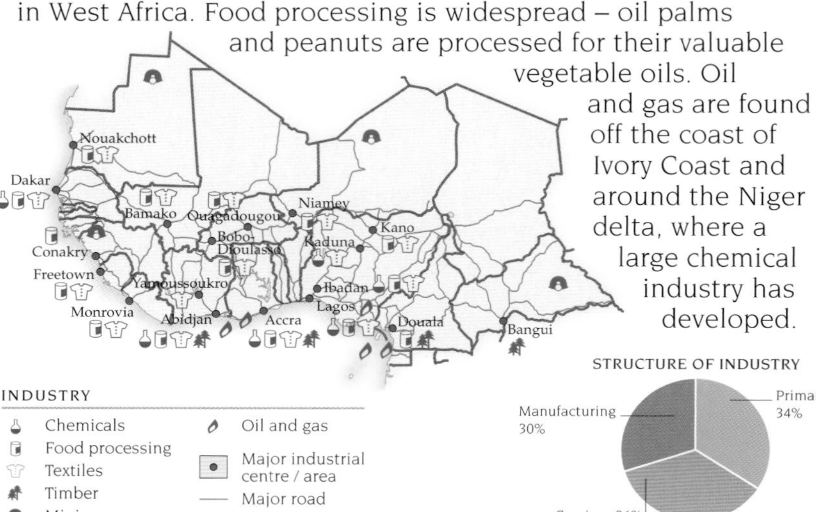
Nouakchott
Dakar
Bamako
Ouagadougou
Niamey
Kano
Bobo-Dioulasso
Kaduna
Conakry
Freetown
Yamoussoukro
Ibadan
Lagos
Monrovia
Abidjan
Accra
Douala
Bangui
INDUSTRY
Chemicals
Food processing
Textiles
Timber
Mining
Oil and gas
Major industrial centre / area
Major road
STRUCTURE OF INDUSTRY
Manufacturing 30%
Primary 34%
Services 36%

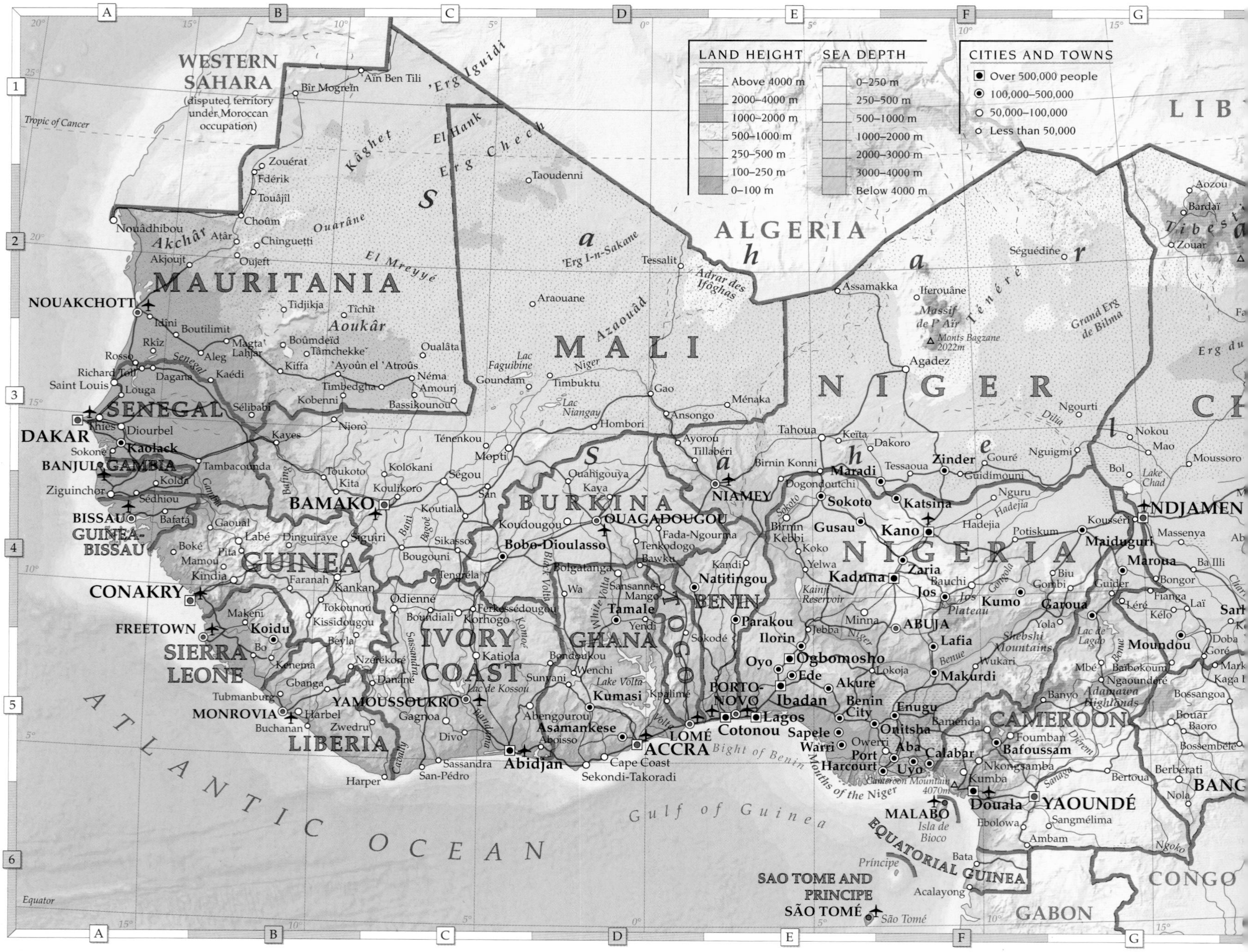

FARMING AND LAND USE

Well-watered land along the coast allows a wide variety of crops to be grown, including cocoa and oil palms, both of which provide important cash crops. In the drier north, goats and sheep are grazed, and subsistence crops such as yams, millet and cassava are grown.

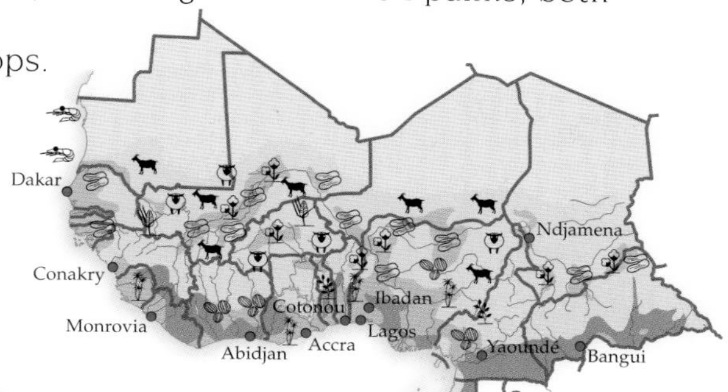
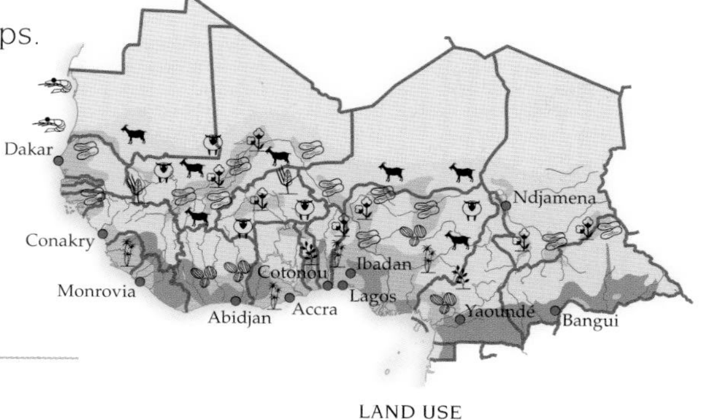

Dakar
Conakry
Monrovia
Abidjan
Accra
Cotonou
Ibadan
Lagos
Yaoundé
Bangui
Ndjamena

FARMING AND LAND USE

- Goats
- Sheep
- Shellfish
- Cassava
- Cocoa
- Cotton
- Millet
- Oil palms
- Peanuts
- Cropland
- Desert
- Forest
- Pasture
- Wetland
- Major conurbation

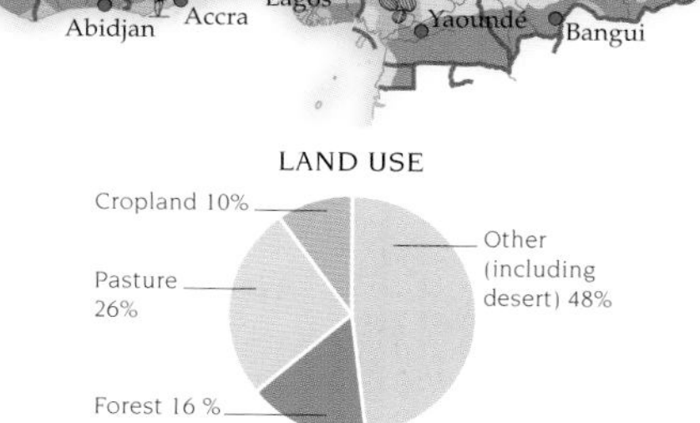

LAND USE
Cropland 10%
Pasture 26%
Forest 16 %
Other (including desert) 48%

CLIMATE

The climate differs immensely from the hot desert north, through to the tropical rainforest south. July is the wet season, and rainfall is heavy in the south, while the desert areas remain dry throughout the year.

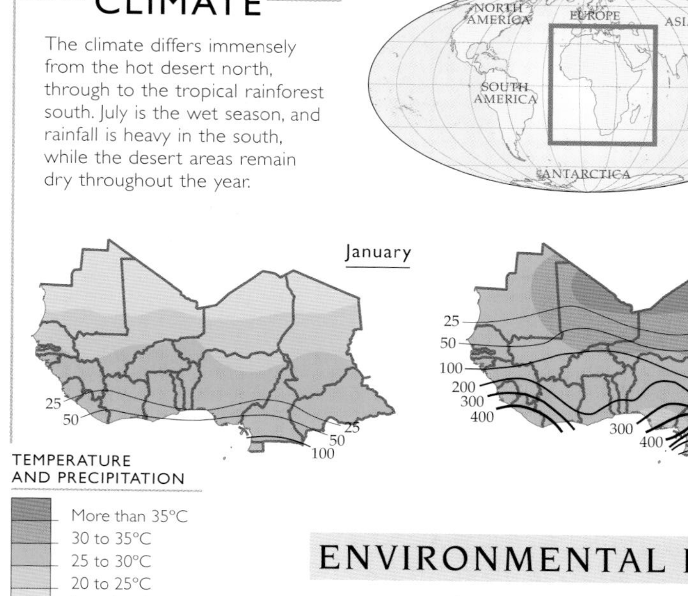

AFRICA
West Africa
NORTH AMERICA
EUROPE
ASIA
SOUTH AMERICA
AUSTRALASIA AND OCEANIA
ANTARCTICA
January
July
25
50
100
200
300
400

TEMPERATURE AND PRECIPITATION

- More than 35°C
- 30 to 35°C
- 25 to 30°C
- 20 to 25°C
- Less than 20°C
- 100 Precipitation (mm)

POPULATION

Most of the population lives in the southern coastal regions. In the drier north, settlement becomes more sporadic, and nomadic tribespeople are best suited to live in the desert north. Nigeria is the most populated country in Africa and Lagos is one of the continent's larger cities, although West Africa's population remains mainly rural.

INHABITANTS PER SQ KM

- More than 200
- 100–200
- 50–100
- 10–50
- Less than 10
- Capital city
- Major city

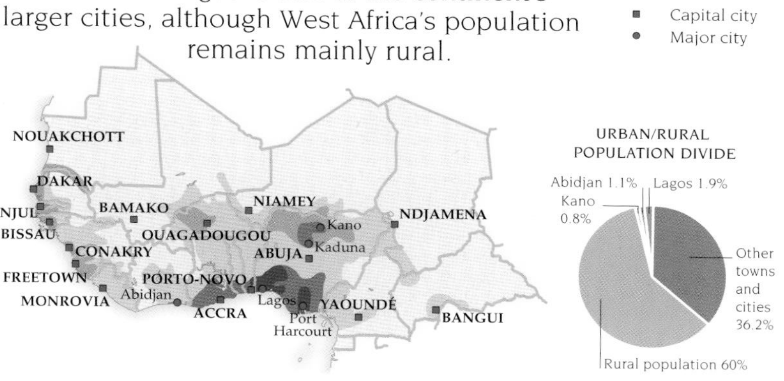

NOUAKCHOTT
DAKAR
BANJUL
BISSAU
BAMAKO
CONAKRY
FREETOWN
MONROVIA
Abidjan
OUAGADOUGOU
NIAMEY
Kano
Kaduna
ABUJA
PORTO-NOVO
ACCRA
Lagos
Port Harcourt
YAOUNDÉ
NDJAMENA
BANGUI
URBAN/RURAL POPULATION DIVIDE
Abidjan 1.1%
Lagos 1.9%
Kano 0.8%
Other towns and cities 36.2%
Rural population 60%

ENVIRONMENTAL ISSUES

Persistent droughts are the main concerns in the north of the region. The problem is made worse by a shortage of wood needed for fuel, which leads to the cutting down of any available trees for fuelwood. In the tropical south, the timber industry is destroying much of the ancient forest. In 2007 huge floods affected almost all of the region.

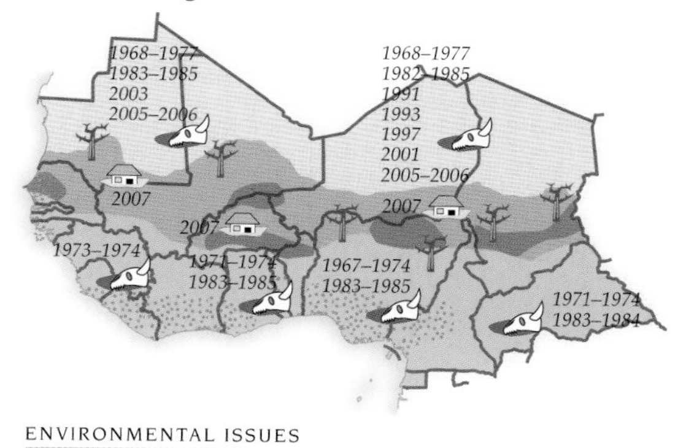

1968–1977
1983–1985
2003
2005–2006
2007
1973–1974
1971–1974
1983–1985
1967–1974
1983–1985
1968–1977
1982–1985
1991
1993
1997
2001
2005–2006
2007
1971–1974
1983–1984

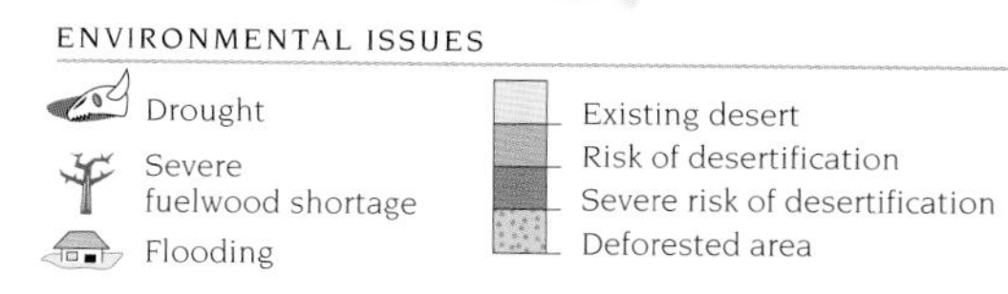

ENVIRONMENTAL ISSUES
Drought
Severe fuelwood shortage
Flooding
Existing desert
Risk of desertification
Severe risk of desertification
Deforested area

THE LANDSCAPE

Large differences in rainfall from north to south have led to a varied landscape. The wet coastal regions contain tropical rainforest. To the north, savannah grasslands, arid Sahel scrubland and barren desert lie in successive bands. The Niger is one of the larger rivers and is unusual because it has two deltas; one at the sea, and one inland.

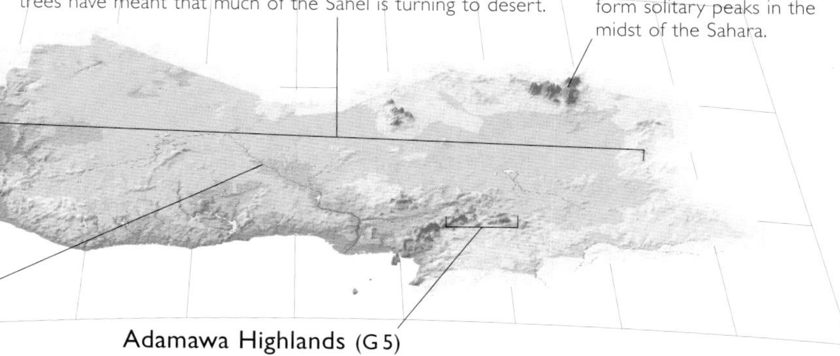

Sahel (E 3)
The band of semi-desert stretching from Senegal to Sudan along the southern boundary of the Sahara is called the Sahel. Frequent droughts in recent years, and excessive cutting of trees have meant that much of the Sahel is turning to desert.

Tibesti mountains (G 2)
These mountains in north-western Chad are a chain of extinct volcanoes which now form solitary peaks in the midst of the Sahara.

River Niger (D 3)
The River Niger is West Africa's longest river. When it reaches the sea, it flows through a vast delta of mud flats and mangrove swamps. Great oil deposits have been found here.

Adamawa Highlands (G 5)
This mountainous spine separates West Africa from the vast Congo Basin to the southeast.

East Africa

BURUNDI, DJIBOUTI, ERITREA, ETHIOPIA, KENYA, RWANDA, SOMALIA, SOUTH SUDAN, SUDAN, TANZANIA, UGANDA

Much of East Africa is covered by long grass, scrub and scattered trees, called savannah. This land is grazed by both domestic animals and a great variety of wild animals including lions, giraffes and elephants. The east of the region is known as the Horn of Africa, because it is shaped like an animal horn. Along with Sudan, the countries there have recently been devastated by civil wars, and periods of drought and famine. In contrast, Kenya in the south is more stable but still has to battle with corruption.

FARMING AND LAND USE

Much of the north and east is too dry for farming, but in Sudan, cotton is grown on land irrigated by the River Nile. The Lake Victoria basin and rich volcanic soils of the highlands in Kenya, Uganda and Tanzania support staple food crops, and those grown for export, such as tea and coffee. Kenya also grows high-quality vegetables, like mangetout, and exports them by air to supermarkets abroad. Sheep, goats and cattle are herded on the savannah.

Khartoum, Addis Ababa, Mogadishu, Kampala, Nairobi, Mombasa, Dar es Salaam

LAND USE

Cropland 9%, Pasture 40%, Other 26%, Forest 25%

FARMING AND LAND USE

- Cattle
- Fishing
- Goats
- Sheep
- Bananas
- Coffee
- Cotton
- Dates
- Market gardening
- Sugarcane
- Sisal
- Tea
- Cropland
- Desert
- Forest
- Pasture
- Wetland
- Major conurbation

INDUSTRY

East Africa has few mineral resources, and industry is mainly based on processing raw materials. Coffee, tea, sugarcane and sisal, are harvested and processed before being exported. Textile production is widespread, but is only on a small scale. Tourism is increasingly important in Kenya and Tanzania; each year, many thousands of people visit the wildlife reserves there.

Port Sudan, Khartoum, Asmara, Addis Ababa, Dire Dawa

Mogadishu
Kampala
Kigali
Bujumbura
Nairobi
Arusha
Mombasa
Dodoma
Dar es Salaam

INDUSTRY

- Cement manufacturing
- Chemicals
- Food processing
- Textiles
- Tourism
- Major industrial centre / area
- Major road

STRUCTURE OF INDUSTRY

Primary 38%, Services 44%, Manufacturing 18%

THE LANDSCAPE

The south of East Africa is savannah grassland, broken by the rugged mountains – some of them active volcanoes – and large fresh and saltwater lakes that make up part of the Great Rift Valley. The River Nile has its source here, flowing through lakes Victoria, Kyoga and Albert as it takes much-needed water to the arid desert areas in the north.

Great Rift Valley (D 6) (D 4)
The Great Rift Valley is like a deep scar running 7,000 km from north to south through East Africa. It has been formed by the movements of two of the Earth's plates over millions of years. If these movements continue, East Africa may eventually become an island, separated by the ocean from the rest of the continent.

Sudd (B 4)
The north of Sudan is rocky desert, but in the south, the waters of the White Nile run into a swampy area called the Sudd where much of its water disperses and evaporates.

River Juba (E 5)
This river rises in the highlands of Ethiopia and flows some 1,200 km southwards to the Indian Ocean. It, and the River Shebeli, which joins it about 30 km from the coast, are the only permanent rivers in Somalia.

Lake Victoria (C 5)
Lake Victoria is Africa's largest lake and the second largest freshwater lake in the world. It lies on the Equator, between Kenya, Tanzania and Uganda, and covers 68,880 sq km. Its only outlet is the River Nile in the north.

Kilimanjaro (D 6)
This old volcano, made up of alternating layers of lava and ash, is Africa's highest mountain, rising to 5,895 m. Although it lies only three degrees from the Equator, its peak is permanently covered with snow.

ENVIRONMENTAL ISSUES

Rapid population growth has created a need for increasing amounts of land for farming. This, as well as the need for fuelwood, has led to tree cover being stripped, allowing the soil to be washed or blown away. Over the past 30 years, eastern Africa has been stricken by many catastrophic droughts which have made desertification worse, and brought much human suffering.

ENVIRONMENTAL ISSUES

- Drought
- Severe fuelwood shortage
- Flooding
- Existing desert
- Risk of desertification
- Severe risk of desertification

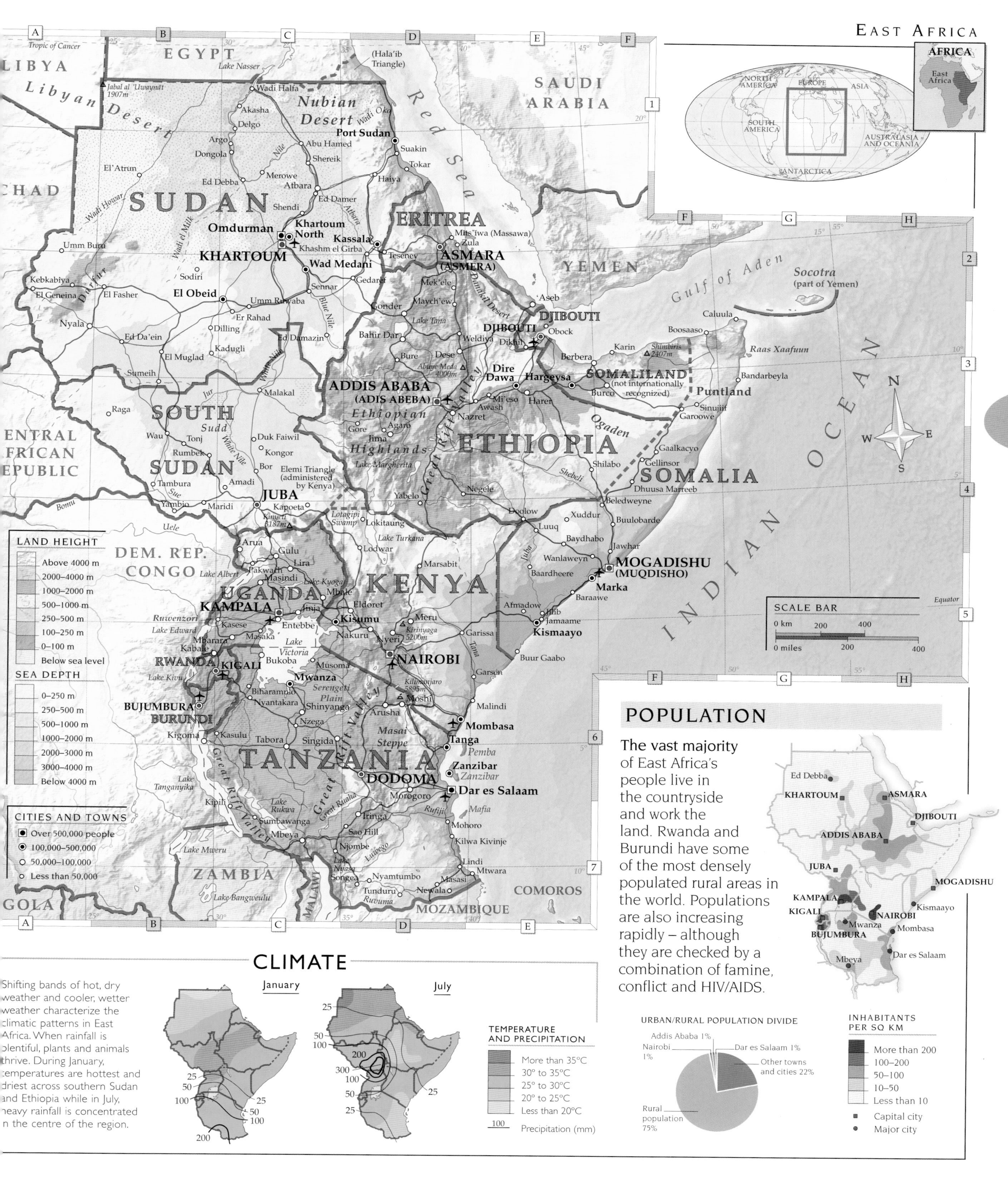
AFRICA
East Africa
EGYPT
LIBYA
SUDAN
SOUTH SUDAN
ERITREA
DJIBOUTI
ETHIOPIA
SOMALIA
SOMALILAND (not internationally recognized)
Puntland
KENYA
UGANDA
RWANDA
BURUNDI
TANZANIA
SAUDI ARABIA
YEMEN
DEM. REP. CONGO
ZAMBIA
MALAWI
MOZAMBIQUE
COMOROS
INDIAN OCEAN
Red Sea
Gulf of Aden
KHARTOUM
ASMARA (ASMERA)
ADDIS ABABA (ADIS ABEBA)
JUBA
MOGADISHU (MUQDISHO)
NAIROBI
KAMPALA
KIGALI
BUJUMBURA
DODOMA
LAND HEIGHT
Above 4000 m
2000–4000 m
1000–2000 m
500–1000 m
250–500 m
100–250 m
0–100 m
Below sea level
SEA DEPTH
0–250 m
250–500 m
500–1000 m
1000–2000 m
2000–3000 m
3000–4000 m
Below 4000 m
CITIES AND TOWNS
Over 500,000 people
100,000–500,000
50,000–100,000
Less than 50,000
SCALE BAR
0 km 200 400
0 miles 200 400
January
July
TEMPERATURE AND PRECIPITATION
More than 35°C
30° to 35°C
25° to 30°C
20° to 25°C
Less than 20°C
100 Precipitation (mm)
URBAN/RURAL POPULATION DIVIDE
Addis Ababa 1%
Nairobi 1%
Dar es Salaam 1%
Other towns and cities 22%
Rural population 75%
INHABITANTS PER SQ KM
More than 200
100–200
50–100
10–50
Less than 10
Capital city
Major city

POPULATION

The vast majority of East Africa's people live in the countryside and work the land. Rwanda and Burundi have some of the most densely populated rural areas in the world. Populations are also increasing rapidly – although they are checked by a combination of famine, conflict and HIV/AIDS.

CLIMATE

Shifting bands of hot, dry weather and cooler, wetter weather characterize the climatic patterns in East Africa. When rainfall is plentiful, plants and animals thrive. During January, temperatures are hottest and driest across southern Sudan and Ethiopia while in July, heavy rainfall is concentrated in the centre of the region.

SOUTHERN AFRICA

ANGOLA, BOTSWANA, COMOROS, CONGO, DEM. REP. CONGO, GABON, LESOTHO, MADAGASCAR, MALAWI, MOZAMBIQUE, NAMIBIA, SOUTH AFRICA, SWAZILAND, ZAMBIA, ZIMBABWE

Southern Africa contains the richest deposits of valuable minerals on the continent. South Africa is the wealthiest and most industrialized country in the region. Most of the surrounding countries rely on it for trade and work. Racial segregation under apartheid operated from 1948 until 1994, when South Africa held its first multiracial elections.

FARMING AND LAND USE

Most of southern Africa's farmers grow just enough food to feed their families, though much of the farmland is in the hands of a few wealthy landowners. In the tropical north, oil palms and rubber are grown on large commercial plantations. Fruits are cultivated in the south, and tea and coffee are important in the east. Cattle farming is widespread across the dry grasslands.

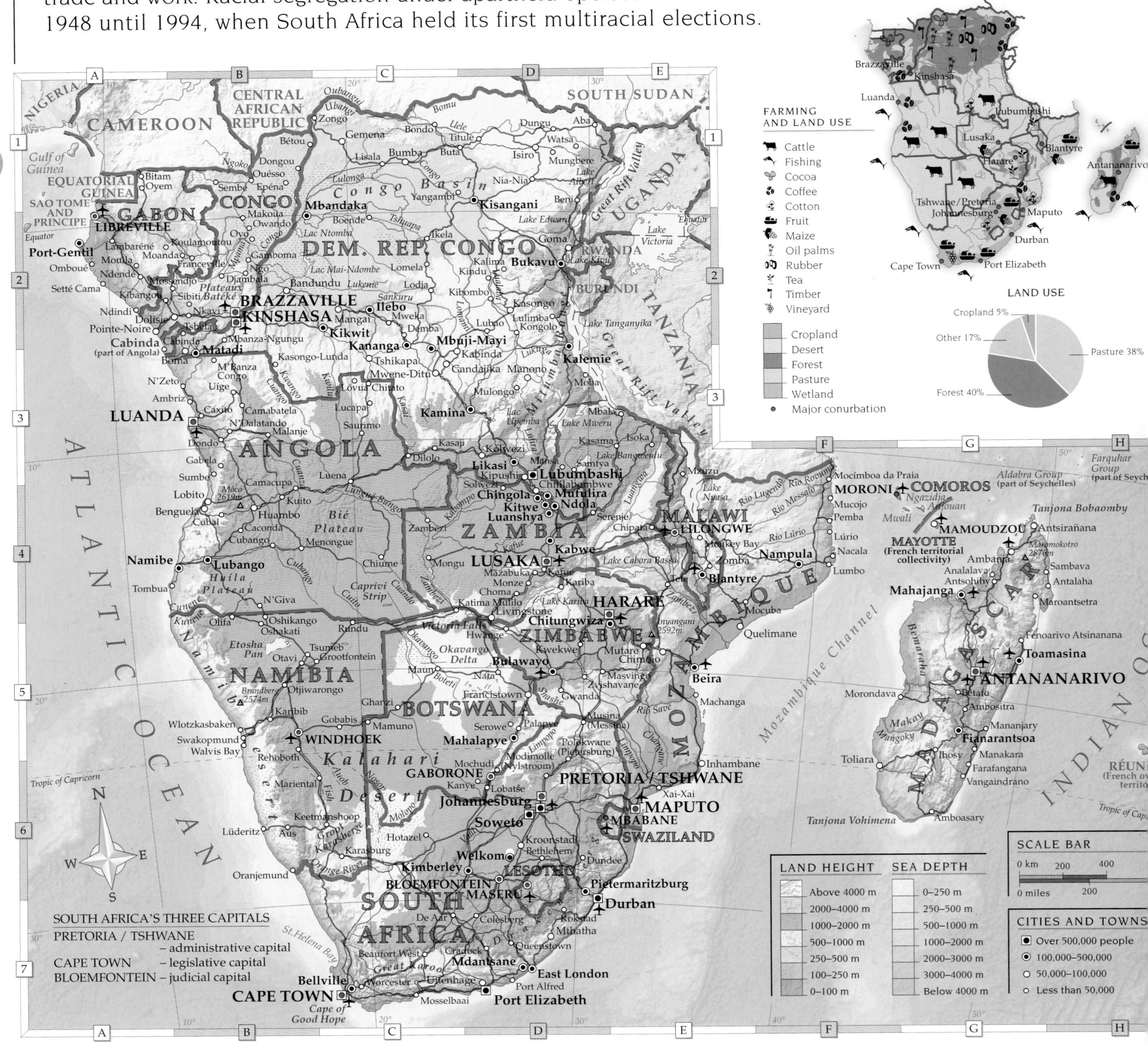
FARMING AND LAND USE
Cattle
Fishing
Cocoa
Coffee
Cotton
Fruit
Maize
Oil palms
Rubber
Tea
Timber
Vineyard
Cropland
Desert
Forest
Pasture
Wetland
Major conurbation
Brazzaville
Kinshasa
Luanda
Lubumbashi
Lusaka
Harare
Blantyre
Antananarivo
Tshwane/Pretoria
Johannesburg
Maputo
Durban
Cape Town
Port Elizabeth
LAND USE
Cropland 5%
Other 17%
Pasture 38%
Forest 40%
SOUTH AFRICA'S THREE CAPITALS
PRETORIA / TSHWANE – administrative capital
CAPE TOWN – legislative capital
BLOEMFONTEIN – judicial capital
LAND HEIGHT
Above 4000 m
2000–4000 m
1000–2000 m
500–1000 m
250–500 m
100–250 m
0–100 m
SEA DEPTH
0–250 m
250–500 m
500–1000 m
1000–2000 m
2000–3000 m
3000–4000 m
Below 4000 m
SCALE BAR
0 km 200 400
0 miles 200
CITIES AND TOWNS
Over 500,000 people
100,000–500,000
50,000–100,000
Less than 50,000
CAMEROON
CENTRAL AFRICAN REPUBLIC
SOUTH SUDAN
UGANDA
EQUATORIAL GUINEA
SAO TOME AND PRINCIPE
GABON
LIBREVILLE
CONGO
DEM. REP. CONGO
BRAZZAVILLE
KINSHASA
RWANDA
BURUNDI
TANZANIA
ANGOLA
LUANDA
Cabinda (part of Angola)
ZAMBIA
LUSAKA
MALAWI
LILONGWE
MOZAMBIQUE
MAPUTO
ZIMBABWE
HARARE
NAMIBIA
WINDHOEK
BOTSWANA
GABORONE
SOUTH AFRICA
PRETORIA / TSHWANE
LESOTHO
MASERU
SWAZILAND
MBABANE
CAPE TOWN
MADAGASCAR
ANTANANARIVO
COMOROS
MORONI
MAYOTTE (French territorial collectivity)
MAMOUDZOU
Aldabra Group (part of Seychelles)
Farquhar Group (part of Seychelles)
ATLANTIC OCEAN
INDIAN OCEAN
Gulf of Guinea
Mozambique Channel
Congo Basin
Kalahari Desert
Great Rift Valley
Lake Victoria
Lake Tanganyika
Lake Nyasa
Lake Kariba
Okavango Delta
Caprivi Strip
Bié Plateau
Huíla Plateau
Etosha Pan
Namib Desert
Cape of Good Hope
Tropic of Capricorn
Equator

AFRICA

Southern Africa

NORTH AMERICA EUROPE ASIA SOUTH AMERICA AUSTRALASIA AND OCEANIA ANTARCTICA

CLIMATE

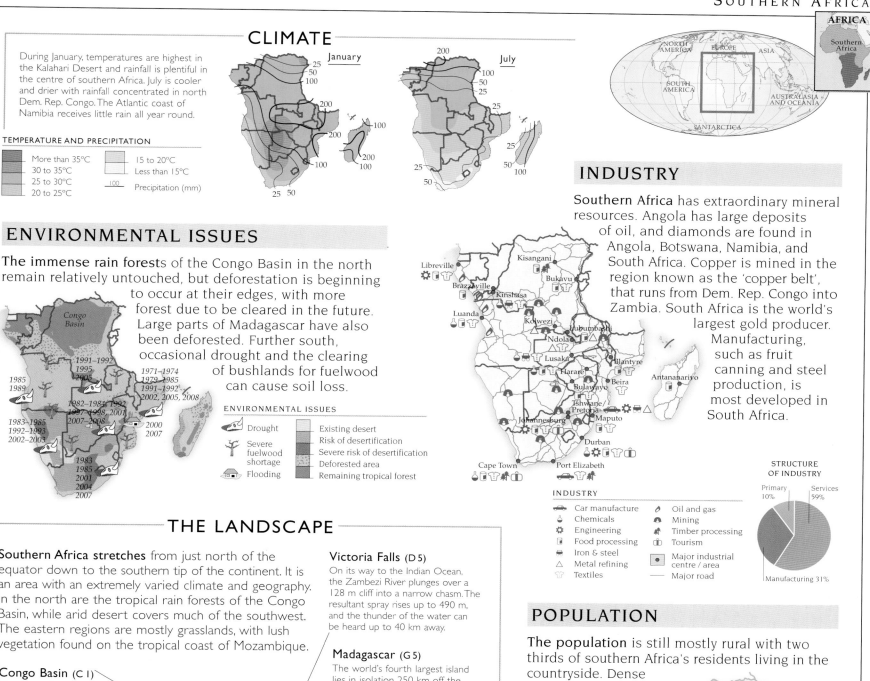

During January, temperatures are highest in the Kalahari Desert and rainfall is plentiful in the centre of southern Africa. July is cooler and drier with rainfall concentrated in north Dem. Rep. Congo. The Atlantic coast of Namibia receives little rain all year round.

January

July

TEMPERATURE AND PRECIPITATION

- More than 35°C
- 30 to 35°C
- 25 to 30°C
- 20 to 25°C
- 15 to 20°C
- Less than 15°C
- 100 Precipitation (mm)

ENVIRONMENTAL ISSUES

The immense rain forests of the Congo Basin in the north remain relatively untouched, but deforestation is beginning to occur at their edges, with more forest due to be cleared in the future. Large parts of Madagascar have also been deforested. Further south, occasional drought and the clearing of bushlands for fuelwood can cause soil loss.

Congo Basin

ENVIRONMENTAL ISSUES

- Drought
- Severe fuelwood shortage
- Flooding
- Existing desert
- Risk of desertification
- Severe risk of desertification
- Deforested area
- Remaining tropical forest

INDUSTRY

Southern Africa has extraordinary mineral resources. Angola has large deposits of oil, and diamonds are found in Angola, Botswana, Namibia, and South Africa. Copper is mined in the region known as the 'copper belt', that runs from Dem. Rep. Congo into Zambia. South Africa is the world's largest gold producer. Manufacturing, such as fruit canning and steel production, is most developed in South Africa.

INDUSTRY

- Car manufacture
- Chemicals
- Engineering
- Food processing
- Iron & steel
- Metal refining
- Textiles
- Oil and gas
- Mining
- Timber processing
- Tourism
- Major industrial centre / area
- Major road

STRUCTURE OF INDUSTRY

Primary 10%, Services 59%, Manufacturing 31%

THE LANDSCAPE

Southern Africa stretches from just north of the equator down to the southern tip of the continent. It is an area with an extremely varied climate and geography. In the north are the tropical rain forests of the Congo Basin, while arid desert covers much of the southwest. The eastern regions are mostly grasslands, with lush vegetation found on the tropical coast of Mozambique.

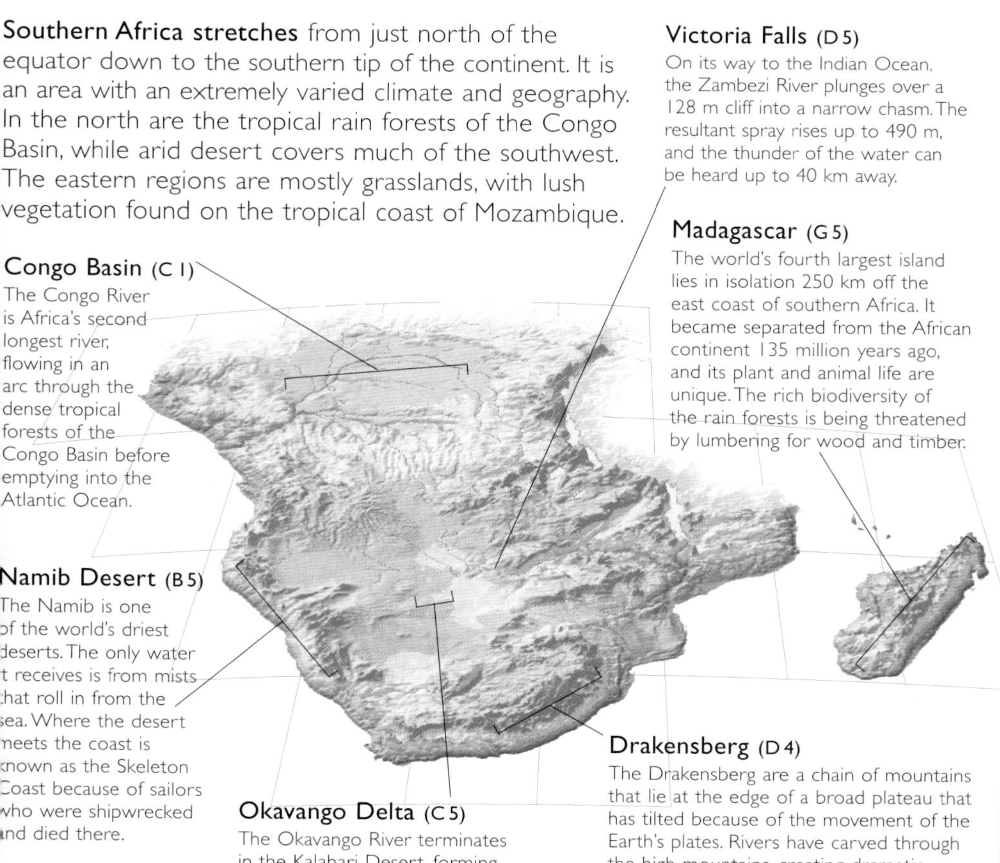

Congo Basin (C 1)
The Congo River is Africa's second longest river, flowing in an arc through the dense tropical forests of the Congo Basin before emptying into the Atlantic Ocean.

Namib Desert (B 5)
The Namib is one of the world's driest deserts. The only water it receives is from mists that roll in from the sea. Where the desert meets the coast is known as the Skeleton Coast because of sailors who were shipwrecked and died there.

Okavango Delta (C 5)
The Okavango River terminates in the Kalahari Desert, forming a vast, swampy inland delta.

Victoria Falls (D 5)
On its way to the Indian Ocean, the Zambezi River plunges over a 128 m cliff into a narrow chasm. The resultant spray rises up to 490 m, and the thunder of the water can be heard up to 40 km away.

Madagascar (G 5)
The world's fourth largest island lies in isolation 250 km off the east coast of southern Africa. It became separated from the African continent 135 million years ago, and its plant and animal life are unique. The rich biodiversity of the rain forests is being threatened by lumbering for wood and timber.

Drakensberg (D 4)
The Drakensberg are a chain of mountains that lie at the edge of a broad plateau that has tilted because of the movement of the Earth's plates. Rivers have carved through the high mountains, creating dramatic gorges and waterfalls.

POPULATION

The population is still mostly rural with two thirds of southern Africa's residents living in the countryside. Dense tropical rain forest in the north and arid desert in the southwest have kept habitation to a bare minimum. Malawi is the most densely populated country in the region.

Luanda 1.4%, Kinshasa 2.4%, Cape Town 1.2%, Other towns and cities 34%, Rural population 61%

INHABITANTS PER SQ KM

- More than 100
- 50–100
- 10–50
- Less than 10
- Capital city
- Major city

Continental Europe

Europe is the world's second smallest continent, occupying the western tip of the vast Eurasian landmass. To the north and west are old highlands, with the high peaks of the Alps in the south. Most people live on the densely populated North European Plain, which runs from southern England, through northern France, across Germany into Russia.

5,400 km
5,050 km

Cross-section through Europe

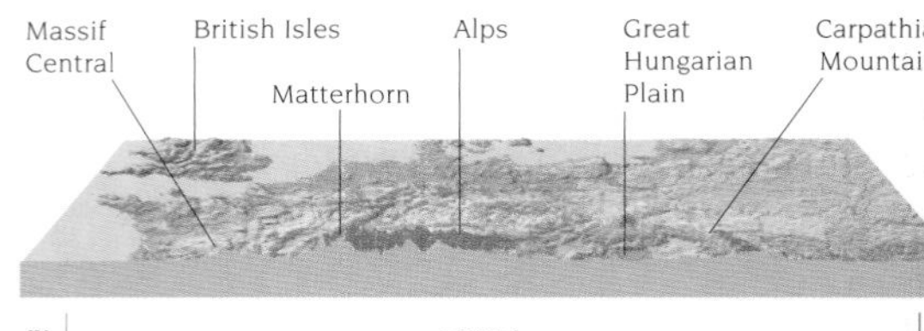
Massif Central
British Isles
Matterhorn
Alps
Great Hungarian Plain
W
2,500 km

In the west, the land rises up from the Atlantic coast towards the Massif Central in France, and the high peaks of the Alps. Between the Alps and the Carpathian Mountains is the Great Hungarian Plain, where the River Danube flows on its way to the Black Sea.

Physical Europe

The ancient mountains of northwest Europe were scoured and smoothed by glaciers in the last Ice Age. The Alps are newer and more jagged – pushed up when Africa collided with Europe. In between is the North European Plain, where thick layers of fertile soils allow many different crops to be grown.

ELEVATION

- Above 4000 m
- 2000–4000 m
- 1000–2000 m
- 500–1000 m
- 250–500 m
- 100–250 m
- 0–100 m
- Below sea level

cross-section

SCALE 1:31,000,000

0 km 300 600

0 miles 300 600

1 The Frozen North

Europe's northern coastline stretches deep into the Arctic Circle. Here in Norway, icebergs drift into the deep, wide-bottomed fjords.

The North European Plain 2

The North European Plain has low, rolling hills and plains. Much of the area is cultivated and used for growing crops like wheat and sugar beet.

3 Ancient Highlands

Some of the world's oldest rocks are found in northwest Europe. Erosion by glaciers in the last Ice Age created smoothed hills such as the mountains of Wales.

The Alps 5

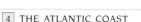

The Alps are Europe's major mountain chain. They formed about 65-million years ago. The Matterhorn is one of the most dramatic peaks.

4 The Atlantic Coast

On Europe's Atlantic coast, the force of waves and winds has created striking landforms like this huge sand dune in southwest France.

POLITICAL EUROPE

Europe's population increased rapidly during the 18th and 19th centuries, following the Industrial Revolution. In the 20th century, Europe suffered a series of wars which redrew the political map. From 1989–1991, communist governments in eastern Europe and the former Soviet Union collapsed, as political reform swept through the countries behind the 'Iron Curtain'. In 2013, Croatia became the 28th country to join the European Union.

EUROPEAN UNION
six original members, 1957
nine further members, 1973 – 1995
ten further members, 2004
two new members, 2007
one new member, 2013
NORTH AMERICA
EUROPE
ASIA
AFRICA
SOUTH AMERICA
AUSTRALASIA and OCEANIA
ANTARCTICA
REYKJAVIK
ICELAND
Arctic Circle
Novaya Zemlya
Barents Sea
White Sea
Norwegian Sea
Faeroe Islands (to Denmark)
Shetland Islands
Orkney Islands
Outer Hebrides
North Sea
NORWAY
SWEDEN
FINLAND
Gulf of Bothnia
OSLO
STOCKHOLM
HELSINKI
TALLINN
ESTONIA
Åland
Gotland
Lake Vänern
Lake Onega
Lake Ladoga
Northern Dvina
RUSSIAN FEDERATION
MOSCOW
Ural Mountains
Volga
UNITED KINGDOM
IRELAND
DUBLIN
Isle of Man (to UK)
LONDON
Channel Islands (to UK)
DENMARK
COPENHAGEN
Baltic Sea
RIGA
LATVIA
LITHUANIA
VILNIUS
MINSK
BELARUS
KALININGRAD (part of Russ. Fed)
NETHERLANDS
AMSTERDAM
THE HAGUE
BERLIN
WARSAW
BELGIUM
BRUSSELS
GERMANY
POLAND
Elbe
LUXEMBOURG
PRAGUE
CZECH REPUBLIC
KIEV
UKRAINE
Dniester
Dnieper
PARIS
Seine
Loire
FRANCE
Bay of Biscay
LIECHTENSTEIN
BERN
SWITZERLAND
VIENNA
Danube
SLOVAKIA
BRATISLAVA
AUSTRIA
BUDAPEST
HUNGARY
MOLDOVA
CHISINAU
Sea of Azov
ROMANIA
SLOVENIA
LJUBLJANA
ZAGREB
CROATIA
Po
Rhône
BELGRADE
SERBIA
BOSNIA AND HERZ.
SARAJEVO
BUCHAREST
SAN MARINO
MONACO
Corsica
ITALY
Adriatic Sea
ROME
VATICAN CITY
MONT.
PODGORICA
KOS.
PRISHTINE
SOFIA
BULGARIA
SKOPJE
MACEDONIA
TIRANA
ALBANIA
Black Sea
Caucasus
TURKEY
ASIA
GREECE
ATHENS
Ionian Sea
Crete
Tyrrhenian Sea
Sicily
Sardinia
MALTA
VALLETTA
ATLANTIC OCEAN
LISBON
PORTUGAL
MADRID
SPAIN
ANDORRA
The Basque Country
Ebro
Majorca
Ibiza
Minorca
Balearic Islands
Gibraltar (to UK)
Ceuta (part of Spain)
Melilla (part of Spain)
Mediterranean Sea
AFRICA
POPULATION
Capital cities
Above 500,000
100,000 to 500,000
50,000 to 100,000
SCALE 1:27,500,000
0 km 300 600
0 miles 300 600
Largest city MOSCOW 10.1 million people
POPULATION DENSITY People per sq km)
Below 49
50–99
100–149
150–199
200–299
Above 300
STANDARD OF LIVING (UN Human Development Index)
low
high

REGIONAL IDENTITY

Throughout Europe, there is a growing call to recognize regional cultural identity. The Basque region, straddling southwest France and Spain, is one example.

RURAL LIFE

Away from Europe's bustling cities, traditional rural lifestyles survive. Here in Ireland, a winter shelter is being made for cattle.

STANDARDS OF LIVING

Living standards are generally much lower in eastern Europe than in the wealthier west. Homelessness and unemployment are still problems, even in the most prosperous countries.

POPULATION

More than 730 million people live in Europe, and its population is highly urbanized. In Belgium and the Netherlands, almost 90% of people live in cities. In the south and east, more people still live in rural areas. The northern countries have the smallest populations, because much of the land is too cold to be habitable.

SPREADING CITIES

Amsterdam, in the Netherlands, is part of a conurbation, a large built-up area where several towns or cities have merged together to form a single urban area.

European Geography

Europe is blessed with a temperate climate, ample mineral reserves, and good transport links. During the 18th and 19th centuries the continent was transformed, as new methods of production made industry and farming more efficient and productive. Today, in many countries, 'heavy' industries have been replaced by hi-tech and service industries. Agriculture is still important and many crops thrive on Europe's fertile plains.

Industry

Western Europe has some of the world's wealthiest countries. In countries such as France, Germany and the UK, traditional industries like iron and steel-making are now being replaced by light industries such as electronics, and services like finance and insurance. In Eastern Europe, industry was subsidized by the communist governments for years. Many factories are old fashioned and need investment to improve their equipment and production methods.

ECONOMIC ACTIVITY
Aerospace
Car/vehicle manufacture
Chemicals
Coal
Defence
Electronics
Engineering
Finance
Food processing
Hi-tech industry
Iron & steel
Oil and gas
Printing & publishing
Textiles
Timber processing
ICELAND
Barents Sea
Norwegian Sea
North Sea
ATLANTIC OCEAN
NORWAY
SWEDEN
FINLAND
RUSSIAN FEDERATION
ASIA
UNITED KINGDOM
IRELAND
Glasgow
Newcastle upon Tyne
Manchester
Birmingham
London
Oslo
Stockholm
Gothenburg
Helsinki
St Petersburg
ESTONIA
LATVIA
LITHUANIA
Yaroslavl'
Nizhniy Novgorod
Moscow
Tula
Perm'
Ufa
Samara
Saratov
Volgograd
Baltic Sea
DENMARK
Hamburg
Amsterdam
Kaliningrad (part of Russ. Fed.)
NETH.
GERMANY
Berlin
POLAND
Warsaw
BELARUS
Brussels
BELG.
Cologne
LUX.
Frankfurt am Main
Prague
CZECH REP.
Kraków
Kiev
UKRAINE
Dnipropetrovs'k
Rostov-on-Don
Kryvyy Rih
Paris
FRANCE
Stuttgart
LIECH.
Munich
SLOVAKIA
Zürich
SWITZ.
AUSTRIA
HUNGARY
MOLDOVA
Lyon
Milan
SLVN.
ROMANIA
Bilbao
Toulouse
Turin
CROATIA
BOSNIA AND HERZ.
SERBIA
Bucharest
Lisbon
PORTUGAL
SPAIN
Madrid
ANDORRA
Barcelona
SAN MARINO
MONTENEGRO
ITALY
Rome
KOSOVO
BULGARIA
Sofia
MACED.
Istanbul
Black Sea
TURKEY
Naples
ALBANIA
GREECE
Athens
Mediterranean Sea
AFRICA
MALTA
GNI per capita (US$)
Below 4,999
5,000-9,999
10,000-24,999
25,000-39,999
40,000-54,999
Above 55,000
Industrial centre

Mineral Resources

Europe has few sizeable reserves of metallic minerals; most were used up by industry during the 19th century Oil, gas and coal are found in large quantities – gas in the North Sea and oil in the Volga basin. Coal, though abundant, is being steadily depleted.

MINERAL RESOURCES

- Bauxite
- Chromium
- Copper
- Iron
- Manganese
- Nickel
- Uranium
- Oil/gas fiel
- Coal field

OIL AND GA

Oil and gas reserves are plentifu in the Russian Federation. Sout of Rostov-on-Don, oil is pumpe from the ground and pipe to nearby refineries

CAR MANUFACTURE

Germany is one of the world's largest and oldest manufacturer of cars. Companies like BMW, Mercedes-Benz and Volkswagen export cars across the world.

FINANCE

London, Frankfurt and Paris are among the most important financial centres in the world. Many banks and financial institutions have their headquarters here. At the London Stock Exchange, people buy and sell stocks and shares.

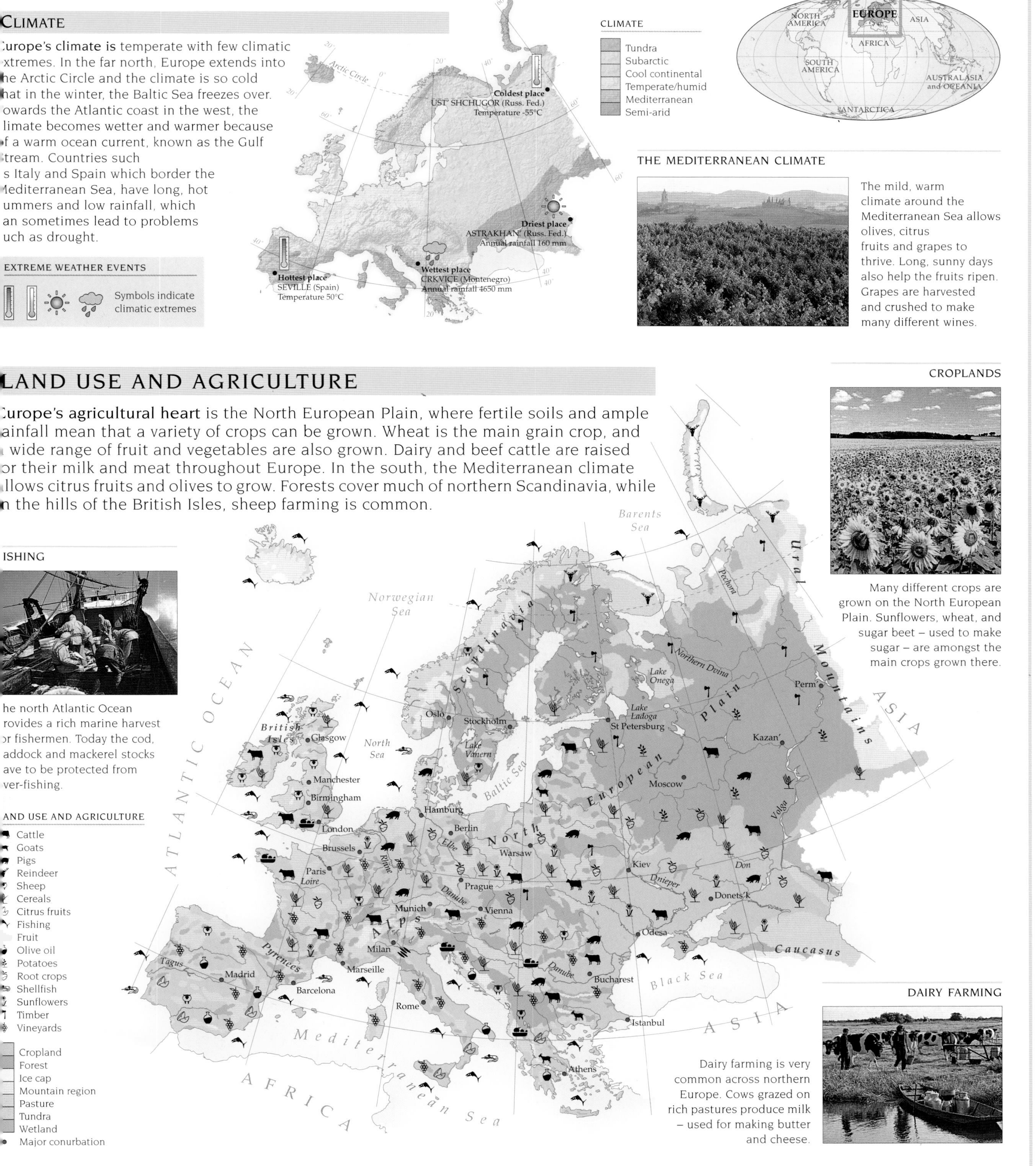
CLIMATE
Tundra
Subarctic
Cool continental
Temperate/humid
Mediterranean
Semi-arid
NORTH AMERICA
EUROPE
ASIA
AFRICA
SOUTH AMERICA
AUSTRALASIA and OCEANIA
ANTARCTICA
Arctic Circle
Coldest place
UST' SHCHUGOR (Russ. Fed.)
Temperature -55°C
Driest place
ASTRAKHAN' (Russ. Fed.)
Annual rainfall 160 mm
Hottest place
SEVILLE (Spain)
Temperature 50°C
Wettest place
CRKVICE (Montenegro)
Annual rainfall 4650 mm
EXTREME WEATHER EVENTS
Symbols indicate climatic extremes
Barents Sea
Norwegian Sea
ATLANTIC OCEAN
North Sea
Baltic Sea
Scandinavia
British Isles
North European Plain
Ural Mountains
ASIA
Alps
Pyrenees
Caucasus
Black Sea
Mediterranean Sea
AFRICA
Glasgow
Manchester
Birmingham
London
Brussels
Paris
Oslo
Stockholm
Hamburg
Berlin
Warsaw
Prague
Munich
Vienna
Milan
Marseille
Barcelona
Madrid
Rome
Bucharest
Istanbul
Athens
Odesa
Kiev
Donets'k
Moscow
St Petersburg
Kazan'
Perm
Lake Onega
Lake Ladoga
Lake Vänern
Northern Dvina
Pechora
Volga
Don
Dnieper
Danube
Rhine
Elbe
Loire
Tagus
LAND USE AND AGRICULTURE
Cattle
Goats
Pigs
Reindeer
Sheep
Cereals
Citrus fruits
Fishing
Fruit
Olive oil
Potatoes
Root crops
Shellfish
Sunflowers
Timber
Vineyards
Cropland
Forest
Ice cap
Mountain region
Pasture
Tundra
Wetland
Major conurbation

CLIMATE

Europe's climate is temperate with few climatic extremes. In the far north, Europe extends into the Arctic Circle and the climate is so cold that in the winter, the Baltic Sea freezes over. Towards the Atlantic coast in the west, the climate becomes wetter and warmer because of a warm ocean current, known as the Gulf Stream. Countries such as Italy and Spain which border the Mediterranean Sea, have long, hot summers and low rainfall, which can sometimes lead to problems such as drought.

THE MEDITERRANEAN CLIMATE

The mild, warm climate around the Mediterranean Sea allows olives, citrus fruits and grapes to thrive. Long, sunny days also help the fruits ripen. Grapes are harvested and crushed to make many different wines.

LAND USE AND AGRICULTURE

Europe's agricultural heart is the North European Plain, where fertile soils and ample rainfall mean that a variety of crops can be grown. Wheat is the main grain crop, and a wide range of fruit and vegetables are also grown. Dairy and beef cattle are raised for their milk and meat throughout Europe. In the south, the Mediterranean climate allows citrus fruits and olives to grow. Forests cover much of northern Scandinavia, while in the hills of the British Isles, sheep farming is common.

FISHING

The north Atlantic Ocean provides a rich marine harvest for fishermen. Today the cod, haddock and mackerel stocks have to be protected from over-fishing.

CROPLANDS

Many different crops are grown on the North European Plain. Sunflowers, wheat, and sugar beet – used to make sugar – are amongst the main crops grown there.

DAIRY FARMING

Dairy farming is very common across northern Europe. Cows grazed on rich pastures produce milk – used for making butter and cheese.

NORTHERN EUROPE

DENMARK, ESTONIA, FINLAND, ICELAND, LATVIA, LITHUANIA, NORWAY, SWEDEN

Denmark, Sweden and Norway are together known as Scandinavia. These countries, along with the North Atlantic island of Iceland, have similar languages and cultures. Finland has a very different language and a separate identity from its Scandinavian neighbours. Estonia, Latvia and Lithuania, known as the Baltic states, were part of the Soviet Union until 1989, when each became an independent country.

INDUSTRY

In Scandinavia, many natural resources are used in industry: timber for paper and furniture; iron ore for steel and cars; and fish and natural gas from the seas. Hydro-electric power is generated by water flowing down steep mountain slopes. The Baltic states still rely on Russia to supply their raw materials and energy.

INDUSTRY

- Car manufacture
- Chemicals
- Engineering
- Fish processing
- Hydro-electric power
- Shipbuilding
- Timber processing
- Tourism
- Major industrial centre / area
- Major road

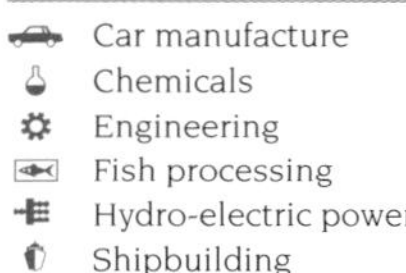

STRUCTURE OF INDUSTRY

Primary 4%, Services 65%, Manufacturing 31%

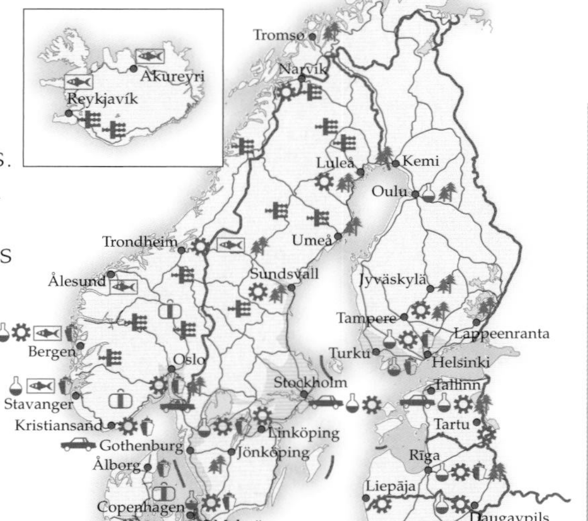

Tromsø
Narvik
Akureyri
Reykjavík
Luleå
Kemi
Oulu
Trondheim
Umeå
Ålesund
Sundsvall
Jyväskylä
Tampere
Lappeenranta
Bergen
Oslo
Turku
Helsinki
Stockholm
Tallinn
Stavanger
Kristiansand
Linköping
Tartu
Gothenburg
Jönköping
Ålborg
Riga
Liepāja
Copenhagen
Daugavpils
Odense
Malmö
Kaunas
Vilnius
Kaliningrad

FARMING AND LAND USE

Southern Denmark and Sweden are the most producti areas, with pig farming, dairy-farming and crops such a wheat, barley and potatoes. Sheep farming is importan in southern Norway and Iceland. In the Baltic states, cereals, potatoes and sugar beet are the main crops an cattle graze on damp pasture.

FARMING AND LAND USE

- Cattle
- Fishing
- Pigs
- Sheep
- Cereals
- Root crops
- Timber
- Pasture
- Cropland
- Forest
- Ice cap
- Mountain region
- Tundra
- Major conurbation

LAND USE

Pasture 3%, Cropland 11%, Forest 49%, Other (including mountains) 37%

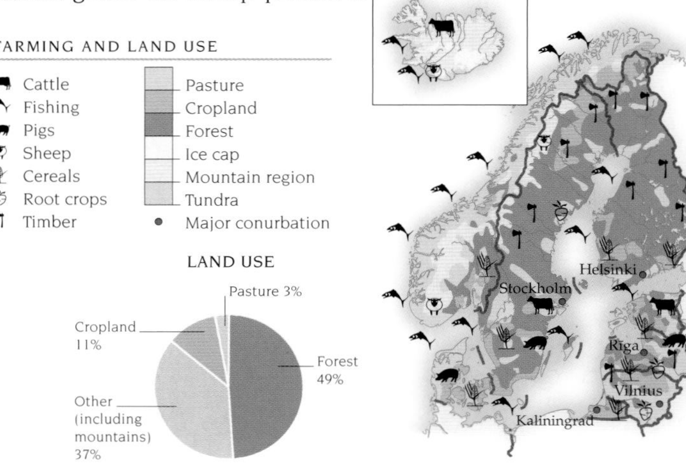

Helsinki
Stockholm
Riga
Vilnius
Kaliningrad

THE LANDSCAPE

The north and west of Scandinavia is extremely rugged and mountainous, with landscapes eroded by ice. In the south of Scandinavia the land is flatter, with fertile soils deposited by glaciers. Much of Finland, Norway and Swede is covered by dense forests. The Baltic states are much lower, with rounded hills and many lakes and marshes.

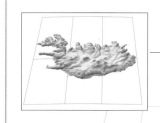

The land of ice and fire. Iceland is one of the world's most active volcanic areas. There are about 200 volcanoes on the island, along with bubbling hot springs, mud-holes, and geysers which spurt boiling water and steam high into the air.

Fjords Norway has many fjords: deep, wide valleys carved by glaciers, drowned by seawater when the ice melted at the end of the last Ice Age.

Baltic Sea (D7) Ships from Finland, Sweden and the Baltic states use the Baltic Sea as their route to the north Atlantic Ocean. In winter, much of the sea is frozen.

Glacial lakes Finland and Sweden have many thousands of lakes. During the last Ice Age, glaciers scoured hollows which filled with water when the ice melted.

Courland Spit (D This wide sandspit ru 100 km along the Ba of Lithuania and the enclave of Kaliningrad It encloses a huge lag

POPULATION

The population is distributed mainly along the warmer and flatter southern and coastal areas. Population totals and densities are low for all of the countries, and Iceland has the lowest population density in Europe, with just three people per sq km. Many Scandinavians have holiday homes on the islands, along the lake shores, or in coastal areas.

REYKJAVÍK
Trondheim
Bergen
Tampere
HELSINKI
Uppsala
Espoo
OSLO
STOCKHOLM
TALLINN
Gothenburg
RIGA
Århus
Malmö
COPENHAGEN
VILNIUS
Kaliningrad

INHABITANTS PER SQ KM

- More than 200
- 100–200
- 50–100
- Less than 50
- Capital city
- Major city

URBAN/RURAL POPULATION DIVIDE

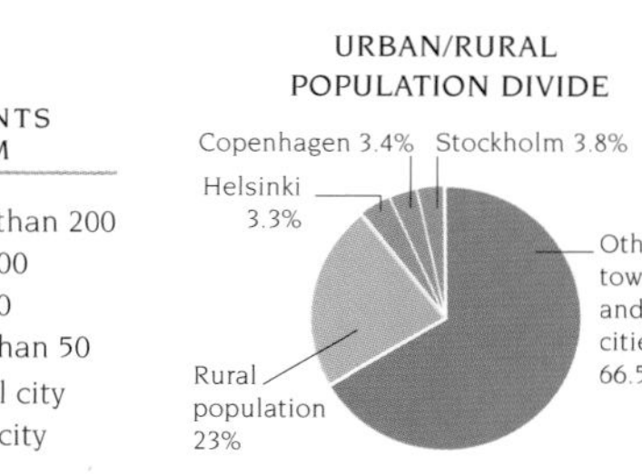

Copenhagen 3.4%
Stockholm 3.8%
Helsinki 3.3%
Other towns and cities 66.5%
Rural population 23%

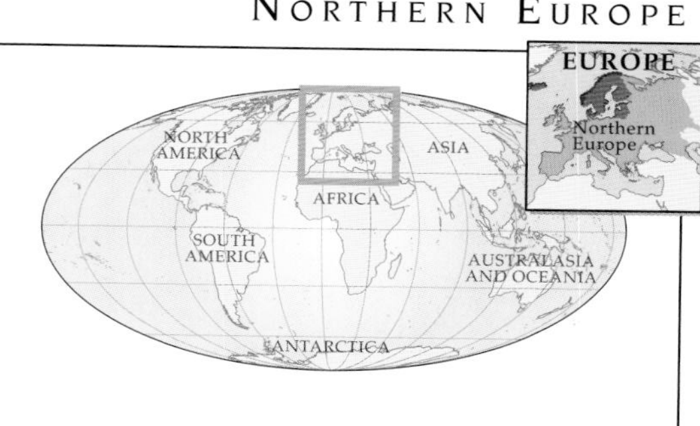
EUROPE
Northern Europe
NORTH AMERICA
ASIA
AFRICA
SOUTH AMERICA
AUSTRALASIA AND OCEANIA
ANTARCTICA

ENVIRONMENTAL ISSUES

Northern Europe has been badly affected by industrial pollution from other parts of Europe. Polluted air moves north, and mixes with the rain to create acid rain. This poisons forests and lakes, destroying the plants and animals living in them. Renewable energy plays a major role in this region, hydro-electric, geothermal and wind power are all exploited.

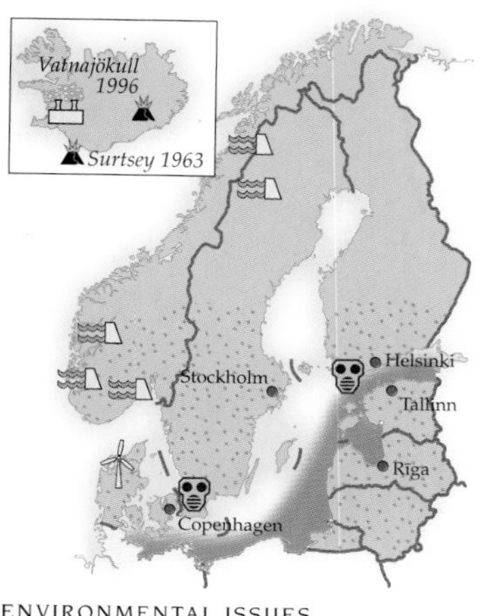
Vatnajökull 1996
Surtsey 1963
Stockholm
Helsinki
Tallinn
Riga
Copenhagen

ENVIRONMENTAL ISSUES

- Major dams
- Urban air pollution
- Volcanic eruption
- Wind farm
- Geothermal power
- Affected by acid rain
- Sea pollution
- Major industrial centre

CLIMATE

Warm ocean currents flowing north along the coasts of Norway and Iceland make the climate mild and wet. Away from the sea, the climate is generally colder, and drier.

January

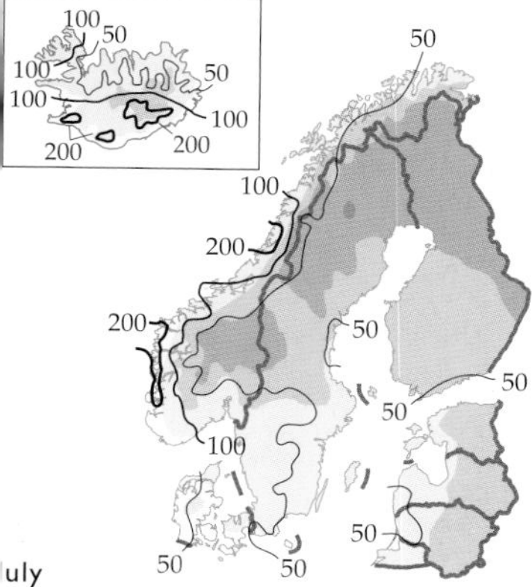

uly

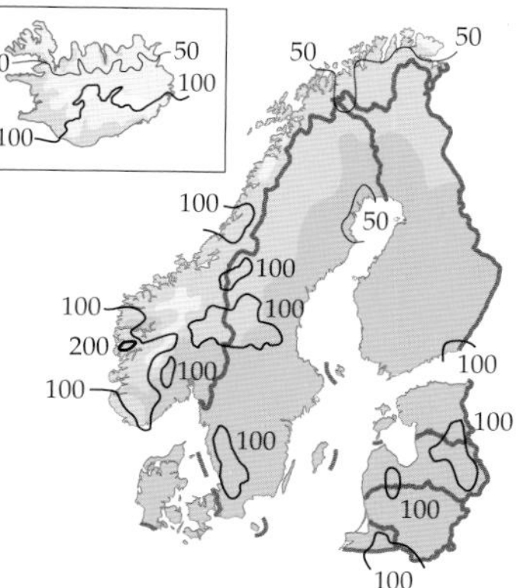

EMPERATURE AND PRECIPITATION

- More than 15°C
- 10 to 15°C
- 5 to 10°C
- 0 to 5°C
- 0 to -5°C
- -5 to -10°C
- -10 to -15°C
- Less than -15°C
- 100 Precipitation (mm)

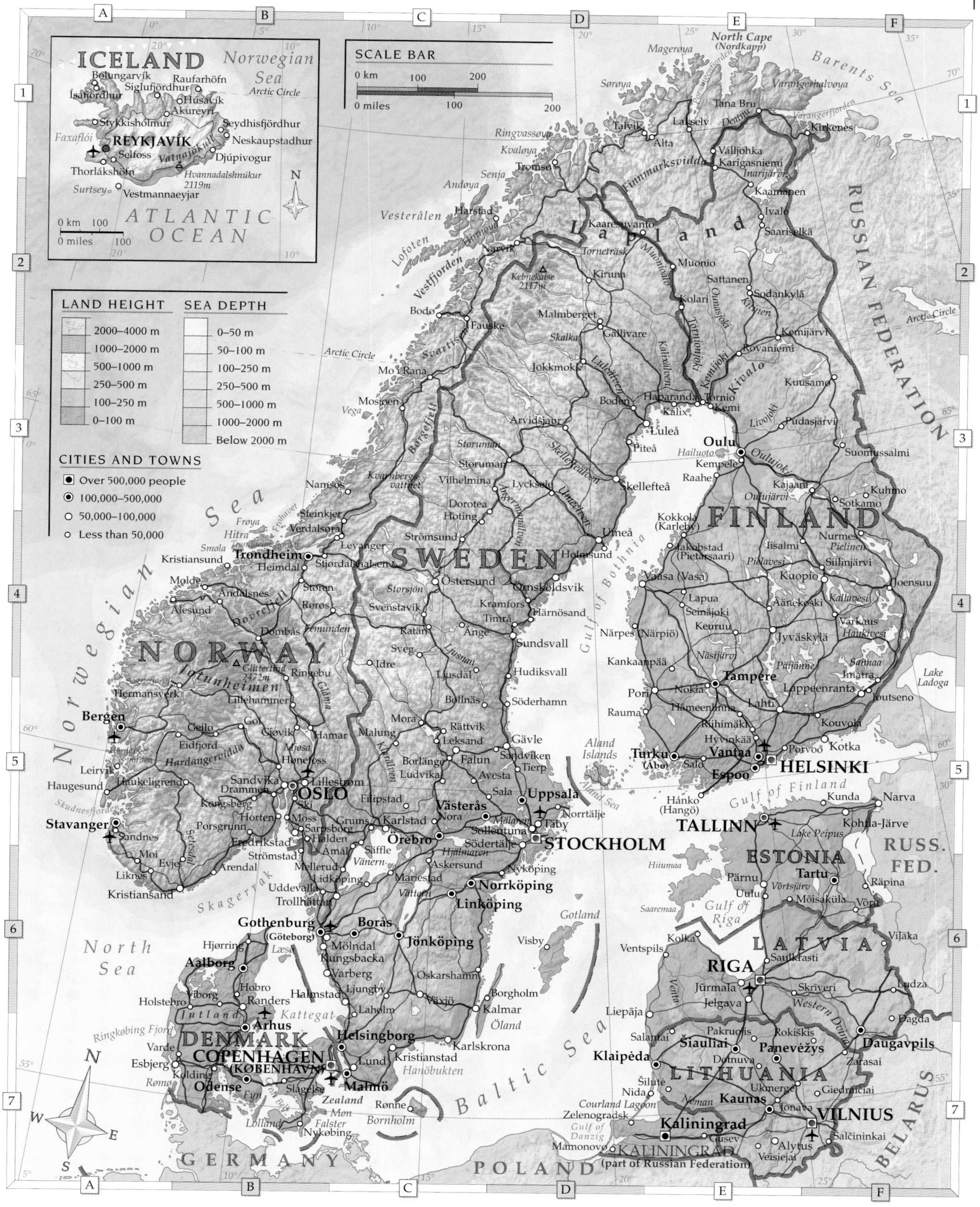

SCALE BAR

0 km 100 200
0 miles 100 200

LAND HEIGHT	SEA DEPTH
2000–4000 m	0–50 m
1000–2000 m	50–100 m
500–1000 m	100–250 m
250–500 m	250–500 m
100–250 m	500–1000 m
0–100 m	1000–2000 m
	Below 2000 m

CITIES AND TOWNS

- Over 500,000 people
- 100,000–500,000
- 50,000–100,000
- Less than 50,000

THE LOW COUNTRIES

BELGIUM, LUXEMBOURG, NETHERLANDS

Belgium, Luxembourg and the Netherlands are called the Low Countries because most of their land is flat and low-lying. Much of the Netherlands lies below sea level, and over hundreds of years the Dutch have built dykes and dams to prevent flooding, and have pumped water off large areas of land to reclaim them from the sea. The Low Countries are Europe's most densely populated countries, but most of their people have a high living standard.

ENVIRONMENTAL ISSUES

Huge land reclamation projects in the Netherlands, such as the IJsselmeer project, have created some new land for agricultural use, and also for houses, roads and open spaces. However, because of this work, sea-level rise is a major threat to large parts of the Netherlands.

ENVIRONMENTAL ISSUES

- Urban air pollution
- Built-up areas
- Reclaimed land
- Polluted river
- Major industrial centre

Amsterdam
IJssel
Lek
Rotterdam
Rhine
Bergse Maas
Antwerp
Brussels
Meuse

CLIMATE

The Low Countries share a similar climate, with mild winters and warm summers. Only in the upland Ardennes region does rainfall increase and temperatures decrease.

TEMPERATURE AND PRECIPITATION

- More than 15°C
- 10 to 15°C
- 5 to 10°C
- 0 to 5°C
- Less than 0°C
- 100 Precipitation (mm)

January
Less than 50
100

July
Less than 50
100

NETHERLANDS' TWO CAPITALS
AMSTERDAM - capital
THE HAGUE - seat of govern[ment]

CITIES AND TOWNS

- Over 500,000 people
- 100,000–500,000
- 50,000–100,000
- Less than 50,000

LAND HEIGH[T]

- 500–1000 m
- 250–500 m
- 100–250 m
- 0–100 m
- Below sea le[vel]

SEA DEPTH

- 0–100 m

SCALE BAR
0 km 25 50
0 miles 25 50

NETHERLANDS
BELGIUM
LUXEMBOURG
GERMANY
FRANCE
North Sea
West Frisian Islands (Waddeneilanden)

EUROPE
Low Countries
NORTH AMERICA
ASIA
AFRICA
SOUTH AMERICA
AUSTRALASIA AND OCEANIA
ANTARCTICA

POPULATION

More than 27 million people live in the Low Countries and nine out of every ten people live in a town or city. The largest urban area – known as the *Randstad Holland* – is in the Netherlands. It runs in an unbroken line from Rotterdam in the south, to Amsterdam in the west. Even most rural areas in the Low Countries are densely populated.

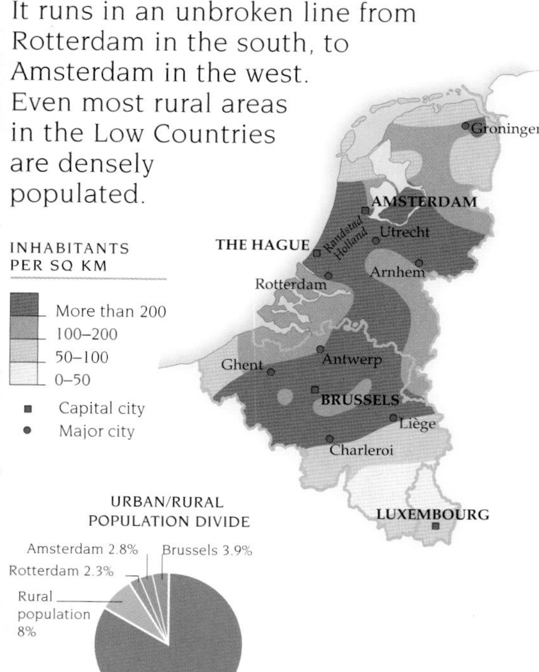
Groningen
AMSTERDAM
Randstad Holland
Utrecht
THE HAGUE
Arnhem
Rotterdam
Ghent
Antwerp
BRUSSELS
Liège
Charleroi
LUXEMBOURG

INHABITANTS PER SQ KM

- More than 200
- 100–200
- 50–100
- 0–50
- ■ Capital city
- ● Major city

URBAN/RURAL POPULATION DIVIDE

Amsterdam 2.8%
Brussels 3.9%
Rotterdam 2.3%
Rural population 8%
Other towns and cities 83%

FARMING AND LAND USE

The Low Countries' fertile soils and flat plains provide excellent conditions for farming. The main crops grown are barley, potatoes, and flax for making linen. In the Netherlands, much farmland is used for dairy-farming. The country is also famous for growing flowers, which are exported around the world. Flowers and vegetables are grown either in open fields or in enormous greenhouses, which allow production all year round.

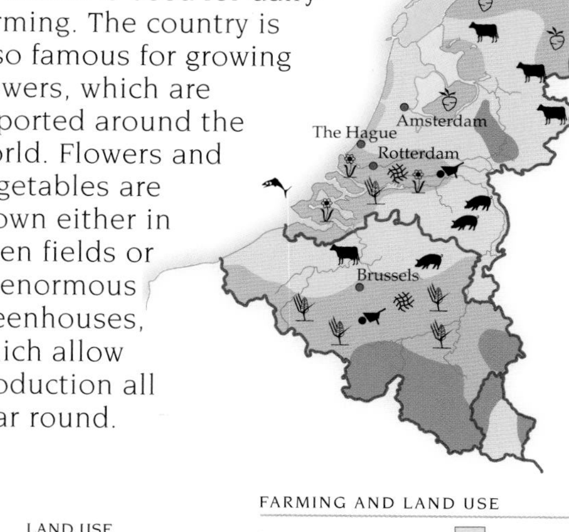
Amsterdam
The Hague
Rotterdam
Brussels

LAND USE

Forest 16%
Other (including urban) 29%
Pasture 26%
Cropland 29%

FARMING AND LAND USE

- Cattle
- Pigs
- Cereals
- Flax
- Flowers
- Market gardening
- Sugar beet
- Pasture
- Cropland
- Forest
- Wetland
- ● Major conurbation

THE LANDSCAPE

The Low Countries are largely flat and low-lying. The ancient hills of the Ardennes, in the far southeast, are the only higher region. They rise to heights of more than 500 m. Two major rivers – the Meuse and the Rhine – flow across the Low Countries to their mouths in the North Sea. At the coast, the River Rhine deposits large quantities of sediment to form a delta.

Polders
In the Netherlands, land has been reclaimed from the sea since the Middle Ages by building dykes and drainage ditches. These areas of land are called polders. They are very fertile.

The River Rhine (E4)
The River Rhine erodes and carries large amounts of sediment along its course. When it reaches the Netherlands it divides into three rivers. As they approach the North Sea, the rivers slow down, depositing the sediment to form a delta.

Low-lying Netherlands
Over two-thirds of the Netherlands lies at or below sea level. This makes flooding a constant threat in coastal areas.

Flanders (B 6)
The plains of Flanders in western Belgium have fertile soils which were deposited by glaciers during the last Ice Age. They provide excellent land for growing crops.

Heathlands
The heathlands on the Dutch-Belgian border have thin, sandy soils. The only plants which grow well here are heathers and gorse.

The Ardennes (D 8)
The hills of the Ardennes were formed over 300 million years ago. They have many deep valleys, which have been eroded by rivers like the Meuse.

INDUSTRY

The Low Countries are an important centre for the hi-tech and electronics industries. Good transport links to the rest of Europe allow them to sell their products in other countries. The built-up area stretching from Amsterdam in the Netherlands to Antwerp in Belgium has the greatest number of factories. Luxembourg is also an important banking centre; many international banks have their headquarters in its capital city.

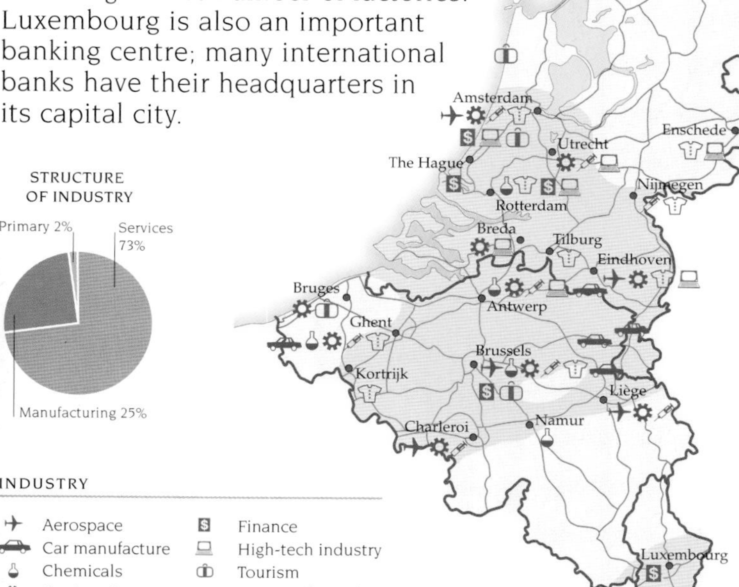
Groningen
Amsterdam
Enschede
Utrecht
The Hague
Nijmegen
Rotterdam
Breda
Tilburg
Eindhoven
Bruges
Antwerp
Ghent
Brussels
Kortrijk
Liège
Namur
Charleroi
Luxembourg

STRUCTURE OF INDUSTRY

Primary 2%
Services 73%
Manufacturing 25%

INDUSTRY

- Aerospace
- Car manufacture
- Chemicals
- Engineering
- Pharmaceuticals
- Textiles
- Finance
- High-tech industry
- Tourism
- Major industrial centre / area
- Major road

THE BRITISH ISLES

IRELAND, UNITED KINGDOM

The British Isles lie off the northwest coast of mainland Europe. They are made up of two large islands and over 5,000 smaller ones. Politically, the region is divided into two countries: the United Kingdom – England, Wales, Scotland and Northern Ireland – and Ireland. In 2014, Scotland will hold a referendum to decide whether it should separate from the UK and become an independent nation.

FARMING AND LAND USE

The English lowlands and the wide, flat stretches of land in East Anglia are the agricultural heartland of the United Kingdom. The country is no longer self-sufficient in food, but wheat, potatoes and other vegetables, and fruits, are widely grown. In Ireland, and in central and southern England, dairy and beef cattle feed off grassy pastures. In the hilly and mountainous areas, sheep farming is more usual.

Glasgow
Liverpool
Manchester
Birmingham
London

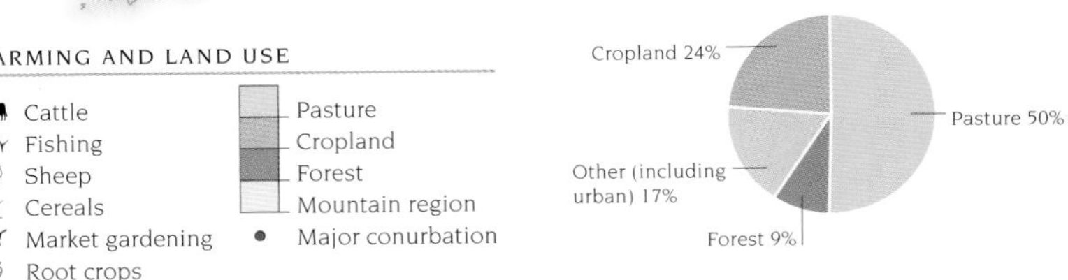
FARMING AND LAND USE
Cattle
Fishing
Sheep
Cereals
Market gardening
Root crops
Pasture
Cropland
Forest
Mountain region
Major conurbation
LAND USE
Cropland 24%
Pasture 50%
Other (including urban) 17%
Forest 9%

THE LANDSCAPE

Low rolling hills, high moorlands, and small fields with high hedges are all typical of the British Isles. Ireland is known as the Emerald Isle, because heavy rainfall gives it a lush, green appearance. Scotland and Wales are mountainous; the rocks forming the mountains there are some of the oldest in the world.

Indented coastlines
The west coast of the British Isles faces the Atlantic Ocean, and over 3,000 km of open sea to the North American continent. Storms and high waves constantly batter the hard, rocky coastline, giving it a jagged outline.

Ben Nevis (C4)
This mountain is the highest point in the British Isles. It is 1,343 m above sea level.

The Lake District (D5)
The Lake District National Park has England's highest peak, Scafell Pike, at 978 m (E4), its deepest lake, Wast Water (80 m), and its largest lake, Windermere (16 km long).

The Pennines (D6)
The Pennines are a chain of high hills, topped by moorland. They run for over 400 km, and are known as the 'backbone of England'.

The Burren (A6)
The Burren is a large area of limestone rock in the west of Ireland. Its flat surfaces are known as limestone 'pavements'. There are also many caves and sinkholes in the area.

Rias
Rias are river valleys that have been drowned by rising sea levels. The southern coast of southwest England has many good examples.

The Fens (E6)
This is the flattest area in England. Much of the land here has been reclaimed from the sea.

INDUSTRY

The United Kingdom's traditional industries, such as coal mining, steel-making, and textiles, have declined in recent years. Today, newer industries make cars, chemicals, electronic and hi-tech goods. Service industries, especially banking and insurance, have grown in importance. The country's hugely valuable North Sea oil and gas fields are expected to remain in production until around 2050.

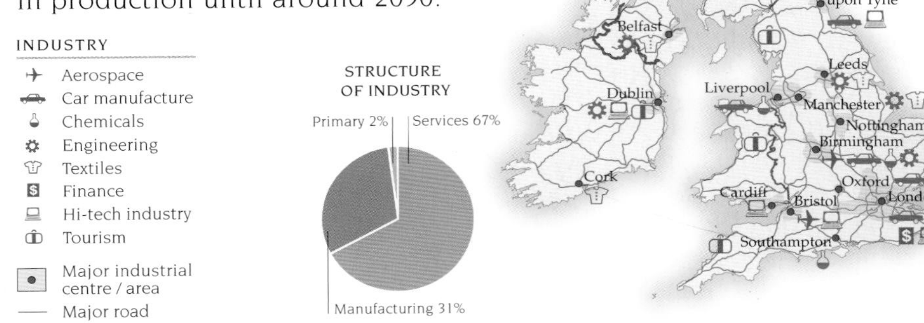
INDUSTRY
Aerospace
Car manufacture
Chemicals
Engineering
Textiles
Finance
Hi-tech industry
Tourism
Major industrial centre / area
Major road
STRUCTURE OF INDUSTRY
Primary 2%
Services 67%
Manufacturing 31%
Aberdeen
Dundee
Edinburgh
Glasgow
Newcastle upon Tyne
Belfast
Leeds
Dublin
Liverpool
Manchester
Nottingham
Birmingham
Cork
Oxford
Cardiff
Bristol
London
Southampton

POPULATION

The United Kingdom is densely populated, with most of the people living in urban areas. The southeast is the most crowded part of the country. The Scottish Highlands are less populated today than they were 200 years ago. Ireland is still mainly rural, with many Irish people making their living from farming.

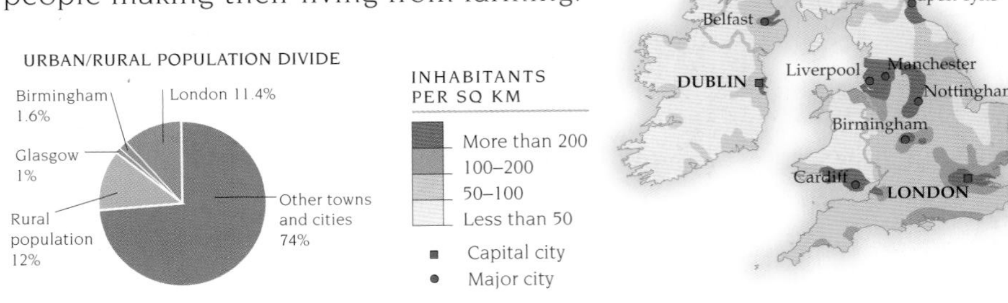
URBAN/RURAL POPULATION DIVIDE
Birmingham 1.6%
London 11.4%
Glasgow 1%
Rural population 12%
Other towns and cities 74%
INHABITANTS PER SQ KM
More than 200
100–200
50–100
Less than 50
Capital city
Major city
Glasgow
Edinburgh
Newcastle upon Tyne
Belfast
DUBLIN
Liverpool
Manchester
Nottingham
Birmingham
Cardiff
LONDON

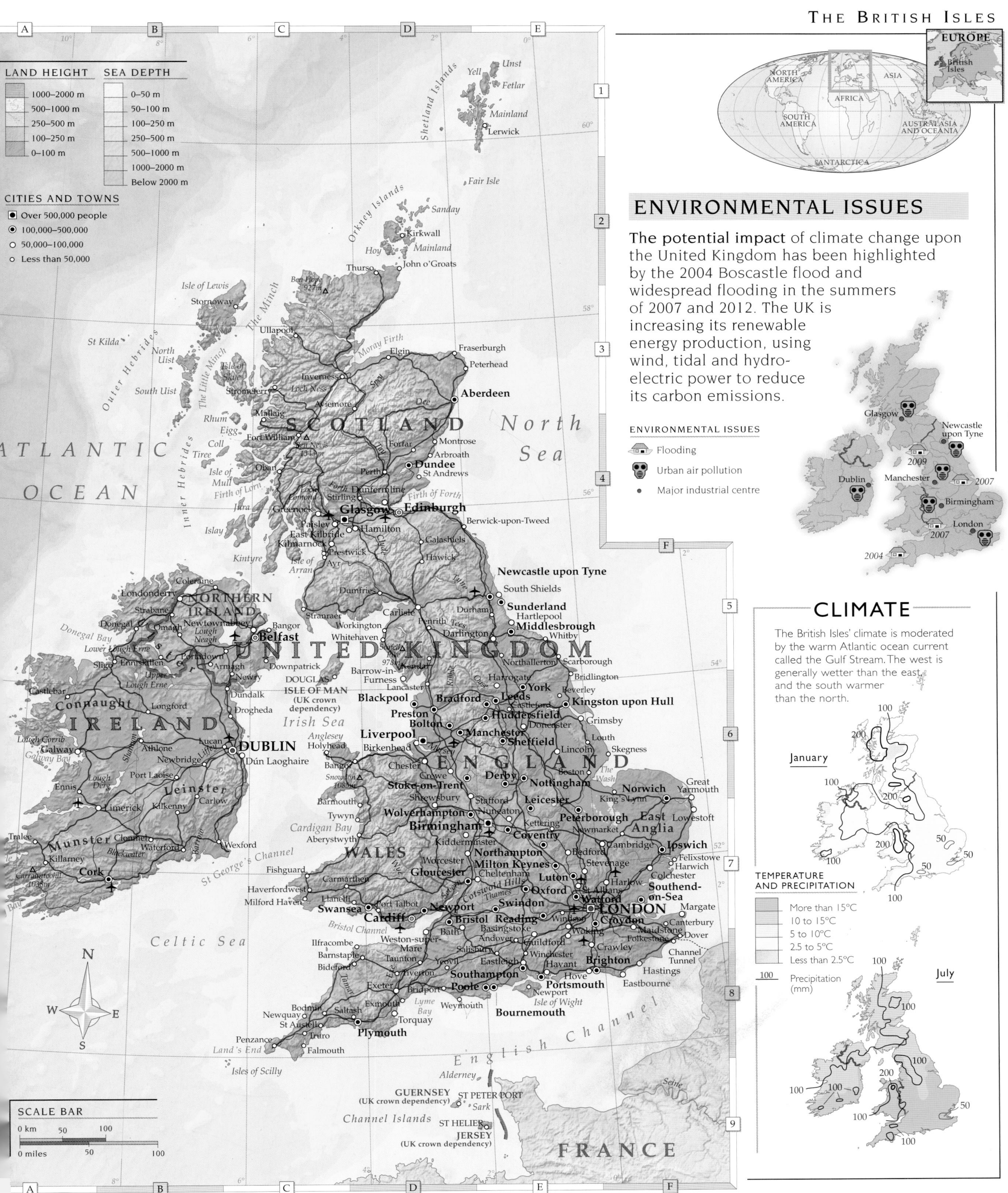
LAND HEIGHT
1000–2000 m
500–1000 m
250–500 m
100–250 m
0–100 m
SEA DEPTH
0–50 m
50–100 m
100–250 m
250–500 m
500–1000 m
1000–2000 m
Below 2000 m
CITIES AND TOWNS
Over 500,000 people
100,000–500,000
50,000–100,000
Less than 50,000
ATLANTIC OCEAN
North Sea
Irish Sea
Celtic Sea
English Channel
St George's Channel
Bristol Channel
SCOTLAND
NORTHERN IRELAND
UNITED KINGDOM
IRELAND
ENGLAND
WALES
FRANCE
Shetland Islands
Orkney Islands
Outer Hebrides
Inner Hebrides
Isle of Lewis
Stornoway
Ben Nevis 1343m
Ben Hope 927m
Kirkwall
Lerwick
Inverness
Aberdeen
Dundee
Perth
Stirling
Glasgow
Edinburgh
Londonderry
Belfast
Bangor
DOUGLAS
ISLE OF MAN
(UK crown dependency)
DUBLIN
Dún Laoghaire
Galway
Limerick
Cork
Waterford
Wexford
Newcastle upon Tyne
Sunderland
Middlesbrough
Carlisle
Leeds
York
Bradford
Kingston upon Hull
Liverpool
Manchester
Sheffield
Nottingham
Leicester
Birmingham
Wolverhampton
Coventry
Norwich
Cambridge
Ipswich
Oxford
LONDON
Brighton
Southampton
Portsmouth
Bournemouth
Bristol
Cardiff
Swansea
Exeter
Plymouth
Land's End
Isles of Scilly
Isle of Wight
Alderney
GUERNSEY
(UK crown dependency)
ST PETER PORT
Sark
ST HELIER
JERSEY
(UK crown dependency)
Channel Islands
Channel Tunnel
SCALE BAR
0 km 50 100
0 miles 50 100
N
S
E
W
EUROPE
British Isles
NORTH AMERICA
SOUTH AMERICA
AFRICA
ASIA
AUSTRALASIA AND OCEANIA
ANTARCTICA
ENVIRONMENTAL ISSUES
The potential impact of climate change upon the United Kingdom has been highlighted by the 2004 Boscastle flood and widespread flooding in the summers of 2007 and 2012. The UK is increasing its renewable energy production, using wind, tidal and hydro-electric power to reduce its carbon emissions.
ENVIRONMENTAL ISSUES
Flooding
Urban air pollution
Major industrial centre
Glasgow
Newcastle upon Tyne
2009
Manchester
2007
Dublin
Birmingham
London
2007
2004
CLIMATE
The British Isles' climate is moderated by the warm Atlantic ocean current called the Gulf Stream. The west is generally wetter than the east, and the south warmer than the north.
January
July
TEMPERATURE AND PRECIPITATION
More than 15°C
10 to 15°C
5 to 10°C
2.5 to 5°C
Less than 2.5°C
Precipitation (mm)

IRELAND

IRELAND, NORTHERN IRELAND

Ireland faces the north Atlantic Ocean and is one of the remotest parts of the European Union. Since 1921 the island has been divided into two separate states: Northern Ireland, which is part of the United Kingdom, and Ireland, which has its own government in Dublin. The eastern side of the island has more people and industry. In the west, traditional ways of life based on farming remain strong and the native Irish language is still spoken by some people.

INDUSTRY

Ireland has few mineral resources, around 15% of its electricity is produced by burning peat. In the last 20 years the European Union has given money to help the Irish economy and many new factories have been set up, mainly in the area around Dublin. Hi-tech industries expanded rapidly, as a result of low set-up costs and tax benefits.

INDUSTRY

- Aerospace
- Brewing
- Chemicals
- Engineering
- Food processing
- Textiles
- Hi-tech industry
- Tourism
- Major industrial centre / area
- Major road

FARMING AND LAND USE

Potatoes were once the traditional staple food of the Irish; potatoes and cereals flourish in the drier east. The climate is too wet for many types of crop, particularly in the west, where the soils are thin and the land is mostly used for sheep grazing. In bog areas a type of soil called peat is cut from the ground and dried to be burned as fuel.

FARMING AND LAND USE

- Cattle
- Sheep
- Cereals
- Potatoes
- Cropland
- Forest
- Pasture
- Major conurbation

POPULATION

The population of Ireland has actually fallen over the last century as a result of mass emigration, mainly to North America. The rate of people leaving the country to live abroad is still high, although one of Europe's highest birth rates and economic immigration are finally causing the population to rise again, with one person in every three being less than 20-years old.

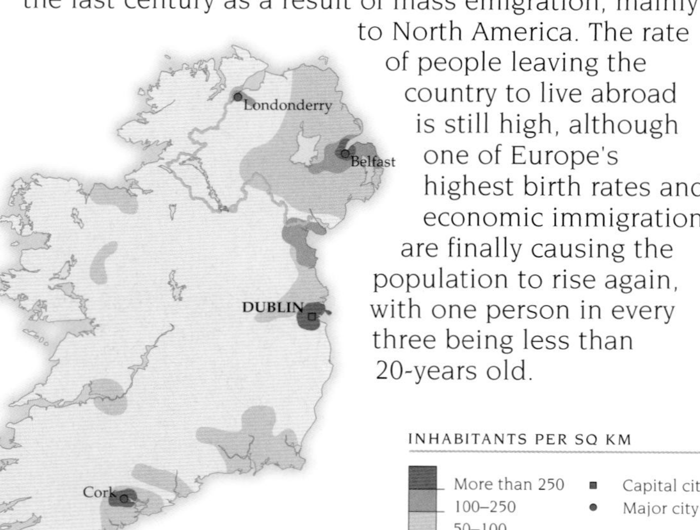
Londonderry
Belfast
DUBLIN
Cork

INHABITANTS PER SQ KM

- More than 250
- 100–250
- 50–100
- Less than 50
- Capital city
- Major city

THE LANDSCAPE

Ireland's mountains are nearly all close to the sea. They form a ring of high ground – broken in only a few places – encircling a lower lying plain which fills the central areas. Hundreds of lakes, large areas of bogland and low, grassy hills cover this central plain. The west coast follows an extremely irregular line, with many long bays and headlands.

High cliffs (C 2)
The cliffs of Donegal are some of the highest in Europe. Slieve League has been half cut away by sea erosion, so that the cliff rises vertically, all the way up from the shore to its 670 m summit.

Lakes made by glaciers
The central plain is covered with lakes of many different sizes. Most of these lakes were formed by huge blocks of ice which remained lying around as the last Ice Age came to an end, slowly melting over hundreds of years to leave sunken pits in the land surface.

Flooded river valleys (A 6)
Dingle Bay extends deep inland. Rising seas have flooded the old river valley. Bays formed when the sea floods a river valley are known as rias.

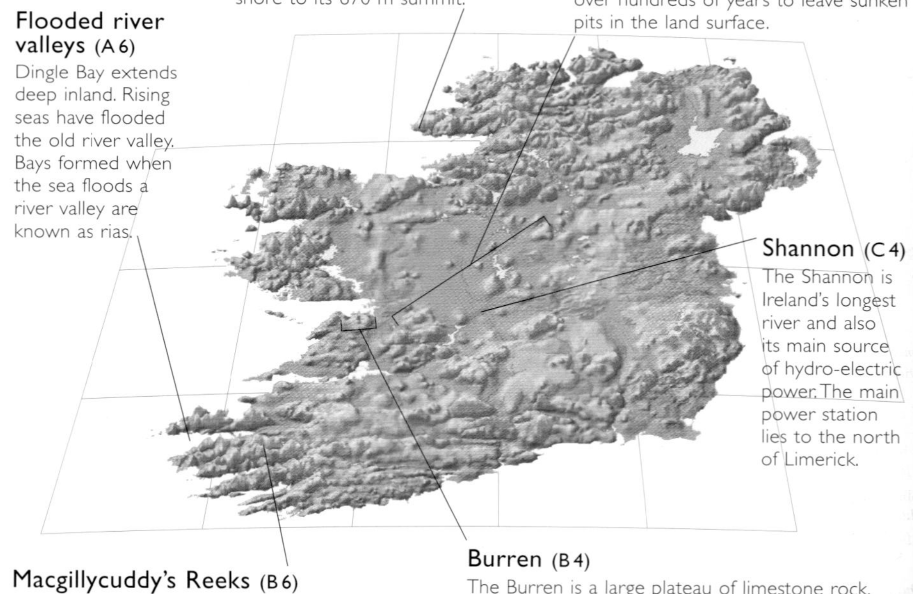

Shannon (C 4)
The Shannon is Ireland's longest river and also its main source of hydro-electric power. The main power station lies to the north of Limerick.

Macgillycuddy's Reeks (B 6)
This is the highest mountain range in Ireland. The jagged peaks and steep-sided valleys were cut from the highly resistant rocks by glacial erosion, during the last Ice Age.

Burren (B 4)
The Burren is a large plateau of limestone rock. Limestone is permeable, which means that water sinks below the surface and flows underground. The bare rock is visible at the surface in many places, where it is called a limestone pavement.

ENVIRONMENTAL ISSUES

Ireland has many areas of natural bog, which have been formed over hundreds of years by decomposing plants. Many of these wet bog areas are now under threat. The bogs are being damaged by an increase in peat cutting for fuel, while large areas are being drained and planted with coniferous trees to provide timber. Ireland's biodiversity is under threat due to habitat loss. Habitat is being fragmented by infrastructure and is under pressure from intensive agriculture and urban development.

CLIMATE

Ireland's location in the path of the Gulf Stream ocean current produces warm, moist air masses which pass over the country from the west. Rainfall is abundant, which allows many plants to grow – giving Ireland the name the 'Emerald Isle'.

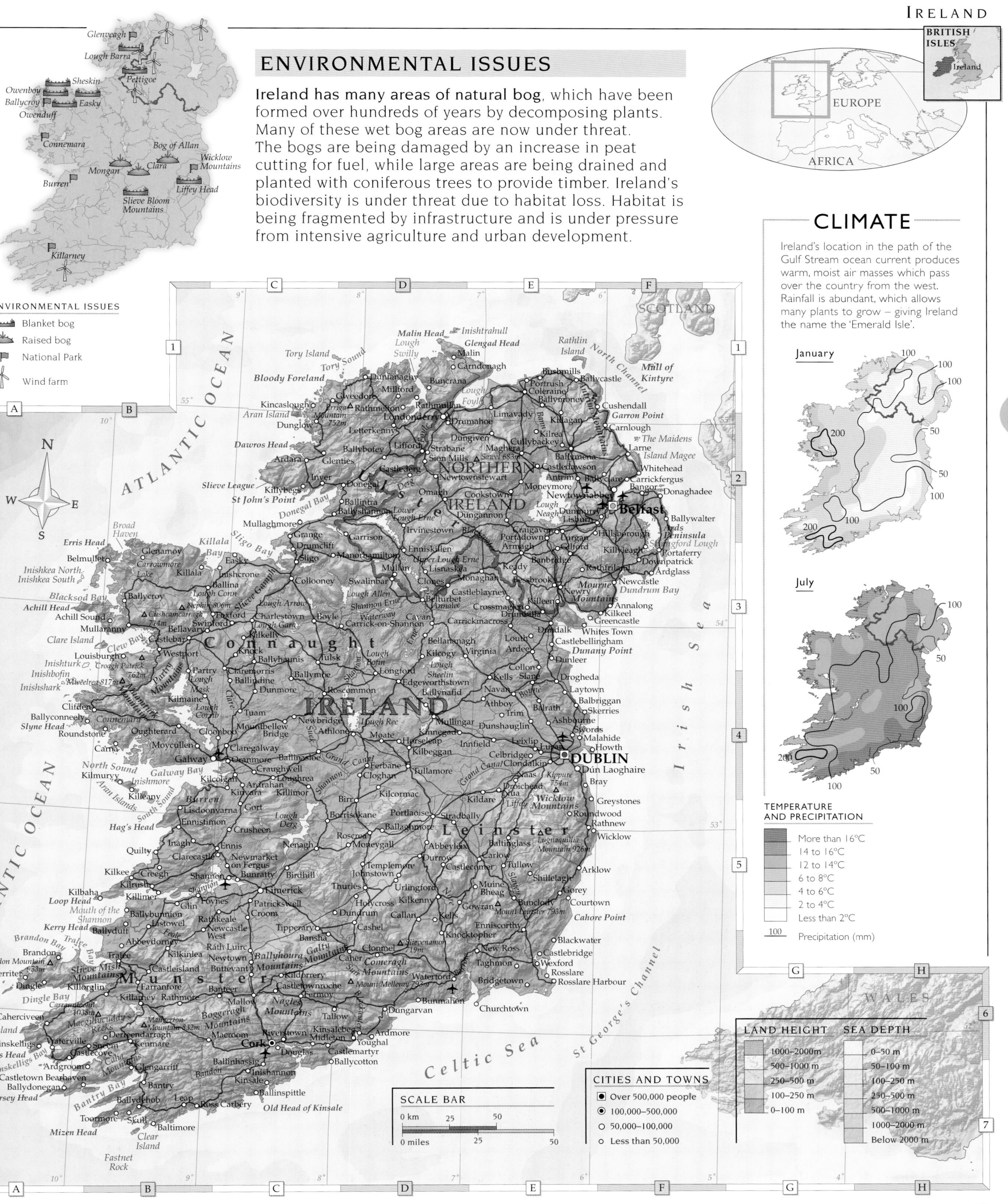
ENVIRONMENTAL ISSUES
Blanket bog
Raised bog
National Park
Wind farm
Glenveagh
Lough Barra
Sheskin
Pettigoe
Owenboy
Ballycroy
Easky
Owenduff
Connemara
Bog of Allan
Wicklow Mountains
Clara
Mongan
Burren
Liffey Head
Slieve Bloom Mountains
Killarney
BRITISH ISLES
Ireland
EUROPE
AFRICA
January
July
TEMPERATURE AND PRECIPITATION
More than 16°C
14 to 16°C
12 to 14°C
6 to 8°C
4 to 6°C
2 to 4°C
Less than 2°C
Precipitation (mm)
ATLANTIC OCEAN
NORTHERN IRELAND
IRELAND
SCOTLAND
WALES
Irish Sea
Celtic Sea
St George's Channel
North Channel
Connaught
Ulster
Leinster
Munster
DUBLIN
Belfast
Cork
Galway
Limerick
Waterford
SCALE BAR
0 km 25 50
0 miles 25 50
CITIES AND TOWNS
Over 500,000 people
100,000–500,000
50,000–100,000
Less than 50,000
LAND HEIGHT
1000–2000m
500–1000 m
250–500 m
100–250 m
0–100 m
SEA DEPTH
0–50 m
50–100 m
100–250 m
250–500 m
500–1000 m
1000–2000 m
Below 2000 m

Scotland

Scotland occupies the northern third of Britain and has three main regions: the northern highlands and islands, the Southern Uplands and, between these two mountain areas, the central lowlands, where around three quarters of the population live and work. Scotland was once an independent country and, after nearly 300 years of union with England, has regained its own parliament, with certain autonomous powers. In 2014, Scotland will hold a vote to decide whether to become independent from the UK.

FARMING AND LAND USE

The eastern side of Scotland has a drier climate than the west and is suitable for growing cereal crops and vegetables. Most of the mountain areas are too wet and barren for arable farming and are put to a variety of uses, which include sheep and deer farming, game keeping, forestry, tourism and recreation. Scottish fishermen currently land about two-thirds of all the fish caught by the UK.

FARMING AND LAND USE

- Cattle
- Deer
- Fishing
- Sheep
- Cereals
- Root crops
- Timber
- Cropland
- Forest
- Mountains
- Pasture
- Major conurbation

Aberdeen, Dundee, Edinburgh, Glasgow

INDUSTRY

A century ago, the area around the River Clyde was one of the great industrial regions of the world. The old heavy industries have since declined and been replaced by hi-tech and electronics industries, earning the area the name of 'Silicon Glen'. North Sea oil has brought many jobs and attracted new, oil-based industries such as chemicals and plastics production to the east coast.

INDUSTRY

- Aerospace
- Brewing
- Chemicals
- Engineering
- Fish processing
- Food processing
- Textiles
- Oil and gas
- Hi-tech industry
- Printing and publishing
- Tourism
- Major industrial centre / area
- Major road

Stornoway, Wick, Banff, Inverness, Peterhead, Aberdeen, Fort William, Perth, Dundee, Glasgow, Dunfermline, Greenock, Edinburgh, Paisley, Kilmarnock, East Kilbride, Ayr, Prestwick, Dumfries, Lerwick

ENVIRONMENTAL ISSUES

During a storm in January 1993, the Braer oil tanker struck the cliffs of southern Shetland. The ship broke up, shedding its entire load of crude oil into the sea. Although the oil was washed away within weeks, it did have some long-term effects upon the shellfish industry. Due to its favourable landscape, Scotland has seen a significant rise in the number of wind farms built in recent years.

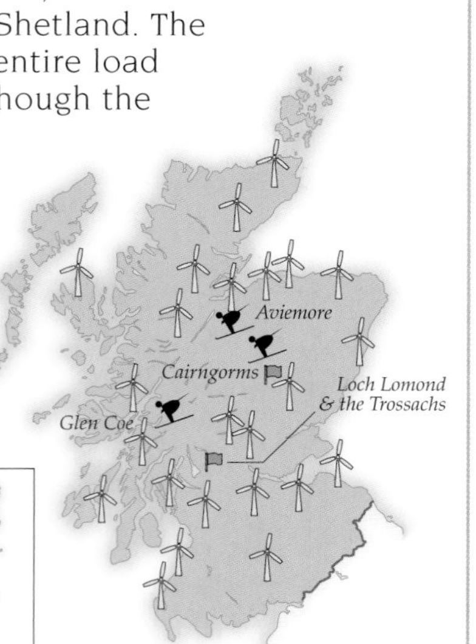
Aviemore
Cairngorms
Loch Lomond & the Trossachs
Glen Coe
Braer – 1993

ENVIRONMENTAL ISSUES

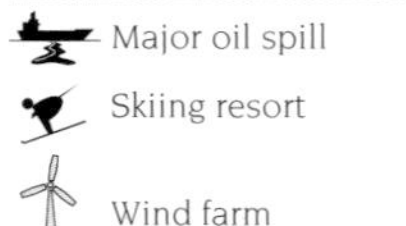

- Major oil spill
- Skiing resort
- Wind farm
- National Park

THE LANDSCAPE

Much of Scotland is rugged and mountainous. During the last Ice Age, around 18,000 years ago, glaciers and great sheets of ice attacked Scotland's hard, ancient rocks, leaving behind a landscape of high moorlands and steep-sided mountains separated by deep valleys, often filled by lakes known as lochs.

Glen Mor (D 3)
Glen Mor is a deep valley which runs right across Scotland. It marks a major line of rock fracture, known as a fault. Much of the fault line is filled by Loch Ness (D 3) and Loch Linnhe (C 4).

Grampians (D 4)
The Grampians are Britain's largest and highest mountain region. They include the spectacular Cairngorm range (E 3) and, to the west, Ben Nevis (D 4), the highest point in the British Isles, at 1,343 m.

Hebrides (A 2), (B 6)
The Inner and Outer Hebrides comprise several large islands and hundreds of small ones. Many of these were formed following the last Ice Age, as the sea level rose, cutting off parts of the mountainous landscape from the mainland.

Firth of Forth (E 5)
The Firth of Forth is one of several great sea inlets, known as firths, along the Scottish coast. They include the Firths of Clyde (D 6), Tay (F 5) and Moray (E 3).

Lochs (D 5)
The many sea lochs (fjords) of the west coast were formed as the sea level rose after the last Ice Age, flooding the deep valleys that had been cut by glaciers. The sea lochs cause the coast to follow a highly irregular line.

Rannoch Moor (D 5)
Rannoch Moor is the largest wild moorland in Scotland. A great ice sheet covered the area during the last Ice Age, leaving behind a vast expanse of bleak, bare ground, pitted with small depressions.

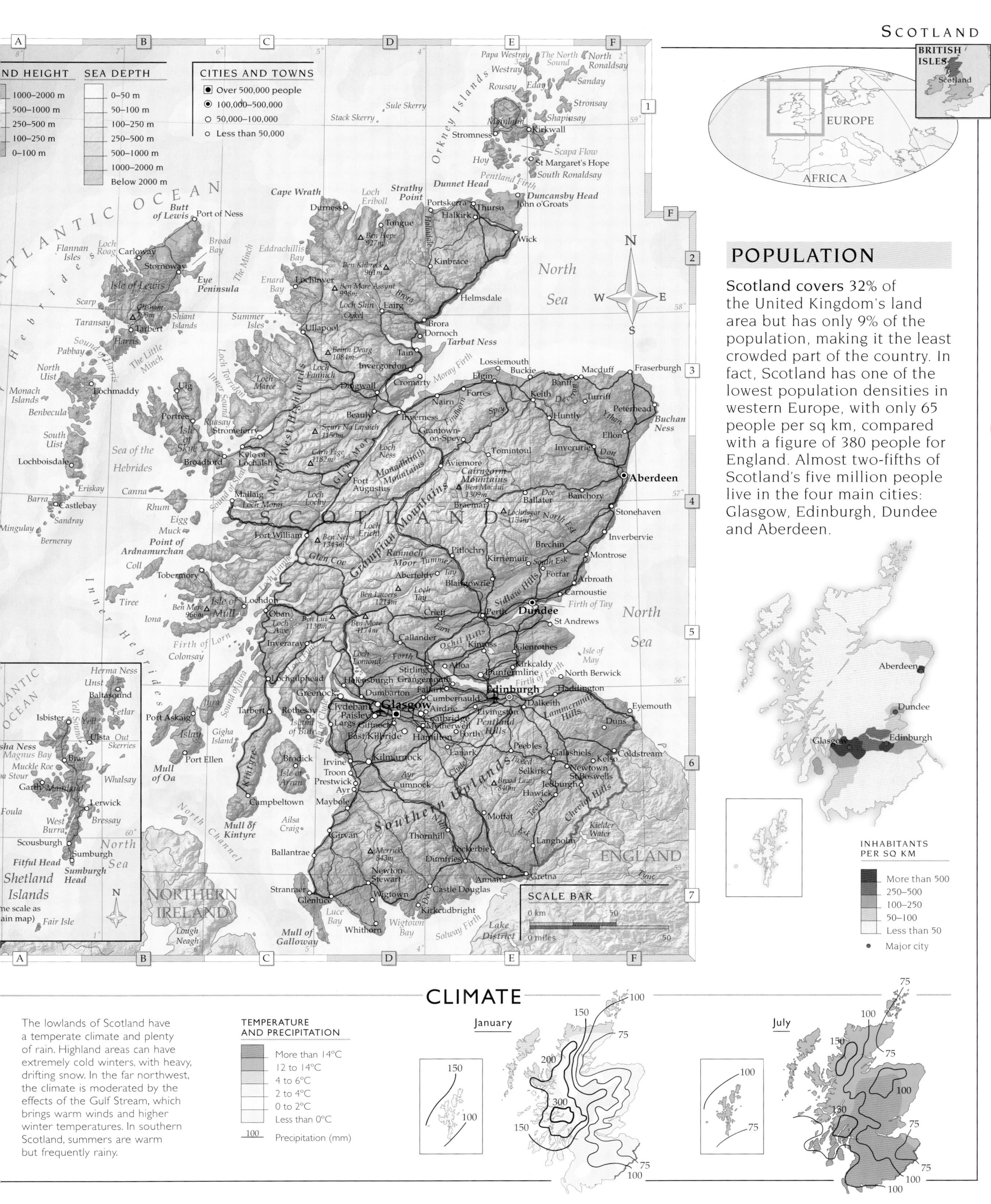
ND HEIGHT
1000–2000 m
500–1000 m
250–500 m
100–250 m
0–100 m
SEA DEPTH
0–50 m
50–100 m
100–250 m
250–500 m
500–1000 m
1000–2000 m
Below 2000 m
CITIES AND TOWNS
Over 500,000 people
100,000–500,000
50,000–100,000
Less than 50,000
BRITISH ISLES
Scotland
EUROPE
AFRICA
ATLANTIC OCEAN
North Sea
Orkney Islands
Shetland Islands
Hebrides
Inner Hebrides
Sea of the Hebrides
The Minch
The Little Minch
Moray Firth
Firth of Forth
Firth of Lorn
Firth of Clyde
Solway Firth
North Channel
Pentland Firth
SCOTLAND
Grampian Mountains
North West Highlands
Cairngorm Mountains
Monadhliath Mountains
Southern Uplands
Cheviot Hills
Sidlaw Hills
Ochil Hills
Pentland Hills
Lammermuir Hills
Ben Nevis 1343m
Ben Macdui 1309m
Lochnagar 1154m
Ben Lawers 1214m
Ben More 1174m
Ben Lui 1130m
Ben More 966m
Ben Hope 927m
Ben Klibreck 961m
Ben More Assynt 998m
Beinn Dearg 1084m
Sgurr Na Lapaich 1150m
Carn Eige 1182m
Clisham 799m
Merrick 843m
Broad Law 840m
Loch Ness
Loch Lomond
Loch Tay
Loch Rannoch
Loch Ericht
Loch Shin
Loch Maree
Loch Awe
Loch Fyne
Cape Wrath
Dunnet Head
Duncansby Head
John o'Groats
Strathy Point
Tarbat Ness
Buchan Ness
Butt of Lewis
Isle of Lewis
Harris
North Uist
Benbecula
South Uist
Barra
Skye
Rhum
Eigg
Muck
Canna
Coll
Tiree
Mull
Iona
Colonsay
Jura
Islay
Isle of Arran
Kintyre
Mull of Kintyre
Mull of Galloway
Mull of Oa
Point of Ardnamurchan
Aberdeen
Dundee
Edinburgh
Glasgow
Inverness
Perth
Stirling
Fort William
Oban
Stornoway
Kirkwall
Lerwick
Thurso
Wick
Ullapool
Aviemore
Pitlochry
Dumfries
Stranraer
Ayr
Kilmarnock
Paisley
Greenock
Dunfermline
Kirkcaldy
St Andrews
Montrose
Arbroath
Peterhead
Fraserburgh
Elgin
Nairn
Gretna
Berwick
Galashiels
Hawick
Moffat
Lockerbie
Campbeltown
NORTHERN IRELAND
ENGLAND
Lake District
SCALE BAR
0 km 50
0 miles 50
POPULATION
Scotland covers 32% of the United Kingdom's land area but has only 9% of the population, making it the least crowded part of the country. In fact, Scotland has one of the lowest population densities in western Europe, with only 65 people per sq km, compared with a figure of 380 people for England. Almost two-fifths of Scotland's five million people live in the four main cities: Glasgow, Edinburgh, Dundee and Aberdeen.
Aberdeen
Dundee
Glasgow
Edinburgh
INHABITANTS PER SQ KM
More than 500
250–500
100–250
50–100
Less than 50
Major city
CLIMATE
The lowlands of Scotland have a temperate climate and plenty of rain. Highland areas can have extremely cold winters, with heavy, drifting snow. In the far northwest, the climate is moderated by the effects of the Gulf Stream, which brings warm winds and higher winter temperatures. In southern Scotland, summers are warm but frequently rainy.
TEMPERATURE AND PRECIPITATION
More than 14°C
12 to 14°C
4 to 6°C
2 to 4°C
0 to 2°C
Less than 0°C
100 Precipitation (mm)
January
July

Northern England & Wales

The Industrial Revolution of the 18th and 19th centuries began in northern England, exploiting rich local resources to begin a new era of mass production. Today, these industries have declined, but despite a number of difficult years, northern England is becoming more prosperous again. Similarly, south Wales was once a major coal-mining and heavy industrial area but this has largely been replaced by new service industries. The magnificent scenery throughout this region attracts many tourists and outdoor enthusiasts.

Industry

Traditional industries such as iron and steel, coal-mining and textiles have been in decline for many years. More recently, the type of industries have changed to light engineering and hi-tech industries, producing microchips and computers, together with service industries such as insurance and retailing, printing and publishing. Tourism is important; large numbers of people visit the area's stunning national parks each year.

INDUSTRY

- Aerospace
- Brewing
- Car manufacture
- Ceramics
- Chemicals
- Engineering
- Fish processing
- Food processing
- Iron & steel
- Metal refining
- Pharmaceuticals
- Shipbuilding
- Textiles
- Oil refining
- Hi-tech industry
- Printing and publishing
- Tourism
- Major industrial centre / area
- Major road

Farming and Land Use

The eastern lowlands have an ideal climate for arable crops, while oats and potatoes grow in the north and west. The southwest is used mainly for grazing cattle and sheep, which also graze rough in the upland areas of the Pennines and Wales. Forestry is increasingly important in mountain areas.

FARMING AND LAND USE

- Cattle
- Sheep
- Cereals
- Market gardening
- Root crops
- Cropland
- Forest
- Pasture
- Major conurbation

Environmental Issues

Some of the UK's most dramatic scenery is found in this area, and national parks have long been established to protect the environment. These parks have proved so popular that in some places tourists are in danger of destroying the environment. Coal-fired power stations in the region power the large cities, but recently there has been an increase in renewable energy production.

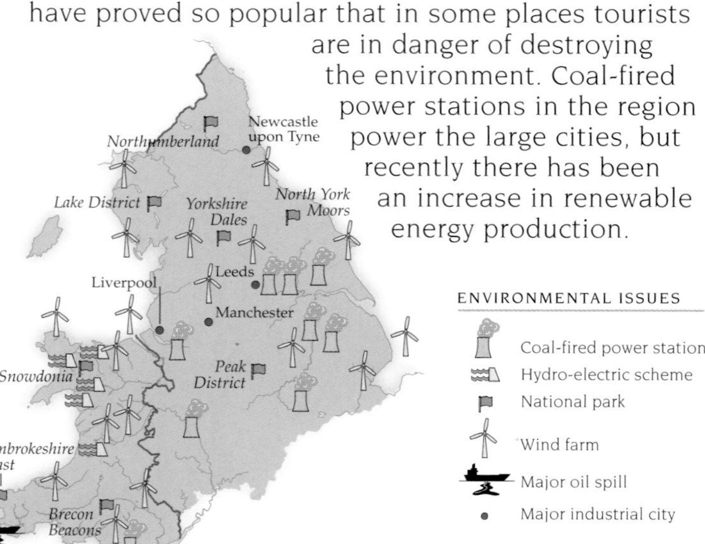
Newcastle upon Tyne
Northumberland
Lake District
Yorkshire Dales
North York Moors
Leeds
Liverpool
Manchester
Snowdonia
Peak District
Pembrokeshire Coast
Brecon Beacons
Milford Haven – 1996

ENVIRONMENTAL ISSUES

- Coal-fired power station
- Hydro-electric scheme
- National park
- Wind farm
- Major oil spill
- Major industrial city

The Landscape

The Pennines form the backbone of northern England. Likewise, the Cambrian Mountains, including the spectacular landscape of Snowdonia, run the length of central Wales. To the east, the Aire and Ouse rivers have cut a broad flood plain between the Pennines and the North York Moors, while in the far northwest, Cumbria's Lake District has many long, deep lakes, which were formed during the last Ice Age.

Limestone pavements

Bare 'pavements' of weathered limestone are also known as karst scenery. They have a block-like appearance, with deep cracks between the blocks that have been dissolved by rainwater.

Spurn Head (F 4)

Spurn Head is a long sand bar (called a spit) at the mouth of the Humber estuary. It was formed by waves which deposited sand across the mouth of the bay. Constant erosion has often made Spurn Head almost inaccessible from the mainland.

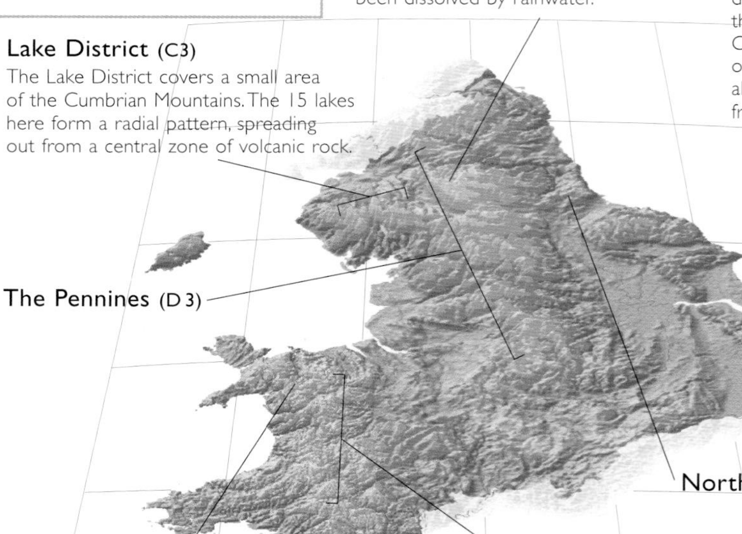
The Pennines (D 3)
North York Moors (E

Lake District (C3)

The Lake District covers a small area of the Cumbrian Mountains. The 15 lakes here form a radial pattern, spreading out from a central zone of volcanic rock.

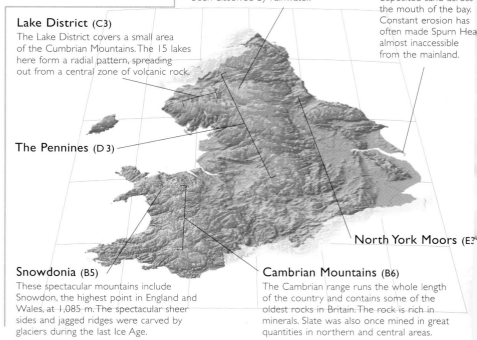

Snowdonia (B5)

These spectacular mountains include Snowdon, the highest point in England and Wales, at 1,085 m. The spectacular sheer sides and jagged ridges were carved by glaciers during the last Ice Age.

Cambrian Mountains (B6)

The Cambrian range runs the whole length of the country and contains some of the oldest rocks in Britain. The rock is rich in minerals. Slate was also once mined in great quantities in northern and central areas.

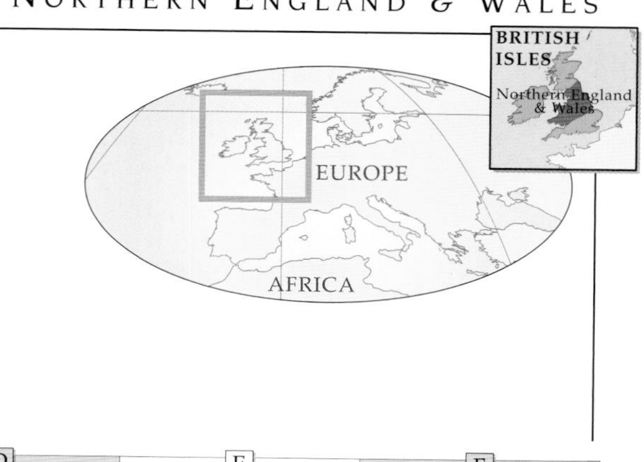
BRITISH ISLES
Northern England & Wales
EUROPE
AFRICA

POPULATION

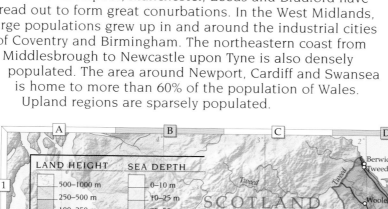

The cities of Liverpool, Manchester, Leeds and Bradford have spread out to form great conurbations. In the West Midlands, large populations grew up in and around the industrial cities of Coventry and Birmingham. The northeastern coast from Middlesbrough to Newcastle upon Tyne is also densely populated. The area around Newport, Cardiff and Swansea is home to more than 60% of the population of Wales. Upland regions are sparsely populated.

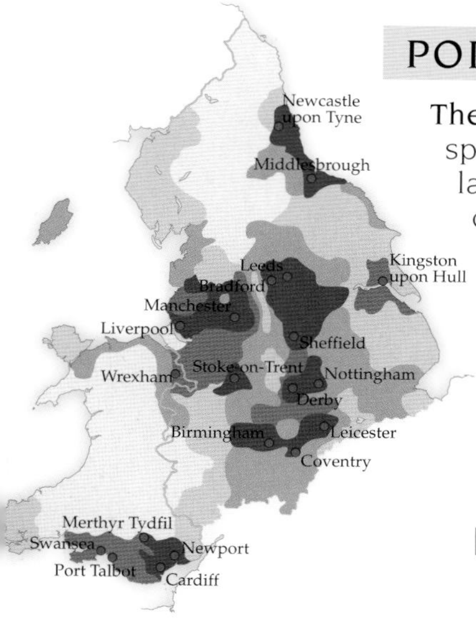

Newcastle upon Tyne
Middlesbrough
Leeds
Bradford
Kingston upon Hull
Manchester
Liverpool
Sheffield
Wrexham
Stoke-on-Trent
Nottingham
Derby
Birmingham
Leicester
Coventry
Merthyr Tydfil
Swansea
Newport
Port Talbot
Cardiff

INHABITANTS PER SQ KM

More than 500
250–500
100–250
50–100
Less than 50
• Major city

CLIMATE

Northern England tends to be cooler and wetter than the south, especially in the summer months. High rainfall totals are recorded in the upland areas of the west. The east, in the 'rainshadow' of the Pennines, is drier.

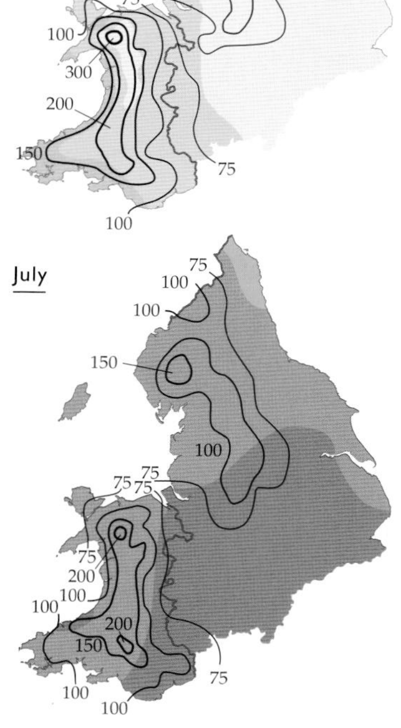
January 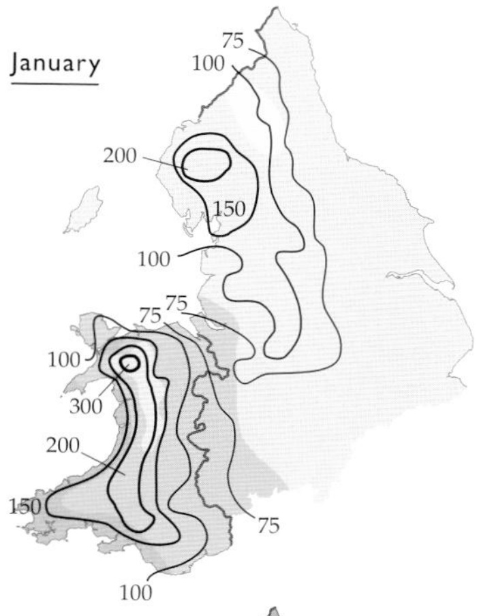
75
100
200
150
100
75
100
300
200
150
75
100
July
75
100
150
100
75
75
200
100
200
150
100
100
75

TEMPERATURE AND PRECIPITATION

More than 16°C
14 to 16°C
12 to 14°C
4 to 6°C
2 to 4°C
Less than 2°C
100 Precipitation (mm)

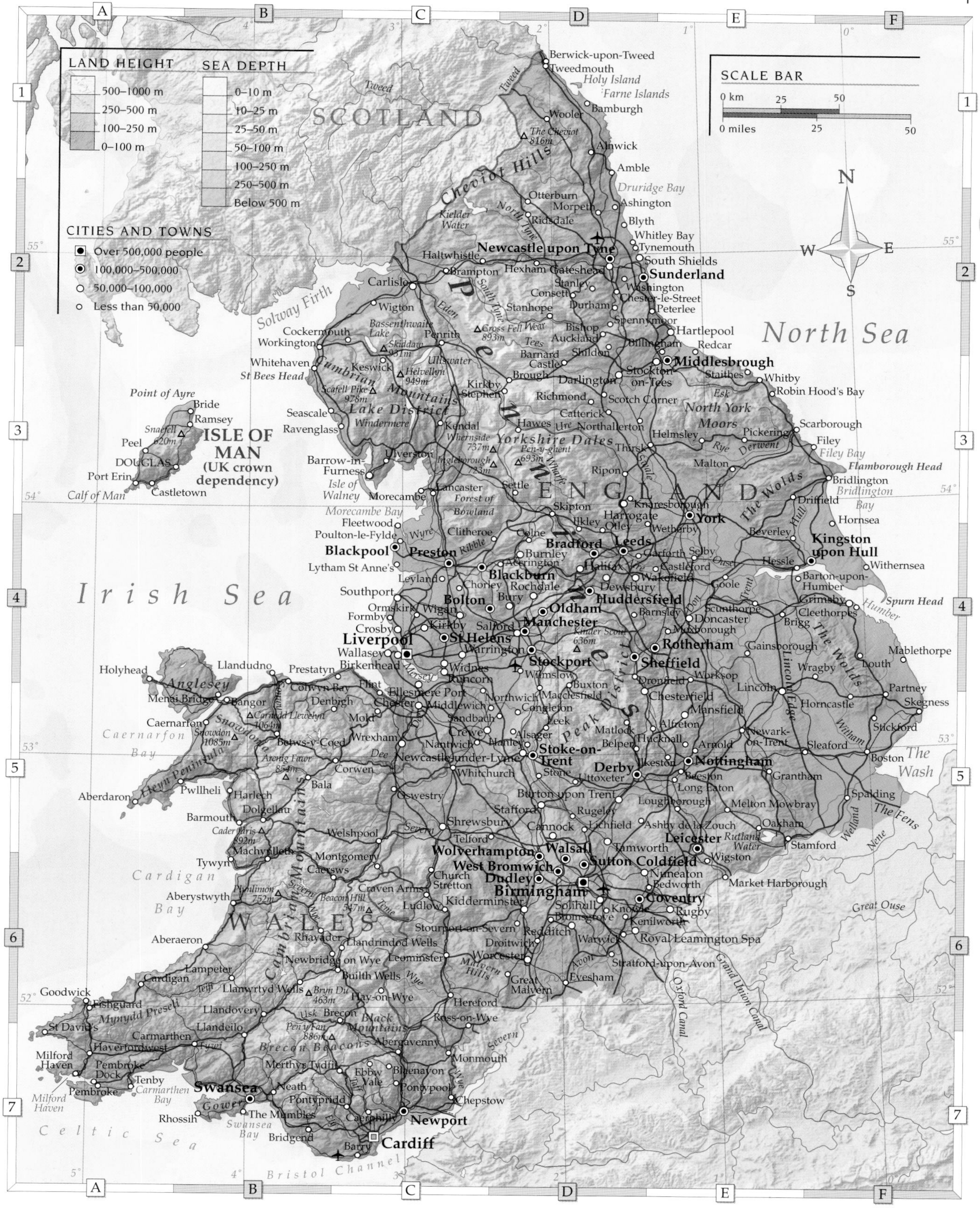

LAND HEIGHT

500–1000 m
250–500 m
100–250 m
0–100 m

SEA DEPTH

0–10 m
10–25 m
25–50 m
50–100 m
100–250 m
250–500 m
Below 500 m

CITIES AND TOWNS

Over 500,000 people
100,000–500,000
50,000–100,000
Less than 50,000

SCALE BAR

0 km 25 50
0 miles 25 50

N
W E
S

SCOTLAND
ENGLAND
WALES
ISLE OF MAN (UK crown dependency)
Irish Sea
North Sea
Celtic Sea
Bristol Channel
Cardigan Bay
Caernarfon Bay
Solway Firth
Morecambe Bay
The Wash
Liverpool
Manchester
Leeds
Bradford
Sheffield
York
Newcastle upon Tyne
Sunderland
Middlesbrough
Kingston upon Hull
Nottingham
Derby
Leicester
Stoke-on-Trent
Birmingham
Coventry
Wolverhampton
Cardiff
Swansea
Newport

SOUTHERN ENGLAND

The southern counties of England, and particularly Greater London, are the most densely populated part of the British Isles. There are more industries and more jobs here than anywhere else in the UK. In contrast, the counties of the far west and east are much less heavily populated and more rural, although towns in the eastern counties have been growing rapidly since the 1980s. Following the completion of the Channel Tunnel, the UK has had a direct rail link to Europe.

INDUSTRY

London is one of the world's top financial centres and is also a leading centre for other service industries including insurance, the media and publishing. Many car manufacturers are based in southern England, though the numbers of people employed have greatly decreased. Several cities, including Cambridge and Swindon, are centres for hi-tech industry. Thousands of tourists visit the historic and cultural centres in southern England every year.

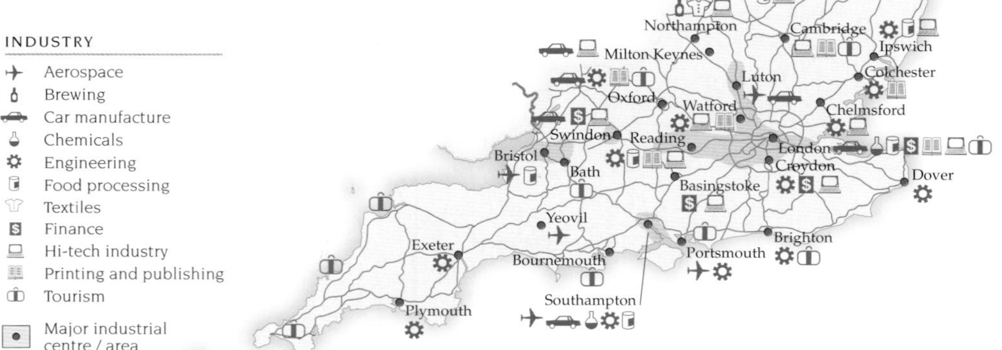

INDUSTRY
Aerospace
Brewing
Car manufacture
Chemicals
Engineering
Food processing
Textiles
Finance
Hi-tech industry
Printing and publishing
Tourism
Major industrial centre / area
Major road
Norwich
Peterborough
Northampton
Cambridge
Ipswich
Milton Keynes
Luton
Colchester
Oxford
Watford
Chelmsford
Swindon
Reading
Bristol
London
Croydon
Bath
Dover
Basingstoke
Yeovil
Brighton
Exeter
Bournemouth
Portsmouth
Southampton
Plymouth

ENVIRONMENTAL ISSUES

The large and growing population of southern England has increased pressure for the development of 'green belt' land, designed to protect the countryside surrounding large cities. Alternatives include infilling in urban areas, 'brownfield' redevelopment and building on flood plains. The proposed expansion of Heathrow airport has been cancelled.

ENVIRONMENTAL ISSUES
'Green belt' areas
National Park
Wind farm
Major town/city
The Broads
Cambridge
Oxford
London
Bristol
Heathrow
Exmoor
New Forest
South Downs
Southampton
Dartmoor
Bournemouth

FARMING AND LAND USE

Fertile soils and reliable rainfall mean that a wide range of crops can be grown in southern England. Large arable farms growing wheat and barley are found in the flat eastern counties, and a great variety of soft and orchard fruits and vegetables are grown in market gardens in the far southeast. Beef and dairy cattle and large flocks of sheep are grazed throughout the south.

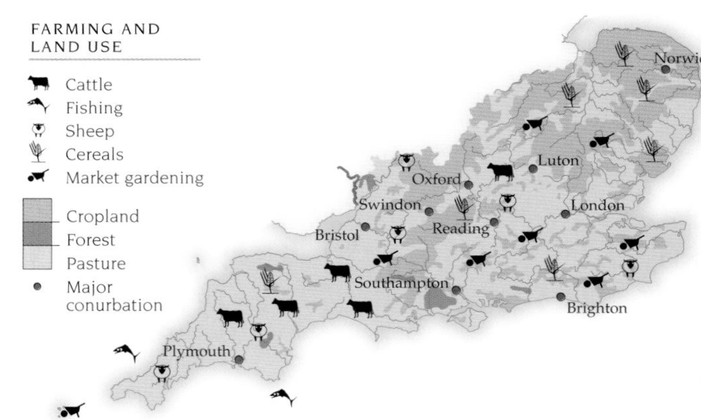

FARMING AND LAND USE
Cattle
Fishing
Sheep
Cereals
Market gardening
Cropland
Forest
Pasture
Major conurbation
Norwich
Oxford
Luton
Swindon
London
Bristol
Reading
Southampton
Brighton
Plymouth

THE LANDSCAPE

The landscape of southern England is very varied. Cornwall in the far west has craggy hills, and a jagged coastline shaped by the Atlantic Ocean. The Cotswolds and the North and South Downs are gentle hills, while towards the east, the land becomes flatter. Near the east coast, low-lying areas are occasionally prone to flooding.

Chalk hills The rounded hills of the Chilterns (F 3) are made from chalk. Because chalk is a porous rock, water quickly seeps through it, so few rivers can be seen in chalk areas.

The Broads (H 2)
The Broads in Norfolk are a series of wide waterways flowing across flat meadows. The channels were cut by peat cutters and are not 'natural'. They then flooded, forming shallow inland lakes.

Steep cliffs
The coasts of north Devon and Cornwall are battered by great waves from the Atlantic Ocean. The force of the waves weakens the rock at the foot of the cliffs, causing them to be 'undercut'. The top layer of rock breaks off and the cliffs recede.

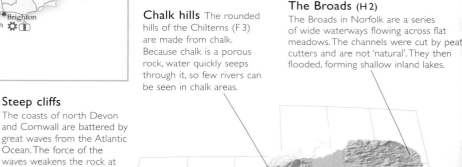

Dartmoor (B 5)
Dartmoor is the visible part of a great dome of granite rock. It was formed when molten rock seeped into and cooled in the Earth's crust. Because granite is so hard it erodes very slowly, so outcrops of rock known as *tors* can be seen all over Dartmoor.

River Thames (F 3)
The Thames has its source close to the Cotswolds, and meanders through Oxford and London before reaching the North Sea in a wide estuary.

CLIMATE

Southern England has a warm, temperate climate. The eastern counties are more windy and exposed, and low rainfall means that drought has become a major problem in the far southeast.

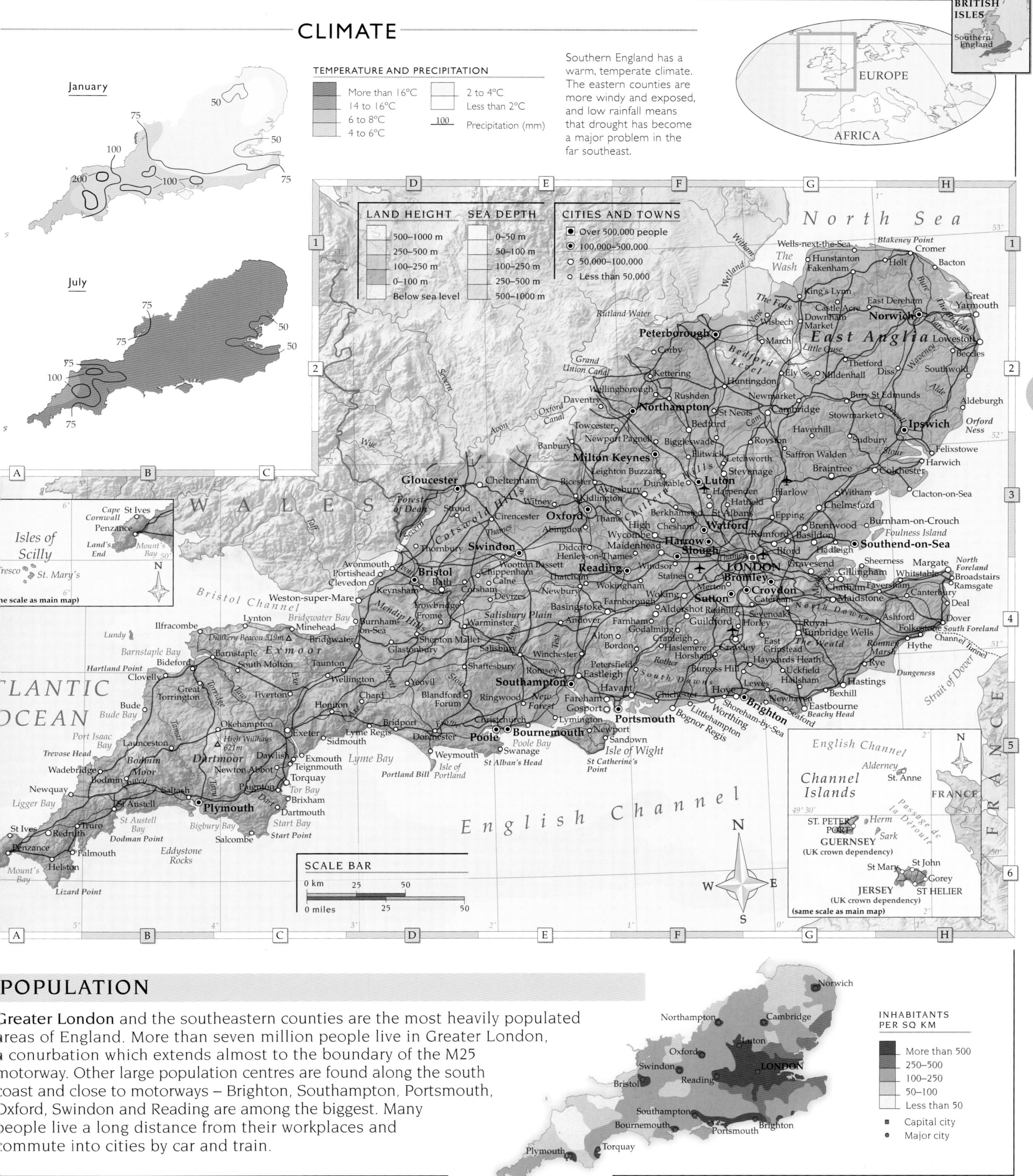
BRITISH ISLES
Southern England
EUROPE
AFRICA
January
July
TEMPERATURE AND PRECIPITATION
More than 16°C
14 to 16°C
6 to 8°C
4 to 6°C
2 to 4°C
Less than 2°C
100 Precipitation (mm)
LAND HEIGHT
500–1000 m
250–500 m
100–250 m
0–100 m
Below sea level
SEA DEPTH
0–50 m
50–100 m
100–250 m
250–500 m
500–1000 m
CITIES AND TOWNS
Over 500,000 people
100,000–500,000
50,000–100,000
Less than 50,000
North Sea
East Anglia
The Wash
WALES
Bristol Channel
ATLANTIC OCEAN
English Channel
Isles of Scilly
Channel Islands
FRANCE
LONDON
Southend-on-Sea
Peterborough
Northampton
Milton Keynes
Luton
Watford
Harrow
Slough
Croydon
Bromley
Sutton
Reading
Oxford
Swindon
Gloucester
Bristol
Southampton
Portsmouth
Bournemouth
Poole
Brighton
Plymouth
Norwich
Ipswich
Cambridge
Isle of Wight
Dartmoor
Exmoor
Salisbury Plain
North Downs
South Downs
The Weald
Cotswold Hills
Mendip Hills
Chiltern Hills
ST. PETER PORT
GUERNSEY
(UK crown dependency)
JERSEY
ST HELIER
(UK crown dependency)
(same scale as main map)
SCALE BAR
0 km 25 50
0 miles 25 50
INHABITANTS PER SQ KM
More than 500
250–500
100–250
50–100
Less than 50
Capital city
Major city

POPULATION

Greater London and the southeastern counties are the most heavily populated areas of England. More than seven million people live in Greater London, a conurbation which extends almost to the boundary of the M25 motorway. Other large population centres are found along the south coast and close to motorways – Brighton, Southampton, Portsmouth, Oxford, Swindon and Reading are among the biggest. Many people live a long distance from their workplaces and commute into cities by car and train.

FRANCE

ANDORRA, FRANCE, MONACO

France has helped to shape the history and culture of Europe for centuries. Today, as a founder-member of the European Union, France is a keen supporter of the eventual political and economic integration of Europe's different countries. France is Western Europe's leading farming nation, and one of the world's top industrial powers. Its cultural attractions and scenery draw tourists from around the world.

FARMING AND LAND USE

France is able to produce a variety of crops because of its rich soils and mild climate. Wheat is grown in many parts of the north, along with potatoes and other vegetables. Fields of maize and sunflowers and fruit orchards, are found in the south, while grapes for the famous wine industry are grown across the country. Beef and dairy cattle are grazed on low-lying pasture.

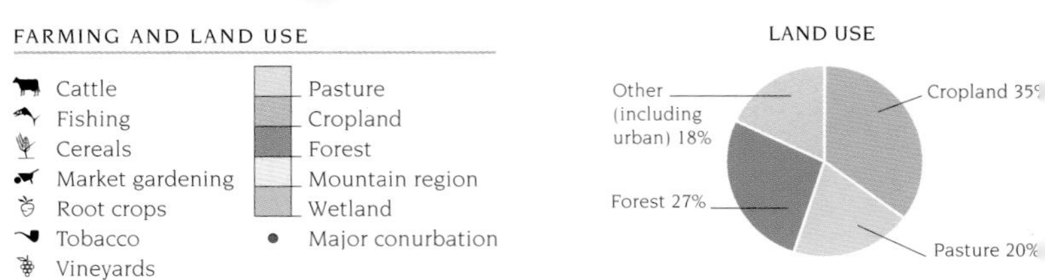
FARMING AND LAND USE
Cattle
Fishing
Cereals
Market gardening
Root crops
Tobacco
Vineyards
Pasture
Cropland
Forest
Mountain region
Wetland
Major conurbation
LAND USE
Other (including urban) 18%
Cropland 35%
Forest 27%
Pasture 20%

THE LANDSCAPE

The north and west of France is made up of mainly flat, grassy plains or low hills. Wooded mountains line the country's borders in the south and east, and much of central France is taken up by the Massif Central, an enormous plateau, cut by deep river valleys and scattered with extinct volcanoes. Three major rivers, the Loire, Seine and Garonne drain the lowland basins.

Paris Basin
The Paris Basin is a saucer-shaped hollow made up of layers of hard and soft rock, covered with very fertile soils. It runs across about 100,000 sq km of northern France.

Alps (E5)
The western end of the European Alpine mountain chain stretches into southeast France. The French Alps can be crossed by several passes, which give access to Italy and Switzerland.

Normandy
The coast of Normandy is lined with high chalk cliffs.

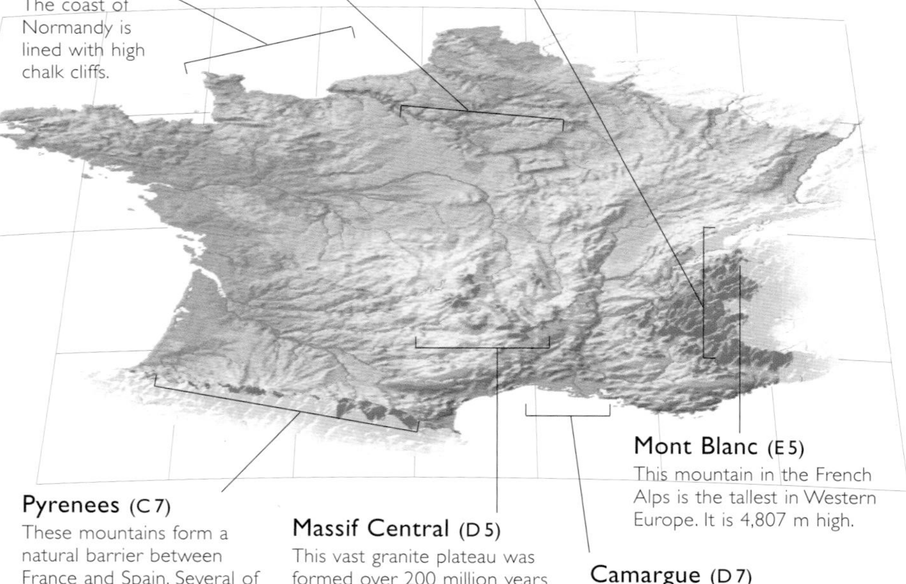

Pyrenees (C7)
These mountains form a natural barrier between France and Spain. Several of their peaks reach heights of over 3,000 m. The Pyrenees are difficult to cross, due to their height, and because they have few low passes.

Massif Central (D5)
This vast granite plateau was formed over 200 million years ago. Volcanic activity here only stopped within the last 10,000 years and the region's rounded hills are the worn down remains of volcanic mountains.

Camargue (D7)
The Camargue is an area of marshes, pastures, sand dunes and salt flats at the mouth of the River Rhône. Rare animal and plant species are found there.

Mont Blanc (E5)
This mountain in the French Alps is the tallest in Western Europe. It is 4,807 m high.

INDUSTRY

France is one of the world's top manufacturing nations, with a variety of both traditional and hi-tech industries. Cars, machinery and electronic products are exported worldwide, along with luxury goods such as perfumes, fashions and fine wines. Extensive use of nuclear power has allowed France to become the world's largest net exporter of electricity.

Lille
Amiens
Le Havre
Rouen
Caen
Brest
Reims
Metz
Paris
Strasbourg
Rennes
Angers
Orléans
Mulhouse
Nantes
Tours
Bourges
Limoges
Clermont-Ferrand
Lyon
Bordeaux
St-Etienne
Grenoble
Toulouse
Marseille
Nice
Toulon

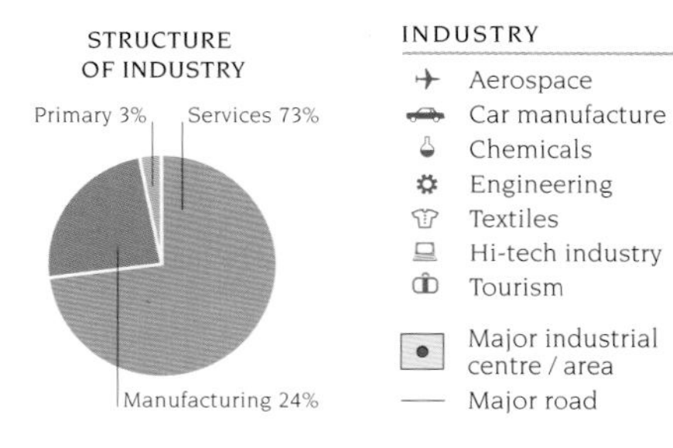
STRUCTURE OF INDUSTRY
Primary 3%
Services 73%
Manufacturing 24%
INDUSTRY
Aerospace
Car manufacture
Chemicals
Engineering
Textiles
Hi-tech industry
Tourism
Major industrial centre / area
Major road

POPULATION

In the past 50 years, most people have moved from the countryside into urban areas. Paris and its suburbs, the industrial cities, and the Côte d'Azur in the southeast are the most economically developed parts of France and now have the biggest populations.

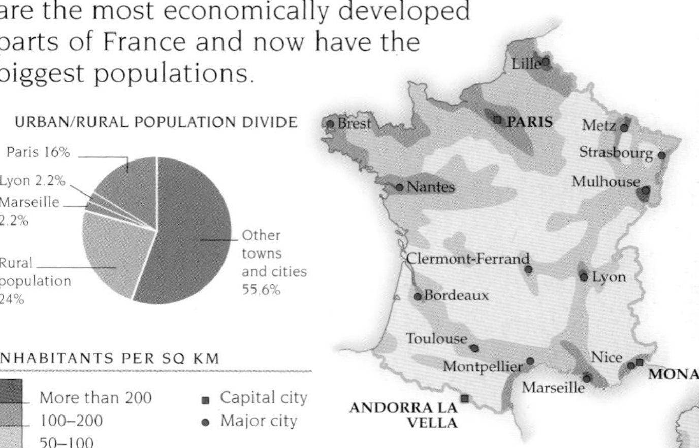
URBAN/RURAL POPULATION DIVIDE
Paris 16%
Lyon 2.2%
Marseille 2.2%
Rural population 24%
Other towns and cities 55.6%
INHABITANTS PER SQ KM
More than 200
100–200
50–100
Less than 50
Capital city
Major city
Lille
Brest
PARIS
Metz
Strasbourg
Mulhouse
Nantes
Clermont-Ferrand
Lyon
Bordeaux
Toulouse
Montpellier
Nice
Marseille
MONACO
ANDORRA LA VELLA

EUROPE

France

NORTH AMERICA · SOUTH AMERICA · AFRICA · ASIA · AUSTRALASIA AND OCEANIA · ANTARCTICA

ENVIRONMENTAL ISSUES

Nuclear power station
Sea pollution
Polluted rivers
Major industrial centre

ENVIRONMENTAL ISSUES

Many of France's coastal areas have been polluted by industry and tourism. A summer heatwave in 2003 severeley affected France, with temperatures of up to 40°C contributing to the deaths of an estimated 15,000 people. France's reliance on nuclear energy – over 75% of its electricity is generated by nuclear power – means that it suffers less from the pollution caused by burning fossil fuels than many other countries in Europe.

CLIMATE

In winter, the coldest areas of France are the mountains of the Massif Central, and the Alps. Summers are hottest on the Mediterranean coast.

TEMPERATURE AND PRECIPITATION

More than 20°C
15 to 20°C
10 to 15°C
5 to 10°C
0 to 5°C
0 to -5°C
Less than -5°C
100 Precipitation (mm)

January

July

SCALE BAR

km 50 100

miles 50 100

LAND HEIGHT

Above 4000 m
2000–4000 m
1000–2000 m
500–1000 m
250–500 m
100–250 m
0–100 m

SEA DEPTH

0–50 m
50–100 m
100–250 m
250–500 m
500–1000 m
1000–2000 m
Below 2000 m

CITIES AND TOWNS

Over 500,000 people
100,000–500,000
50,000–100,000
Less than 50,000

UNITED KINGDOM · BELGIUM · LUXEMBOURG · GERMANY · SWITZERLAND · ITALY · MONACO · ANDORRA · SPAIN · FRANCE

English Channel · Bay of Biscay · Gulf of Lion · Ligurian Sea · Mediterranean Sea · Tyrrhenian Sea

Corsica (Corse) · Sardinia (Sardegna) (part of Italy) · Scale: same as main map

Spain and Portugal

PORTUGAL, SPAIN

Spain and Portugal occupy the Iberian Peninsula, which is cut off from the rest of Europe by the Pyrenees. Over the centuries, Iberia has been invaded and settled by many different peoples. The Moors, who arrived from North Africa in the 8th century, ruled much of Spain for almost 800 years and their influence can still be seen in Spanish culture. Portugal has modernized it's economy since joining the European Union, and both countries have changed their currencies to the euro.

INDUSTRY

Madrid, Barcelona and the northern ports are Spain's industrial centres. Here, iron ore from Spanish mines is used to make steel, and factories produce cars, machinery and chemicals. Portugal exports textiles, clothing and footwear, along with fish such as sardines and tuna, caught off the Atlantic coast. In both countries, tourism is very important to the economy.

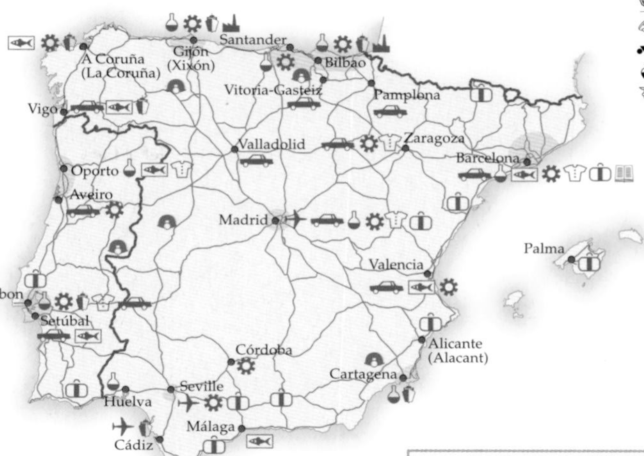

A Coruña
(La Coruña)
Gijón
(Xixón)
Santander
Bilbao
Vitoria-Gasteiz
Pamplona
Vigo
Zaragoza
Valladolid
Barcelona
Oporto
Aveiro
Madrid
Palma
Valencia
Lisbon
Setúbal
Alicante
(Alacant)
Córdoba
Cartagena
Seville
Huelva
Málaga
Cádiz

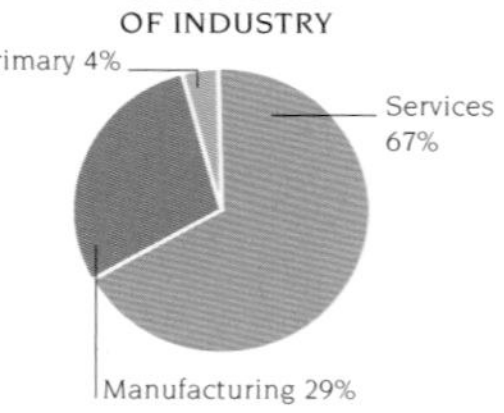

STRUCTURE OF INDUSTRY
Primary 4%
Services 67%
Manufacturing 29%

INDUSTRY
Aerospace
Car manufacture
Chemicals
Engineering
Fish processing
Shipbuilding
Steel
Textiles
Mining
Tourism
Publishing

Major industrial centre / area
Major road

POPULATION

Gijón
(Xixón)
Bilbao
Vigo
Zaragoza
Barcelona
Tarragona
Oporto
MADRID
Palma
LISBON
Valencia
Alicante
(Alacant)
Seville
Granada
Cartagena
Cádiz
Malaga

In the first half of the 20th century, most Spaniards lived in villages or small towns, scattered around the country. Today, tourism and industry have drawn most of the population to the cities and coastal areas. Most Portuguese live in cities, but one third still live in rural areas along the coast or in the river valleys.

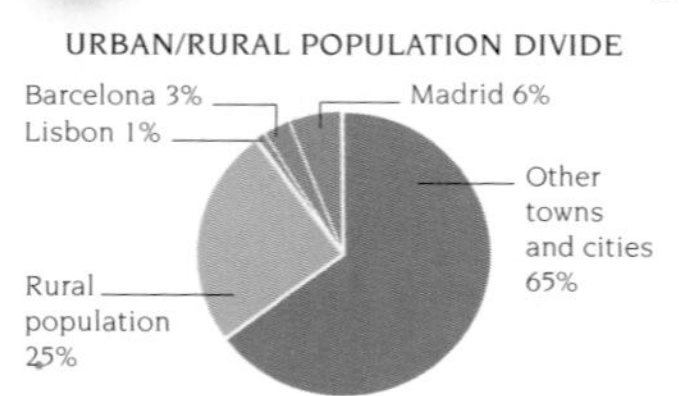

URBAN/RURAL POPULATION DIVIDE
Barcelona 3%
Lisbon 1%
Madrid 6%
Other towns and cities 65%
Rural population 25%

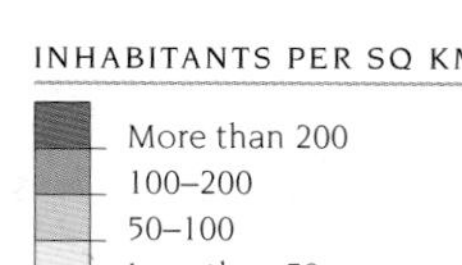

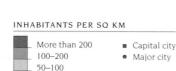

INHABITANTS PER SQ KM
More than 200
100–200
50–100
Less than 50
Capital city
Major city

FARMING AND LAND USE

Cereals, especially wheat and barley, are Iberia's chief crops. In the dry south of Spain, the land is irrigated to grow citrus fruits, especially oranges, and vegetables. In both countries, olive trees and vineyards occupy large areas of land; olive oil and wine are important exports. Cork oak trees from Iberia's forests supply 80% of the world's cork.

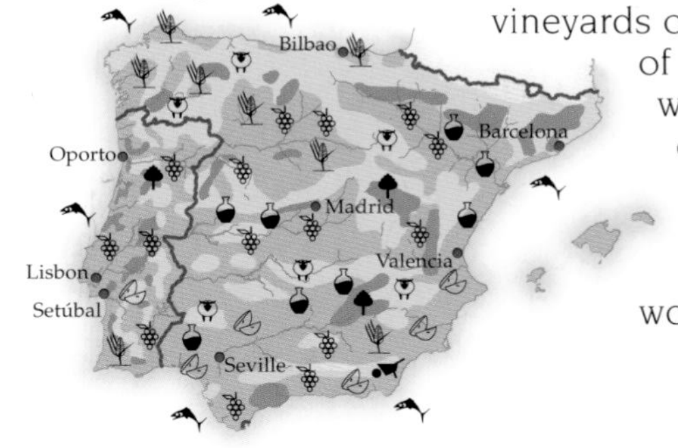

Bilbao
Oporto
Barcelona
Madrid
Valencia
Lisbon
Setúbal
Seville

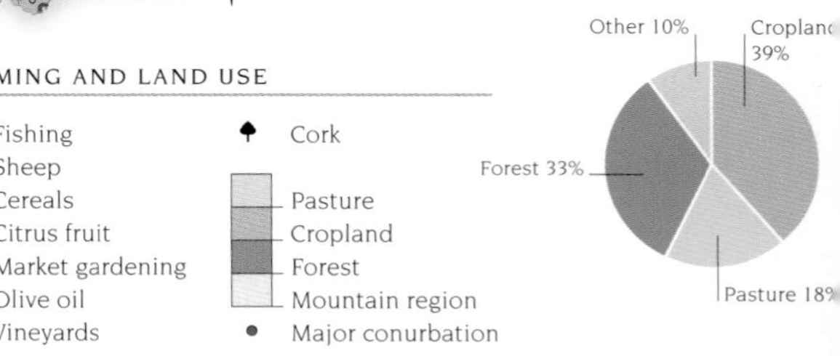

FARMING AND LAND USE
Fishing
Sheep
Cereals
Citrus fruit
Market gardening
Olive oil
Vineyards
Cork
Pasture
Cropland
Forest
Mountain region
Major conurbation
LAND USE
Other 10%
Cropland 39%
Forest 33%
Pasture 18%

THE LANDSCAPE

Most of inland Spain is taken up by the Meseta a dry, almost treeless plateau surrounded by steep mountain ranges. The only lowlands, apart from narrow strips along the Mediterranean coast are the valleys of the Ebro, Tagus, Guadiana and Guadalquivir rivers. Portugal's coast is lined by wide plains. Inland, the River Tagus divides the country in two. To the north the land is hilly and wooded; to the south it is low-lying and drier.

Westward-flowing rivers
The Duero, Tagus and Guadalquivir rivers flow across the Meseta on their courses to the Atlantic Ocean.

River Ebro (E 2)
The River Ebro carries vital irrigation water to Spain's northeastern plains before flowing into the Mediterranean Sea.

Cordillera Cantábrica (C 1)
These rugged, forested mountains rise on Spain's Atlantic coast. They form the northern edge of the Meseta.

The Pyrenees (F 2)
These high mountains form a natural boundary with France.

River Duero (D 2)

River Tagus (B 4)

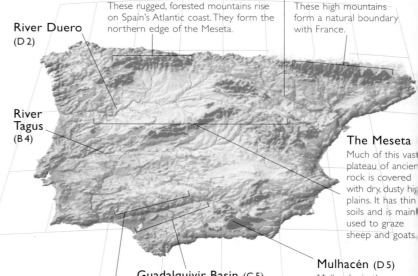

The Meseta
Much of this vast plateau of ancient rock is covered with dry, dusty high plains. It has thin soils and is mainly used to graze sheep and goats.

Sierra Morena (C 5)
The southern end of the Meseta is marked by this low range of mountains.

Guadalquivir Basin (C 5)
The River Guadalquivir has deposited layers of rich soil called alluvium on its flood plain, making this one of Spain's most fertile regions.

Mulhacén (D 5)
Mulhacén, in the snow-capped Sierra Nevada range in southern Spain is 3,481 m high. It is Iberia's tallest mountain

ENVIRONMENTAL ISSUES

Soil erosion – where the top layer of soil has been worn away by wind and rain – has affected much of the Iberian Peninsula. This is caused by farming, combined with drought and deforestation. In Spain, a national tree-planting scheme has been started to combat this problem. Industrial and tourist development along the Mediterranean coast of Spain, and in the Balearic Islands, has damaged natural habitats on both land and sea.

CLIMATE

Northern Spain is wetter and cooler than the south. On the central plateau, summers are very hot and dry, and winters often freezing. The north of Portugal is cooled by winds blowing off the Atlantic Ocean. The south is warmer, with dry, mild winters.

EUROPE
Spain and Portugal
NORTH AMERICA
ASIA
AFRICA
SOUTH AMERICA
AUSTRALASIA AND OCEANIA
ANTARCTICA
ENVIRONMENTAL ISSUES
Major oil spill
Overbuilding
Soil degradation
Severe soil degradation
Polluted rivers
Sea pollution
Aegean Sea 1992
Prestige 2002
Douro
Ebro
Guadiana
Guadalquivir
Segura
Costa Brava
Majorca
Ibiza
Costa Blanca
Costa del Sol
TEMPERATURE AND PRECIPITATION
More than 25°C
20 to 25°C
15 to 20°C
10 to 15°C
5 to 10°C
0 to 5°C
0 to -5°C
-5 to -10°C
Less than -10°C
100 Precipitation (mm)
January
July
Bay of Biscay
Costa Verde
FRANCE
ANDORRA
Pyrenees
Gulf of Lion
Cordillera Cantábrica
Sistema Ibérico
Sistema Central
Sierra de Gredos
Sierra de Guadarrama
Sierra Morena
Sistemas Béticos
Sierra Nevada
Serra da Estrela
SPAIN
PORTUGAL
MADRID
LISBON (LISBOA)
A Coruña (La Coruña)
Gijón (Xixón)
Oviedo
Santander
Bilbao
Donostia/San Sebastián
Vitoria-Gasteiz
Pamplona (Iruña)
León
Burgos
Logroño
Valladolid
Zaragoza
Lleida (Lérida)
Barcelona
L'Hospitalet de Llobregat
Sabadell
Terrassa
Tarragona
Salamanca
Getafe
Vigo
Ourense (Orense)
Oporto (Porto)
Vila Nova de Gaia
Matosinhos
Coimbra
Badajoz
Castellón de la Plana
Valencia
Albacete
Alicante (Alacant)
Elche (Elx)
Murcia
Cartagena
Córdoba
Jaén
Seville (Sevilla)
Huelva
Granada
Málaga
Cádiz
Algeciras
GIBRALTAR (UK dependent territory)
Ceuta (part of Spain)
MOROCCO
ALGERIA
Strait of Gibraltar
Gulf of Cadiz (Golfo de Cádiz)
Mediterranean Sea
Gulf of Valencia
Costa del Azahar
Costa Blanca
Costa Brava
Costa del Sol
Balearic Islands (Islas Baleares)
Majorca (Mallorca)
Minorca (Menorca)
Ibiza
Formentera
Palma
Galicia
Asturias
Cantabria
The Basque Country (País Vasco)
Navarra
La Rioja
Aragón
Cataluña (Catalonia)
Castilla-León
Castilla-La Mancha
Extremadura
Andalusia (Andalucía)
Murcia
País Valenciano
Algarve
Monte Perdido 3348m
Mulhacén 3481m
Javalambre 2020m
Alto da Torre 1993m
Cabo Fisterra
Cabo de São Vicente
Tagus
LAND HEIGHT
2000–4000 m
1000–2000 m
500–1000 m
250–500 m
100–250 m
0–100 m
SEA DEPTH
0–250 m
250–500 m
500–1000 m
1000–2000 m
2000–3000 m
3000–4000 m
Below 4000 m
CITIES AND TOWNS
Over 500,000 people
100,000–500,000
50,000–100,000
Less than 50,000
SCALE BAR
0 km 50 100
0 miles 50 100

GERMANY AND THE ALPINE STATES

AUSTRIA, GERMANY, LIECHTENSTEIN, SLOVENIA, SWITZERLAND

Germany lies at the heart of Europe and is the biggest industrial power in the continent. In 1945, Germany was divided into two separate countries, East and West Germany, which were reunited in 1990. To the south, the snow-capped peaks of the Alps, Europe's highest mountains, tower over the Alpine states – Switzerland, Austria, Liechtenstein and the former Yugoslavian state of Slovenia.

INDUSTRY

Germany is a leading manufacturer of cars, chemicals, machinery and transport equipment. Switzerland and Liechtenstein, with few raw materials, make high-value products such as watches and pharmaceuticals, and provide services such as banking. The Alpine states are a popular tourist location all year round.

INDUSTRY

- Aerospace
- Car manufacture
- Chemicals
- Engineering
- Iron & steel
- Shipbuilding
- Pharmaceuticals
- Finance
- Hi-tech industry
- Tourism
- Major industrial centre / area
- Major road

STRUCTURE OF INDUSTRY

Primary 1%
Services 68%
Manufacturing 31%

POPULATION

Western and central Germany are the most densely populated areas in this region – particularly in and around the Rhine and Ruhr valleys, where there are many industries. In the south, the steep slopes of the Alps and permanent snow cover on the higher peaks means that most large towns and cities are in scattered lowland areas.

INHABITANTS PER SQ KM

- More than 200
- 100–200
- 50–100
- Less than 50
- Capital city
- Major city

URBAN/RURAL POPULATION DIVIDE

Hamburg 1.8%
Berlin 3.5%
Viena 1.7%
Rural population 16%
Other towns and cities 77%

FARMING AND LAND USE

Germany produces three-quarters of its own food. Crop farming is widespread, with cereals and root crops grown in flat, fertile areas. Cattle and pig farming supplies meat and dairy products. Across the Alps, the mountains limit farming, although vines are grown on the warmer, south-facing slopes. The rich pastures of the lower slopes are used to graze beef and dairy cattle.

FARMING AND LAND USE

- Cattle
- Pigs
- Cereals
- Root crops
- Vineyards
- Pasture
- Cropland
- Forest
- Mountain region
- Major conurbation

LAND USE

Forest 33%
Other (including mountains) 20%
Pasture 18%
Cropland 29%

THE LANDSCAPE

To the north, flat plains and heathlands surround the North Sea coast. Further south are Germany's central uplands, which are lower and older than the jagged peaks of the Alps, which began to form about 65 million years ago. From its source in the Black Forest, the River Danube flows eastward across Germany and Austria on its course to the Black Sea. The other major river, the Rhine, flows northward.

The River Rhine (B5)
The Rhine is Germany's main waterway. It is an important transport route to and from northern ports. It twists and turns across 1,320 km of Europe, from its source in southeast Switzerland, to the North Sea.

The Danube (B7)
The Danube is Europe's second longest river, flowing 2,840 km.

Lake Constance (B7)
Lake Constance covers 540 sq km and is Germany's largest lake, although its waters are shared by Austria and Switzerland.

The Harz mountains (C4)
These rugged, wooded mountains are much older than the Alps. They were formed over 300 million years ago.

Karst region (E8)
Most of the water in this limestone region of Slovenia flows underground, through huge caves and caverns.

The Alps (C8)
The Alps were formed when the African Plate collided with the Eurasian Plate, pushing up and crushing huge amounts of rock, to form mountains.

EUROPE
Germany and the Alpine States
NORTH AMERICA
SOUTH AMERICA
AFRICA
ASIA
AUSTRALASIA AND OCEANIA
ANTARCTICA
ENVIRONMENTAL ISSUES
The large number of industries in Germany, especially in the east of the country, has led to high levels of pollution in cities, and in rivers like the Rhine. Acid rain from car fumes and industrial pollution has poisoned many of Germany's forests. The popularity of the Alps as a year-round tourist destination puts great demands on the environment. The development of new resorts has destroyed the natural habitats of many plants and animals.
ENVIRONMENTAL ISSUES
Urban air pollution
Flooding
Winter tourist resort
Affected by acid rain
Polluted rivers
Major industrial centre
Elbe
2006
Berlin
Bitterfeld
Ruhr Valley
Leipzig
2002
Frankfurt am Main
Rhine
Munich
Danube
Interlaken
Zermatt
St. Moritz
Badgastein
CLIMATE
Winter temperatures decrease eastwards, and the high Alpine region is coldest. Rainfall is higher in the summer. Climate variations in the Alps are common, due to turbulent air flows.
January
July
TEMPERATURE AND PRECIPITATION
More than 20°C
15 to 20°C
10 to 15°C
5 to 10°C
0 to 5°C
0 to -5°C
-5 to -10°C
Less than -10°C
100 Precipitation (mm)
SCALE BAR
CITIES AND TOWNS
Over 500,000 people
100,000–500,000
50,000–100,000
Less than 50,000
LAND HEIGHT
Above 4000 m
2000–4000 m
1000–2000 m
500–1000 m
250–500 m
100–250 m
0–100 m
SEA DEPTH
0–10 m
10–25 m
25–50 m
50–100 m
DENMARK
SWEDEN
GERMANY
POLAND
CZECH REPUBLIC
AUSTRIA
SWITZERLAND
LIECHTENSTEIN
SLOVAKIA
HUNGARY
SLOVENIA
CROATIA
ITALY
BOSNIA AND HERZEGOVINA
North Sea
Baltic Sea
Gulf of Venice
BERLIN
VIENNA (WIEN)
BERN
VADUZ
LJUBLJANA
Hamburg
Munich (München)
Cologne (Köln)
Frankfurt am Main
Stuttgart
Dresden
Leipzig
Hanover (Hannover)
Nuremberg (Nürnberg)
Salzburg
Innsbruck
Graz
Linz
Zürich
Basel
Geneva (Genève)

ITALY

ITALY, SAN MARINO, VATICAN CITY

Italy has played an important role in Europe since the Romans based their mighty empire here over 2,000 years ago. The famous boot shape divides into two very different halves. Northern Italy has a varied range of industries and agriculture. Beautiful cities like Venice, Florence, and Rome draw tourists from all over the world. Southern Italy is poorer and less developed than the north, with a hotter, drier climate and less productive land.

THE LANDSCAPE

Italy is a peninsula jutting south from mainland Europe into the Mediterranean Sea. In northern and central Italy the land is mainly mountainous. Most of the flat land is in the Po Valley and along the eastern coast. Italy lies within an earthquake zone, which makes the land unstable, and there are also a number of active volcanoes.

Po Valley (C2)
The basin of the River Po has the best soils in Italy. Rich alluvium is washed from the mountains by the river to form a wide plain.

Italian lakes
Great lakes like Garda (B3) and Como (B2) fill several south-facing valleys once occupied by glaciers.

The Dolomites (D2)
These high mountains are part of the same range as the Alps. They were formed 65 million years ago.

Earthquakes
The southern Apennines, as well as coastal areas of southwestern Italy, often experience earthquakes and mudslides.

The Apennines (C4)
This mountain range forms the 'backbone' of Italy, dividing the rocky west coast from the flatter, sandy east coast.

Tyrrhenian Sea (C6)
This sea, which divides the Italian mainland from Sardinia, is gradually filling with sediment from the rivers which flow into it.

Sardinia
The island of Sardinia is made from very old rocks which were thrust up to form mountains.

Sicily
Sicily is the largest island in the Mediterranean. It has a famous active volcano called Mount Etna, and often experiences earthquakes

Gulf of Taranto (F7)
During earthquakes, great blocks of land have broken away and sunk into the sea, forming the Gulf's square shape.

FARMING AND LAND USE

The Po Valley is a broad, flat plain in the north of Italy. It contains the most fertile land in the country, and wheat and rice are the main cereal crops grown here. Grapes for wine are grown everywhere in Italy. In much of the south, the land must be irrigated to support crops. Where there is enough water, citrus fruits, olives, and many kinds of tomatoes are grown.

LAND USE
Cropland 37%
Pasture 15%
Forest 34%
Other 14%

FARMING AND LAND USE
Cattle
Pigs
Sheep
Cereals
Citrus fruits
Olive oil
Rice
Vineyards
Pasture
Cropland
Forest
Mountain region
Major conurbation

INDUSTRY

Italian industry is located mainly in the north. Design is extremely important to Italians and they are proud of the elegant designs of their furniture, clothes and shoes. Though many firms are small, they are very efficient. Italy has few mineral resources so it needs to import raw materials to make cars, engines and other hi-tech products.

INDUSTRY
Car manufacture
Chemicals
Iron & steel
Textiles
Finance
Hi-tech industry
Tourism
Major industrial centre / area
Major road

STRUCTURE OF INDUSTRY

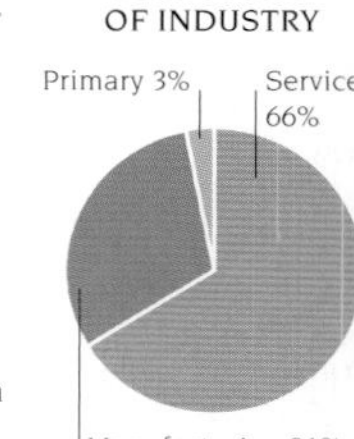
Primary 3%
Services 66%
Manufacturing 31%

POPULATION

Most of Italy's population lives in the north, mainly in and around the Po Valley, which is home to over 25 million people. Most people here have a high standard of living. Southern Italy is much more rural; towns are smaller and life is often much harder.

URBAN/RURAL POPULATION DIVIDE

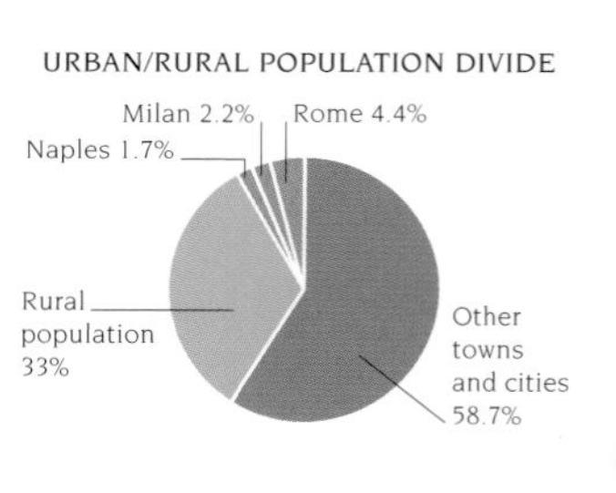
Milan 2.2%
Rome 4.4%
Naples 1.7%
Rural population 33%
Other towns and cities 58.7%

INHABITANTS PER SQ KM

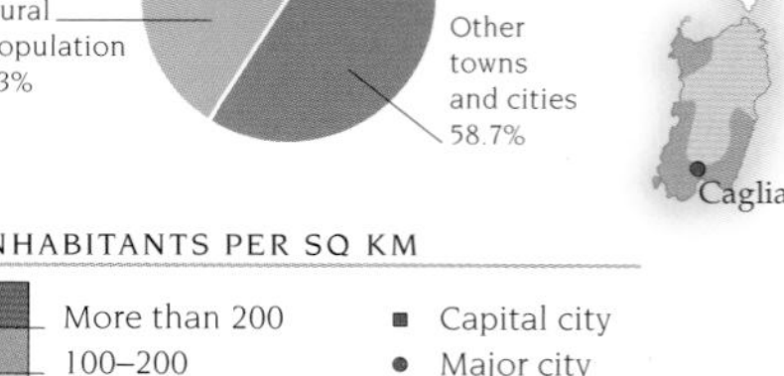
More than 200
100–200
50–100
0–50
Capital city
Major city

ENVIRONMENTAL ISSUES
Sewage and chemical by-products from industry have polluted the Mediterranean and Adriatic seas. Southern Italy is subject to natural dangers like volcanoes, earthquakes and mudslides. Mount Etna is one of the most active volcanoes in the world.
ENVIRONMENTAL ISSUES
Catastrophic earthquakes
Urban air pollution
Affected by acid rain
Sea pollution
Severe sea pollution
Major industrial centre
Turin
Milan
Genoa
Gemona del Friuli 1976
Emilia 2012
Ancona 1972
Colfiorito 1997
Tuscania 1971
L'Aquila 2009
Rome
Isernia 1984
Foggia 2002
Naples
Irpino 1980
Palermo
Belice 1968
Sicily
Etna
Syracuse 1990
CLIMATE
The Alpine north has cold winters, often with snow. Further south, temperatures are higher. Sicily has Italy's highest temperatures, due to warm African winds.
January
July
TEMPERATURE AND PRECIPITATION
More than 25°C
20 to 25°C
15 to 20°C
10 to 15°C
5 to 10°C
0 to 5°C
0 to -5°C
-5 to -10°C
Less than -10°C
100 Precipitation (mm)
Less than 50
EUROPE
Italy
NORTH AMERICA
SOUTH AMERICA
AFRICA
ASIA
AUSTRALASIA AND OCEANIA
ANTARCTICA
GERMANY
SWITZERLAND
LIECHTENSTEIN
AUSTRIA
SLOVENIA
CROATIA
SAN MARINO
VATICAN CITY
MALTA
TUNISIA
Lake Constance
Lake Geneva
Brenner Pass 1374m
Mont Blanc 4807m
Great Saint Bernard Pass 2469m
Gran Paradiso 4061m
Dolomites
Lombardy (Lombardia)
Piedmont (Piemonte)
Milan (Milano)
Turin (Torino)
Genoa (Genova)
Venice (Venezia)
Padua (Padova)
Florence (Firenze)
ROME (ROMA)
Naples (Napoli)
Tuscany (Toscana)
Campania
Apulia (Puglia)
Sardegna (Sardinia)
Sicilia (Sicily)
Corsica (Corse) (part of France)
Mount Etna 3340m
Vesuvius 1277m
Punta La Marmora 1834m
Ligurian Sea
Tyrrhenian Sea
Adriatic Sea
Ionian Sea
Mediterranean Sea
Gulf of Genoa
Gulf of Venice
Gulf of Gaeta
Gulf of Salerno
Gulf of Taranto
Strait of Bonifacio
Strait of Sicily
Strait of Messina
Strait of Otranto
Malta Channel
Aeolian Islands
Stromboli
Lipari
Vulcano
Egadi Is.
Pantelleria
Pelagie
Isola d' Ustica
Ponziane Is.
Capri
Elba
Archipelago Toscano
Dalmatia
Istra
La Sila
SCALE BAR
0 km 40 80
0 miles 40 80
CITIES AND TOWNS
Over 500,000 people
100,000–500,000
50,000–100,000
Less than 50,000
LAND HEIGHT
Above 4000 m
2000–4000 m
1000–2000 m
500–1000 m
250–500 m
100–250 m
0–100 m
SEA DEPTH
0–50 m
50–100 m
100–250 m
250–500 m
500–1000 m
1000–2000 m
Below 2000 m

Central Europe

CZECH REPUBLIC, HUNGARY, POLAND, SLOVAKIA

Central Europe has been invaded many times throughout history. The countries have changed shape frequently as their borders have shifted backwards and forwards. From the end of the Second World War until 1989, they were ruled by communist governments, which were supported by the Soviet Union. In 1993, the state of Czechoslovakia voted to split into two separate nations, called the Czech Republic and Slovakia.

FARMING AND LAND USE

Central Europe's main crops are cereals such as maize, wheat and rye, along with sugar beet and potatoes. In Hungary, sweet peppers grow, helped by the warm summers and mild winters. They are used to make paprika. Grapes are also grown, to make wine. Large areas of the plains of Hungary and Poland are used for rearing pigs and cattle. Trees for timber grow in the mountains of Slovakia and the Czech Republic.

FARMING AND LAND USE
Cattle
Pigs
Cereals
Root crops
Potatoes
Timber
Vineyards
Pasture
Cropland
Forest
Major conurbation

LAND USE

Cropland 47%
Other 11%
Forest 29%
Pasture 13%

INDUSTRY

Brown coal, or lignite, is central Europe's main fuel, and one of Poland's major exports. A variety of minerals are mined in the mountains of the Czech Republic and Slovakia. Hungary has a wide range of industries producing vehicles, metals, and chemicals, as well as textiles and electrical goods. The Czech Republic is famous for its breweries and glass-making.

STRUCTURE OF INDUSTRY

Primary 3%
Services 65%
Manufacturing 32%

INDUSTRY
Brewing
Car manufacture
Chemicals
Engineering
Food processing
Iron & steel
Coal mining
Major industrial centre / area
Major road

THE LANDSCAPE

The high Carpathian Mountains sweep across northern Slovakia. The lower Sudeten Mountains lie on the border of the Czech Republic and Poland. Together, these mountains form a barrier which divides the Great Hungarian Plain and the River Danube basin in the south from Poland and the vast rolling lowlands of the North European Plain.

Pomerania (C2)
This is a sandy coastal area with lakes formed by glaciers. It stretches west from the River Vistula to just beyond the German border.

River Vistula (F4)
Poland's largest river is the Vistula. It flows northwards, passing through the capital, Warsaw, on its way to the Baltic Sea.

North European Plain

Hot springs
The Sudeten mountains (C5) are famous for their hot mineral springs. These occur where water heated deep within the Earth's crust finds its way to the surface along fractures in the rock.

River Danube (D7)
The River Danube forms the border between Slovakia and Hungary for over 162 km. It then turns south to flow across the Great Hungarian Plain.

Great Hungarian Plain (E8)
This huge plain covers almost half of Hungary's land area. It is a mixture of farmland and steppe.

Tatra Mountains (E6)
The Tatra Mountains are a small range at the northern end of the Carpathian Mountains. They include Gerlachovský Stít, which is Central Europe's highest point at 2,655 m.

ENVIRONMENTAL ISSUES

The growth of heavy industries that took place under communist rule has caused terrible environmental pollution in some places. Hungary's oil and Poland's brown coal have a high sulphur content. Burning these fuels to produce electricity causes air pollution, and the sulphur dioxide produced combines with moisture in the air, leading to acid rain.

ENVIRONMENTAL ISSUES
Severe industrial pollution
Flooding
Urban air pollution
Affected by acid rain
Polluted rivers
Major industrial centre

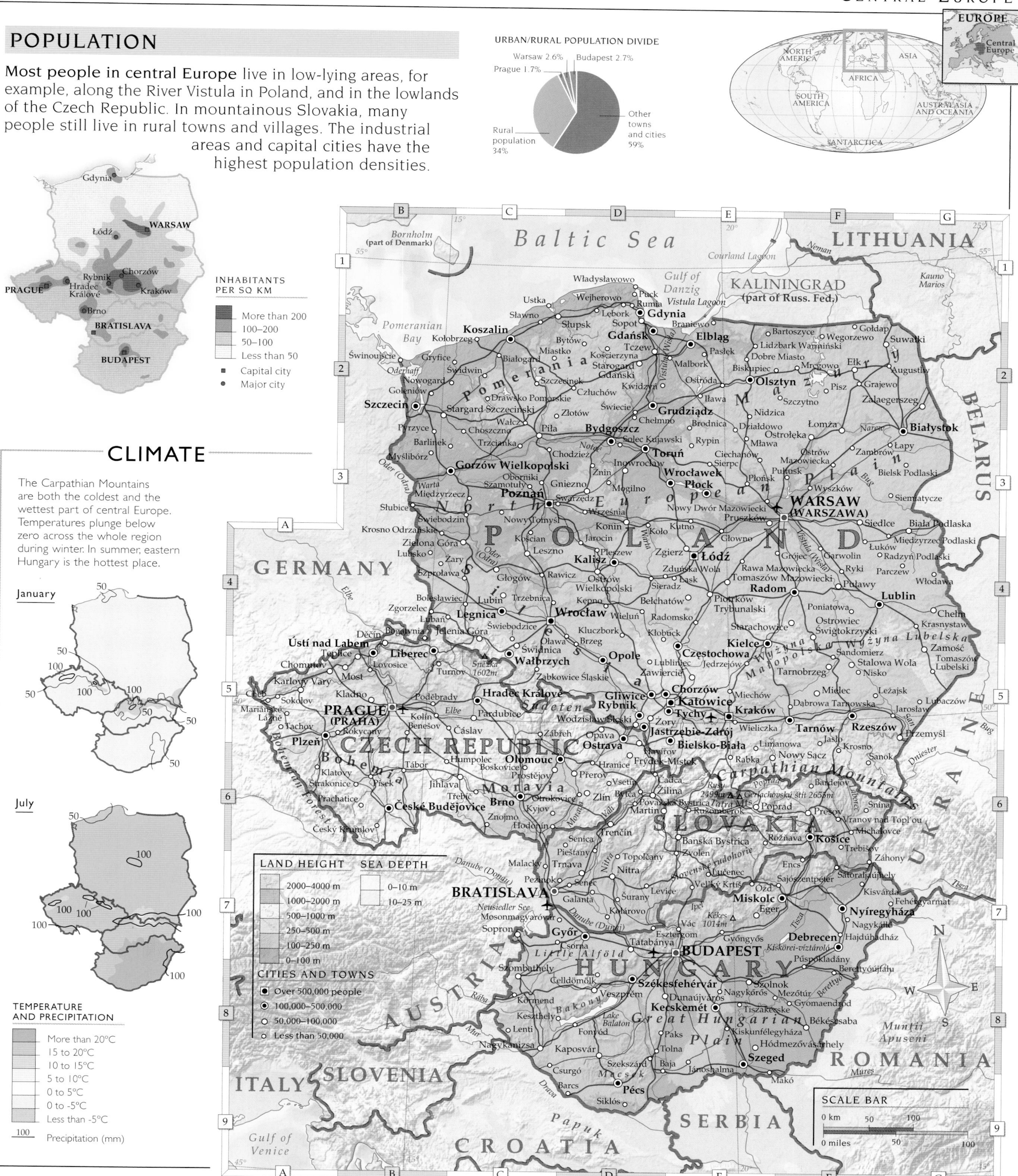
EUROPE
Central Europe
NORTH AMERICA
ASIA
AFRICA
SOUTH AMERICA
AUSTRALASIA AND OCEANIA
ANTARCTICA
URBAN/RURAL POPULATION DIVIDE
Warsaw 2.6%
Budapest 2.7%
Prague 1.7%
Other towns and cities 59%
Rural population 34%
INHABITANTS PER SQ KM
More than 200
100–200
50–100
Less than 50
Capital city
Major city
Gdynia
WARSAW
Łódź
Rybnik
Chorzów
PRAGUE
Hradec Králové
Kraków
Brno
BRATISLAVA
BUDAPEST
January
July
TEMPERATURE AND PRECIPITATION
More than 20°C
15 to 20°C
10 to 15°C
5 to 10°C
0 to 5°C
0 to -5°C
Less than -5°C
100 Precipitation (mm)
Baltic Sea
LITHUANIA
KALININGRAD (part of Russ. Fed.)
BELARUS
POLAND
GERMANY
CZECH REPUBLIC
SLOVAKIA
UKRAINE
HUNGARY
AUSTRIA
SLOVENIA
ITALY
CROATIA
SERBIA
ROMANIA
Carpathian Mountains
LAND HEIGHT
2000–4000 m
1000–2000 m
500–1000 m
250–500 m
100–250 m
0–100 m
SEA DEPTH
0–10 m
10–25 m
CITIES AND TOWNS
Over 500,000 people
100,000–500,000
50,000–100,000
Less than 50,000
SCALE BAR
0 km 50 100
0 miles 50 100

POPULATION

Most people in central Europe live in low-lying areas, for example, along the River Vistula in Poland, and in the lowlands of the Czech Republic. In mountainous Slovakia, many people still live in rural towns and villages. The industrial areas and capital cities have the highest population densities.

CLIMATE

The Carpathian Mountains are both the coldest and the wettest part of central Europe. Temperatures plunge below zero across the whole region during winter. In summer, eastern Hungary is the hottest place.

Southeast Europe

ALBANIA, BOSNIA AND HERZEGOVINA, BULGARIA, CROATIA, GREECE, KOSOVO, MACEDONIA, MONTENEGRO, SERBIA

Southeast Europe extends inland from the coasts of the Aegean, Adriatic and Black seas. Ancient Greece was the birthplace of European civilization. Albania and Bulgaria were ruled by communists for over 50 years, until the early 1990s. The rest of the region was part of a communist union of states called Yugoslavia. The collapse of this union in 1991 led to a civil war, after which seven separate countries emerged.

THE LANDSCAPE

Southeast Europe is largely mountainous, with ranges running from northwest to southeast. The Dinaric Alps run parallel to the Dalmatian coast, and the Pindus Mountains continue this line into Greece. In the Aegean Sea, the drowned peaks of an old mountain chain form thousands of islands.

Earthquakes

Bulgaria, Greece, and Macedonia lie in earthquake zones. Major earthquakes have hit the Ionian Islands in 1953, and Macedonia in 1963.

Great Hungarian Plain (D 1)

The Vojvodina region of Serbia is the southern part of the Great Hungarian Plain. The plain is flat and fertile soils allow grain crops like corn and wheat to be grown.

Dinaric Alps (C 2)

Balkan Mountains (F 3)

The mountains form a spur running east to west through Bulgaria and separate the two main rivers, the Danube and the Maritsa.

Dalmatian coast (B 2)

The Dalmatian coast has many long, narrow islands near the shore. These were formed as the Adriatic Sea flooded the river valleys which ran parallel to the coast.

Greek Islands

The Peloponnese (E 6)

The Peloponnese is a mountainous peninsula linked to the Greek mainland only by a narrow strip of land, only 6 km wide, called the Isthmus of Corinth.

Greek Islands

There are two groups of Greek Islands, the Ionian Islands to the west of mainland Greece, and the more numerous islands to the east in the Aegean Sea.

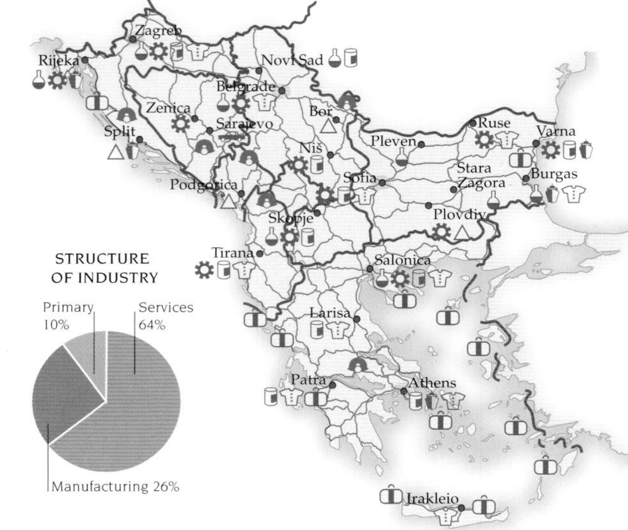
Rijeka
Zagreb
Novi Sad
Belgrade
Zenica
Bor
Split
Sarajevo
Nis
Pleven
Ruse
Varna
Stara Zagora
Burgas
Podgorica
Sofia
Plovdiv
Skopje
Tirana
Salonica
Larisa
Patra
Athens
Irakleio
STRUCTURE OF INDUSTRY
Primary 10%
Services 64%
Manufacturing 26%

FARMING AND LAND USE

Cereals like wheat, and fruits, vegetables and grapes are grown in the fertile north of the region. The band of mountains across southeast Europe is used mainly for grazing sheep and goats. Further south, and in coastal areas, the warm Mediterranean climate is ideal for growing grapes, olives and tobacco.

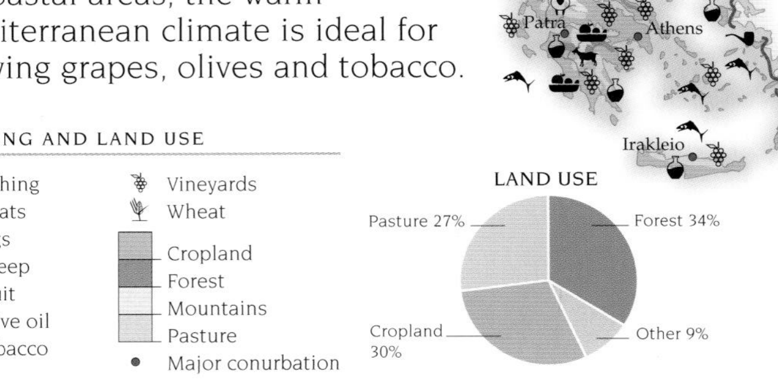
FARMING AND LAND USE
Fishing
Goats
Pigs
Sheep
Fruit
Olive oil
Tobacco
Vineyards
Wheat
Cropland
Forest
Mountains
Pasture
Major conurbation
LAND USE
Pasture 27%
Forest 34%
Cropland 30%
Other 9%

INDUSTRY

Mainland Greece and the many islands in the Aegean Sea are centres of a thriving tourist trade, while tourism on the Black Sea coast continues to grow. The Dalmatian coast's growing tourist industry is recovering after the civil war in former Yugoslavia disrupted it, and other industries. Heavy industries like chemicals, engineering and shipbuilding remain an important source of income in Bulgaria.

INDUSTRY
Car manufacture
Chemicals
Engineering
Food processing
Metal refining
Shipbuilding
Textiles
Mining
Tourism
Major industrial centre / area
Major road

POPULATION

Greece's population is two thirds urban; over 35% live in the capital, Athens and in Salonica. In Bulgaria, most people live in cities. About half of Albania's and Macedonia's people are still rural. Since the civil war, the different ethnic groups in Bosnia and Herzegovina, Montenegro, Serbia and Croatia have lived apart from one another.

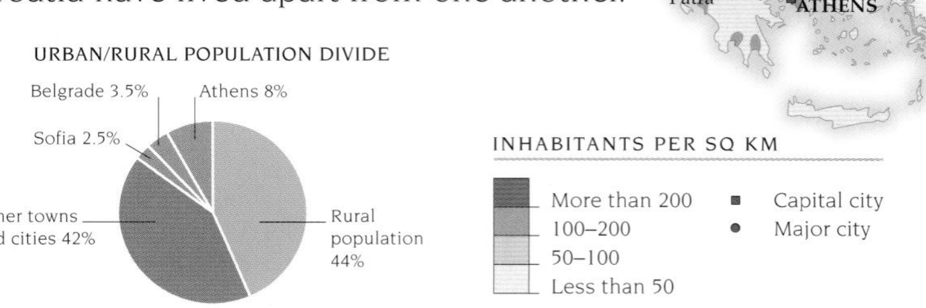
URBAN/RURAL POPULATION DIVIDE
Belgrade 3.5%
Athens 8%
Sofia 2.5%
Other towns and cities 42%
Rural population 44%
INHABITANTS PER SQ KM
More than 200
100–200
50–100
Less than 50
Capital city
Major city

CLIMATE
Southeastern Europe's climate varies from north to south. Continental climates are found in the north; winters are cold and dry, while towards the south, winters are milder and summers much hotter. Europe's wettest place is found in the mountains in Bosnia and Herzegovina.
January
July
TEMPERATURE AND PRECIPITATION
More than 25°C
20 to 25°C
15 to 20°C
10 to 15°C
5 to 10°C
0 to 5°C
0 to -5°C
Less than -5°C
100 Precipitation (mm)
EUROPE
Southeast Europe
NORTH AMERICA
SOUTH AMERICA
AFRICA
ASIA
AUSTRALASIA AND OCEANIA
ANTARCTICA
SCALE BAR
0 km 50 100
0 miles 50 100
CITIES AND TOWNS
Over 500,000 people
100,000–500,000
50,000–100,000
Less than 50,000
AUSTRIA
SLOVENIA
HUNGARY
CROATIA
BOSNIA AND HERZEGOVINA
SERBIA
ROMANIA
BULGARIA
MONTENEGRO
KOSOVO (disputed)
ALBANIA
MACEDONIA
GREECE
TURKEY
MOLDOVA
UKRAINE
SAN MARINO
ZAGREB
BELGRADE (BEOGRAD)
SARAJEVO
PODGORICA
PRISHTINË
SKOPJE
TIRANA (TIRANË)
SOFIA (SOFIYA)
ATHENS (ATHINA)
Adriatic Sea
Ionian Sea
Black Sea
Aegean Sea
Sea of Crete (Kritikó Pélagos)
Mediterranean Sea
Strait of Otranto
Sea of Marmara
Thracian Sea
Mirtoan Sea
Danube
Balkan Mountains
Rhodope Mountains
Pindus Mountains
Dinaric Alps
Crete (Kriti)
Rhodes (Rodos)
Cyclades (Kyklades)
Dodecanese (Dodekanisa)
LAND HEIGHT
2000–4000 m
1000–2000 m
500–1000 m
250–500 m
100–250 m
0–100 m
SEA DEPTH
0–50 m
50–100 m
100–250 m
250–500 m
500–1000 m
1000–2000 m
Below 2000 m
ENVIRONMENTAL ISSUES
Emissions from industry and traffic fumes have polluted the air in Athens and Zagreb. In Athens, smog from vehicle exhausts can be severe as it gets trapped in the city's natural basin. The situation is made worse because many residents drive, rather than use public transport. Earthquakes are possible; Macedonia's capital city, Skopje, was badly hit in 1963.
Zagreb
Belgrade
Danube
Sofia
Skopje 1963
Salonica 1978
Athens
ENVIRONMENTAL ISSUES
Catastrophic earthquake
Urban air pollution
Risk of wild fire
Sea pollution
Severe sea pollution
Polluted river
Major town

Eastern Europe

BELARUS, MOLDOVA, ROMANIA, UKRAINE

Much of Eastern Europe, which extends north from the River Danube and the Black Sea, is covered by open grasslands called steppe. Ukraine's excellent farmland and large mineral reserves make it one of the strongest new countries to emerge from the former Soviet Union. Moldova and Belarus were also part of the USSR, until they became independent in 1991. Romania joined the Europen Union in 2007.

POPULATION

Many Romanians still live in rural areas, although Bucharest, the capital, is home to six times as many people as the next largest city. In Ukraine, two-thirds of the population live in cities such as those in the Donbass industrial area. Most of Belarus's people are city dwellers. Moldova is the most rural country in Eastern Europe; over half live in the countryside.

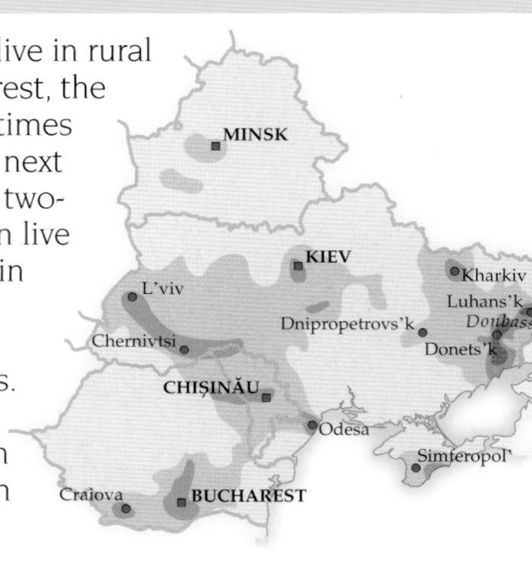

MINSK
KIEV
L'viv
Kharkiv
Luhans'k
Donbass
Dnipropetrovs'k
Donets'k
Chernivtsi
CHIŞINĂU
Odesa
Simferopol'
Craiova
BUCHAREST

URBAN/RURAL POPULATION DIVIDE

Bucharest 2.3%
Kiev 3.1%
Minsk 2.1%
Rural population 36%
Other towns and cities 56.5%

INHABITANTS PER SQ KM

More than 200
100–200
50–100
Less than 50
Capital city
Major city

INDUSTRY

In Ukraine, most industry is based around the country's mineral reserves. The Donbass region has Europe's largest coalfield and is an important centre for iron and steel production. Belarus's main industries are chemicals, machine building and food-processing. Romania's manufacturing industries are growing, with the help of foreign investment.

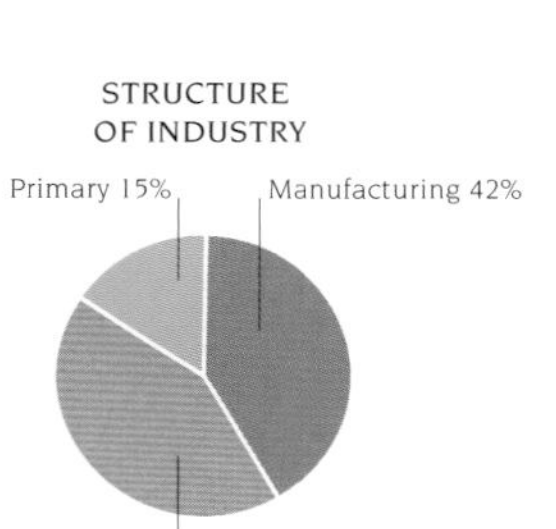

STRUCTURE OF INDUSTRY
Primary 15%
Manufacturing 42%
Services 43%

INDUSTRY
Aerospace
Car manufacture
Chemicals
Engineering
Food processing
Iron & steel
Textiles
Coal
Mining
Oil and gas
Tourism
Major industrial centre / area
Major road

THE LANDSCAPE

Flat or rolling grasslands, marshes and river flood plains cover almost all of Ukraine and Belarus. The Carpathian Mountains cross the southwestern corner of Ukraine and continue in a large arc-shaped chain of high peaks at the heart of Romania. Along the southern part of this chain, the Carpathians are called the Transylvanian Alps.

Pripet Marshes (C 3)
The Pripet Marshes in Belarus and Ukraine form the largest area of marshland in Europe.

The steppes
The steppes are great, wide grasslands which are found across eastern Europe and central Asia. Over 70% of the Ukrainian landscape is steppe. Little rain falls throughout the steppes.

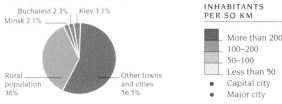

Carpathian Mountains (C 5)
The Carpathians are the largest mountain range in Eastern Europe. They are a rich source of timber and minerals.

Dnieper (E 5) **and Dniester** (D 5) **rivers**
The Dnieper and Dniester run south and east towards the Black Sea. They flow slowly across huge areas of low-lying land.

The Crimea (F 6)
This peninsula divides the Sea of Azov from the Black Sea. The steep mountains of Kryms'ki Hory run along the southeastern coast of the Crimea.

FARMING AND LAND USE

The black soils found across much of Ukraine are very fertile and the country is a big producer of cereals, sugar beet, and sunflowers, which are grown for their oil. In Moldova and southern Romania, the warm summers are ideal for growing grapes for wine, along with sunflowers and a variety of vegetables. Cattle and pigs are farmed throughout Eastern Europe.

Minsk
Brest
Kiev
L'viv
Kharkiv
Dnipropetrovs'k
Donets'k
Chişinău
Braşov
Simferopol'
Bucharest

LAND USE

Other 11%
Forest 24%
Pasture 15%
Cropland 50%

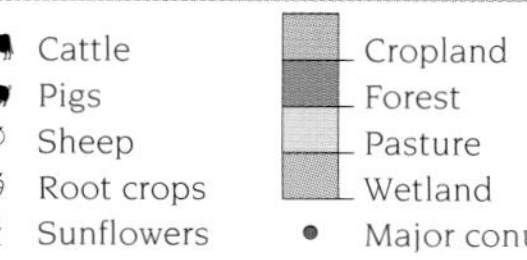

FARMING AND LAND USE
Cattle
Pigs
Sheep
Root crops
Sunflowers
Vineyards
Wheat
Cropland
Forest
Pasture
Wetland
Major conurbation

CLIMATE

The climate is continental, with warm, dry summers and very cold, dry winters. Temperatures are higher along the fringes of the Black Sea, while the Carpathian Mountains are colder and wetter all year round.

ENVIRONMENTAL ISSUES

The worst nuclear accident in history happened at Chornobyl' nuclear power station in northern Ukraine in 1986. Around 70% of the nuclear fallout was received by Belarus, contaminating its farmland, forests and water supplies. Four million Ukrainians still live in dangerously radioactive areas.

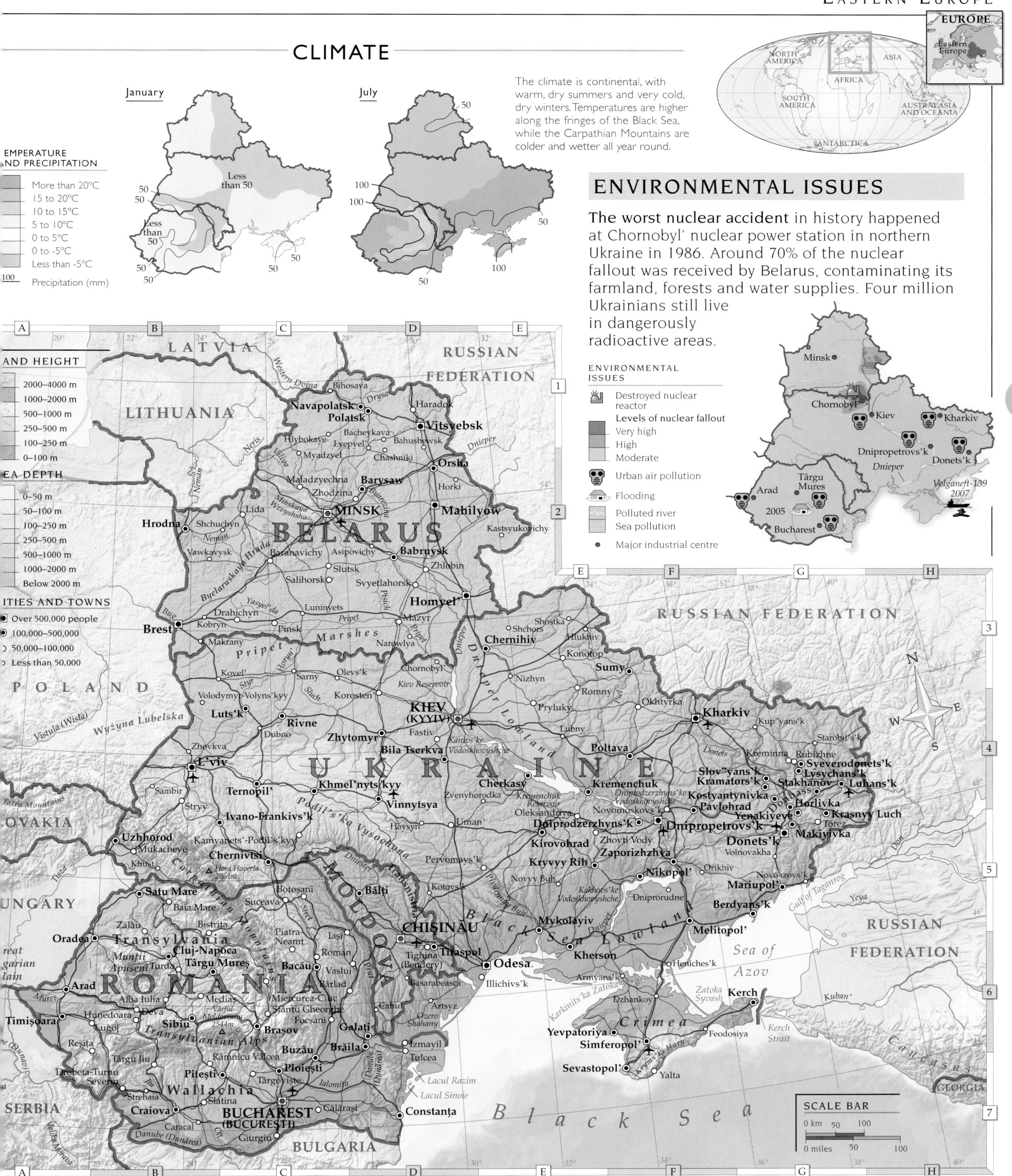
EUROPE
Eastern Europe
NORTH AMERICA
SOUTH AMERICA
AFRICA
ASIA
AUSTRALASIA AND OCEANIA
ANTARCTICA
January
July
Less than 50
EMPERATURE
ND PRECIPITATION
More than 20°C
15 to 20°C
10 to 15°C
5 to 10°C
0 to 5°C
0 to -5°C
Less than -5°C
Precipitation (mm)
ENVIRONMENTAL ISSUES
Destroyed nuclear reactor
Levels of nuclear fallout
Very high
High
Moderate
Urban air pollution
Flooding
Polluted river
Sea pollution
Major industrial centre
Minsk
Chornobyl'
Kiev
Kharkiv
Dnipropetrovs'k
Donets'k
Dnieper
Târgu Mures
Arad
2005
Bucharest
Volganeft-139
2007
AND HEIGHT
2000–4000 m
1000–2000 m
500–1000 m
250–500 m
100–250 m
0–100 m
EA DEPTH
0–50 m
50–100 m
100–250 m
250–500 m
500–1000 m
1000–2000 m
Below 2000 m
ITIES AND TOWNS
Over 500,000 people
100,000–500,000
50,000–100,000
Less than 50,000
LATVIA
LITHUANIA
RUSSIAN FEDERATION
BELARUS
MINSK
POLAND
UKRAINE
KIEV (KYYIV)
MOLDOVA
CHIŞINĂU
ROMANIA
BUCHAREST (BUCUREŞTI)
BULGARIA
SERBIA
UNGARY
OVAKIA
GEORGIA
Black Sea
Sea of Azov
Crimea
Transylvania
Wallachia
Pripet Marshes
SCALE BAR
0 km 50 100
0 miles 50 100

European Russia

RUSSIAN FEDERATION

European Russia is separated from the Asiatic part of the Russian Federation by the Ural Mountains. It is home to two-thirds of the country's population. Russia was the largest and most powerful republic of the communist Soviet Union, which collapsed in 1991. Though new businesses were set up when communism ended, many old state industries closed down, causing unemployment and further hardship for many people.

POPULATION

Three-quarters of European Russia's people live in towns and cities, most in a broad band stretching south from Saint Petersburg to Moscow, and eastwards to the Urals. The capital, Moscow, and Saint Petersburg are very crowded cities. Living conditions there are cramped, with two families often sharing one flat. The southeast is also heavily populated. Over 12 million people live in the cities and towns which line the banks of the River Volga.

INHABITANTS PER SQ KM

- More than 100
- 50–100
- 10–50
- Less than 10
- Capital city
- Major city

INDUSTRY

European Russia is rich in natural resources. Minerals are mined on the Kola Peninsula, and in the Urals, while dense forests are felled and processed in many of the larger northern cities. The Volga basin is one of Europe's largest sources of oil and gas. Moscow, and the cities near the Volga are centres of skilled labour for a wide range of manufacturing industries like cars, chemicals and heavy engineering and steel production.

INDUSTRY

- Car manufacture
- Chemicals
- Engineering
- Iron & steel
- Textiles
- Mining
- Oil & gas
- Timber processing
- Major industrial centre/area
- Major road

THE LANDSCAPE

European Russia lies on the North European Plain, a huge, rolling lowland with wide river basins. The northern half of the plain, which was once covered by glaciers, has many lakes and swamps. The River Volga drains much of the plain as it flows south to the Caspian Sea. The Caucasus and Ural mountains form natural boundaries in the south and east.

Northern European Russia (C 3)
Northern European Russia reaches into the Arctic Circle. It is a region of pine and birch forests, marshes and tundra. There are also tens of thousands of lakes, including the biggest in Europe, Ladoga, which covers about 17,700 sq km.

Ural Mountains (E 5)
The Ural Mountains run from north to south, stretching almost 4,020 km.

Lake Ladoga (B 4)

Valdai Hills (A 5)
The Valdai Hills are a high, swampy region of the North European Plain. Two of Europe's biggest rivers, the Volga and the Western Dvina, have their sources here.

Caucasus (A 9)
This massive barrier of mountains stretches from the Black Sea to the Caspian Sea. It includes El'brus, the highest peak in Europe, at 5,642 m.

Caspian Sea (C 9)

River Volga (C 7)
The River Volga flows for 3,688 km, making it Europe's longest river and Russia's most important inland waterway. It is used for transport and to generate hydro-electric power.

The North European Plain (C 4)
The North European Plain sweeps west from the Ural Mountains all the way to the River Rhine in Germany. In European Russia it includes a number of hill ranges, such as the Volga Uplands and the Central Russian Upland.

FARMING AND LAND USE

Russia's best farmland lies within this region. Big crops of wheat, barley and oats, potatoes and sunflowers are produced in the fertile black soil which forms a thick band across the country to the south of Moscow. The far north is cold and frozen, with bare mountains and tundra making cultivation impossible. Further south there are extensive forests, and rough pastures used for herding and hunting.

FARMING AND LAND USE

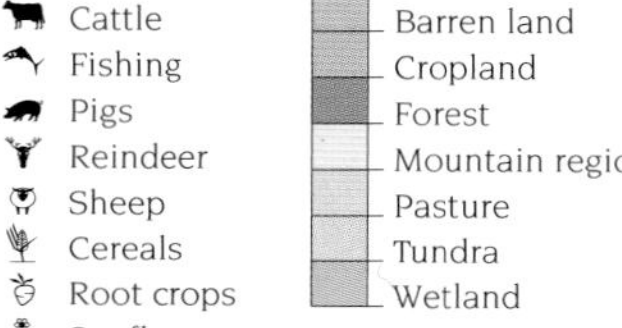
Cattle
Fishing
Pigs
Reindeer
Sheep
Cereals
Root crops
Sunflowers
Timber
Barren land
Cropland
Forest
Mountain region
Pasture
Tundra
Wetland
Major conurbation

EUROPE
European Russia
NORTH AMERICA
SOUTH AMERICA
AFRICA
ASIA
AUSTRALASIA AND OCEANIA
ANTARCTICA
ENVIRONMENTAL ISSUES
The many factories in European Russia have caused widespread pollution, Dzerzhinsk is said to be the most polluted town on earth. Several of Russia's older nuclear power stations have been declared unsafe, but are yet to be shut down. Waste from these power stations, as well as from nuclear submarines, has for many years been dumped in the Barents Sea and off Novaya Zemlya.
ENVIRONMENTAL ISSUES
Nuclear waste dump site
Unstable nuclear reactor
Urban air pollution
Polluted rivers
Sea pollution
Major industrial centre
CLIMATE
Winters are extremely cold and dry; temperatures plunge well below zero in the north and east. Summer brings much warmer and wetter weather, especially in the south, while along the northern coast, it remains relatively cold. Rainfall is highest in the Caucasus.
January
July
TEMPERATURE AND PRECIPITATION
More than 20°C
15 to 20°C
10 to 15°C
5 to 10°C
0 to 5°C
0 to -5°C
-5 to -10°C
-10 to -15°C
Less than -15°C
Precipitation (mm)
CITIES AND TOWNS
Over 500,000 people
100,000–500,000
50,000–100,000
Less than 50,000
LAND HEIGHT
Above 4000 m
2000–4000 m
1000–2000 m
500–1000 m
250–500 m
100–250 m
0–100 m
Below sea level
SEA DEPTH
0–50 m
50–100 m
100–250 m
250–500 m
500–1000 m
1000–2000 m
Below 2000 m
SCALE BAR
0 km 100 200
0 miles 100 200
ARCTIC OCEAN
Barents Sea
Kara Sea (Karskoye More)
RUSSIAN FEDERATION
North European Plain
Ural Mountains
Kirghiz Steppe
KAZAKHSTAN
Caspian Sea
MOSCOW (MOSKVA)
Saint Petersburg (Sankt-Peterburg)
FINLAND
Kola Peninsula (Kol'skiy Poluostrov)

The Mediterranean

The Mediterranean Sea separates Europe from Africa. It stretches more than 4,000 km from east to west and is almost completely enclosed by land. Many great civilizations, including the Greek and Roman empires grew up around the Mediterranean. It has been a crossroads of international trade routes for many centuries. More than 100 million people live in the 28 countries which border the sea and their numbers are increased by the large crowds of tourists who regularly visit the area.

ENVIRONMENTAL ISSUES

Sea pollution is widespread in the Mediterranean, especially near the large coastal resorts where raw sewage and industrial effluent is pumped out to sea and often ends up on the beaches. Oil refining and oil spills have also furthered pollution.

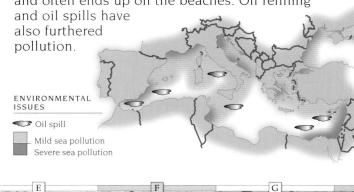

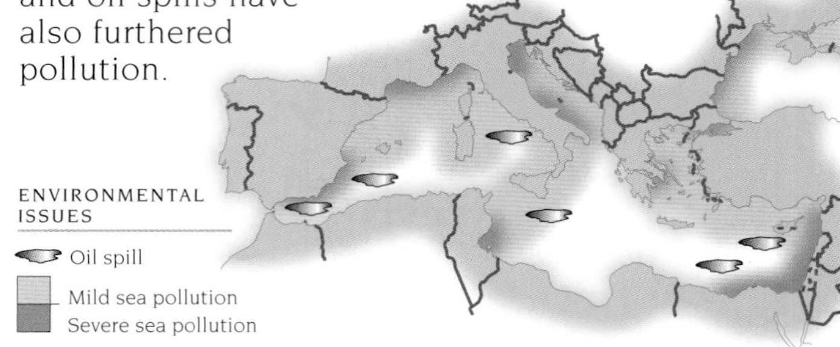
ENVIRONMENTAL ISSUES
Oil spill
Mild sea pollution
Severe sea pollution

SCALE BAR

0 km 100 200

0 miles 100 200

MALTA

0 km 10

0 miles 10

CYPRUS

TURKISH REPUBLIC OF NORTHERN CYPRUS (recognized only by Turkey)

0 km 25

0 miles 25

LAND HEIGHT	SEA DEPTH
Above 4000 m	0–250 m
2000–4000 m	250–500 m
1000–2000 m	500–1000 m
500–1000 m	1000–2000 m
250–500 m	2000–3000 m
100–250 m	3000–4000 m
0–100 m	Below 4000 m
Below sea level	

CITIES AND TOWNS

- Over 500,000 people
- 100,000–500,000
- 50,000–100,000
- Less than 50,000

EUROPE
Mediterranean
NORTH AMERICA
ASIA
AFRICA
SOUTH AMERICA
AUSTRALASIA AND OCEANIA
ANTARCTICA

THE LANDSCAPE

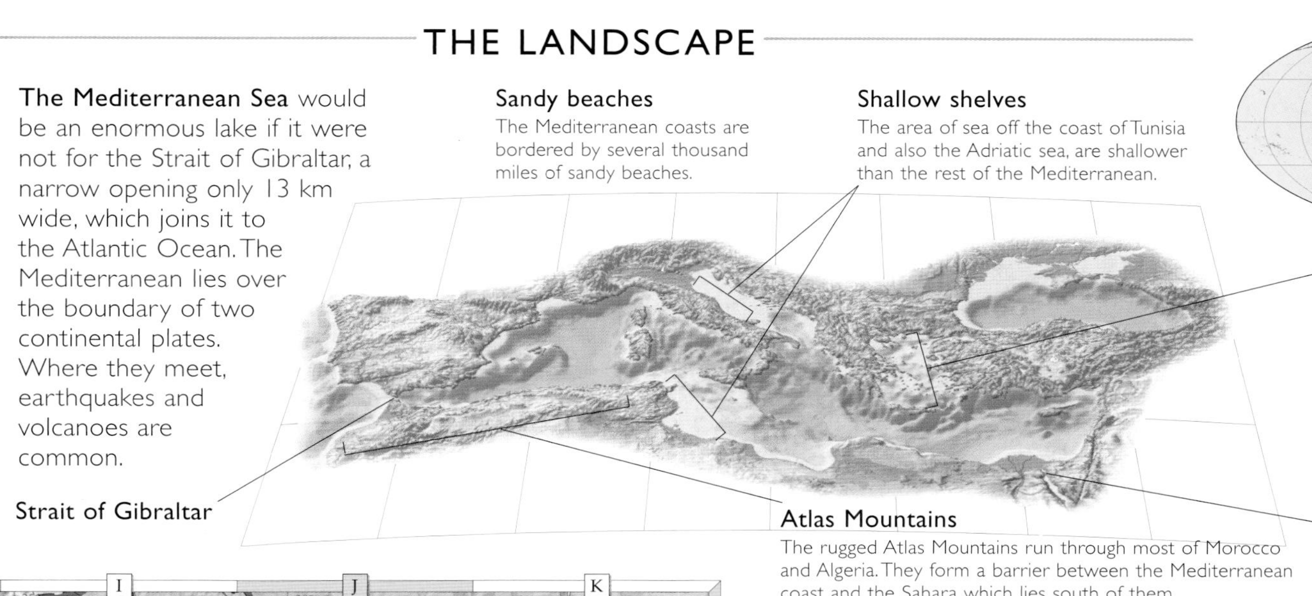

The Mediterranean Sea would be an enormous lake if it were not for the Strait of Gibraltar, a narrow opening only 13 km wide, which joins it to the Atlantic Ocean. The Mediterranean lies over the boundary of two continental plates. Where they meet, earthquakes and volcanoes are common.

Sandy beaches
The Mediterranean coasts are bordered by several thousand miles of sandy beaches.

Shallow shelves
The area of sea off the coast of Tunisia and also the Adriatic sea, are shallower than the rest of the Mediterranean.

Greek islands
Greece has thousands of islands which lie both in the Mediterranean and in the smaller Aegean Sea. Some of them are the remains of old volcanoes which have left black sand on the beaches.

Suez Canal
The Suez Canal links the Mediterranean to the Gulf of Suez and the Red Sea. Before it was built, ships had to sail around the whole of Africa to reach Asia.

Strait of Gibraltar

Atlas Mountains
The rugged Atlas Mountains run through most of Morocco and Algeria. They form a barrier between the Mediterranean coast and the Sahara which lies south of them.

I
J
K
1
2
3
4
5
6
Bălţi
MOLD.
UKRAINE
CHIŞINĂU
Carpathian Mountains
Dniester
Kakhovs'ke Vodoskhovyshche
Dnieper
Berdyans'k
Odesa
Sea of Azov
Crimea
Kerch
RUSS. FED.
Galaţi
Sevastopol'
BUCHAREST (BUCUREŞTI)
Danube
Constanţa
Black Sea
N
W
E
S
Varna
Burgas
Plovdiv
Erdine
Bosporus
Zonguldak
Küre Dağları
Samsun
Istanbul
Sea of Marmara
Kızıl Irmak
Bursa
ANKARA
Eskişehir
Balıkesir
TURKEY
Lesbos
Kayseri
Lake Tuz (Tuz Gölü)
İzmir
Chios
Andros
Samos
Anatolia
Konya
Taurus Mountains
Gaziantep
Dodecanese (Dodekánisa)
Cyclades
Adana
Antalya
Mersin
Gulf of Antalya
Rhodes
Karpathos
TURKISH REPUBLIC OF NORTHERN CYPRUS (recognized only by Turkey)
NICOSIA
Aleppo (Halab)
Crete
CYPRUS
Larnaca
Limassol
LEBANON
BEIRUT (BEYROUTH)
SYRIA
DAMASCUS (DIMASHQ)
Haifa
ISRAEL
Tel Aviv-Yafo
AMMAN
Sidi Barrani
Nile Delta
Port Said
Gaza
JERUSALEM
Dead Sea
Alexandria
Suez Canal
JORDAN
Qattara Depression
CAIRO
Suez
Giza
Gulf of Suez
Al 'Aqabah
Elat
▽-133m
EGYPT
Nile
Sinai
SAUDI ARABIA

TOURISM

The tourist industry in and around the Mediterranean is one of the most highly developed in the world. More than half the world's income from tourism is generated here. Resorts have grown up along the northwest coast of Africa, and in Egypt, in southern Spain, France, Italy, Greece and Turkey. Tourism brings huge economic benefits, but the ever-increasing number of visitors has also damaged the environment.

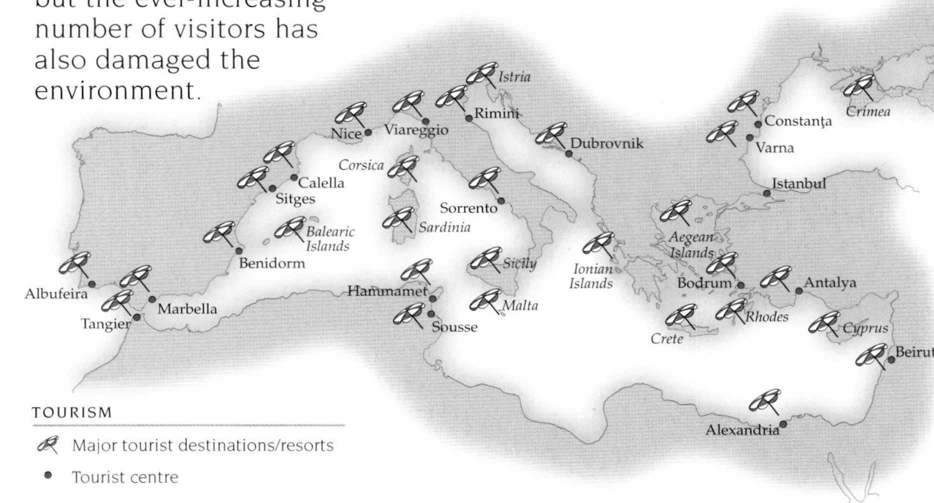
Istria
Crimea
Nice
Viareggio
Rimini
Constanţa
Dubrovnik
Varna
Corsica
Calella
Sitges
Istanbul
Sorrento
Sardinia
Balearic Islands
Benidorm
Aegean Islands
Sicily
Ionian Islands
Albufeira
Hammamet
Bodrum
Antalya
Malta
Tangier
Marbella
Sousse
Rhodes
Cyprus
Crete
Beirut
Alexandria
TOURISM
Major tourist destinations/resorts
Tourist centre

INDUSTRY

The Mediterranean has a large fishing industry, although most of the fishing is small-scale. Tuna and sardines are caught throughout the region and mussels are farmed off the coast of Italy. Fish canning and packing takes place at most of the larger ports. Small oil and gas reserves are extracted off the coast of North Africa and near Greece, Spain and Italy.

Genoa
Marseille
Livorno
Constanţa
Barcelona
Rome
Istanbul
Naples
Valencia
Izmir
Palermo
Piraeus
Antalya
Málaga
Tunis
Algiers
Valletta
Oran
Sfax
Beruit
Tripoli
Tel Aviv-Yafo
Benghazi
Alexandria
Port Said
Cairo
INDUSTRY
Fishing ports
Oil and gas
Major city

CONTINENTAL ASIA

9,700 km
6,500 km

Asia is the world's largest continent, and has the greatest range of physical extremes. Some of the highest, lowest, and coldest places on Earth are found in Asia: Mount Everest in the Himalayas is the highest, the Dead Sea in the west is the lowest, and the frozen wastes of northern Siberia are among the coldest. More people live in Asia than on any other continent – 1.3 billion of them in China, and 1.2 billion in India.

CROSS-SECTION THROUGH ASIA

Persian Gulf, Arabian Peninsula, Iranian Plateau, Himalayas, Plateau of Tibet, Mouth of the Ganges, Yellow River, Taiwan

W — 7,800 km —

The Arabian Peninsula and the mountainous Iranian Plateau are divided by the Persian Gulf, fed by the Tigris and Euphrates rivers. Further east, the land begins to rise, the mountains spreading north to the Plateau of Tibet, and south to the Himalayas. The plains to the south of the Himalayas are drained by the Indus and Ganges, and to the east of the Plateau of Tibet by the Yellow River.

PHYSICAL ASIA

Northern Asia is made up of old mountains and ancient, stable plateaus. The jagged Himalayan mountains dominate the central part of the continent, along with the Plateau of Tibet, which stretches north into China. In Southeast Asia, there are many islands. Volcanoes and earthquakes are common, and some of the islands are volcanically-formed.

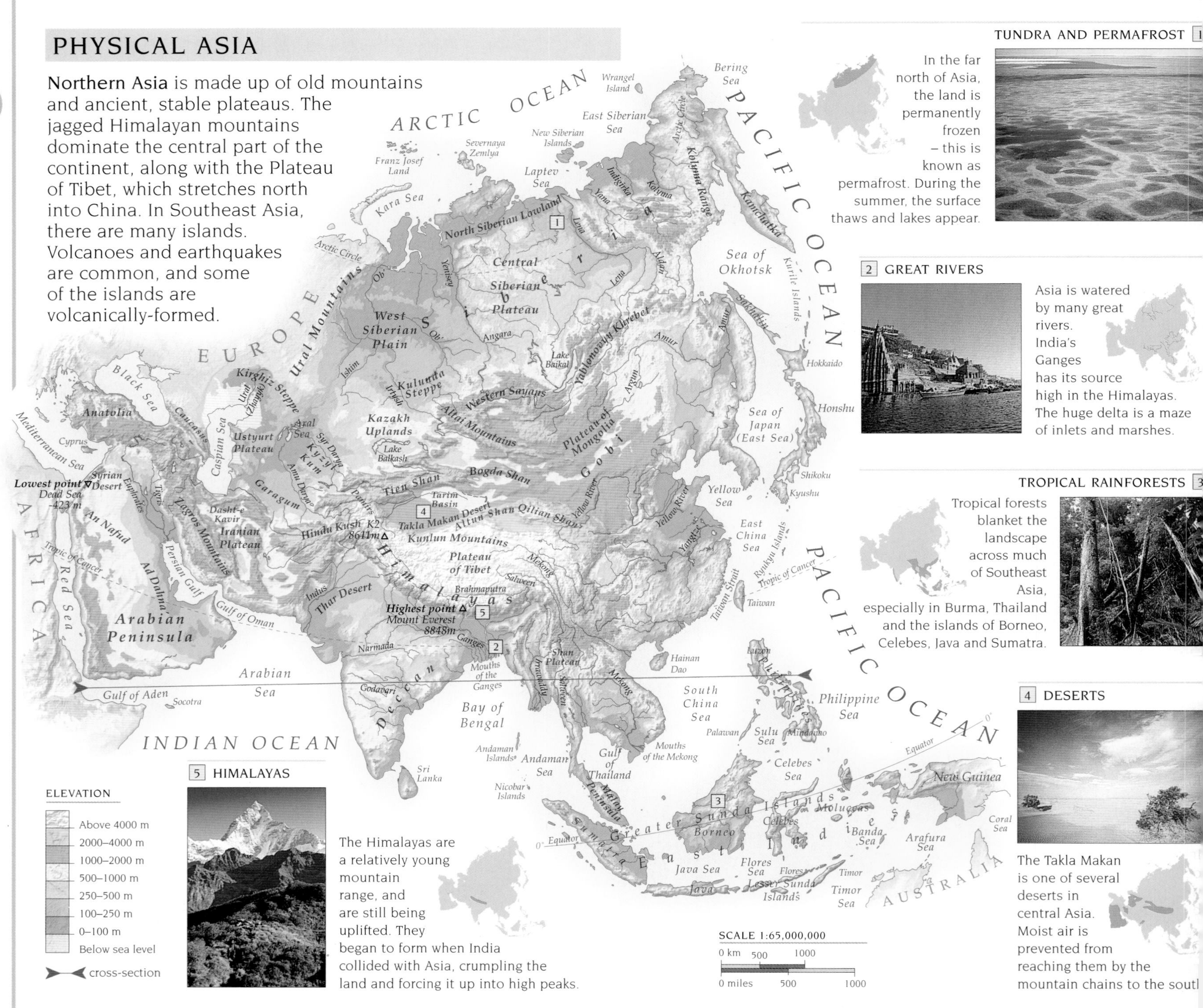

ARCTIC OCEAN
PACIFIC OCEAN
INDIAN OCEAN
EUROPE
AFRICA
AUSTRALIA
Bering Sea
Wrangel Island
East Siberian Sea
New Siberian Islands
Severnaya Zemlya
Franz Josef Land
Laptev Sea
Kara Sea
North Siberian Lowland
Central Siberian Plateau
West Siberian Plain
Ural Mountains
Kirghiz Steppe
Kulunda Steppe
Kazakh Uplands
Western Sayans
Altai Mountains
Plateau of Mongolia
Gobi
Lake Baikal
Yablonovyy Khrebet
Sea of Okhotsk
Kurile Islands
Sakhalin
Kamchatka
Hokkaido
Honshu
Shikoku
Kyushu
Sea of Japan (East Sea)
Yellow Sea
East China Sea
Taiwan
Ryukyu Islands
Tropic of Cancer
Black Sea
Caspian Sea
Aral Sea
Anatolia
Cyprus
Mediterranean Sea
Ustyurt Plateau
Garagum
Kyzyl Kum
Lake Balkash
Tien Shan
Bogda Shan
Tarim Basin
Takla Makan Desert
Altun Shan
Qilian Shan
Kunlun Mountains
Plateau of Tibet
Hindu Kush
K2 8611m
Pamirs
Lowest point Dead Sea -423m
Syrian Desert
An Nafud
Dasht-e Kavir
Iranian Plateau
Zagros Mountains
Persian Gulf
Gulf of Oman
Arabian Peninsula
Ad Dahna
Red Sea
Gulf of Aden
Socotra
Arabian Sea
Thar Desert
Highest point Mount Everest 8848m
Himalayas
Brahmaputra
Ganges
Mouths of the Ganges
Narmada
Godavari
Deccan
Bay of Bengal
Sri Lanka
Andaman Islands
Andaman Sea
Nicobar Islands
Shan Plateau
Mekong
Salween
Yangtze
Yellow River
Hainan Dao
South China Sea
Gulf of Thailand
Mouths of the Mekong
Malay Peninsula
Sumatra
Borneo
Java
Java Sea
Palawan
Sulu Sea
Mindanao
Luzon
Philippine Sea
Philippines
Celebes Sea
Celebes
Moluccas
Banda Sea
Flores Sea
Flores
Lesser Sunda Islands
Timor
Timor Sea
Arafura Sea
New Guinea
Coral Sea
Equator
Greater Sunda Islands
Indonesia

1 TUNDRA AND PERMAFROST

In the far north of Asia, the land is permanently frozen – this is known as permafrost. During the summer, the surface thaws and lakes appear.

2 GREAT RIVERS

Asia is watered by many great rivers. India's Ganges has its source high in the Himalayas. The huge delta is a maze of inlets and marshes.

3 TROPICAL RAINFORESTS

Tropical forests blanket the landscape across much of Southeast Asia, especially in Burma, Thailand and the islands of Borneo, Celebes, Java and Sumatra.

4 DESERTS

The Takla Makan is one of several deserts in central Asia. Moist air is prevented from reaching them by the mountain chains to the south

5 HIMALAYAS

The Himalayas are a relatively young mountain range, and are still being uplifted. They began to form when India collided with Asia, crumpling the land and forcing it up into high peaks.

ELEVATION

- Above 4000 m
- 2000–4000 m
- 1000–2000 m
- 500–1000 m
- 250–500 m
- 100–250 m
- 0–100 m
- Below sea level
- cross-section

SCALE 1:65,000,000

0 km 500 1000

0 miles 500 1000

POLITICAL ASIA

Asia is a continent of many contrasts: in its lands, its peoples and its traditions. The break up of the Soviet Union, which once stretched south from Russia to Iran, produced the new central Asian republics of Kazakhstan, Kyrgyzstan, Tajikistan, Turkmenistan and Uzbekistan. The countries in southwest Asia are mainly Muslim, and include monarchies, republics and theocracies. India is the world's largest democracy, while China is a communist power regaining its economic influence in the world.

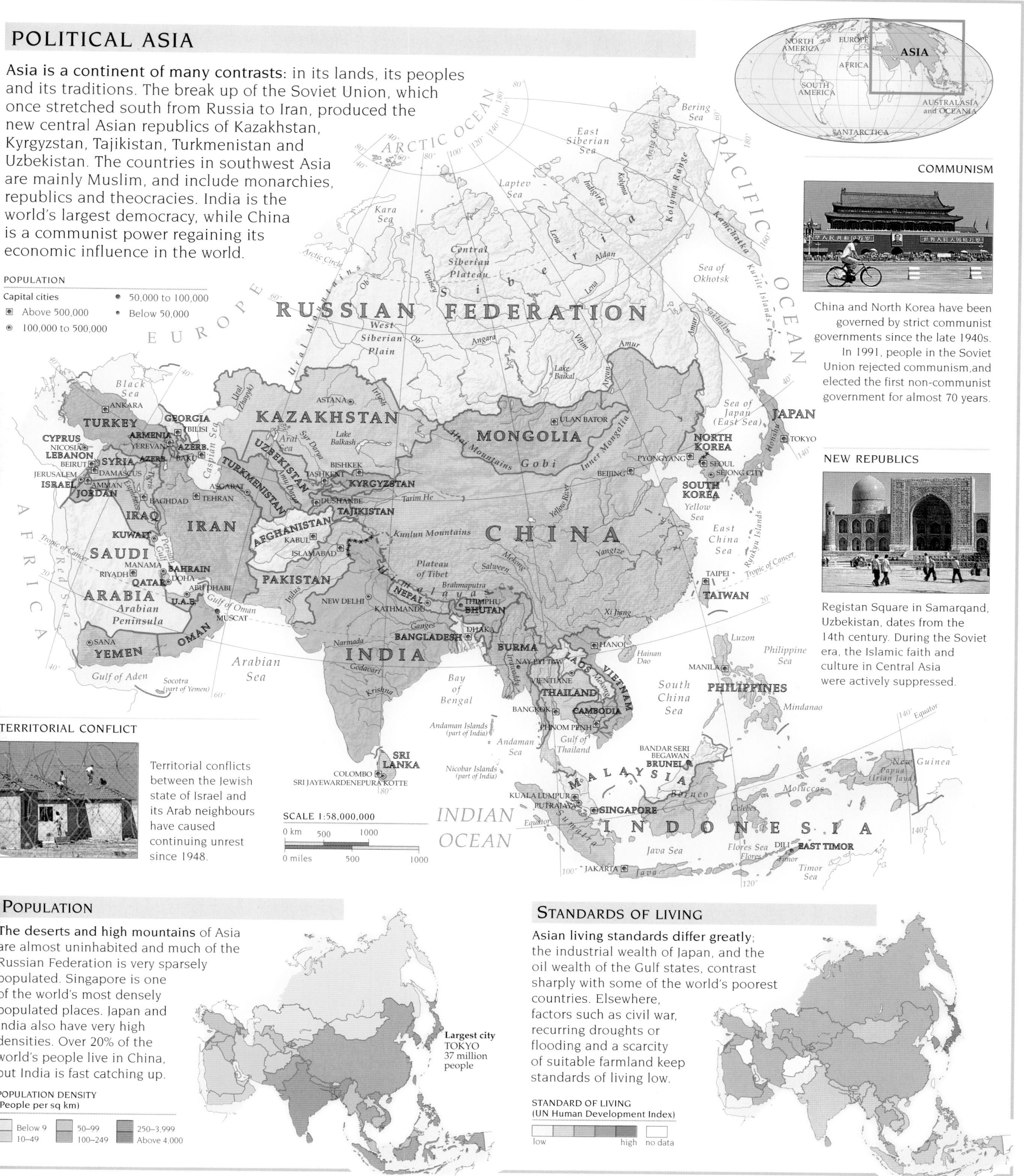
POPULATION
Capital cities
Above 500,000
100,000 to 500,000
50,000 to 100,000
Below 50,000
RUSSIAN FEDERATION
KAZAKHSTAN
MONGOLIA
CHINA
INDIA
IRAN
TURKEY
SAUDI ARABIA
PAKISTAN
AFGHANISTAN
UZBEKISTAN
TURKMENISTAN
KYRGYZSTAN
TAJIKISTAN
GEORGIA
ARMENIA
AZERB.
CYPRUS
LEBANON
SYRIA
ISRAEL
JORDAN
IRAQ
KUWAIT
BAHRAIN
QATAR
U.A.E.
OMAN
YEMEN
NEPAL
BHUTAN
BANGLADESH
SRI LANKA
BURMA
THAILAND
LAOS
VIETNAM
CAMBODIA
MALAYSIA
SINGAPORE
BRUNEI
INDONESIA
EAST TIMOR
PHILIPPINES
TAIWAN
NORTH KOREA
SOUTH KOREA
JAPAN
ARCTIC OCEAN
PACIFIC OCEAN
INDIAN OCEAN
EUROPE
AFRICA
Arabian Sea
Bay of Bengal
South China Sea
SCALE 1:58,000,000
0 km 500 1000
0 miles 500 1000
NORTH AMERICA
SOUTH AMERICA
EUROPE
AFRICA
ASIA
AUSTRALASIA and OCEANIA
ANTARCTICA

COMMUNISM

China and North Korea have been governed by strict communist governments since the late 1940s. In 1991, people in the Soviet Union rejected communism,and elected the first non-communist government for almost 70 years.

NEW REPUBLICS

Registan Square in Samarqand, Uzbekistan, dates from the 14th century. During the Soviet era, the Islamic faith and culture in Central Asia were actively suppressed.

TERRITORIAL CONFLICT

Territorial conflicts between the Jewish state of Israel and its Arab neighbours have caused continuing unrest since 1948.

POPULATION

The deserts and high mountains of Asia are almost uninhabited and much of the Russian Federation is very sparsely populated. Singapore is one of the world's most densely populated places. Japan and India also have very high densities. Over 20% of the world's people live in China, but India is fast catching up.

POPULATION DENSITY
People per sq km)

Below 9 · 10–49 · 50–99 · 100–249 · 250–3,999 · Above 4,000

Largest city
TOKYO
37 million people

STANDARDS OF LIVING

Asian living standards differ greatly; the industrial wealth of Japan, and the oil wealth of the Gulf states, contrast sharply with some of the world's poorest countries. Elsewhere, factors such as civil war, recurring droughts or flooding and a scarcity of suitable farmland keep standards of living low.

STANDARD OF LIVING
(UN Human Development Index)

low · high · no data

Asian Geography

Asia's forbidding mountain ranges, barren deserts, and fertile plains have affected the way in which people settled the continent. Intensive agriculture is found in the more fertile areas, and the largest concentrations of people grew up near fertile land and close to great rivers. Asia's mineral wealth has brought people to the more inhospitable parts of the continent: the deserts of southwest Asia for oil, and frozen Siberia for oil, gas and minerals.

Mineral resources

Over half of the world's oil and gas reserves are in Asia, most importantly around the Persian Gulf and in western Siberia. Coal in Siberia and China has provided power for steel industries. Metallic minerals are also abundant: tin in Southeast Asia, and platinum and nickel in Siberia.

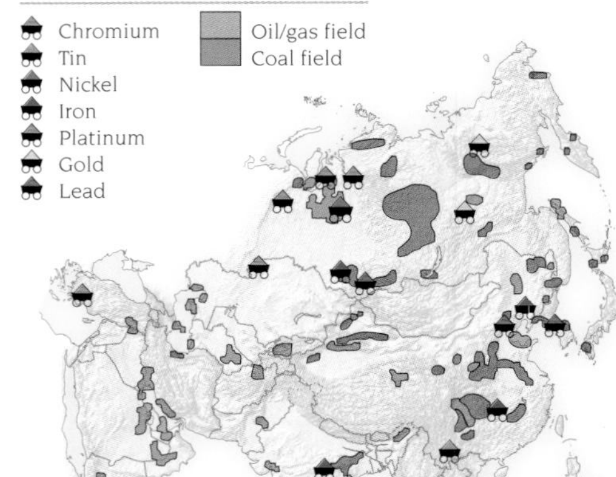
MINERAL RESOURCES
Chromium
Tin
Nickel
Iron
Platinum
Gold
Lead
Oil/gas field
Coal field

Industry

Many people in Asia still rely on agriculture as a source of income, and some countries have very few industries. Heavy industry dominates eastern China and Russia, but Japan is the most industrially productive country. In recent years, booming 'tiger' economies have developed in countries such as Taiwan, that border the Pacific Ocean.

INDUSTRY

- Aerospace
- Brewing
- Car/vehicle manufacture
- Cement
- Chemicals
- Coal
- Electronics
- Engineering
- Finance
- Food processing
- Hi-tech industry
- Iron & steel
- Mining
- Oil & gas
- Pharmaceuticals
- Printing & publishing
- Shipbuilding
- Textiles
- Timber processing

GNI per capita (US$)

- Below 999
- 1,000-1,999
- 2,000-4,999
- 5,000-9,999
- 10,000-19,999
- Above 20,000
- • Industrial centre

Oil and gas

The discovery of oil in The Gulf has generated enormous wealth, and produced rapid industrial and social change in countries such as Saudi Arabia, U.A.E. and Kuwait that control the oil supplies.

High-tech industries

Japan is a world-leading producer of electronic and hi-tech goods like computers, cameras and hi-fi equipment. Taiwan, South Korea and Singapore also produce electronic goods.

Finance

Mumbai (Bombay) is India's leading industrial city and has a thriving stock market. Modern office blocks stand close to sprawling slums.

Industrial complexes

Noril'sk is one of several Soviet-era industrial complexes built in Russia. It is a processing center for the rich mineral reserves found nearby.

Traditional industries

Traditional industries and methods of working are still important to less industrialized nations. Here in Vietnam, seawater has been evaporated by the sun, and the salt is collected for market.

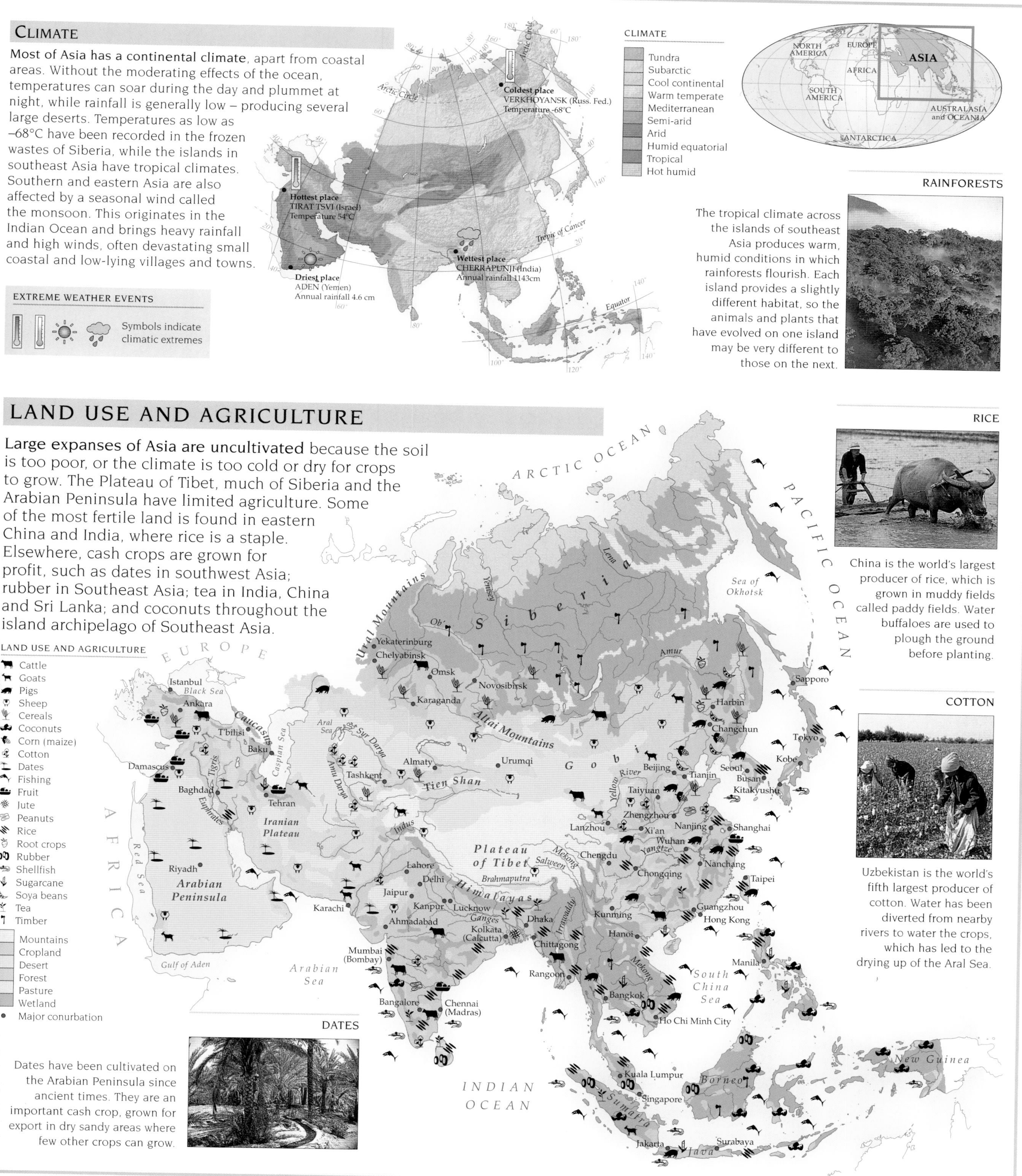
CLIMATE
Tundra
Subarctic
Cool continental
Warm temperate
Mediterranean
Semi-arid
Arid
Humid equatorial
Tropical
Hot humid
Coldest place
VERKHOYANSK (Russ. Fed.)
Temperature -68°C
Hottest place
TIRAT TSVI (Israel)
Temperature 54°C
Driest place
ADEN (Yemen)
Annual rainfall 4.6 cm
Wettest place
CHERRAPUNJI (India)
Annual rainfall 1143cm
Arctic Circle
Tropic of Cancer
Equator
NORTH AMERICA
EUROPE
ASIA
AFRICA
SOUTH AMERICA
AUSTRALASIA and OCEANIA
ANTARCTICA
EXTREME WEATHER EVENTS
Symbols indicate climatic extremes
LAND USE AND AGRICULTURE
Cattle
Goats
Pigs
Sheep
Cereals
Coconuts
Corn (maize)
Cotton
Dates
Fishing
Fruit
Jute
Peanuts
Rice
Root crops
Rubber
Shellfish
Sugarcane
Soya beans
Tea
Timber
Mountains
Cropland
Desert
Forest
Pasture
Wetland
Major conurbation
ARCTIC OCEAN
PACIFIC OCEAN
INDIAN OCEAN
EUROPE
AFRICA
Siberia
Gobi
Ural Mountains
Altai Mountains
Tien Shan
Himalayas
Plateau of Tibet
Iranian Plateau
Arabian Peninsula
Arabian Sea
South China Sea
Sea of Okhotsk
Black Sea
Caspian Sea
Aral Sea
Red Sea
Gulf of Aden
Caucasus
Yenisey
Lena
Ob'
Amur
Syr Darya
Amu Darya
Indus
Ganges
Brahmaputra
Tigris
Euphrates
Yellow River
Yangtze
Mekong
Salween
Irrawaddy
Istanbul
Ankara
T'bilisi
Baku
Damascus
Baghdad
Tehran
Riyadh
Karachi
Yekaterinburg
Chelyabinsk
Omsk
Novosibirsk
Karaganda
Almaty
Tashkent
Urumqi
Lahore
Delhi
Jaipur
Kanpur
Lucknow
Ahmadabad
Kolkata (Calcutta)
Dhaka
Chittagong
Mumbai (Bombay)
Bangalore
Chennai (Madras)
Rangoon
Bangkok
Ho Chi Minh City
Hanoi
Kunming
Chengdu
Chongqing
Lanzhou
Xi'an
Zhengzhou
Taiyuan
Beijing
Tianjin
Nanjing
Wuhan
Shanghai
Nanchang
Guangzhou
Hong Kong
Taipei
Manila
Harbin
Changchun
Seoul
Busan
Kitakyushu
Kobe
Tokyo
Sapporo
Kuala Lumpur
Singapore
Jakarta
Surabaya
Sumatra
Java
Borneo
New Guinea
RAINFORESTS
RICE
COTTON
DATES

CLIMATE

Most of Asia has a continental climate, apart from coastal areas. Without the moderating effects of the ocean, temperatures can soar during the day and plummet at night, while rainfall is generally low – producing several large deserts. Temperatures as low as –68°C have been recorded in the frozen wastes of Siberia, while the islands in southeast Asia have tropical climates. Southern and eastern Asia are also affected by a seasonal wind called the monsoon. This originates in the Indian Ocean and brings heavy rainfall and high winds, often devastating small coastal and low-lying villages and towns.

The tropical climate across the islands of southeast Asia produces warm, humid conditions in which rainforests flourish. Each island provides a slightly different habitat, so the animals and plants that have evolved on one island may be very different to those on the next.

LAND USE AND AGRICULTURE

Large expanses of Asia are uncultivated because the soil is too poor, or the climate is too cold or dry for crops to grow. The Plateau of Tibet, much of Siberia and the Arabian Peninsula have limited agriculture. Some of the most fertile land is found in eastern China and India, where rice is a staple. Elsewhere, cash crops are grown for profit, such as dates in southwest Asia; rubber in Southeast Asia; tea in India, China and Sri Lanka; and coconuts throughout the island archipelago of Southeast Asia.

China is the world's largest producer of rice, which is grown in muddy fields called paddy fields. Water buffaloes are used to plough the ground before planting.

Uzbekistan is the world's fifth largest producer of cotton. Water has been diverted from nearby rivers to water the crops, which has led to the drying up of the Aral Sea.

Dates have been cultivated on the Arabian Peninsula since ancient times. They are an important cash crop, grown for export in dry sandy areas where few other crops can grow.

Russia and Kazakhstan

Russia lies partly in Europe, but mostly in Asia. The land to the east of the Ural Mountains is called Siberia. This immense stretch of grasslands, thick, evergreen forest and tundra is crossed by giant rivers. Vast areas of Siberia are almost untouched by human activity, yet in the industrial regions set up under communism (1922–1991), air, water and soil are heavily polluted with harmful substances. Along with the former Soviet state of Kazakhstan, Siberia is rich in a huge variety of minerals.

INDUSTRY

The discovery of gold in the 19th century opened Siberia up to economic and industrial development. Later, vast reserves of oil, coal and gas were found, especially in the west, which is now the main centre for oil extraction. Gold and diamonds are mined in the east. In Kazakhstan, mining and other industries are growing, with the help of foreign investors.

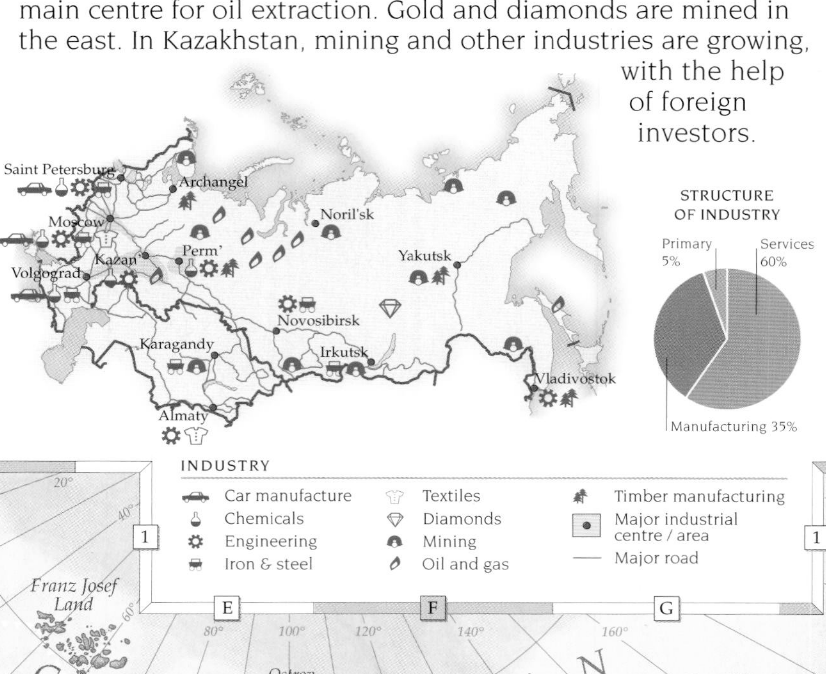

Saint Petersburg
Archangel
Moscow
Noril'sk
Perm'
Kazan
Volgograd
Yakutsk
Novosibirsk
Karagandy
Irkutsk
Vladivostok
Almaty
STRUCTURE OF INDUSTRY
Primary 5%
Services 60%
Manufacturing 35%
INDUSTRY
Car manufacture
Chemicals
Engineering
Iron & steel
Textiles
Diamonds
Mining
Oil and gas
Timber manufacturing
Major industrial centre / area
Major road

LAND HEIGHT
- above 4000 m
- 2000–4000 m
- 1000–2000 m
- 500–1000 m
- 250–500 m
- 100–250 m
- 0–100 m
- Below sea level

SEA DEPTH
- 0–250 m
- 250–500 m
- 500–1000 m
- 1000–2000 m
- 2000–3000 m
- 3000–4000 m
- Below 4000 m

SCALE BAR
0 km 200 400
0 miles 200 400

CITIES AND TOWNS
- Over 500,000 people
- 100,000–500,000
- 50,000–100,000
- Less than 50,000

THE LANDSCAPE

East of the Ural Mountains lies the West Siberian Plain – the world's biggest area of flat ground. The plain gradually rises to the Central Siberian Plateau, and then again to highlands in the southeast. Great coniferous forests called *taiga* stretch across most of this land. The far north of Siberia extends into the Arctic Circle. There, the landscape is made up of frozen plains called tundra. Much of Kazakhstan is covered by huge rolling grasslands, or steppe; in the south are arid sandy deserts.

Tundra and *taiga*

Stubby birch trees, dwarf bushes, moss and lichen huddle close to the ground in the frozen tundra wastes of northern Russia. They lie between the permanent ice and snow of the Arctic, and the thick *taiga* forests which cover an area greater than the Amazon rainforest.

The Caspian Sea (A 5)

The Caspian Sea covers 371,000 sq km and is the world's largest expanse of inland water. It is fed by the Volga and Ural rivers, which flow in from the plains of the north.

West Siberian Plain (D 4)

This vast, flat expanse is covered with a network of marshes and streams. The Ob' river, which winds its way north across the plains, is frozen for up to half the year.

Lake Baikal (F 5)

Lake Baikal is the deepest lake in the world, and the largest freshwater one – it is more than 1.6 km deep, and covers 32,500 sq km. It is fed by 336 rivers and contains around 20% of all the fresh water in the world.

CLIMATE

Russia and Kazakhstan have strongly continental climates, and their distance away from seas and oceans means that temperatures fluctuate wildly, both daily and seasonally. Temperatures in eastern Siberia have been known to reach -68°C.

January

July

TEMPERATURE AND PRECIPITATION

- More than 30°C
- 25 to 30°C
- 20 to 25°C
- 15 to 20°C
- 10 to 15°C
- 5 to 10°C
- 0 to 5°C
- 0 to -5°C
- -5 to -10°C
- -10 to -15°C
- Less than -15°C
- 100 Precipitation (mm)

FARMING AND LAND USE

Siberia's harsh climate has restricted farming to the south, where there are a few areas warm enough to grow cereal crops, such as wheat and oats, and to raise cattle on the small pockets of pasture. The rest of the region is used for hunting, herding reindeer, and forestry – the *taiga* forests contain the world's biggest timber reserves. In Kazakhstan, big herds of cattle, goats and sheep are raised for wool and meat, and wheat is cultivated in the fertile north.

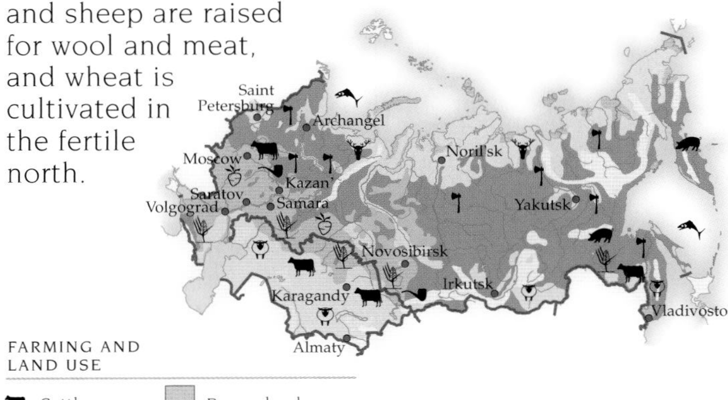

Saint Petersburg
Archangel
Noril'sk
Moscow
Kazan'
Saratov
Samara
Volgograd
Yakutsk
Novosibirsk
Irkutsk
Karagandy
Vladivostok
Almaty

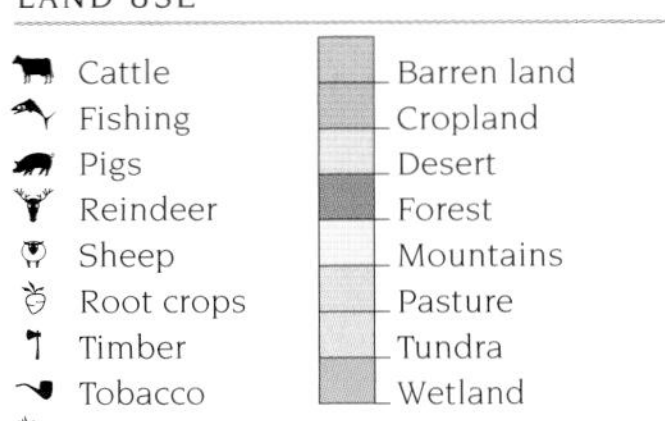

FARMING AND LAND USE
Cattle
Fishing
Pigs
Reindeer
Sheep
Root crops
Timber
Tobacco
Wheat
Barren land
Cropland
Desert
Forest
Mountains
Pasture
Tundra
Wetland
Major conurbation

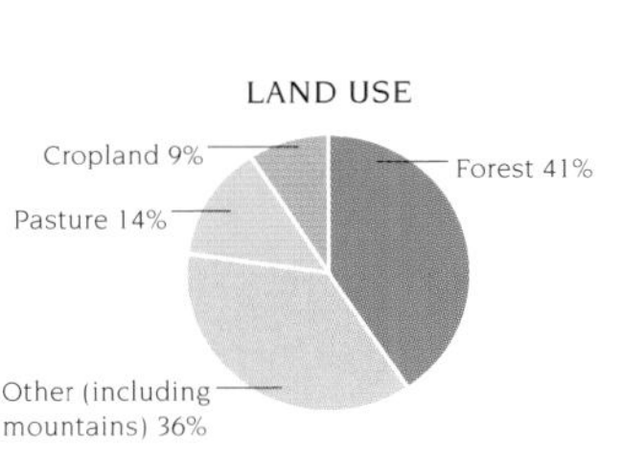

LAND USE
Cropland 9%
Pasture 14%
Forest 41%
Other (including mountains) 36%

POPULATION

Siberia has some of the world's largest areas of uninhabited land – the bitingly cold climate and harsh living conditions have kept the population small. The industrial cities in the west hold the most people. Despite its huge size, Kazakhstan has only 16 million people; just over half live in urban areas.

Saint Petersburg
MOSCOW
Nizhniy Novgorod
Saratov
Kazan'
Volgograd
Samara
Yakutsk
Omsk
Novosibirsk
ASTANA
Khabarovsk
Irkutsk
Karagandy
Almaty
Vladivostok

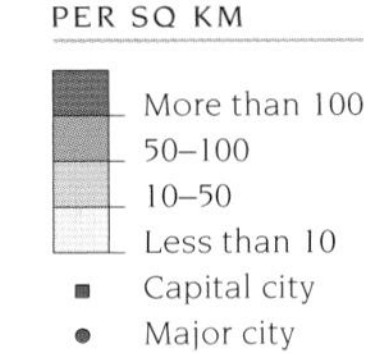

INHABITANTS PER SQ KM
More than 100
50–100
10–50
Less than 10
Capital city
Major city

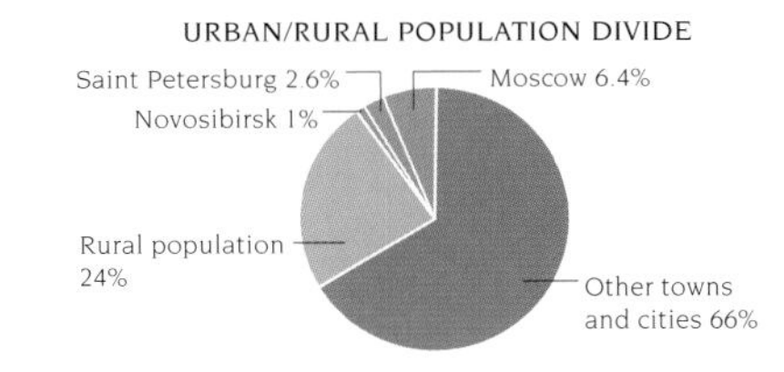

URBAN/RURAL POPULATION DIVIDE
Saint Petersburg 2.6%
Moscow 6.4%
Novosibirsk 1%
Rural population 24%
Other towns and cities 66%

ENVIRONMENTAL ISSUES

Decades of industrial development during the communist regime brought new industries to undeveloped parts of the region, like Siberia. This industrial development has now led to environmental degradation on a massive scale and river, air and land pollution in Russia is among the worst in the world.

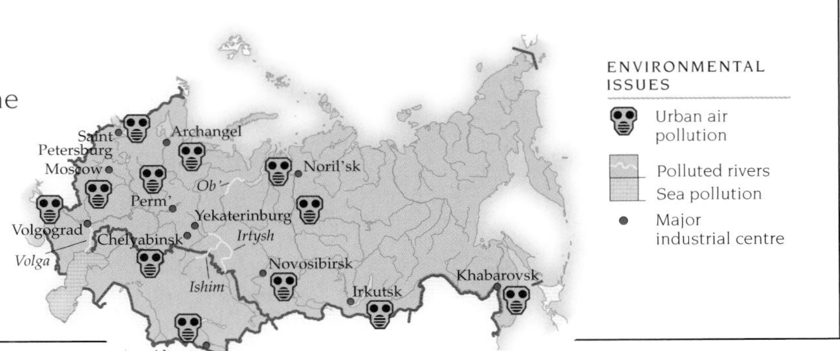

Saint Petersburg
Archangel
Moscow
Noril'sk
Ob'
Perm'
Volgograd
Yekaterinburg
Irtysh
Chelyabinsk
Volga
Novosibirsk
Ishim
Khabarovsk
Irkutsk
Almaty
ENVIRONMENTAL ISSUES
Urban air pollution
Polluted rivers
Sea pollution
Major industrial centre

TURKEY AND THE CAUCASUS

ARMENIA, AZERBAIJAN, GEORGIA, TURKEY

Turkey and the Caucasus lie partly in Europe, partly in Asia. Turkey has a long Islamic tradition, and although the country is now a secular (non-religious) one, most Turks are Muslims. Turkey is becoming more industrialized, although one third of its workforce is still employed in agriculture. The countries of the Caucasus were under Russian rule for 70 years, until 1991. They are home to more than 50 different ethnic groups.

INDUSTRY

Turkey has a wide range of industries, including tourism and growing trade links with Europe. Azerbaijan has large oil reserves and is able to export oil. The other states use imported fuel and hydro-electric power generated by their rushing rivers. Georgia produces industrial machinery and chemicals. Armenia's economy is recovering from the conflict with Azerbaijan.

FARMING AND LAND USE

With its warm climate and good soils, Turkey is able to produce all of its own food. Cattle and goats are kept on the central plateau. Along the Mediterranean coast, farmers grow olives, figs, grapes and peaches. Hazelnuts are cultivated along the shores of the Black Sea. Across the Caucasus, the limited fertile land is used to grow wine grapes, tobacco and cotton.

FARMING AND LAND USE

- Livestock
- Fishing
- Cotton
- Fruit
- Hazelnuts
- Root crops
- Tobacco
- Vineyards
- Pasture
- Cropland
- Forest
- Major conurbation

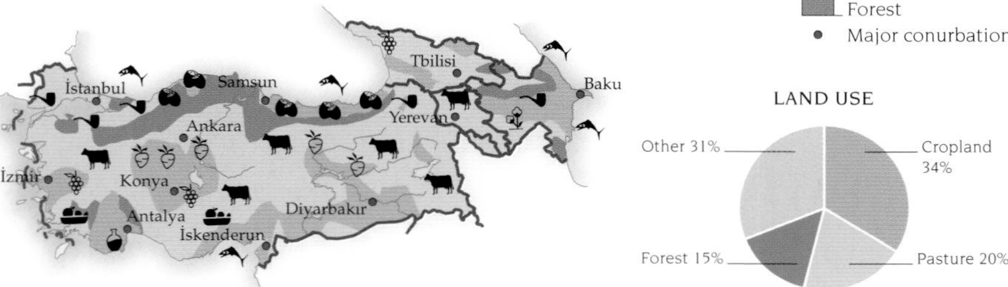

İstanbul
Samsun
Tbilisi
Baku
Ankara
Yerevan
İzmir
Konya
Antalya
İskenderun
Diyarbakır

LAND USE

Other 31%
Cropland 34%
Forest 15%
Pasture 20%

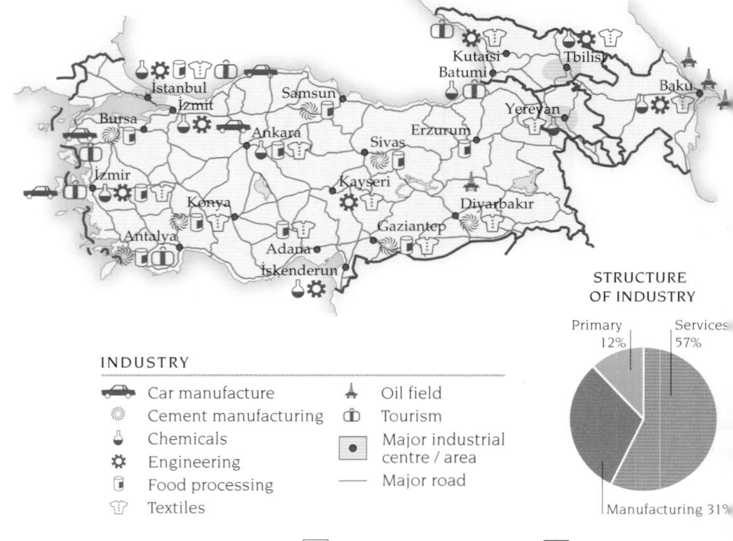

Kutaisi
Batumi
Tbilisi
Baku
İstanbul
İzmit
Samsun
Bursa
Ankara
Sivas
Erzurum
Yerevan
İzmir
Konya
Kayseri
Diyarbakır
Gaziantep
Antalya
Adana
İskenderun

STRUCTURE OF INDUSTRY

Primary 12%
Services 57%
Manufacturing 31%

INDUSTRY

- Car manufacture
- Cement manufacturing
- Chemicals
- Engineering
- Food processing
- Textiles
- Oil field
- Tourism
- Major industrial centre / area
- Major road

THE LANDSCAPE

A huge semi-arid plateau called Anatolia runs across the centre of Turkey. It is rimmed by several mountain ranges along the Black Sea coast, and the steep Taurus Mountains in the south. A narrow strip of lowland separates the Caucasus and the Lesser Caucasus mountains in the northeast.

Anatolia
Anatolia has large areas of soft limestone rock. Over a long period of time, layers of rock have been worn away by water to produce strange landscapes with caves, and tall, isolated rock pinnacles.

Caucasus Mountains (H 1)

Lesser Caucasus (H 2)

Earthquakes
In 1988, 25,000 people were killed in an earthquake in the west of Armenia.

Between two continents
The city of Istanbul (B2) in Turkey is divided in two by a narrow channel of water called the Bosporus. One part of the city is in Europe, the other in Asia. The two parts are linked by bridges.

Taurus Mountains (D 5)
The Taurus Mountains were formed around 60 to 65 million years ago. Weathering has formed caves and deep gorges.

Lake Van (H 4)
Lake Van is one of the shallow salt lakes found in Anatolia. Salt lakes develop in hot, dry areas where large quantities of water evaporate, leaving behind salty deposits.

A
B
2
3
4
5
BULGARIA
GREECE
Kırklareli
Edirne
Çorlu
Tekirdağ
Bosporus
İstanbul
İzmit
Adapazarı
Sea of Marmara
Yalova
Bandırma
Çanakkale
Bursa
Bilecik
Dardanelles
Balıkesir
Edremit
Ayvalık
Bozüyük
Eskişehir
Kütahya
Simav
Gediz
Lesbos
(Lésvos)
Akhisar
Manisa
Menemen
Chios
İzmir
Uşak
Afyon
Ödemiş
Alaşehir
Sámos
Aydın
Nazilli
Denizli
Dinar
Söke
Tavas
Burdur
Isparta
Milas
Muğla
Bodrum
Marmaris
Dalaman
Fethiye
Dodecanese
(Dodekánisa)
Rhodes
(Ródos)
Kaş
Finike
Kárpathos
Mediterranean Se

POPULATION

Over 75% of Turks live in large towns or cities, mostly in the western half of the country. The eastern and southeastern parts of Anatolia are home to the Kurdish people. The Caucasian republics became more industrialized under Russian rule, and today, two thirds of their people live in urban places.

İstanbul
Zonguldak
TBILISI
Samsun
Trabzon
YEREVAN
BAKU
Bursa
ANKARA
İzmir
Konya
Adana

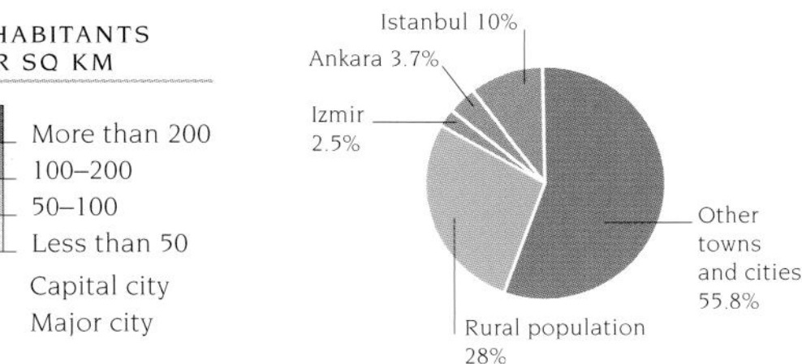
URBAN/RURAL
POPULATION DIVIDE
INHABITANTS PER SQ KM
More than 200
100–200
50–100
Less than 50
Capital city
Major city
Istanbul 10%
Ankara 3.7%
Izmir 2.5%
Other towns and cities 55.8%
Rural population 28%

ENVIRONMENTAL ISSUES

Turkey has built many large dams to use water from rivers – especially the Euphrates – to irrigate its farmland. Syria and Iraq, which lie downstream, have opposed the dams, because they will have less water flowing into their countries. The safety of old-style nuclear plants such as Metsamor in Armenia has caused concern.

Tbilisi
1998
İstanbul
Yerevan
Bursa
Metsamor
1999
Ankara
Erzurum
Atatürk Dam
Euphrates

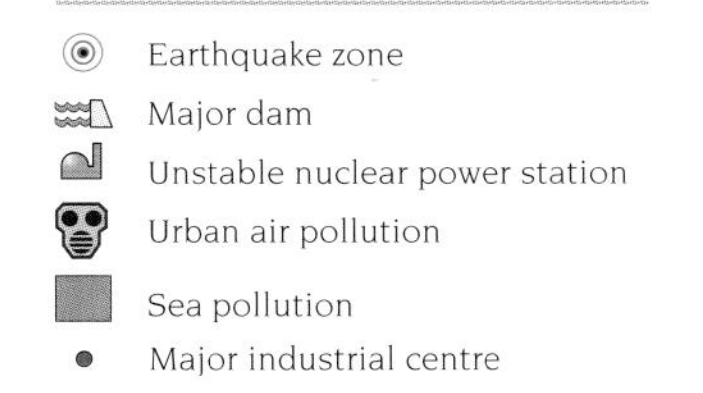
ENVIRONMENTAL ISSUES
Earthquake zone
Major dam
Unstable nuclear power station
Urban air pollution
Sea pollution
Major industrial centre

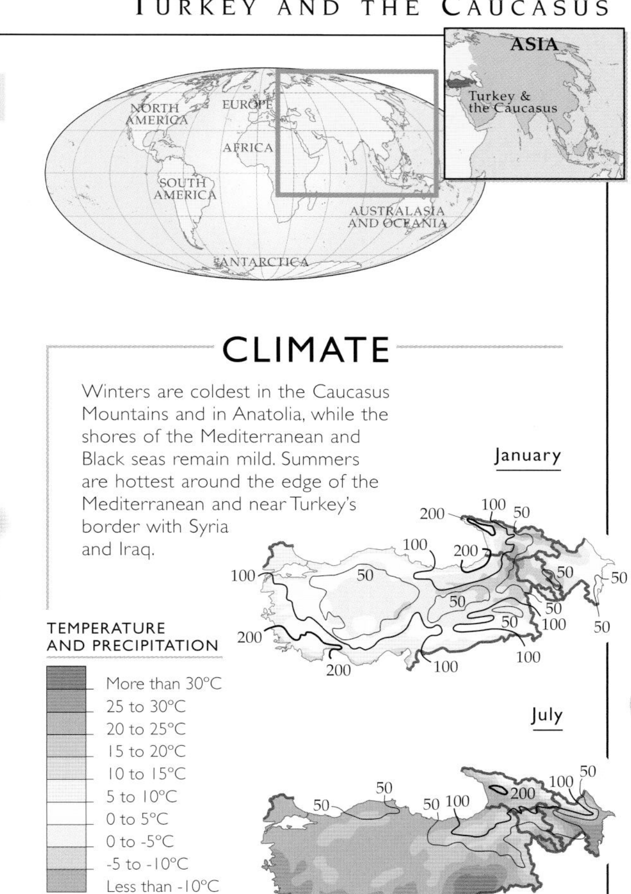
ASIA
Turkey & the Caucasus
NORTH AMERICA
EUROPE
AFRICA
SOUTH AMERICA
AUSTRALASIA AND OCEANIA
ANTARCTICA
January
July
TEMPERATURE AND PRECIPITATION
More than 30°C
25 to 30°C
20 to 25°C
15 to 20°C
10 to 15°C
5 to 10°C
0 to 5°C
0 to -5°C
-5 to -10°C
Less than -10°C
100 Precipitation (mm)

CLIMATE

Winters are coldest in the Caucasus Mountains and in Anatolia, while the shores of the Mediterranean and Black seas remain mild. Summers are hottest around the edge of the Mediterranean and near Turkey's border with Syria and Iraq.

SCALE BAR
0 km 75 150
0 miles 75 150

CITIES AND TOWNS
- Over 500,000 people
- 100,000–500,000
- 50,000–100,000
- Less than 50,000

LAND HEIGHT	SEA DEPTH
Above 4000 m	0–50 m
2000–4000 m	50–100 m
1000–2000 m	100–250 m
500–1000 m	250–500 m
250–500 m	500–1000 m
100–250 m	1000–2000 m
0–100 m	Below 2000 m
Below sea level	

Southwest Asia

BAHRAIN, IRAN, IRAQ, ISRAEL, JORDAN, KUWAIT, LEBANON, OMAN, QATAR, SAUDI ARABIA, SYRIA, UNITED ARAB EMIRATES, YEMEN

Most of southwest Asia is barren desert, yet the world's first cities developed here, over 5,000 years ago. It was also the birthplace of three major religions: Islam, Judaism and Christianity. In recent years, the discovery of oil has brought great wealth to much of the region, but it has been torn by internal conflicts and wars between neighbouring countries. Most people here are Muslims, although Israel is the world's only Jewish state.

ENVIRONMENTAL ISSUES

Water shortages are common because of the hot, dry climate and the lack of rivers. Desalination plants convert sea water into fresh water, and are found along the Red Sea and Gulf coasts. Lack of water also makes the risk of desertification greater. Iran has had many catastrophic earthquakes; in 2003 an earthquake in Bam killed 26,000 people.

ENVIRONMENTAL ISSUES

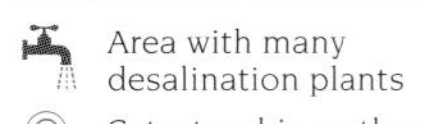

Area with many desalination plants

Catastrophic earthquake

Urban air pollution

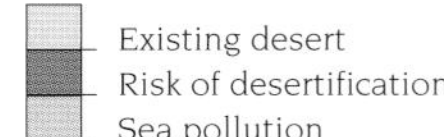

Existing desert

Risk of desertification

Sea pollution

Major industrial centre

INDUSTRY

Oil has made the previously poor Arab states very wealthy. Oil and natural gas continue to be the main source of income for many of the countries here, although other industries are being developed to support their economies when these resources run out. Iran is famous for its carpets, which are woven from wool or silk.

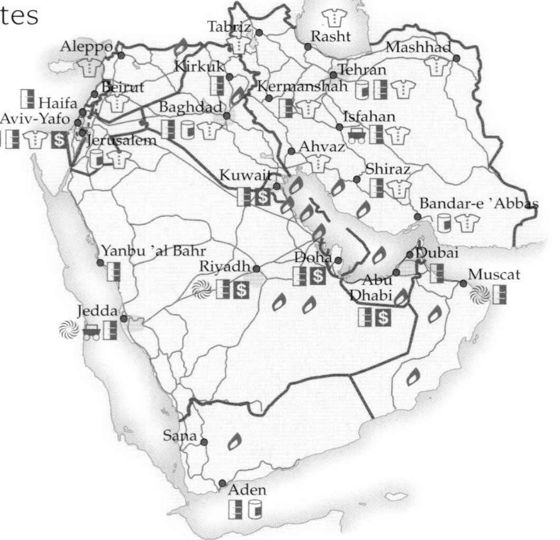

Tabriz
Rasht
Mashhad
Aleppo
Kirkuk
Tehran
Beirut
Kermanshah
Haifa
Tel Aviv-Yafo
Baghdad
Isfahan
Jerusalem
Ahvaz
Kuwait
Shiraz
Bandar-e 'Abbas
Yanbu 'al Bahr
Riyadh
Doha
Dubai
Abu Dhabi
Muscat
Jedda
Sana
Aden

INDUSTRY

Cement manufacturing

Food processing

Iron and steel

Oil refining

Textiles

Oil and gas

Finance

Major industrial centre / area

Major road

STRUCTURE OF INDUSTRY

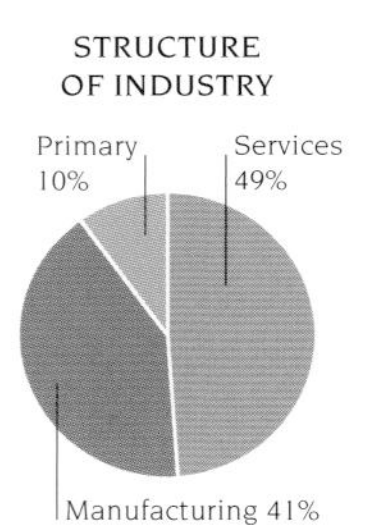

Primary 10%
Services 49%
Manufacturing 41%

THE LANDSCAPE

Great desert plateaus, both sandy and rocky, cover much of southwest Asia. On the enormous Arabian Peninsula, which covers an area almost the size of India, narrow, sandy plains along the Red Sea and south coast rise to dry mountains. In the centre is a vast, high plateau that slopes gently down to the flat shores of the Persian Gulf. The mountainous areas of Iran experience frequent earthquakes.

Wadis

Valleys or riverbeds, called *wadis*, are found in the Saudi Arabian desert. Usually they are dry, but after heavy rains, they are briefly filled by fast flowing rivers.

Oases

Oases are areas within a desert where water is available for plants, and human use. They are usually formed when a fault, or split, in the rock allows water to come to the surface. Oases can be no bigger than a few palm trees, or cover several hundred sq km.

Syrian Desert (B 2)

The Syrian Desert extends from the Jordan valley in the west, to the fertile plains of the Tigris and Euphrates rivers in the east. It is mainly a rocky desert, as the sand has been swept away by winds and occasional heavy rainstorms.

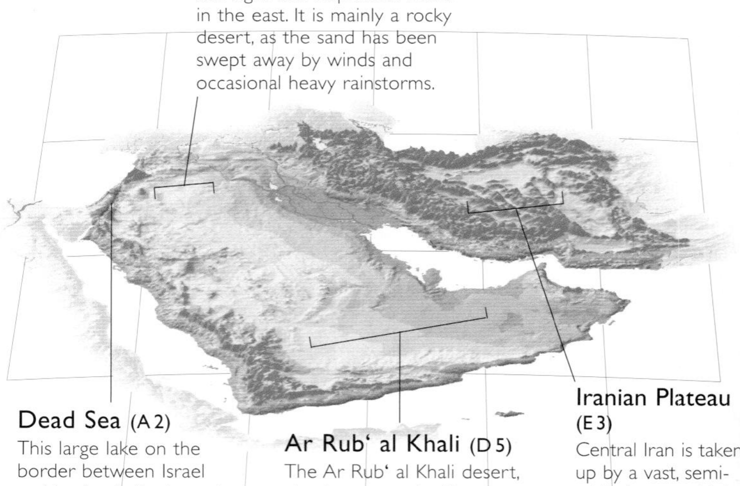

Dead Sea (A 2)

This large lake on the border between Israel and Jordan is the lowest point on the Earth's surface – its shores lie 423 m below sea level. It is also the world's saltiest body of water, and can support no life forms.

Ar Rub' al Khali (D 5)

The Ar Rub' al Khali desert, also known as the 'Empty Quarter', is the largest uninterrupted stretch of sand on Earth. It covers some 650,000 sq km and is one of the world's driest and most hostile deserts.

Iranian Plateau (E 3)

Central Iran is taken up by a vast, semi-arid plateau, which rises steeply from the coastal lowlands bordering the Persian Gulf. It is ringed by the high Zagros and Elburz mountains.

FARMING AND LAND USE

The best farmland is found along the Mediterranean coast, and in the fertile valleys of the Tigris, Euphrates and Jordan rivers. Wheat is the main cereal crop, and cotton, dates, citrus and orchard fruits are grown for export. Elsewhere, modern irrigation techniques have created patches of fertile land in the desert. Dates, wheat and coffee are cultivated in the oases and along the Persian Gulf coast.

LAND USE

Forest 2%

Other (including desert) 47%

Pasture 45%

Cropland 6%

FARMING AND LAND USE

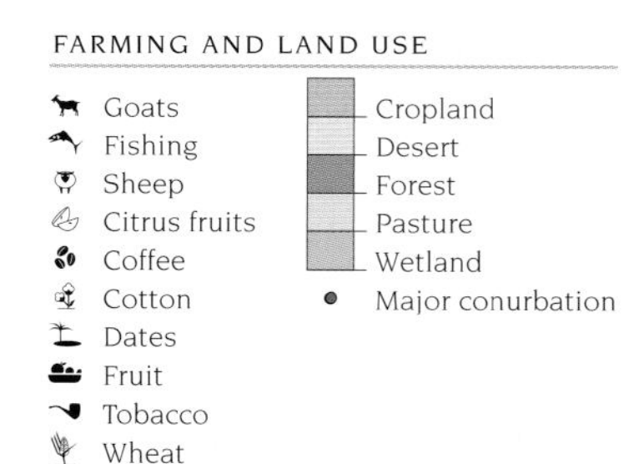

Goats

Fishing

Sheep

Citrus fruits

Coffee

Cotton

Dates

Fruit

Tobacco

Wheat

Cropland

Desert

Forest

Pasture

Wetland

Major conurbation

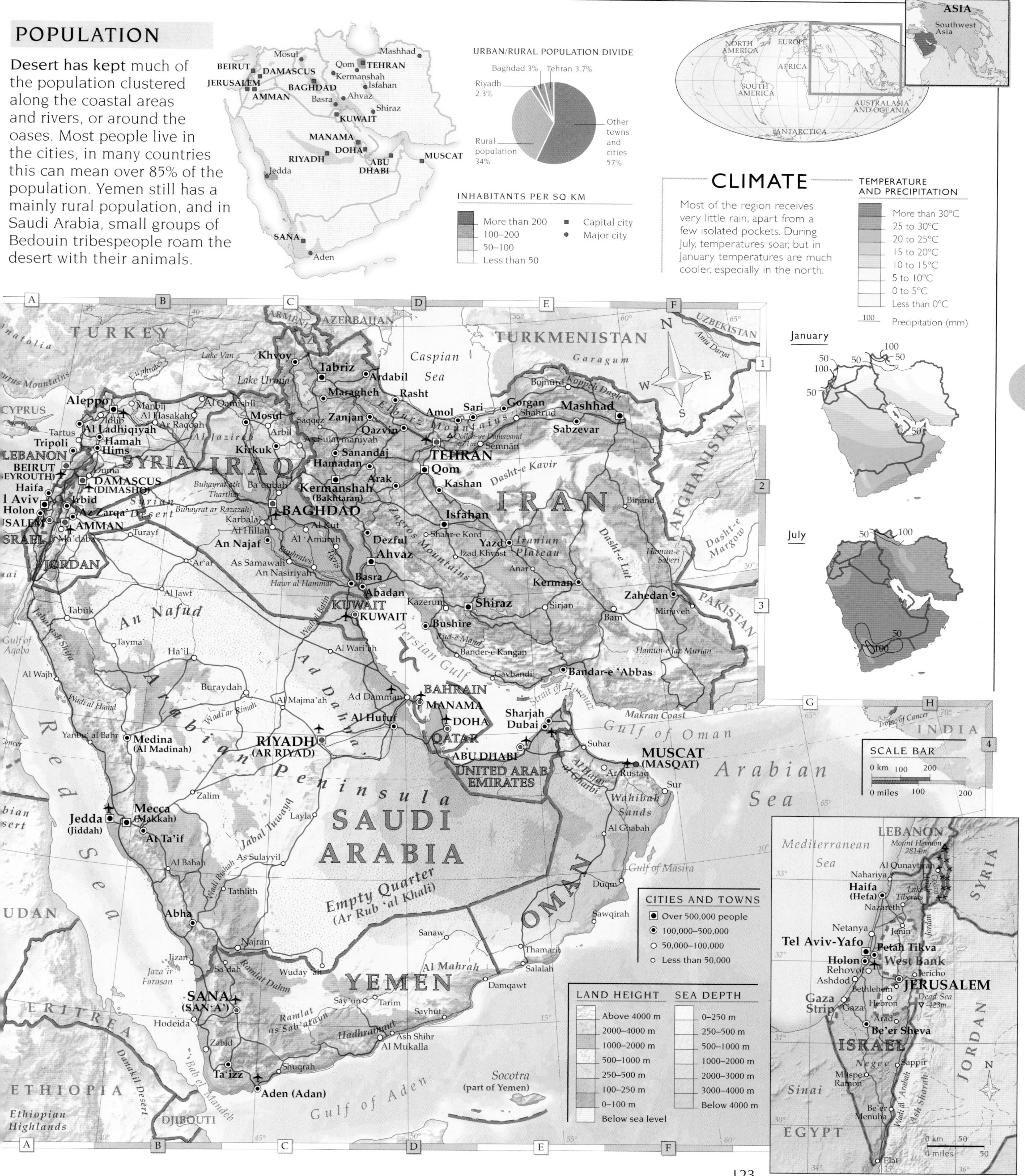
POPULATION
Desert has kept much of the population clustered along the coastal areas and rivers, or around the oases. Most people live in the cities, in many countries this can mean over 85% of the population. Yemen still has a mainly rural population, and in Saudi Arabia, small groups of Bedouin tribespeople roam the desert with their animals.
URBAN/RURAL POPULATION DIVIDE
Baghdad 3%
Tehran 3.7%
Riyadh 2.3%
Rural population 34%
Other towns and cities 57%
INHABITANTS PER SQ KM
More than 200
100–200
50–100
Less than 50
Capital city
Major city
ASIA
Southwest Asia
NORTH AMERICA
EUROPE
AFRICA
SOUTH AMERICA
AUSTRALASIA AND OCEANIA
ANTARCTICA
CLIMATE
Most of the region receives very little rain, apart from a few isolated pockets. During July, temperatures soar, but in January temperatures are much cooler, especially in the north.
TEMPERATURE AND PRECIPITATION
More than 30°C
25 to 30°C
20 to 25°C
15 to 20°C
10 to 15°C
5 to 10°C
0 to 5°C
Less than 0°C
100 Precipitation (mm)
January
July
TURKEY
SYRIA
IRAQ
IRAN
TURKMENISTAN
AFGHANISTAN
PAKISTAN
LEBANON
ISRAEL
JORDAN
KUWAIT
BAHRAIN
QATAR
UNITED ARAB EMIRATES
OMAN
SAUDI ARABIA
YEMEN
ERITREA
ETHIOPIA
DJIBOUTI
INDIA
Caspian Sea
Persian Gulf
Gulf of Oman
Arabian Sea
Red Sea
Gulf of Aden
Arabian Peninsula
Empty Quarter (Ar Rub 'al Khali)
An Nafud
Zagros Mountains
Elburz Mountains
Iranian Plateau
Dasht-e Kavir
Dasht-e Lut
Syrian Desert
TEHRAN
BAGHDAD
DAMASCUS
BEIRUT
AMMAN
RIYADH (AR RIYAD)
MANAMA
DOHA
ABU DHABI
MUSCAT (MASQAT)
SANA (SAN'A')
Socotra (part of Yemen)
CITIES AND TOWNS
Over 500,000 people
100,000–500,000
50,000–100,000
Less than 50,000
SCALE BAR
LAND HEIGHT
Above 4000 m
2000–4000 m
1000–2000 m
500–1000 m
250–500 m
100–250 m
0–100 m
Below sea level
SEA DEPTH
0–250 m
250–500 m
500–1000 m
1000–2000 m
2000–3000 m
3000–4000 m
Below 4000 m
Mediterranean Sea
JERUSALEM
Tel Aviv-Yafo
Haifa (Hefa)
Gaza Strip
West Bank
Be'er Sheva
Dead Sea
Sinai
EGYPT

CENTRAL ASIA

AFGHANISTAN, KYRGYZSTAN, TAJIKISTAN, TURKMENISTAN, UZBEKISTAN

Central Asia is a land of hot, dry deserts and high, rugged mountains. It lies on the ancient Silk Road, an important trade route between China and Europe for over 400 years, until the 15th century. All of the countries here, apart from Afghanistan, were part of the Soviet Union from the 1920s, until 1991, when they gained independence. Since then, their people have re-established their local languages and Islamic faith, all of which were restricted under Russian rule.

INDUSTRY

Fossil fuels, especially coal, natural gas and oil, are extracted and processed throughout Central Asia. Agriculture supplies the raw materials for many industries, including food and textile processing, and the manufacture of leather goods and clothing. The region is famous for its colourful traditional carpets, hand-woven from the wool of the Karakul sheep. The Fergana Valley, southeast of Tashkent, is the main industrial area.

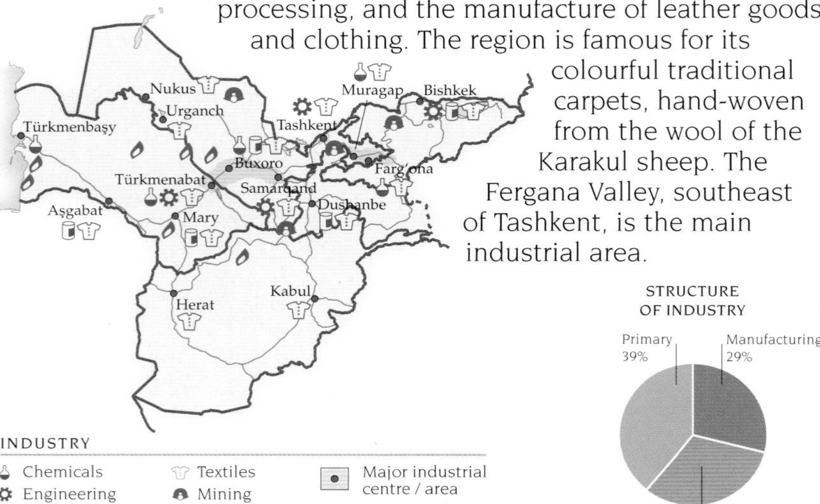
Nukus
Urganch
Türkmenbaşy
Buxoro
Türkmenabat
Samarqand
Aşgabat
Mary
Tashkent
Muragap
Bishkek
Farg'ona
Dushanbe
Kabul
Herat
INDUSTRY
Chemicals
Engineering
Food processing
Textiles
Mining
Oil and gas
Major industrial centre / area
Major road

STRUCTURE OF INDUSTRY

Primary 39%
Manufacturing 29%
Services 32%

POPULATION

The peoples of Central Asia are mostly rural farmers, living in the river valleys and in oases. There are few large cities. A few still lead a traditional nomadic lifestyle, moving from place to place with their animals, in search of new pastures. Large areas of Afghanistan, the western deserts and the mountain regions in the east, are virtually uninhabited.

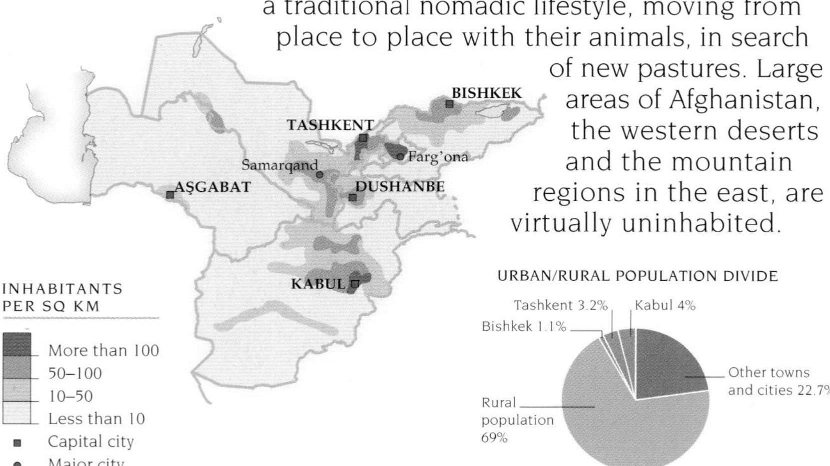
BISHKEK
TASHKENT
Farg'ona
Samarqand
AŞGABAT
DUSHANBE
KABUL
INHABITANTS PER SQ KM
More than 100
50–100
10–50
Less than 10
Capital city
Major city

URBAN/RURAL POPULATION DIVIDE

Tashkent 3.2%
Kabul 4%
Bishkek 1.1%
Other towns and cities 22.7%
Rural population 69%

FARMING AND LAND USE

Farming is concentrated around the fertile river valleys in the east, like the Fergana Valley. A variety of cereals, and fruits, including peaches, melons and apricots, are grown. In drier areas, animal breeding is important, with goats, sheep and cattle supplying wool, meat and hides. Big crops of cotton, which is a major export, are produced on land irrigated by the Amu Darya river.

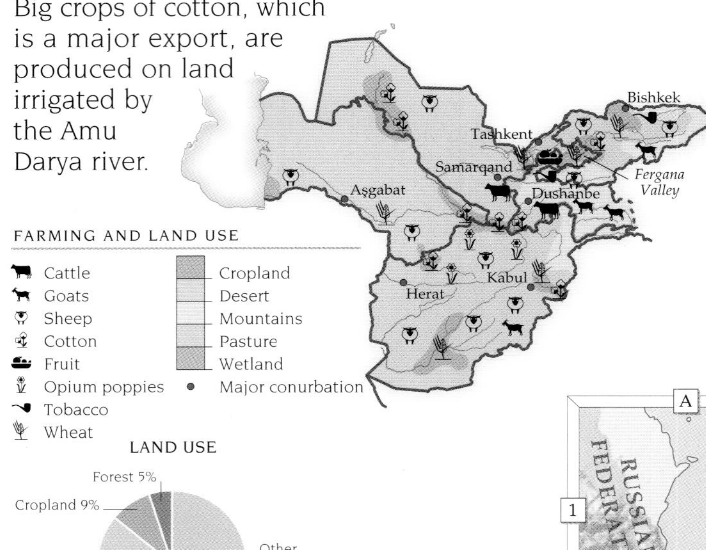
Bishkek
Tashkent
Samarqand
Fergana Valley
Aşgabat
Dushanbe
Herat
Kabul

FARMING AND LAND USE

Cattle
Goats
Sheep
Cotton
Fruit
Opium poppies
Tobacco
Wheat
Cropland
Desert
Mountains
Pasture
Wetland
Major conurbation

LAND USE

Forest 5%
Cropland 9%
Other (including mountains and deserts) 35%
Pasture 51%

THE LANDSCAPE

Two of the world's great deserts, the Garagum and the Kyzyl Kum, cover much of the western portion of Central Asia. In the east, a belt of high mountain ranges – the Hindu Kush, the Tien Shan and the Pamirs – tower above the land. Few rivers cross the deserts, apart from the Amu Darya, which flows from the Pamirs to the shrinking Aral Sea.

The Aral Sea (D 1)
The Aral Sea was once the fourth largest lake in the world, but it has shrunk by 75% since 1960. Diversion of its water for irrigation has made the lake shallower, so its waters evaporate faster.

Garagum (D 3)
The sandy desert of the Garagum occupies over 70% of Turkmenistan. Its surface consists of wind-sculpted dunes and depressions. Human settlement is limited to the desert's fringes.

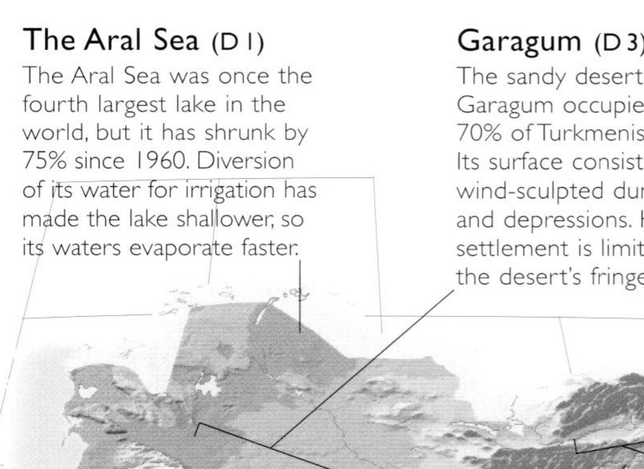

Tien Shan (H 2)

Fergana Valley (G 3)
Stresses and strains in the Earth created the Fergana Valley, a deep depression encircled by high mountains. The valley's fertile soils are irrigated by water from the Syr Darya river, and underground sources.

Amu Darya river (E 3)

Hindu Kush (G 4)

Pamirs (G 4)
The Pamirs lie mainly in Tajikistan. Their highest point, at 7,495 m, is Qullai Ismoili Somoni, previously known as Communism Peak because it was the highest peak in the former Soviet Union.

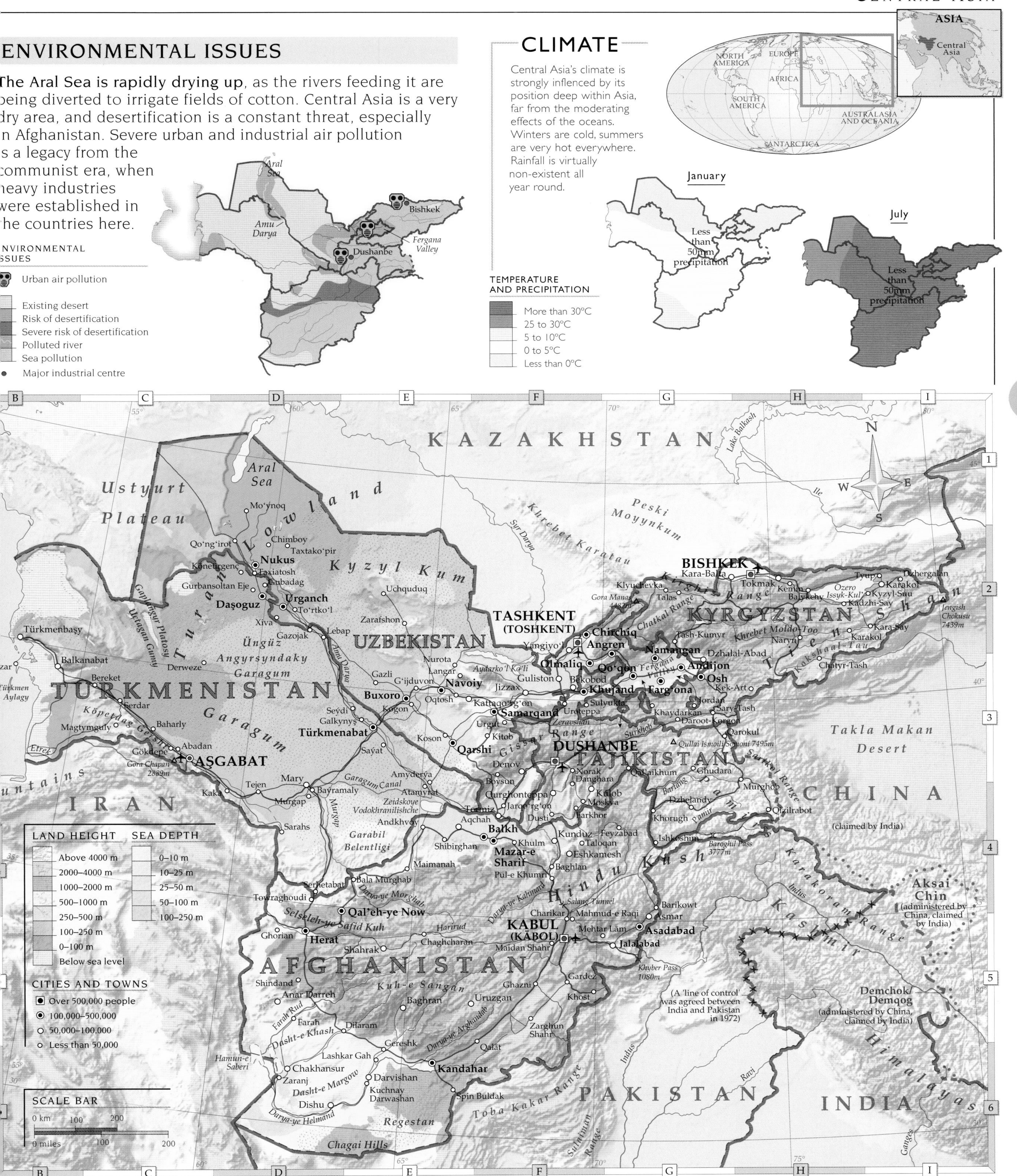
ENVIRONMENTAL ISSUES
The Aral Sea is rapidly drying up, as the rivers feeding it are being diverted to irrigate fields of cotton. Central Asia is a very dry area, and desertification is a constant threat, especially in Afghanistan. Severe urban and industrial air pollution is a legacy from the communist era, when heavy industries were established in the countries here.
ENVIRONMENTAL ISSUES
Urban air pollution
Existing desert
Risk of desertification
Severe risk of desertification
Polluted river
Sea pollution
Major industrial centre
Aral Sea
Amu Darya
Bishkek
Dushanbe
Fergana Valley
CLIMATE
Central Asia's climate is strongly inflenced by its position deep within Asia, far from the moderating effects of the oceans. Winters are cold, summers are very hot everywhere. Rainfall is virtually non-existent all year round.
ASIA
Central Asia
NORTH AMERICA
EUROPE
AFRICA
SOUTH AMERICA
AUSTRALASIA AND OCEANIA
ANTARCTICA
January
July
Less than 50mm precipitation
TEMPERATURE AND PRECIPITATION
More than 30°C
25 to 30°C
5 to 10°C
0 to 5°C
Less than 0°C
KAZAKHSTAN
UZBEKISTAN
TURKMENISTAN
KYRGYZSTAN
TAJIKISTAN
AFGHANISTAN
IRAN
CHINA
PAKISTAN
INDIA
Aral Sea
Ustyurt Plateau
Turan Lowland
Kyzyl Kum
Garagum
Peski Moyynkum
Takla Makan Desert
Hindu Kush
Karakoram Range
Kashmir
Himalayas
Tien Shan
Pamirs
Aksai Chin (administered by China, claimed by India)
Demchok/Demqoq (administered by China, claimed by India)
(A 'line of control' was agreed between India and Pakistan in 1972)
(claimed by India)
TASHKENT (TOSHKENT)
BISHKEK
DUSHANBE
AŞGABAT
KABUL (KĀBOL)
Samarqand
Buxoro
Nukus
Urganch
Daşoguz
Türkmenbaşy
Türkmenabat
Mary
Herat
Kandahar
Mazar-e Sharif
Jalalabad
Osh
Namangan
Andijon
Farg'ona
Khujand
Qarshi
Termiz
Jengish Chokusu 7439m
Qullai Ismoili Somoni 7495m
Khyber Pass 1080m
Salang Tunnel
LAND HEIGHT
Above 4000 m
2000–4000 m
1000–2000 m
500–1000 m
250–500 m
100–250 m
0–100 m
Below sea level
SEA DEPTH
0–10 m
10–25 m
25–50 m
50–100 m
100–250 m
CITIES AND TOWNS
Over 500,000 people
100,000–500,000
50,000–100,000
Less than 50,000
SCALE BAR
0 km 100 200
0 miles 100 200

South Asia

BANGLADESH, BHUTAN, INDIA, NEPAL, PAKISTAN, SRI LANKA

South Asia is a land of many contrasts. Its landscape ranges from the mighty peaks of the Himalayas in the north, through vast plains and arid desert, to tropical forests and palm-fringed beaches in the south. More than one-fifth of the world's people live here, and a long history of foreign invasions has left a mosaic of hugely different cultures, religions and traditions, and thousands of languages and dialects.

FARMING AND LAND USE

Over 60% of the population is involved in agriculture, but most farms are small, and produce only enough food to feed one family. Grains are the staple food crops – rice in the wetter parts of the east and west, corn and millet on the Deccan plateau, and wheat in the north. Groundnuts are widely grown as a source of cooking oil. Cash crops include tea, which is grown on plantations, and jute.

FARMING AND LAND USE

Cattle
Fishing
Goats
Cereals
Groundnuts
Jute
Rice
Tea
Cropland
Desert
Forest
Pasture
Wetland
Major conurbation

LAND USE

Pasture 5%
Forest 21%
Other 24%
Cropland 50%

INDUSTRY

Industry has expanded in India in recent years, and in the cities a variety of goods are produced and processed, including cars, aeroplanes, chemicals, food and drink. Service industries such as tourism and banking are also growing. Elsewhere, small-scale cottage industries serve the needs of local people, but many products, mainly silk and cotton textiles, clothing, leather and jewellery, are also exported.

STRUCTURE OF INDUSTRY

Primary 23%
Services 49%
Manufacturing 28%

INDUSTRY

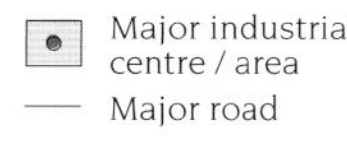

Aerospace
Car manufacture
Chemicals
Electronics
Engineering
Food processing
Iron and steel
Textiles
Mining
High-tech industry
Finance
Tourism
Major industrial centre / area
Major road

THE LANDSCAPE

A massive, towering wall of snow-capped mountains stretches in an arc across the north, isolating South Asia from the rest of the continent. The huge floodplains and deltas of the Indus, Ganges and Brahmaputra rivers separate the mountains from the rest of the peninsula: a great rolling plateau, bordered on either side by coastal hills called the Eastern and Western Ghats.

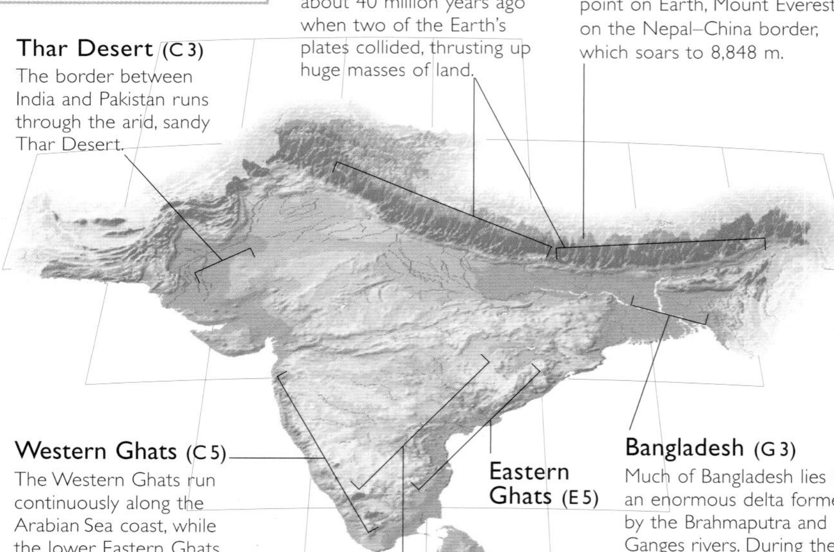

Himalayas (E 2)
The Himalayas are the highest mountain system in the world. They were formed about 40 million years ago when two of the Earth's plates collided, thrusting up huge masses of land.

Mount Everest (F 3)
The northern ranges of the Himalayas average 7,000 m in height. They include the highest point on Earth, Mount Everest on the Nepal–China border, which soars to 8,848 m.

Thar Desert (C 3)
The border between India and Pakistan runs through the arid, sandy Thar Desert.

Western Ghats (C 5)
The Western Ghats run continuously along the Arabian Sea coast, while the lower Eastern Ghats are interrupted by rivers that follow the gentle slope of the Deccan plateau and flow across broad lowlands into the Bay of Bengal. This is one of the wettest regions in the world.

Eastern Ghats (E 5)

Deccan plateau (D 5)
This giant plateau makes up most of central and southern India. Its volcanic rock has been deeply cut by rivers such as the Krishna, creating stepped valleys called *traps*.

Bangladesh (G 3)
Much of Bangladesh lies in an enormous delta formed by the Brahmaputra and Ganges rivers. During the summer monsoon, the rivers become swollen by the torrential rains – and meltwater from the Himalayas – and the delta floods. Over the years, millions of people have drowned or been made homeless by heavy flooding.

POPULATION

Most of South Asia's people live in villages scattered across the fertile river floodplains, in mountain valleys or along the coasts, but increasing numbers are migrating to the cities in search of work. Overcrowding is a serious problem in both rural and urban areas; in many cities, thousands of people are forced to live in slums, or on the streets.

INHABITANTS PER SQ KM

More than 200
100–200
50–100
Less than 50
Capital city
Major city

URBAN/RURAL POPULATION DIVIDE

Kolkata 1%
Mumbai 1.2%
Delhi 0.8%
Other towns and cities 23%
Rural population 74%

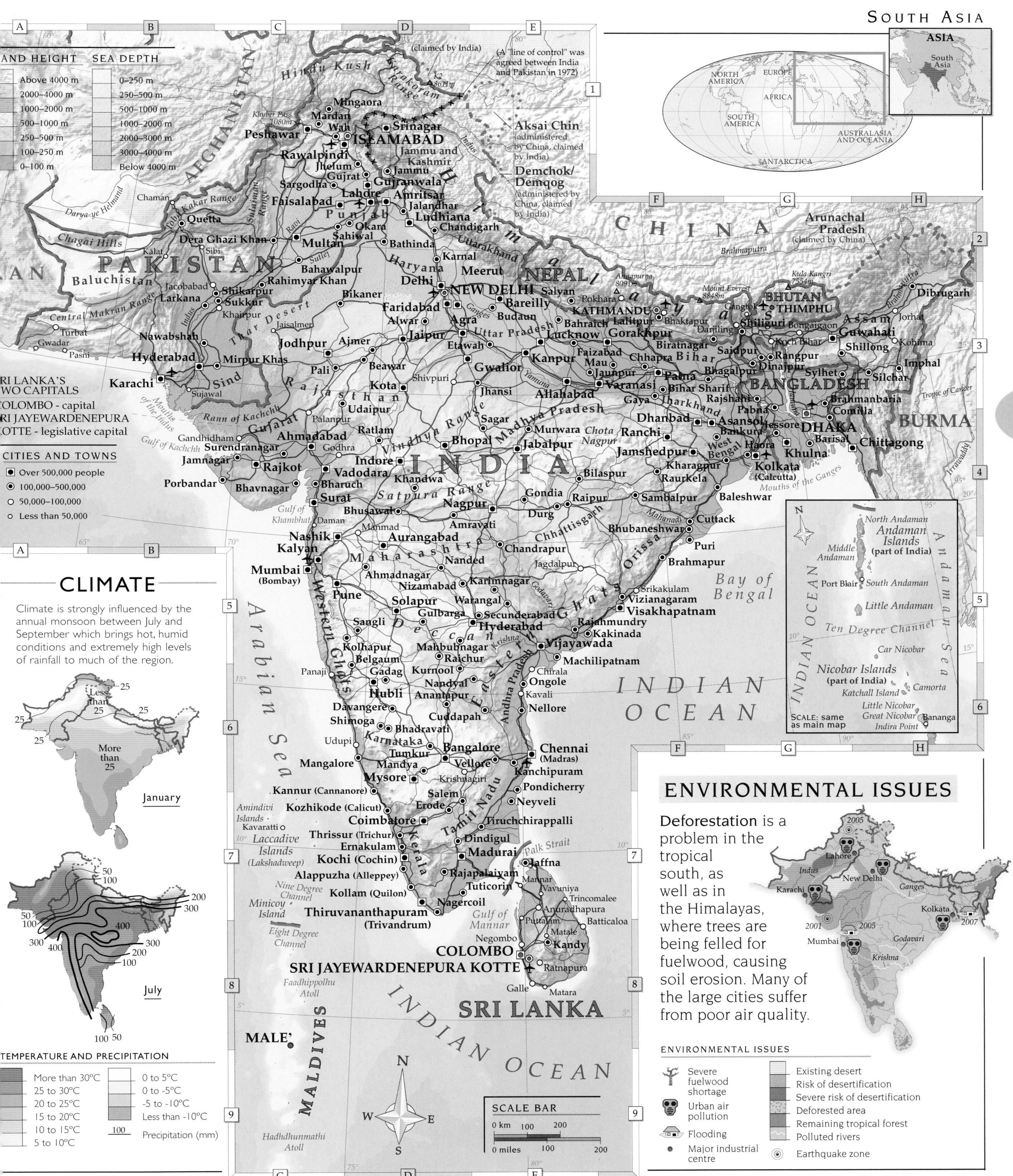
LAND HEIGHT
Above 4000 m
2000–4000 m
1000–2000 m
500–1000 m
250–500 m
100–250 m
0–100 m
SEA DEPTH
0–250 m
250–500 m
500–1000 m
1000–2000 m
2000–3000 m
3000–4000 m
Below 4000 m
SRI LANKA'S TWO CAPITALS
COLOMBO - capital
SRI JAYEWARDENEPURA KOTTE - legislative capital
CITIES AND TOWNS
Over 500,000 people
100,000–500,000
50,000–100,000
Less than 50,000
ASIA
South Asia
NORTH AMERICA
EUROPE
AFRICA
SOUTH AMERICA
AUSTRALASIA AND OCEANIA
ANTARCTICA
(claimed by India)
(A "line of control" was agreed between India and Pakistan in 1972)
Aksai Chin (administered by China, claimed by India)
Demchok/ Demqog (administered by China, claimed by India)
Arunachal Pradesh (claimed by China)
AFGHANISTAN
PAKISTAN
INDIA
NEPAL
BHUTAN
BANGLADESH
BURMA
CHINA
SRI LANKA
MALDIVES
ISLAMABAD
NEW DELHI
KATHMANDU
THIMPHU
DHAKA
COLOMBO
SRI JAYEWARDENEPURA KOTTE
MALE'
Hindu Kush
Karakoram Range
Himalayas
Jammu and Kashmir
Punjab
Baluchistan
Sind
Thar Desert
Rajasthan
Gujarat
Haryana
Uttarakhand
Uttar Pradesh
Madhya Pradesh
Bihar
Jharkhand
West Bengal
Assam
Chhattisgarh
Orissa
Maharashtra
Karnataka
Andhra Pradesh
Tamil Nadu
Kerala
Deccan
Western Ghats
Eastern Ghats
Vindhya Range
Satpura Range
Chota Nagpur
Arabian Sea
Bay of Bengal
INDIAN OCEAN
Gulf of Khambhat
Gulf of Kachchh
Rann of Kachchh
Mouths of the Indus
Mouths of the Ganges
Gulf of Mannar
Palk Strait
Laccadive Islands (Lakshadweep)
Amindivi Islands
Minicoy Island
Nine Degree Channel
Eight Degree Channel
Faadhippolhu Atoll
Hadhdhunmathi Atoll
Tropic of Cancer
Peshawar
Rawalpindi
Srinagar
Lahore
Amritsar
Faisalabad
Multan
Quetta
Karachi
Hyderabad
Delhi
Jaipur
Agra
Lucknow
Kanpur
Varanasi
Patna
Kolkata (Calcutta)
Ahmadabad
Surat
Mumbai (Bombay)
Pune
Nagpur
Bhopal
Indore
Hyderabad
Visakhapatnam
Vijayawada
Chennai (Madras)
Bangalore
Mysore
Coimbatore
Madurai
Kochi (Cochin)
Thiruvananthapuram (Trivandrum)
Jaffna
Kandy
Chittagong
Khulna
Guwahati
SCALE: same as main map
North Andaman
Andaman Islands (part of India)
Middle Andaman
Port Blair
South Andaman
Little Andaman
Ten Degree Channel
Car Nicobar
Nicobar Islands (part of India)
Camorta
Katchall Island
Little Nicobar
Great Nicobar
Indira Point
Bananga
Andaman Sea
SCALE BAR
0 km 100 200
0 miles 100 200
CLIMATE
Climate is strongly influenced by the annual monsoon between July and September which brings hot, humid conditions and extremely high levels of rainfall to much of the region.
January
July
Less than 25
More than 25
TEMPERATURE AND PRECIPITATION
More than 30°C
25 to 30°C
20 to 25°C
15 to 20°C
10 to 15°C
5 to 10°C
0 to 5°C
0 to -5°C
-5 to -10°C
Less than -10°C
Precipitation (mm)
ENVIRONMENTAL ISSUES
Deforestation is a problem in the tropical south, as well as in the Himalayas, where trees are being felled for fuelwood, causing soil erosion. Many of the large cities suffer from poor air quality.
ENVIRONMENTAL ISSUES
Severe fuelwood shortage
Urban air pollution
Flooding
Major industrial centre
Existing desert
Risk of desertification
Severe risk of desertification
Deforested area
Remaining tropical forest
Polluted rivers
Earthquake zone

EAST ASIA

CHINA, MONGOLIA, TAIWAN

China is the world's fourth largest country and its most populous – over 1.3 billion people live there. Under its communist government, which came to power in 1949, China has become a major industrial nation, but most of its people still live and work on the land, as they have for thousands of years. Taiwan also has a booming economy and exports its products around the world. Mongolia is a vast, remote country with a small population, many of whom are nomads.

INDUSTRY

Chemicals, iron and steel, engineering and textiles are the main industries in China's east coast cities, and in industrial centres like Shenyang. Shanghai, Hong Kong and Beijing are also important financial centres. In the interior, large deposits of coal support the heavy industries in major cities such as Chengdu and Wuhan. Taiwan specializes in textiles and shoe manufacture, along with electronic goods. Mongolia's economy is mainly agricultural.

INDUSTRY

- Aerospace
- Car manufacture
- Chemicals
- Electronics
- Electronic goods
- Engineering
- Food processing
- Iron & steel
- Shipbuilding
- Textiles
- Coal
- Mining
- Finance
- Major industrial centre / area
- Major road

STRUCTURE OF INDUSTRY

Services 37%
Manufacturing 50%
Primary 13%

POPULATION

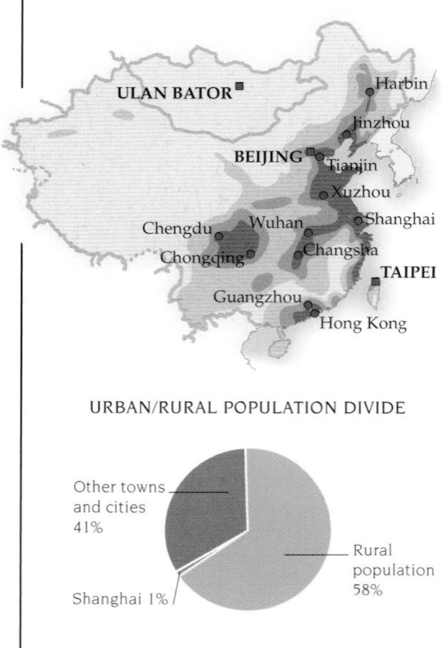
ULAN BATOR
Harbin
Jinzhou
BEIJING
Tianjin
Xuzhou
Shanghai
Chengdu
Wuhan
Chongqing
Changsha
TAIPEI
Guangzhou
Hong Kong
URBAN/RURAL POPULATION DIVIDE
Other towns and cities 41%
Rural population 58%
Shanghai 1%

Most of China's people live in the eastern part of the country, where the climate, landscape and soils are most favourable. Chinese cities are home to over 690 million people, surpassing the rural population for the first time in 2011. Taiwan's lowlands are very densely populated. In Mongolia, one third of the people live in the countryside.

INHABITANTS PER SQ KM

- More than 200
- 100–200
- 50–100
- Less than 50
- Capital city
- Major city

FARMING AND LAND USE

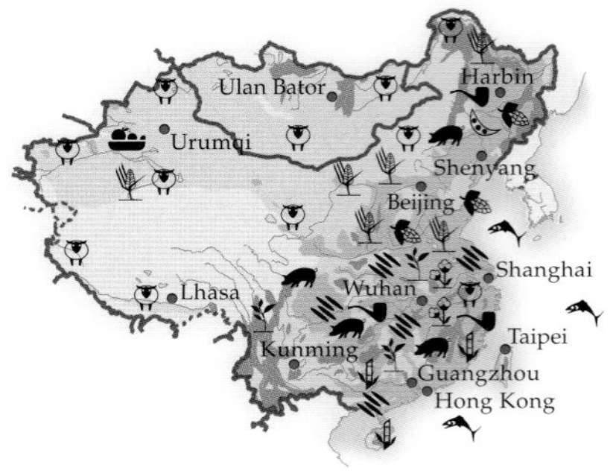
Ulan Bator
Harbin
Urumqi
Shenyang
Beijing
Shanghai
Lhasa
Wuhan
Taipei
Kunming
Guangzhou
Hong Kong

Despite its size, about 90% of China is unsuitable for farming. Either the soils and climate are poor, or the landscape is too mountainous. In the north and west, most farmers make their living by herding animals. On the fertile eastern plains, soya beans, wheat, corn and cotton are grown. Further south, rice becomes the main crop, and pigs are raised in large numbers.

FARMING AND LAND USE

- Fishing
- Pigs
- Sheep
- Corn (maize)
- Cotton
- Fruit
- Rice
- Soya beans
- Sugarcane
- Tea
- Tobacco
- Wheat
- Cropland
- Desert
- Forest
- Mountain region
- Pasture
- Major conurbation

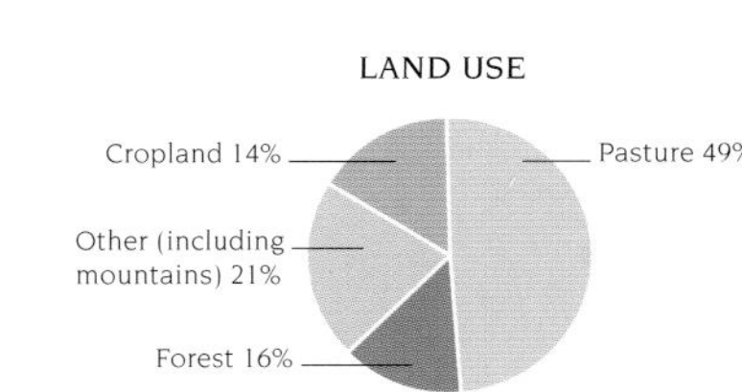
LAND USE
Cropland 14%
Pasture 49%
Other (including mountains) 21%
Forest 16%

THE LANDSCAPE

China's landscape divides into three areas. The vast Plateau of Tibet in the southwest is the highest and largest plateau on Earth. It contains both dry deserts and pockets of pasture surrounded by high mountains. Northwest China has dry highlands. The great plains of eastern China were formed from soils deposited by rivers like the Yellow River over thousands of years. Most of Mongolia is dry, grassland steppe and cold, arid desert.

Tien Shan mountains (B 2)

The Tien Shan, or 'Heavenly Mountains' reach heights of 7,443 m. They surround fields of permanent ice and spectacular glaciers.

Gobi (E 2) and Takla Makan (B 3) deserts

The arid landscapes of the Gobi and Takla Makan deserts are made up of bare rock surfaces and huge areas of shifting sand dunes. They are hot in summer, but unlike most other deserts are extremely cold in winter.

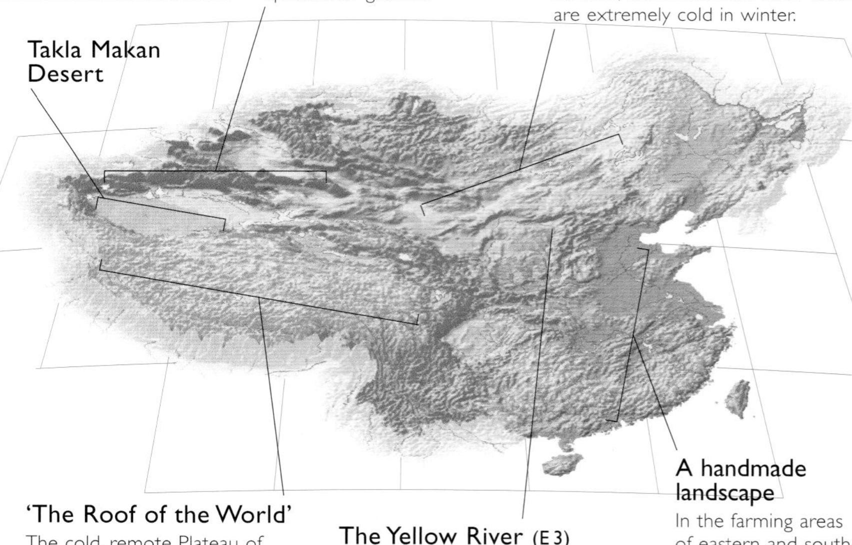

Takla Makan Desert

'The Roof of the World'

The cold, remote Plateau of Tibet (C 4) averages 4,000 m in height. Many of China's great rivers have their sources here. The world's highest human settlement, a town called Wenquan, is found in the east of the plateau. It lies 5,099 m above sea level.

The Yellow River (E 3)

The Yellow River (Huang He) is the world's muddiest river, carrying hundreds of lorry loads of sediment to the sea every minute. The river has burst its banks many times throughout history, causing enormous damage and claiming millions of human lives.

A handmade landscape

In the farming areas of eastern and southern China, terraces have been carved into the hillsides to make them flat enough to grow rice and other crops. This method of farming has been used for over 7,000 years.

ENVIRONMENTAL ISSUES

China is now the world's largest emitter of greenhouse gases. Its rapid economic growth has had a huge impact upon the environment. The Yangtze and Yellow Rivers are badly polluted. Urbanization is increasing, with over 00 cities in China having populations above 1 million. The Three Gorges Dam is the largest hydro-electric project in the world.

ENVIRONMENTAL ISSUES

- Polluted river
- Sea pollution
- Major dam
- Urban air pollution
- Industrial city

CLIMATE

Two air masses control climate; one cold and dry from Siberia, and one moist and warm from the Pacific. Winters are long and cold away from the coast – especially on the Plateau of Tibet.

TEMPERATURE AND PRECIPITATION

- More than 30°C
- 20 to 30°C
- 10 to 20°C
- 0 to 10°C
- 0 to -10°C
- -10 to -20°C
- Less than -20°C
- 100 Precipitation (mm)

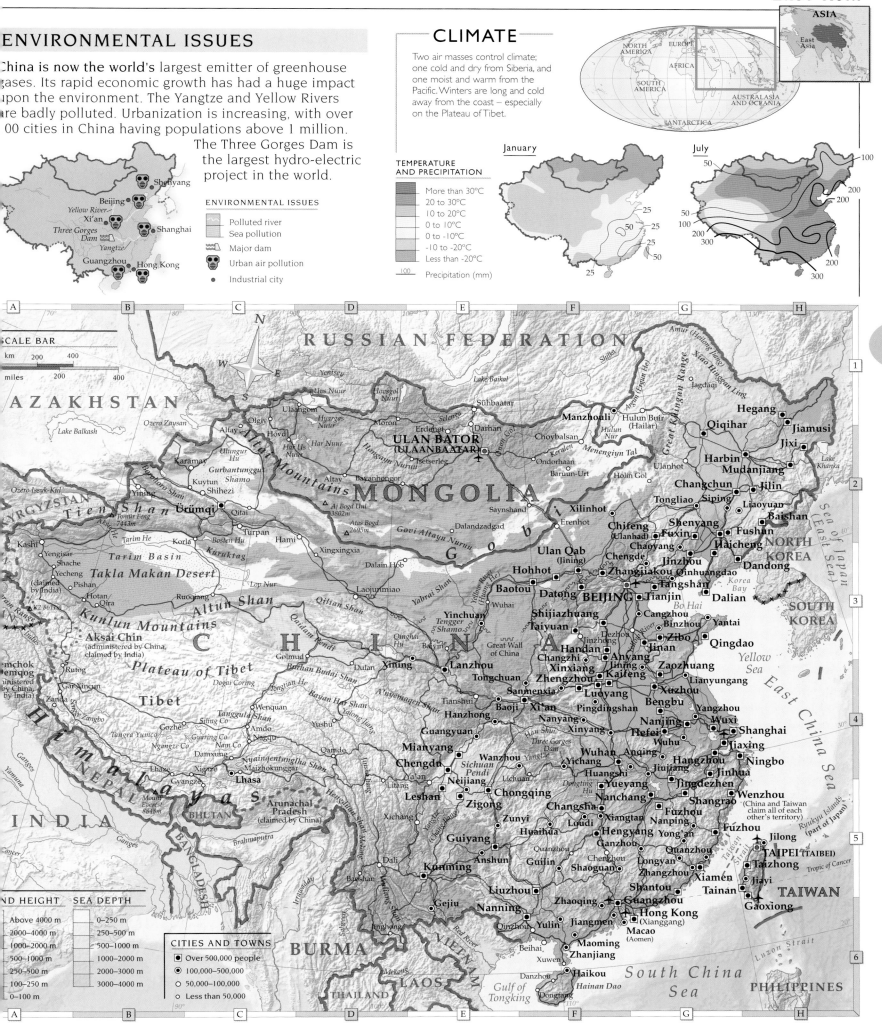

January

July

SCALE BAR

LAND HEIGHT

- Above 4000 m
- 2000–4000 m
- 1000–2000 m
- 500–1000 m
- 250–500 m
- 100–250 m
- 0–100 m

SEA DEPTH

- 0–250 m
- 250–500 m
- 500–1000 m
- 1000–2000 m
- 2000–3000 m
- 3000–4000 m

CITIES AND TOWNS

- Over 500,000 people
- 100,000–500,000
- 50,000–100,000
- Less than 50,000

Southeast Asia

BRUNEI, BURMA, CAMBODIA, EAST TIMOR, INDONESIA, LAOS, MALAYSIA, PHILIPPINES, SINGAPORE, THAILAND, VIETNAM

Southeast Asia is made up of a mainland area and many thousands of tropical islands. The region has great natural wealth – from precious stones to oil – and has recently experienced fast industrial growth. Some countries here, especially Singapore and Malaysia, have become prosperous, but Laos and Cambodia remain poor, and are still recovering from years of terrible warfare.

ENVIRONMENTAL ISSUES

In Burma, Malaysia and Indonesia, ancient rainforests are being cut down faster than they can grow back. On 26th of December, 2004 a tsunami devastated the west of the region, it is estimated that over 225,000 people died around the Indian Ocean.

Rangoon
Bangkok
Manila
Kuala Lumpur
Singapore
Jakarta
Surabaya

ENVIRONMENTAL ISSUES

- Urban air pollution
- Deforested area
- Remaining tropical forest
- Major industrial centre

POPULATION

On the mainland, the population is concentrated in the river valleys, plateaus or plains. Upland areas are inhabited by small groups of hill peoples. Most people still live in rural areas, but the cities are growing fast. In Indonesia and the Philippines, the population is unevenly distributed. Some islands, such as Java, are densely settled; others are barely occupied.

NAY PYI TAW
HANOI
VIENTIANE
Da Nang
Rangoon
MANILA
BANGKOK
PHNOM PENH
Ho Chi Minh
Davao
KUALA LUMPUR
BANDAR SERI BEGAWAN
Medan
PUTRAJAYA
SINGAPORE
Manado
Palembang
JAKARTA
Surabaya
DILI

INHABITANTS PER SQ KM

- More than 200
- 100–200
- 50–100
- Less than 50
- Capital city
- Major city

URBAN/RURAL POPULATION DIVIDE

Bangkok 1.2%
Jakarta 1.5%
Manilla 1.8%
Rural population 37%
Other towns and cities 58.5%

INDUSTRY

Industries based on the processing of raw materials, like metallic minerals, timber, oil and gas and agricultural produce, are important here, but manufacturing has grown dramatically in recent years. Many foreign firms, attracted by low labour costs, have invested in the region. Malaysia and Singapore are major producers of electronic goods like disk drives for computers.

Mandalay
Hanoi
Rangoon
Da Nang
Manila
Bangkok
Phnom Penh
Ho Chi Minh
Davao
Medan
Kuala Lumpur
Singapore
Palembang
Jakarta
Bandung
Surabaya
Semarang

STRUCTURE OF INDUSTRY

Primary 19%
Services 45%
Manufacturing 36%

INDUSTRY

- Chemicals
- Engineering
- Food processing
- Textiles
- Mining
- Oil and gas
- Timber
- Finance
- Hi-tech
- Tourism
- Major industrial centre / area
- Major road

THE LANDSCAPE

On the mainland, a belt of mountain ranges, cloaked in thick forest, runs north–south. The mountains are cut through by the wide valleys of five great rivers. On their route to the sea, these rivers have deposited sediment, forming immense, fertile flood plains and deltas. To the southeast of the mainland lies a huge arc of over 20,000 mountainous, volcanic islands.

Borneo (D7)
Borneo is the world's third-largest island, with a total area of 757,050 sq km. Lying on the Equator and in the path of two monsoons, the island is hot, and one of the wettest places on Earth. The landscape contains thickly-forested central highlands and swampy lowlands.

Asian Tsunami (A6)
On December 26th, 2004 the second largest earthquake ever recorded occured under the sea off the west coast of Sumatra. This triggered a huge Tsunami wave, up to 30 m high in places, that devastated coastal communities causing the deaths of over 225,000 people in eleven countries.

Philippines (E4)
The Philippines' 7,000 islands are mountainous and volcanic with narrow coastal plains.

Papua (Irian Jaya) (I7)
Papua is a province of Indonesia. Its dense rainforests are some of the last unexplored areas on Earth and are inhabited by many rare plant and animal species.

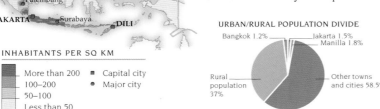

Volcanoes
Indonesia is the most active volcanic region in the world; Java alone has over 50 active volcanoes out of the country's total of more than 220.

Indonesia (C7)
Indonesia is an archipelago of 13,677 islands, scattered over almost 5,000 km. The islands lie on the boundary between two of the Earth's tectonic plates and frequently experience earthquakes.

A
INDIA
Brahmaputra
Myitkyina
Banmauk
BURMA
Falam
Monywa
Mandalay
Sagaing
Pakokku
Taunggyi
Minbu
Sittwe
Ramree Island
NAY PYI TAW
Cheduba Island
Pyay
Thandwe
Hinthada
Rangoon
Pathein
Mawlamyine
Mouths of the Irrawaddy
Andaman Islands
(part of India)
Andaman Sea
Nicobar Islands
(part of India)
Bandaaceh
Sigli
Meulaboh
Pematangsiantar
Pulau Simeulue
Pulau Nias
Kepulauan Banyak
Equator
INDIA
SCALE BAR
0 km
200
400
0 miles
200
1
2
3
4
5
6
7
8

FARMING AND LAND USE
The staple crop here is rice, which grows in low-lying flooded fields called paddies, or on terraces cut into the hillsides. Sugarcane, coconuts, bananas and pineapples are widely grown as cash crops, and Malaysia produces 25% of the world's rubber. Freshwater and marine fish are caught in large quantities; fish is one of the main foods in this region.
FARMING AND LAND USE
Cattle
Fishing
Pigs
Shellfish
Coconuts
Fruit
Rice
Rubber
Sugarcane
Timber
Cropland
Forest
Pasture
Wetland
Major conurbation
LAND USE
Pasture 4%
Cropland 21%
Forest 51%
Other 24%
ASIA
Southeast Asia
NORTH AMERICA
EUROPE
AFRICA
SOUTH AMERICA
AUSTRALASIA AND OCEANIA
ANTARCTICA
CLIMATE
Southeast Asia's climate is strongly affected by the monsoon, which brings warm, humid air and high rainfall to mainland Southeast Asia during July, and to maritime southeast Asia during January.
January
July
TEMPERATURE AND PRECIPITATION
More than 30°C
20 to 30°C
10 to 20°C
Less than 10°C
100 Precipitation (mm)
LAND HEIGHT
Above 4000 m
2000–4000 m
1000–2000 m
500–1000 m
250–500 m
100–250 m
0–100 m
SEA DEPTH
0–250 m
250–500 m
500–1000 m
1000–2000 m
2000–3000 m
3000–4000 m
Below 4000 m
CITIES AND TOWNS
Over 500,000 people
100,000–500,000
50,000–100,000
Less than 50,000
MALAYSIA'S TWO CAPITALS
KUALA LUMPUR - capital
PUTRAJAYA - administrative capital
CHINA
TAIWAN
PHILIPPINES
VIETNAM
CAMBODIA
MALAYSIA
BRUNEI
INDONESIA
EAST TIMOR
PALAU
PAPUA NEW GUINEA
PACIFIC OCEAN
South China Sea
Philippine Sea
Celebes Sea
Sulu Sea
Java Sea
Flores Sea
Banda Sea
Arafura Sea
Timor Sea
Savu Sea
PARACEL ISLANDS (disputed by China, Taiwan & Vietnam)
SPRATLY ISLANDS (disputed by China, Malaysia, Philippines, Taiwan & Vietnam)
Ryukyu Islands (part of Japan)
HANOI
MANILA
KUALA LUMPUR
PUTRAJAYA
SINGAPORE
JAKARTA
BANDAR SERI BEGAWAN
DILI
Borneo
Kalimantan
Sarawak
Sabah
Celebes (Sulawesi)
Moluccas (Maluku)
Papua (Irian Jaya)
New Guinea
Mindanao
Luzon
Java
Equator

Japan and Korea

JAPAN, NORTH KOREA, SOUTH KOREA

Japan is a curved chain of over 4,000 islands in the Pacific Ocean. To the west, Korea juts out from northern China. Japan has few natural resources but it has become one of the world's most successful industrial nations due to investment in new technology and a highly efficient workforce. North Korea is a communist state with limited contact with the outside world, while South Korea is a democracy with major international trade links.

THE LANDSCAPE

Most of Japan is covered by forested mountains and hills, among which are many short, fast-flowing rivers and small lakes. Only about a quarter of the land is suitable for building and farming and new land has been created by cutting back hillsides and reclaiming land from the sea. North and South Korea are mostly mountainous, with some coastal plains.

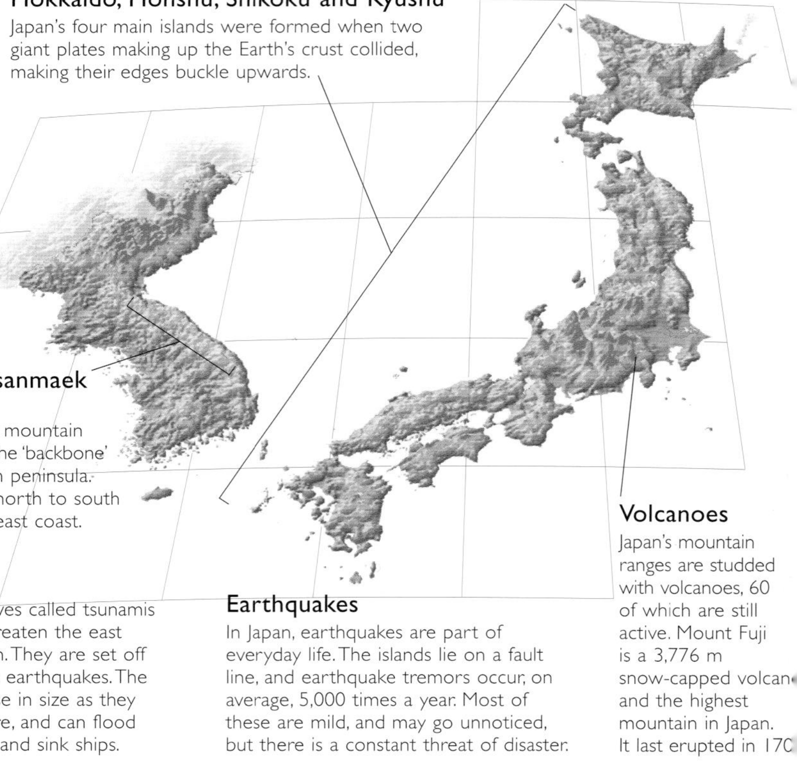

Hokkaido, Honshu, Shikoku and Kyushu
Japan's four main islands were formed when two giant plates making up the Earth's crust collided, making their edges buckle upwards.

T'aebaek-sanmaek (C5)
This wooded mountain range forms the 'backbone' of the Korean peninsula. It runs from north to south close to the east coast.

Tsunamis
Huge sea waves called tsunamis frequently threaten the east coast of Japan. They are set off by submarine earthquakes. The waves increase in size as they near the shore, and can flood coastal areas and sink ships.

Earthquakes
In Japan, earthquakes are part of everyday life. The islands lie on a fault line, and earthquake tremors occur, on average, 5,000 times a year. Most of these are mild, and may go unnoticed, but there is a constant threat of disaster.

Volcanoes
Japan's mountain ranges are studded with volcanoes, 60 of which are still active. Mount Fuji is a 3,776 m snow-capped volcan and the highest mountain in Japan. It last erupted in 170

FARMING AND LAND USE

Modern farming methods allow Japan to grow much of its own food, despite a shortage of farmland. Rice is the main crop grown throughout the region. Japan has a large fishing fleet; the Japanese eat more fish than any other nation. In North Korea, farming is controlled by the government.

FARMING AND LAND USE

- Cattle
- Fishing
- Pigs
- Fruit
- Rice
- Soya beans
- Tea
- Tobacco
- Cropland
- Forest
- Pasture
- Major conurbation

LAND USE

Pasture 1%
Cropland 16%
Other (including mountains) 18%
Forest 65%

POPULATION

Most of Japan's 128 million people live in crowded cities on the coasts of the four main islands. The Kanto Plain around Tokyo is Japan's biggest area of flat land, and the most populous part of the country. In South Korea, a quarter of the population lives in the capital, Seoul. Most North Koreans live on the coastal plains.

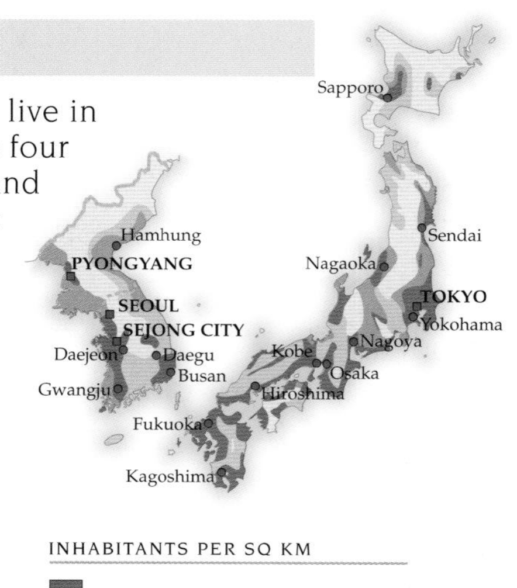
Sapporo
Hamhung
PYONGYANG
SEOUL
SEJONG CITY
Daejeon
Daegu
Busan
Gwangju
Fukuoka
Kagoshima
Hiroshima
Kobe
Osaka
Nagoya
Nagaoka
Sendai
TOKYO
Yokohama

URBAN/RURAL POPULATION DIVIDE

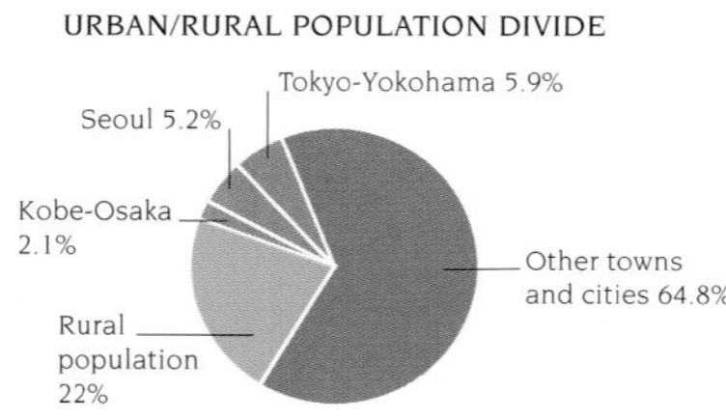
Tokyo-Yokohama 5.9%
Seoul 5.2%
Kobe-Osaka 2.1%
Rural population 22%
Other towns and cities 64.8%

INHABITANTS PER SQ KM

- More than 200
- 100–200
- 50–100
- Less than 50
- Capital city
- Major city

INDUSTRY

Japan is a world leader in hi-tech electronic goods like computers, televisions and cameras, as well as cars. South Korea also has a thriving economy. It produces ships, cars, hi-tech goods, shoes and clothes for worldwide export. Both countries have to import most of their raw materials and energy. North Korea has little trade with other countries, but it is rich in minerals such as coal and silver.

STRUCTURE OF INDUSTRY

Primary 2%
Services 70%
Manufacturing 28%

INDUSTRY

- Car manufacture
- Chemicals
- Engineering
- Food processing
- Iron & steel
- Shipbuilding
- Textiles
- Mining
- Finance
- Hi-tech
- Research & Development
- Major industrial centre / area
- Major road

ENVIRONMENTAL ISSUES
Industrial pollution from Korea and China has produced acid rain, and pollution in Japanese cities has led to people wearing masks to filter the air. Russia regularly dumps nuclear waste into the Sea of Japan. In 2011, a tsunami destroyed much of the coastal region around Sendai.
ENVIRONMENTAL ISSUES
Catastrophic earthquake
Nuclear waste dump site
Urban air pollution
Affected by acid rain
Site of nuclear accident
Major industrial area
Sea of Japan / East Sea
Seoul
Kobe 1995
Osaka
Tokyo
Tohoku 2011
1999/2011
CLIMATE
Korea has hot summers and dry, very cold winters, especially in the north, where snow is common. In Japan, winters are less cold than on the Asian mainland; summers are hot, wet and humid.
January
July
Less than 50
TEMPERATURE AND PRECIPITATION
More than 20°C
15 to 20°C
10 to 15°C
5 to 10°C
0 to 5°C
0 to -5°C
Less than -5°C
Precipitation (mm)
ASIA
Japan and Korea
NORTH AMERICA
EUROPE
AFRICA
SOUTH AMERICA
AUSTRALASIA AND OCEANIA
ANTARCTICA
SCALE BAR
CHINA
NORTH KOREA
SOUTH KOREA
JAPAN
PACIFIC OCEAN
Sea of Japan/ East Sea
Sea of Okhotsk
East China Sea
Yellow Sea
Hokkaido
Honshu
Shikoku
Kyushu
Kurile Islands (administered by Russian Federation, claimed by Japan)
(North and South Korea have been divided by a ceasefire agreement since 1953)
Liancourt Rocks (under South Korean control)
PYONGYANG
SEOUL (SOUL)
SEJONG CITY
TOKYO
Sapporo
Sendai
Osaka
Kyoto
Nagoya
Hiroshima
Fukuoka
Busan
Ryukyu Islands (part of Japan)
Philippine Sea
SOUTH KOREA'S TWO CAPITALS
SEOUL - capital
SEJONG CITY - administrative capital
LAND HEIGHT
2000–4000 m
1000–2000 m
500–1000 m
250–500 m
100–250 m
0–100 m
SEA DEPTH
0–250 m
250–500 m
500–1000 m
1000–2000 m
2000–3000 m
3000–4000 m
Below 4000 m
CITIES AND TOWNS
Over 500,000 people
100,000–500,000
50,000–100,000
Less than 50,000

AUSTRALASIA & OCEANIA

7,300 km

9,800 km

Australasia and Oceania encompasses the ancient land mass of Australia, the islands of New Zealand, and the scattering of thousands of small islands that stretch out into the Pacific Ocean. Indigenous peoples of the South Pacific, such as the Aborigines, Maoris, Polynesians, Micronesians and Melanesians, inhabit the region. In Australia and New Zealand, they live alongside people of European origin who settled in the 18th century, and more recent arrivals from East and Southeast Asia.

PACIFIC ISLANDS

Micronesia is one of the Pacific's island nations, consisting of a group of volcanic islands, low-lying coral reefs and lagoons. Many of the smaller Pacific islands are only a few metres above sea level.

LAND USE AND AGRICULTURE

Much of the centre of Australia is a dry, barren desert and unsuitable for agriculture. At its fringes, sheep farming is practised, and Australia and New Zealand alike are massive producers of wool and lamb. The Pacific islands export many exotic fruits and crops – especially oil palms and coconut palms. Oil from the palms is processed and sold, as well as the fruits themselves. Small-scale fishing is common, but larger scale operations are run by foreign fishing fleets, especially the Japanese, who fish tuna from the deeper waters of the Pacific.

SHEEP FARMING

New Zealand and Australia are the world's biggest producers of wool. In New Zealand, sheep outnumber people by 12 to 1.

POPULATION

Capital cities
- Above 500,000
- 100,000 to 500,000
- 50,000 to 100,000
- Below 50,000

State capitals
- Above 500,000
- 100,000 to 500,000
- 50,000 to 100,000

BORDERS
- full international border
- indication of maritime country extent
- indication of maritime dependent territory extent
- state border

Mariana Islands
Saipan
HAGÅTÑA (AGANA)
Guam (to USA)
MICRON
Yap
NGERULMUD
Babeldaob
PALAU

PAPUA
Bismarck Sea
New Britain
New Guinea
PORT MORESBY
Arafura Sea
Torres Strait
Darwin
Arnhem Land
Gulf of Carpentaria
Cape York Peninsula
Great Barrier Reef
Timor Sea
INDIAN OCEAN
Kimberley Plateau
NORTHERN TERRITORY
Tanami Desert
QUEENSLAND
Great Sandy Desert
Simpson Desert
Uluru (Ayers Rock)
AUSTRALIA
Hamersley Range
Gibson Desert
Lake Eyre North
SOUTH AUSTRALIA
WESTERN AUSTRALIA
Lake Torrens
Tropic of Capricorn
Great Victoria Desert
Lake Everard
Lake Gairdner
Nullarbor Plain
Great Australian Bight
Adelaide
Kangaroo Island
Perth

New Guinea
Port Moresby
Honiara
Torres Strait
Timor Sea
Darwin
Coral Sea
Port Vila
Suva
Great Barrier Reef
Townsville
PACIFIC OCEAN
INDIAN OCEAN
Brisbane
Newcastle
Sydney
Canberra
Adelaide
Melbourne
Auckland
Wellington
Christchurch
Perth
Hobart
Tasman Sea

LAND USE AND AGRICULTURE
- Cattle
- Sheep
- Coconuts
- Coffee
- Fishing
- Fruit
- Shellfish
- Sugarcane
- Timber
- Vineyards
- Wheat
- Cropland
- Desert
- Forest
- Mountain region
- Pasture
- Major conurbation

COCONUTS

Coconuts are grown throughout the islands of the Pacific, and the white flesh is dried in the sun to produce copra. Copra is a valuable export crop for many islands.

MINERAL RESOURCES

Mineral resources are not widespread, but where they are found, t is in great abundance. Most of the small Pacific islands have no nineral resources, but Australia has enormous reserves of bauxite and iron ore, and also sizeable reserves of gold and zinc. Copper s found in Papua New Guinea, and New Caledonia has large nickel reserves. There are ample supplies of fossil fuels and although coal is plentiful in eastern Australia, oil and gas are found only in isolated pockets around Australia's coast.

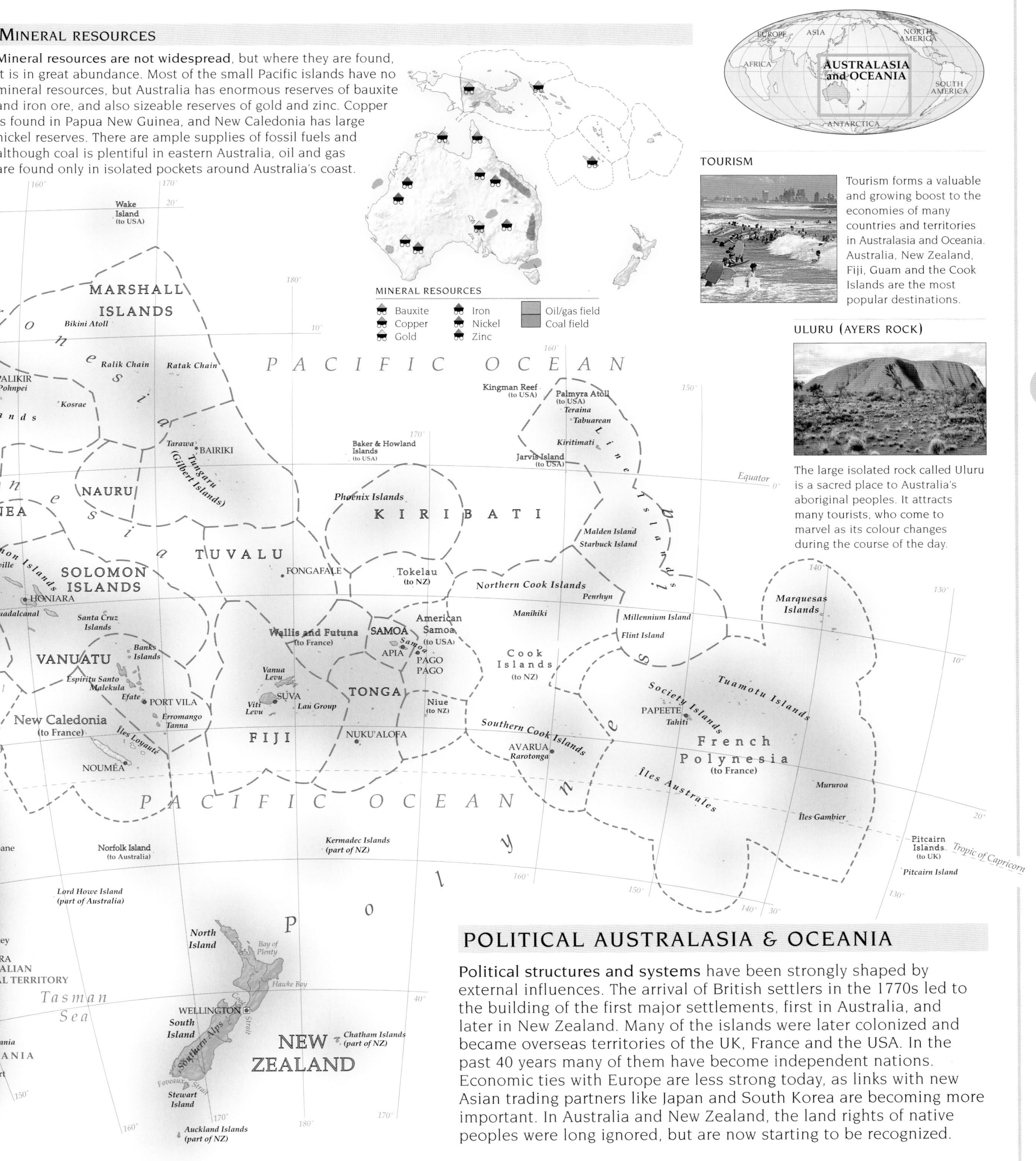

MINERAL RESOURCES
Bauxite
Copper
Gold
Iron
Nickel
Zinc
Oil/gas field
Coal field
EUROPE
ASIA
NORTH AMERICA
AFRICA
AUSTRALASIA and OCEANIA
SOUTH AMERICA
ANTARCTICA
Wake Island (to USA)
MARSHALL ISLANDS
Bikini Atoll
Ralik Chain
Ratak Chain
PALIKIR
Pohnpei
Kosrae
NAURU
Tarawa
BAIRIKI
Tungaru (Gilbert Islands)
PACIFIC OCEAN
Kingman Reef (to USA)
Palmyra Atoll (to USA)
Teraina
Tabuaerean
Kiritimati
Jarvis Island (to USA)
Baker & Howland Islands (to USA)
Equator
Phoenix Islands
KIRIBATI
Malden Island
Starbuck Island
Line Islands
TUVALU
FONGAFALE
Tokelau (to NZ)
Northern Cook Islands
Penrhyn
Manihiki
Millennium Island
Flint Island
Marquesas Islands
SOLOMON ISLANDS
HONIARA
Santa Cruz Islands
VANUATU
Banks Islands
Espiritu Santo
Malekula
Efate
PORT VILA
Erromango
Tanna
Wallis and Futuna (to France)
SAMOA
APIA
American Samoa (to USA)
PAGO PAGO
Cook Islands (to NZ)
Vanua Levu
Viti Levu
SUVA
Lau Group
TONGA
Niue (to NZ)
FIJI
NUKU'ALOFA
Southern Cook Islands
AVARUA
Rarotonga
Society Islands
PAPEETE
Tahiti
Tuamotu Islands
French Polynesia (to France)
New Caledonia (to France)
Îles Loyauté
NOUMÉA
Îles Australes
Mururoa
Îles Gambier
Pitcairn Islands (to UK)
Pitcairn Island
Tropic of Capricorn
Norfolk Island (to Australia)
Kermadec Islands (part of NZ)
Lord Howe Island (part of Australia)
Polynesia
North Island
Bay of Plenty
Hawke Bay
Tasman Sea
WELLINGTON
Cook Strait
South Island
Southern Alps
NEW ZEALAND
Chatham Islands (part of NZ)
Foveaux Strait
Stewart Island
Auckland Islands (part of NZ)

TOURISM

Tourism forms a valuable and growing boost to the economies of many countries and territories in Australasia and Oceania. Australia, New Zealand, Fiji, Guam and the Cook Islands are the most popular destinations.

ULURU (AYERS ROCK)

The large isolated rock called Uluru is a sacred place to Australia's aboriginal peoples. It attracts many tourists, who come to marvel as its colour changes during the course of the day.

POLITICAL AUSTRALASIA & OCEANIA

Political structures and systems have been strongly shaped by external influences. The arrival of British settlers in the 1770s led to the building of the first major settlements, first in Australia, and later in New Zealand. Many of the islands were later colonized and became overseas territories of the UK, France and the USA. In the past 40 years many of them have become independent nations. Economic ties with Europe are less strong today, as links with new Asian trading partners like Japan and South Korea are becoming more important. In Australia and New Zealand, the land rights of native peoples were long ignored, but are now starting to be recognized.

AUSTRALIA

Australia is the world's sixth-largest country, and also the smallest, flattest continent, with the lowest rainfall. Most Australians are of European, mainly British, origin. However, since 1945 almost six million settlers from more than 170 countries have made Australia their home. The Aboriginal peoples, now only a tiny minority, were the first inhabitants. Recently, there have been several moves to restore their ancient lands.

FARMING AND LAND USE

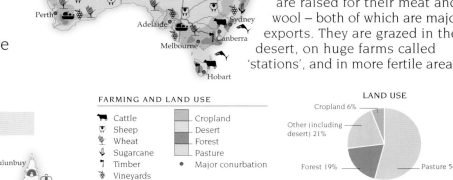

Away from the coasts, much of the land is too dry for agriculture. Fields of sugarcane grow close to the east coast, and grapes for the thriving wine industry are cultivated in the south and west, along with wheat. Vast numbers of cattle and sheep are raised for their meat and wool – both of which are major exports. They are grazed in the desert, on huge farms called 'stations', and in more fertile areas

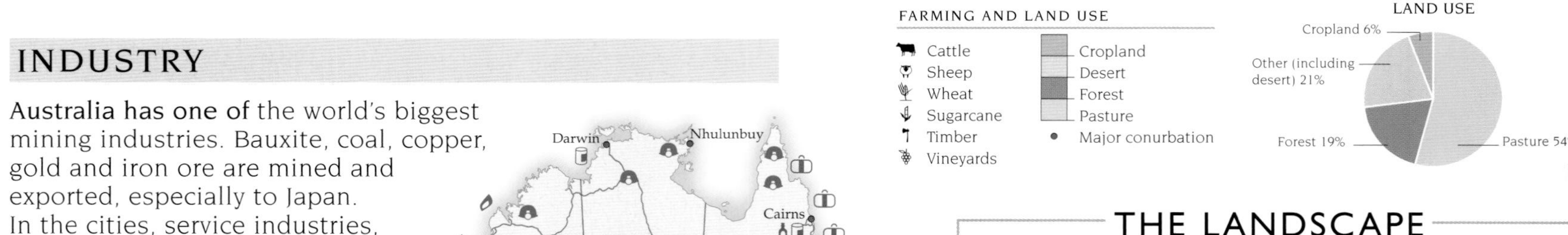
FARMING AND LAND USE
Cattle
Sheep
Wheat
Sugarcane
Timber
Vineyards
Cropland
Desert
Forest
Pasture
Major conurbation
LAND USE
Cropland 6%
Other (including desert) 21%
Forest 19%
Pasture 54%

INDUSTRY

Australia has one of the world's biggest mining industries. Bauxite, coal, copper, gold and iron ore are mined and exported, especially to Japan. In the cities, service industries, particularly tourism, are growing fast; Australia's sunshine and dramatic scenery are attracting an increasing number of overseas visitors.

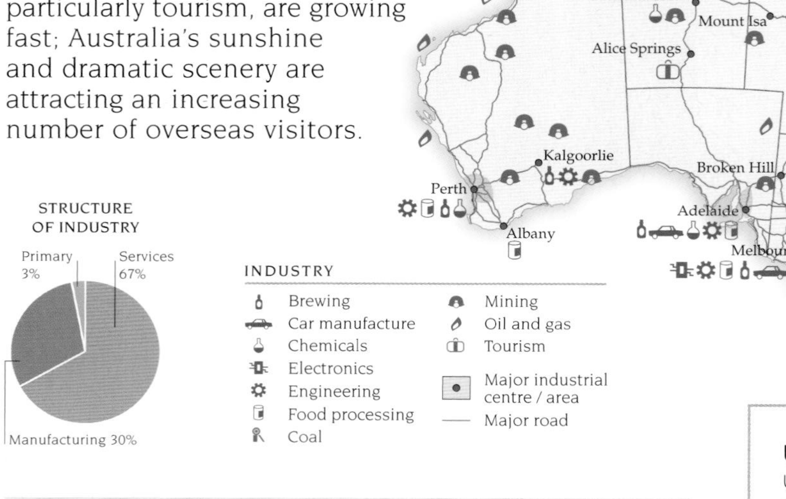
STRUCTURE OF INDUSTRY
Primary 3%
Services 67%
Manufacturing 30%
INDUSTRY
Brewing
Car manufacture
Chemicals
Electronics
Engineering
Food processing
Coal
Mining
Oil and gas
Tourism
Major industrial centre / area
Major road

THE LANDSCAPE

Most of Australia is dry, flat and barren; all of the wetter fertile land is found along its coastline. Huge sun-baked deserts, fringed by semi-arid plains of scrub and grassland cover most of the west and centre of the country. In the east, the land rises to the highlands of the Great Dividing Range, which run the whole length of the east coast. The tropical north coast has rainforests and mangrove swamps.

Blue Mountains (G 6)
The Blue Mountains lie towards the southern end of the Great Dividing Range. They get their name from the blue haze of oil droplets given off by the eucalyptus trees covering their slopes.

Great Barrier Reef (G 2)
This spectacular coral reef, which stretches for over 2,000 km off the coast of Queensland, is the largest living structure on Earth. The reef has built up over millions of years and its waters are home to thousands of different species of coral and marine animals.

Uluru (Ayers Rock) (D 4)
Uluru is an enormous block of red sandstone, standing almost in the middle of Australia. It is the world's biggest free-standing rock – 9.4 km around the base, and 867 m high. It is the summit of a sandstone hill that is buried beneath the sands of the desert.

Simpson Desert (E 4)
The Simpson Desert covers around 130,000 sq km. It contains long, parallel lines of sand dunes and is scattered with large salt pans and salt lakes, which were created when old rivers evaporated. They are now fed by the seasonal rains.

Murray River (F 5)
Together with its tributaries, the Murray River is Australia's main river system. It winds slowly westwards for more than 2,500 km from the Great Dividing Range to the Indian Ocean. It is fed by snow from mountains in the far southeast.

Great Dividing Range (H 5)
These highlands separate the desert regions from the fertile eastern plains. Rivers and streams have eroded them, creating deep valleys and gorges.

POPULATION

Despite its vast size, Australia is sparsely populated. The desert 'outback', which covers most of the interior, is too dry and barren to support many people. About 85% of the population live in the cities and towns on the east and southeast coasts, and around Perth in the west.

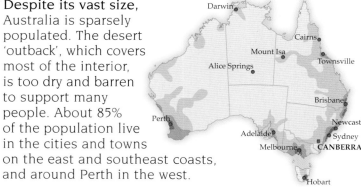

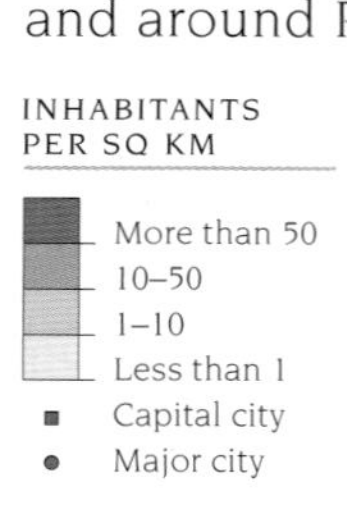
INHABITANTS PER SQ KM
More than 50
10–50
1–10
Less than 1
Capital city
Major city

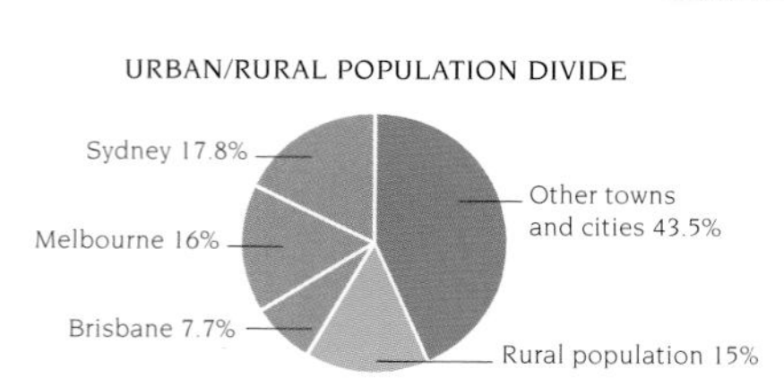
URBAN/RURAL POPULATION DIVIDE
Sydney 17.8%
Melbourne 16%
Brisbane 7.7%
Other towns and cities 43.5%
Rural population 15%

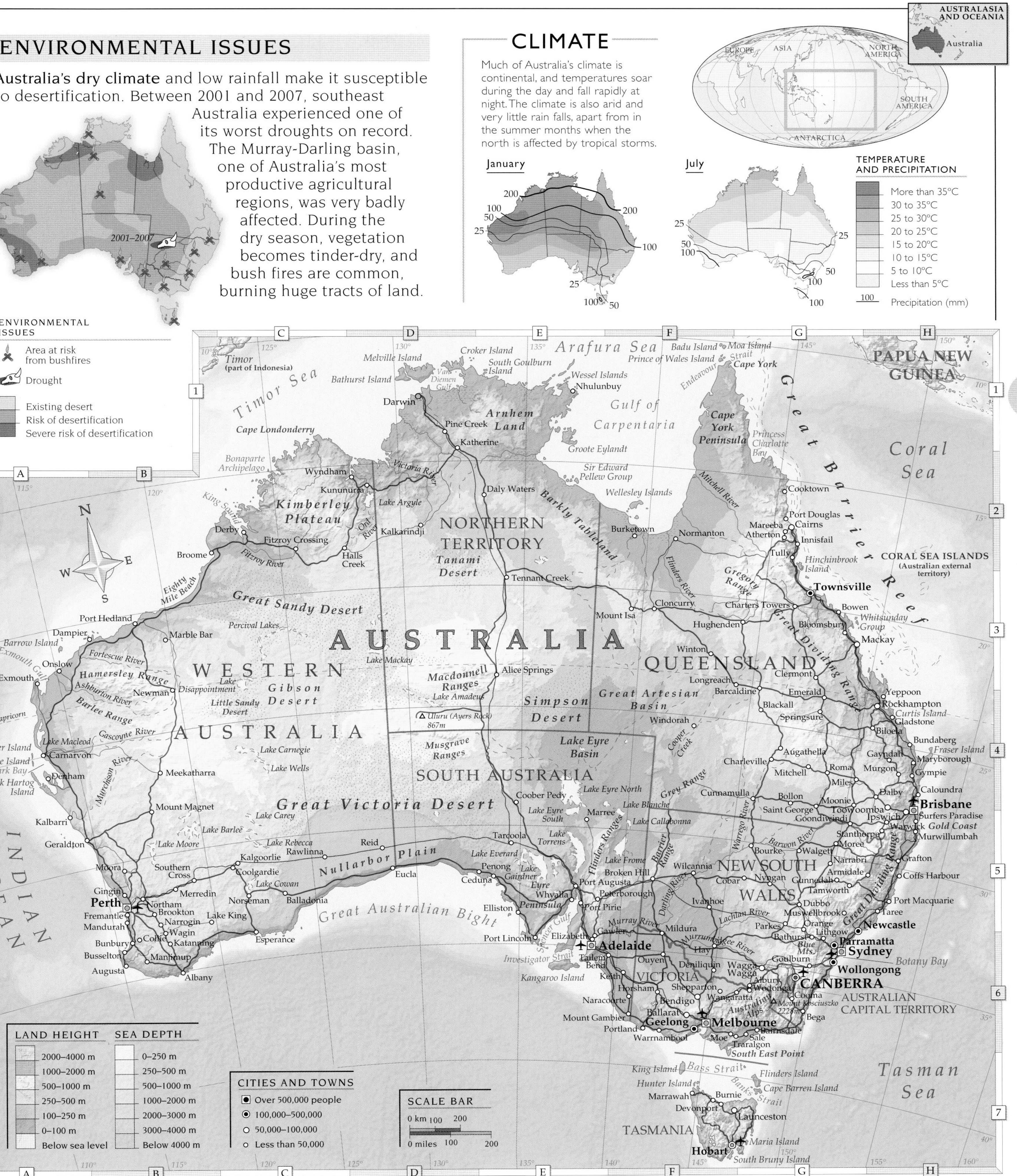

ENVIRONMENTAL ISSUES

Australia's dry climate and low rainfall make it susceptible to desertification. Between 2001 and 2007, southeast Australia experienced one of its worst droughts on record. The Murray-Darling basin, one of Australia's most productive agricultural regions, was very badly affected. During the dry season, vegetation becomes tinder-dry, and bush fires are common, burning huge tracts of land.

CLIMATE

Much of Australia's climate is continental, and temperatures soar during the day and fall rapidly at night. The climate is also arid and very little rain falls, apart from in the summer months when the north is affected by tropical storms.

AUSTRALASIA AND OCEANIA
Australia
EUROPE
ASIA
NORTH AMERICA
SOUTH AMERICA
ANTARCTICA
2001–2007
ENVIRONMENTAL ISSUES
Area at risk from bushfires
Drought
Existing desert
Risk of desertification
Severe risk of desertification
January
July
TEMPERATURE AND PRECIPITATION
More than 35°C
30 to 35°C
25 to 30°C
20 to 25°C
15 to 20°C
10 to 15°C
5 to 10°C
Less than 5°C
Precipitation (mm)
LAND HEIGHT
2000–4000 m
1000–2000 m
500–1000 m
250–500 m
100–250 m
0–100 m
Below sea level
SEA DEPTH
0–250 m
250–500 m
500–1000 m
1000–2000 m
2000–3000 m
3000–4000 m
Below 4000 m
CITIES AND TOWNS
Over 500,000 people
100,000–500,000
50,000–100,000
Less than 50,000
SCALE BAR
0 km 100 200
0 miles 100 200
AUSTRALIA
WESTERN AUSTRALIA
NORTHERN TERRITORY
SOUTH AUSTRALIA
QUEENSLAND
NEW SOUTH WALES
VICTORIA
TASMANIA
AUSTRALIAN CAPITAL TERRITORY
CORAL SEA ISLANDS (Australian external territory)
PAPUA NEW GUINEA
Timor (part of Indonesia)
Arafura Sea
Timor Sea
Gulf of Carpentaria
Coral Sea
Great Barrier Reef
Tasman Sea
INDIAN OCEAN
Great Australian Bight
Bass Strait
Great Sandy Desert
Gibson Desert
Great Victoria Desert
Simpson Desert
Tanami Desert
Nullarbor Plain
Great Artesian Basin
Lake Eyre Basin
Kimberley Plateau
Arnhem Land
Cape York Peninsula
Great Dividing Range
Macdonnell Ranges
Musgrave Ranges
Barkly Tableland
Uluru (Ayers Rock) 867m
Darwin
Perth
Adelaide
Melbourne
Sydney
Brisbane
CANBERRA
Hobart
Alice Springs
Townsville
Newcastle
Wollongong
Geelong
Gold Coast
Cairns
Kalgoorlie
Broome
Tennant Creek
Mount Isa
Launceston

NEW ZEALAND

New Zealand is one of the most remote populated places in the world. The first people to settle on the islands were the Maori, a Polynesian people. When European settlers arrived during the 19th century, the Maori became a minority, and now only make up about 8% of the population. With a small population and rich natural resources, New Zealand's people have high living standards. The country's magnificent rugged scenery is popular with tourists.

ENVIRONMENTAL ISSUES

New Zealand is one of the world's least polluted countries – largely due to its low population and lack of heavy industries, although air quality is occasionally poor in Auckland and Christchurch. Environment-friendly geothermal energy is tapped to make electricity in the volcanic region of North Island. Recently, logging companies have begun to exploit the rich forest reserves, although this has been widely opposed.

Auckland
Hamilton
Wellington
Christchurch 2010
Christchurch
Dunedin

ENVIRONMENTAL ISSUES
- Geothermal power generation
- Logging activity
- Urban air pollution
- Major industrial centre
- Catastrophic earthquake

INDUSTRY

Hi-tech industries such as electronics and computing are growing in the major cities of Auckland and Wellington, although agricultural products such as meat, wool and milk are still among New Zealand's major exports, and large pine forests supply wood for paper pulp and timber. The exciting scenery and varied climate draw tourists from all over the world, especially for walking and adventure holidays.

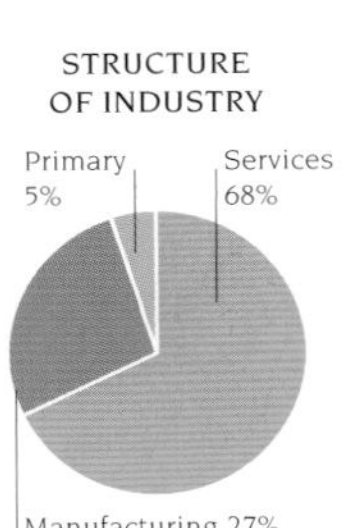
STRUCTURE OF INDUSTRY
Primary 5%
Services 68%
Manufacturing 27%

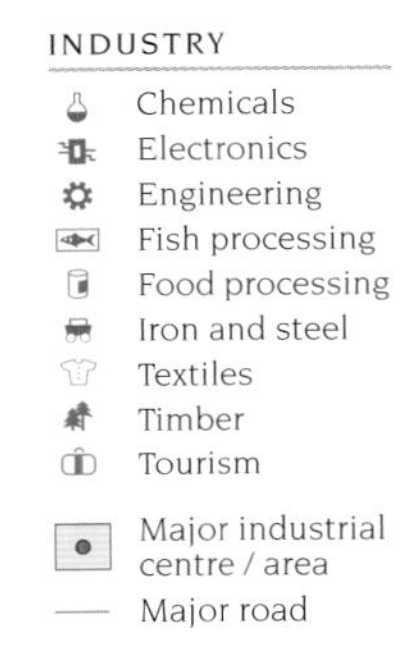
INDUSTRY
Chemicals
Electronics
Engineering
Fish processing
Food processing
Iron and steel
Textiles
Timber
Tourism
Major industrial centre / area
Major road

Whangarei
Auckland
Tauranga
Hamilton
New Plymouth
Napier
Hastings
Wellington
Nelson
Blenheim
Christchurch
Timaru
Dunedin
Invercargill

THE LANDSCAPE

Two large, mountainous islands form New Zealand's main land areas. A large crack or fault – the Alpine Fault, in the west of South Island – is the boundary between two plates in the Earth's crust. Land either side of the fault tends to move, causing earthquakes. Volcanoes, many of them still active, are also found, on both islands. South Island has many high peaks, several more than 3,000 m high.

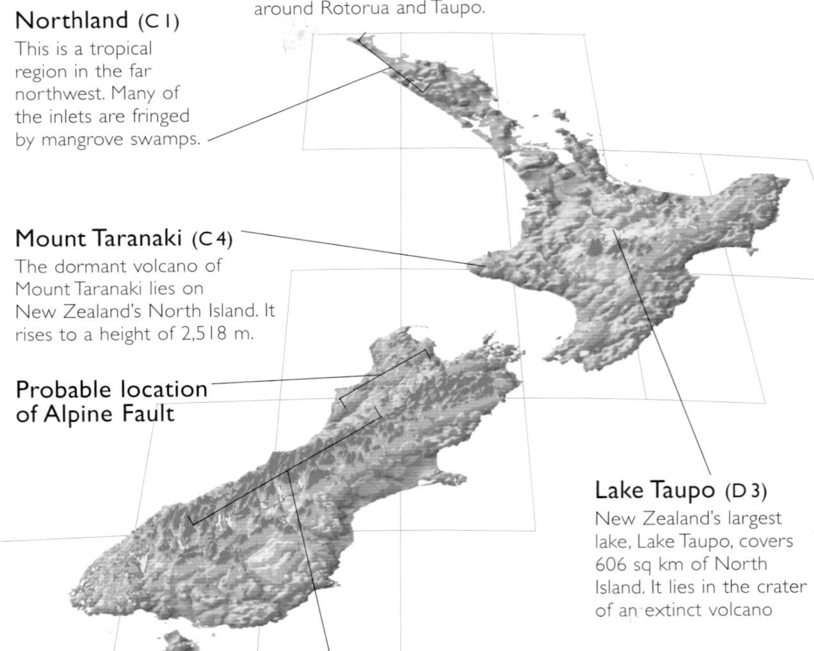

Geysers and boiling mud
Geysers occur when hot volcanic rocks come into contact with underground water. The water boils and turns to steam forcing the water above it to burst through the Earth's surface into the air. There are many geysers and boiling mud pools in the areas around Rotorua and Taupo.

Northland (C 1)
This is a tropical region in the far northwest. Many of the inlets are fringed by mangrove swamps.

Mount Taranaki (C 4)
The dormant volcano of Mount Taranaki lies on New Zealand's North Island. It rises to a height of 2,518 m.

Probable location of Alpine Fault

Lake Taupo (D 3)
New Zealand's largest lake, Lake Taupo, covers 606 sq km of North Island. It lies in the crater of an extinct volcano

Southern Alps
New Zealand's Southern Alps stretch more than 483 km down the backbone of South Island. They were formed by the collision of the Indo-Australian and Pacific plates. Heavy snowfalls here, brought by westerly winds, feed the Fox Glacier which moves at a speed of 0.5–4.5 m a day.

POPULATION

Most of the population is descended from European settlers, although immigrants from Asia and from the Pacific islands are increasing. About one-third of New Zealand's 4 million people live in Auckland on North Island, which also has the largest Polynesian population of any city in the Pacific. Elsewhere, the population is clustered along the coasts, where the land is lower.

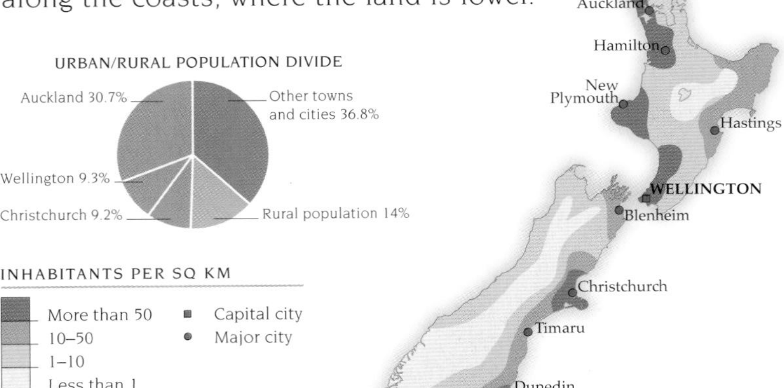
URBAN/RURAL POPULATION DIVIDE
Auckland 30.7%
Other towns and cities 36.8%
Wellington 9.3%
Christchurch 9.2%
Rural population 14%
INHABITANTS PER SQ KM
More than 50
10–50
1–10
Less than 1
Capital city
Major city
Auckland
Hamilton
New Plymouth
Hastings
WELLINGTON
Blenheim
Christchurch
Timaru
Dunedin
Invercargill

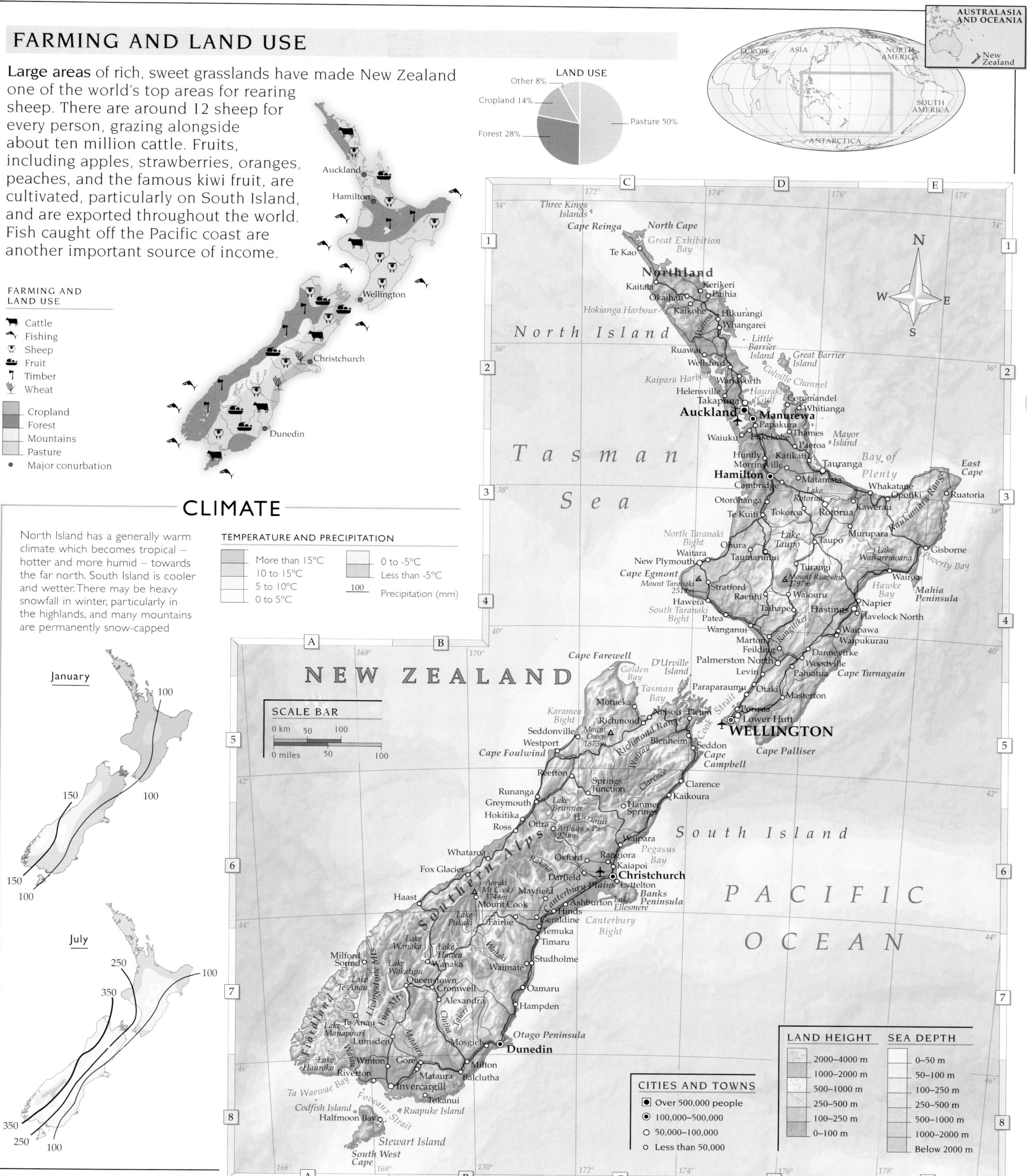
FARMING AND LAND USE
Large areas of rich, sweet grasslands have made New Zealand one of the world's top areas for rearing sheep. There are around 12 sheep for every person, grazing alongside about ten million cattle. Fruits, including apples, strawberries, oranges, peaches, and the famous kiwi fruit, are cultivated, particularly on South Island, and are exported throughout the world. Fish caught off the Pacific coast are another important source of income.
FARMING AND LAND USE
Cattle
Fishing
Sheep
Fruit
Timber
Wheat
Cropland
Forest
Mountains
Pasture
Major conurbation
Auckland
Hamilton
Wellington
Christchurch
Dunedin
LAND USE
Other 8%
Cropland 14%
Forest 28%
Pasture 50%
AUSTRALASIA AND OCEANIA
New Zealand
EUROPE
ASIA
NORTH AMERICA
SOUTH AMERICA
ANTARCTICA
CLIMATE
North Island has a generally warm climate which becomes tropical – hotter and more humid – towards the far north. South Island is cooler and wetter. There may be heavy snowfall in winter, particularly in the highlands, and many mountains are permanently snow-capped
TEMPERATURE AND PRECIPITATION
More than 15°C
10 to 15°C
5 to 10°C
0 to 5°C
0 to -5°C
Less than -5°C
100 Precipitation (mm)
January
July
NEW ZEALAND
North Island
South Island
Tasman Sea
PACIFIC OCEAN
SCALE BAR
0 km 50 100
0 miles 50 100
Cape Reinga
North Cape
Northland
Auckland
Manurewa
Hamilton
Tauranga
Rotorua
Taupo
Gisborne
Napier
Hastings
New Plymouth
Palmerston North
WELLINGTON
Nelson
Blenheim
Christchurch
Southern Alps
Aoraki (Mt Cook) 3744m
Dunedin
Invercargill
Stewart Island
Cook Strait
Foveaux Strait
CITIES AND TOWNS
Over 500,000 people
100,000–500,000
50,000–100,000
Less than 50,000
LAND HEIGHT
2000–4000 m
1000–2000 m
500–1000 m
250–500 m
100–250 m
0–100 m
SEA DEPTH
0–50 m
50–100 m
100–250 m
250–500 m
500–1000 m
1000–2000 m
Below 2000 m

Southwest Pacific

The many thousands of islands in the Pacific Ocean are scattered across an enormous area. The original inhabitants, the Polynesians, Melanesians and Micronesians, settled the islands following the last Ice Age. In the 1700s Europeans arrived. They colonized all of the Pacific islands, introducing their culture, languages and religion. Today, many, though not all, of the islands have become independent. Their economies are simple, based largely on fishing and agriculture. Many are increasingly relying on their beautiful scenery and tropical climates to attract tourists and give a valuable boost to their economies.

LANDSCAPE

Most of the Pacific islands are extremely small, the largest land mass is the half of the island of New Guinea occupied by Papua New Guinea. The edges of the Indo-Australian and Pacific plates meet on the western edge of the area, leading to much volcanic and earthquake activity. Many of the islands are coral atolls, originally formed by volcanic activity, and some are no more than a few metres above sea level.

New Guinea (A 2)

A mountainous spine runs through the centre of the island, separating the northern coast from the dense forests and mangroves found in the south.

Pacific Ocean

The Pacific Ocean is the Earth's oldest and deepest ocean. Its name means peaceful, though it is far from being so; the highest wave ever recorded on open ocean – 34 m – occurred during a hurricane in the Pacific.

Kavachi

Kavachi is a submarine volcano lying off the coast of New Georgia, in the Solomon Islands. It still erupts every few years.

Ring of Fire

The 'Ring of Fire' is the term used to describe the string of volcanoes which surround the entire Pacific Ocean and erupt frequently because of intense stress and movement from within the Earth. The ring crosses the south Pacific, running between Vanuatu and New Caledonia, along the edge of the Solomon Islands, and between New Britain and New Guinea.

Sea trenches

Deep trenches mark the sea floor boundary where the Indo-Australian plate 'dives' under the Pacific plate.

Coral atolls

Volcanic activity in the Pacific has led to the creation of many islands. These islands become fringed with a ring of coral. When the islands subside beneath the sea once again, only the circle of coral is left, forming an atoll.

INDUSTRY

Today, the main industry for many of the Pacific islands is tourism. Food processing and small-scale textile industries are also common on many islands.

INDUSTRY
Brewing
Food processing
Textiles
Timber processing
Mining
Tourism
Major industrial centre
Major road

Rabaul
Madang
Mount Hagen
Lae
Port Moresby
Honiara
Port Vila
Suva
Nouméa

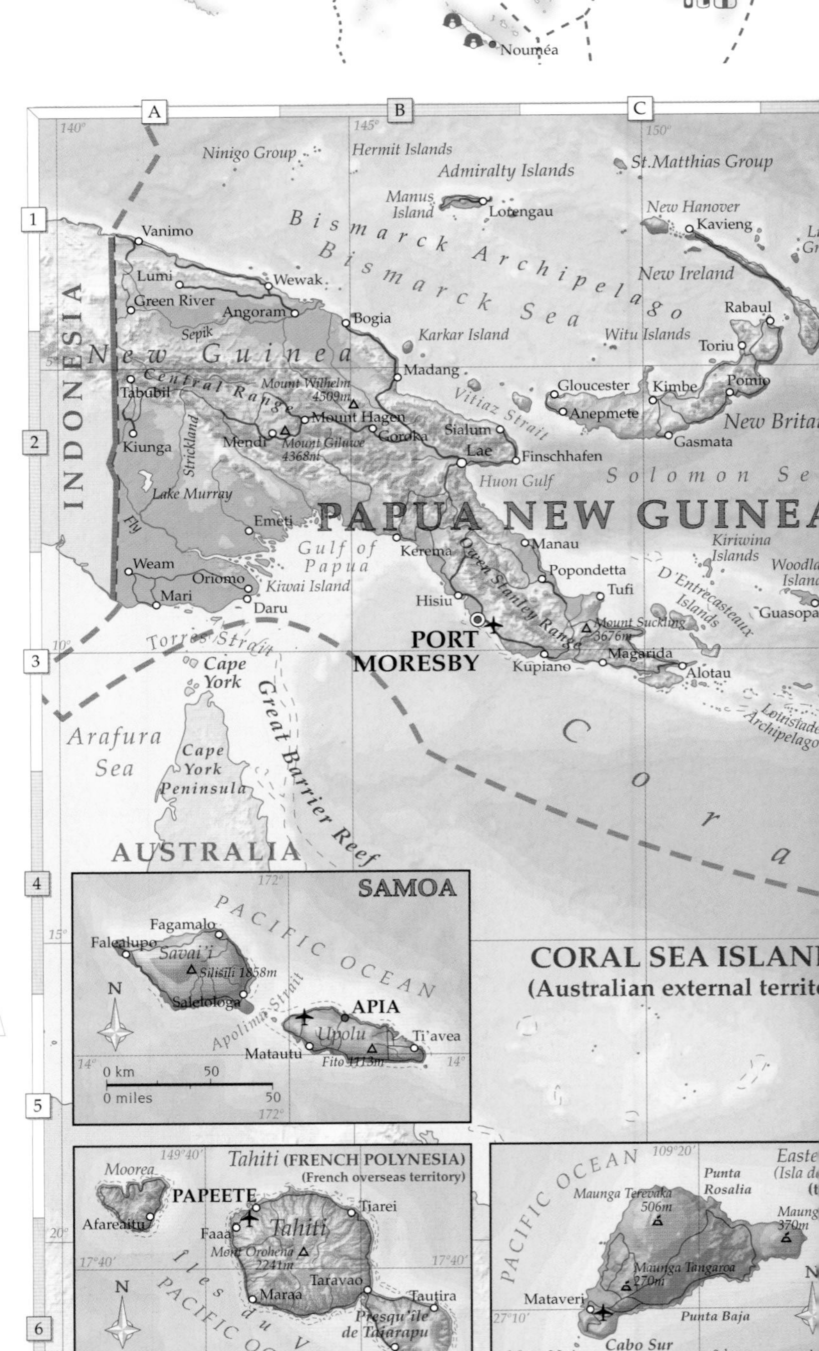
Ninigo Group
Hermit Islands
Admiralty Islands
St.Matthias Group
Manus Island
Lorengau
New Hanover
Kavieng
Vanimo
Bismarck Archipelago
Bismarck Sea
New Ireland
Lumi
Wewak
Green River
Angoram
Bogia
Rabaul
Sepik
Karkar Island
Witu Islands
Toriu
INDONESIA
New Guinea
Madang
Central Range
Tabubil
Mount Wilhelm 4509m
Gloucester
Kimbe
Pomio
Mount Hagen
Anepmete
Vitiaz Strait
Goroka
Sialum
New Britain
Kiunga
Mendi
Mount Giluwe 4368m
Lae
Gasmata
Finschhafen
Huon Gulf
Solomon Sea
Lake Murray
Strickland
Fly
Emeti
PAPUA NEW GUINEA
Gulf of Papua
Kerema
Manau
Kiriwina Islands
Weam
Oriomo
Kiwai Island
Popondetta
D'Entrecasteaux Islands
Mari
Daru
Hisiu
Tufi
Owen Stanley Range
Guasopa
Mount Suckling 3676m
Torres Strait
PORT MORESBY
Cape York
Kupiano
Magarida
Alotau
Louisiade Archipelago
Arafura Sea
Great Barrier Reef
Cape York Peninsula
Coral Sea
AUSTRALIA
SAMOA
PACIFIC OCEAN
Fagamalo
Falealupo
Savai'i
Silisili 1858m
Salelologa
Apolima Strait
APIA
Upolu
Ti'avea
Matautu
Fito 1113m
0 km 50
0 miles 50
CORAL SEA ISLANDS
(Australian external territory)
Tahiti (FRENCH POLYNESIA)
(French overseas territory)
Moorea
Afareaitu
PAPEETE
Faaa
Tiarei
Tahiti
Mont Orohena 2241m
Taravao
Maraa
Tautira
Presqu'île de Taiarapu
Teahupoo
Iles du Vent
PACIFIC OCEAN
0 km 30
0 miles 30
Punta Rosalia
Maunga Terevaka 506m
Maunga Tangaroa 270m
Mataveri
Punta Baja
Cabo Sur
Motu Nui
0 km
0 miles

FARMING AND LAND USE

Most farming that takes place on the Pacific islands is at a subsistence level, and many people keep pigs and chickens. A few crops are grown for export, especially oil palms, and coconuts, which are dried in the sun to produce copra. Many islanders make their living from the rich fishing grounds of the Pacific. The thick forests of Papua New Guinea are increasingly cut down for timber.

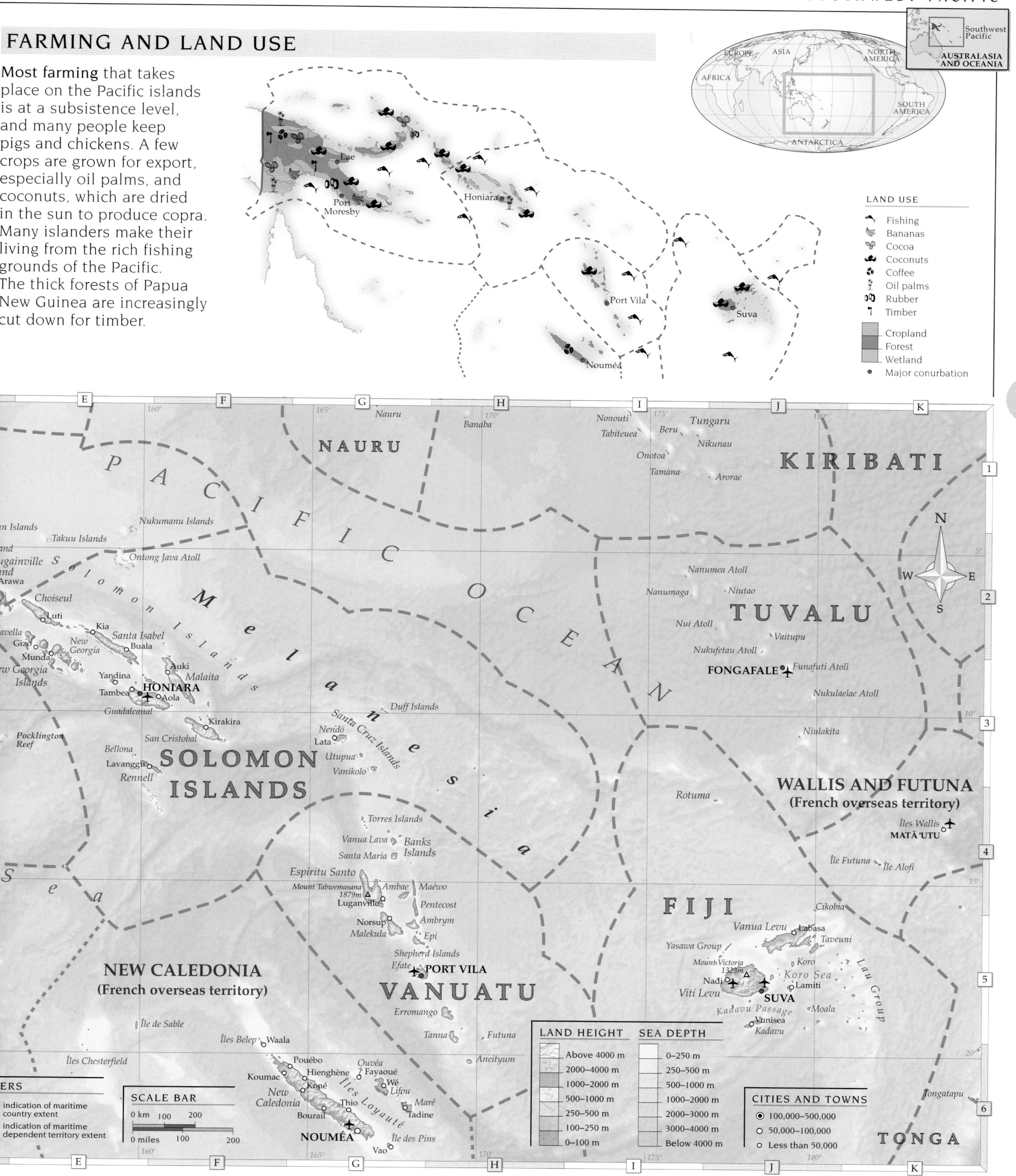

Southwest Pacific
AUSTRALASIA AND OCEANIA
EUROPE
ASIA
AFRICA
NORTH AMERICA
SOUTH AMERICA
ANTARCTICA
Lae
Port Moresby
Honiara
Port Vila
Suva
Nouméa
LAND USE
Fishing
Bananas
Cocoa
Coconuts
Coffee
Oil palms
Rubber
Timber
Cropland
Forest
Wetland
Major conurbation
PACIFIC OCEAN
Melanesia
NAURU
Nauru
Banaba
Nonouti
Tabiteuea
Beru
Tungaru
Nikunau
Onotoa
Tamana
Arorae
KIRIBATI
Nukumanu Islands
Takuu Islands
Ontong Java Atoll
Solomon Islands
Bougainville Island
Arawa
Choiseul
Luti
Kia
Santa Isabel
Buala
New Georgia
Gizo
Munda
New Georgia Islands
Auki
Malaita
Yandina
Tambea
HONIARA
Aola
Guadalcanal
Kirakira
San Cristobal
Pocklington Reef
Bellona
Lavanggu
Rennell
SOLOMON ISLANDS
Duff Islands
Santa Cruz Islands
Nendö
Lata
Utupua
Vanikolo
Nanumea Atoll
Nanumaga
Niutao
TUVALU
Nui Atoll
Vaitupu
Nukufetau Atoll
FONGAFALE
Funafuti Atoll
Nukulaelae Atoll
Niulakita
Rotuma
WALLIS AND FUTUNA
(French overseas territory)
Îles Wallis
MATĀ'UTU
Île Futuna
Île Alofi
Torres Islands
Vanua Lava
Banks Islands
Santa Maria
Espiritu Santo
Mount Tabwemasana 1879m
Ambae
Maéwo
Luganville
Pentecost
Norsup
Ambrym
Malekula
Epi
Shepherd Islands
Efate
PORT VILA
VANUATU
Erromango
Tanna
Futuna
Aneityum
FIJI
Cikobia
Vanua Levu
Labasa
Taveuni
Yasawa Group
Mount Victoria 1323m
Koro
Koro Sea
Nadi
Lamiti
Viti Levu
SUVA
Lau Group
Kadavu Passage
Moala
Vunisea
Kadavu
NEW CALEDONIA
(French overseas territory)
Île de Sable
Îles Chesterfield
Îles Belep
Waala
Pouébo
Hienghène
Ouvéa
Fayaoué
Koumac
Koné
Wé
Lifou
New Caledonia
Îles Loyauté
Thio
Maré
Bourail
Tadine
NOUMÉA
Île des Pins
Vao
Tongatapu
TONGA
N
S
E
W
LAND HEIGHT
Above 4000 m
2000–4000 m
1000–2000 m
500–1000 m
250–500 m
100–250 m
0–100 m
SEA DEPTH
0–250 m
250–500 m
500–1000 m
1000–2000 m
2000–3000 m
3000–4000 m
Below 4000 m
CITIES AND TOWNS
100,000–500,000
50,000–100,000
Less than 50,000
SCALE BAR
0 km 100 200
0 miles 100 200
indication of maritime country extent
indication of maritime dependent territory extent

ANTARCTICA

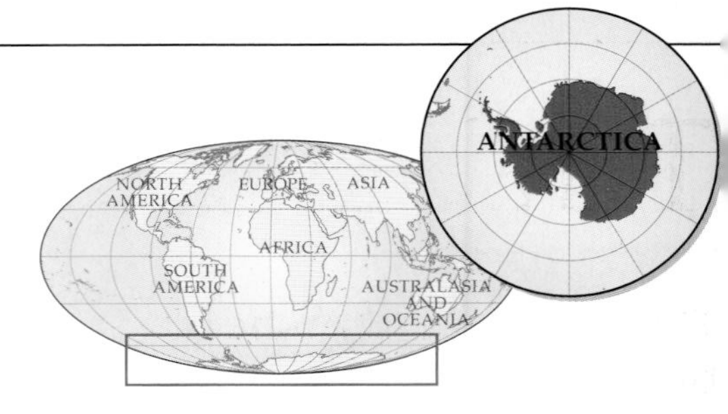
NORTH AMERICA
EUROPE
ASIA
AFRICA
SOUTH AMERICA
AUSTRALASIA AND OCEANIA
ANTARCTICA

The continent of Antarctica has no permanent human population and very few animals can survive on the frozen land, although the surrounding seas teem with fish and mammals. Even in the summer the temperature is rarely above freezing and the sea-ice only partly melts; in winter, temperatures plummet to –80°C. The only people who live in Antarctica are teams of scientists who study the wildlife and monitor the ice for changes in the Earth's atmosphere.

○ Research Station

Ice shelf

LAND HEIGHT	SEA DEPTH
Above 4000 m	0–250 m
2000–4000 m	250–500 m
1000–2000 m	500–1000 m
500–1000 m	1000–2000 m
250–500 m	2000–3000 m
100–250 m	3000–4000 m
0–100 m	Below 4000 m

ATLANTIC OCEAN

SOUTH GEORGIA (to UK)

SOUTH SANDWICH ISLANDS (to UK)

South Sandwich Trench

America-Antarctica Ridge

Atlantic-Indian Basin

Scotia Sea

Antarctic Circle

Lazarev Sea

Orcadas (Argentina)

South Orkney Islands

Signy (UK)

Drake Passage

Weddell Plain

South Shetland Islands

Sanae (South Africa)
Georg von Neumayer (Germany)
Maitri (India)
Novolazarevskaya (Russian Federation)
Dronning Maud Land
Lutzow-Holm Bay
Syowa (Japan)
Molodezhnaya (Russian Federation)
SOUTHERN OCEAN
Multinational Stations
Esperanza (Argentina)
Capitan Arturo Prat (Chile)
Halley (UK)
Weddell Sea
Coats Land
Enderby Land
Kemp Land
Mawson (Australia)
Palmer (USA)
Antarctic Peninsula
Belgrano II (Argentina)
Berkner Island
Rothera (UK)
San Martin (Argentina)
Palmer Land
Ronne Ice Shelf
Alexander Island
Lambert Glacier
Mackenzie Bay
Cape Darnley
Zhongshan (China)
Prydz Bay
ANTARCTICA
Princess Elizabeth Land
Davis (Australia)
Bellingshausen Sea
Vinson Massif 4897m
PETER I ISLAND (to Norway)
Davis Sea
Amundsen-Scott (USA)
South Pole
East
Ellsworth Land
West
Transantarctic Mountains
Mirny (Russian Federation)
Antarctica
Antarctica
Vostok (Russian Federation)
South Geomagnetic Pole
Shackleton Ice Shelf
Limit of winter pack ice
Limit of summer pack ice
Marie Byrd Land
Mount Kirkpatrick 4528m
Mount Markham 4351m
Amundsen Sea
Mount Sidley 4181m
Ross Ice Shelf
Wilkes Land
Casey (Australia)
Mount Siple 3100m
Roosevelt Island
Scott Base (NZ)
Victoria Land
Cape Poinsett
SOUTHERN OCEAN
McMurdo Base (USA)
Mount Erebus 3794m
Ross Sea
Terre Adélie
Amundsen Plain
Cape Adare
George V Land
Dumont d'Urville (France)
Leningradskaya (Russian Federation)
SCALE BAR
0 km 500 1000
0 miles 500 1000

THE LANDSCAPE

Antarctica is the world's most southerly continent. It is also the world's coldest continent and its highest, mainly due to the great ice sheet – up to 2 km thick in parts – which lies over the mountains of the Antarctic Peninsula and the plateau of East Antarctica.

Frozen seas
During the cold winter months, the seas surrounding Antarctica freeze, almost doubling the size of the continent.

Lambert Glacier (E4)
The Lambert Glacier is the world's largest series of glaciers. It is 80 km wide at the coast and reaches more than 300 km inland.

Transantarctic Mountains (C5)
The Transantarctic Mountains run across the continent, splitting it into East and West Antarctica.

Ice sheet
A massive sheet of ice, about 4,800 m thick at its deepest point, covers almost the entire area of Antarctica. It contains most of the fresh water on Earth. The weight of the ice pushes the land down below sea level.

The Ross Ice Shelf (C5)
The Ross Sea is part of the Southern Ocean. This deep bay is covered by a thick sheet of ice which floats on the ocean.

RESOURCES

The mountains of Antarctica have rich mineral reserves. Gold, iron and coal are found, and there is natural gas in the surrounding seas. The unique and abundant marine wildlife is Antarctica's greatest resource. Colonies of penguins breed on the ice sheet, and whales, seals and many bird and fish species thrive in the icy waters.

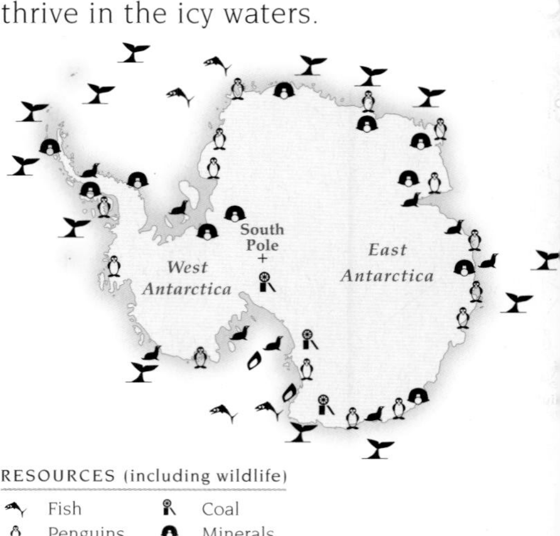
South Pole
West Antarctica
East Antarctica

RESOURCES (including wildlife)

Fish — Penguins — Seals — Whales — Coal — Minerals — Gas

THE ARCTIC

The ice-covered Arctic Ocean is encircled by the most northerly parts of Europe, North America and Asia. Very few people live in the often freezing conditions. Those who do, including the Sami of northern Scandinavia, the Siberian Yugyt and Nenet people and the Canadian Inuit, were nomads who lived by hunting and herding. Some live like this today, but many have now settled in small towns.

THE LANDSCAPE

The Arctic Ocean is the smallest ocean in the world, covering a total area of 15,100,000 sq km. The ocean is divided into two large basins, divided by three great underwater mountain ranges including the Lomonosov Ridge which is more than 3,000 m high on average.

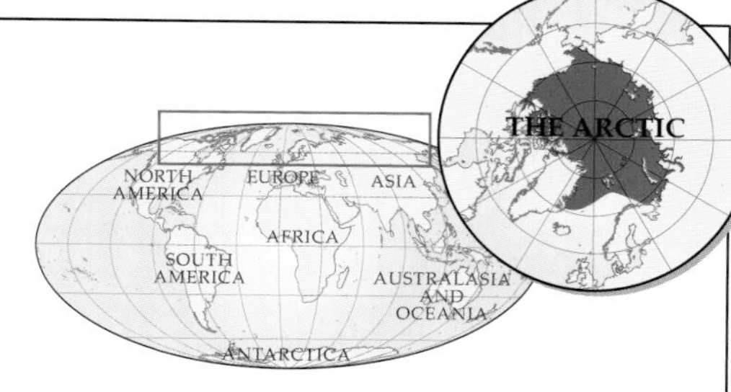
THE ARCTIC
NORTH AMERICA
EUROPE
ASIA
AFRICA
SOUTH AMERICA
AUSTRALASIA AND OCEANIA
ANTARCTICA

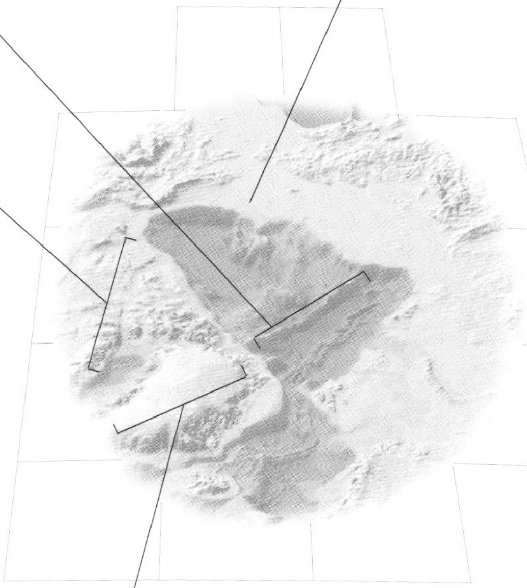

Pack-ice
Much of the Arctic Ocean is permanently covered by pack-ice. When the ice breaks up, it forms enormous floating ice-masses called icebergs.

Lomonosov Ridge (C 4)

Arctic islands (A 4)
In the far north of Canada, there are many thousands of islands including Baffin Island and Victoria Island. Many of them are almost entirely surrounded by pack-ice.

Greenland (A 3)
Greenland is the world's largest island. It is covered by a huge ice sheet, more than 1,683,400 sq km across. The weight of the ice has pushed most of the land below sea level.

Sastrugi
Snow, blown by strong winds can scratch deep patterns in the snow. These patterns are known as sastrugi and line up with the direction of the wind.

SCALE BAR
0 km 250 500
0 miles 250 500

CITIES AND TOWNS
100,000–500,000
50,000–100,000
Less than 50,000

SEA DEPTH
0–250 m
250–500 m
500–1000 m
1000–2000 m
2000–3000 m
3000–4000 m
Below 4000 m

RESOURCES

Coal, oil and gas are found beneath the Arctic Ocean and in Canada, Alaska and Russia. Fears about damage to the environment and the cost of extracting these resources have restricted the quantities removed. Overfishing has reduced fish stocks to very low levels. Quotas have been put in place to allow them to revive.

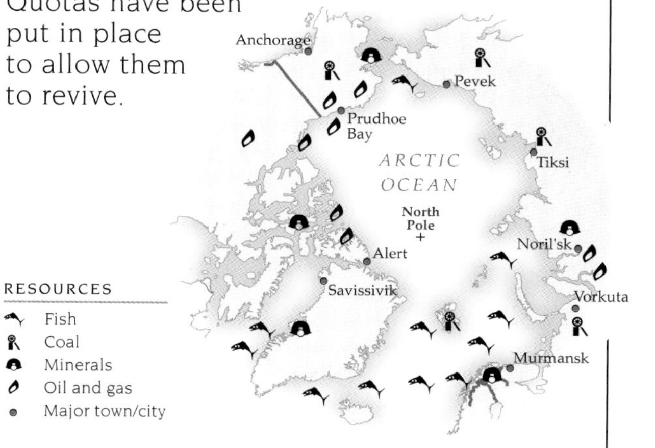

RESOURCES
Fish
Coal
Minerals
Oil and gas
Major town/city

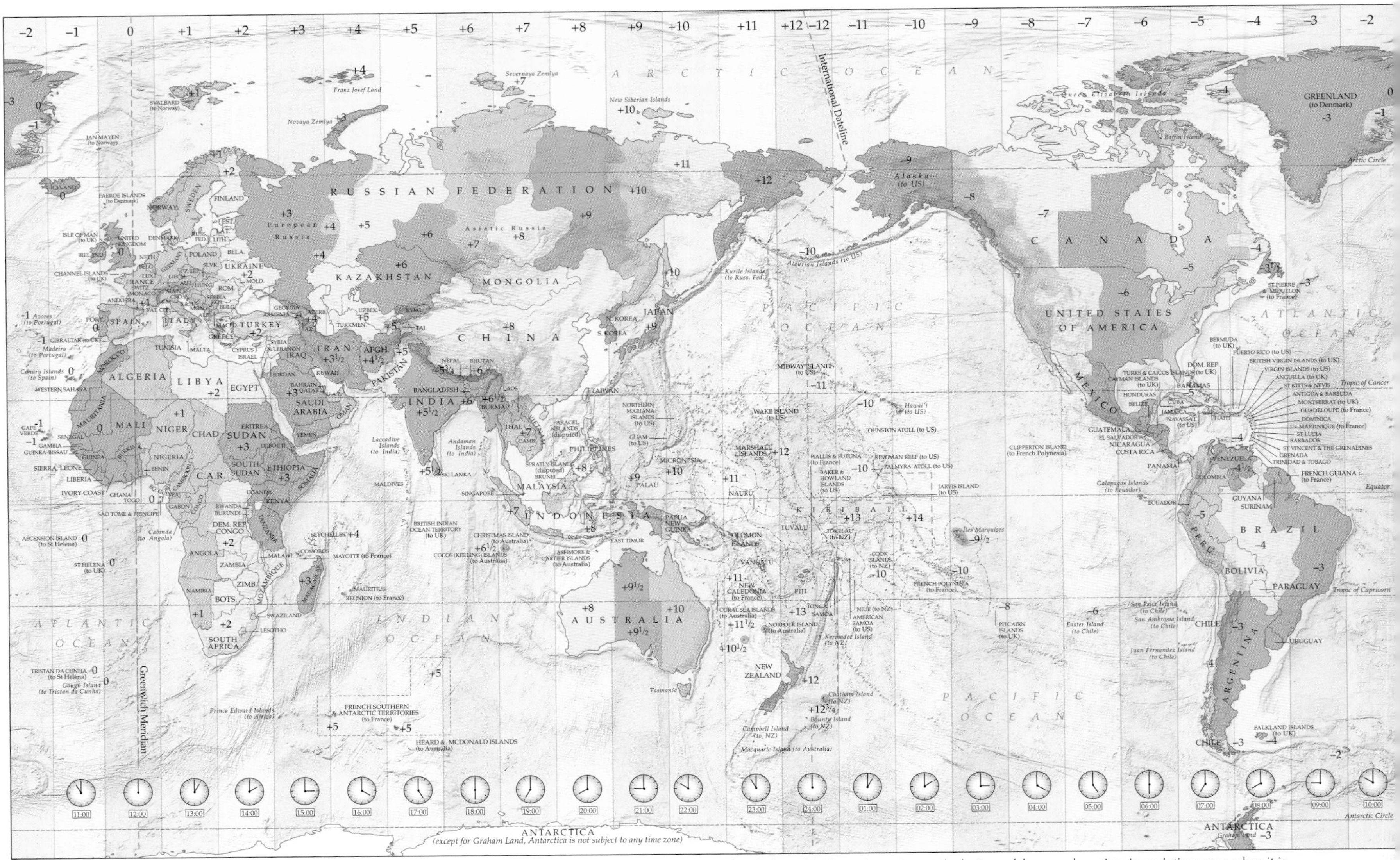

The numbers along the top of the map (+2/-2 etc.), indicate the number of hours each time zone is ahead or behind UTC (Coordinated Universal Time)

The clocks and 24-hour times given at the bottom of the map show time in each time zone when it is 12.00 hours noon UTC

Time Zones

The Earth is a rotating sphere, and because of this the Sun only shines on half of its surface at any one time. This means that it is morning, evening and night time in different parts of the world (*see diagram below*). Because of these differences, each country or part of a country uses a local time. A region of Earth's surface which uses a single local time is called a time zone. There are 24 one-hour time zones around the world, arranged roughly in vertical longitudinal bands.

Day and night around the world

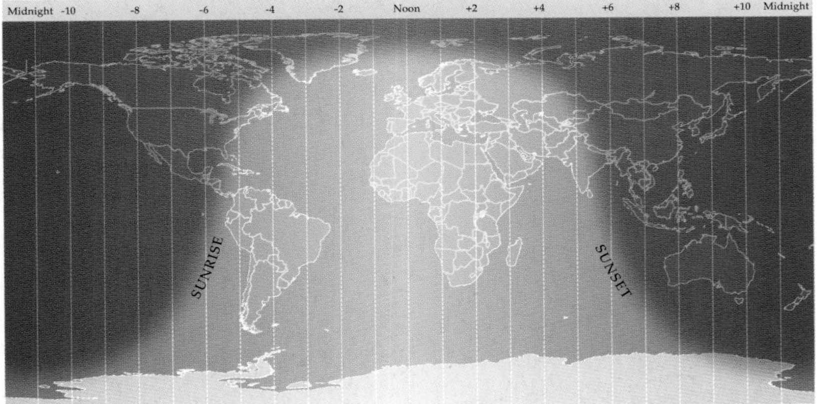
Midnight -10
-8
-6
-4
-2
Noon
+2
+4
+6
+8
+10
Midnight
SUNRISE
SUNSET

Standard Time

Standard time is the official local time in a particular country or part of a country. Although time zones are arranged roughly in longitudinal bands, in many places the borders of a zone do not fall exactly along a line of longitude, as can be seen on the map, but are determined by geographical factors or by borders between countries.

Most countries have just one time zone, but some large countries (such as the USA, Canada and Russia) are split between several time zones, so standard time varies across those countries. For example, mainland USA crosses four time zones and so has four standard times, called the Eastern, Central, Mountain and Pacific standard times. China is unusual in that just one standard time is used for the whole country, even though it extends across 60° of longitude from west to east.

Coordinated Universal Time (UTC)

Coordinated Universal Time (UTC) is an international reference used to set the local time in each time zone. For example, Australian Western Standard Time (the local time in Western Australia) is set 8 hours ahead of UTC (it is UTC+8), so if it were 12.00 noon UTC in London, UK, it would be 8.00pm in Perth, Western Australia. UTC has replaced Greenwich Mean Time (GMT) because UTC is based on an atomic clock, which is more accurate and convenient than GMT. Greenwich Mean Time was determined by the Sun's position in the sky relative to the 0° line of longitude, also known as the Greenwich Meridian, which runs through Greenwich, UK.

The International Dateline

The International Dateline is an imaginary line from pole to pole that roughly corresponds to the 180° line of longitude. It is an arbitrary marker between calendar days. The dateline is needed because of the use of local times around the world rather than a single universal time. When moving from west to east across the dateline, travellers have to set their watches back one day. Those travelling in the opposite direction, from east to west, must add a day.

Daylight saving time

Daylight saving is a summertime adjustment to the local time in a country or region, designed to increase the hours of daylight that occur during people's normal waking hours. To follow the system, clocks are advanced by an hour on a pre-decided date in spring and reverted back in autumn. About half of the world's nations use daylight saving.

ᴀRGEST COUNTRIES

ssian Federation	17,075,200 sq km (6,592,735 sq miles)
ıada	9,984,670 sq km (3,885,171 sq miles)
A	9,826,675 sq km (3,794,100 sq miles)
na	9,596,960 sq km (3,705,386 sq miles)
zil	8,511,965 sq km (3,286,470 sq miles)
stralia	7,686,850 sq km (2,967,893 sq miles)
ia	3,287,590 sq km (1,269,339 sq miles)
entina	2,766,890 sq km (1,068,296 sq miles)
zakhstan	2,717,300 sq km (1,049,150 sq miles)
eria	2,381,740 sq km (919,590 sq miles)

ᴍALLEST COUNTRIES

ican City	0.44 sq km (0.17 sq miles)
naco	1.95 sq km (0.75 sq miles)
ıru	21 sq km (8.1 sq miles)
alu	26 sq km (10 sq miles)
Marino	61 sq km (24 sq miles)
chtenstein	160 sq km (62 sq miles)
rshall Islands	181 sq km (70 sq miles)
Kitts & Nevis	261 sq km (101 sq miles)
dives	300 sq km (116 sq miles)
ta	316 sq km (122 sq miles)

OST POPULOUS COUNTRIES

na	1,353,600,000
ia	1,258,400,000
A	315,800,000
onesia	244,800,000
zil	198,400,000
istan	180,000,000
eria	166,600,000
gladesh	152,400,000
ssian Federation	142,700,000
an	126,400,000

AST POPULOUS COUNTRIES

ican City	800
ıru	9400
alu	10,700
au	21,100
naco	30,500
Marino	32,400
chtenstein	37,000
Kitts & Nevis	51,000
rshall Islands	69,700
minica	73,000

OST DENSELY POPULATED COUNTRIES

naco	15,641 per sq km (40,667 people per sq mile)
gapore	8689 per sq km (22,591 people per sq mile)
rain	1983 per sq km (5155 people per sq mile)
ican City	1907 per sq km (4958 people per sq mile)
ta	1250 per sq km (3250 people per sq mile)
gladesh	1138 per sq km (2958 people per sq mile)
dives	1000 per sq km (2600 people per sq mile)
wan	722 per sq km (1877 people per sq mile)
ıritius	699 per sq km (1817 people per sq mile)
bados	698 per sq km (1815 people per sq mile)

OST SPARSELY POPULATED COUNTRIES

ngolia	2 per sq km (4 people per sq mile)
nibia	3 per sq km (7 people per sq mile)
stralia	3 per sq km (7 people per sq mile)
inam	3 per sq km (8 people per sq mile)
and	3 per sq km (8 people per sq mile)
swana	4 per sq km (9 people per sq mile)
ıritania	4 per sq km (9 people per sq mile)
ıada	4 per sq km (9 people per sq mile)
ya	4 per sq km (9 people per sq mile)
yana	4 per sq km (10 people per sq mile)

Richest countries (GNI per capita, in US$)

Monaco	183,150
Liechtenstein	137,070
Norway	88,890
Qatar	80,440
Luxembourg	78,130
Switzerland	76,380
Denmark	60,390
Sweden	54,230
San Marino	50,670
Neth	49,730

Poorest countries (GNI per capita, in US$)

Congo, Dem. Rep.	190
Liberia	240
Burundi	250
Somalia	288
Malawi	340
Sierra Leone	340
Niger	360
Ethiopia	400
Eritrea	430
Madagascar	430

Most widely spoken languages

1. Chinese (Mandarin)	6. Arabic
2. English	7. Bengali
3. Hindi, Hindustani, Urdu	8. Portuguese
4. Spanish	9. Malay-Indonesian
5. Russian	10. French

Largest deserts

Sahara	9,065,000 sq km (3,450,000 sq miles)
Gobi	1,295,000 sq km (500,000 sq miles)
Empty Quarter (Ar Rub al Khali)	750,000 sq km (289,600 sq miles)
Great Victorian	647,000 sq km (249,800 sq miles)
Sonoran	311,000 sq km (120,000 sq miles)
Kalahari	310,800 sq km (120,000 sq miles)
Garagum	300,000 sq km (115,800 sq miles)
Takla Makan	260,000 sq km (100,400 sq miles)
Namib	135,000 sq km (52,100 sq miles)
Thar	130,000 sq km (33,670 sq miles)

NB – *Most of Antarctica is a polar desert, with only 50 mm (2 inches) of precipitation annually*

Largest islands

Greenland	2,200,000 sq km (849,400 sq miles)
New Guinea	808,000 sq km (312,000 sq miles)
Borneo	757,050 sq km (292,222 sq miles)
Madagascar	594,000 sq km (229,300 sq miles)
Sumatra	524,000 sq km (202,300 sq miles)
Baffin Island	476,000 sq km (183,800 sq miles)
Honshu	230,000 sq km (88,800 sq miles)
Britain	229,800 sq km (88,700 sq miles)
Victoria Island	212,000 sq km (81,900 sq miles)
Ellesmere Island	196,000 sq km (75,700 sq miles)

Highest mountains (Height above sea level)

Everest	8848 m (29,029 ft)
K2	8611 m (28,253 ft)
Kanchenjunga I	8598 m (28,210 ft)
Makalu I	8463 m (27,767 ft)
Cho Oyu	8201 m (26,907 ft)
Dhaulagiri I	8167 m (26,796 ft)
Manaslu I	8163 m (26,783 ft)
Nanga Parbat I	8126 m (26,661 ft)
Annapurna I	8091 m (26,547 ft)
Gasherbrum I	8068 m (26,471 ft)

Deepest ocean features

Challenger Deep, Mariana Trench (Pacific)	10,916 m (35,814 ft)
Vityaz III Depth, Tonga Trench (Pacific)	10,882 m (35,704 ft)
Vityaz Depth, Kurile-Kamchatka Trench (Pacific)	10,542 m (34,588 ft)
Cape Johnson Deep, Philippine Trench (Pacific)	10,497 m (34,441 ft)
Kermadec Trench (Pacific)	10,047 m (32,964 ft)
Ramapo Deep, Japan Trench (Pacific)	9984 m (32,758 ft)
Milwaukee Deep, Puerto Rico Trench (Atlantic)	9200 m (30,185 ft)
Argo Deep, Torres Trench (Pacific)	9165 m (30,070 ft)
Meteor Depth, South Sandwich Trench (Atlantic)	9144 m (30,000 ft)
Planet Deep, New Britain Trench (Pacific)	9140 m (29,988 ft)

Largest bodies of inland water (Area & depth)

Caspian Sea	371,000 sq km (143,243 sq miles)	980 m (3215 ft)
Lake Superior	83,270 sq km (32,151 sq miles)	393 m (1289 ft)
Lake Victoria	68,880 sq km (26,560 sq miles)	100 m (328 ft)
Lake Huron	60,700 sq km (23,436 sq miles)	229 m (751 ft)
Lake Michigan	58,020 sq km (22,402 sq miles)	281 m (922 ft)
Lake Tanganyika	32,900 sq km (12,703 sq miles)	1435 m (4700 ft)
Great Bear Lake	31,790 sq km (12,274 sq miles)	319 m (1047 ft)
Lake Baikal	30,500 sq km (11,776 sq miles)	1741 m (5712 ft)
Great Slave Lake	28,440 sq km (10,981 sq miles)	140 m (459 ft)
Lake Erie	25,680 sq km (9915 sq miles)	60 m (197 ft)

Longest rivers

Nile (NE Africa)	6695 km (4160 miles)
Amazon (South America)	6516 km (4049 miles)
Yangtze (China)	6299 km (3915 miles)
Mississippi/Missouri (US)	5969 km (3710 miles)
Ob'-Irtysh (Russ. Fed.)	5570 km (3461 miles)
Yellow River (China)	5464 km (3395 miles)
Congo (Central Africa)	4667 km (2900 miles)
Mekong (Southeast Asia)	4425 km (2749 miles)
Lena (Russian Federation)	4400 km (2734 miles)
Mackenzie (Canada)	4250 km (2640 miles)
Yenisey (Russian Federation)	4090 km (2541 miles)

Greatest waterfalls (Mean flow of water)

Boyoma (Congo)	17,000 cu.m/sec (600,400 cu. ft/sec)
Khône (Laos/Cambodia)	11,600 cu.m/sec (410,000 cu. ft/sec)
Niagara (USA/Canada)	5500 cu.m/sec (195,000 cu. ft/sec)
Grande (Uruguay)	4500 cu.m/sec (160,000 cu. ft/sec)
Paulo Afonso (Brazil)	2800 cu.m/sec (100,000 cu. ft/sec)
Urubupunga (Brazil)	2750 cu.m/sec (97,000 cu. ft/sec)
Iguaçu (Argentina/Brazil)	1700 cu.m/sec (62,000 cu. ft/sec)
Maribondo (Brazil)	1500 cu.m/sec (53,000 cu. ft/sec)
Victoria (Zimbabwe)	1100 cu.m/sec (39,000 cu. ft/sec
Kabalega (Uganda)	1200 cu.m/sec (42,000 cu. ft/sec)
Churchill (Canada)	1000 cu.m/sec (35,000 cu. ft/sec)
Cauvery (India)	900 cu.m/sec (33,000 cu. ft/sec)

Highest waterfalls

Angel (Venezuela)	979 m (3212 ft)
Tugela (South Africa)	948 m (3110 ft)
Utigard (Norway)	800 m (2625 ft)
Mongefossen (Norway)	774 m (2539 ft)
Mtarazi (Zimbabwe)	762 m (2500 ft)
Yosemite (USA)	739 m (2425 ft)
Ostre Mardola Foss (Norway)	657 m (2156 ft)
Tyssestrengane (Norway)	646 m (2119 ft)
*Cuquenan (Venezuela)	610 m (2001 ft)
Sutherland (New Zealand)	580 m (1903 ft)
*Kjellfossen (Norway)	561 m (1841 ft)

** indicates that the total height is a single leap*

	GENERAL FACTS				
Country	**Capital city**	**Land area (sq km)**	**Main languages spoken**	**Unit of currency**	**Populatio (2012–201**
NORTH AMERICA					
Antigua & Barbuda	St John's	442	English, English patois	East Caribbean dollar	9
Bahamas	Nassau	13 940	English, English Creole, French Creole	Bahamian dollar	40
Barbados	Bridgetown	430	Bajan (Barbadian English), English	Barbados dollar	30
Belize	Belmopan	22 966	English Creole, Spanish, English, Mayan, Garifuna (Carib)	Belizean dollar	30
Canada	Ottawa	9 984 670	English, French, Chinese, Italian, German, Ukrainian, Portuguese, Inuktitut, Cree	Canadian dollar	34 70
Costa Rica	San José	51 100	Spanish, English Creole, Bribri, Cabecar	Costa Rican colón	4 80
Cuba	Havana	110 860	Spanish	Cuban peso	11 20
Dominica	Roseau	754	French Creole, English	East Caribbean dollar	7
Dominican Republic	Santo Domingo	48 380	Spanish, French Creole	Dominican Republic peso	10 20
El Salvador	San Salvador	21 040	Spanish	Salvadorean colón, US $	6 30
Grenada	St George's	340	English, English Creole	East Caribbean dollar	11
Guatemala	Guatemala City	108 890	Quiché, Mam, Cakchiquel, Kekchí, Spanish	Quetzal	15 10
Haiti	Port-au-Prince	27 750	French Creole, French	Gourde	10 30
Honduras	Tegucigalpa	112 090	Spanish, Garífuna (Carib), English Creole	Lempira	7 90
Jamaica	Kingston	10 990	English Creole, English	Jamaican dollar	2 80
Mexico	Mexico City	1 972 550	Spanish, Nahuatl, Mayan, Zapotec, Mixtec, Otomi, Totonac, Tzotzil, Tzeltal	Mexican peso	116 10
Nicaragua	Managua	129 494	Spanish, English Creole, Miskito	Córdoba oro	6 00
Panama	Panama City	78 200	English Creole, Spanish, Amerindian languages, Chibchan languages	Balboa, US dollar	3 60
St Kitts & Nevis	Basseterre	261	English, English Creole	East Caribbean dollar	5
St Lucia	Castries	620	English, French Creole	East Caribbean dollar	16
St Vincent & the Grenadines	Kingstown	389	English, English Creole	East Caribbean dollar	10
Trinidad & Tobago	Port-of-Spain	5 128	English Creole, English, Hindi, French, Spanish	Trinidad and Tobago dollar	1 40
United States	Washington D.C.	9 826 675	English, Spanish, Chinese, French, German, Tagalog, Vietnamese, Italian, Korean, Russian, Polish	US dollar	315 80
SOUTH AMERICA					
Argentina	Buenos Aires	2 766 890	Spanish, Italian, Amerindian languages	Argentine peso	41 10
Bolivia	La Paz/Sucre	1 098 580	Aymara, Quechua, Spanish	Boliviano	10 20
Brazil	Brasília	8 511 965	Portuguese, German, Italian, Spanish, Polish, Japanese, Amerindian languages	Real	198 40
Chile	Santiago	756 950	Spanish, Amerindian languages	Chilean peso	17 40
Colombia	Bogotá	1 138 910	Spanish, Wayuu, Páez, other Amerindian languages	Colombian peso	47 60
Ecuador	Quito	283 560	Spanish, Quechua, other Amerindian languages	US dollar	14 90
Guyana	Georgetown	214 970	English Creole, Hindi, Tamil, Amerindian languages, English	Guyanese dollar	80
Paraguay	Asunción	406 750	Guaraní, Spanish, German	Guaraní	6 70
Peru	Lima	1 285 200	Spanish, Quechua, Aymara	Nuevo sol	29 70
Surinam	Paramaribo	163 270	Sranan (creole), Dutch, Javanese, Sarnami Hindi, Saramaccan, Chinese, Carib	Surinamese dollar	50
Uruguay	Montevideo	176 220	Spanish	Uruguayan peso	3 40
Venezuela	Caracas	912 050	Spanish, Amerindian languages	Bolívar fuerte	29 90
AFRICA					
Algeria	Algiers	2 381 740	Arabic, Tamazight (Kabyle, Shawia, Tamashek), French	Algerian dinar	36 50
Angola	Luanda	1 246 700	Portuguese, Umbundu, Kimbundu, Kikongo	Readjusted kwanza	20 20
Benin	Porto-Novo	112 620	Fon, Bariba, Yoruba, Adja, Houeda, Somba, French	CFA franc	9 40
Botswana	Gaborone	600 370	Setswana, English, Shona, San, Khoikhoi, isiNdebele	Pula	2 10
Burkina	Ouagadougou	274 200	Mossi, Fulani, French, Tuareg, Dyula, Songhai	CFA franc	17 50
Burundi	Bujumbura	27 830	Kirundi, French, Kiswahili	Burundian franc	8 70
Cameroon	Yaoundé	475 400	Bamileke, Fang, Fulani, French, English	CFA franc	20 50
Cape Verde	Praia	4 033	Portuguese Creole, Portuguese	Escudo	50
Central African Republic	Bangui	622 984	Sango, Banda, Gbaya, French	CFA franc	4 60
Chad	N'Djamena	1 284 000	French, Sara, Arabic, Maba	CFA franc	11 80
Comoros	Moroni	2 170	Arabic, Comoran, French	Comoros franc	80
Congo, Democratic Republic	Kinshasa	2 345 410	Kiswahili, Tshiluba, Kikongo, Lingala, French	Congolese franc	69 60

POPULATION					HEALTH AND EDUCATION					ECONOMIC DEVELOPMENT			TECHNOLOGICAL DEVELOPMENT		
lation ity q km 2–)	Birth rate per 1000 population (2010–2012)	Death rate per 1000 population (2009–2012)	Life expectancy at birth (years; 2010–2015)		Medical doctors per 10 000 people (2004–2012)	Infant mortality (deaths per 1000 live births; 2010–2011)	Adult literacy rate (percentage of adults over 15; 2005–2012)		Average calorie intake per person (2009)	GNI per person (US$; 2011)	Annual electricity consumption per person (kWh; 2010)	Annual military expenditure as percentage of GDP (2009–2012)	Mobile telephones per 1000 population (2010–2011)	Internet users per 1000 population (2010–2011)	ICT Dev. Index (IDI), compiled by the ITU (2011)
			Male	Female			Male	Female							
205	16	7	74	78	1.8	7	98.4	99.4	2 373	12 060	1 230	0.7	1 964	820	43
40	15	5	73	79	28.2	14	95.0	96.7	2 750	21 970	5 790	0.7	861	650	-
698	11	9	74	80	18.1	17	99.0	99.0	3 021	12 660	3 448	0.7	1 270	718	34
13	24	4	75	78	8.3	14	76.7	77.1	2 680	3 690	1 990	1.1	700	140	-
4	11	7	79	83	19.8	5	99.0	99.0	3 399	45 560	14 808	1.4	797	830	22
94	16	4	77	82	13.0	9	95.9	96.4	2 886	7 660	1 889	0.7	922	421	71
101	10	7	77	81	67.2	5	99.0	99.0	3 258	5 550	1 229	3.1	117	232	106
98	16	7	73	79	5.1	11	94.0	94.0	3 147	7 090	1 274	0.0	1 640	513	-
211	21	6	71	77	18.4	22	89.4	89.7	2 491	5 240	1 335	0.6	872	355	93
304	20	7	68	77	16.0	14	87.1	82.3	2 574	3 480	890	1.0	1 335	177	103
322	19	6	74	78	6.6	9	-	-	2 456	7 220	1 648	-	1 167	335	-
139	32	5	68	75	9.3	25	80.6	70.3	2 244	2 870	587	0.4	1 404	117	-
374	26	9	61	64	2.6	70	53.4	44.6	1 979	700	22	0.2	415	84	-
71	26	5	71	76	3.7	20	84.8	84.7	2 694	1 970	607	1.1	1 040	159	107
259	15	7	71	76	4.1	20	81.6	91.4	2 807	4 980	1 077	0.5	1 081	315	89
61	19	5	75	80	19.6	14	94.4	91.9	3 146	9 240	1 888	0.5	824	362	79
51	23	5	71	77	3.7	23	78.1	77.9	2 517	1 170	433	0.6	822	106	113
47	20	5	74	79	15.3	17	94.7	93.5	2 606	7 910	1 820	1.1	1 886	427	66
142	14	7	73	78	11.7	7	-	-	2 546	12 480	2 520	-	1 527	760	-
267	13	6	72	78	4.7	14	89.5	90.6	2 710	6 680	2 068	0.0	1 230	420	64
304	17	7	70	75	5.3	19	-	-	2 914	6 100	1 212	0.0	1 205	430	59
273	15	8	67	74	11.8	24	99.2	98.4	2 751	15 040	6 172	0.5	1 356	552	61
32	13	8	76	81	24.2	7	99.0	99.0	3 688	48 450	12 564	4.7	927	779	15
15	17	8	72	80	32.1	12	97.8	99.4	2 918	9 740	2 687	0.7	1 349	477	56
9	26	7	65	69	12.2	42	95.8	86.8	2 172	2 040	586	1.5	828	300	98
23	15	6	71	77	17.6	17	90.2	90.4	3 173	10 720	2 327	1.4	1 243	450	60
23	14	6	76	82	10.3	8	98.6	98.5	2 908	12 280	3 218	3.2	1297	539	55
46	19	5	70	78	1.5	17	93.3	93.5	2 717	6 110	1 026	3.3	985	404	76
54	20	5	73	79	16.9	18	93.3	90.5	2 267	4 140	991	3.5	1045	314	82
4	18	6	67	73	2.1	25	99.0	99.0	2 718	2 900	684	1.2	699	320	99
17	24	5	71	75	11.0	21	94.8	92.9	2 518	2 970	1 063	1.1	994	239	97
23	20	5	72	77	9.2	15	94.9	84.6	2 563	5 500	1 022	1.2	1 104	365	86
3	18	7	68	74	9.1	27	95..4	94.0	2 548	7 640	2 606	1.1	1 789	320	-
19	14	9	74	81	37.4	9	97.6	98.6	2 808	11 860	2 762	1.9	1 408	514	50
34	20	5	72	78	19.5	16	95.7	95.4	3 014	11 920	3 361	0.8	978	402	77
15	20	5	72	75	12.1	31	81.3	63.9	3 239	4 470	937	4.6	990	140	104
16	41	14	50	53	1.7	98	82.7	58.1	2 079	4 060	269	3.5	484	148	-
85	39	12	55	59	0.6	73	55.2	30.3	2 592	780	96	1.5	853	35	141
4	23	13	54	51	3.4	36	84.0	84.9	2 164	7 480	1 556	2.1	1 428	70	108
64	43	12	55	57	0.6	93	36.7	21.6	2 647	570	48	1.3	453	30	151
339	34	14	50	53	0.3	88	72.9	61.8	1 604	250	22	3.2	223	11	-
44	36	14	51	54	0.8	84	78.9	63.0	2 457	1 210	269	1.4	524	50	138
124	20	5	71	78	5.7	29	89.3	79.4	2 644	3 540	525	0.5	792	320	101
7	35	16	48	51	0.5	106	69.3	43.2	2 181	470	31	1.8	406	22	153
9	44	16	49	52	0.4	99	45.0	24.2	2 074	690	9	2.3	318	19	154
359	37	9	60	63	1.5	63	80.2	69.7	2 139	770	52	2.8	287	55	130
31	43	16	47	51	1.1	112	76.9	57.0	1 585	190	89	1.5	231	12	146

Country	GENERAL FACTS				
	Capital city	Land area (sq km)	Main languages spoken	Unit of currency	Populatio (2012–20
Congo	Brazzaville	342 000	Kongo, Teke, Lingala, French	CFA franc	4 200
Djibouti	Djibouti	22 000	Somali, Afar, French, Arabic	Djibouti franc	900
Egypt	Cairo	1 001 450	Arabic, French, English, Berber	Egyptian pound	84 000
Equatorial Guinea	Malabo	28 051	Spanish, Fang, Bubi, French	CFA franc	700
Eritrea	Asmara	121 320	Tigrinya, English, Tigre, Afar, Arabic, Saho, Bilen, Kunama, Nara, Hadareb	Nakfa	5 600
Ethiopia	Addis Ababa	1 127 127	Amharic, Tigrinya, Galla, Sidamo, Somali, English, Arabic	Birr	86 500
Gabon	Libreville	267 667	Fang, French, Punu, Sira, Nzebi, Mpongwe	CFA franc	1 600
Gambia	Banjul	11 300	Mandinka, Fulani, Wolof, Jola, Soninke, English	Dalasi	1 800
Ghana	Accra	238 540	Twi, Fanti, Ewe, Ga, Adangbe, Gurma, Dagomba (Dagbani)	Cedi	25 500
Guinea	Conakry	245 857	Pulaar, Malinké, Soussou, French	Guinea franc	10 500
Guinea-Bissau	Bissau	36 120	Portuguese Creole, Balante, Fulani, Malinké, Portuguese	CFA franc	1 600
Ivory Coast	Yamoussoukro	322 460	Akan, French, Krou, Voltaïque	CFA franc	20 600
Kenya	Nairobi	582 650	Kiswahili, English, Kikuyu, Luo, Kalenjin, Kamba	Kenya shilling	42 700
Lesotho	Maseru	30 355	English, Sesotho, isiZulu	Loti, S African rand	2 200
Liberia	Monrovia	111 370	Kpelle, Vai, Bassa, Kru, Grebo, Kissi, Gola, Loma, English	Liberian dollar	4 200
Libya	Tripoli	1 759 540	Arabic, Tuareg	Libyan dinar	6 500
Madagascar	Antananarivo	587 040	Malagasy, French, English	Ariary	21 900
Malawi	Lilongwe	118 480	Chewa, Lomwe, Yao, Ngoni, English	Malawi kwacha	15 900
Mali	Bamako	1 240 000	Bambara, Fulani, Senufo, Soninke, French	CFA franc	16 300
Mauritania	Nouakchott	1 030 700	Hassaniyah Arabic, Wolof, French	Ouguiya	3 600
Mauritius	Port Louis	1 860	French Creole, Hindi, Urdu, Tamil, Chinese, English, French	Mauritian rupee	1 300
Morocco	Rabat	446 300	Arabic, Tamazight (Berber), French, Spanish	Moroccan dirham	32 600
Mozambique	Maputo	801 590	Makua, Xitsonga, Sena, Lomwe, Portuguese	New metical	24 500
Namibia	Windhoek	825 418	Ovambo, Kavango, English, Bergdama, German, Afrikaans	Namibian $, S African rand	2 400
Niger	Niamey	1 267 000	Hausa, Djerma, Fulani, Tuareg, Teda, French	CFA franc	16 600
Nigeria	Abuja	923 768	Hausa, English, Yoruba, Ibo	Naira	166 600
Rwanda	Kigali	26 338	Kinyarwanda, French, Kiswahili, English	Rwanda franc	11 300
São Tomé & Príncipe	São Tomé	1 001	Portuguese Creole, Portuguese	Dobra	200
Senegal	Dakar	196 190	Wolof, Pulaar, Serer, Diola, Mandinka, Malinké, Soninké, French	CFA franc	13 100
Seychelles	Victoria	455	French Creole, English, French	Seychelles rupee	9
Sierra Leone	Freetown	71 740	Mende, Temne, Krio, English	Leone	6 100
Somalia	Mogadishu	637 657	Somali, Arabic, English, Italian	Somali shilin	9 800
South Africa	Pretoria/Cape Town/Bloemfontein	1 219 912	English, isiZulu, isiXhosa, Afrikaans, Sepedi, Setswana, 5 other official languages	Rand	50 700
South Sudan	Juba	644 329	Arabic, Dinka, Nuer, Zande, Bari, Shilluk, Lotuko	South Sudan pound	10 700
Sudan	Khartoum	1 861 481	Arabic, Nubian, Beja, Fur	New Sudanese pound	35 000
Swaziland	Mbabane	17 363	English, siSwati, isiZulu, Xitsonga	Lilangeni	1 200
Tanzania	Dodoma	945 087	Kiswahili, Sukuma, Chagga, Nyamwezi, Hehe, Makonde, Yao, Sandawe, English	Tanzanian shilling	47 700
Togo	Lomé	56 785	Ewe, Kabye, Gurma, French	CFA franc	6 300
Tunisia	Tunis	163 610	Arabic, French	Tunisian dinar	10 700
Uganda	Kampala	236 040	Luganda, Nkole, Chiga, Lango, Acholi, Teso, Lugbara, English	New Uganda shilling	35 600
Western Sahara (occupied by Morocco)	Laâyoune	266 000	Arabic, Tamazight (Berber), Spanish	Moroccan dirham	53
Zambia	Lusaka	752 614	Bemba, Tonga, Nyanja, Lozi, Lala-Bisa, Nsenga, English	Zambian kwacha	13 900
Zimbabwe	Harare	390 580	Shona, isiNdebele, English	US $, S African rand*	13 000
EUROPE					
Albania	Tirana	28 748	Albanian, Greek	Lek	3 200
Andorra	Andorra la Vella	468	Spanish, Catalan, French, Portuguese	Euro	8
Austria	Vienna	83 858	German, Croatian, Slovenian, Hungarian (Magyar)	Euro	8 400
Belarus	Minsk	207 600	Belarussian, Russian	Belarussian rouble	9 500
Belgium	Brussels	30 510	Dutch, French, German	Euro	10 800
Bosnia & Herzegovina	Sarajevo	51 129	Bosnian, Serbian, Croatian	Marka	3 700
Bulgaria	Sofia	110 910	Bulgarian, Turkish, Romani	Lev	7 400
Croatia	Zagreb	56 542	Croatian	Kuna	4 400

* Zimbabwe dollar suspended in 2009; US dollar, South African rand, euro, UK pound and Botswanan pula now legal t

POPULATION					HEALTH AND EDUCATION					ECONOMIC DEVELOPMENT			TECHNOLOGICAL DEVELOPMENT		
…ulation …ity …sq km …2– …)	Birth rate per 1000 population (2010–2012)	Death rate per 1000 population (2009–2012)	Life expectancy at birth (years; 2010–2015)		Medical doctors per 10 000 people (2004–2012)	Infant mortality (deaths per 1000 live births; 2010–2011)	Adult literacy rate (percentage of adults over 15; 2005–2012)		Average calorie intake per person (2009)	GNI per person (US$; 2011)	Annual electricity consumption per person (kWh; 2010)	Annual military expenditure as percentage of GDP (2009–2012)	Mobile telephones per 1000 population (2010–2011)	Internet users per 1000 population (2010–2011)	ICT Dev. Index (IDI), compiled by the ITU (2011)
			Male	Female			Male	Female							
12	35	11	57	59	1.0	61	89.6	78.4	2 056	2 270	140	1.4	938	56	140
39	29	10	57	60	2.3	73	79.9	61.4	2 419	1 270	408	3.5	213	70	128
84	23	5	72	76	28.3	19	80.3	63.5	3 349	2 600	1 521	1.9	1 011	387	83
25	36	14	50	53	3.0	81	97.1	90.6	-	14 540	138	0.1	591	60	-
48	36	8	60	64	0.5	42	78.7	57.5	1 640	430	44	4.2	45	62	152
78	31	9	58	62	0.2	68	49.1	28.9	2 097	400	52	1.1	167	11	150
6	27	9	62	64	2.8	54	91.9	84.9	2 745	7 980	933	1.2	1 173	80	111
180	38	9	58	60	0.4	57	60.0	40.4	2 643	610	122	0.7	789	109	125
111	31	8	64	66	0.9	50	73.2	61.2	2 934	1 410	225	0.3	848	141	117
43	38	13	53	56	1.0	81	52.0	30.0	2 652	440	87	1.6	440	13	148
57	38	16	47	50	0.5	92	68.2	40.6	2 476	600	40	1.6	562	27	-
65	34	12	55	58	1.4	86	65.2	46.6	2 670	1 100	184	1.5	861	22	129
75	37	10	57	59	1.8	55	90.6	84.2	2 092	820	151	1.5	675	280	114
72	28	15	50	48	0.5	65	83.3	95.6	2 371	1 220	160	2.4	562	42	-
44	39	11	56	59	0.1	74	64.8	56.8	2 261	240	85	0.9	492	30	149
4	23	4	73	78	19.0	13	95.6	82.7	3 157	12 320	4 131	2.8	1 557	170	-
38	35	6	65	69	1.6	43	67.4	61.6	2 117	430	54	0.7	407	19	143
169	44	12	55	55	0.2	58	81.1	68.5	2 318	340	119	1.1	257	33	144
13	46	14	51	53	0.5	99	43.4	20.3	2 624	610	33	1.8	683	20	145
4	33	9	57	61	1.3	75	64.9	51.2	2 856	1 000	203	3.8	936	45	136
699	12	7	70	77	10.9	13	90.9	86.2	2 993	8 240	1 822	0.1	990	350	74
73	19	6	70	75	6.2	30	68.9	43.9	3 264	2 970	747	3.3	1 133	510	90
31	37	14	50	52	0.3	92	70.8	42.9	2 112	470	456	0.9	328	43	147
3	26	8	62	63	3.7	29	89.0	88.5	2 151	4 700	1 567	3.4	964	120	109
13	48	13	55	56	0.2	73	42.9	15.1	2 489	360	55	1.0	295	13	155
183	40	14	52	53	4.0	88	72.1	50.4	2 711	1 200	126	1.0	586	284	122
453	41	12	54	57	0.2	44	74.8	67.5	2 188	570	29	1.2	406	70	133
208	31	8	64	66	4.5	53	93.9	84.7	2 734	1 360	159	0.5	683	202	-
68	37	9	59	61	0.6	50	61.8	38.7	2 479	1 070	180	1.7	733	175	124
336	17	7	69	79	15.0	12	91.4	92.3	2 426	11 130	2 989	0.9	1 457	432	70
85	38	15	48	49	0.2	114	53.6	31.4	2 162	340	26	0.9	356	3	-
16	43	15	50	53	0.4	108	49.7	25.8	1 762	288	29	0.9	69	13	-
42	21	15	53	54	7.6	41	90.7	87.0	3 017	6 960	4 378	1.3	1 268	210	91
17	-	-	-	-	-	102	40.0	16.0	-	-	149	2.9	-	-	-
19	32	9	61	65	2.8	62	80.1	62.0	2 326	1 300	149	1.3	561	190	-
70	29	14	50	49	1.7	55	88.1	86.8	2 249	3 300	781	3.0	637	181	116
54	41	10	58	60	0.1	50	79.0	67.5	2 137	540	77	1.1	555	120	139
116	32	11	56	59	0.5	66	71.2	43.6	2 363	560	103	1.6	504	35	134
69	19	6	73	77	11.9	14	86.4	71.0	3 314	4 070	1 262	1.3	1169	391	85
178	45	12	54	55	1.2	63	82.6	64.6	2 260	510	70	1.6	484	130	132
2	31	9	60	64	-	58	-	-	-	2 500	171	-	-	-	-
19	46	15	49	50	0.6	69	80.7	61.7	1 879	1 160	610	1.6	606	115	135
34	29	13	54	53	0.6	51	94.7	89.9	2 219	640	1 079	1.6	721	157	115
117	13	6	74	80	11.1	16	97.3	94.7	2 903	3 980	1 563	1.5	964	490	80
183	10	8	80	85	39.1	3	99.0	99.0	-	41 130	-	0.0	755	810	-
102	9	9	78	84	48.5	4	99.0	99.0	3 800	48 300	7 767	0.9	1 548	798	19
46	12	14	65	76	37.6	4	99.0	99.0	3 186	5 830	3 279	1.1	1 119	396	46
329	12	10	77	83	30.1	4	99.0	99.0	3 721	46 160	8 124	1.1	1 166	780	23
72	8	10	73	78	16.4	8	99.4	96.5	3 070	4 780	2 849	1.4	845	600	63
67	10	15	70	77	37.3	11	98.7	98.0	2 791	6 550	4 261	1.5	1 407	510	51
78	9	12	73	80	26.0	5	99.0	98.2	3 130	13 850	3 474	1.7	1 164	707	42

	GENERAL FACTS				
Country	**Capital city**	**Land area (sq km)**	**Main languages spoken**	**Unit of currency**	**Population (2012–201**
Cyprus	Nicosia	9 250	Greek, Turkish	Euro, Turkish lira	1 100
Czech Republic	Prague	78 866	Czech, Slovak, Hungarian (Magyar)	Czech koruna	10 600
Denmark	Copenhagen	43 094	Danish	Danish krone	5 600
Estonia	Tallinn	45 226	Estonian, Russian	Euro	1 300
Finland	Helsinki	337 030	Finnish, Swedish, Sámi	Euro	5 400
France	Paris	547 030	French, Provençal, German, Breton, Catalan, Basque	Euro	63 500
Germany	Berlin	357 021	German, Turkish	Euro	82 000
Greece	Athens	131 940	Greek, Turkish, Macedonian, Albanian	Euro	11 400
Hungary	Budapest	93 030	Hungarian (Magyar)	Forint	9 900
Iceland	Reykjavík	103 000	Icelandic	Icelandic króna	300
Ireland	Dublin	70 280	English, Irish Gaelic	Euro	4 600
Italy	Rome	301 230	Italian, German, French, Rhaeto-Romanic, Sardinian	Euro	61 000
Kosovo (disputed)	Prishtinë	10 908	Albanian, Serbian, Bosniak, Gorani, Roma, Turkish	Euro	1 800
Latvia	Riga	64 589	Latvian, Russian	Lats	2 200
Liechtenstein	Vaduz	160	German, Alemannish dialect, Italian	Swiss franc	37
Lithuania	Vilnius	65 200	Lithuanian, Russian	Litas	3 300
Luxembourg	Luxembourg-Ville	2 586	Luxembourgish, German, French	Euro	500
Macedonia	Skopje	25 333	Macedonian, Albanian, Turkish, Romani, Serbian	Macedonian denar	2 100
Malta	Valletta	316	Maltese, English	Euro	400
Moldova	Chisinau	33 843	Moldovan, Ukrainian, Russian	Moldovan leu	3 500
Monaco	Monaco-Ville	1.95	French, Italian, Monégasque, English	Euro	30
Montenegro	Podgorica	13 812	Montenegrin, Serbian, Albanian, Bosniak, Croatian	Euro	600
Netherlands	Amsterdam/The Hague	41 526	Dutch, Frisian	Euro	16 700
Norway	Oslo	324 220	Norwegian (*Bokmål* "book language" and *Nynorsk* "new Norsk"), Sámi	Norwegian krone	5 000
Poland	Warsaw	312 685	Polish	Zloty	38 300
Portugal	Lisbon	92 391	Portuguese	Euro	10 700
Romania	Bucharest	237 500	Romanian, Hungarian (Magyar), Romani, German	New Romanian leu	21 400
Russian Federation	Moscow	17 075 200	Russian, Tatar, Ukrainian, Chavash, various other national languages	Russian rouble	142 700
San Marino	San Marino	61	Italian	Euro	32
Serbia	Belgrade	77 453	Serbian, Hungarian (Magyar)	Serbian dinar	9 800
Slovakia	Bratislava	48 845	Slovak, Hungarian (Magyar), Czech	Euro	5 500
Slovenia	Ljubljana	20 253	Slovenian	Euro	2 000
Spain	Madrid	504 782	Spanish, Catalan, Galician, Basque	Euro	46 800
Sweden	Stockholm	449 964	Swedish, Finnish, Sámi	Swedish krona	9 500
Switzerland	Bern	41 290	German, Swiss-German, French, Italian, Romansch	Swiss franc	7 700
Ukraine	Kiev	603 700	Ukrainian, Russian, Tatar	Hryvna	44 900
United Kingdom	London	244 820	English, Welsh, Scottish Gaelic, Irish Gaelic	Pound sterling	62 800
Vatican City	Vatican City	0.44	Italian, Latin	Euro	
ASIA					
Afghanistan	Kabul	647 500	Pashtu, Tajik, Dari, Farsi, Uzbek, Turkmen	Afghani	33 400
Armenia	Yerevan	29 800	Armenian, Azeri, Russian	Dram	3 100
Azerbaijan	Baku	86 600	Azeri, Russian	New manat	9 400
Bahrain	Manama	620	Arabic	Bahraini dinar	1 400
Bangladesh	Dhaka	144 000	Bengali, Urdu, Chakma, Marma (Magh), Garo, Khasi, Santhali, Tripuri, Mro	Taka	152 400
Bhutan	Thimphu	47 000	Dzongkha, Nepali, Assamese	Ngultrum	800
Brunei	Bandar Seri Begawan	5 770	Malay, English, Chinese	Brunei dollar	400
Burma (Myanmar)	Nay Pyi Taw	678 500	Burmese, Shan, Karen, Rakhine, Chin, Yangbye, Kachin, Mon	Kyat	48 700
Cambodia	Phnom Penh	181 040	Khmer, French, Chinese, Vietnamese, Cham	Riel	14 500
China	Beijing	9 596 960	Mandarin, Wu, Cantonese, Hsiang, Min, Hakka, Kan	Renminbi (known as yuan)	1 353 600
East Timor	Dili	14 874	Tetum (Portuguese/Austronesian), Bahasa Indonesia, Portuguese	US dollar	1 200
Georgia	Tbilisi	69 700	Georgian, Russian, Azeri, Armenian, Mingrelian, Ossetian, Abkhazian	Lari	4 300

POPULATION					HEALTH AND EDUCATION					ECONOMIC DEVELOPMENT			TECHNOLOGICAL DEVELOPMENT		
ation ty q km –	Birth rate per 1000 population (2010–2012)	Death rate per 1000 population (2009–2012)	Life expectancy at birth (years; 2010–2015)		Medical doctors per 10 000 people (2004–2012)	Infant mortality (deaths per 1000 live births; 2010–2011)	Adult literacy rate (percentage of adults over 15; 2005–2012)		Average calorie intake per person (2009)	GNI per person (US$; 2011)	Annual electricity consumption per person (kWh; 2010)	Annual military expenditure as percentage of GDP (2009–2012)	Mobile telephones per 1000 population (2010–2011)	Internet users per 1000 population (2010–2011)	ICT Dev. Index (IDI), compiled by the ITU (2011)
			Male	Female			Male	Female							
119	12	7	78	82	25.8	3	99.0	97.3	2 678	29 450	4 346	2.2	977	577	44
134	10	10	75	81	36.7	3	99.0	99.0	3 305	18 520	5 998	1.1	1 234	730	32
132	11	9	77	81	34.2	3	99.0	99.0	3 378	60 390	6 084	1.5	1 285	900	3
29	11	11	70	80	33.3	4	99.0	99.0	3 163	15 200	6 156	1.7	1 390	765	24
18	11	9	77	83	29.1	2	99.0	99.0	3 240	48 420	16 142	1.5	1 660	894	5
115	13	9	78	85	33.8	2	99.0	99.0	3 531	42 420	7 252	2.2	948	796	18
235	8	10	78	83	36.0	3	99.0	99.0	3 549	43 980	6 726	1.3	1 323	830	16
87	9	10	78	83	61.7	3	98.3	96.1	3 661	25 030	5 247	2.8	1 065	530	33
107	9	13	71	78	30.3	5	99.0	98.9	3 477	12 730	3 690	1.0	1 173	590	41
3	14	6	80	84	34.6	2	99.0	99.0	3 376	35 020	52 537	0.0	1 061	950	4
67	16	6	78	83	31.7	3	99.0	99.0	3 617	38 580	5 447	0.6	1 084	768	20
207	9	10	79	85	34.9	3	99.0	98.7	3 627	35 330	5 050	1.6	1 579	568	29
165	18	7	68	72	10.8	9	96.6	87.5	-	3 520	3 294	-	845	-	-
34	9	14	69	79	29.9	8	99.0	99.0	2 923	12 350	2 958	1.0	1 029	717	36
231	11	7	79	84	13.1	2	99.0	99.0	-	137 070	-	0.0	1 018	850	-
51	11	14	67	78	36.1	5	99.0	99.0	3 486	12 280	2 608	1.0	1 513	651	35
193	11	7	78	83	27.8	2	99.0	99.0	3 637	78 130	12 942	0.5	1 483	909	7
82	11	9	73	77	26.3	10	98.7	95.9	2 983	4 730	3 419	1.3	1 072	567	54
1 250	10	8	78	82	32.3	5	91.2	93.5	3 438	18 620	3 936	0.7	1 249	692	26
104	12	13	66	73	36.4	16	99.0	98.1	2 707	1 980	945	0.3	1 048	380	62
15 641	7	8	78	85	70.6	3	99.0	99.0	-	183 150	-	0.0	897	750	-
43	12	10	73	77	21.0	7	99.0	97.4	2 887	7 060	4 916	2.0	1 853	400	-
492	11	8	79	83	28.6	4	99.0	99.0	3 261	49 730	6 639	1.4	1 154	923	6
16	12	8	79	83	41.6	3	99.0	99.0	3 453	88 890	25 855	1.6	1 156	940	13
126	10	10	72	81	21.6	5	99.0	99.0	3 392	12 480	3 506	1.9	1 310	649	31
116	9	10	77	83	38.7	3	96.9	93.6	3 617	21 250	4 681	2.0	1 154	553	37
93	9	12	71	78	22.7	11	98.3	97.1	3 487	7 910	2 204	1.1	1 092	440	52
8	13	14	63	75	43.1	9	99.0	99.0	3 172	10 400	6 044	3.9	1 793	490	38
532	10	7	81	86	48.8	2	99.0	99.0	-	50 670	-	-	1 118	496	-
127	9	14	72	77	21.1	6	99.0	96.7	2 823	5 680	3 959	2.1	1 254	422	48
112	11	10	72	80	30.0	7	99.0	99.0	2 881	16 070	4 803	1.1	1 093	744	39
99	11	9	76	83	25.1	2	99.0	99.0	3 275	23 610	6 289	1.4	1 066	720	25
94	10	8	79	85	39.6	4	98.5	97.0	3 239	30 990	5 742	1.0	1 132	676	28
23	12	10	80	84	37.7	2	99.0	99.0	3 125	53 230	14 983	1.3	1 186	910	2
194	10	8	80	85	40.7	4	99.0	99.0	3 454	76 380	7 687	0.8	1 314	852	10
74	11	15	64	75	35.2	11	99.0	99.0	3 198	3 120	3 312	2.5	1 230	306	67
260	13	9	78	82	27.7	5	99.0	99.0	3 432	37 780	5 281	2.6	1 308	820	9
1 907	-	-	79	84	-	-	99.0	99.0	-	-	-	0.0	-	-	-
51	43	16	49	49	2.1	103	43.1	12.6	1 539	410	85	4.7	543	50	-
104	15	9	71	77	28.5	18	99.0	99.0	2 806	3 360	1 587	4.0	1 036	320	-
109	19	6	68	74	33.8	39	99.0	99.0	3 072	5 290	1 459	4.9	1 087	500	68
1 983	19	3	75	76	14.4	9	92.8	90.2	-	15 920	9 840	3.6	1 280	770	40
1 138	20	6	69	70	3.6	38	61.3	52.2	2 481	770	249	1.3	561	50	-
17	20	7	66	70	0.2	44	65.0	38.7	-	2 070	2 400	1.0	656	210	118
76	19	3	76	81	14.2	6	96.8	93.6	3 088	31 800	8 258	2.5	1 092	560	57
74	17	8	64	68	4.6	50	94.8	98.9	2 493	578	114	4.8	26	10	131
82	22	8	62	65	2.3	43	82.8	65.9	2 382	830	139	1.5	962	31	121
145	12	7	72	76	18.2	16	97.1	91.3	3 036	4 940	2 732	2.0	732	383	78
82	38	8	62	64	1.0	46	63.6	53.0	2 076	2 730	-	2.6	532	9	-
62	12	12	71	77	42.4	20	99.0	99.0	2 743	2 860	1 657	3.0	1 023	366	73

Country	Capital city	Land area (sq km)	Main languages spoken	Unit of currency	Populatio (2012–201
	GENERAL FACTS				
India	New Delhi	3 287 590	Hindi, English, Urdu, Bengali, Marathi, Telugu, Tamil, Bihari, Gujarati, Kanarese	Indian rupee	1 258 400
Indonesia	Jakarta	1 919 440	Javanese, Sundanese, Madurese, Bahasa Indonesia, Dutch	Rupiah	244 800
Iran	Tehran	1 648 000	Farsi, Azeri, Luri, Gilaki, Mazanderani, Kurdish, Turkmen, Arabic, Baluchi	Iranian rial	75 600
Iraq	Baghdad	437 072	Arabic, Kurdish, Turkic languages, Armenian, Assyrian	New Iraqi dinar	33 700
Israel	Jerusalem (disputed)	20 770	Hebrew, Arabic, Yiddish, German, Russian, Polish, Romanian, Persian	Shekel	7 700
Japan	Tokyo	377 835	Japanese, Korean, Chinese	Yen	126 400
Jordan	Amman	92 300	Arabic	Jordanian dinar	6 500
Kazakhstan	Astana	2 717 300	Kazakh, Russian, Ukrainian, German, Uzbek, Tatar, Uighur	Tenge	16 400
Kuwait	Kuwait City	17 820	Arabic, English	Kuwaiti dinar	2 900
Kyrgyzstan	Bishkek	198 500	Kyrgyz, Russian, Uzbek, Tatar, Ukrainian	Som	5 400
Laos	Vientiane	236 800	Lao, Mon-Khmer, Yao, Vietnamese, Chinese, French	New kip	6 400
Lebanon	Beirut	10 400	Arabic, French, Armenian, Assyrian	Lebanese pound	4 300
Malaysia	Kuala Lumpur/Putrajaya	329 750	Bahasa Malaysia, Malay, Chinese, Tamil, English	Ringgit	29 300
Maldives	Male'	300	Dhivehi (Maldivian), Sinhala, Tamil, Arabic	Rufiyaa	300
Mongolia	Ulan Bator	1 565 000	Khalkha Mongolian, Kazakh, Chinese, Russian	Tugrik (tögrög)	2 800
Nepal	Kathmandu	140 800	Nepali, Maithili, Bhojpuri	Nepalese rupee	31 000
North Korea	Pyongyang	120 540	Korean	North Korean won	24 600
Oman	Muscat	212 460	Arabic, Baluchi, Farsi, Hindi, Punjabi	Omani rial	2 900
Pakistan	Islamabad	803 940	Punjabi, Sindhi, Pashtu, Urdu, Baluchi, Brahui	Pakistani rupee	180 000
Philippines	Manila	300 000	Filipino, English, Tagalog, Cebuano, Ilocano, Hiligaynon, many other local languages	Philippine peso	96 500
Qatar	Doha	11 437	Arabic	Qatar riyal	1 900
Saudi Arabia	Riyadh	1 960 582	Arabic	Saudi riyal	28 700
Singapore	Singapore	648	Mandarin, Malay, Tamil, English	Singapore dollar	5 300
South Korea	Seoul/Sejong City	98 480	Korean	South Korean won	48 600
Sri Lanka	Colombo/Sri Jayewardenepura Kotte	65 610	Sinhala, Tamil, Sinhala-Tamil, English	Sri Lanka rupee	21 200
Syria	Damascus	184 180	Arabic, French, Kurdish, Armenian, Circassian, Turkic languages, Assyrian, Aramaic	Syrian pound	21 100
Taiwan	Taipei	35 980	Amoy Chinese, Mandarin Chinese, Hakka Chinese	Taiwan dollar	23 300
Tajikistan	Dushanbe	143 100	Tajik, Uzbek, Russian	Somoni	7 100
Thailand	Bangkok	514 000	Thai, Chinese, Malay, Khmer, Mon, Karen, Miao	Baht	69 900
Turkey	Ankara	780 580	Turkish, Kurdish, Arabic, Circassian, Armenian, Greek, Georgian, Ladino	Turkish lira	74 500
Turkmenistan	Ashgabat	488 100	Turkmen, Uzbek, Russian, Kazakh, Tatar	New manat	5 200
United Arab Emirates	Abu Dhabi	82 880	Arabic, Farsi, Indian and Pakistani languages, English	UAE dirham	8 100
Uzbekistan	Tashkent	447 400	Uzbek, Russian, Tajik, Kazakh	Som	28 100
Vietnam	Hanoi	329 560	Vietnamese, Chinese, Thai, Khmer, Muong, Nung, Miao, Yao, Jarai	Dông	89 700
Yemen	Sana	527 970	Arabic	Yemeni rial	25 600
AUSTRALASIA & OCEANIA					
Australia	Canberra	7 686 850	English, Italian, Cantonese, Greek, Arabic, Vietnamese, Aboriginal languages	Australian dollar	22 900
Fiji	Suva	18 270	Fijian, English, Hindi, Urdu, Tamil, Telugu	Fiji dollar	900
Kiribati	Bairiki (Tarawa Atoll)	717	English, Kiribati	Australian dollar	103
Marshall Islands	Majuro	181	Marshallese, English, Japanese, German	US dollar	69
Micronesia	Palikir (Pohnpei Island)	702	Trukese, Pohnpeian, Kosraean, Yapese, English	US dollar	106
Nauru	None	21	Nauruan, Kiribati, Chinese, Tuvaluan, English	Australian dollar	9
New Zealand	Wellington	268 680	English, Maori	New Zealand dollar	4 500
Palau	Ngerulmud	458	Palauan, English, Japanese, Angaur, Tobi, Sonsorolese	US dollar	21
Papua New Guinea	Port Moresby	462 840	Pidgin English, Papuan, English, Motu, around 800 native languages	Kina	7 200
Samoa	Apia	2 860	Samoan, English	Tala	200
Solomon Islands	Honiara	28 450	English, Pidgin English, Melanesian Pidgin, around 120 native languages	Solomon Islands dollar	600
Tonga	Nuku'alofa	748	English, Tongan	Pa'anga (Tongan dollar)	106
Tuvalu	Fongafale (Funafuti Atoll)	26	Tuvaluan, Kiribati, English	Australian $, Tuvaluan $	10
Vanuatu	Port Vila	12 200	Bislama (Melanesian pidgin), English, French, other indigenous languages	Vatu	300

POPULATION					HEALTH AND EDUCATION					ECONOMIC DEVELOPMENT			TECHNOLOGICAL DEVELOPMENT		
pulation nsity r sq km 12–13)	Birth rate per 1000 population (2010–2012)	Death rate per 1000 population (2009–2012)	Life expectancy at birth (years; 2010–2015)		Medical doctors per 10 000 people (2004–2012)	Infant mortality (deaths per 1000 live births; 2010–2011)	Adult literacy rate (percentage of adults over 15; 2005–2012)		Average calorie intake per person (2009)	GNI per person (US$; 2011)	Annual electricity consumption per person (kWh; 2010)	Annual military expenditure as percentage of GDP (2009–2012)	Mobile telephones per 1000 population (2010–2011)	Internet users per 1000 population (2010–2011)	ICT Dev. Index (IDI), compiled by the ITU (2011)
			Male	Female			Male	Female							
423	22	8	64	68	6.5	48	75.2	50.8	2 321	1 410	596	2.5	720	101	119
136	18	7	68	72	2.0	27	95.6	89.7	2 646	2 940	596	0.7	1 031	180	95
46	17	5	72	75	8.9	22	89.3	80.7	3 143	4 520	2 375	2.6	749	210	87
77	35	6	68	73	6.9	31	86.0	70.6	2 197	2 640	1 184	5.1	781	50	-
379	21	5	80	84	31.1	4	99.0	99.0	3 569	28 930	6 627	6.8	1 217	700	27
336	8	10	80	87	21.4	2	99.0	99.0	2 723	45 180	7 857	1.0	1 050	795	8
73	25	4	72	75	24.5	18	95.8	89.2	2 977	4 380	1 963	4.7	1 182	349	75
6	23	9	62	73	38.4	29	99.0	99.0	3 284	8 220	4 250	1.0	1 557	450	49
163	18	3	74	76	17.9	10	95.0	91.8	3 681	48 900	18 370	3.2	1 751	742	-
27	27	7	64	72	24.7	33	99.0	99.0	2 791	920	1 354	0.8	1 164	200	-
28	22	6	66	69	2.7	42	82.5	63.2	2 377	1 130	370	0.3	872	90	120
420	15	7	71	75	35.4	19	93.4	86.0	3 153	9 110	3 440	4.4	786	520	65
89	20	5	73	77	9.4	5	95.4	90.7	2 902	8 420	3 884	1.6	1 270	610	58
1 000	17	4	76	79	16.0	14	98.4	98.4	2 720	6 530	707	4.0	1 657	340	72
2	23	6	65	73	27.6	26	96.9	97.9	2 434	2 320	1 280	0.9	1 051	200	84
227	24	6	68	70	2.1	41	73.0	48.3	2 443	540	95	1.4	438	90	137
204	14	10	66	72	32.9	26	99.0	99.0	2 078	555	724	22.3	41	-	-
14	18	4	71	76	19.0	8	90.0	80.9	-	19 260	5 161	6.0	1 690	680	53
233	27	7	65	67	8.1	70	68.6	40.3	2 423	1 120	404	3	616	90	127
324	25	6	66	73	11.5	23	95.0	95.8	2 580	2 210	569	1.1	993	290	94
173	12	2	79	78	27.6	7	96.5	95.4	-	80 440	11 933	2.5	1 231	862	30
14	22	4	73	76	9.4	15	90.4	81.3	3 076	17 820	7 418	8.4	1 912	475	47
8 689	10	5	79	84	18.3	2	98.0	93.8	-	42 930	7 903	3.6	1 502	710	12
492	10	5	77	84	20.2	4	99.0	99.0	3 200	20 870	9 242	2.8	1 085	838	1
327	18	7	72	78	4.9	14	92.6	90.0	2 426	2 580	423	2.6	870	150	105
115	22	4	74	78	15.0	14	89.9	76.9	3 212	2 750	1 604	4.2	632	225	96
722	9	7	76	83	16.0	4	99.0	96.3	2 673	20 690	9 412	2.5	1 241	720	-
50	28	6	65	71	19.0	52	99.0	99.0	2 106	870	1 816	1.0	906	130	-
137	12	7	71	78	3.2	11	95.9	92.6	2 862	4 420	2 123	1.6	1 116	237	92
97	18	5	72	77	17.1	12	96.4	85.3	3 666	10 410	2 190	2.3	887	421	69
11	21	8	61	69	23.9	47	99.0	99.0	2 878	4 110	2 250	1.6	688	50	110
97	13	1	76	78	19.3	6	89.5	91.5	3 245	40 760	17 116	3.6	1 486	700	45
63	21	5	66	72	25.6	44	99.0	99.0	2 618	1 510	1 597	3.5	916	302	102
276	16	5	73	77	12.2	19	95.3	91.1	2 690	1 260	957	2.2	1 434	351	81
45	38	6	65	68	3.0	57	81.2	46.8	2 109	1 070	235	3.5	470	149	126
3	13	7	80	84	29.9	4	99.0	99.0	3 261	46 200	9 925	1.9	1 083	790	21
49	21	7	67	72	4.3	15	95.9	92.9	2 996	3 680	922	1.9	837	280	88
145	23	7	66	71	3.8	39	99.0	99.0	2 866	2 110	232	0.0	136	100	-
385	30	12	70	75	4.4	22	93.6	93.7	-	3 910	-	0.0	70	35	-
151	24	6	68	70	1.8	34	-	-	-	2 900	-	0.0	248	200	-
449	28	11	62	69	7.1	32	-	-	-	3 433	3 667	0.0	650	60	-
17	14	7	79	83	27.4	5	99.0	99.0	3 172	29 350	9 587	1.1	1 092	860	17
42	11	5	69	76	13.8	15	-	-	-	7 250	-	0.0	749	270	-
16	30	7	61	66	0.5	47	63.9	57.3	2 193	1 480	514	0.5	342	20	142
71	24	5	70	76	4.8	17	99.0	98.6	2 997	3 190	583	0.0	914	70	-
21	31	6	67	70	2.2	23	-	-	2 439	1 110	136	0.0	498	60	123
148	27	6	70	75	5.6	13	99.0	99.0	-	3 580	358	0.9	526	250	100
411	23	11	63	68	10.9	27	-	-	-	5 010	-	0.0	216	300	112
25	29	5	70	74	1.2	12	84.3	80.8	2 841	2 870	208	0.0	558	80	-

GLOSSARY

This glossary defines certain geographical and technical terms used in this Atlas.

Acid rain Rain, sleet, snow or mist that has absorbed waste gases from fossil-fuelled power stations and vehicle exhausts, becoming acidic and poisonous.

Alluvium Material deposited by a river, such as silt, sand and mud.

Archipelago A group, or chain, of islands.

Atoll A circular or horseshoe-shaped coral reef enclosing a shallow area of water (lagoon).

Aquifer A body of rock that can absorb water. It may be a source of water for wells or springs.

Bar, coastal An offshore strip of sand or shingle, either above or below the water.

Biodiversity The quantity of different animal or plant species in a given area.

Birth rate The number of live births per 1000 individuals annually within a population.

Cash crop Agricultural produce grown for sale, often for foreign export, rather than to be consumed within the country or area in which it was grown.

Climate The long-term trends in weather conditions for an area.

Coniferous forest A type of forest containing trees or shrubs, like pines and firs, which have needles instead of leaves. They are found in temperate zones.

Continental plates The huge interlocking plates which make up the Earth's surface. A plate boundary is an area where two plates meet, and is the point at which earthquakes occur most frequently.

Conurbation A large urban area created by the merging of several towns.

Coral reef An underwater barrier created by colonies of coral polyps. The polyps secrete a protective skeleton of calcium carbonate, and reefs develop as live polyps build on the skeletons of dead generations.

Core The layers of liquid rock and solid iron at the centre of the Earth.

Crust The hard, thin outer shell of the Earth. The crust floats on the mantle, which is softer, but more dense.

Deciduous forest A type of broadleaf forest found in temperate regions.

Deforestation Cutting down trees or forest for timber or farmland. It can lead to soil erosion, flooding and landslides.

Delta A low-lying, fan-shaped area at a river mouth, formed by the deposition of successive layers of sediment. Slowing as it enters the sea, a river deposits sediment and may, as a result, split into many smaller channels called distributaries.

Deposition The laying down of material broken down by erosion or weathering and transported by the wind, water or gravity.

Desertification The spread of desert conditions into a region which was not previously a desert.

Drainage basin The land drained by a river and its tributaries.

Drought A long period of continuously low rainfall.

Earthquake A trembling or shaking of the ground caused by the sudden movement of rocks in the Earth's crust – and sometimes deeper than the crust. Earthquakes occur most frequently along continental plate boundaries.

Economy The organization of a country's finances, exports, imports, industry, agriculture and services.

Ecosytem A community of species dependent on each other and on the habitat in which they live.

Equator The 0° line of latitude. Equatorial climates are hot and there is plenty of rain.

Erosion The wearing down of the land surface by running water, waves, moving ice, wind and weather.

Estuary The mouth of a river, where the salt water from the sea meets the fresh water of the river.

Fault A crack or fracture in the Earth along which there has been movement of the rock masses relative to one another.

Fjord A coastal valley that has been was sculpted by glacial action.

Flood plain The broad, flat part of a river valley, next to the river itself, formed by sediment deposited during flooding.

Geyser A fountain of hot water or steam that erupts periodically as a result of underground streams coming into contact with hot rocks.

GDP Gross Domestic Product. The total value of goods and services produced by a country, excluding income from foreign countries.

GIS Geographical Information System. A computerized system for the collection, storage and retrieval of geographical data.

Glacier A huge mass of ice made up of compacted and frozen snow which moves slowly, eroding and depositing rock.

Glaciation The moulding of the land by a glacier or ice sheet.

GNI Gross National Income. The total value of goods and services produced by a country.

Groundwater Water that has seeped into the pores, cavities and cracks of rocks or into soil and water held in an aquifer or permeable rock.

Gully A deep, narrow chasm eroded in the landscape by a fast-flowing stream.

Heavy industry Industry that uses large amounts of energy and raw materials to produce heavy goods, such as machinery, ships or locomotives.

Humidity The moisture content of the air.

Hurricane A Violent tropical storm, also known as a cyclone in the Indian Ocean and a typhoon in the Pacific Ocean.

Hydro-electric power Energy produced by harnessing the rapid movement of water down steep mountain slopes to drive turbines to generate electricity.

Ice Age Periods of time in the past when much of the Earth's surface was covered by massive ice sheets. The most recent Ice Age began two million years ago and ended 10,000 years ago.

Iceberg A floating mass of ice that has broken off from a glacier or ice sheet.

Ice sheet A massive area of ice, thousands of metres thick.

Irrigation The artificial supply of water to dry areas – mainly for agricultural use. Water is carried or pumped to the area through pipes or ditches.

Lagoon A shallow stretch of coastal salt water behind a partial barrier such as a sandbank or coral reef.

Latitude The distance north or south of the Equator, measured in degrees, and shown on a globe as imaginary circles running around the Earth parallel to the Equator.

Lava The molten rock, magma, which erupts onto the Earth's surface through a volcano, or through a fault or crack in the Earth's crust. Lava refers to the rock both in its liquid and its later, solidified form.

Load The material that is carried by a river or stream.

Longitude The distance, measured in degrees, east or west of the Prime Meridian.

Limestone A type of rock, formed by sediment, through which water can pass.

Magma Underground, molten rock, which is very hot and highly charged with gas. It originates in the Earth's lower crust or mantle.

Mantle The layer of the Earth's interior between the crust and the core. It is about 2,900 km thick.

Map projection A mathematical formula that is used to show the curved surface of the Earth on a flat map.

Market gardening The intensive growing of fruit and vegetables close to large local markets.

Meander A loop-like bend in a river. As a river nears the sea, it tends to wind more and more. The bigger the river and the shallower its slope, the more likely it is that meanders will form.

Mediterranean climate A temperate climate of hot, dry summers and warm, damp winters.

Meltwater Water which has melted from glaciers or ice sheets.

Mestizo A person of mixed native American and European origin.

Mineral A chemical compound that occurs naturally in the Earth.

Monsoon Winds that change direction according to the seasons. They are most common in South and East Asia, where they blow from the southwest in summer, bringing heavy rainfall, and the northeast in winter.

Moraine Sand and gravel that have been deposited by a glacier or ice sheet.

Nomads (nomadic) Wandering communities who move around in search of suitable pasture for their herds of animals.

Oasis A fertile area in a desert, usually watered by an underground aquifer.

Pack ice Ice masses more than three metres thick which form on the sea surface and are not attached to a landmass.

Pacific Rim The name given to the economically dynamic countries bordering the Pacific Ocean.

Peat Decomposed vegetation found in bogs. It can be dried and used as fuel.

Per capita A latin term meaning 'for each person'.

Plantation A large farm on which only one crop is usually grown, e.g. bananas or coffee.

Plain A flat, level region of land, often relatively low-lying.

Plateau A large area of high, flat land. When surrounded by steep slopes it is called a tableland.

Peninsula A thin strip of land surrounded on three of its sides by water. Large examples include Italy, Florida and Korea.

Permafrost Permanently frozen ground, in which temperatures have remained below 0°C for more than two years.

Precipitation The fall of moisture from the atmosphere onto the surface of the Earth, as dew, hail, rain, sleet or snow.

Prairie A Spanish-American term for grassy plains, with few or no trees.

Prime Meridian 0° longitude. Also known as the Greenwich Meridian because it runs through Greenwich in England.

Rainforest Dense forests in tropical zones with high rainfall, temperature and humidity.

Rainshadow An area downwind from high terrain which has little or no rainfall because it has fallen upon the high relief.

Remote-sensing A way of obtaining information about the environment by using unmanned equipment, such as a satellite, which relays the information to a point where it is collected.

Ria A flooded V-shaped river valley or estuary flooded by a rise in sea level or sinking land.

Rift valley A long, narrow depression in the Earth's crust, formed by the sinking of rocks between two faults.

Savannah Open grassland, where an annual dry season prevents the growth of most trees. They lie between the tropical rainforest and hot desert regions.

Scale The relationship between distance on a map and on the Earth's surface.

Sediment Grains of rock transported and deposited by rivers, sea, ice or wind.

Semi-arid Areas between deserts and better-watered areas, where there is sufficient moisture to support a little more vegetation than in a true desert.

Service industry An industry that supplies services, such as banking, rather than producing manufactured goods.

Shanty town An area in or around a city where people live in temporary shacks, usually without basic facilities such as running water.

Silt Small particles, finer than sand, often carried by water and deposited on river banks, at river mouths and harbours.

Soil A thin layer of rock particles mixed with the remains of dead plants and animals. Soil occurs naturally on the surface of the Earth and provides a medium for plants to grow.

Soil erosion The wearing away of soil more quickly than it is replaced by natural processes. Over-grazing and the clearing of land for farming speeds up the process.

Sorghum A type of grass found in South America, similar to sugar cane.

Spit A narrow bank of shingle or sand extending out from the sea shore. Spits are made out of material transported along the coast by currents, wind and waves.

Staple crop The main food crop grown in a region, for example rice in Southeast Asia.

Steppe Large areas of dry grassland in the northern hemisphere – particularly found in southeast Europe and central Asia.

Subsistence farming A method of farming where enough food is produced to feed farmers and their families but not providing any extra to generate an income.

Taiga A Russian name given to the belt of coniferous forest found in Russia, which borders tundra in the north and mixed forests and grasslands in the south.

Temperate The mild, variable climate found in areas between the tropics and cold polar regions.

Terrace Steps cut into steep slopes to create flat surfaces for cultivating crops.

Tropics An area between the Equator and the Tropic of Cancer and Tropic of Capricorn that has heavy rainfall and high temperatures, and lacks any clear seasonal variation.

Tundra The land area lying in the very cold northern regions of Europe, Asia and Canada, where winters are long and cold and the ground beneath the surface is permanently frozen.

U-shaped valley A river valley that has been deepened and widened by a glacier. They are flat-bottomed and steep-sided, and usually much deeper than river valleys.

V-shaped valley A typical valley eroded by a river in its upper course.

Volcano An opening or vent in the Earth's crust where magma erupts. Volcanos are caused by the movement of the Earth's plates. When the plates collide or spread apart, magma is forced to the surface, at or near the place where the plates meet.

Watershed The dividing line between one drainage basin and another.

INDEX

A

Aachen *101 A5* W Germany
Aalborg *83 B6* N Denmark
Aalen *101 C6* S Germany
Aalsmeer *84 D4* C Netherlands
Aalst *84 C6* C Belgium
Aalten *84 F4* E Netherlands
Aalter *84 B6* NW Belgium
Äänekoski *83 E4* W Finland
Aare *101 B8* ≈ W Switzerland
Aba *76 E1* NE Dem. Rep. Congo
Aba *72 F5* S Nigeria
Abadan *123 D3* SW Iran
Abadan *125 C3* C Turkmenistan
Abadla *70 C2* W Algeria
Abakan *118 E5* S Russian Federation
Abashiri *133 G1* NE Japan
Abbeville *97 D1* N France
Abbeydorney *89 B6* SW Ireland
Abbeyleix *89 D5* C Ireland
Abéché *72 H3* SE Chad
Abengourou *72 D5* E Ivory Coast
Aberaeron *93 B6* SW Wales, United Kingdom
Aberdaron *93 A5* NW Wales, United Kingdom
Aberdeen *91 F4* NE Scotland, United Kingdom
Aberdeen *43 C3* South Dakota, N USA
Aberdeen *49 B2* Washington, NW USA
Aberfeldy *91 D4* C Scotland, United Kingdom
Abergavenny *93 C7* SE Wales, United Kingdom
Aberystwyth *93 B6* W Wales, United Kingdom
Abha *123 B6* SW Saudi Arabia
Abidjan *72 C5* S Ivory Coast
Abilene *44 G3* Texas, SW USA
Abingdon *95 E3* S England, United Kingdom
Åbo *see* Turku
Aboisso *72 D5* SE Ivory Coast
Abou-Déïa *72 H4* SE Chad
Abrantes *99 B4* C Portugal
Abruzzese, Appennino *103 D5* ▲▲ C Italy
Absaroka Range *47 D3* ▲▲ Montana/Wyoming, NW USA
Abu Dhabi *123 E4* ● test
Abu Hamed *75 C1* N Sudan
Abuja *72 F4* ● C Nigeria
Abunã, Rio *63 D5* ≈ Bolivia/Brazil
Abuye Meda *75 D3* ▲ C Ethiopia
Acalayong *72 F6* SW Equatorial Guinea
Acaponeta *53 D4* C Mexico
Acapulco *53 F6* S Mexico
Accra *72 D5* ● SE Ghana
Accrington *93 D4* NW England, United Kingdom
Achacachi *65 A2* W Bolivia
Achara *121 G2 cultural region* SW Georgia
Achill Head *89 A3 headland* W Ireland
Achill Sound *89 B3* W Ireland
Acklins Island *57 E3 island* SE Bahamas
Aconcagua, Cerro *65 A5* ▲ W Argentina
A Coruña *99 B1* NW Spain
Acre *63 C5 state* W Brazil
Ada *43 D8* Oklahoma, C USA
Adamawa Highlands *72 G5 plateau* NW Cameroon
Adams, Mount *49 B3* ▲ Washington, NW USA
Adan *see* Aden
Adana *121 D5* S Turkey
Adapazarı *120 B2* NW Turkey
Adare, Cape *142 C6 cape* Antarctica
Ad Dahna *123 C4 desert* E Saudi Arabia
Ad Damman *123 D4* NE Saudi Arabia
Addis Ababa *75 D3* ● C Ethiopia
Adelaide *137 E6 state capital* South Australia
Aden *123 C7* SW Yemen
Aden, Gulf of *75 F2 gulf* SW Arabian Sea
Adige *103 C2* ≈ N Italy
Adirondack Mountains *37 D3* ▲▲ New York, NE USA
Adis Abeba *see* Addis Ababa
Adıyaman *121 E4* SE Turkey
Admiralty Islands *141 B1 island group* N Papua New Guinea
Adra *99 E6* S Spain
Adrar *70 D3* C Algeria
Adrian *40 E5* Michigan, N USA
Adriatic Sea *112 F2 sea* N Mediterranean Sea
Adycha *118 G3* ≈ NE Russian Federation
Aegean Sea *107 F5 sea* NE Mediterranean Sea
Aeolian Islands *103 D7 island group* S Italy
Afareaitu *141 A5* W French Polynesia
Afghanistan *125 D5* ◆ *islamic state* C Asia
Afmadow *75 E5* S Somalia
Africa *66 continent*
Africa, Horn of *66 physical region* Ethiopia/Somalia
Afyon *120 B3* W Turkey
Agadez *72 F3* C Niger
Agadir *70 B2* SW Morocco
Agana *see* Hagåtña
Agaro *75 D4* C Ethiopia
Agat *51* W Guam
Agathónisi *107 F6 island* Dodecanese, Greece
Agde *97 D6* S France
Agen *97 C6* SW France
Agialousa *see* Yenierenköy
Ágios Nikólaos *107 F7* Crete, Greece
Agra *127 D3* N India
Ağrı *121 G3* NE Turkey
Agrigento *103 C8* Sicily, Italy
Agropoli *103 D6* S Italy
Aguadilla *51* W Puerto Rico
Aguadulce *55 G7* S Panama
Aguán, Río *55 D2* ≈ N Honduras
Agua Prieta *53 C2* NW Mexico
Aguascalientes *53 E4* C Mexico
Aguilas *99 E5* SE Spain
Aguililla *53 E5* SW Mexico
Ahaggar *70 E4 high plateau region* SE Algeria
Ahmadabad *127 C4* W India
Ahmadnagar *127 D5* W India
Ahuachapán *55 B4* W El Salvador
Ahvaz *123 D3* SW Iran
Aiken *39 G4* South Carolina, SE USA
Ailsa Craig *91 C6 island* SW Scotland, United Kingdom
'Aïn Ben Tili *72 C1* N Mauritania
Aiquile *65 B2* C Bolivia
Airdrie *91 D6* S Scotland, United Kingdom
Aire *93 D4* ≈ N England, United Kingdom
Aïr, Massif de l' *72 F2* ▲▲ NC Niger
Aix-en-Provence *97 E6* SE France
Ajaccio *97 G6* Corsica, France
Aj Bogd Uul *129 D2* ▲ SW Mongolia
Ajdabiya *70 G2* NE Libya
Ajmer *127 D3* N India
Ajo *44 B3* Arizona, SW USA
Akasha *75 C1* N Sudan
Akchâr *72 A2 desert* W Mauritania
Akhaltsikhe *121 G2* SW Georgia
Akhdar, Al Jabal al *70 G2 hill range* NE Libya
Akhisar *120 A3* W Turkey
Akhmim *70 I3* C Egypt
Akhtubinsk *111 B7* SW Russian Federation
Akimiski Island *35 C3 island* Nunavut, C Canada
Akita *133 F3* C Japan
Akjoujt *72 B2* W Mauritania
Akkeshi *133 H1* NE Japan
Aklavik *33 E3* Northwest Territories, NW Canada
Akmola *see* Astana
Akpatok Island *35 E1 island* Nunavut, E Canada
Akron *40 F6* Ohio, N USA
Akrotiri Sovereign Base Area *112 C6 UK air base* S Cyprus
Aksai Chin *129 B3 disputed region* China/India
Aksaray *121 D4* C Turkey
Akşehir *120 C4* W Turkey
Aksu He *129 B2* ≈ China/Kyrgyzstan
Aktau *118 A5* W Kazakhstan
Aktobe *118 B4* NW Kazakhstan
Akure *72 E5* SW Nigeria
Akureyri *83 A1* N Iceland
Alabama *39 D5* ⬖ *state* S USA
Alabama River *39 D5* ≈ Alabama, S USA
Alaca *121 D3* N Turkey
Alacant *see* Alicante
Alagoas *63 H5 state* E Brazil
Alajuela *55 E6* C Costa Rica
Alakanuk *50 D2* Alaska, USA
Al 'Alamayn *70 I2* N Egypt
Al 'Amarah *123 C3* E Iraq
Alamo *47 B6* Nevada, W USA
Alamogordo *44 D3* New Mexico, SW USA
Alamosa *47 F6* Colorado, C USA
Aland Islands *83 D5 island group* SW Finland
Aland Sea *83 D5 strait* Baltic Sea/Gulf of Bothnia
Alanya *121 C5* S Turkey
Alappuzha *127 D7* SW India (see also Alleppey)
Al 'Aqabah *112 K6* SW Jordan
A Laracha *99 B1* NW Spain
Alaşehir *120 A4* W Turkey
Alaska *50 D2* ⬖ *state* NW USA
Alaska, Gulf of *50 D3 gulf* Canada/USA
Alaska Peninsula *50 D3 peninsula* Alaska, USA
Alaska Range *50 E2* ▲▲ Alaska, USA
Alazeya *118 H2* ≈ NE Russian Federation
Albacete *99 E4* C Spain
Al Bāḩah *123 B5* SW Saudi Arabia
Alba Iulia *109 B6* W Romania
Albania *107 C3* ◆ *republic* SE Europe
Albany *137 B6* Western Australia
Albany *39 F5* Georgia, SE USA
Albany *49 B3* Oregon, NW USA
Albany *35 C4* ≈ Ontario, S Canada
Albany *37 E4 state capital* New York, NE USA
Al Bayda' *70 H2* NE Libya
Albergaria-a-Velha *99 B3* N Portugal
Albert *97 D1* N France
Alberta *33 F6* ⬖ *province* SW Canada
Albert, Lake *75 B5* ◎ Dem. Rep. Congo/Uganda
Albert Lea *43 E4* Minnesota, N USA
Albi *97 D6* S France
Albuquerque *44 D2* New Mexico, SW USA
Albury *137 G6* New South Wales, SE Australia
Alcácer do Sal *99 B4* W Portugal
Alcalá de Henares *99 D3* C Spain
Alcamo *103 C8* Sicily, Italy
Alcañiz *99 F3* NE Spain
Alcántara, Embalse de *99 B4* ⊠ W Spain
Alcoi *see* Alcoy
Alcoy *99 F4* E Spain
Aldabra Group *76 G3 island group* SW Seychelles
Aldan *118 G3* ≈ NE Russian Federation
Alde *95 H2* ≈ E England, United Kingdom
Aldeburgh *95 H2* E England, United Kingdom
Alderney *95 H5 island* Channel Islands
Aldershot *95 F4* S England, United Kingdom
Aleg *72 B3* SW Mauritania
Aleksin *111 A5* W Russian Federation
Alençon *97 C3* N France
'Alenuihaha Channel *51 D2 channel* Hawaii, USA, C Pacific Ocean
Aleppo *123 B1* NW Syria
Alert *33 H1* Ellesmere Island, Nunavut, N Canada
Alès *97 D6* S France
Alessandria *103 B2* N Italy
Ålesund *83 A4* S Norway
Aleutian Basin *15 undersea feature* Bering Sea
Aleutian Islands *50 B2 island group* Alaska, USA
Aleutian Trench *15 undersea feature* S Bering Sea
Alexander Archipelago *50 E4 island group* Alaska, USA
Alexander City *39 E5* Alabama, S USA
Alexander Island *142 A4 island* Antarctica
Alexandra *139 B7* South Island, New Zealand
Alexandria *70 I2* N Egypt
Alexandria *39 B5* Louisiana, S USA
Alexandria *43 D3* Minnesota, N USA
Alexandroúpoli *107 F4* NE Greece
Alfeiós *107 D6* ≈ S Greece
Alfreton *93 E5* C England, United Kingdom
Alga *118 B4* NW Kazakhstan
Algarve *99 B5 cultural region* S Portugal
Algeciras *99 C6* SW Spain
Algemesí *99 F4* E Spain
Algeria *70 C3* ◆ *republic* N Africa
Al Ghabah *123 F5* C Oman
Alghero *103 A5* Sardinia, Italy
Algiers *70 E1* ● N Algeria
Algona *43 E4* Iowa, C USA
Al Hajar al Gharbi *123 E4* ▲▲ N Oman
Al Hasakah *123 B1* NE Syria
Al Hillah *123 C2* C Iraq
Al Hufuf *123 D4* NE Saudi Arabia
Aliákmonas *107 E4* ≈ N Greece
Alíartos *107 E5* C Greece
Ali-Bayramli *121 J2* SE Azerbaijan
Alicante *99 F5* SE Spain
Alice *44 G5* Texas, SW USA
Alice Springs *137 E3* Northern Territory, C Australia
Aligandí *55 I6* NE Panama
Alindao *72 H5* S Central African Republic
Aliquippa *37 B5* Pennsylvania, NE USA
Al Isma'iliyah *70 I2* N Egypt
Al Jaghbub *70 H3* NE Libya
Al Jawf *123 B3* NW Saudi Arabia
Al Jazirah *123 B2 physical region* Iraq/Syria
Al Kharijah *70 I3* C Egypt
Al Khums *70 F2* NW Libya
Alkmaar *84 C3* NW Netherlands
Al Kufrah *70 H4* SE Libya
Al Kut *123 C2* E Iraq
Al Lādhiqīyah *123 A2* W Syria
Allahabad *127 E3* N India
Allegheny Mountains *39 G2* ▲▲ NE USA
Allegheny Plateau *37 C4* ▲▲ New York/Pennsylvania, NE USA
Allen, Lough *89 D3* ◎ NW Ireland
Allentown *37 D5* Pennsylvania, NE USA
Alleppey *127 D7* SW India (see also Alappuzha)
Alliance *43 A4* Nebraska, C USA
Alloa *91 D5* C Scotland, United Kingdom
Alma-Ata *see* Almaty
Almada *99 A4* W Portugal
Al Madinah *see* Medina
Al Mahrah *123 D6* ▲▲ E Yemen
Al Majma'ah *123 C4* C Saudi Arabia
Almansa *99 F4* C Spain
Almaty *118 C6* SE Kazakhstan
Almelo *84 F3* E Netherlands
Almendra, Embalse de *99 C3* ⊠ NW Spain
Almendralejo *99 C4* W Spain
Almere *84 D3* C Netherlands
Almería *99 E6* S Spain
Al'met'yevsk *111 D6* W Russian Federation
Al Minya *70 I3* C Egypt
Almirante *55 F6* NW Panama
Al Mukalla *123 D7* SE Yemen
Alnwick *93 D1* N England, United Kingdom
Alofi, Île *141 K4 island* S Wallis and Futuna
Alónnisos *107 E5 island* Vóreioi Sporádes, Greece
Álora *99 D6* S Spain
Alor, Kepulauan *131 F8 island group* E Indonesia
Alotau *141 C3* SE Papua New Guinea
Alpena *40 E3* Michigan, N USA
Alpha Cordillera *143 B4 undersea feature* Arctic Ocean
Alphen aan den Rijn *84 C4* C Netherlands
Alpine *44 E4* Texas, SW USA
Alps *78* ▲▲ C Europe
Al Qamishli *123 B1* NE Syria
Alqueva, Barragem do *99 B4* ⊠ Portugal/Spain
Al Qunaytirah *123 H5* SW Syria
Alsace *97 F2 cultural region* NE France, Europe
Alsager *93 D5* W England, United Kingdom
Alsdorf *101 A5* W Germany
Alta *83 D1* N Norway
Altai Mountains *129 C2* ▲▲ Asia/Europe
Altamaha River *39 F5* ≈ Georgia, SE USA
Altamira *63 F4* NE Brazil
Altamura *103 E6* SE Italy
Altar, Desierto de *53 A1 desert* Mexico/USA
Altay *129 C2* NW China
Altay *129 D2* W Mongolia
Alton *95 F4* S England, United Kingdom
Alton *40 B7* Illinois, N USA
Altoona *37 C5* Pennsylvania, NE USA
Altun Shan *129 C3* ▲▲ NW China
Alturas *49 C5* California, W USA
Altus *43 C8* Oklahoma, C USA
Al 'Uwaynat *70 F4* SW Libya
Alva *43 C7* Oklahoma, C USA
Alvarado *53 G5* E Mexico
Alvin *44 H4* Texas, SW USA
Al Wajh *123 A4* NW Saudi Arabia
Alwar *127 D3* N India
Al Wari'ah *123 C3* N Saudi Arabia
Alytus *83 E7* S Lithuania
Alzette *84 E9* ≈ S Luxembourg
Amadeus, Lake *137 D4 seasonal lake* Northern Territory, C Australia
Amadi *75 C4* S South Sudan
Amadjuak Lake *33 I3* ◎ Baffin Island, Nunavut, N Canada
Amakusa-nada *133 C8 gulf* SW Japan
Åmål *83 C5* S Sweden
Amami-gunto *133 A7 island group* SW Japan
Amami-o-shim *133 A7 island* S Japan
Amantea *103 E7* SW Italy
Amapá *63 F3 state* NE Brazil
Amarapura *131 A2* C Burma (Myanmar)
Amarillo *44 F2* Texas, SW USA
Amay *84 D7* E Belgium
Amazon *63 F3* ≈ Brazil/Peru
Amazonas *63 C4 state* N Brazil
Amazon Basin *63 E4 basin* N South America
Amazon, Mouths of the *63 G3 delta* NE Brazil
Ambae *141 G4 island* C Vanuatu
Ambam *72 F6* S Cameroon
Ambanja *76 G4* N Madagascar
Ambarchik *118 H2* NE Russian Federation
Ambérieu-en-Bugey *97 E5* E France
Amble *93 D2* N England, United Kingdom
Amboasary *76 G6* S Madagascar
Ambon *131 G7* E Indonesia
Ambositra *76 G5* SE Madagascar
Amboy *49 D8* California, W USA
Ambriz *76 B3* NW Angola
Ambrym *141 G5 island* C Vanuatu
Amchitka Island *50 A2 island* Aleutian Islands, Alaska, USA
Amdo *129 C4* W China
Ameland *84 D1 island* N Netherlands
America-Antarctica Ridge *142 B2 undersea feature* S Atlantic Ocean
American Falls Reservoir *47 C4* ⊠ Idaho, NW USA
American Samoa *51 US* ◇ W Polynesia
Amersfoort *84 D4* C Netherlands
Ames *43 E5* Iowa, C USA
Amga *118 G4* ≈ NE Russian Federation
Amherst *35 F5* Nova Scotia, SE Canada
Amiens *97 D1* N France
Amindivi Islands *127 C7 island group* SW India
Amistad Reservoir *44 F4* ⊠ Mexico/USA
Amman *123 A2* ● NW Jordan
Ammassalik *143 A6* S Greenland
Ammochostos *see* Famagusta
Amol *123 D1* N Iran
Amorgós *107 F6 island* Cyclades, Greece
Amos *35 D4* Québec, SE Canada
Amourj *72 C3* SE Mauritania
Ampato, Nevado *63 B6* ▲ S Peru
Amposta *99 F3* NE Spain
Amravati *127 D4* C India
Amritsar *127 D2* N India
Amstelveen *84 D4* C Netherlands
Amsterdam *84 C4* ● C Netherlands
Am Timan *72 H4* SE Chad
Amu Darya *125 D3* ≈ C Asia
Amund Ringnes Island *33 H2 island* Nunavut, N Canada
Amundsen Gulf *33 F3 gulf* Northwest Territories, N Canada
Amundsen Plain *142 B6 undersea feature* S Pacific Ocean
Amundsen-Scott *142 C4 US research station* Antarctica
Amundsen Sea *142 A5 sea* S Pacific Ocean
Amuntai *131 E7* C Indonesia
Amur *118 H5* ≈ China/Russian Federation
Amyderya *125 E4* NE Turkmenistan
Anabar *118 F3* ≈ NE Russian Federation
Anaconda *47 C2* Montana, NW USA
Anacortes *49 B1* Washington, NW USA
Anadyr' *118 H2* ≈ NE Russian Federation
Anadyr, Gulf of *118 I1 gulf* NE Russian Federation
Anáfi *107 F6 island* Cyclades, Greece
Analalava *76 G4* NW Madagascar
Anamur *121 C5* S Turkey
Anantapur *127 D6* S India
Anápolis *63 G6* C Brazil
Anar *123 E3* C Iran
Anar Darreh *125 D5* W Afghanistan
Anatolia *121 C4 plateau* C Turkey
Añatuya *65 B4* N Argentina
Anchorage *50 E3* Alaska, USA
Ancona *103 D4* C Italy
Ancud *65 A7* S Chile
Åndalsnes *83 B4* S Norway
Andalucía *99 D5 cultural region* S Spain Europe
Andalucia *see* Andalusia
Andalusia *39 E6* Alabama, S USA
Andaman Islands *127 H4 island group* India, NE Indian Ocean
Andaman Sea *127 H5 sea* NE Indian Ocean
Andenne *84 D7* SE Belgium
Anderlues *84 C7* S Belgium
Andersen Air Force Base *51 air base* NE Guam
Anderson *40 D6* Indiana, N USA
Andes *63 B5* ▲▲ W South America
Andhra Pradesh *127 E6 cultural region* E India
Andijon *125 G3* E Uzbekistan
Andkhvoy *125 E4* N Afghanistan
Andong *133 C6* E South Korea
Andorra *97 C7* ◆ *monarchy* SW Europe
Andorra la Vella *97 B7* ● C Andorra
Andover *95 E4* S England, United Kingdom
Andøya *83 C2 island* C Norway
Andreanof Islands *50 A2 island group* Aleutian Islands, Alaska, USA
Andrews *44 F3* Texas, SW USA
Andria *103 E6* SE Italy
Ándros *107 F5 island* Cyclades, SE Greece
Andros Island *57 C2 island* NW Bahamas
Andros Town *57 D2* NW Bahamas
Aneityum *141 H6 island* S Vanuatu
Anepmete *141 C2* E Papua New Guinea
Angara *118 E4* ≈ C Russian Federation
Angarsk *118 F5* S Russian Federation
Ånge *83 C4* C Sweden
Ángel de la Guarda, Isla *53 B2 island* NW Mexico
Angeles *131 F3* Luzon, N Philippines
Angel Falls *63 D2 waterfall* E Venezuela
Ångermanälven *83 D3* ≈ N Sweden
Angermünde *101 E3* NE Germany
Angers *97 C3* NW France
Anglesey *93 B4 island* NW Wales, United Kingdom
Anglet *97 B6* SW France
Angleton *44 H5* Texas, SW USA
Ang Nam Ngum *131 B3* ◎ C Laos
Angola *76 B3* ◆ *republic* SW Africa
Angola Basin *15 undersea feature* E Atlantic Ocean
Angoram *141 B1* NW Papua New Guinea
Angostura, Presa de la *53 H6* ⊠ SE Mexico
Angoulême *97 C5* W France
Angoumois *97 C5 cultural region* W France
Angren *125 G3* E Uzbekistan
Anguilla *57 J4* ◇ E West Indies
Anguilla Cays *57 C2 islets* SW Bahamas
Animas *44 C3* New Mexico, SW USA
Anjou *97 C3 cultural region* NW France
Anjouan *76 G4 island* SE Comoros
Anju *133 A5* W North Korea
Ankara *121 C3* ● C Turkey
Ankeny *43 E5* Iowa, C USA
Anklam *101 D2* NE Germany
Annaba *70 E1* NE Algeria
An Nafud *123 B3 desert* NW Saudi Arabia
An Najaf *123 C3* S Iraq
Annalee *89 D3* ≈ N Ireland
Annalong *89 F3* S Northern Ireland, United Kingdom
Annan *91 E7* S Scotland, United Kingdom
Annapolis *39 H1 state capital* Maryland, NE USA
Annapurna *127 F2* ▲ C Nepal
Ann Arbor *40 E5* Michigan, N USA
An Nasiriyah *123 C3* SE Iraq
Annecy *97 E5* E France
Anniston *39 E4* Alabama, S USA
Anqing *129 G4* E China
Anshun *129 E5* S China
Anson *44 G3* Texas, SW USA
Ansongo *72 D3* E Mali
Antakya *121 E5* S Turkey
Antalaha *76 H4* NE Madagascar
Antalya *120 B5* SW Turkey
Antalya, Gulf of *120 B5 gulf* SW Turkey
Antananarivo *76 G5* ● C Madagascar
Antarctica *142 C4 continent*
Antarctic Peninsula *142 A4 peninsula* Antarctica
Antequera *99 D5* S Spain
Antibes *97 F6* SE France
Anticosti, Île d' *35 F4 island* Québec, E Canada
Antigua *57 J5 island* S Antigua and Barbuda
Antigua and Barbuda *57 J4* ◆ *commonwealth republic* E West Indies
Antikythira *107 E7 island* S Greece
Antofagasta *65 A3* N Chile
Antony *97 D2* N France
Antrim *89 E2* NE Northern Ireland, United Kingdom
Antrim Mountains *89 E1* ▲▲ NE Northern Ireland, United Kingdom
Antsirañana *76 G4* N Madagascar
Antsohihy *76 G4* NW Madagascar
Antwerp *84 C6* N Belgium
Antwerpen *see* Antwerp
Anuradhapura *127 E7* C Sri Lanka
Anyang *129 F3* C China
A'nyêmaqên Shan *129 D4* ▲▲ C China
Anzio *103 C5* C Italy
Aola *141 F3* C Solomon Islands
Aomori *133 G3* C Japan
Aoraki *139 B6* ▲ South Island, New Zealand
Aosta *103 A2* NW Italy
Aoukâr *72 B2 plateau* C Mauritania
Aouk, Bahr *72 H4* ≈ Central African Republic/Chad
Aozou *72 G2* N Chad
Apalachee Bay *39 E6 bay* Florida, SE USA
Apalachicola River *39 E6* ≈ Florida, SE USA
Apaporis, Río *63 C3* ≈ Brazil/Colombia
Apatity *111 B2* NW Russian Federation
Apeldoorn *84 E4* E Netherlands
Apennines *103 C3* ▲▲ Italy/San Marino
Apia *141 B5* ● SE Samoa
Apkhazeti *121 G2 cultural region* SW Georgia
Apolima Strait *141 A5 strait* C Pacific Ocean
Apostle Islands *40 B2 island group* Wisconsin, N USA
Appalachian Mountains *39 F3* ▲▲ E USA
Appingedam *84 F2* NE Netherlands
Appleton *40 C4* Wisconsin, N USA
Apra Heights *51* W Guam
Apuseni, Munţii *109 B6* ▲▲ W Romania
Aqaba, Gulf of *123 A3 gulf* NE Red Sea
Aqchah *125 F4* N Afghanistan
Aquitaine *97 B6 region* SW France
'Arabah, Wadi al *123 H7 dry watercourse* Israel/Jordan
Arabian Basin *15 undersea feature* N Arabian Sea
Arabian Peninsula *123 C4 peninsula* SW Asia
Arabian Sea *114 sea* NW Indian Ocean
Aracaju *63 I5* E Brazil
'Arad *123 H6* S Israel
Arad *109 A6* W Romania
Arafura Sea *131 H8 sea* W Pacific Ocean
Aragón *99 E3 cultural region* E Spain
Araguaia, Río *63 F5* ≈ C Brazil
Araguari *63 G7* SE Brazil
Arak *123 D2* W Iran
Arakan Yoma *131 A2* ▲▲ W Burma (Myanmar)
Aral Sea *125 D1 inland sea* Kazakhstan/Uzbekistan
Aral'sk *118 B5* SW Kazakhstan
Aranda de Duero *99 D2* N Spain
Aran Island *89 C2 island* NW Ireland
Aran Islands *89 B4 island group* W Ireland
Aranjuez *99 D3* C Spain
Araouane *72 D2* N Mali
'Ar'ar *123 B3* NW Saudi Arabia
Ararat, Mount *121 G3* ▲ E Turkey
Aras *121 I3* ≈ SW Asia
Arawa *141 D2* Bougainville Island, NE Papua New Guinea
Arbil *123 C2* N Iraq
Arbroath *91 E5* E Scotland, United Kingdom
Arcachon *97 B5* SW France
Arcata *49 A5* California, W USA
Archangel *111 C3* NW Russian Federation
Archidona *99 D5* S Spain
Arco *103 C2* N Italy
Arco *47 C3* Idaho, NW USA
Arctic Ocean *143 C3 ocean*
Arda *107 F3* ≈ Bulgaria/Greece
Ardabil *123 D1* NW Iran
Ardara *89 C2* N Ireland
Ardas *107 F3* ≈ Bulgaria/Greece
Ardèche *97 D6 cultural region* E France Europe
Ardee *89 E3* NE Ireland
Ardennes *84 D8 plateau* Belgium/France/Luxembourg W Europe
Ardglass *89 F3* E Northern Ireland, United Kingdom
Ardgroom *89 B7* S Ireland
Ardmore *89 D6* S Ireland
Ardmore *43 D8* Oklahoma, C USA
Ardnamurchan, Point of *91 B4 headland* N Scotland, United Kingdom
Ardrahan *89 C4* W Ireland

⬖ Administrative region ◆ Country ● Country capital ◇ Dependent territory ○ Dependent territory capital ▲▲ Mountain range ▲ Mountain △ Volcano ≈ River ◎ Lake ⊠ Reservoir

Ards Peninsula *89 F2 peninsula* E Northern Ireland, United Kingdom
Arecibo *51* C Puerto Rico
Arenal, Volcán *55 E6* NW Costa Rica
Arendal *83 B6* S Norway
Arenig Fawr *93 B5* ▲ NW Wales, United Kingdom
Arenys de Mar *99 G2* NE Spain
Areópoli *107 E6* S Greece
Arequipa *63 C6* SE Peru
Arezzo *103 C4* C Italy
Argenteuil *97 D2* N France
Argentina *65 A6* ◆ *republic* S South America
Argentine Basin *14 undersea feature* SW Atlantic Ocean
Arghandab, Darya-ye *125 E5* SE Afghanistan
Argo *75 C1* N Sudan
Argun *129 F1* China/Russian Federation
Argyle, Lake *137 D2 salt lake* Western Australia
Århus *83 B7* C Denmark
Arica *65 A2* N Chile
Arizona *44 A2* ⬖ *state* SW USA
Arkansas *39 B3* ⬖ *state* S USA
Arkansas City *43 D7* Kansas, C USA
Arkansas River *39 B4* C USA
Arkhangel'sk *see* Archangel
Arklow *89 E5* SE Ireland
Arles *97 E6* SE France
Arlington *44 H3* Texas, SW USA
Arlington *39 H1* Virginia, NE USA
Arlon *84 E9* SE Belgium
Armagh *89 E3* S Northern Ireland, United Kingdom
Armagnac *97 C6 cultural region* S France
Armenia *63 B2* W Colombia
Armenia *121 H2* ◆ *republic* SW Asia
Armidale *137 H5* New South Wales, SE Australia
Armstrong *35 B4* Ontario, S Canada
Armyans'k *109 F6* S Ukraine
Arnedo *99 E2* N Spain
Arnhem *84 E4* SE Netherlands
Arnhem Land *137 E1 physical region* Northern Territory, N Australia
Arno *103 C3* C Italy
Arnold *93 E5* C England, United Kingdom
Arnold *49 C6* California, W USA
Arnold *43 G6* Missouri, C USA
Arorae *141 J1 atoll* Tungaru, W Kiribati
Arran, Isle of *91 C6 island* SW Scotland, United Kingdom
Ar Raqqah *123 B2* N Syria
Arras *97 D1* N France
Arriaga *53 G5* SE Mexico
Ar Riyad *see* Riyadh
Arrow, Lough *89 C3* N Ireland
Ar Rub 'al Khali *see* Empty Quarter
Ar Rustaq *123 F4* N Oman
Árta *107 D5* W Greece
Artashat *121 H3* S Armenia
Artemisa *57 B2* W Cuba
Artesia *44 E3* New Mexico, SW USA
Arthur's Pass *139 C6 pass* C New Zealand
Artigas *65 C5* N Uruguay
Art'ik *121 H2* W Armenia
Artois *97 D1 cultural region* N France
Artsyz *109 D6* SW Ukraine
Artvin *121 G2* NE Turkey
Arua *75 C5* NW Uganda
Aruba *57 G7 Dutch* ◇ S West Indies
Aru, Kepulauan *131 H7 island group* E Indonesia
Arunachal Pradesh *127 F2 cultural region* NE India Asia
Arusha *75 D6* N Tanzania
Arviat *33 H5* Nunavut, C Canada
Arvidsjaur *83 D3* N Sweden
Arys' *118 C6* S Kazakhstan
Asadabad *125 G5* E Afghanistan
Asahi-dake *133 G1* ▲ Hokkaidō, N Japan
Asahikawa *133 F1* N Japan
Asamankese *72 D5* SE Ghana
Asansol *127 F4* NE India
Ascension Island *26 St. Helena* ◇ C Atlantic Ocean
Ascoli Piceno *103 D4* C Italy
'Aseb *75 E3* SE Eritrea
Aşgabat *125 C3* ● C Turkmenistan
Ashbourne *89 E4* E Ireland
Ashburton *139 C6* South Island, New Zealand
Ashburton River *137 B4* Western Australia
Ashby de la Zouch *93 D5* C England, United Kingdom
Ashdod *123 G6* W Israel
Asheville *39 F3* North Carolina, SE USA
Ashford *95 G4* SE England, United Kingdom
Ashington *93 D2* N England, United Kingdom
Ashland *49 B4* Oregon, NW USA
Ashland *40 B2* Wisconsin, N USA
Ash Sharah *123 H7* W Jordan
Ash Shihr *123 D7* SE Yemen
Ashtabula *40 F5* Ohio, N USA
Asia *114 continent*
Asinara *103 A5 island* W Italy
Asipovichy *109 D2* C Belarus
Aşkale *121 F3* NE Turkey
Askersund *83 C6* C Sweden
Asmar *125 G5* E Afghanistan
Asmara *75 D2* ● C Eritrea
Asmera *see* Asmara
Aspermont *44 F3* Texas, SW USA
Assad, Lake *121 E5* N Syria
Assam *127 G3 cultural region* NE India Asia
Assamakka *72 E2* NW Niger
As Samawah *123 C3* S Iraq
Assen *84 F2* NE Netherlands
Assenede *84 B6* NW Belgium
As Sulaymaniyah *123 C2* NE Iraq
As Sulayyil *123 C5* S Saudi Arabia
Astana *118 C5* ● N Kazakhstan
Asti *103 B2* NW Italy
Astorga *99 C2* N Spain
Astrakhan' *111 B8* SW Russian Federation
Asturias *99 C1 cultural region* NW Spain
Astypálaia *107 F6 island* Cyclades, Greece
Asunción *65 C4* ● S Paraguay
Aswan *70 J4* SE Egypt
Asyut *70 I3* C Egypt
Atacama Desert *65 A3 desert* N Chile
Atamyrat *125 E4* E Turkmenistan
Aṭâr *72 B2* W Mauritania
Atas Bogd *129 D2* ▲ SW Mongolia
Atascadero *49 B8* California, W USA
Atatürk Baraji *121 F4* S Turkey
Atbara *75 C2* NE Sudan
Atbara *75 D2* Eritrea/Sudan
Atbasar *118 C5* N Kazakhstan
Atchison *43 E6* Kansas, C USA
Ath *84 B7* SW Belgium
Athabasca *33 G6* Alberta, SW Canada
Athabasca *33 F6* Alberta, SW Canada
Athabasca, Lake *33 G5* Alberta/Saskatchewan, SW Canada
Athboy *89 E4* E Ireland
Athens *107 E5* ● C Greece
Athens *39 F4* Georgia, SE USA
Athens *40 F7* Ohio, N USA
Athens *44 H3* Texas, SW USA
Atherton *137 G2* Queensland, NE Australia
Athina *see* Athens
Athlone *89 D4* C Ireland
Ati *72 H3* C Chad
Atikokan *35 A4* Ontario, S Canada
Atka *118 H3* E Russian Federation
Atka *50 B2* Atka Island, Alaska, USA
Atlanta *44 I3* Texas, SW USA
Atlanta *39 E4 state capital* Georgia, SE USA
Atlantic *39 I3* North Carolina, SE USA
Atlantic City *37 D6* New Jersey, NE USA
Atlantic Ocean *14 ocean*
Atlas Mountains *70 C2* NW Africa
Atlasovo *118 I3* E Russian Federation
Atlas, Tell *70 D2* N Algeria
Atlin *33 E5* British Columbia, W Canada
At Ta'if *123 B5* W Saudi Arabia
Attawapiskat *35 C3* Ontario, C Canada
Attawapiskat *35 C3* Ontario, S Canada
Attu Island *50 A1 island* Aleutian Islands, Alaska, USA
Atyrau *118 B4* W Kazakhstan
Aubagne *97 E7* SE France
Aubange *84 E9* SE Belgium
Auburn *37 D3* New York, NE USA
Auburn *49 B2* Washington, NW USA
Auch *97 C6* S France
Auckland *139 D2* North Island, New Zealand
Audincourt *97 F3* E France
Augathella *137 G4* Queensland, E Australia
Augsburg *101 C7* S Germany
Augusta *137 B6* Western Australia
Augusta *39 F4* Georgia, SE USA
Augusta *37 G3 state capital* Maine, NE USA
Augustów *105 G2* NE Poland
Auki *141 F3* Malaita, N Solomon Islands
Aunu'u Island *51 island* W American Samoa
Auob *76 C6* Namibia/South Africa
Aurangabad *127 D5* C India
Auray *97 B3* NW France
Aurès, Massif de l' *112 D4* NE Algeria
Aurillac *97 D5* C France
Aurora *47 F5* Colorado, C USA
Aurora *40 C5* Illinois, N USA
Aurora *43 E7* Missouri, C USA
Aus *76 B6* SW Namibia
Austin *43 E4* Minnesota, N USA
Austin *47 B5* Nevada, W USA
Austin *44 G4 state capital* Texas, SW USA
Australes, Îles *135 island group* SW French Polynesia
Australia *137 D3* ◆ *commonwealth republic*
Australian Alps *137 G6* SE Australia
Australian Capital Territory *137 G6* ⬖ *territory* SE Australia
Austria *101 E8* ◆ *republic* C Europe
Auvergne *97 D5 cultural region* C France Europe
Auxerre *97 D3* C France
Avarua *135* ○ Rarotonga, S Cook Islands
Aveiro *99 B3* W Portugal
Avellino *103 D6* S Italy
Avesta *83 C5* C Sweden
Aveyron *97 C6* S France
Avezzano *103 D5* C Italy
Aviemore *91 D4* N Scotland, United Kingdom
Avignon *97 E6* SE France
Ávila *99 D3* C Spain
Avilés *99 C1* NW Spain
Avon *95 D4* SW England, United Kingdom
Avon *95 E4* C England, United Kingdom
Avonmouth *95 D4* SW England, United Kingdom
Avranches *97 B2* N France
Awaji-shima *133 E6 island* SW Japan
Awash *75 E3* NE Ethiopia
Awbari *70 F3* SW Libya
Awe, Loch *91 C5* W Scotland, United Kingdom
Axe *95 D5* SW England, United Kingdom
Axel *84 B6* SW Netherlands
Axel Heiberg Island *33 G1 island* Nunavut, N Canada
Ayacucho *63 C6* S Peru
Ayagoz *118 D6* E Kazakhstan
Ayamonte *99 B5* SW Spain
Aydarko'l Ko'li *125 F3* C Uzbekistan
Aydın *120 A4* SW Turkey
Ayers Rock *see* Uluru
Aylesbury *95 F3* SE England, United Kingdom
Ayorou *72 D3* W Niger
'Ayoûn el 'Atroûs *72 B3* SE Mauritania
Ayr *91 D6* W Scotland, United Kingdom
Ayr *91 D6* W Scotland, United Kingdom
Ayre, Point of *93 A3 headland* N Isle of Man
Ayteke Bi *118 B5* SW Kazakhstan
Aytos *107 F3* E Bulgaria
Ayvalık *120 A3* W Turkey
Azahar, Costa del *99 F4 coastal region* E Spain
Azaouâd *72 D2 desert* C Mali
Azerbaijan *121 I2* ◆ *republic* SE Asia
Azoum, Bahr *72 H4 seasonal river* SE Chad
Azov *118 A4* SW Russian Federation
Azov, Sea of *109 F6 sea* NE Black Sea
Aztec *44 C1* New Mexico, SW USA
Azuaga *99 C5* W Spain
Azuero, Península de *55 G7 peninsula* S Panama
Azul *65 C6* E Argentina
Az Zagazig *70 I2* N Egypt
Az Zarqā' *123 A2* NW Jordan
Az Zāwiyah *70 F2* NW Libya

B

Baardheere *75 E5* SW Somalia
Baarle-Hertog *84 D5* N Belgium
Baarn *84 D4* C Netherlands
Babayevo *111 B4* NW Russian Federation
Babeldaob *131 H5 island* N Palau
Bab el Mandeb *123 B7 strait* Gulf of Aden/Red Sea
Babruysk *109 D3* E Belarus
Babuyan Channel *131 F3 channel* N Philippines
Babuyan Island *131 F3 island* N Philippines
Bacabal *63 G4* E Brazil
Bacău *109 C6* NE Romania
Bacheykava *109 D2* N Belarus
Back *33 G4* Nunavut, N Canada
Bacton *95 H1* E England, United Kingdom
Badajoz *99 B4* W Spain
Baden-Baden *101 B6* SW Germany
Bad Freienwalde *101 E3* NE Germany
Badgastein *101 D8* NW Austria
Bad Hersfeld *101 C5* C Germany
Bad Homburg vor der Höhe *101 B5* W Germany
Bad Ischl *101 E7* N Austria
Bad Krozingen *101 B7* SW Germany
Badlands *43 A4 physical region* North Dakota/South Dakota, N USA
Badu Island *137 F1 island* Queensland, NE Australia
Bad Vöslau *101 F7* NE Austria
Badwater Basin *49 D7 depression* California, W USA
Baengynyeong-do *133 A5 island* NW South Korea
Bafatá *72 A4* C Guinea-Bissau
Baffin Bay *33 I2 bay* Canada/Greenland
Baffin Island *33 I3 island* Nunavut, NE Canada
Bafing *72 B4* W Africa
Bafoussam *72 F5* W Cameroon
Bafra *121 D2* N Turkey
Bagaces *55 E5* NW Costa Rica
Bagé *63 F9* S Brazil
Baghdad *123 C2* ● C Iraq
Baghlan *125 F4* NE Afghanistan
Baghran *125 E5* S Afghanistan
Bago *131 A3* SW Burma (Myanmar)
Bagoé *72 C4* Ivory Coast/Mali
Baguio *131 F3* Luzon, N Philippines
Bagzane, Monts *72 F3* ▲ N Niger
Bahamas *57 D2* ◆ *commonwealth republic* N West Indies
Baharly *125 C3* C Turkmenistan
Bahawalpur *127 C2* E Pakistan
Bahia *63 G5 state* E Brazil
Bahía Blanca *65 B6* E Argentina
Bahir Dar *75 D3* N Ethiopia
Bahraich *127 E3* N India
Bahrain *123 D4* ◆ *monarchy* SW Asia
Bahushewsk *109 D2* NE Belarus
Baia Mare *109 B5* NW Romania
Baïbokoum *72 G5* SW Chad
Baie-Comeau *35 F4* Québec, SE Canada
Baikal, Lake *118 F5* S Russian Federation
Bailén *99 D5* S Spain
Ba Illi *72 G4* SW Chad
Bainbridge *39 E6* Georgia, SE USA
Bairiki *135* ● Tarawa, NW Kiribati
Bairnsdale *137 G6* Victoria, SE Australia
Baishan *129 H2* NE China
Baiyin *129 E3* N China
Baja *105 E8* S Hungary
Baja, Punta *141 C6 headland* Easter Island, Chile
Bajram Curri *107 D3* N Albania
Bakala *72 H5* C Central African Republic
Baker *49 C3* Oregon, NW USA
Baker and Howland Islands *135 US* ◇ W Polynesia
Baker Lake *33 H4* Nunavut, N Canada
Bakersfield *49 C8* California, W USA
Bakhtaran *see* Kermanshah
Baki *see* Baku
Bakony *105 D8* W Hungary
Baku *121 J2* ● E Azerbaijan
Bala *93 B5* NW Wales, United Kingdom
Balabac Strait *131 E5 strait* Malaysia/Philippines
Balaguer *99 G2* NE Spain
Balaitous *97 B7* ▲ France/Spain
Balakovo *111 C7* W Russian Federation
Bala Murghab *125 E4* NW Afghanistan
Balashov *111 B6* W Russian Federation
Balaton, Lake *105 D8* W Hungary
Balbina, Represa *63 E3* NW Brazil
Balboa *55 H6* C Panama
Balbriggan *89 E4* E Ireland
Balcarce *65 C6* E Argentina
Balclutha *139 B8* South Island, New Zealand
Baldy Mountain *47 D1* ▲ Montana, NW USA
Baldy Peak *44 C3* ▲ Arizona, SW USA
Baleares, Islas *see* Balearic Islands
Balearic Islands *99 G4 island group* Spain, W Mediterranean Sea
Baleine, Rivière à la *35 E2* Québec, E Canada
Balen *84 D6* N Belgium
Baleshwar *127 F4* E India
Bali *131 E8 island* C Indonesia
Balıkesir *120 A3* W Turkey
Balikpapan *131 E7* C Indonesia
Balkanabat *125 B3* W Turkmenistan
Balkan Mountains *107 E3* Bulgaria/Serbia
Balkash *118 C6* SE Kazakhstan
Balkash, Lake *118 C6* SE Kazakhstan
Balkh *125 F4* N Afghanistan
Balladonia *137 C5* Western Australia
Ballaghmore *89 D5* C Ireland
Ballantrae *91 C7* W Scotland, United Kingdom
Ballarat *137 F6* Victoria, SE Australia
Ballater *91 E4* NE Scotland, United Kingdom
Ballina *89 C3* W Ireland
Ballinasloe *89 C4* W Ireland
Ballindine *89 C4* NW Ireland
Ballinger *44 G4* Texas, SW USA
Ballinhassig *89 C7* S Ireland
Ballinskelligs *89 A6* SW Ireland
Ballinskelligs Bay *89 A7 inlet* SW Ireland
Ballinspittle *89 C7* S Ireland
Ballintra *89 D2* NW Ireland
Ballybofey *89 D2* NW Ireland
Ballybunnion *89 B5* SW Ireland
Ballycastle *89 E1* N Northern Ireland, United Kingdom
Ballyclare *89 F2* E Northern Ireland, United Kingdom
Ballyconneely *89 B4* W Ireland
Ballycotton *89 C7* S Ireland
Ballycroy *89 B3* NW Ireland
Ballydehob *89 B7* S Ireland
Ballydonegan *89 A7* S Ireland
Ballyduff *89 B5* SW Ireland
Ballyferriter *89 A6* SW Ireland
Ballyhaunis *89 C3* W Ireland
Ballyhoura Mountains *89 C6* S Ireland
Ballymena *89 E2* NE Northern Ireland, United Kingdom
Ballymoe *89 C4* W Ireland
Ballymoney *89 E1* NE Northern Ireland, United Kingdom
Ballynafid *89 D4* C Ireland
Ballyshannon *89 C2* NW Ireland
Ballywalter *89 F2* E Northern Ireland, United Kingdom
Balrath *89 E4* E Ireland
Balsas *63 G4* E Brazil
Balsas, Río *53 E5* S Mexico
Baltasound *91 B5* NE Scotland, United Kingdom
Bălți *109 D5* N Moldova
Baltic Sea *83 D7 sea* N Europe
Baltimore *89 B7* S Ireland
Baltimore *39 H1* Maryland, NE USA
Baltinglass *89 E5* E Ireland
Baluchistan *127 B3 province* SW Pakistan
Balykchy *125 H2* NE Kyrgyzstan
Bam *123 F3* SE Iran
Bamako *72 C4* ● SW Mali
Bambari *72 H5* C Central African Republic
Bamberg *101 C5* SE Germany
Bamburgh *93 D1* N England, United Kingdom
Bamenda *72 F5* W Cameroon
Banaba *141 H1 island* W Kiribati
Bananga *127 H6* Nicobar Islands, India
Banbridge *89 E3* SE Northern Ireland, United Kingdom
Banbury *95 E3* S England, United Kingdom
Banchory *91 F4* NE Scotland, United Kingdom
Bandaaceh *131 A5* Sumatra, W Indonesia
Bandama *72 C5* S Ivory Coast
Bandarbeyla *75 G3* NE Somalia
Bandar-e 'Abbas *123 E4* S Iran
Bandar-e Būshehr *123 D3* S Iran
Bandar-e Kangan *123 D3* S Iran
Bandar Lampung *131 B7* W Indonesia
Bandar Seri Begawan *131 D5* ● N Brunei
Banda Sea *131 G7 sea* E Indonesia
Bandırma *120 A2* NW Turkey
Bandon *89 B7* S Ireland
Bandundu *76 B2* W Dem. Rep. Congo
Bandung *131 C8* Java, C Indonesia
Banff *91 E3* NE Scotland, United Kingdom
Bangalore *127 D6* S India
Bangassou *72 I5* SE Central African Republic
Banggai, Kepulauan *131 F6 island group* C Indonesia
Banghazi *see* Benghazi
Bangka, Pulau *131 C7 island* W Indonesia
Bangkok *131 B4* ● C Thailand
Bangladesh *127 G3* ◆ *republic* S Asia
Bangor *93 B5* NW Wales, United Kingdom
Bangor *89 F2* E Northern Ireland, United Kingdom
Bangor *37 G2* Maine, NE USA
Bangui *72 H5* ● SW Central African Republic
Bangweulu, Lake *76 D3* N Zambia
Bani *72 C4* S Mali
Bani Suwayf *70 I3* N Egypt
Banja Luka *107 C2* Republika Srpska, NW Bosnia and Herzegovina
Banjarmasin *131 E7* C Indonesia
Banjul *72 A3* ● W Gambia
Banks Island *33 F3 island* Northwest Territories, NW Canada
Banks Islands *141 G4 island group* N Vanuatu
Banks Lake *49 C2* Washington, NW USA
Banks Peninsula *139 C6 peninsula* South Island, New Zealand
Banks Strait *137 G7 strait* SW Tasman Sea
Bankura *127 F4* NE India
Banmauk *131 A2* N Burma (Myanmar)
Bann *89 E2* N Northern Ireland, United Kingdom
Ban Nadou *131 C3* S Laos
Bansha *89 C6* S Ireland
Banská Bystrica *105 E6* C Slovakia
Banteer *89 C6* S Ireland
Bantry *89 B7* SW Ireland
Bantry Bay *89 B7 bay* SW Ireland
Banyak, Kepulauan *131 A6 island group* NW Indonesia
Banyo *72 F5* NW Cameroon
Banyoles *99 H2* NE Spain
Baoji *129 E4* C China
Baoro *72 G5* W Central African Republic
Baoshan *129 D5* SW China
Baotou *129 F3* N China
Ba'qubah *123 C2* C Iraq
Baraawe *75 E5* S Somalia
Baranavichy *109 C3* SW Belarus
Barbados *57 K6* ◆ *commonwealth republic* SE West Indies
Barbastro *99 F2* NE Spain
Barbate de Franco *99 C6* S Spain
Barbuda *57 J4 island* N Antigua and Barbuda
Barcaldine *137 G3* Queensland, E Australia
Barcelona *99 G2* E Spain
Barcelona *63 D1* NE Venezuela
Barcs *105 D9* SW Hungary
Bardaï *72 G2* N Chad
Bardejov *105 F6* E Slovakia
Bareilly *127 E3* N India
Barendrecht *84 C4* SW Netherlands
Barentin *97 C2* N France
Barents Sea *111 C2 sea* Arctic Ocean
Bar Harbor *37 G2* Mount Desert Island, Maine, NE USA
Bari *103 E6* SE Italy
Barikowt *125 G4* NE Afghanistan
Barillas *55 A2* NW Guatemala
Barinas *63 C2* W Venezuela
Barisal *127 G4* S Bangladesh
Barisan, Pegunungan *131 B7* Sumatera, W Indonesia
Barito, Sungai *131 E7* Borneo, C Indonesia
Barkly Tableland *137 E2 plateau* Northern Territory/Queensland, N Australia
Bârlad *109 C6* E Romania
Bar-le-Duc *97 E2* NE France
Barlee, Lake *137 B5* Western Australia
Barlee Range *137 B4* Western Australia
Barletta *103 E5* SE Italy
Barlinek *105 C3* NW Poland
Barmouth *93 B5* NW Wales, United Kingdom
Barnard Castle *93 D3* N England, United Kingdom
Barnaul *118 D5* C Russian Federation
Barnsley *93 D4* N England, United Kingdom
Barnstaple *95 B4* SW England, United Kingdom
Barnstaple Bay *95 B4 bay* SW England, United Kingdom
Baroghil Pass *125 G4 pass* Afghanistan/Pakistan
Barquisimeto *63 C1* NW Venezuela
Barra *91 A4 island* NW Scotland, United Kingdom
Barra de Río Grande *55 E4* E Nicaragua
Barranca *63 B5* W Peru
Barrancabermeja *63 B2* N Colombia
Barranquilla *63 B1* N Colombia
Barreiro *99 A4* W Portugal
Barrier Range *137 F5 hill range* New South Wales, SE Australia
Barrier Reef *55 C1 reef* E Belize
Barrow *50 E1* Alaska, USA
Barrow *89 D6* SE Ireland
Barrow-in-Furness *93 C3* NW England, United Kingdom
Barrow Island *137 A3 island* Western Australia
Barry *93 C7* S Wales, United Kingdom
Barstow *49 D8* California, W USA
Bartang *125 G4* SE Tajikistan
Bartın *121 C2* NW Turkey
Bartlesville *43 D7* Oklahoma, C USA
Barton-upon-Humber *93 F4* N England, United Kingdom
Bartoszyce *105 E2* NE Poland
Baruun-Urt *129 F2* E Mongolia
Barú, Volcán *55 F6* W Panama
Barva, Volcán *55 E6* NW Costa Rica
Barwon River *137 G5* New South Wales, SE Australia
Barysaw *109 D2* NE Belarus
Basarabeasca *109 D6* SE Moldova
Basel *101 B7* NW Switzerland
Basilan *131 F5 island* SW Philippines
Basildon *95 G3* E England, United Kingdom
Basingstoke *95 E4* S England, United Kingdom
Basque Country, The *99 E1 cultural region* N Spain Europe
Basra *123 D3* SE Iraq
Bassano del Grappa *103 C2* NE Italy
Bassenthwaite Lake *93 C2* NW England, United Kingdom
Basseterre *57 J4* ● C Saint Kitts and Nevis
Basse-Terre *57 J5* ○ SW Guadeloupe
Bassett *43 C4* Nebraska, C USA
Bassikounou *72 C3* SE Mauritania
Bass Strait *137 F7 strait* SE Australia
Bassum *101 B3* NW Germany
Bastia *97 G5* Corsica, France
Bastogne *84 E8* SE Belgium
Bata *72 F6* NW Equatorial Guinea
Batangas *131 F4* Luzon, N Philippines
Batdambang *131 C4* NW Cambodia
Batéké, Plateaux *76 B2 plateau* S Congo
Bath *95 D4* SW England, United Kingdom
Bath *37 G3* Maine, NE USA
Bathinda *127 D2* NW India
Bathurst *137 G6* New South Wales, SE Australia
Bathurst *35 F4* New Brunswick, SE Canada
Bathurst Island *137 C1 island* Northern Territory, N Australia
Bathurst Island *33 G2 island* Parry Islands, Nunavut, N Canada
Batin, Wadi al *123 C3 dry watercourse* SW Asia
Batman *121 G4* SE Turkey
Batna *70 E1* NE Algeria
Baton Rouge *39 C6 state capital* Louisiana, S USA
Batticaloa *127 E8* E Sri Lanka
Battipaglia *103 D6* S Italy
Battle Mountain *47 B5* Nevada, W USA
Batumi *121 G2* W Georgia
Batu Pahat *131 C6* W Malaysia
Bauchi *72 F4* NE Nigeria
Bautzen *101 E4* E Germany
Bavaria *101 C7 cultural region* SE Germany Europe
Bavarian Alps *101 C7* Austria/Germany
Bavispe, Río *53 C2* NW Mexico
Bawiti *70 I3* N Egypt
Bawku *72 D4* N Ghana
Bayamo *57 D3* E Cuba
Bayamón *51* E Puerto Rico
Bayan Har Shan *129 D4* C China
Bayanhongor *129 D2* C Mongolia
Bayano, Lago *55 H6* E Panama
Bayard *44 C3* New Mexico, SW USA
Bay City *40 E4* Michigan, N USA
Bay City *44 H5* Texas, SW USA
Baydhabo *75 E5* SW Somalia
Bayern *see* Bavaria
Bayeux *97 C2* N France
Bay Islands *55 D2 island group* N Honduras
Baymak *111 D7* W Russian Federation
Bayonne *97 B6* SW France
Baýramaly *125 D4* S Turkmenistan
Bayreuth *101 C5* SE Germany
Baytown *44 I4* Texas, SW USA
Baza *99 E5* S Spain
Beachy Head *95 G5 headland* SE England, United Kingdom
Beacon *37 E4* New York, NE USA
Beacon Hill *93 C6 hill* E Wales, United Kingdom
Beagle Channel *65 B9 channel* Argentina/Chile
Bear Lake *47 D4* Idaho/Utah, NW USA
Beas de Segura *99 E5* S Spain
Beata, Isla *57 F5 island* SW Dominican Republic
Beatrice *43 D5* Nebraska, C USA
Beatty *47 B6* Nevada, W USA
Beaufort Sea *50 F1 sea* Arctic Ocean
Beaufort West *76 C7* SW South Africa
Beauly *91 D3* N Scotland, United Kingdom
Beaumont *44 I4* Texas, SW USA
Beaune *97 E4* C France
Beauvais *97 D2* N France
Beaver Falls *37 A5* Pennsylvania, NE USA
Beaver Island *40 C3 island* Michigan, N USA
Beaver River *43 B7* Oklahoma, C USA
Beaverton *49 B3* Oregon, NW USA
Beawar *127 D3* N India

⬖ Administrative region ◆ Country ● Country capital ◇ Dependent territory ○ Dependent territory capital Mountain range ▲ Mountain Volcano River Lake Reservoir

Beccles 95 H2 E England, United Kingdom
Béchar 70 D2 W Algeria
Beckley 39 G2 West Virginia, NE USA
Bedford 95 F2 E England, United Kingdom
Bedford 40 D7 Indiana, N USA
Bedford Level 95 F2 *physical region* E England, United Kingdom
Bedum 84 F2 NE Netherlands
Bedworth 93 D6 C England, United Kingdom
Be'er Menuha 123 H7 S Israel
Beernem 84 B6 NW Belgium
Be'er Sheva 123 G6 S Israel
Beesel 84 E6 SE Netherlands
Beeston 93 E5 C England, United Kingdom
Beeville 44 G5 Texas, SW USA
Bega 137 G6 New South Wales, SE Australia
Beihai 129 F6 S China
Beijing 129 F3 ● E China
Beilen 84 E3 NE Netherlands
Beinn Dearg 91 D3 ▲ N Scotland, United Kingdom
Beira 76 E5 C Mozambique
Beirut 123 A2 ● W Lebanon
Beja 99 B5 SE Portugal
Béjar 99 C3 N Spain
Békéscsaba 105 F8 SE Hungary
Bekobod 125 F3 E Uzbekistan
Belarus 109 C2 ◆ *republic* E Europe
Bełchatów 105 E4 C Poland
Belcher Islands 35 C2 *island group* Nunavut, SE Canada
Beledweyne 75 F4 C Somalia
Belém 63 G3 N Brazil
Belén 55 D5 SW Nicaragua
Belen 44 D2 New Mexico, SW USA
Belep, Îles 141 F6 *island group* W New Caledonia
Belfast 89 F2 *National region capital,* E Northern Ireland, United Kingdom
Belfield 43 A2 North Dakota, N USA
Belfort 97 F3 E France
Belgaum 127 D6 W India
Belgium 84 B7 ◆ *monarchy* NW Europe
Belgorod 111 A6 W Russian Federation
Belgrade 107 D2 ● N Serbia
Belgrano II 142 B4 *Argentinian research station* Antarctica
Belitung, Pulau 131 C7 *island* W Indonesia
Belize 55 B2 ◆ *commonwealth republic* Central America
Belize 55 B1 ≈ Belize/Guatemala
Belize City 55 C1 NE Belize
Belkofski 50 C3 Alaska, USA
Bellananagh 89 D3 N Ireland
Bellavary 89 B3 NW Ireland
Belle Île 97 A3 *island* NW France
Belle Isle, Strait of 35 G3 *strait* Newfoundland and Labrador, E Canada
Belleville 40 B7 Illinois, N USA
Bellevue 43 D5 Nebraska, C USA
Bellevue 49 B2 Washington, NW USA
Bellingham 49 B1 Washington, NW USA
Bellingshausen Sea 142 A4 *sea* Antarctica
Bellinzona 101 B8 S Switzerland
Bello 63 B2 W Colombia
Bellona 141 E3 *island* S Solomon Islands
Bellville 76 C7 SW South Africa
Belmopan 55 B2 ● C Belize
Belmullet 89 B3 W Ireland
Belo Horizonte 63 G7 SE Brazil
Belomorsk 111 B3 NW Russian Federation
Beloretsk 111 D6 W Russian Federation
Belorussia *see* Belarus
Belozersk 111 B4 NW Russian Federation
Belper 93 D5 C England, United Kingdom
Belton 44 H4 Texas, SW USA
Belturbet 89 D3 N Ireland
Belukha, Gora 118 D5 ▲ Kazakhstan/ Russian Federation
Belyy, Ostrov 118 D2 *island* N Russian Federation
Bemaraha 76 G5 ⛰ W Madagascar
Bemidji 43 E2 Minnesota, N USA
Bemmel 84 E4 SE Netherlands
Benavente 99 C2 N Spain
Benbecula 91 A3 *island* NW Scotland, United Kingdom
Bend 49 B4 Oregon, NW USA
Bendery *see* Tighina
Bendigo 137 F6 Victoria, SE Australia
Benešov 105 B5 W Czech Republic
Benevento 103 D6 S Italy
Bengbu 129 G4 E China
Benghazi 70 G2 NE Libya
Bengkulu 131 B7 Sumatra, W Indonesia
Benguela 76 B4 W Angola
Ben Hope 91 D2 ▲ N Scotland, United Kingdom
Beni 76 D1 NE Dem. Rep. Congo
Benidorm 99 F4 SE Spain
Beni-Mellal 70 C2 C Morocco
Benin 72 D4 ◆ *republic* W Africa
Benin, Bight of 72 E5 *gulf* W Africa
Benin City 72 E5 SW Nigeria
Beni, Río 65 A2 ≈ N Bolivia
Ben Klibreck 91 C2 ▲ N Scotland, United Kingdom
Ben Lawers 91 D5 ▲ C Scotland, United Kingdom
Ben Lui 91 C5 ▲ C Scotland, United Kingdom
Ben Macdui 91 E4 ▲ C Scotland, United Kingdom
Ben More 91 B5 ▲ W Scotland, United Kingdom
Ben More 91 D5 ▲ C Scotland, United Kingdom
Ben More Assynt 91 D2 ▲ N Scotland, United Kingdom
Ben Nevis 91 C4 ▲ N Scotland, United Kingdom
Benson 44 C3 Arizona, SW USA
Benton 39 B4 Arkansas, C USA
Benton Harbor 40 D5 Michigan, N USA
Benue 72 F5 ≈ Cameroon/Nigeria
Beograd *see* Belgrade
Berat 107 D4 C Albania
Berau, Teluk 131 H7 *bay* Papua, E Indonesia
Berbera 75 F3 NW Somalia
Berbérati 72 G5 SW Central African Republic
Berck-Plage 97 D1 N France
Berdyans'k 109 G6 SE Ukraine
Bereket 125 C3 W Turkmenistan
Berettyó 105 F8 ≈ Hungary/Romania
Berettyóújfalu 105 F7 E Hungary
Berezniki 111 D5 NW Russian Federation
Berga 99 G2 NE Spain
Bergamo 103 B2 N Italy
Bergen 101 D2 NE Germany
Bergen 84 C3 NW Netherlands
Bergen 83 A5 S Norway
Bergerac 97 C5 SW France
Bergeyk 84 D6 S Netherlands
Bergse Maas 84 D5 ≈ S Netherlands
Beringen 84 D6 NE Belgium
Bering Sea 50 B1 *sea* N Pacific Ocean
Bering Strait 50 D1 *strait* Bering Sea/Chukchi Sea
Berja 99 E6 S Spain
Berkeley 49 B7 California, W USA
Berkhamsted 95 F3 SE England, United Kingdom
Berkner Island 142 B4 *island* Antarctica
Berlin 101 D3 ● NE Germany
Berlin 37 F3 New Hampshire, NE USA
Bermejo, Río 65 B3 ≈ N Argentina
Bermeo 99 E1 N Spain
Bermuda 26 UK ◇ NW Atlantic Ocean
Bern 101 A8 ● W Switzerland
Bernau 101 D3 NE Germany
Bernburg 101 D4 C Germany
Berner Alpen 101 A8 ⛰ SW Switzerland
Berneray 91 A4 *island* NW Scotland, United Kingdom
Bernier Island 137 A4 *island* Western Australia
Berry 97 D3 *cultural region* C France
Berry Islands 57 C1 *island group* N Bahamas
Bertoua 72 G5 E Cameroon
Berwick-upon-Tweed 93 D1 N England, United Kingdom
Besançon 97 E4 E France
Bessbrook 89 E3 S Northern Ireland, United Kingdom
Betafo 76 G5 C Madagascar
Betanzos 99 B1 NW Spain
Bethlehem 76 D6 C South Africa
Bethlehem 37 D5 Pennsylvania, NE USA
Bethlehem 123 H6 C West Bank
Béticos, Sistemas 99 D5 ⛰ S Spain
Bétou 76 C1 N Congo
Bette, Picco 70 G4 ▲ S Libya
Betws-y-Coed 93 B5 N Wales, United Kingdom
Beulah 40 D3 Michigan, N USA
Beveren 84 C6 N Belgium
Beverley 93 F4 E England, United Kingdom
Bexhill 95 G4 SE England, United Kingdom
Beyla 72 C4 SE Guinea
Beyrouth *see* Beirut
Beyşehir Gölü 120 B4 ◎ C Turkey
Béziers 97 D6 S France
Bhadravati 127 D6 SW India
Bhagalpur 127 F3 NE India
Bhaktapur 127 F3 C Nepal
Bharuch 127 C4 W India
Bhavnagar 127 C4 W India
Bhopal 127 D4 C India
Bhubaneshwar 127 F4 E India
Bhusawal 127 D4 C India
Bhutan 127 G3 ◆ *monarchy* S Asia
Biak, Pulau 131 H6 *island* E Indonesia
Biała Podlaska 105 G3 E Poland
Białogard 105 C2 NW Poland
Białystok 105 G2 NE Poland
Biarritz 97 B6 SW France
Bicester 95 E3 C England, United Kingdom
Biddeford 37 F3 Maine, NE USA
Bideford 95 B4 SW England, United Kingdom
Biel 101 A8 W Switzerland
Bielefeld 101 B4 NW Germany
Bielsko-Biała 105 E5 S Poland
Bielsk Podlaski 105 G3 E Poland
Biên Hoa 131 C4 S Vietnam
Bienville, Lac 35 D3 ◎ Québec, C Canada
Bié Plateau 76 C4 *plateau* C Angola
Big Bend National Park 44 E5 *national park* Texas, S USA
Bigbury Bay 95 B6 *bay* SW England, United Kingdom
Big Cypress Swamp 39 G8 *wetland* Florida, SE USA
Biggleswade 95 F2 C England, United Kingdom
Bighorn Mountains 47 E3 ⛰ Wyoming, C USA
Bighorn River 47 E3 ≈ Montana/ Wyoming, NW USA
Big Sioux River 43 D4 ≈ Iowa/South Dakota, N USA
Big Smoky Valley 47 B6 *valley* Nevada, W USA
Big Spring 44 F3 Texas, SW USA
Bihać 107 B2 NW Bosnia and Herz.
Bihar 127 F3 *cultural region* N India Asia
Biharamulo 75 C6 NW Tanzania
Bihar Sharif 127 F3 NE India
Bihosava 109 C1 NW Belarus
Bijelo Polje 107 D3 E Montenegro
Bikaner 127 D3 NW India
Bikin 118 H5 SE Russian Federation
Bilaspur 127 E4 C India
Biläsuvar 121 I3 SE Azerbaijan
Bila Tserkva 109 D4 N Ukraine
Bilauktaung Range 131 B4 ⛰ Burma (Myanmar)/Thailand
Bilbao 99 E1 N Spain
Bilecik 120 B3 NW Turkey
Billingham 93 E2 N England, United Kingdom
Billings 47 E2 Montana, NW USA
Bilma, Grand Erg de 72 G2 *desert* NE Niger
Biloela 137 H4 Queensland, E Australia
Biloxi 39 C6 Mississippi, S USA
Biltine 72 H3 E Chad
Bilzen 84 D6 NE Belgium
Bimini Islands 57 C1 *island group* W Bahamas
Binche 84 C7 S Belgium
Binghamton 37 D4 New York, NE USA
Bingöl 121 F3 E Turkey
Bintulu 131 D6 C Malaysia
Binzhou 129 G3 E China
Bío Bío, Río 65 A6 ≈ C Chile
Bioco, Isla de 72 F6 *island* NW Equatorial Guinea
Birak 70 F3 C Libya
Birao 72 I4 NE Central African Republic
Biratnagar 127 F3 SE Nepal
Birdhill 89 C5 S Ireland
Birhar Sharif 127 F3 N India
Birjand 123 F2 E Iran
Birkenfeld 101 A6 SW Germany
Birkenhead 93 C4 NW England, United Kingdom
Birmingham 93 D6 C England, United Kingdom
Birmingham 39 D4 Alabama, S USA
Bir Mogreïn 72 B1 N Mauritania
Birnin Kebbi 72 E4 NW Nigeria
Birnin Konni 72 E3 SW Niger
Birobidzhan 118 H5 SE Russian Federation
Birr 89 D4 C Ireland
Birsk 111 D6 W Russian Federation
Birżebbuġa 112 B6 SE Malta
Bisbee 44 C4 Arizona, SW USA
Biscay, Bay of 97 B4 *bay* France/Spain
Bishah, Wadi 123 B5 *dry watercourse* C Saudi Arabia
Bishkek 125 H2 ● N Kyrgyzstan
Bishop 49 C7 California, W USA
Bishop Auckland 93 D2 N England, United Kingdom
Biskra 70 E1 NE Algeria
Biskupiec 105 F2 NE Poland
Bislig 131 G5 S Philippines
Bismarck 43 B2 *state capital* North Dakota, N USA
Bismarck Archipelago 141 B1 *island group* NE Papua New Guinea
Bismarck Sea 141 B1 *sea* W Pacific Ocean
Bissau 72 A4 ● W Guinea-Bissau
Bistriţa 109 B6 N Romania
Bitam 76 A1 N Gabon
Bitburg 101 A5 SW Germany
Bitlis 121 G4 SE Turkey
Bitola 107 D4 S Macedonia
Bitonto 103 E6 SE Italy
Bitterfeld 101 D4 E Germany
Bitterroot Range 47 C2 ⛰ Idaho/ Montana, NW USA
Biu 72 G4 E Nigeria
Biwa-ko 133 E6 ◎ Honshu, SW Japan
Bizerte 70 F1 N Tunisia
Bjørnøya 143 D5 *island* N Norway
Blackall 137 G4 Queensland, E Australia
Blackburn 93 C4 NW England, United Kingdom
Black Drin 107 D3 ≈ Albania/Macedonia
Blackfoot 47 D4 Idaho, NW USA
Black Forest 101 B7 ⛰ SW Germany
Black Hills 43 A4 ⛰ South Dakota/ Wyoming, N USA
Black Mountain 47 D5 ▲ Colorado, C USA
Black Mountains 93 C6 ⛰ SE Wales, United Kingdom
Blackpool 93 C4 NW England, United Kingdom
Black Range 44 D3 ⛰ New Mexico, SW USA
Black River 131 B2 ≈ China/Vietnam
Black Rock Desert 47 A4 *desert* Nevada, W USA
Black Sea 78 *sea* Asia/Europe
Black Sea Lowland 109 E6 *depression* SE Europe
Blacksod Bay 89 A3 *inlet* W Ireland
Black Volta 72 D4 ≈ W Africa
Blackwater 89 E6 SE Ireland
Blackwater 89 D6 ≈ S Ireland
Blackwater 89 E2 ≈ Ireland/Northern Ireland, United Kingdom
Blaenavon 93 C7 SE Wales, United Kingdom
Blagoevgrad 107 E3 W Bulgaria
Blagoveshchensk 118 H5 SE Russian Federation
Blairgowrie 91 E5 C Scotland, United Kingdom
Blakeney Point 95 G1 *headland* E England, United Kingdom
Blanca, Bahía 65 B6 *bay* E Argentina
Blanca, Costa 99 F5 *physical region* SE Spain
Blanche, Lake 137 F4 ◎ South Australia
Blanc, Mont 97 F5 ▲ France/Italy
Blanco, Cape 49 A4 *headland* Oregon, NW USA
Blandford Forum 95 D5 S England, United Kingdom
Blanes 99 H2 NE Spain
Blankenberge 84 B5 NW Belgium
Blankenheim 101 A5 W Germany
Blanquilla, Isla 57 I7 *island* N Venezuela
Blantyre 76 E4 S Malawi
Blaricum 84 D4 C Netherlands
Blenheim 139 C5 South Island, New Zealand
Blida 70 D1 N Algeria
Bloemfontein 76 D6 ● C South Africa
Blois 97 C3 C France
Bloody Foreland 89 C1 *headland* NW Ireland
Bloomfield 44 C1 New Mexico, SW USA
Bloomington 40 B6 Illinois, N USA
Bloomington 40 D7 Indiana, N USA
Bloomington 43 E3 Minnesota, N USA
Bloomsburg 37 D5 Pennsylvania, NE USA
Bloomsbury 137 G3 Queensland, NE Australia
Bluefield 39 G2 West Virginia, NE USA
Bluefields 55 E4 SE Nicaragua
Blue Mountains 137 G6 ⛰ New South Wales, SE Australia
Blue Mountains 49 C3 ⛰ Oregon/ Washington, NW USA
Blue Nile 75 C3 ≈ Ethiopia/Sudan
Bluff 47 D6 Utah, W USA
Blumenau 63 F8 S Brazil
Blyth 93 D2 N England, United Kingdom
Blythe 49 E9 California, W USA
Blytheville 39 C3 Arkansas, C USA
Bo 72 B5 S Sierra Leone
Boaco 55 D4 S Nicaragua
Boa Vista 63 E3 NW Brazil
Bobaomby, Tanjona 76 G4 *headland* N Madagascar
Bobo-Dioulasso 72 C4 SW Burkina
Boca Raton 39 G8 Florida, SE USA
Bocay 55 D3 N Nicaragua
Bocholt 101 A4 W Germany
Bochum 101 A4 W Germany
Bodaybo 118 F4 E Russian Federation
Boden 83 D3 N Sweden
Bodmin 95 B5 SW England, United Kingdom
Bodmin Moor 95 B5 *moorland* SW England, United Kingdom
Bodø 83 C2 C Norway
Bodrum 120 A4 SW Turkey
Boende 76 C2 C Dem. Rep. Congo
Bofin, Lough 89 D3 ◎ N Ireland
Bogalusa 39 C6 Louisiana, S USA
Bogatynia 105 B4 SW Poland
Boğazlıyan 121 D3 C Turkey
Boggeragh Mountains 89 C6 ⛰ S Ireland
Bogia 141 B1 N Papua New Guinea
Bognor Regis 95 F5 SE England, United Kingdom
Bogor 131 C8 Java, C Indonesia
Bogotá 63 B2 ● C Colombia
Bo Hai 129 G3 *gulf* NE China
Bohemia 105 B6 *cultural region* W Czech Republic
Bohemian Forest 101 D6 ⛰ C Europe
Bohol Sea 131 F5 *sea* S Philippines
Bohoro Shan 129 B2 ⛰ NW China
Boise 47 B3 *state capital* Idaho, NW USA
Boise City 43 A7 Oklahoma, C USA
Boizenburg 101 C3 N Germany
Bojnūrd 123 E1 N Iran
Boké 72 A4 W Guinea
Bol 72 G3 W Chad
Bolesławiec 105 C4 SW Poland
Bolgatanga 72 D4 N Ghana
Bolivia 65 A2 ◆ *republic* W South America
Bollene 97 E6 SE France
Bollnäs 83 C5 C Sweden
Bollon 137 G4 Queensland, C Australia
Bologna 103 C3 N Italy
Bol'shevik, Ostrov 118 F2 *island* Severnaya Zemlya, N Russian Federation
Bol'shezemel'skaya Tundra 111 E3 *physical region* NW Russian Federation
Bol'shoy Lyakhovskiy, Ostrov 118 G2 *island* NE Russian Federation
Bolton 93 C4 NW England, United Kingdom
Bolu 121 C2 NW Turkey
Bolungarvík 83 A1 NW Iceland
Bolus Head 89 A6 *headland* SW Ireland
Bolzano 103 C1 N Italy
Boma 76 B3 W Dem. Rep. Congo
Bombay *see* Mumbai
Bomu 76 C1 ≈ Central African Republic/Dem. Rep. Congo
Bonaire 57 H7 *Dutch* ◇ S Caribbean Sea
Bonanza 55 E3 NE Nicaragua
Bonaparte Archipelago 137 B2 *island group* Western Australia
Bon, Cap 112 E4 *headland* N Tunisia
Bondo 76 C1 N Dem. Rep. Congo
Bondoukou 72 D5 E Ivory Coast
Bone, Teluk 131 F7 *bay* Celebes, C Indonesia
Bongaigaon 127 G3 NE India
Bongo, Massif des 72 H4 ⛰ NE Central African Republic
Bongor 72 G4 SW Chad
Bonifacio 97 G6 Corsica, France
Bonifacio, Strait of 103 A5 *strait* C Mediterranean Sea
Bonin Trench 15 *undersea feature* NW Pacific Ocean
Bonn 101 A5 W Germany
Boonville 37 D3 New York, NE USA
Boosaaso 75 F3 N Somalia
Boothia, Gulf of 33 H3 *gulf* Nunavut, NE Canada
Boothia Peninsula 33 H3 *peninsula* Nunavut, NE Canada
Boppard 101 B5 W Germany
Boquete 55 F6 W Panama
Boquillas 53 D2 NE Mexico
Bor 107 D2 E Serbia
Bor 75 C4 S South Sudan
Borah Peak 47 B3 ▲ Idaho, NW USA
Borås 83 C6 S Sweden
Bordeaux 97 B5 SW France
Bordj Omar Driss 70 E3 E Algeria
Bordon 95 F4 S England, United Kingdom
Børgefjelt 83 C3 ⛰ C Norway
Borger 84 F2 NE Netherlands
Borger 44 F2 Texas, SW USA
Borgholm 83 C6 S Sweden
Borisoglebsk 111 B6 W Russian Federation
Borlänge 83 C5 C Sweden
Borne 84 F4 E Netherlands
Borneo 131 D7 *island* Brunei/Indonesia/Malaysia
Bornholm 83 C7 *island* E Denmark
Borovichi 111 A4 W Russian Federation
Borriana 99 F3 E Spain
Borrisokane 89 C5 S Ireland
Bosanski Novi 107 B1 Republika Srpska, NW Bosnia and Herzegovina
Boskovice 105 C6 SE Czech Republic
Bosna 107 C2 ≈ N Bosnia and Herzegovina
Bosna I Hercegovina, Federacija 107 C2 *republic* Bosnia and Herzegovina
Bosnia and Herzegovina 107 C2 ◆ *republic* SE Europe
Boso-hanto 133 G6 *peninsula* S Japan
Bosporus 120 B2 *strait* NW Turkey
Bossangoa 72 H5 C Central African Republic
Bossembélé 72 H5 C Central African Republic
Bossier City 39 B5 Louisiana, S USA
Bosten Hu 129 C3 ◎ NW China
Boston 93 F5 E England, United Kingdom
Boston 37 F4 *state capital* Massachusetts, NE USA
Boston Mountains 39 B3 ⛰ Arkansas, C USA
Botany Bay 137 H6 *inlet* New South Wales, SE Australia
Boteti 76 C5 ≈ N Botswana
Bothnia, Gulf of 83 D4 *gulf* N Baltic Sea
Botoşani 109 C5 NE Romania
Botrange 84 E7 ▲ E Belgium
Botswana 76 C5 ◆ *republic* S Africa
Bouar 72 G5 W Central African Republic
Bou Craa 70 B3 NW Western Sahara
Bougainville Island 141 D2 *island* NE Papua New Guinea
Bougaroun, Cap 112 D4 *headland* NE Algeria
Bougouni 72 C4 SW Mali
Boujdour 70 A3 W Western Sahara
Boulder 47 F5 Colorado, C USA
Boulder 47 D2 Montana, NW USA
Boulogne-sur-Mer 97 D1 N France
Boûmdeïd 72 B3 S Mauritania
Boundiali 72 C4 N Ivory Coast
Bountiful 47 D5 Utah, W USA
Bourail 141 G6 C New Caledonia
Bourbonnais 97 D4 *cultural region* C France
Bourg-en-Bresse 97 E4 E France
Bourges 97 D4 C France
Bourgogne *see* Burgundy
Bourke 137 G5 New South Wales, SE Australia
Bournemouth 95 E5 S England, United Kingdom
Boutilimit 72 A3 SW Mauritania
Bowen 137 G3 Queensland, NE Australia
Bowland, Forest of 93 C3 *forest* N England, United Kingdom
Bowling Green 39 E3 Kentucky, S USA
Bowling Green 40 E5 Ohio, N USA
Bowman 43 A2 North Dakota, N USA
Boxmeer 84 E5 SE Netherlands
Boyle 89 C3 C Ireland
Boyne 89 E4 ≈ E Ireland
Boysun 125 F3 S Uzbekistan
Bozeman 47 D3 Montana, NW USA
Bozüyük 120 B3 NW Turkey
Brač 107 B3 *island* S Croatia
Bradford 93 D4 N England, United Kingdom
Bradford 37 B4 Pennsylvania, NE USA
Brady 44 G4 Texas, SW USA
Brae 91 A6 NE Scotland, United Kingdom
Braemar 91 E4 NE Scotland, United Kingdom
Braga 99 B2 NW Portugal
Bragança 99 C2 NE Portugal
Brahmanbaria 127 G3 E Bangladesh
Brahmapur 127 F5 E India
Brahmaputra 127 H3 ≈ S Asia
Brăila 109 D7 E Romania
Braine-le-Comte 84 C7 SW Belgium
Brainerd 43 E2 Minnesota, N USA
Braintree 95 G3 SE England, United Kingdom
Brampton 35 D6 Ontario, S Canada
Brampton 93 C2 NW England, United Kingdom
Brandberg 76 B5 ▲ NW Namibia
Brandenburg 101 D3 NE Germany
Brandon 33 H7 Manitoba, S Canada
Brandon 89 A6 SW Ireland
Brandon Bay 89 A6 *bay* SW Ireland
Brandon Mountain 89 A6 ▲ SW Ireland
Braniewo 105 E2 NE Poland
Brasília 63 G6 ● C Brazil
Braşov 109 C6 C Romania
Bratislava 105 D7 ● W Slovakia
Bratsk 118 F5 C Russian Federation
Braunschweig 101 C4 N Germany
Brava, Costa 99 H2 *coastal region* NE Spain
Bravo, Río 53 D2 ≈ Mexico/USA North America
Brawley 49 D9 California, W USA
Bray 89 E4 E Ireland
Brazil 63 C4 ◆ *federal republic* South America
Brazil Basin 14 *undersea feature* W Atlantic Ocean
Brazilian Highlands 63 G6 ⛰ E Brazil
Brazos River 44 H4 ≈ Texas, SW USA
Brazzaville 76 B2 ● S Congo
Brechin 91 E4 E Scotland, United Kingdom
Brecht 84 C5 N Belgium
Brecon 93 C6 E Wales, United Kingdom
Brecon Beacons 93 B7 ⛰ S Wales, United Kingdom
Breda 84 D5 S Netherlands
Bree 84 D6 NE Belgium
Bregalnica 107 E3 ≈ E Macedonia
Bremen 101 B3 NW Germany
Bremerhaven 101 B3 NW Germany
Bremerton 49 B2 Washington, NW USA
Brenham 44 H4 Texas, SW USA
Brenner Pass 101 C8 *pass* Austria/Italy
Brentwood 95 G3 E England, United Kingdom
Brescia 103 C2 N Italy
Bressanone 103 C1 N Italy
Bressay 91 B6 *island* NE Scotland, United Kingdom
Brest 109 B3 SW Belarus
Brest 97 A2 NW France
Bretagne *see* Brittany
Brewton 39 D6 Alabama, S USA
Bria 72 H5 C Central African Republic
Briançon 97 F5 SE France
Bride 93 B3 N Isle of Man
Bridgend 93 B7 S Wales, United Kingdom
Bridgeport 49 C6 California, W USA
Bridgeport 37 E5 Connecticut, NE USA
Bridgetown 57 K6 ● SW Barbados
Bridgetown 89 E6 SE Ireland
Bridgwater 95 D4 SW England, United Kingdom
Bridgwater Bay 95 C4 *bay* SW England, United Kingdom
Bridlington 93 F3 E England, United Kingdom
Bridlington Bay 93 F3 *bay* E England, United Kingdom
Bridport 95 D5 S England, United Kingdom
Brig 101 B8 SW Switzerland
Brigg 93 E4 N England, United Kingdom
Brigham City 47 D4 Utah, W USA
Brighton 95 F5 SE England, United Kingdom
Brighton 47 F5 Colorado, C USA
Brindisi 103 F6 SE Italy
Brisbane 137 H4 *state capital* Queensland, E Australia
Bristol 95 D4 SW England, United Kingdom
Bristol 37 E4 Connecticut, NE USA
Bristol 39 F3 Virginia, NE USA North America
Bristol Bay 50 C2 *bay* Alaska, USA
Bristol Channel 95 C4 *inlet* England/ Wales, United Kingdom
British Columbia 33 E5 ◐ *province* SW Canada
British Indian Ocean Territory 27 *UK* ◇ C Indian Ocean
British Isles 78 *island group* NW Europe
British Virgin Islands 57 I4 *UK* ◇ E West Indies
Brittany 97 B2 *cultural region* NW France Europe
Brive-la-Gaillarde 97 C5 C France
Brixham 95 C5 SW England, United Kingdom
Brno 105 C6 SE Czech Republic
Broad Bay 91 C2 *bay* NW Scotland, United Kingdom
Broadford 91 C4 N Scotland, United Kingdom
Broad Haven 89 B2 *inlet* NW Ireland
Broad Law 91 E6 ▲ S Scotland, United Kingdom
Broadstairs 95 H4 SE England, United Kingdom
Broads, The 95 H2 *wetland* E England, United Kingdom
Brockton 37 F4 Massachusetts, NE USA
Brodeur Peninsula 33 H3 *peninsula* Baffin Island, Nunavut, NE Canada
Brodick 91 C6 W Scotland, United Kingdom
Brodnica 105 E2 C Poland
Broek-in-Waterland 84 D3 C Netherlands
Broken Hill 137 F5 New South Wales, SE Australia
Bromley 95 F4 SE England, United Kingdom
Bromsgrove 93 D6 W England, United Kingdom
Brookhaven 39 C5 Mississippi, S USA
Brookings 43 D3 South Dakota, N USA
Brooks Range 50 E2 ⛰ Alaska, USA

◐ Administrative region ◆ Country ● Country capital ◇ Dependent territory ○ Dependent territory capital ⛰ Mountain range ▲ Mountain Volcano ≈ River ◎ Lake Reservoir

Brookton *137 B5* Western Australia
Broome *137 C2* Western Australia
Broomfield *47 F5* Colorado, C USA
Brora *91 D3* N Scotland, United Kingdom
Brora *91 D2* ≈ N Scotland, United Kingdom
Brough *93 D3* NW England, United Kingdom
Brownfield *44 F3* Texas, SW USA
Brownsville *44 H6* Texas, SW USA
Brownwood *44 G4* Texas, SW USA
Bruges *84 B6* NW Belgium
Brugge *see* Bruges
Brummen *84 E4* E Netherlands
Brunei *131 D5* ◆ *monarchy* SE Asia
Brunner, Lake *139 C6* ◎ South Island, New Zealand
Brunswick *39 G6* Georgia, SE USA
Brunswick *37 G3* Maine, NE USA
Brus Laguna *55 E2* E Honduras
Brussel *see* Brussels
Brussels *84 C6* ● C Belgium
Bruxelles *see* Brussels
Bryan *44 H4* Texas, SW USA
Bryansk *111 A6* W Russian Federation
Bryn Du *93 B6 hill* E Wales, United Kingdom
Brzeg *105 D4* S Poland
Buala *141 E2* E Solomon Islands
Bucaramanga *63 C2* N Colombia
Buchanan *72 B5* SW Liberia
Buchanan, Lake *44 G4* ⊠ Texas, SW USA
Buchan Ness *91 F3 headland* NE Scotland, United Kingdom
Bucharest *109 C7* ● S Romania
Buckie *91 E3* NE Scotland, United Kingdom
București *see* Bucharest
Bucyrus *40 E6* Ohio, N USA
Budapest *105 E7* ● N Hungary
Budaun *127 E3* N India
Bude *95 B5* SW England, United Kingdom
Bude Bay *95 B5 bay* SW England, United Kingdom
Buenaventura *63 B3* W Colombia
Buena Vista *65 B2* C Bolivia
Buenos Aires *65 C5* ● E Argentina
Buenos Aires *55 F6* SE Costa Rica
Buenos Aires, Lago *65 A8* ◎ Argentina/Chile
Buffalo *37 B3* New York, NE USA
Buffalo *43 A3* South Dakota, N USA
Buffalo *44 H4* Texas, SW USA
Buffalo Narrows *33 G6* Saskatchewan, C Canada
Bug *109 B3* ≈ E Europe
Buguruslan *111 D6* W Russian Federation
Builth Wells *93 C6* E Wales, United Kingdom
Bujalance *99 D5* S Spain
Bujanovac *107 D3* SE Serbia
Bujumbura *75 B6* ● W Burundi
Buka Island *141 D2 island* NE Papua New Guinea
Bukavu *76 D2* E Dem. Rep. Congo
Bukoba *75 C5* NW Tanzania
Bülach *101 B7* NW Switzerland
Bulawayo *76 D5* SW Zimbabwe
Bulgaria *107 E3* ◆ *republic* SE Europe
Bullhead City *44 A2* Arizona, SW USA
Bull Shoals Lake *43 F7* ⊠ Arkansas/Missouri, C USA
Bulukumba *131 E7* Celebes, C Indonesia
Bumba *76 C1* N Dem. Rep. Congo
Bunbury *137 B6* Western Australia
Bunclody *89 E5* SE Ireland
Buncrana *89 D1* NW Ireland
Bundaberg *137 H4* Queensland, E Australia
Bungo-suido *133 D7 strait* SW Japan
Bunmahon *89 D6* S Ireland
Bunratty *89 C5* W Ireland
Bünyan *121 D3* C Turkey
Buon Ma Thuot *131 C4* S Vietnam
Buraydah *123 C4* N Saudi Arabia
Burco *75 F3* NW Somalia
Burdur *120 B4* SW Turkey
Burdur Gölü *120 B4 salt lake* SW Turkey
Bure *75 D3* N Ethiopia
Bure *95 H1* ≈ E England, United Kingdom
Burgas *107 G3* E Bulgaria
Burgaski Zaliv *120 A1 gulf* E Bulgaria
Burgess Hill *95 F4* SE England, United Kingdom
Burgos *99 D2* N Spain
Burgundy *97 E4 region* E France
Burhan Budai Shan *129 D4* ▲▲ C China
Burjassot *99 F4* E Spain
Burkburnett *44 G2* Texas, SW USA
Burketown *137 F2* Queensland, NE Australia
Burkina *72 C4* ◆ *republic* W Africa
Burkina Faso *see* Burkina
Burley *47 C4* Idaho, NW USA
Burlington *47 G5* Colorado, C USA
Burlington *43 F5* Iowa, C USA
Burlington *37 E3* Vermont, NE USA
Burma *131 A2* ◆ *military dictatorship* SE Asia
Burnham-on-Crouch *95 G3* SE England, United Kingdom
Burnham-on-Sea *95 D4* SW England, United Kingdom
Burnie *137 F7* Tasmania, SE Australia
Burnley *93 D4* NW England, United Kingdom
Burns *49 C4* Oregon, NW USA
Burnside *33 G4* ≈ Nunavut, NW Canada
Burns Junction *49 C4* Oregon, NW USA
Burnsville *43 E3* Minnesota, N USA
Burren *89 B5 physical region* W Ireland
Bursa *120 B3* NW Turkey
Burton upon Trent *93 D5* C England, United Kingdom
Burundi *75 B6* ◆ *republic* C Africa
Buru, Pulau *131 F7 island* E Indonesia
Bury *93 D4* NW England, United Kingdom
Bury St Edmunds *95 G2* E England, United Kingdom
Busan *133 C6* SE South Korea
Bushmills *89 E1* N Northern Ireland, United Kingdom
Busselton *137 B6* Western Australia
Buta *76 D1* N Dem. Rep. Congo
Bute, Island of *91 C6 island* SW Scotland, United Kingdom
Butler *37 B5* Pennsylvania, NE USA
Buton, Pulau *131 F7 island* C Indonesia
Butte *47 C2* Montana, NW USA
Buttevant *89 C6* S Ireland
Button Islands *35 E1 island group* Nunavut, NE Canada
Butuan *131 F5* S Philippines
Buulobarde *75 F4* C Somalia
Buur Gaabo *75 E5* S Somalia
Buxoro *125 E3* C Uzbekistan
Buxton *93 D5* C England, United Kingdom
Buynaksk *111 B9* SW Russian Federation
Büyükmenderes Nehri *120 A4* ≈ SW Turkey
Buzău *109 C7* SE Romania
Buzuluk *111 C6* W Russian Federation
Byarezina *109 D2* ≈ C Belarus
Bydgoszcz *105 D3* C Poland
Byelaruskaya Hrada *109 C3 ridge* N Belarus
Bytča *105 D6* N Slovakia
Bytów *105 D2* N Poland

C

Caazapá *65 C4* S Paraguay
Caballo Reservoir *44 D3* ⊠ New Mexico, SW USA
Cabanaquinta *99 C1* N Spain
Cabanatuan *131 F3* N Philippines
Cabinda *76 B2* NW Angola
Cabinda *76 B3 province* NW Angola
Cabora Bassa, Lake *76 E4* ⊠ NW Mozambique
Caborca *53 B2* NW Mexico
Cabo Rojo *51* Puerto Rico
Cabot Strait *35 G4 strait* E Canada
Cabras Island *51 island* W Guam
Cabrera, Illa de *99 G4 island* Balearic Islands, Spain
Cáceres *99 C4* W Spain
Cachimbo, Serra do *63 E4* ▲▲ C Brazil
Caconda *76 B4* C Angola
Čadca *105 D6* N Slovakia
Cader Idris *93 B5* ▲ NW Wales, United Kingdom
Cadillac *40 D4* Michigan, N USA
Cadiz *131 F4* C Philippines
Cádiz *99 C6* SW Spain
Cádiz, Golfo de *see* Cadiz, Gulf of
Cadiz, Gulf of *99 B6 gulf* Portugal/Spain
Caen *97 C2* N France
Caernarfon *93 B5* NW Wales, United Kingdom
Caernarfon Bay *93 A5 bay* NW Wales, United Kingdom
Caerphilly *93 C7* S Wales, United Kingdom
Caersws *93 B6* C Wales, United Kingdom
Cafayate *65 B4* N Argentina
Cagayan de Oro *131 F5* S Philippines
Cagliari *103 A6* Sardinia, Italy
Caguas *57 I4* E Puerto Rico
Caha Mountains *89 B7* ▲▲ SW Ireland
Caher *89 D6* S Ireland
Caherciveen *89 A6* SW Ireland
Cahore Point *89 E5 headland* SE Ireland
Cahors *97 C6* S France
Cahul *109 D6* S Moldova
Caicos Passage *57 F3 strait* Bahamas/Turks and Caicos Islands
Cairngorm Mountains *91 E4* ▲▲ C Scotland, United Kingdom
Cairns *137 G2* Queensland, NE Australia
Cairo *70 I2* ● N Egypt
Cajamarca *63 B5* NW Peru
Calabar *72 F5* S Nigeria
Calahorra *99 E2* N Spain
Calais *97 D1* N France
Calais *37 H2* Maine, NE USA
Calama *65 A3* N Chile
Călărași *109 C7* SE Romania
Calatayud *99 E3* NE Spain
Calbayog *131 F4* C Philippines
Calcasieu Lake *39 B6* ◎ Louisiana, S USA
Calcutta *see* Kolkata
Caldas da Rainha *99 A4* W Portugal
Caldera *65 A4* N Chile
Caldwell *47 B3* Idaho, NW USA
Caledonia *55 C1* N Belize
Caleta Olivia *65 B8* SE Argentina
Calf of Man *93 A4 island* SW Isle of Man
Calgary *33 G7* Alberta, SW Canada
Cali *63 B3* W Colombia
Calicut *127 D7* SW India (see also Kozhikode)
Caliente *47 C6* Nevada, W USA
California *49 C8* ◈ *state* W USA
California, Gulf of *53 B2 gulf* W Mexico
Callabonna, Lake *137 F5* ◎ South Australia
Callan *89 D5* S Ireland
Callander *91 D5* C Scotland, United Kingdom
Callao *63 B5* W Peru
Callosa de Segura *99 F5* E Spain
Calne *95 E4* S England, United Kingdom
Caloundra *137 H4* Queensland, E Australia
Caltanissetta *103 D8* sw Italy
Caluula *75 G3* NE Somalia
Cam *95 F2* ≈ E England, United Kingdom
Camabatela *76 B3* NW Angola
Camacupa *76 B4* C Angola
Camagüey *57 D3* C Cuba
Camagüey, Archipiélago de *57 D3 island group* C Cuba
Camargue *97 E6 physical region* SE France
Ca Mau *131 C5* S Vietnam
Cambodia *131 C4* ◆ *republic* SE Asia
Cambrai *97 D1* N France
Cambrian Mountains *93 B6* ▲▲ C Wales, United Kingdom
Cambridge *139 D3* North Island, New Zealand
Cambridge *95 G2* E England, United Kingdom
Cambridge *39 I2* Maryland, NE USA
Cambridge *40 F6* Ohio, NE USA
Cambridge Bay *33 G4* Victoria Island, Nunavut, NW Canada
Camden *39 B4* Arkansas, C USA
Cameroon *72 F5* ◆ *republic* W Africa
Cameroon Mountain *72 E5* ▲ SW Cameroon
Camocim *63 H4* E Brazil
Camorta *127 H6 island* SE India
Campamento *55 D3* C Honduras
Campbell, Cape *139 D5 headland* SW New Zealand
Campbell Plateau *15 undersea feature* SW Pacific Ocean
Campbell River *33 E7* Vancouver Island, British Columbia, SW Canada
Campbeltown *91 C6* W Scotland, United Kingdom
Campeche *53 H4* SE Mexico
Campeche, Bay of *53 G4 bay* E Mexico
Câm Pha *131 C2* N Vietnam
Campina Grande *63 I5* E Brazil
Campinas *63 G7* S Brazil
Campobasso *103 D5* C Italy
Campo de Criptana *99 D4* C Spain
Campo Grande *63 F7* SW Brazil
Campos dos Goytacazes *63 H7* SE Brazil
Camp Verde *44 B2* Arizona, SW USA
Cam Ranh *131 D4* S Vietnam
Canada *28* ◆ *commonwealth republic* N North America
Canada Basin *143 B3 undersea feature* Arctic Ocean
Canadian *44 F2* Texas, SW USA
Canadian River *44 E2* ≈ SW USA
Canadian Shield *35 B3 physical region* Canada
Çanakkale *120 A2* W Turkey
Cananea *53 B2* NW Mexico
Canarreos, Archipiélago de los *57 B3 island group* W Cuba
Canary Islands *70 A2 island group* Spain, NE Atlantic Ocean
Cañas *55 E5* NW Costa Rica
Canaveral, Cape *39 G7 headland* Florida, SE USA
Canavieiras *63 H6* E Brazil
Canberra *137 G6* ● Australian Capital Territory, SE Australia
Cancún *53 I4* SE Mexico
Cangzhou *129 G3* E China
Caniapiscau *35 E2* ≈ Québec, E Canada
Caniapiscau, Réservoir de *35 E3* ⊠ Québec, C Canada
Canik Dağları *121 E2* ▲▲ N Turkey
Çankırı *121 C2* N Turkey
Canna *91 B4 island* NW Scotland, United Kingdom
Cannanore *127 D7* SW India (see also Kannur)
Cannes *97 F6* SE France
Cannock *93 D5* C England, United Kingdom
Canoas *63 F9* S Brazil
Canon City *47 F6* Colorado, C USA
Cantabria *99 D1 cultural region* N Spain
Cantábrica, Cordillera *99 C1* ▲▲ N Spain
Canterbury *95 H4* SE England, United Kingdom
Canterbury Bight *139 C6 bight* South Island, New Zealand
Canterbury Plains *139 C6 plain* South Island, New Zealand
Can Tho *131 C4* S Vietnam
Canton *39 C5* Mississippi, S USA
Canton *40 F6* Ohio, N USA
Canton *see* Guangzhou
Canyon *44 F2* Texas, SW USA
Canyon *47 D3* Wyoming, C USA
Cape Barren Island *137 G7 island* Furneaux Group, Tasmania, SE Australia
Cape Breton Island *35 G5 island* Nova Scotia, SE Canada
Cape Charles *39 I2* Virginia, NE USA
Cape Coast *72 D5* S Ghana
Cape Girardeau *43 G7* Missouri, C USA
Capelle aan den IJssel *84 C4* SW Netherlands
Cape May *37 D6* New Jersey, NE USA
Cape Town *76 C7* ● SW South Africa
Cape Verde *67* ◆ *republic* E Atlantic Ocean
Cape York Peninsula *137 F1 peninsula* Queensland, N Australia
Cap-Haïtien *57 F4* N Haiti
Capira *55 H6* C Panama
Capitán Arturo Prat *142 A3 Chilean research station* South Shetland Islands, Antarctica
Capitán Pablo Lagerenza *65 C3* N Paraguay
Capri *103 D6* S Italy
Caprivi Strip *76 C4 cultural region* NE Namibia
Captain Cook *51 D3* Hawaii, USA, C Pacific Ocean
Caquetá, Río *63 B3* ≈ Brazil/Colombia
Caracal *109 B7* S Romania
Caracaraí *63 E3* W Brazil
Caracas *63 D1* ● N Venezuela
Caratasca, Laguna de *55 E2 lagoon* NE Honduras
Carbondale *40 B8* Illinois, N USA
Carbonia *103 A6* W Italy
Carcassonne *97 D6* S France
Cárdenas *57 C2* W Cuba
Cardiff *93 C7 National region capital,* S Wales, United Kingdom
Cardigan *93 A6* SW Wales, United Kingdom
Cardigan Bay *93 A6 bay* W Wales, United Kingdom
Carey *47 C4* Idaho, NW USA
Carey, Lake *137 C5* ◎ Western Australia
Caribbean Sea *57 F6 sea* W Atlantic Ocean
Carlisle *93 C2* NW England, United Kingdom
Carlow *89 E5* SE Ireland
Carloway *91 B2* NW Scotland, United Kingdom
Carlsbad *44 E3* New Mexico, SW USA
Carlsbad Caverns *44 D3 cave* New Mexico, SW USA North America
Carmarthen *93 B7* SW Wales, United Kingdom
Carmarthen Bay *93 A7 inlet* SW Wales, United Kingdom
Carmaux *97 D6* S France
Carmel *40 D6* Indiana, N USA
Carmelita *55 B1* N Guatemala
Carmen *53 H5* SE Mexico
Carmona *99 C5* SW Spain
Carna *89 B4* W Ireland
Carnarvon *137 A4* Western Australia
Carndonagh *89 D1* NW Ireland
Carnedd Llywelyn *93 B5* ▲ NW Wales, United Kingdom
Carnegie, Lake *137 C4 salt lake* Western Australia
Carn Eige *91 C4* ▲ N Scotland, United Kingdom
Car Nicobar *127 H5 island* SE India
Carnlough *89 F2* E Northern Ireland, United Kingdom
Carnoustie *91 E5* E Scotland, United Kingdom
Carolina *63 G4* E Brazil
Carolina *51* E Puerto Rico
Carpathian Mountains *105 F6* ▲▲ E Europe
Carpentaria, Gulf of *137 E1 gulf* N Australia
Carpi *103 C3* N Italy
Carrara *103 B3* C Italy
Carrauntoohil *89 A6* ▲ SW Ireland
Carrickfergus *89 F2* NE Northern Ireland, United Kingdom
Carrickmacross *89 E3* N Ireland
Carrick-on-Shannon *89 D3* NW Ireland
Carrizo Springs *44 G5* Texas, SW USA
Carrizozo *44 D3* New Mexico, SW USA
Carrowmore Lake *89 B3* ◎ NW Ireland
Carson City *47 A5 state capital* Nevada, W USA
Carson Sink *47 A5 salt flat* Nevada, W USA
Cartagena *63 B1* NW Colombia
Cartagena *99 F5* SE Spain
Cartago *55 E6* C Costa Rica
Carthage *43 E7* Missouri, C USA
Carthage *44 I3* Texas, SW USA
Cartwright *35 G3* Newfoundland and Labrador, E Canada
Caruthersville *43 G7* Missouri, C USA
Casablanca *70 C1* NW Morocco
Casa Grande *44 B3* Arizona, SW USA
Cascade Range *49 B3* ▲▲ Oregon/Washington, NW USA
Cascais *99 A4* C Portugal
Caserta *103 D5* S Italy
Casey *142 E5 Australian research station* Antarctica
Cashel *89 D5* S Ireland
Čáslav *105 C5* C Czech Republic
Casper *47 E4* Wyoming, C USA
Caspian Depression *111 B8 depression* Kazakhstan/Russian Federation
Caspian Sea *114 inland sea* Asia/Europe
Casteggio *103 B2* N Italy
Castellón de la Plana *99 F3* E Spain
Castelnaudary *97 C6* S France
Castelo Branco *99 B4* C Portugal
Castelsarrasin *97 C6* S France
Castelvetrano *103 C8* Sicily, Italy
Castilla-La Mancha *99 E4 cultural region* NE Spain Europe
Castilla-León *99 C2 cultural region* NW Spain
Castle Acre *95 G1* E England, United Kingdom
Castlebar *89 B3* W Ireland
Castlebay *91 A4* NW Scotland, United Kingdom
Castlebellingham *89 E3* NE Ireland
Castleblayney *89 E3* N Ireland
Castlebridge *89 E6* SE Ireland
Castlecomer *89 D5* SE Ireland
Castlecove *89 A6* SW Ireland
Castledawson *89 E2* C Northern Ireland, United Kingdom
Castlederg *89 D2* W Northern Ireland, United Kingdom
Castle Douglas *91 D7* S Scotland, United Kingdom
Castleford *93 E4* N England, United Kingdom
Castleisland *89 B6* SW Ireland
Castlemartyr *89 C6* S Ireland
Castletown *93 A4* SE Isle of Man
Castletown Bearhaven *89 B7* SW Ireland
Castletownroche *89 C6* S Ireland
Castricum *84 C3* W Netherlands
Castries *57 K6* ● N Saint Lucia
Castro *65 A7* W Chile
Castrovillari *103 E7* SW Italy
Castuera *99 C4* W Spain
Catacamas *55 D3* C Honduras
Catalonia *99 G2 cultural region* N Spain Europe
Cataluña *see* Catalonia
Catania *103 D8* Sicily, Italy
Catanzaro *103 E7* SW Italy
Catarroja *99 F4* E Spain
Caterham *95 G4* SE England, United Kingdom
Cathedral Caverns *39 D4 cave* Alabama, S USA
Cat Island *57 E2 island* C Bahamas
Catskill Mountains *37 D4* ▲▲ New York, NE USA
Catterick *93 D3* N England, United Kingdom
Caucasus *121 G1* ▲▲ Georgia/Russian Federation
Cavally *72 C5* ≈ Ivory Coast/Liberia Africa
Cavan *89 D3* N Ireland
Caviana de Fora, Ilha *63 G3 island* N Brazil
Caxito *76 B3* NW Angola
Cayenne *63 F2* ○ NE French Guiana
Cayes *57 E4* SW Haiti
Cayman Brac *57 C4 island* E Cayman Islands
Cayman Islands *56 B4* UK ◇ W West Indies
Cay Sal *57 C2 islet* SW Bahamas
Cazorla *99 E5* S Spain
Ceará *63 H4 state* C Brazil
Cébaco, Isla *55 G7 island* SW Panama
Cebu *131 F4* C Philippines
Cecina *103 B4* C Italy
Cedar City *47 C6* Utah, W USA
Cedar Falls *43 F4* Iowa, C USA
Cedar Rapids *43 F5* Iowa, C USA
Cedar River *40 A4* ≈ Iowa/Minnesota, C USA
Cedros, Isla *53 A3 island* W Mexico
Ceduna *137 E5* South Australia
Cefalù *103 D8* Sicily, Italy
Celbridge *89 E4* E Ireland
Celebes *131 E7 island* C Indonesia
Celebes Sea *131 E6 sea* Indonesia/Philippines
Celje *101 E8* C Slovenia
Celldömölk *105 D8* W Hungary
Celle *101 C3* N Germany
Celtic Sea *87 B8 sea* SW British Isles
Cenderawasih, Teluk *131 H7 bay* E Indonesia
Cenon *97 B5* SW France
Central African Republic *72 H5* ◆ *republic* C Africa
Central, Cordillera *57 F4* ▲▲ C Dominican Republic
Central, Cordillera *55 G6* ▲▲ C Panama
Central, Cordillera *131 F3* ▲▲ Luzon, N Philippines
Central, Cordillera *51* ▲▲ Puerto Rico
Centralia *49 B2* Washington, NW USA
Central Makran Range *127 B3* ▲▲ W Pakistan
Central Pacific Basin *15 undersea feature* C Pacific Ocean
Central Range *141 A2* ▲▲ NW Papua New Guinea
Central Russian Upland *111 A6* ▲▲ W Russian Federation
Central Siberian Plateau *118 E3* ▲▲ N Russian Federation
Central, Sistema *99 D3* ▲▲ C Spain
Central Valley *49 B6 valley* California, W USA
Ceram Sea *131 G7 sea* E Indonesia
Cerignola *103 E5* SE Italy
Çerkes *121 C2* N Turkey
Cernay *97 F3* NE France
Cerro de Pasco *63 B5* C Peru
Cervera *99 G2* NE Spain
Cesena *103 C3* N Italy
České Budějovice *105 B6* S Czech Republic
Český Krumlov *105 B6* S Czech Republic
Ceuta *99 C6* S Spain
Cévennes *97 D6* ▲▲ S France
Ceyhan *121 D5* S Turkey
Ceylanpinar *121 F5* SE Turkey
Chachapoyas *63 A4* NW Peru
Chad *72 G3* ◆ *republic* C Africa
Chad, Lake *72 G3* ◎ Chad/Niger/Nigeria
Chadron *43 A4* Nebraska, C USA
Chagai Hills *127 B2* ▲▲ Afghanistan/Pakistan
Chaghcharan *125 E5* C Afghanistan
Chajul *55 A3* W Guatemala
Chakhansur *125 D6* SW Afghanistan
Chalatenango *55 B3* N El Salvador
Chalki *107 G6 island* SE Greece
Chalkida *107 E5* E Greece
Chalkidiki *107 E4 peninsula* NE Greece
Challans *97 B4* NW France
Châlons-en-Champagne *97 E2* NE France
Chalon-sur-Saône *97 E4* C France
Chaman *127 B2* SW Pakistan
Chambersburg *37 C5* Pennsylvania, NE USA
Chambéry *97 E5* E France
Champagne *97 E2 cultural region* N France
Champaign *40 C6* Illinois, N USA
Champasak *131 C3* S Laos
Champerico *55 A3* SW Guatemala
Champlain, Lake *37 E2* ◎ Canada/USA
Champotón *53 H4* SE Mexico
Chañaral *65 A4* N Chile
Chandeleur Islands *39 D6 island group* Louisiana, S USA
Chandigarh *127 D2* N India
Chandrapur *127 E5* C India
Changane *76 E5* ≈ S Mozambique
Changchun *129 G2* NE China
Chang Jiang *129 D4* ≈ SW China
Changsha *129 F5* S China
Changyŏn *133 A5* SW North Korea
Changzhi *129 F4* C China
Chaniá *107 E7* SE Greece
Chañi, Nevado de *65 A3* ▲ NW Argentina
Channel Islands *95 G6 island group* S English Channel
Channel Islands *49 B9 island group* California, W USA
Channel-Port aux Basques *35 G4* Newfoundland, Newfoundland and Labrador, SE Canada
Channel Tunnel *95 H4 tunnel* France/United Kingdom
Chantada *99 B2* NW Spain
Chanute *43 D7* Kansas, C USA
Chaoyang *129 G3* NE China
Chapala, Lago de *53 E5* ◎ C Mexico
Chapan, Gora *125 C3* ▲ C Turkmenistan
Chapayevsk *111 C6* W Russian Federation
Chard *95 D5* SW England, United Kingdom
Charente *97 C5 cultural region* W France
Charente *97 C5* ≈ W France
Chari *72 H4* ≈ Central African Republic/Chad
Charikar *125 F5* NE Afghanistan
Chariton River *43 F6* ≈ Missouri, C USA
Charleroi *84 C7* S Belgium
Charlesbourg *35 E5* Québec, SE Canada
Charles Island *35 D1 island* Nunavut, NE Canada
Charleston *40 C7* Illinois, N USA
Charleston *39 G5* South Carolina, SE USA
Charleston *39 F2 state capital* West Virginia, NE USA
Charlestown *89 C3* NW Ireland
Charleville *137 G4* Queensland, E Australia
Charleville-Mézières *97 E2* N France
Charlotte *39 G3* North Carolina, SE USA
Charlotte Amalie *57 I4* ○ N Virgin Islands (USA)
Charlotte Harbor *39 F8 inlet* Florida, SE USA
Charlottesville *39 H2* Virginia, NE USA
Charlottetown *35 G5* Prince Edward Island, SE Canada
Charters Towers *137 G3* Queensland, NE Australia
Chartres *97 D3* C France
Chashniki *109 D2* N Belarus
Châteaubriant *97 B3* NW France
Châteaudun *97 D3* C France
Châteauroux *97 D4* C France
Château-Thierry *97 D2* N France
Châtelet *84 C7* S Belgium
Châtellerault *97 C4* W France
Chatham *95 G4* SE England, United Kingdom
Chatkal Range *125 G2* ▲▲ Kyrgyzstan/Uzbekistan
Chattahoochee River *39 E5* ≈ SE USA
Chattanooga *39 D4* Tennessee, S USA
Chatyr-Tash *125 H3* C Kyrgyzstan
Chaumont *97 E3* N France
Chaves *99 B2* N Portugal
Chaykovskiy *111 D6* NW Russian Federation
Cheb *105 A5* W Czech Republic
Cheboksary *111 C6* W Russian Federation
Cheboygan *40 D3* Michigan, N USA
Chech, Erg *72 C1 desert* Algeria/Mali
Cheduba Island *131 A3 island* W Burma (Myanmar)
Chelm *105 G4* SE Poland
Chelmno *105 D2* C Poland
Chelmsford *95 G3* E England, United Kingdom
Cheltenham *95 D3* C England, United Kingdom
Chelyabinsk *118 C4* C Russian Federation
Chemnitz *101 D5* E Germany
Chemult *49 B4* Oregon, NW USA
Chengde *129 G3* E China
Chengdu *129 E4* C China
Chennai *127 E6* S India
Chenzhou *129 F5* S China
Cheonan *133 B6* W South Korea
Chepstow *93 C7* SE Wales, United Kingdom
Cher *97 D4* ≈ C France
Cherbourg *97 B1* N France
Cherepovets *111 B4* NW Russian Federation

hergui, Chott ech *112 B5 salt lake* NW Algeria
herkasy *109 E4* C Ukraine
herkessk *111 A8* SW Russian Federation
hernihiv *109 E3* NE Ukraine
hernivtsi *109 C5* W Ukraine
herry Hill *37 D5* New Jersey, NE USA
herskiy *118 H2* NE Russian Federation
herskogo, Khrebet *118 G3* ⛰ NE Russian Federation
hesapeake Bay *39 I2 inlet* NE USA
hesham *95 F3* C England, United Kingdom
hëshskaya Guba *143 E6 bay* NW Russian Federation
hester *93 C5* C England, United Kingdom
hesterfield *93 E5* C England, United Kingdom
hesterfield, Îles *141 E6 island group* NW New Caledonia
hester-le-Street *93 D2* N England, United Kingdom
hetumal *53 I4* SE Mexico
heviot Hills *95 D1 hill range* England/ Scotland, United Kingdom
heviot, The *93 C1* ▲ NE England, United Kingdom
heyenne *47 F4 state capital* Wyoming, C USA
heyenne River *43 B3* ≈ South Dakota/ Wyoming, N USA
hhapra *127 F3* N India
hhattisgarh *127 E4 state* E India
hiang Mai *131 B3* NW Thailand
hiapa de Corzo *53 H5* SE Mexico
hiba *133 G5* S Japan
hibougamau *35 D4* Québec, SE Canada
hicago *40 C5* Illinois, N USA
hichester *95 F5* SE England, United Kingdom
hickasha *43 C8* Oklahoma, C USA
hiclayo *63 B5* NW Peru
hico *49 B6* California, W USA
hico, Río *65 B7* ≈ SE Argentina
hico, Río *65 A8* ≈ S Argentina
hicoutimi *35 E4* Québec, SE Canada
hieti *103 D5* C Italy
hifeng *129 G2* N China (see also Ulanhad)
hihuahua *53 D2* NW Mexico
hildress *44 F2* Texas, SW USA
hile *65 A4* ◆ *republic* SW South America
hile Chico *65 A8* W Chile
hililabombwe *76 D4* C Zambia
hillán *65 A6* C Chile
hillicothe *40 E7* Ohio, N USA
hiloé, Isla de *65 A7 island* W Chile
hilpancingo *53 F5* S Mexico
hiltern Hills *95 F3 hill range* S England, United Kingdom
himán *55 H6* E Panama
himbote *63 B5* W Peru
himboy *125 D2* NW Uzbekistan
himney Rock *43 A5 rock* Nebraska, C USA
himoio *76 E5* C Mozambique
hina *129 C3* ◆ *republic* E Asia
hinandega *55 C4* NW Nicaragua
hindwinn *131 A1* ≈ N Burma (Myanmar)
hingola *76 D4* C Zambia
hinguetti *72 B2* C Mauritania
hin Hills *131 A2* ⛰ W Burma (Myanmar)
hinle *44 C1* Arizona, SW USA
hioggia *103 D2* NE Italy
hios *107 F5* E Greece
hios *107 F5 island* E Greece
hipata *76 E4* E Zambia
hippenham *95 D4* S England, United Kingdom
hippewa River *40 A3* ≈ Wisconsin, N USA
hiputneticook Lakes *37 H2 lakes* Canada/USA
hiquimula *55 B3* SE Guatemala
hirala *127 E6* E India
hirchiq *125 F2* E Uzbekistan
hiriqui Gulf *55 F7 gulf* SW Panama
hiriquí, Laguna de *55 F6 lagoon* NW Panama
hirripó Grande, Cerro *55 F6* ▲ SE Costa Rica
hisec *55 B2* C Guatemala
hisholm *43 E2* Minnesota, N USA
hişinău *109 D6* ● C Moldova
hita *118 G5* S Russian Federation
hitato *76 C3* NE Angola
hitina *50 E3* Alaska, USA
hitose *133 G2* NE Japan
hitré *55 G7* S Panama
hittagong *127 H4* SE Bangladesh
hitungwiza *76 E5* NE Zimbabwe
hiume *76 C4* E Angola
hlef *70 D1* NW Algeria
hodzież *105 C3* C Poland
hoele Choel *65 B6* C Argentina
hoiseul *141 E2 island* NW Solomon Islands
holet *97 B4* NW France
holuteca *55 C4* S Honduras
holuteca, Río *55 D4* ≈ SW Honduras
homa *76 D4* S Zambia
homutov *105 A5* NW Czech Republic
h'ongjin *133 C3* NE North Korea
hongju *133 A5* W North Korea
hongqing *129 E5* C China
honos, Archipiélago de los *65 A7 island group* S Chile
horley *93 C4* NW England, United Kingdom
hornobyl' *109 D3* N Ukraine
Chorzów *105 E5* S Poland
Ch'osan *133 A4* N North Korea
Choshi *133 G5* S Japan
Choszczno *105 C3* NW Poland
Chota Nagpur *127 E4 plateau* N India
Choûm *72 B2* C Mauritania
Choybalsan *129 F2* E Mongolia
Christchurch *139 C6* South Island, New Zealand
Christchurch *95 E5* S England, United Kingdom
Christiansted *51* S Virgin Islands (USA)
Chubut, Río *65 B7* ≈ SE Argentina
Chucunaque, Río *55 I6* ≈ E Panama
Chugoku-sanchi *133 D6* ⛰ Honshū, SW Japan
Chukchi Plain *143 C2 undersea feature* Arctic Ocean
Chukchi Plateau *143 B2 undersea feature* Arctic Ocean
Chukchi Sea *118 H1 sea* Arctic Ocean
Chukot Range *118 H1* ⛰ NE Russian Federation
Chula Vista *49 D9* California, W USA
Chulucanas *63 A4* NW Peru
Chulym *118 E5* ≈ C Russian Federation
Chuncheon *133 B5* N South Korea
Chungju *133 B6* C South Korea
Chunya *118 F4* ≈ C Russian Federation
Chuquicamata *65 A3* N Chile
Chur *101 C8* E Switzerland
Churchill *33 H5* Manitoba, C Canada
Churchill *35 A2* ≈ Manitoba/ Saskatchewan, C Canada
Churchill *35 F3* ≈ Newfoundland and Labrador, E Canada
Church Stretton *93 C6* W England, United Kingdom
Churchtown *89 E6* SE Ireland
Chuska Mountains *44 C1* ⛰ Arizona/ New Mexico, SW USA
Chusovoy *111 D5* NW Russian Federation
Chuy *65 D5* E Uruguay
Cide *121 C2* N Turkey
Ciechanów *105 E3* C Poland
Ciego de Ávila *57 D3* C Cuba
Cienfuegos *57 C3* C Cuba
Cieza *99 E5* SE Spain
Cihanbeyli *121 C4* C Turkey
Cikobia *141 J4 island* N Fiji
Cilacap *131 D8* C Indonesia
Cimarron River *43 C7* ≈ Kansas/ Oklahoma, C USA
Cincinnati *40 D7* Ohio, N USA
Ciney *84 D8* SE Belgium
Cinto, Monte *97 F7* ▲ Corse, France, C Mediterranean Sea
Cipolletti *65 B6* C Argentina
Cirebon *131 C8* S Indonesia
Cirencester *95 E3* C England, United Kingdom
Cirò Marina *103 E7* S Italy
Citrus Heights *49 B6* California, W USA
Ciudad Bolívar *63 D2* E Venezuela
Ciudad Camargo *53 D3* N Mexico
Ciudad Darío *55 D4* W Nicaragua
Ciudad del Este *65 C4* SE Paraguay
Ciudad Guayana *63 D2* NE Venezuela
Ciudad Guzmán *53 E5* SW Mexico
Ciudad Hidalgo *53 H6* SE Mexico
Ciudad Juárez *53 C1* N Mexico
Ciudad Lerdo *53 D3* C Mexico
Ciudad Madero *53 F4* C Mexico
Ciudad Mante *53 F4* C Mexico
Ciudad Miguel Alemán *53 E3* C Mexico
Ciudad Obregón *53 C3* NW Mexico
Ciudad Real *99 D4* C Spain
Ciudad-Rodrigo *99 C3* N Spain
Ciudad Valles *53 F4* C Mexico
Ciudad Victoria *53 F3* C Mexico
Ciutadella *99 H3* Majorca, Spain
Civitanova Marche *103 D4* C Italy
Civitavecchia *103 C5* C Italy
Clacton-on-Sea *95 H3* E England, United Kingdom
Clare *89 C4* ≈ W Ireland
Clarecastle *89 C5* W Ireland
Claregalway *89 C4* W Ireland
Clare Island *89 A3 island* W Ireland
Claremont *37 F3* New Hampshire, NE USA
Claremore *43 D7* Oklahoma, C USA
Claremorris *89 C3* W Ireland
Clarence *139 C5* South Island, New Zealand
Clarence *139 C5* ≈ South Island, New Zealand
Clarence Town *57 E2* C Bahamas
Clarinda *43 E5* Iowa, C USA
Clarión, Isla *53 A5 island* W Mexico
Clark Fork *47 C2* ≈ Idaho/Montana, NW USA
Clark Hill Lake *39 F4* ⊟ Georgia/South Carolina, SE USA
Clarksburg *39 G1* West Virginia, NE USA
Clarksdale *39 C4* Mississippi, S USA
Clarksville *39 D3* Tennessee, S USA
Clayton *44 E1* New Mexico, SW USA
Clear Island *89 B7 island* S Ireland
Clearlake *49 B6* California, W USA
Clearwater *39 F7* Florida, SE USA
Clearwater Mountains *47 B2* ⛰ Idaho, NW USA
Clearwater River *47 B2* ≈ Idaho, NW USA
Cleburne *44 G3* Texas, SW USA
Cleethorpes *93 F4* E England, United Kingdom
Clermont *137 G3* Queensland, E Australia
Clermont-Ferrand *97 D5* C France
Clevedon *95 D4* SW England, United Kingdom
Cleveland *40 F5* Ohio, N USA
Cleveland *39 E4* Tennessee, S USA
Clew Bay *89 B3 inlet* W Ireland
Clifden *89 B4* W Ireland
Clifton *44 C3* Arizona, SW USA
Clinton *39 C5* Mississippi, S USA
Clinton *43 C8* Oklahoma, C USA
Clisham *91 B2* ▲ NW Scotland, United Kingdom
Clitheroe *93 C4* NW England, United Kingdom
Cloghan *89 D4* C Ireland
Cloncurry *137 F3* Queensland, C Australia
Clondalkin *89 E4* E Ireland
Clones *89 D3* N Ireland
Clonmel *89 D6* S Ireland
Cloonboo *89 C4* W Ireland
Cloppenburg *101 B3* NW Germany
Cloquet *43 E2* Minnesota, N USA
Cloud Peak *47 E3* ▲ Wyoming, C USA
Clovelly *95 B4* SW England, United Kingdom
Clovis *44 E2* New Mexico, SW USA
Cluj-Napoca *109 B6* NW Romania
Clutha *139 B7* ≈ South Island, New Zealand
Clyde *91 E6* ≈ W Scotland, United Kingdom
Clydebank *91 D5* W Scotland, United Kingdom
Clyde, Firth of *91 C6 inlet* S Scotland, United Kingdom
Coari *63 D4* N Brazil
Coast Mountains *33 E5* ⛰ Canada/USA
Coast Ranges *49 B4* ⛰ W USA
Coatbridge *91 D6* S Scotland, United Kingdom
Coats Island *33 I4 island* Nunavut, NE Canada
Coats Land *142 B3 physical region* Antarctica
Coatzacoalcos *53 G5* E Mexico
Cobán *55 B3* C Guatemala
Cobar *137 G5* New South Wales, SE Australia
Cobija *65 A1* NW Bolivia
Coburg *101 C5* SE Germany
Cochabamba *65 B2* C Bolivia
Cochin *127 D7* SW India (see also Kochi)
Cochrane *35 C4* Ontario, S Canada
Cochrane *65 A8* S Chile
Cockburn Town *57 F3* ○ Turks and Caicos Islands, C West Indies
Cockermouth *93 B2* NW England, United Kingdom
Coconino Plateau *44 B1 plain* Arizona, SW USA
Coco, Río *55 E3* ≈ Honduras/Nicaragua
Cocos Basin *15 undersea feature* E Indian Ocean
Cocos Island *51 island* S Guam
Cod, Cape *37 G4 headland* Massachusetts, NE USA
Codfish Island *139 A8 island* SW New Zealand
Cody *47 E3* Wyoming, C USA
Coeur d'Alene *47 B2* Idaho, NW USA
Coevorden *84 F3* NE Netherlands
Coffs Harbour *137 H5* New South Wales, SE Australia
Cognac *97 C4* W France
Coiba, Isla de *55 F7 island* SW Panama
Coihaique *65 A7* S Chile
Coimbatore *127 D7* S India
Coimbra *99 B3* W Portugal
Coín *99 D6* S Spain
Colby *43 B6* Kansas, C USA
Colchester *95 G3* E England, United Kingdom
Coldstream *91 F6* SE Scotland, United Kingdom
Coleman *44 G3* Texas, SW USA
Coleraine *89 E1* N Northern Ireland, United Kingdom
Colesberg *76 D7* South Africa
Colima *53 D5* S Mexico
Coll *91 B4 island* W Scotland, United Kingdom
College Station *44 H4* Texas, SW USA
Collie *137 B6* Western Australia
Collon *89 E3* NE Ireland
Collooney *89 C3* NW Ireland
Colmar *97 F3* NE France
Colne *93 D4* NW England, United Kingdom
Cologne *101 A5* W Germany
Colombia *63 B3* ◆ *republic* N South America
Colombo *127 E8* ● W Sri Lanka
Colón *55 H6* C Panama
Colón, Archipiélago de *see* Galapagos Islands
Colonsay *91 B5 island* W Scotland, United Kingdom
Colorado *47 E5* ◐ *state* C USA
Colorado City *44 F3* Texas, SW USA
Colorado Plateau *44 B1 plateau* W USA
Colorado, Río *65 B6* ≈ E Argentina
Colorado River *44 A2* ≈ Mexico/USA
Colorado River *44 H4* ≈ Texas, SW USA
Colorado Springs *47 F5* Colorado, C USA
Columbia *39 H1* Maryland, NE USA
Columbia *43 F6* Missouri, C USA
Columbia *39 D3* Tennessee, S USA
Columbia *39 G4 state capital* South Carolina, SE USA
Columbia River *49 C2* ≈ Canada/USA
Columbia Basin *49 C2 basin* Washington, NW USA
Columbia Plateau *47 B4 plateau* Idaho/ Oregon, NW USA
Columbine *47 E5* Colorado, C USA North America
Columbus *39 E5* Georgia, SE USA
Columbus *40 D7* Indiana, N USA
Columbus *39 D4* Mississippi, S USA
Columbus *43 D5* Nebraska, C USA
Columbus *40 E6 state capital* Ohio, N USA
Colville Channel *139 D2 channel* North Island, New Zealand
Colville River *50 E1* ≈ Alaska, USA
Colwyn Bay *93 B4* N Wales, United Kingdom
Comacchio *103 C3* N Italy
Comalcalco *53 G5* SE Mexico
Comarapa *65 B2* C Bolivia
Comayagua *55 C3* W Honduras
Comeragh Mountains *89 D6* ⛰ S Ireland
Comilla *127 G4* E Bangladesh
Comino *see* Kemmuna
Comitán *53 H5* SE Mexico
Como *103 B2* N Italy
Comodoro Rivadavia *65 B7* SE Argentina
Como, Lake *103 B2* ◎ N Italy
Comoros *76 G4* ◆ *republic* W Indian Ocean
Compiègne *97 D2* N France
Conakry *72 B4* ● SW Guinea
Concan *44 G5* Texas, SW USA
Concarneau *97 A3* NW France
Concepción *65 B2* E Bolivia
Concepción *65 A6* C Chile
Concepción *65 C3* C Paraguay
Concepción, Volcán *55 D5* ⌆ SW Nicaragua
Conchos, Río *53 D2* ≈ NW Mexico
Concord *49 B7* California, W USA
Concord *37 F3 state capital* New Hampshire, NE USA
Concordia *65 C5* E Argentina
Concordia *43 D6* Kansas, C USA
Condega *55 D4* NW Nicaragua
Congleton *93 D5* W England, United Kingdom
Congo *76 B2* ◆ *republic* C Africa
Congo *76 B2* ≈ C Africa
Congo Basin *76 C1 drainage basin* W Dem. Rep. Congo
Democratic Republic of Congo *76 C2* ◆ *republic* C Africa
Connaught *89 B3 cultural region* W Ireland
Connecticut *37 E4* ◐ *state* NE USA
Connecticut *37 E3* ≈ Canada/USA
Connemara *89 B4 physical region* W Ireland
Conn, Lough *89 B3* ◎ W Ireland
Conroe *44 H4* Texas, SW USA
Consett *93 D2* N England, United Kingdom
Consolación del Sur *57 B2* W Cuba
Constance, Lake *101 B7* ◎ Austria/ Germany/Switzerland
Constanța *109 D7* SE Romania
Constantine *70 E1* NE Algeria
Conwy *93 B5* ≈ N Wales, United Kingdom
Coober Pedy *137 E4* South Australia
Cookeville *39 E3* Tennessee, S USA
Cook Islands *135 NZ* ◇ S Pacific Ocean
Cook, Mount *see* Aoraki
Cookstown *89 E2* C Northern Ireland, United Kingdom
Cook Strait *139 D5 strait* New Zealand
Cooktown *137 G2* Queensland, NE Australia
Coolgardie *137 C5* Western Australia
Cooma *137 G6* New South Wales, SE Australia
Coon Rapids *43 E3* Minnesota, N USA
Cooper Creek *137 F4 seasonal river* Queensland/South Australia
Coos Bay *49 A4* Oregon, NW USA
Copacabana *65 A2* W Bolivia
Copenhagen *83 B7* ● E Denmark
Copiapó *65 A4* N Chile
Copperas Cove *44 G4* Texas, SW USA
Coppermine *see* Kugluktuk
Coquimbo *65 A5* N Chile
Coral Harbour *33 I4* Southampton Island, Nunavut, NE Canada
Coral Sea *141 C4 sea* SW Pacific Ocean
Coral Sea Islands *141 B4 Australian* ◇ SW Pacific Ocean
Corby *95 F2* C England, United Kingdom
Corcovado, Golfo *65 A7 gulf* S Chile
Cordele *39 F5* Georgia, SE USA
Córdoba *65 B5* C Argentina
Córdoba *53 F5* E Mexico
Córdoba *99 D5* S Spain
Cordova *50 E3* Alaska, USA
Corfu *107 C5* W Greece
Corfu *107 C5 island* Ionian Islands, Greece
Coria *99 C3* W Spain
Corinth *107 E5* S Greece
Corinth *39 D4* Mississippi, S USA
Corinth, Gulf of *107 E5 gulf* C Greece
Corinth, Isthmus of *107 D5 isthmus* S Greece
Corinto *55 C4* NW Nicaragua
Cork *89 C6* S Ireland
Çorlu *120 A2* NW Turkey
Corner Brook *35 G4* Newfoundland, Newfoundland and Labrador, E Canada
Corn Islands *55 F4 island group* SE Nicaragua
Cornwall, Cape *95 A6 headland* SW England, United Kingdom
Cornwallis Island *33 G2 island* Parry Islands, Nunavut, N Canada
Coro *63 C1* NW Venezuela
Corocoro *65 A2* W Bolivia
Coromandel *139 D2* North Island, New Zealand
Corona *44 D2* New Mexico, SW USA
Coronado, Bahía de *55 E6 bay* S Costa Rica
Coronel Dorrego *65 B6* E Argentina
Corozal *55 C1* N Belize
Corpus Christi *44 H5* Texas, SW USA
Corrales *44 D2* New Mexico, SW USA
Corrib, Lough *89 B4* ◎ W Ireland
Corrientes *65 C4* NE Argentina
Corsham *95 D4* S England, United Kingdom
Corsica *97 F7 island* SE France
Corsicana *44 H3* Texas, SW USA
Cortegana *99 B5* S Spain
Cortés *55 F6* SE Costa Rica
Cortez *47 E6* Colorado, C USA
Cortina d'Ampezzo *103 D2* NE Italy
Coruche *99 B4* C Portugal
Çoruh Nehri *121 F2* ≈ Georgia/Turkey
Çorum *121 D2* N Turkey
Corvallis *49 B3* Oregon, NW USA
Corwen *93 C5* N Wales, United Kingdom
Cosenza *103 E7* SW Italy
Cosne-Cours-sur-Loire *97 D3* C France
Costa Rica *55 E5* ◆ *republic* Central America
Cotagaita *65 B3* S Bolivia
Côte d'Azur *97 F7 physical region* SE France
Côte d'Or *97 E3 cultural region* C France
Cotonou *72 E5* S Benin
Cotswold Hills *95 D3 hill range* S England, United Kingdom
Cottbus *101 E4* E Germany
Council Bluffs *43 D5* Iowa, C USA
Courland Lagoon *83 D7 lagoon* Lithuania/Russian Federation
Courtown *89 E5* E Ireland
Coutances *97 B2* N France
Couvin *84 C8* S Belgium
Coventry *93 D6* C England, United Kingdom
Covilhã *99 B3* E Portugal
Cowan, Lake *137 C5* ◎ Western Australia
Cozumel, Isla *53 I4 island* SE Mexico
Cradock *76 D7* S South Africa
Craig *47 E5* Colorado, C USA
Craigavon *89 E2* C Northern Ireland, United Kingdom
Craiova *109 B7* SW Romania
Cranbrook *33 F7* British Columbia, SW Canada
Cranleigh *95 F4* SE England, United Kingdom
Craughwell *89 C4* W Ireland
Craven Arms *93 C6* W England, United Kingdom
Crawley *95 F4* SE England, United Kingdom
Creegh *89 B5* W Ireland
Cremona *103 B2* N Italy
Cres *107 B2 island* W Croatia
Crescent City *49 A5* California, W USA
Creston *43 E5* Iowa, C USA
Creston *47 E4* Wyoming, C USA
Crestview *39 D6* Florida, SE USA
Crete *107 F7 island* SE Greece
Créteil *97 D2* N France
Crete, Sea of *107 F6 sea* Greece, Aegean Sea
Creuse *97 C4* ≈ C France
Crewe *93 C5* C England, United Kingdom
Crieff *91 D5* C Scotland, United Kingdom
Crimea *109 F6 peninsula* SE Ukraine
Cristóbal *55 H6* C Panama
Crna Reka *107 D4* ≈ S Macedonia
Croagh Patrick *89 B3* ▲ W Ireland
Croatia *107 B1* ◆ *republic* SE Europe
Croker Island *137 D1 island* Northern Territory, N Australia
Cromarty *91 D3* N Scotland, United Kingdom
Cromer *95 H1* E England, United Kingdom
Cromwell *139 B7* South Island, New Zealand
Crooked Island *57 E2 island* SE Bahamas
Crooked Island Passage *57 E2 channel* SE Bahamas
Crooked River *49 C4* ≈ Oregon, NW USA
Crookston *43 D2* Minnesota, N USA
Croom *89 C5* SW Ireland
Crosby *93 C4* NW England, United Kingdom
Cross Fell *93 C2* ▲ N England, United Kingdom
Crossmaglen *89 E3* S Northern Ireland, United Kingdom
Crotone *103 E7* SW Italy
Croydon *95 F4* SE England, United Kingdom
Crozet Islands *15 island group* W French Southern and Antarctic Territories
Crusheen *89 C5* W Ireland
Cruz Bay *51* E Virgin Islands (USA)
Crystal Falls *40 C3* Michigan, N USA
Csorna *105 D7* NW Hungary
Csurgó *105 D8* SW Hungary
Cuando *76 C4* ≈ S Africa
Cuango *76 B3* ≈ Angola/ Dem. Rep. Congo
Cuanza *76 B3* ≈ C Angola
Cuauhtémoc *53 D2* N Mexico
Cuautla *53 F5* S Mexico
Cuba *57 D3* ◆ *republic* W West Indies
Cubal *76 B4* W Angola
Cubango *76 B4* SW Angola
Cubango *76 B4* ≈ S Africa
Cúcuta *63 C2* N Colombia
Cuddapah *127 E6* S India
Cuenca *63 B4* S Ecuador
Cuenca *99 E3* C Spain
Cuernavaca *53 F5* S Mexico
Cuiabá *63 E6* SW Brazil
Cuijck *84 E5* SE Netherlands
Cuito *76 C4* ≈ SE Angola
Culebra *51* E Puerto Rico
Culebra, Isla de *51 island* E Puerto Rico
Culiacán *53 C3* C Mexico
Cullera *99 F4* E Spain
Cullman *39 D4* Alabama, S USA
Cullybackey *89 E2* NE Northern Ireland, United Kingdom
Cumberland *39 H1* Maryland, NE USA
Cumberland, Lake *39 E3* ⊟ Kentucky, S USA
Cumberland Sound *33 J3 inlet* Baffin Island, Nunavut, NE Canada
Cumbernauld *91 D5* S Scotland, United Kingdom
Cumbrian Mountains *93 C3* ⛰ NW England, United Kingdom
Cumnock *91 D6* W Scotland, United Kingdom
Cumpas *53 C2* NW Mexico
Cuneo *103 A3* NW Italy
Cunnamulla *137 G4* Queensland, E Australia
Curaçao *57 H7 Dutch* ◇ S Caribbean Sea
Curicó *65 A6* C Chile
Curitiba *63 F8* S Brazil
Curtis Island *137 H4 island* Queensland, SE Australia
Cusco *63 C6* C Peru
Cushcamcarragh *89 B3* ▲ NW Ireland
Cushendall *89 E1* N Northern Ireland, United Kingdom
Cusset *97 D4* C France
Cuttack *127 F4* E India
Cuxhaven *101 B2* NW Germany
Cyclades *107 F6 island group* SE Greece
Cyprus *112 C5* ◆ *republic* E Mediterranean Sea
Cyrenaica *70 H2 cultural region* NE Libya
Czech Republic *105 B6* ◆ *republic* C Europe
Częstochowa *105 D2* S Poland
Człuchów *105 D2* NW Poland

D

Dąbrowa Tarnowska *105 F5* S Poland
Daegu *133 C6* SE South Korea
Daejeon *133 B6* C South Korea
Dagana *72 A3* N Senegal
Dagda *83 F6* SE Latvia
Dagupan *131 F3* N Philippines
Dahm, Ramlat *123 C6 desert* NW Yemen
Daimiel *99 D4* C Spain
Dakar *72 A3* ● W Senegal
Dakoro *72 E3* S Niger
Dalain Hob *129 E3* N China
Dalaman *120 A5* SW Turkey
Dalandzadgad *129 E2* S Mongolia
Da Lat *131 C4* S Vietnam
Dalby *137 H4* Queensland, E Australia
Dale City *39 H2* Virginia, NE USA
Dalhart *44 E1* Texas, SW USA
Dali *129 D5* SW China
Dalian *129 G3* NE China
Dalkeith *91 E5* SE Scotland, United Kingdom
Dallas *44 H3* Texas, SW USA
Dalmatia *107 B2 cultural region* S Croatia
Dalton *39 E4* Georgia, SE USA
Daly Waters *137 E2* Northern Territory, N Australia
Daman *127 C4* W India
Damara *72 H5* S Central African Republic
Damascus *123 B4* ● SW Syria
Damavand, Qolleh-ye *123 D2* ▲ N Iran
Dampier *137 B3* Western Australia
Dampier, Selat *131 G6 strait* Papua, E Indonesia
Damqawt *123 E6* E Yemen
Damxung *129 C4* W China
Danakil Desert *75 E3 desert* E Africa
Danané *72 C5* W Ivory Coast
Da Nang *131 C4* S Vietnam
Danbury *37 E4* Connecticut, NE USA
Dandong *129 G3* NE China
Daneborg *143 B6* Tunu, N Greenland
Danforth *37 G2* Maine, NE USA
Danghara *125 F4* SW Tajikistan
Dangrek, Chuor Phnum *131 C4* ⛰ Cambodia/Thailand
Dangriga *55 C2* E Belize
Daniel *47 D4* Wyoming, C USA
Danlí *55 D3* S Honduras
Dannenberg *101 C3* N Germany
Dannevirke *139 D4* North Island, New Zealand
Danube *78* ≈ C Europe
Danubian Plain *107 E2 lowlands* N Bulgaria
Danville *39 G3* Virginia, NE USA
Danzhou *129 F6* S China
Danzig, Gulf of *105 D1 gulf* N Poland
Dardanelles *120 A3 strait* Sea of Marmara, Mediterranean Sea
Dar es Salaam *75 D6* E Tanzania
Darfield *139 C6* South Island, New Zealand

◐ Administrative region ◆ Country ● Country capital ◇ Dependent territory ○ Dependent territory capital ⛰ Mountain range ▲ Mountain ⌆ Volcano ≈ River ◎ Lake ⊟ Reservoir

Darfur 75 B3 cultural region W Sudan
Darhan 129 E2 N Mongolia
Darien, Gulf of 63 B2 gulf S Caribbean Sea
Darién, Serranía del 55 I6 Colombia/Panama
Darjiling 127 G3 NE India
Darling River 137 F5 New South Wales, SE Australia
Darlington 93 D3 N England, United Kingdom
Darmstadt 101 B5 SW Germany
Darnah 70 H2 NE Libya
Darnley, Cape 142 E4 cape Antarctica
Daroca 99 E3 NE Spain
Daroot-Korgon 125 G3 SW Kyrgyzstan
Dart 95 C5 SW England, United Kingdom
Dartmoor 95 B5 moorland SW England, United Kingdom
Dartmouth 35 G5 Nova Scotia, SE Canada
Dartmouth 95 C5 SW England, United Kingdom
Daru 141 A3 SW Papua New Guinea
Darvishan 125 E6 S Afghanistan
Darwin 137 D1 territory capital Northern Territory, N Australia
Darwin, Isla 63 A6 island Galapagos Islands, Ecuador
Daşoguz 125 D2 N Turkmenistan
Datong 129 F3 C China
Daugavpils 83 F7 SE Latvia
Dauphiné 97 E6 cultural region E France
Davangere 127 D6 W India
Davao 131 F5 S Philippines
Davao Gulf 131 G5 gulf S Philippines
Davenport 43 F5 Iowa, C USA
Daventry 95 E2 C England, United Kingdom
David 55 F7 W Panama
Davis 142 E4 Australian research station Antarctica
Davis Sea 142 E4 sea Antarctica
Davis Strait 33 J2 strait Baffin Bay/Labrador Sea
Dawei 131 B4 S Burma (Myanmar)
Dawlish 95 C5 SW England, United Kingdom
Dawros Head 89 C2 headland N Ireland
Dax 97 B6 SW France
Dayton 40 E6 Ohio, N USA
Daytona Beach 39 G7 Florida, SE USA
De Aar 76 C7 C South Africa
Dead Sea 123 H6 salt lake Israel/Jordan
Deal 95 H4 SE England, United Kingdom
Dean, Forest of 95 D3 forest C England, United Kingdom
Deán Funes 65 B5 C Argentina
Death Valley 49 D7 valley California, W USA
Deatnu 83 E1 Finland/Norway
De Bilt 84 D4 C Netherlands
Debrecen 105 F7 E Hungary
Decatur 39 D4 Alabama, S USA
Decatur 40 B6 Illinois, N USA
Deccan 127 D5 plateau C India
Děčín 105 B5 NW Czech Republic
Dedemsvaart 84 E3 E Netherlands
Dee 91 E4 NE Scotland, United Kingdom
Dee 93 F2 England/Wales, United Kingdom
Dee 93 C5 S Scotland, United Kingdom
Deering 50 D1 Alaska, USA
Deggendorf 101 D6 SE Germany
Değirmenlik 112 D6 N Cyprus
Deinze 84 B6 NW Belgium
Dékoa 72 H5 C Central African Republic
De Land 39 G7 Florida, SE USA
Delano 49 C8 California, W USA
Delaware 40 E6 Ohio, N USA
Delaware 37 D6 ◆ state NE USA
Delaware Bay 37 D6 bay NE USA
Delft 84 C4 W Netherlands
Delfzijl 84 F2 NE Netherlands
Delgo 75 C1 N Sudan
Delhi 127 D3 N India
Delicias 53 D2 N Mexico
Delmenhorst 101 B3 NW Germany
Del Rio 44 F5 Texas, SW USA
Delta 47 C5 Utah, W USA
Deltona 39 G7 Florida, SE USA
Demba 76 C2 C Dem. Rep. Congo
Dembia 72 I5 SE Central African Republic
Demchok 129 A4 disputed region China/India
Deming 44 D3 New Mexico, SW USA
Demmin 101 D2 NE Germany
Demopolis 39 D5 Alabama, S USA
Demqog see Demchok
Denali see McKinley, Mount
Denbigh 93 B5 NE Wales, United Kingdom
Dender 84 B7 W Belgium
Denekamp 84 F3 E Netherlands
Denham 137 A4 Western Australia
Den Ham 84 F3 E Netherlands
Den Helder 84 C2 NW Netherlands
Dénia 99 F4 E Spain
Deniliquin 137 F6 New South Wales, SE Australia
Denison 43 D5 Iowa, C USA
Denison 44 H2 Texas, SW USA
Denizli 120 B4 SW Turkey
Denmark 83 B7 ◆ monarchy N Europe
Denov 125 F3 S Uzbekistan
Denpasar 131 E8 Bali, C Indonesia
Denton 44 H3 Texas, SW USA
D'Entrecasteaux Islands 141 C3 island group SE Papua New Guinea
Denver 47 F5 state capital Colorado, C USA
De Queen 39 A4 Arkansas, C USA
Dera Ghazi Khan 127 C2 C Pakistan
Derbent 111 B9 SW Russian Federation
Derby 137 C2 Western Australia
Derby 93 D5 C England, United Kingdom
Derg 89 D2 Ireland/Northern Ireland, United Kingdom
Derg, Lough 89 C5 W Ireland
De Ridder 39 B6 Louisiana, S USA
Déroute, Passage de la 95 G5 strait Channel Islands/France
Derreendarragh 89 B6 SW Ireland
Derwent 93 E3 N England, United Kingdom
Derweze 125 C3 C Turkmenistan
Deschutes River 49 B3 Oregon, NW USA
Dese 75 E3 N Ethiopia
Deseado, Río 65 B8 S Argentina
Des Moines 43 E5 state capital Iowa, C USA
Desna 111 A6 Russian Federation/Ukraine
Dessau 101 D4 E Germany
Detroit 40 E5 Michigan, N USA
Detroit Lakes 43 D2 Minnesota, N USA
Deurne 84 E5 SE Netherlands
Deva 109 B6 W Romania
Deventer 84 E4 E Netherlands
Deveron 91 E3 NE Scotland, United Kingdom
Devils Lake 43 C2 North Dakota, N USA
Devizes 95 E4 S England, United Kingdom
Devon Island 33 H2 island Parry Islands, Nunavut, NE Canada
Devonport 137 F7 Tasmania, SE Australia
Devrek 121 C2 N Turkey
Dewsbury 93 D4 N England, United Kingdom
Dexter 43 G7 Missouri, C USA
Dezful 123 D2 SW Iran
Dezhou 129 G3 E China
Dhaka 127 G4 ● C Bangladesh
Dhanbad 127 F4 NE India
Dhekelia Sovereign Air Base 112 D6 UK air base SE Cyprus
Dhuusa Marreeb 75 F4 C Somalia
Diamantina, Chapada 63 H5 E Brazil
Dibrugarh 127 H3 NE India
Dickinson 43 B2 North Dakota, N USA
Didcot 95 E3 C England, United Kingdom
Didymoteicho 107 F4 NE Greece
Diekirch 84 E8 C Luxembourg
Diepenbeek 84 D6 NE Belgium
Diepholz 101 B3 NW Germany
Dieppe 97 C1 N France
Dieren 84 E4 E Netherlands
Differdange 84 E9 SW Luxembourg
Digne 97 E6 SE France
Digoin 97 E4 C France
Digul, Sungai 131 I7 Papua, E Indonesia
Dijon 97 E4 C France
Dikhil 75 E3 SW Djibouti
Dikson 118 E2 N Russian Federation
Dikti 107 F7 Crete, Greece
Dilaram 125 E5 SW Afghanistan
Dili 131 F8 ● C East Timor
Dilia 72 G3 SE Niger
Dilling 75 C3 C Sudan
Dillon 47 C3 Montana, NW USA
Dilolo 76 C3 S Dem. Rep. Congo
Dimashq see Damascus
Dimitrovgrad 107 F3 S Bulgaria
Dimitrovgrad 111 C6 W Russian Federation
Dimovo 107 E2 NW Bulgaria
Dinajpur 127 G3 NW Bangladesh
Dinan 97 B2 NW France
Dinant 84 D8 S Belgium
Dinar 120 B4 SW Turkey
Dinaric Alps 107 C2 Bosnia and Herzegovina/Croatia
Dindigul 127 D7 SE India
Dingle 89 A6 SW Ireland
Dingle Bay 89 A6 bay SW Ireland
Dinguiraye 72 B4 N Guinea
Dingwall 91 D3 N Scotland, United Kingdom
Diourbel 72 A3 W Senegal
Dire Dawa 75 E3 E Ethiopia
Dirk Hartog Island 137 A4 island Western Australia
Disappointment, Lake 137 B3 salt lake Western Australia
Dishu 125 D6 S Afghanistan
Diss 95 H2 E England, United Kingdom
Divinópolis 63 G7 SE Brazil
Divo 72 C5 S Ivory Coast
Diyarbakır 121 F4 SE Turkey
Djambala 76 B2 C Congo
Djanet 70 E4 SE Algeria
Djelfa 70 E1 N Algeria
Djéma 72 I5 E Central African Republic
Djerba 70 F2 island E Tunisia
Djérem 72 G5 C Cameroon
Djibouti 75 E3 ● E Djibouti
Djibouti 75 E3 ◆ republic E Africa
Djourab, Erg du 72 H3 desert N Chad
Djúpivogur 83 B1 SE Iceland
Dnieper 78 E Europe
Dnieper Lowland 109 E4 lowlands Belarus/Ukraine
Dniester 109 D5 Moldova/Ukraine
Dniprodzerzhyns'k 109 F5 E Ukraine
Dniprodzerzhyns'ke Vodoskhovyshche 109 F5 C Ukraine
Dnipropetrovs'k 109 F5 E Ukraine
Dniprorudne 109 F5 SE Ukraine
Doba 72 G4 S Chad
Döbeln 101 D4 E Germany
Doberai Peninsula 131 G7 peninsula E Indonesia
Dobre Miasto 105 E2 NE Poland
Dobrich 107 G2 NE Bulgaria
Dodecanese 107 F6 island group SE Greece
Dodekánisa see Dodecanese
Dodge City 43 C7 Kansas, C USA
Dodman Point 95 B6 headland SW England, United Kingdom
Dodoma 75 D6 ● C Tanzania
Dogai Coring 129 C4 W China
Dogo 133 D6 island Oki-shoto, SW Japan
Dogondoutchi 72 E3 SW Niger
Doğubayazıt 121 H3 E Turkey
Doğu Karadeniz Dağları 121 F2 NE Turkey
Doha 123 D4 ● C Qatar
Dokkum 84 E2 N Netherlands
Dôle 97 E4 E France
Dolgellau 93 B5 NW Wales, United Kingdom
Dolisie 76 B2 S Congo
Dolomites 103 C2 NE Italy
Dolores 65 C6 E Argentina
Dolores 55 B2 N Guatemala
Dolores 65 C5 SW Uruguay
Dolores Hidalgo 53 E4 C Mexico
Dombås 83 B4 S Norway
Domeyko 65 A4 N Chile
Dominica 57 K5 ◆ republic E West Indies
Dominican Republic 57 F5 ◆ republic C West Indies
Don 111 B7 SW Russian Federation
Don 91 F4 NE Scotland, United Kingdom
Don 93 E4 N England, United Kingdom
Donaghadee 89 F2 E Northern Ireland, United Kingdom
Donau see Danube
Donauwörth 101 C6 S Germany
Donawitz 101 E7 SE Austria
Donbass 109 G5 industrial region Russian Federation/Ukraine
Don Benito 99 C4 W Spain
Doncaster 93 E4 N England, United Kingdom
Dondo 76 B3 NW Angola
Donegal 89 D2 NW Ireland
Donegal Bay 89 C2 bay NW Ireland
Donets 111 A7 Russian Federation/Ukraine
Donets'k 109 G5 E Ukraine
Dongfang 129 F6 S China
Donghae 133 C5 NE South Korea
Dongola 75 C1 N Sudan
Dongou 76 B1 NE Congo
Dongting Hu 129 F5 S China
Donostia 99 E1 N Spain (see also San Sebastián)
Doolow 75 E4 E Ethiopia
Door Peninsula 40 C3 peninsula Wisconsin, N USA
Dorchester 95 D5 S England, United Kingdom
Dordogne 97 C5 cultural region SW France Europe
Dordogne 97 C5 W France
Dordrecht 84 C5 SW Netherlands
Dornoch 91 D3 N Scotland, United Kingdom
Dorotea 83 C3 N Sweden
Dorre Island 137 A4 island Western Australia
Dortmund 101 B4 W Germany
Dos Hermanas 99 C5 SW Spain
Dothan 39 E6 Alabama, S USA
Dotnuva 83 E7 C Lithuania
Douai 97 D1 N France
Douala 72 F5 W Cameroon
Douglas 89 C6 S Ireland
Douglas 93 B3 ○ E Isle of Man
Douglas 44 C4 Arizona, SW USA
Douglas 39 F5 Georgia, SE USA
Douglas 47 F4 Wyoming, C USA
Douro 99 B3 Portugal/Spain
Dover 95 H4 SE England, United Kingdom
Dover 37 D6 state capital Delaware, NE USA
Dover, Strait of 97 D1 strait England, United Kingdom/France
Dovrefjell 83 B4 plateau S Norway
Downham Market 95 G2 E England, United Kingdom
Downpatrick 89 F3 SE Northern Ireland, United Kingdom
Dozen 133 D6 island Oki-shoto, SW Japan
Drachten 84 E2 N Netherlands
Dra, Hamada du 70 C2 plateau W Algeria
Drahichyn 109 C3 SW Belarus
Drakensberg 76 D7 Lesotho/South Africa
Drake Passage 65 B9 passage Atlantic Ocean/Pacific Ocean
Dráma 107 E4 NE Greece
Drammen 83 B5 S Norway
Drau see Drava
Drava 105 C9 C Europe
Drave see Drava
Drawsko Pomorskie 105 C2 NW Poland
Dresden 101 D5 E Germany
Driffield 93 E3 E England, United Kingdom
Drina 107 D2 Bosnia and Herzegovina/Serbia
Drinit, Lumi 107 D3 NW Albania
Drobeta-Turnu Severin 109 B7 SW Romania
Drogheda 89 E4 NE Ireland
Droichead Nua 89 E4 E Ireland
Droitwich 93 D6 W England, United Kingdom
Drôme 97 E6 cultural region SE France Europe
Dronfield 93 D4 C England, United Kingdom
Dronning Maud Land 142 C3 physical region Antarctica
Drumahoe 89 D2 NW Northern Ireland, United Kingdom
Drumbilla 89 E3 NE Ireland
Drumcliff 89 C3 N Ireland
Drummondville 35 E5 Québec, SE Canada
Druridge Bay 93 D2 bay N England, United Kingdom
Dryden 35 A4 Ontario, C Canada
Dryden 44 F4 Texas, SW USA
Drysa 109 D1 N Belarus
Duarte, Pico 57 G4 ▲ C Dominican Republic
Dubai 123 E4 NE United Arab Emirates
Dubawnt 33 G5 Nunavut, NW Canada
Dubbo 137 G5 New South Wales, SE Australia
Dublin 89 E4 ● E Ireland
Dublin 39 F5 Georgia, SE USA
Dubno 109 C4 NW Ukraine
Dubois 47 D3 Idaho, NW USA
Du Bois 37 B5 Pennsylvania, NE USA
Dubrovnik 107 C3 SE Croatia
Dubuque 43 F4 Iowa, C USA
Duchesne 47 D5 Utah, W USA
Dudelange 84 E9 S Luxembourg
Dudley 93 D6 C England, United Kingdom
Duero 92 D2 Portugal/Spain
Duffel 84 C6 C Belgium
Duff Islands 141 G3 island group E Solomon Islands
Dugi Otok 107 B2 island W Croatia
Duisburg 101 A4 W Germany
Duiven 84 E4 E Netherlands
Duk Faiwil 75 C4 E South Sudan
Dulan 129 D4 C China
Dulce 44 D1 New Mexico, SW USA
Dulce, Golfo 55 F7 gulf S Costa Rica
Dülmen 101 B4 W Germany
Dulovo 107 F2 NE Bulgaria
Duluth 43 F2 Minnesota, N USA
Duma 123 A2 SW Syria
Dumas 44 F2 Texas, SW USA
Dumbarton 91 D5 W Scotland, United Kingdom
Dumfries 91 E7 S Scotland, United Kingdom
Dumont d'Urville 142 E6 French research station Antarctica
Dumyat 70 I2 N Egypt
Duna see Danube
Dunaj see Danube
Dunany Point 89 E3 headland NE Ireland
Dunărea see Danube
Dunaújváros 105 E8 C Hungary
Dunav see Danube
Duncan 44 C3 Arizona, SW USA
Duncan 43 C8 Oklahoma, C USA
Duncansby Head 91 E2 headland N Scotland, United Kingdom
Dundalk 89 E3 NE Ireland
Dundee 76 D6 E South Africa
Dundee 91 E5 E Scotland, United Kingdom
Dundrum 89 C5 S Ireland
Dundrum Bay 89 F3 inlet NW Irish Sea
Dunedin 139 B7 South Island, New Zealand
Dunfanaghy 89 D1 NW Ireland
Dunfermline 91 E5 C Scotland, United Kingdom
Dungannon 89 E2 C Northern Ireland, United Kingdom
Dungarvan 89 D6 S Ireland
Dungeness 95 H4 headland SE England, United Kingdom
Dungiven 89 E2 N Northern Ireland, United Kingdom
Dunglow 89 C2 NW Ireland
Dungu 76 D1 NE Dem. Rep. Congo
Dunkerque 97 D1 N France
Dunkery Beacon 95 B4 ▲ SW England, United Kingdom
Dunkirk 37 B4 New York, NE USA
Dún Laoghaire 89 E4 E Ireland
Dunleer 89 E3 NE Ireland
Dunmore 89 C4 W Ireland
Dunmurry 89 F2 E Northern Ireland, United Kingdom
Dunnet Head 91 D2 headland N Scotland, United Kingdom
Dunning 43 C5 Nebraska, C USA
Duns 91 F6 SE Scotland, United Kingdom
Dunseith 43 C1 North Dakota, N USA
Dunshaughlin 89 E4 E Ireland
Dunstable 95 F3 E England, United Kingdom
Duqm 123 F5 E Oman
Durance 97 E6 SE France
Durango 53 D4 W Mexico
Durango 47 E6 Colorado, C USA
Durant 43 D9 Oklahoma, C USA
Durban 76 D7 E South Africa
Durg 127 E4 C India
Durham 93 D2 N England, United Kingdom
Durham 39 H3 North Carolina, SE USA
Durness 91 D2 N Scotland, United Kingdom
Durrës 107 C4 W Albania
Durrow 89 D5 C Ireland
Dursey Head 89 A7 headland S Ireland
D'Urville Island 139 C4 island C New Zealand
Dushanbe 125 F3 ● W Tajikistan
Düsseldorf 101 A4 W Germany
Dusti 125 F4 SW Tajikistan
Dutch Harbor 50 B2 Unalaska Island, Alaska, USA
Dyersburg 39 C3 Tennessee, S USA
Dzerzhinsk 111 B5 W Russian Federation
Dzhalal-Abad 125 G3 W Kyrgyzstan
Dzhankoy 109 F6 S Ukraine
Dzhelandy 125 G4 SE Tajikistan
Dzhergalan 125 I2 NE Kyrgyzstan
Dzhugdzhur, Khrebet 118 H4 E Russian Federation
Działdowo 105 E3 C Poland

E

Eagar 44 C2 Arizona, SW USA
Eagle Pass 44 F5 Texas, SW USA
Earn 91 D5 N Scotland, United Kingdom
Easky 89 C3 N Ireland
East Anglia 95 G2 physical region E England, United Kingdom
East Antarctica 142 D4 physical region Antarctica
Eastbourne 95 G5 SE England, United Kingdom
East Cape 139 E3 headland North Island, New Zealand
East China Sea 114 sea W Pacific Ocean
East Dereham 95 G1 E England, United Kingdom
Easter Island 141 D5 island Chile, E Pacific Ocean
Eastern Ghats 127 E5 SE India
Eastern Sayans 118 E5 Mongolia/Russian Federation
East Falkland 65 C9 island E Falkland Islands
East Frisian Islands 101 A2 island group NW Germany
East Grand Forks 43 D2 Minnesota, N USA
East Grinstead 95 G4 SE England, United Kingdom
East Kilbride 91 D6 S Scotland, United Kingdom
East Korea Bay 133 B5 bay E North Korea
Eastleigh 95 E4 S England, United Kingdom
East Liverpool 40 F6 Ohio, N USA
East London 76 D7 S South Africa
Eastmain 35 D4 Québec, C Canada
East Novaya Zemlya Trough 143 E5 undersea feature W Kara Sea
East Pacific Rise 14 undersea feature E Pacific Ocean
East Saint Louis 40 A7 Illinois, N USA
East Sea see Japan, Sea of
East Siberian Sea 143 C2 sea Arctic Ocean
East Timor 131 F8 ◆ republic SE Asia
Eau Claire 40 A3 Wisconsin, N USA
Ebbw Vale 93 C7 SE Wales, United Kingdom
Ebensee 101 E7 N Austria
Eberswalde-Finow 101 D3 E Germany
Ebetsu 133 F2 NE Japan
Ebolowa 72 F6 S Cameroon
Ebro 99 E2 NE Spain
Echo Bay 33 G4 Northwest Territories, NW Canada
Echt 84 E6 SE Netherlands
Ecija 99 C5 SW Spain
Ecuador 63 B3 ◆ republic NW South America
Eday 91 E1 island NE Scotland, United Kingdom
Ed Da'ein 75 B3 W Sudan
Ed Damazin 75 C3 E Sudan
Ed Damer 75 C2 NE Sudan
Ed Debba 75 C2 N Sudan
Eddrachillis Bay 91 C2 bay NW Scotland, United Kingdom
Eddystone Rocks 95 B6 rocks SW England, United Kingdom
Ede 84 E4 C Netherlands
Ede 72 E5 SW Nigeria
Eden 44 G4 Texas, SW USA
Eden 93 C2 NW England, United Kingdom
Edgeley 43 C2 North Dakota, N USA
Edgeworthstown 89 D4 C Ireland
Edinburg 44 G6 Texas, SW USA
Edinburgh 91 E5 National region capital, S Scotland, United Kingdom
Edirne 120 A2 NW Turkey
Edison 37 E5 New Jersey, NE USA
Edmonds 49 B2 Washington, NW USA
Edmonton 33 G6 province capital Alberta, SW Canada
Edmundston 35 F5 New Brunswick, SE Canada
Edolo 103 C2 N Italy
Edremit 120 A3 NW Turkey
Edward, Lake 76 D2 Dem. Rep. Congo/Uganda
Edwards Plateau 44 F4 plain Texas, SW USA
Edzo 33 F5 Northwest Territories, NW Canada
Eeklo 84 B6 NW Belgium
Eemshaven 84 F1 NE Netherlands
Eersel 84 D5 S Netherlands
Efate 141 H5 island C Vanuatu
Effingham 40 C7 Illinois, N USA
Efstrátios, Ágios 107 F5 island E Greece
Egadi Is. 103 B8 island group S Italy
Eger 105 E7 NE Hungary
Éghezèe 84 D7 C Belgium
Egmont, Mount see Taranaki, Mount
Egmont, Cape 139 C4 cape North Island, New Zealand
Egypt 70 I4 ◆ republic NE Africa
Eibar 99 E1 N Spain
Eibergen 84 F4 E Netherlands
Eidfjord 83 A5 S Norway
Eifel 101 A5 plateau W Germany
Eiger 101 B8 ▲ C Switzerland
Eigg 91 B4 island W Scotland, United Kingdom
Eight Degree Channel 127 C8 channel India/Maldives
Eighty Mile Beach 137 B3 beach Western Australia
Eijsden 84 E7 SE Netherlands
Eindhoven 84 D5 S Netherlands
Eisenhüttenstadt 101 E4 E Germany
Eisenstadt 101 F7 E Austria
Eisleben 101 C4 C Germany
Eivissa see Ibiza
Ejea de los Caballeros 99 E2 NE Spain
Elat 123 G7 S Israel
El'Atrun 75 B2 NW Sudan
Elâzığ 121 F3 E Turkey
Elba 103 B4 island Archipelago Toscano, C Italy
Elbe 101 C3 Czech Republic/Germany
Elbert, Mount 47 E5 ▲ Colorado, C USA
Elbląg 105 E2 NE Poland
El'brus 111 A8 ▲ SW Russian Federation
El Burgo de Osma 99 E2 C Spain
Elburz Mountains 123 D2 N Iran
El Cajon 49 D9 California, W USA
El Calafate 65 A8 S Argentina
El Campo 44 H5 Texas, SW USA
El Centro 49 D9 California, W USA
Elche 99 F5 E Spain
El Chichónal, Volcán 53 G5 SE Mexico
Elda 99 F4 E Spain
Eldorado 65 D4 NE Argentina
El Dorado 53 C4 C Mexico
El Dorado 39 B4 Arkansas, C USA
El Dorado 43 D7 Kansas, C USA
Eldoret 75 D5 W Kenya
Elektrostal' 111 B5 W Russian Federation
Elemi Triangle 75 C4 disputed region Kenya/Sudan
Elephant Butte Reservoir 44 D3 New Mexico, SW USA
Eleuthera Island 57 D1 island N Bahamas
El Fasher 75 B3 W Sudan
El Geneina 75 A3 W Sudan
Elgin 91 E3 NE Scotland, United Kingdom
Elgin 40 C5 Illinois, N USA
El Golea 70 D2 C Algeria
El Ḥank 72 C1 cliff N Mauritania
Elida 44 E3 New Mexico, SW USA
Elista 111 B8 SW Russian Federation
Elizabeth 137 E6 South Australia
Elizabeth City 39 I3 North Carolina, SE USA
Elizabethtown 39 E2 Kentucky, S USA
Ełk 105 F2 NE Poland
Elk City 43 C8 Oklahoma, C USA
Elkhart 40 D5 Indiana, N USA
Elk River 43 E3 Minnesota, N USA
Ellef Ringnes Island 33 G2 island Nunavut, N Canada
Ellensburg 49 C2 Washington, NW USA
Ellesmere Island 33 H1 island Queen Elizabeth Islands, Nunavut, N Canada
Ellesmere, Lake 139 C6 South Island, New Zealand
Ellesmere Port 93 C4 C England, United Kingdom
Elliston 137 E5 South Australia
Ellon 91 F3 NE Scotland, United Kingdom
Ellsworth 37 G2 Maine, NE USA
Ellsworth Land 142 A5 physical region Antarctica
El Mahbas 70 B3 SW Western Sahara
Elmira 37 C4 New York, NE USA
El Mreyyé 72 C2 desert E Mauritania
Elmshorn 101 C2 N Germany
El Muglad 75 B3 C Sudan
El Obeid 75 C3 C Sudan
El Oued 70 E2 NE Algeria
Eloy 44 B3 Arizona, SW USA
El Paso 44 D4 Texas, SW USA
El Porvenir 55 H6 N Panama
El Progreso 55 C3 NW Honduras
El Puerto de Santa María 99 C6 SW Spain
El Rama 55 E4 SE Nicaragua
El Real 55 I6 SE Panama
El Reno 43 C8 Oklahoma, C USA
El Salvador 55 B4 ◆ republic Central America
El Sáuz 53 C2 N Mexico
Elst 84 E4 E Netherlands
El Sueco 53 C2 N Mexico
El Tigre 63 D2 Colombia
Elvas 99 B4 C Portugal
El Vendrell 99 G3 NE Spain
Elwell, Lake 47 D1 Montana, NW USA
Elx see Elche
Ely 95 G2 E England, United Kingdom
Ely 47 C5 Nevada, W USA
Ely 93 C7 SE Wales, United Kingdom
El Yunque 55 I1 ▲ E Puerto Rico
Emba 118 B5 W Kazakhstan
Emden 101 B3 NW Germany
Emerald 137 G4 Queensland, E Australia
Emeti 141 A2 SW Papua New Guinea
Emi Koussi 72 H2 ▲ N Chad

◆ Administrative region ◆ Country ● Country capital ◇ Dependent territory ○ Dependent territory capital Mountain range ▲ Mountain Volcano River Lake Reservoir

mmeloord 84 E3 N Netherlands
mmen 84 F3 NE Netherlands
mmendingen 101 B7 SW Germany
mory Peak 44 E5 ▲ Texas, SW USA
mpalme 53 B3 NW Mexico
mperor Seamounts 15 *undersea feature* NW Pacific Ocean
mporia 43 D6 Kansas, C USA
mpty Quarter 123 D6 *desert* SW Asia
ms 101 B3 〰 NW Germany
nard Bay 91 C2 *bay* NW Scotland, United Kingdom
ncarnación 65 C4 S Paraguay
ncinitas 49 D9 California, W USA
ncs 105 F6 NE Hungary
ndeavour Strait 137 F1 *strait* Queensland, NE Australia
nderby Land 142 D3 *physical region* Antarctica
nghien 84 C7 SW Belgium
ngland 87 E6 ◐ *national region* United Kingdom
nglish Channel 87 E8 *channel* NW Europe
nguri 121 G1 〰 NW Georgia
nid 43 C7 Oklahoma, C USA
nnedi 72 H2 *plateau* E Chad
nnis 89 C5 W Ireland
nnis 44 H3 Texas, SW USA
nniscorthy 89 E5 SE Ireland
nniskillen 89 D3 SW Northern Ireland, United Kingdom
nnistimon 89 B5 W Ireland
nns 101 E7 〰 C Austria
nschede 84 F4 E Netherlands
nsenada 53 A1 NW Mexico
ntebbe 75 C5 S Uganda
ntroncamento 99 B4 C Portugal
nugu 72 F5 S Nigeria
péna 76 B1 NE Congo
phrata 37 D5 Pennsylvania, NE USA
pi 141 H5 *island* C Vanuatu
pinal 97 F3 NE France
pping 95 G3 SE England, United Kingdom
quatorial Guinea 72 F6 ◆ *republic* C Africa
rciş 121 G3 E Turkey
rdenet 129 E2 N Mongolia
rdi 72 H2 *plateau* NE Chad
rebus, Mount 142 C6 🌋 Ross Island, Antarctica
reğli 121 D4 S Turkey
renhot 129 F2 NE China
rfurt 101 C5 C Germany
rgene Çayi 120 A2 〰 NW Turkey
rgun He *see* Argun
riboll, Loch 91 D2 *inlet* NW Scotland, United Kingdom
richt, Loch 91 D4 ◎ C Scotland, United Kingdom
rie 37 B4 Pennsylvania, NE USA
rie, Lake 40 F5 ◎ Canada/USA
riskay 91 A4 *island* NW Scotland, United Kingdom
ritrea 75 D2 ◆ *transitional government* E Africa
rlangen 101 C6 S Germany
rmelo 84 E3 C Netherlands
rmióni 107 E6 S Greece
rnakulam 127 D7 SW India
rne 89 D3 〰 Ireland/Northern Ireland, United Kingdom
rode 127 D7 SE India
rquelinnes 84 C7 S Belgium
r-Rachidia 70 C2 E Morocco
r Rahad 75 C3 C Sudan
rrigal Mountain 89 C1 ▲ N Ireland
rris Head 89 A3 *headland* W Ireland
rromango 141 G5 *island* S Vanuatu
rzgebirge *see* Ore Mountains
rzincan 121 F3 E Turkey
rzurum 121 G3 NE Turkey
sbjerg 83 A7 W Denmark
scanaba 40 C3 Michigan, N USA
sch-sur-Alzette 84 E9 S Luxembourg
scondido 49 D9 California, W USA
scudilla Mountain 44 C3 ▲ Arizona, SW USA
scuinapa 53 D4 C Mexico
scuintla 55 A3 S Guatemala
scuintla 53 H6 SE Mexico
sha Ness 91 A6 *headland* NE Scotland, United Kingdom
shkamesh 125 F4 NE Afghanistan
sk 91 E6 〰 England/Scotland, United Kingdom
sk 93 E3 〰 N England, United Kingdom
skişehir 120 B3 W Turkey
smeraldas 63 B3 N Ecuador
spanola 44 D2 New Mexico, SW USA
sperance 137 C5 Western Australia
speranza 53 C3 NW Mexico
speranza 142 A3 *Argentinian research station* Antarctica
spírito Santo 63 G7 *state* E Brazil
spiritu Santo 141 G4 *island* W Vanuatu
spoo 83 E5 S Finland
squel 65 A7 SW Argentina
ssaouira 70 B2 W Morocco
ssen 84 C5 N Belgium
ssen 101 A4 W Germany
stacado, Llano 44 F3 *plain* New Mexico/Texas, SW USA
stados, Isla de los 65 B9 *island* S Argentina
stância 63 I5 E Brazil
stelí 55 D4 NW Nicaragua
stella 99 E2 N Spain
stepona 99 C6 S Spain
stevan 33 H7 Saskatchewan, S Canada
stonia 83 F6 ◆ *republic* NE Europe
strela, Serra da 99 B3 ⛰ C Portugal
Estremoz 99 B4 S Portugal
Esztergom 105 D7 N Hungary
Étalle 84 D9 SE Belgium
Etawah 127 E3 N India
Ethiopia 75 D4 ◆ *republic* E Africa
Ethiopian Highlands 75 D4 *plateau* N Ethiopia
Etna, Mount 103 D8 🌋 Sicily, Italy
Etosha Pan 76 B5 *salt lake* N Namibia
Etrek 125 B3 〰 Iran/Turkmenistan
Ettelbrück 84 E8 C Luxembourg
Euboea 65 E5 *island* C Greece
Eucla 137 D5 Western Australia
Euclid 40 F5 Ohio, N USA
Eufaula Lake 43 E8 ⊡ Oklahoma, C USA
Eugene 49 B4 Oregon, NW USA
Eupen 84 E7 E Belgium
Euphrates 123 C3 〰 SW Asia
Eureka 49 A5 California, W USA
Eureka 47 C1 Montana, NW USA
Eureka 47 B5 Nevada, W USA
Europe 78 *continent*
Eutin 101 C2 N Germany
Evansdale 43 F4 Iowa, C USA
Evanston 40 C5 Illinois, N USA
Evanston 47 D4 Wyoming, C USA
Evansville 40 C8 Indiana, N USA
Eveleth 43 E2 Minnesota, N USA
Everard, Lake 137 D5 *salt lake* South Australia
Everest, Mount 129 B5 ▲ China/Nepal
Everett 49 B2 Washington, NW USA
Everglades City 39 G8 Florida, SE USA
Everglades, The 39 G8 *wetland* Florida, SE USA
Evesham 93 D6 C England, United Kingdom
Evje 83 B6 S Norway
Évora 99 B4 C Portugal
Évreux 97 D2 N France
Évros 107 F4 〰 SE Europe
Évvoia *see* Euboea
'Ewa Beach 51 B1 O'ahu, Hawaii, USA
Excelsior Springs 43 E6 Missouri, C USA
Exe 95 C4 〰 SW England, United Kingdom
Exeter 95 C5 SW England, United Kingdom
Exmoor 95 C4 *moorland* SW England, United Kingdom
Exmouth 137 A3 Western Australia
Exmouth 95 C5 SW England, United Kingdom
Exmouth Gulf 137 A3 *gulf* Western Australia
Extremadura 99 C4 *cultural region* W Spain
Exuma Cays 57 D2 *islets* C Bahamas
Exuma Sound 57 D2 *sound* C Bahamas
Eyemouth 91 F6 SE Scotland, United Kingdom
Eye Peninsula 91 B2 *peninsula* NW Scotland, United Kingdom
Eyre Basin, Lake 137 E4 *salt lake* South Australia
Eyre Mountains 139 B7 ⛰ South Island, New Zealand
Eyre North, Lake 137 E4 *salt lake* South Australia
Eyre Peninsula 137 E5 *peninsula* South Australia
Eyre South, Lake 137 E5 *salt lake* South Australia

F

Faaa 141 A6 W French Polynesia
Faadhippolhu Atoll 127 C8 *atoll* N Maldives
Fabens 44 D4 Texas, SW USA
Fada 72 H2 E Chad
Fada-Ngourma 72 D4 E Burkina
Faenza 103 C3 N Italy
Fagamalo 141 A4 N Samoa
Fagne 84 C8 *hill range* S Belgium
Faguibine, Lac 72 C3 ◎ NW Mali
Fairbanks 50 E2 Alaska, USA
Fairfield 49 B6 California, W USA
Fair Isle 91 A7 *island* NE Scotland, United Kingdom
Fairlie 139 B6 South Island, New Zealand
Fairmont 43 E4 Minnesota, N USA
Faisalabad 127 D2 NE Pakistan
Faizabad 127 E3 N India
Fakenham 95 G1 E England, United Kingdom
Fakfak 131 H7 E Indonesia
Falam 131 A2 W Burma (Myanmar)
Falconara Marittima 103 D4 C Italy
Falcon Reservoir 44 G6 ⊡ Mexico/USA
Falealupo 141 A4 NW Samoa
Falkirk 91 D5 C Scotland, United Kingdom
Falkland Islands 65 C8 *UK* ◇ SW Atlantic Ocean
Fallbrook 49 D9 California, W USA
Falmouth 95 A6 SW England, United Kingdom
Falster 83 B7 *island* SE Denmark
Falun 83 C5 C Sweden
Famagusta 112 D6 E Cyprus
Famagusta Bay 112 D6 *bay* E Cyprus
Famenne 84 D8 *physical region* SE Belgium
Fannich, Loch 91 C3 ◎ NW Scotland, United Kingdom
Fano 103 D3 C Italy
Farafangana 76 G6 SE Madagascar
Farah 125 D5 W Afghanistan
Farah Rud 125 D5 〰 W Afghanistan
Faranah 72 B4 S Guinea
Farasan, Jaza'ir 123 B6 *island group* SW Saudi Arabia
Fareham 95 E5 S England, United Kingdom
Farewell, Cape 139 C4 *headland* South Island, New Zealand
Fargo 43 D2 North Dakota, N USA
Farg'ona 125 G3 E Uzbekistan
Faribault 43 E3 Minnesota, N USA
Faridabad 127 D3 N India
Farkhor 125 F4 SW Tajikistan
Farmington 43 G7 Missouri, C USA
Farmington 44 C1 New Mexico, SW USA
Farnborough 95 F4 S England, United Kingdom
Farne Islands 93 D1 *island group* N England, United Kingdom
Farnham 95 F4 S England, United Kingdom
Faro 99 B5 S Portugal
Farquhar Group 76 H3 *island group* S Seychelles
Farranfore 89 B6 SW Ireland
Fastiv 109 D4 NW Ukraine
Fastnet Rock 89 B7 *island* SW Ireland
Fauske 83 C2 C Norway
Faversham 95 G4 SE England, United Kingdom
Faxaflói 83 A1 *bay* W Iceland
Faya 72 H2 N Chad
Fayaoué 141 G6 C New Caledonia
Fayetteville 39 A3 Arkansas, C USA
Fayetteville 39 H3 North Carolina, SE USA
Fdérik 72 B1 NW Mauritania
Feale 89 B6 〰 SW Ireland
Fear, Cape 39 H4 *headland* Bald Head Island, North Carolina, SE USA
Fécamp 97 C1 N France
Fehérgyarmat 105 G7 E Hungary
Fehmarn 101 C2 *island* N Germany
Fehmarn Belt 101 C2 *strait* Denmark /Germany
Feijó 63 C5 W Brazil
Feilding 139 D4 North Island, New Zealand
Feira de Santana 63 H5 E Brazil
Felanitx 99 H4 E Spain
Felipe Carrillo Puerto 53 I4 SE Mexico
Felixstowe 95 H3 E England, United Kingdom
Femunden 83 B4 ◎ S Norway
Fenoarivo Arsinanana 76 G5 E Madagascar
Fens, The 95 G1 *wetland* E England, United Kingdom
Feodosiya 109 F6 S Ukraine
Ferbane 89 D4 C Ireland
Fergana Valley 125 G3 *basin* Tajikistan/Uzbekistan
Fergus Falls 43 D2 Minnesota, N USA
Ferkessédougou 72 C4 N Ivory Coast
Fermo 103 D4 C Italy
Fermoy 89 C6 SW Ireland
Ferrara 103 C3 N Italy
Ferrol 99 B1 NW Spain
Ferwert 84 E2 N Netherlands
Fethiye 120 B5 SW Turkey
Fetlar 91 B6 *island* NE Scotland, United Kingdom
Feuilles, Rivière aux 35 D2 〰 Québec, E Canada
Feyzabad 125 G4 NE Afghanistan
Fez 70 C1 N Morocco
Fezzan 70 G4 *cultural region* S Libya
Fianarantsoa 76 G5 C Madagascar
Fianga 72 G4 SW Chad
Fier 107 D4 SW Albania
Figeac 97 D5 S France
Figueira da Foz 99 A3 W Portugal
Figueres 99 H2 E Spain
Figuig 70 D2 E Morocco
Fiji 141 I5 ◆ *republic* SW Pacific Ocean
Filadelfia 55 D6 W Costa Rica
Filey 93 F3 N England, United Kingdom
Filey Bay 93 F3 *bay* N England, United Kingdom
Filipstad 83 C5 C Sweden
Finale Ligure 103 B3 NW Italy
Findhorn 91 E3 〰 N Scotland, United Kingdom
Findlay 40 E6 Ohio, N USA
Finger Lakes 37 C4 ◎ New York, NE USA
Finike 120 B5 SW Turkey
Finland 83 E4 ◆ *republic* N Europe
Finland, Gulf of 83 E5 *gulf* E Baltic Sea
Finnmarksvidda 83 D1 *physical region* N Norway
Finschhafen 141 C2 C Papua New Guinea
Finsterwalde 101 D4 E Germany
Fiordland 139 A7 *physical region* South Island, New Zealand
Firenze *see* Florence
Fischbacher Alpen 101 F7 ⛰ E Austria
Fish 76 C6 〰 S Namibia
Fishguard 93 A6 SW Wales, United Kingdom
Fisterra, Cabo 99 A1 *cape* NW Spain
Fitful Head 91 A7 *headland* NE Scotland, United Kingdom
Fito 141 B5 ▲ Upolu, C Samoa
Fitzroy Crossing 137 C2 Western Australia
Fitzroy River 137 C2 〰 Western Australia
Flagstaff 44 B2 Arizona, SW USA
Flamborough Head 93 F3 *headland* E England, United Kingdom
Fläming 105 A3 *hill range* NE Germany
Flanders 84 A6 *cultural region* Belgium/France
Flannan Isles 91 A2 *island group* NW Scotland, United Kingdom
Flathead Lake 47 C2 ◎ Montana, NW USA
Flattery, Cape 49 A1 *headland* Washington, NW USA
Fleetwood 93 C4 NW England, United Kingdom
Flensburg 101 C2 N Germany
Flinders 137 F3 〰 Queensland, N Australia Oceania
Flinders Island 137 G7 *island* Furneaux Group, Tasmania, SE Australia
Flinders Ranges 137 F5 ⛰ South Australia
Flin Flon 33 H6 Manitoba, C Canada
Flint 93 C5 NE Wales, United Kingdom
Flint 40 E4 Michigan, N USA
Flint Island 135 *island* Line Islands, E Kiribati
Flitwick 95 F3 C England, United Kingdom
Florence 103 D3 C Italy
Florence 39 D4 Alabama, S USA
Florence 39 G4 South Carolina, SE USA
Florencia 63 B3 S Colombia
Flores 55 B2 N Guatemala
Flores 131 F8 *island* Nusa Tenggara, C Indonesia
Flores Sea 131 E8 *sea* C Indonesia
Floriano 63 H4 E Brazil
Florianópolis 63 G8 S Brazil
Florida 65 C5 S Uruguay
Florida 39 F6 ◐ *state* SE USA
Florida Keys 39 G9 *island group* Florida, SE USA
Florida, Straits of 39 H9 *strait* Atlantic Ocean/Gulf of Mexico
Florissant 43 G6 Missouri, C USA
Fly 141 A2 〰 Indonesia/Papua New Guinea
Foča 107 C2 SE Bosnia and Herzegovina
Focșani 109 C6 E Romania
Foggia 103 E5 SE Italy
Foix 97 C7 S France
Foleyet 35 C5 Ontario, S Canada
Foligno 103 D4 C Italy
Folkestone 95 H4 SE England, United Kingdom
Fond du Lac 40 C4 Wisconsin, N USA
Fongafale 141 J3 ● SE Tuvalu
Fonseca, Gulf of 55 C4 *gulf* C Central America
Fontainebleau 97 D3 N France
Fontenay-le-Comte 97 C4 NW France
Fonyód 105 D8 W Hungary
Forchheim 101 C6 SE Germany
Forfar 91 E4 E Scotland, United Kingdom
Forlì 103 C3 N Italy
Formby 93 C4 NW England, United Kingdom
Formentera 99 G4 *island* Balearic Islands, E Spain
Formosa 65 C4 NE Argentina
Formosa, Serra 63 F5 ⛰ C Brazil
Forres 91 E3 NE Scotland, United Kingdom
Forrest City 39 C3 Arkansas, C USA
Fort Albany 35 C4 Ontario, C Canada
Fortaleza 65 B1 N Bolivia
Fortaleza 63 H4 NE Brazil
Fort Augustus 91 D4 N Scotland, United Kingdom
Fort Collins 47 F5 Colorado, C USA
Fort Davis 44 E4 Texas, SW USA
Fort-de-France 57 K5 ○ W Martinique
Fort Dodge 43 E4 Iowa, C USA
Fortescue River 137 B3 〰 Western Australia
Fort Frances 35 A4 Ontario, S Canada
Fort Good Hope 33 F4 Northwest Territories, NW Canada
Forth 91 E6 C Scotland, United Kingdom
Forth 91 D5 〰 C Scotland, United Kingdom
Forth, Firth of 91 E5 *estuary* E Scotland, United Kingdom
Fort Lauderdale 39 G8 Florida, SE USA
Fort Liard 33 F5 Northwest Territories, W Canada
Fort Madison 43 F5 Iowa, C USA
Fort McMurray 33 G6 Alberta, C Canada
Fort McPherson 33 E4 Northwest Territories, NW Canada
Fort Morgan 47 F5 Colorado, C USA
Fort Myers 39 G8 Florida, SE USA
Fort Nelson 33 F5 British Columbia, W Canada
Fort Peck Lake 47 E2 ⊡ Montana, NW USA
Fort Pierce 39 G8 Florida, SE USA
Fort Providence 33 F5 Northwest Territories, W Canada
Fort St. John 33 F6 British Columbia, W Canada
Fort Scott 43 E7 Kansas, C USA
Fort Severn 35 B2 Ontario, C Canada
Fort-Shevchenko 118 A5 W Kazakhstan
Fort Simpson 33 F5 Northwest Territories, W Canada
Fort Smith 33 G5 Northwest Territories, W Canada
Fort Smith 39 A3 Arkansas, C USA
Fort Stockton 44 E4 Texas, SW USA
Fort Vermilion 33 F6 Alberta, W Canada
Fort Walton Beach 39 D6 Florida, SE USA
Fort Wayne 40 D6 Indiana, N USA
Fort William 91 C4 N Scotland, United Kingdom
Fort Worth 44 H3 Texas, SW USA
Fort Yukon 50 F2 Alaska, USA
Fougères 97 C2 NW France
Foula 91 A6 *island* NE Scotland, United Kingdom
Foulness Island 95 H3 *island* SE England, United Kingdom
Foulwind, Cape 139 B5 *headland* South Island, New Zealand
Foumban 72 F5 NW Cameroon
Foveaux Strait 139 A8 *strait* S New Zealand
Fowey 95 B5 〰 SW England, United Kingdom
Foxe Basin 33 I3 *sea* Nunavut, N Canada
Foxford 89 C3 NW Ireland
Fox Glacier 139 B6 South Island, New Zealand
Foyle 89 D2 〰 Ireland/Northern Ireland, United Kingdom
Foyle, Lough 89 D1 *inlet* N Ireland
Foynes 89 B5 SW Ireland
Fraga 99 F2 NE Spain
Fram Basin 143 C4 *undersea feature* Arctic Ocean
France 97 C4 ◆ *republic* W Europe
Franceville 76 B2 E Gabon
Franche-Comté 97 E4 *region* E France
Francis Case, Lake 43 C4 ⊡ South Dakota, N USA
Francisco Escárcega 53 H5 SE Mexico
Francistown 76 D5 NE Botswana
Frankfort 39 E2 *state capital* Kentucky, S USA
Frankfurt am Main 101 B5 SW Germany
Frankfurt an der Oder 101 E4 E Germany
Fränkische Alb 101 C6 〰 S Germany
Franklin 39 D3 Tennessee, S USA
Franklin D. Roosevelt Lake 49 C2 ⊡ Washington, NW USA
Franz Josef Land 118 D1 *island group* N Russian Federation
Fraserburgh 91 F3 NE Scotland, United Kingdom
Fraser Island 137 H4 *island* Queensland, E Australia
Fray Bentos 65 C5 W Uruguay
Fredericksburg 39 H2 Virginia, NE USA
Fredericton 35 F5 *province capital* New Brunswick, SE Canada
Frederiksted 51 S Virgin Islands (USA)
Fredonia 44 B1 Arizona, SW USA
Fredrikstad 83 B5 S Norway
Freeport 57 D1 N Bahamas
Freeport 40 B5 Illinois, N USA
Freeport 44 H5 Texas, SW USA
Freetown 72 B4 ● W Sierra Leone
Freiburg im Breisgau 101 B7 SW Germany
Fremantle 137 B5 Western Australia
Fremont 43 D5 Nebraska, C USA
Fremont 40 E6 Ohio, N USA
French Guiana 63 F2 *French* ◇ N South America
French Polynesia 135 *French* ◇ S Pacific Ocean
Fresnillo 53 E4 C Mexico
Fresno 49 C7 California, W USA
Frías 65 B4 N Argentina
Friedrichshafen 101 B7 S Germany
Frobisher Bay *see* Iqaluit
Frohavet 83 B4 *sound* C Norway
Frome 95 D4 SW England, United Kingdom
Frome 95 D5 〰 S England, United Kingdom
Frome, Lake 137 F5 *salt lake* South Australia
Frontera 53 H5 SE Mexico
Frontignan 97 D6 S France
Frøya 83 B4 *island* W Norway
Frýdek-Místek 105 D6 E Czech Republic
Fuengirola 99 D6 S Spain
Fuerte Olimpo 65 C3 NE Paraguay
Fuji, Mount 133 F6 ▲ Honshū, SE Japan
Fukui 133 F6 SW Japan
Fukuoka 133 D7 SW Japan
Fukushima 133 G4 C Japan
Fulda 101 C5 C Germany
Funafuti Atoll 141 J3 *atoll* C Tuvalu
Fundy, Bay of 35 F5 *bay* Canada/USA
Fürth 101 C6 S Germany
Furukawa 133 G4 C Japan
Fushun 129 G2 NE China
Füssen 101 C7 S Germany
Futuna 141 H5 *island* S Vanuatu
Futuna, Île 141 J4 *island* S Wallis and Futuna
Fuxin 129 G2 NE China
Fuzhou 129 G5 SE China
Fyn 83 B7 *island* C Denmark
Fyne, Loch 91 C5 *inlet* W Scotland, United Kingdom

Gaalkacyo 75 F4 C Somalia
Gabela 76 B3 W Angola
Gabès 70 F2 E Tunisia
Gabès, Golfe de 70 F2 *gulf* E Tunisia
Gabon 76 A1 ◆ *republic* C Africa
Gaborone 76 D6 ● SE Botswana
Gabrovo 107 F3 N Bulgaria
Gadag 127 D6 W India
Gadsden 39 E4 Alabama, S USA
Gaeta 103 D5 C Italy
Gaeta, Gulf of 103 C5 *gulf* C Italy
Gafsa 70 E2 W Tunisia
Gagnoa 72 C5 C Ivory Coast
Gagra 121 F1 NW Georgia
Gaillac 97 C6 S France
Gainesville 39 F6 Florida, SE USA
Gainesville 39 F4 Georgia, SE USA
Gainesville 44 H3 Texas, SW USA
Gainsborough 93 E4 E England, United Kingdom
Gairdner, Lake 137 E5 *salt lake* South Australia
Galán, Cerro 65 A4 ▲ NW Argentina
Galanta 105 D7 W Slovakia
Galapagos Islands 63 A7 *island group* Ecuador, E Pacific Ocean
Galashiels 91 E6 SE Scotland, United Kingdom
Galați 109 D7 E Romania
Galesburg 40 B6 Illinois, N USA
Galicia 99 B1 *cultural region* NW Spain Europe
Galkynys 125 E3 NE Turkmenistan
Galle 127 E8 SW Sri Lanka
Gallipoli 103 F6 SE Italy
Gällivare 83 D2 N Sweden
Galloway, Mull of 91 C7 *headland* S Scotland, United Kingdom
Gallup 44 C2 New Mexico, SW USA
Galtat-Zemmour 70 B3 C Western Sahara
Galty Mountains 89 C6 ⛰ S Ireland
Galveston 44 I5 Texas, SW USA
Galway 89 C4 W Ireland
Galway Bay 89 B4 *bay* W Ireland
Gambell 50 D1 Saint Lawrence Island, Alaska, USA
Gambia 72 A3 ◆ *republic* W Africa
Gambia 72 B3 〰 W Africa
Gambier, Îles 135 *island group* E French Polynesia
Gamboma 76 B2 E Congo
Ganado 44 C2 Arizona, SW USA
Gäncä 121 H2 W Azerbaijan
Gandajika 76 C3 S Dem. Rep. Congo
Gander 35 H4 Newfoundland, Newfoundland and Labrador, SE Canada
Gandhidham 127 C4 W India
Gandia 99 F4 E Spain
Ganges 127 G3 〰 Bangladesh/India
Ganges, Mouths of the 127 G4 *delta* Bangladesh/India
Gangneung 133 C5 NE South Korea
Gangtok 127 G3 N India
Gannett Peak 47 D4 ▲ Wyoming, C USA
Ganzhou 129 G5 S China
Gao 72 D3 E Mali
Gaoual 72 B4 N Guinea
Gaoxiong 129 H6 S Taiwan
Gap 97 E6 SE France
Gaplaňgyr Platosy 125 C2 *ridge* Turkmenistan/Uzbekistan
Garabil Belentligi 125 D4 ⛰ Mary Welaýaty, S Turkmenistan
Garabogaz Aylagy 125 B2 *bay* NW Turkmenistan
Garachiné 55 I7 SE Panama
Garagum 125 D3 *desert* C Turkmenistan
Garagum Canal 125 E4 *canal* C Turkmenistan
Gara, Lough 89 C3 ◎ N Ireland
Garda, Lake 103 C2 ◎ NE Italy
Garden City 43 B7 Kansas, C USA
Gardez 125 F5 E Afghanistan
Garforth 93 D4 N England, United Kingdom
Garissa 75 E5 E Kenya
Garonne 97 C5 〰 S France
Garoowe 75 F3 N Somalia
Garoua 72 G4 N Cameroon
Garrison 89 D2 W Northern Ireland, United Kingdom
Garron Point 89 F2 *headland* E Northern Ireland, United Kingdom
Garry Lake 33 H4 ◎ Nunavut, N Canada
Garsen 75 E6 S Kenya
Garth 91 A6 NE Scotland, United Kingdom
Garwolin 105 F4 E Poland
Gar Xincun 129 A4 W China
Gary 40 C5 Indiana, N USA
Gascogne *see* Gascony
Gascony 97 C6 *cultural region* S France
Gascony, Gulf of 97 B6 *gulf* France/Spain
Gascoyne River 137 B4 〰 Western Australia
Gasmata 141 C2 E Papua New Guinea
Gaspé 35 F4 Québec, SE Canada
Gaspé, Péninsule de 35 F4 *peninsula* Québec, SE Canada
Gastonia 39 G3 North Carolina, SE USA
Gatchina 111 A4 NW Russian Federation
Gateshead 93 D2 NE England, United Kingdom
Gatineau 35 D5 Québec, SE Canada
Gatún, Lake 55 G6 ⊡ C Panama
Gavbandi 123 E4 S Iran
Gavere 84 B6 NW Belgium
Gävle 83 D5 C Sweden
Gawler 137 E6 South Australia
Gaya 127 F3 N India
Gayndah 137 H4 Queensland, E Australia
Gaza 123 G6 NE Gaza Strip
Gaza Strip 123 G6 *disputed region* SW Asia
Gaziantep 121 E4 S Turkey
Gazimağusa *see* Famagusta
Gazli 125 E3 C Uzbekistan
Gazojak 125 D2 NE Turkmenistan
Gbanga 72 B5 N Liberia
Gdańsk 105 D2 N Poland
Gdynia 105 D1 N Poland
Gedaref 75 D2 E Sudan
Gediz 120 B3 W Turkey
Gediz Nehri 120 A3 〰 W Turkey
Geel 84 D6 N Belgium
Geelong 137 F6 Victoria, SE Australia
Geilo 83 B5 S Norway
Gejiu 129 E6 S China
Gela 103 D8 Sicily, Italy

Geldermalsen *84 D4* C Netherlands
Geleen *84 E6* SE Netherlands
Gellinsor *75 F4* C Somalia
Gembloux *84 C7* Belgium
Gemena *76 C1* NW Dem. Rep. Congo
Gemona del Friuli *103 D2* NE Italy
General Alvear *65 B5* W Argentina
General Eugenio A. Garay *65 B3* S Paraguay
General Santos *131 F5* S Philippines
Geneva *101 A8* SW Switzerland
Geneva, Lake *101 A8* ◎ France/ Switzerland
Genève *see* Geneva
Genk *84 D6* NE Belgium
Gennep *84 E5* SE Netherlands
Genoa *103 B3* NW Italy
Genoa, Gulf of *103 B3 gulf* NW Italy
Genova *see* Genoa
Gent *see* Ghent
Geogeum-do *133 C7 island* S South Korea
George, Lake *39 G7* ◎ Florida, SE USA
Georgetown *63 E2* ● N Guyana
George Town *57 D2* C Bahamas
George Town *57 B4* ○ SW Cayman Islands
George Town *131 B5* C Malaysia
Georgetown *39 H4* South Carolina, SE USA
George V Land *142 C6 physical region* Antarctica
Georgia *121 G1* ◆ *republic* SW Asia
Georgia *39 E5* ⬖ *state* SE USA
Georgian Bay *40 F3 lake bay* Ontario, S Canada
Georgia, Strait of *49 A1 strait* British Columbia, W Canada
Georg von Neumayer *142 B3 German research station* Antarctica
Gera *101 D5* E Germany
Geraldine *139 C6* South Island, New Zealand
Geraldton *137 B5* Western Australia
Gerede *121 C2* N Turkey
Gereshk *125 E6* SW Afghanistan
Gering *43 A5* Nebraska, C USA
Gerlach *47 A5* Nevada, W USA
Gerlachovský štít *105 E6* ▲ N Slovakia
Germany *101 B5* ◆ *federal republic* N Europe
Gerona *see* Girona
Gerpinnes *84 C7* S Belgium
Gerze *121 D2* N Turkey
Getafe *99 D3* C Spain
Gevaş *121 H4* SE Turkey
Ghana *72 D5* ◆ *republic* W Africa
Ghanzi *76 C5* W Botswana
Ghardaïa *70 E2* N Algeria
Gharyan *70 F2* NW Libya
Ghazni *125 F5* E Afghanistan
Ghent *84 B6* NW Belgium
Ghorian *125 D5* W Afghanistan
Ghudara *125 G3* SE Tajikistan
Giannitsá *107 E4* N Greece
Gibraltar *99 C6 UK* ◇ SW Europe
Gibraltar, Strait of *99 strait* Atlantic Ocean/Mediterranean Sea
Gibson Desert *137 C4 desert* Western Australia
Giedraičiai *83 F7* E Lithuania
Giessen *101 B5* W Germany
Giffnock *91 D6* C Scotland, United Kingdom
Gifu *133 F6* SW Japan
Giganta, Sierra de la *53 B3* ⛰ W Mexico
Gigha Island *91 B6 island* SW Scotland, United Kingdom
G'ijduvon *125 E3* C Uzbekistan
Gijón *99 C1* NW Spain
Gila River *44 A3* ≈ Arizona, SW USA
Gilf Kebir Plateau *70 H4 plateau* SW Egypt
Gilford *89 E3* SE Northern Ireland, United Kingdom
Gillette *47 F3* Wyoming, C USA
Gillingham *95 G4* SE England, United Kingdom
Gilroy *49 B7* California, W USA
Giluwe, Mount *141 B2* ▲ W Papua New Guinea
Gingin *137 B5* Western Australia
Giresun *121 E2* NE Turkey
Girne *112 C6* N Cyprus
Girona *99 H2* NE Spain
Girvan *91 D6* W Scotland, United Kingdom
Gisborne *139 E3* NE New Zealand
Gissar Range *125 F3* ⛰ Tajikistan/ Uzbekistan
Giulianova *103 D4* C Italy
Giurgiu *109 C7* S Romania
Giza *70 I2* N Egypt
Gizo *141 E2* NW Solomon Islands
Gjeravicë *107 D3* ▲ C Kosovo
Gjirokastër *107 D4* S Albania
Gjoa Haven *33 H3* King William Island, Nunavut, NW Canada
Gjøvik *83 B5* S Norway
Glace Bay *35 G5* Cape Breton Island, Nova Scotia, SE Canada
Glacier Peak *49 B2* ▲ Washington, NW USA
Gladstone *137 H4* Queensland, E Australia
Glåma *83 B5* ≈ S Norway
Glasgow *91 D6* S Scotland, United Kingdom
Glastonbury *95 D4* SW England, United Kingdom
Glazov *111 D5* NW Russian Federation
Glenamoy *89 B3* NW Ireland
Glen Coe *91 C4 valley* N Scotland, United Kingdom
Glendale *44 B3* Arizona, SW USA
Glendale *49 C8* California, W USA
Glendive *47 F2* Montana, NW USA
Glengad Head *89 D1 headland* N Ireland
Glengarriff *89 B7* S Ireland
Glenluce *91 D7* SW Scotland, United Kingdom
Glen Mor *91 D4 valley* NW Scotland, United Kingdom
Glenrothes *91 E5* E Scotland, United Kingdom
Glens Falls *37 E3* New York, NE USA
Glenties *89 C2* NW Ireland
Glin *89 B5* SW Ireland
Glittertind *83 B4* ▲ S Norway
Gliwice *105 D5* S Poland
Globe *44 B3* Arizona, SW USA
Głogów *105 C4* SW Poland
Gloucester *141 C2* E Papua New Guinea
Gloucester *95 D3* C England, United Kingdom
Glovers Reef *55 C2 reef* E Belize
Głowno *105 E3* C Poland
Gniezno *105 D3* C Poland
Gobabis *76 C5* E Namibia
Gobi *129 E3 desert* China/Mongolia
Gobo *133 E7* SW Japan
Godalming *95 F4* SE England, United Kingdom
Godavari *127 E5* ≈ C India
Godhra *127 D4* W India
Godoy Cruz *65 A5* W Argentina
Goeree *84 B5 island* SW Netherlands
Goes *84 B5* SW Netherlands
Gogebic Range *40 B2 hill range* Michigan/Wisconsin, N USA
Goiânia *63 G6* C Brazil
Goiás *63 F6 state* C Brazil
Gojome *133 F3* NW Japan
Gökdepe *125 C3* C Turkmenistan
Göksun *121 E4* C Turkey
Gol *83 B5* S Norway
Golan Heights *123 H5* ⛰ SW Syria
Gołdap *105 F2* NE Poland
Gold Beach *49 A4* Oregon, NW USA
Gold Coast *137 H5* ⬖ *cultural region* Queensland, E Australia
Golden Bay *139 C4 bay* South Island, New Zealand
Goldfield *47 B6* Nevada, W USA
Goldsboro *39 H3* North Carolina, SE USA
Goleniów *105 B2* NW Poland
Golmud *129 D3* C China
Goma *76 D2* NE Dem. Rep. Congo
Gombi *72 G4* E Nigeria
Gómez Palacio *53 D3* C Mexico
Gonaïves *57 F4* N Haiti
Gonâve, Île de la *57 E4 island* C Haiti
Gonder *75 D3* NW Ethiopia
Gondia *127 E4* C India
Gongola *72 F4* ≈ E Nigeria
Good Hope, Cape of *76 B7 cape* SW South Africa
Goodland *43 B6* Kansas, C USA
Goodwick *93 A6* SW Wales, United Kingdom
Goole *93 E4* E England, United Kingdom
Goondiwindi *137 G5* Queensland, E Australia
Goor *84 F4* E Netherlands
Goose Green *65 C9* E Falkland Islands
Goose Lake *49 B5* ◎ California/Oregon, W USA
Göppingen *101 C6* SW Germany
Gorakhpur *127 F3* N India
Goré *72 G5* S Chad
Gore *75 D4* C Ethiopia
Gore *139 B8* South Island, New Zealand
Gorey *89 E5* SE Ireland
Gorey *95 H6* Jersey, Channel Islands
Gorgan *123 E1* N Iran
Gori *121 H1* C Georgia
Gorinchem *84 D5* C Netherlands
Goris *121 I3* SE Armenia
Görlitz *101 E4* E Germany
Goroka *141 B2* C Papua New Guinea
Gorontalo *131 F6* Celebes, C Indonesia
Gorssel *84 E4* E Netherlands
Gort *89 C5* W Ireland
Gorzów Wielkopolski *105 C3* W Poland
Goshogawara *133 F3* C Japan
Gosport *95 E5* S England, United Kingdom
Göteborg *see* Gothenburg
Gotha *101 C5* C Germany
Gothenburg *83 B6* S Sweden
Gotland *83 D6 island* SE Sweden
Goto-retto *133 C8 island group* SW Japan
Gotsu *133 D6* SW Japan
Göttingen *101 C4* C Germany
Gouda *84 C4* C Netherlands
Gouin, Réservoir *35 D4* ⊠ Québec, SE Canada
Goulburn *137 G6* New South Wales, SE Australia
Goundam *72 D3* NW Mali
Gouré *72 F3* SE Niger
Governador Valadares *63 H7* SE Brazil
Govi Altayn Nuruu *129 E2* ⛰ S Mongolia
Gower *93 B7 peninsula* S Wales, United Kingdom
Gowran *89 D5* SE Ireland
Goya *65 C4* NE Argentina
Goz Beïda *72 H4* SE Chad
Gozhě *129 C4* W China
Gozo *112 A6 island* N Malta
Gradačac *107 C2* N Bosnia and Herzegovina
Gradaús, Serra dos *63 F5* ⛰ C Brazil
Grafton *137 H5* New South Wales, SE Australia
Grafton *43 D1* North Dakota, N USA
Graham Land *142 A4 physical region* Antarctica
Grajewo *105 F2* NE Poland
Grampian Mountains *91 D4* ⛰ C Scotland, United Kingdom
Granada *55 D5* SW Nicaragua
Granada *99 D5* S Spain
Gran Chaco *65 B3 lowland plain* South America
Grand Bahama Island *57 C1 island* N Bahamas
Grand Canal *89 C4 canal* C Ireland
Grand Canyon *44 B1 canyon* Arizona, SW USA
Grand Cayman *57 C4 island* SW Cayman Islands
Grande, Bahía *65 B8 bay* S Argentina
Grande de Matagalpa, Río *55 E4* ≈ C Nicaragua
Grande Prairie *33 F6* Alberta, W Canada
Grand Erg Occidental *70 D2 desert* W Algeria
Grand Erg Oriental *70 E3 desert* Algeria/Tunisia
Grande, Rio *44 G5* ≈ Mexico/USA
Grande Terre *57 K5 island* E Guadeloupe
Grand Falls *35 H4* Newfoundland, Newfoundland and Labrador, SE Canada
Grand Forks *43 D2* North Dakota, N USA
Grand Island *43 C5* Nebraska, C USA
Grand Junction *47 E5* Colorado, C USA
Grand Rapids *40 D4* Michigan, N USA
Grand Rapids *43 E2* Minnesota, N USA
Grand Union Canal *95 E2 canal* SE England, United Kingdom
Grange *89 C2* N Ireland
Grangemouth *91 D5* C Scotland, United Kingdom
Granite City *40 B7* Illinois, N USA
Granite Peak *47 B4* ▲ Nevada, W USA
Gran Paradiso *103 A2* ▲ NW Italy
Grantham *93 E6* E England, United Kingdom
Grantown-on-Spey *91 E3* N Scotland, United Kingdom
Grants *44 D2* New Mexico, SW USA
Grantsburg *40 A3* Wisconsin, N USA
Grants Pass *49 B4* Oregon, NW USA
Granville *97 B2* N France
Graulhet *97 C6* S France
Grave *84 E5* SE Netherlands
Gravesend *95 G4* SE England, United Kingdom
Grayling *50 D2* Alaska, USA
Graz *101 E8* SE Austria
Great Abaco *57 D1 island* N Bahamas
Great Artesian Basin *137 F4 lowlands* Queensland, C Australia
Great Australian Bight *137 D5 bight* S Australia
Great Barrier Island *139 D2 island* N New Zealand
Great Barrier Reef *137 G2 reef* Queensland, NE Australia
Great Basin *47 B5 basin* W USA
Great Bear Lake *33 F4* ◎ Northwest Territories, NW Canada
Great Belt *83 B7 channel* Baltic Sea/Kattegat
Great Bend *43 C6* Kansas, C USA
Great Dividing Range *134* ⛰ NE Australia
Greater Antilles *57 E5 island group* West Indies
Greater Caucasus *121 I2* ⛰ N Azerbaijan
Great Exhibition Bay *139 C1 inlet* North Island, New Zealand
Great Exuma Island *57 D2 island* C Bahamas
Great Falls *47 D2* Montana, NW USA
Great Hungarian Plain *105 D8 plain* SE Europe
Great Inagua *57 F3 island* S Bahamas
Great Karoo *76 C7 plateau region* S South Africa
Great Khingan Range *129 G1* ⛰ NE China
Great Lakes *40 lakes* Canada/USA
Great Malvern *93 D6* W England, United Kingdom
Great Nicobar *127 H6 island* SE India
Great Ouse *93 F6* ≈ E England, United Kingdom
Great Plains *43 C5 plains* Canada/USA
Great Rift Valley *65 depression* Asia/Africa
Great Ruaha *75 D7* ≈ S Tanzania
Great Saint Bernard Pass *103 A1 pass* Italy/Switzerland
Great Salt Lake *47 C4 salt lake* Utah, W USA
Great Salt Lake Desert *47 C5 plain* Utah, W USA
Great Salt Plains *43 C7 plain* Oklahoma, C USA
Great Sand Sea *70 H3 desert* Egypt/Libya
Great Sandy Desert *137 C3 desert* Western Australia
Great Slave Lake *33 G5* ◎ Northwest Territories, NW Canada
Great Torrington *95 B4* SW England, United Kingdom
Great Victoria Desert *137 C4 desert* South Australia/Western Australia
Great Wall of China *129 E3 ancient monument* N China Asia
Great Yarmouth *95 H2* E England, United Kingdom
Gredos, Sierra de *99 C3* ⛰ W Spain
Greece *107 D5* ◆ *republic* SE Europe
Greeley *47 F5* Colorado, C USA
Green Bay *40 C3* Wisconsin, N USA
Green Bay *40 C3 lake bay* Michigan/ Wisconsin, N USA
Greencastle *89 E3* S Northern Ireland, United Kingdom
Greeneville *39 F3* Tennessee, S USA
Greenfield *37 E4* Massachusetts, NE USA
Green Islands *141 D2 island group* NE Papua New Guinea
Greenland *28 Danish* ◇ NE North America
Greenland Sea *143 C5 sea* Arctic Ocean
Green Mountains *37 E3* ⛰ Vermont, NE USA
Greenock *91 D5* W Scotland, United Kingdom
Green River *141 A1* NW Papua New Guinea
Green River *47 D5* Utah, W USA
Green River *47 D4* Wyoming, C USA
Green River *47 D5* ≈ W USA
Green River *39 D2* ≈ Kentucky, C USA
Greensboro *39 G3* North Carolina, SE USA
Greensburg *37 B5* Pennsylvania, NE USA
Green Valley *44 B3* Arizona, SW USA
Greenville *39 C4* Mississippi, S USA
Greenville *39 H3* North Carolina, SE USA
Greenville *39 F4* South Carolina, SE USA
Greenville *44 H3* Texas, SW USA
Greenwood *39 C4* Mississippi, S USA
Greenwood *39 F4* South Carolina, SE USA
Gregory Range *137 G3* ⛰ Queensland, E Australia
Greifswald *101 D2* NE Germany
Grenada *39 C4* Mississippi, S USA
Grenada *57 J6* ◆ *commonwealth republic* SE West Indies
Grenadines, The *57 K6 island group* Grenada/St Vincent and the Grenadines
Grenoble *97 E5* E France
Gresham *49 B3* Oregon, NW USA
Gretna *91 E7* SW Scotland, United Kingdom
Grevenmacher *84 E9* E Luxembourg
Greybull *47 E3* Wyoming, C USA
Greymouth *139 B6* South Island, New Zealand
Grey Range *137 F4* ⛰ New South Wales/ Queensland, E Australia
Greystones *89 E4* E Ireland
Griffin *39 E5* Georgia, SE USA
Grimari *72 H5* C Central African Republic
Grimsby *93 F4* E England, United Kingdom
Groesbeek *84 E5* SE Netherlands
Grójec *105 F4* C Poland
Groningen *84 F2* NE Netherlands
Groote Eylandt *137 E2 island* Northern Territory, N Australia
Grootfontein *76 C5* N Namibia
Groot Karasberge *76 C6* ⛰ S Namibia
Grosseto *103 C4* C Italy
Grossglockner *101 D8* ▲ W Austria
Groznyy *111 B9* SW Russian Federation
Grudziądz *105 D2* C Poland
Grums *83 C5* C Sweden
Gryazi *111 B6* W Russian Federation
Gryfice *105 C2* NW Poland
Guabito *55 F6* NW Panama
Guadalajara *53 D5* C Mexico
Guadalajara *99 D3* C Spain
Guadalcanal *141 E3 island* C Solomon Islands
Guadalquivir *99 C5* ≈ W Spain
Guadalupe *53 D4* C Mexico
Guadalupe Peak *44 E4* ▲ Texas, SW USA
Guadalupe River *44 H5* ≈ SW USA
Guadarrama, Sierra de *99 E3* ⛰ C Spain
Guadeloupe *57 K5 French* ◇ E West Indies
Guadiana *99 B4* ≈ Portugal/Spain
Guadix *99 D5* S Spain
Guaimaca *55 D3* C Honduras
Gualaco *55 D3* C Honduras
Gualán *55 B3* C Guatemala
Gualeguaychú *65 C5* E Argentina
Guam *51 US* ◇ W Pacific Ocean
Guamúchil *53 C3* C Mexico
Guanabacoa *57 B2* W Cuba
Guanajuato *53 E4* C Mexico
Guanare *63 C2* N Venezuela
Guangyuan *129 E4* C China
Guangzhou *129 F6* S China
Guantánamo *57 E4* SE Cuba
Guaporé, Rio *63 D5* ≈ Bolivia/Brazil
Guarda *99 B3* N Portugal
Guarumal *55 G7* S Panama
Guasave *53 C3* C Mexico
Guasopa *141 D3* SE Papua New Guinea
Guatemala *55 A3* ◆ *republic* Central America
Guatemala Basin *14 undersea feature* E Pacific Ocean
Guatemala City *55 B3* ● C Guatemala
Guaviare, Río *63 C2* ≈ E Colombia
Guayama *51* E Puerto Rico
Guayaquil *63 A4* SW Ecuador
Guayaquil, Gulf of *63 A4 gulf* SW Ecuador
Guaymas *53 B3* NW Mexico
Guaynabo *51* E Puerto Rico
Gubadag *125 D2* N Turkmenistan
Guben *101 E4* E Germany
Gubkin *111 A6* W Russian Federation
Gudauta *121 F1* NW Georgia
Guéret *97 D4* C France
Guernsey *95 G6 UK* ◇ Channel Islands, NW Europe
Guerrero Negro *53 A3* W Mexico
Guiana Basin *14 undersea feature* W Atlantic Ocean
Guiana Highlands *63 E3* ⛰ N South America
Guider *72 G4* N Cameroon
Guidimouni *72 F3* S Niger
Guildford *95 F4* SE England, United Kingdom
Guilin *129 F5* S China
Guimarães *99 B2* N Portugal
Guinea *72 B4* ◆ *republic* W Africa
Guinea-Bissau *72 A4* ◆ *republic* W Africa
Guinea, Gulf of *72 E6 gulf* E Atlantic Ocean
Guiyang *129 E5* S China
Gujarat *127 C4 cultural region* W India, Asia
Gujranwala *127 D2* NE Pakistan
Gujrat *127 D2* E Pakistan
Gulbarga *127 D5* C India
Gulfport *39 C6* Mississippi, S USA
Gulf, The *see* Persian Gulf
Guliston *125 F3* E Uzbekistan
Gulkana *50 E3* Alaska, USA
Gulu *75 C5* N Uganda
Gümüşhane *121 F2* NE Turkey
Güney Doğu Toroslar *121 F4* ⛰ SE Turkey
Gunnbjørn Fjeld *143 A6* ▲ C Greenland
Gunnedah *137 G5* New South Wales, SE Australia
Gunnison *47 E6* Colorado, C USA
Gunnison *47 D5* Utah, W USA
Gunsan *133 B6* W South Korea
Gurbansoltan Eje *125 D2* N Turkmenistan
Gurbantunggut Shamo *129 C2 desert* NW China
Gurktaler Alpen *101 E8* ⛰ S Austria
Gürün *121 E3* C Turkey
Gusau *72 E4* NW Nigeria
Gusev *83 E7* W Russian Federation
Gustavus *50 F4* Alaska, USA
Güstrow *101 D2* NE Germany
Gütersloh *101 B4* W Germany
Guthrie *44 F3* Texas, SW USA
Guwahati *127 G3* NE India
Guyana *63 E2* ◆ *republic* N South America
Guymon *43 B7* Oklahoma, C USA
Güzelyurt *112 C6* N Cyprus
Gwadar *127 A3* SW Pakistan
Gwalior *127 E3* C India
Gwanda *76 D5* SW Zimbabwe
Gweedore *89 C1* NW Ireland
Gyangzê *129 C5* W China
Gyaring Co *129 C4* ◎ W China
Gympie *137 H4* Queensland, E Australia
Gyomaendrőd *105 F8* SE Hungary
Gyöngyös *105 E7* NE Hungary
Győr *105 D7* NW Hungary
Gyumri *121 G2* W Armenia

H

Haacht *84 C6* C Belgium
Haaksbergen *84 F4* E Netherlands
Haarlem *84 C3* W Netherlands
Haast *139 B6* South Island, New Zealand
Hachijo-jima *133 G7 island* Izu-shoto, SE Japan
Hachinohe *133 G3* C Japan
Haddington *91 E5* SE Scotland, United Kingdom
Hadejia *72 F4* N Nigeria
Hadejia *72 F4* ≈ N Nigeria
Hadleigh *95 G3* SE England, United Kingdom
Ha Dong *131 C2* N Vietnam
Hadramaut *123 D7* ⛰ S Yemen
Haeju *133 A5* S North Korea
Hagåtña *51* ○ NW Guam
Hagerman *47 C4* Idaho, NW USA
Hagerstown *39 H1* Maryland, NE USA
Hagondange *97 F2* NE France
Hag's Head *89 B5 headland* W Ireland
Haguenau *97 F2* NE France
Hague, The *84 C4* ● W Netherlands
Haicheng *129 G3* NE China
Haifa *123 G5* N Israel
Haikou *129 F6* S China
Ha'il *123 B3* NW Saudi Arabia
Hailar *see* Hulun Buir
Hailsham *95 G4* SE England, United Kingdom
Hailuoto *83 E3 island* W Finland
Hainan Dao *129 F6 island* S China
Haines *50 F3* Alaska, USA
Hainichen *101 D5* E Germany
Hai Phong *131 C2* N Vietnam
Haiti *57 F4* ◆ *republic* C West Indies
Haiya *75 D2* NE Sudan
Hajdúhadház *105 F7* E Hungary
Hakodate *133 F2* NE Japan
Hala'ib Triangle *75 D1 disputed region* Egypt/Sudan
Halberstadt *101 C4* C Germany
Halden *83 B5* S Norway
Halfmoon Bay *139 B8* Stewart Island, Southland, New Zealand
Halifax *35 G5 province capital* Nova Scotia, SE Canada
Halifax *93 D4* N England, United Kingdom
Halkirk *91 E2* N Scotland, United Kingdom
Halladale *91 D2* ≈ N Scotland, United Kingdom
Halle *84 C7* C Belgium
Halle *101 D4* C Germany
Halle-Neustadt *101 D4* C Germany
Halley *142 B3 UK research station* Antarctica
Halls Creek *137 D2* Western Australia
Halmahera, Pulau *131 G6 island* E Indonesia
Halmahera Sea *131 G6 sea* E Indonesia
Halmstad *83 C6* S Sweden
Ha Long *131 C2* N Vietnam
Haltwhistle *93 C2* N England, United Kingdom
Hamada *133 D6* SW Japan
Hamadan *123 D2* W Iran
Hamah *123 B2* W Syria
Hamamatsu *133 F6* S Japan
Hamar *83 B5* S Norway
Hamburg *101 C3* N Germany
Hamd, Wadi al *123 A4 dry watercourse* W Saudi Arabia
Hämeenlinna *83 E5* S Finland
Hamersley Range *137 B3* ⛰ Western Australia
Hamgyong-sanmaek *133 B4* ⛰ N North Korea
Hamhung *133 B4* C North Korea
Hami *129 D2* NW China
Hamilton *35 D6* Ontario, S Canada
Hamilton *139 D3* North Island, New Zealand
Hamilton *91 D6* S Scotland, United Kingdom
Hamilton *39 D4* Alabama, S USA
Hamim, Wadi al *70 G3* ≈ NE Libya
Hamm *101 B4* W Germany
Hammamet, Golfe de *112 E4 gulf* NE Tunisia
Hammar, Hawr al *123 C3* ◎ SE Iraq
Hammond *40 C5* Indiana, N USA
Hampden *139 B7* South Island, New Zealand
Hamrun *112 B6* C Malta
Hanalei *51 A1* Kaua'i, Hawaii, USA
Handan *129 F4* E China
Hanford *49 C7* California, W USA
Hangayn Nuruu *129 D2* ⛰ C Mongolia
Hangö *see* Hanko
Hangzhou *129 G4* SE China
Hanko *83 E5* SW Finland
Hanley *93 D5* C England, United Kingdom
Hanmer Springs *139 C6* South Island, New Zealand
Hannibal *43 F6* Missouri, C USA
Hannover *see* Hanover
Hanöbukten *83 C7 bay* S Sweden
Hanoi *131 C2* ● N Vietnam
Hanover *101 C4* NW Germany
Han Shui *129 F4* ≈ C China
Hanzhong *129 E4* C China
Haora *127 G4* NE India
Haparanda *83 E3* N Sweden
Haradok *109 D1* N Belarus
Haramachi *133 G4* E Japan
Harare *76 E4* ● NE Zimbabwe
Harbel *72 B5* W Liberia
Harbin *129 H2* NE China
Hardangerfjorden *83 A5 fjord* S Norway
Hardangervidda *83 B5 plateau* S Norway
Hardenberg *84 F3* E Netherlands
Harelbeke *84 B6* W Belgium
Haren *84 F2* NE Netherlands
Harer *75 E3* E Ethiopia
Hargeysa *75 E3* NW Somalia
Harima-nada *133 E6 sea* S Japan
Harirud *125 E5* ≈ Afghanistan/Iran
Harlan *43 D5* Iowa, C USA
Harlech *93 B5* NW Wales, United Kingdom
Harlingen *84 D2* N Netherlands
Harlingen *44 H6* Texas, SW USA
Harlow *95 G3* E England, United Kingdom
Harney Basin *49 C4 basin* Oregon, NW USA
Härnösand *83 D4* C Sweden
Har Nuur *129 D2* ◎ NW Mongolia
Harpenden *95 F3* E England, United Kingdom
Harper *72 C5* NE Liberia
Harricana *35 D4* ≈ Québec, SE Canada
Harris *91 B3 physical region* NW Scotland, United Kingdom
Harrisburg *40 C8* Illinois, N USA
Harrisburg *37 C5 state capital* Pennsylvania, NE USA
Harrisonburg *39 H2* Virginia, NE USA
Harrison, Cape *35 G2 cape* Newfoundland and Labrador, E Canada
Harris, Sound of *91 B3 strait* NW Scotland, United Kingdom
Harrogate *93 D3* N England, United Kingdom
Harrow *95 F3* SE England, United Kingdom
Harstad *83 C2* N Norway
Hartford *37 E4 state capital* Connecticut, NE USA
Hartland Point *95 B4 headland* SW England, United Kingdom
Hartlepool *93 E2* N England, United Kingdom
Hartwell Lake *39 F4* ⊠ Georgia/ South Carolina, SE USA
Har Us Gol *129 D2* ◎ W Mongolia
Har Us Nuur *129 C2* ◎ NW Mongolia
Harvey *43 C2* North Dakota, N USA
Harwich *95 H3* E England, United Kingdom
Haryana *127 D2 state* N India
Harz *101 C4* ⛰ C Germany
Haslemere *95 F4* SE England, United Kingdom
Hasselt *84 D6* NE Belgium

⬖ Administrative region ◆ Country ● Country capital ◇ Dependent territory ○ Dependent territory capital ⛰ Mountain range ▲ Mountain Volcano ≈ River ◎ Lake ⊠ Reservoir

astings 139 E4 North Island, New Zealand
astings 95 G4 SE England, United Kingdom
astings 43 C5 Nebraska, C USA
atch 44 D3 New Mexico, SW USA
atfield 95 F3 E England, United Kingdom
attem 84 E3 E Netherlands
atteras, Cape 39 I3 *headland* North Carolina, SE USA
attiesburg 39 C6 Mississippi, S USA
at Yai 131 B5 SW Thailand
augesund 83 A5 S Norway
aukeligrend 83 B5 S Norway
aukivesi 83 F4 ◎ SE Finland
auraki Gulf 139 D2 *gulf* North Island, N New Zealand
auroko, Lake 139 A8 ◎ SW New Zealand
autes Fagnes 84 E7 ⛰ E Belgium
auts Plateaux 70 D2 *plateau* Algeria/Morocco
auzenberg 101 E6 SE Germany
avana 57 B2 ● W Cuba
avant 95 F5 S England, United Kingdom
avelock 39 H4 North Carolina, SE USA
avelock North 139 E4 North Island, New Zealand
averfordwest 93 A7 SW Wales, United Kingdom
averhill 95 G2 E England, United Kingdom
avířov 105 D5 E Czech Republic
avre 47 D1 Montana, NW USA
avre-St-Pierre 35 F4 Québec, E Canada
awi 51 D2 Hawaii, USA
awaii 51 C1 ◐ *state* USA, C Pacific Ocean
awai'i 51 D3 *island* USA, C Pacific Ocean
awea, Lake 139 B7 ◎ South Island, New Zealand
awera 139 D4 North Island, New Zealand
awes 93 D3 N England, United Kingdom
awick 91 E6 SE Scotland, United Kingdom
awke Bay 139 E4 *bay* North Island, New Zealand
awthorne 47 A6 Nevada, W USA
ay 137 F6 New South Wales, SE Australia
ayden 44 B3 Arizona, SW USA
ayes 35 A2 ≈ Manitoba, C Canada
ay-on-Wye 93 C6 E Wales, United Kingdom
ay River 33 G5 Northwest Territories, W Canada
ays 43 C6 Kansas, C USA
aysyn 109 D5 C Ukraine
aywards Heath 95 G4 SE England, United Kingdom
azar 125 B3 W Turkmenistan
earne 44 H4 Texas, SW USA
earst 35 C4 Ontario, S Canada
ebbronville 44 G6 Texas, SW USA
ebrides, Sea of the 91 B4 *sea* NW Scotland, United Kingdom
ebron 123 H6 S West Bank
eemskerk 84 C3 W Netherlands
eerde 84 E3 E Netherlands
eerenveen 84 E2 N Netherlands
eerhugowaard 84 D3 NW Netherlands
eerlen 84 E6 SE Netherlands
efa *see* Haifa
efei 129 G4 E China
egang 129 H1 NE China
eide 101 B2 N Germany
eidelberg 101 B6 SW Germany
eidenheim an der Brenz 101 C6 S Germany
eilbronn 101 B6 SW Germany
eilong Jiang *see* Amur
eiloo 84 C3 NW Netherlands
eimdal 83 B4 S Norway
ekimhan 121 E3 C Turkey
elena 47 D2 *state capital* Montana, NW USA
elensburgh 91 D5 W Scotland, United Kingdom
elensville 139 D2 North Island, New Zealand
elgoländer Bucht 101 B2 *bay* NW Germany
ellevoetsluis 84 C5 SW Netherlands
ellín 99 E4 C Spain
ells Canyon 49 D3 *valley* Idaho/Oregon, NW USA
elmand, Darya-ye 125 D6 ≈ Afghanistan/Iran
elmond 84 E5 S Netherlands
elmsdale 91 E2 N Scotland, United Kingdom
elmsley 93 E3 N England, United Kingdom
elsingborg 83 C7 S Sweden
elsinki 83 E5 ● S Finland
elston 95 A6 SW England, United Kingdom
elvellyn 93 C3 ▲ NW England, United Kingdom
enderson 47 C7 Nevada, W USA
enderson 44 H3 Texas, SW USA
engduan Shan 129 D5 ⛰ SW China
engelo 84 F4 E Netherlands
engyang 129 F5 S China
eniches'k 109 F6 S Ukraine
enley-on-Thames 95 F3 C England, United Kingdom
ennebont 97 B3 NW France
erat 125 D5 W Afghanistan
eredia 55 E6 C Costa Rica
ereford 93 C6 W England, United Kingdom
Hereford 44 F2 Texas, SW USA
Herford 101 B4 NW Germany
Herk-de-Stad 84 D6 NE Belgium
Herm 95 G6 *island* Channel Islands
Herma Ness 91 B5 *headland* NE Scotland, United Kingdom
Hermansverk 83 B5 S Norway
Hermiston 49 C3 Oregon, NW USA
Hermit Islands 141 B1 *island group* N Papua New Guinea
Hermon, Mount 123 H5 ▲ S Syria
Hermosillo 53 B2 NW Mexico
Herrera del Duque 99 C4 W Spain
Herselt 84 D6 C Belgium
Herstal 84 E7 E Belgium
Hessen 101 C5 *state* C Germany
Hessle 93 F4 N England, United Kingdom
Hettinger 43 B3 North Dakota, N USA
Hexham 93 D2 N England, United Kingdom
Hidalgo del Parral 53 D3 N Mexico
Hida-sanmyaku 133 E5 ⛰ Honshū, S Japan
Hienghène 141 G6 C New Caledonia
High Atlas 70 C2 ⛰ C Morocco
High Point 39 G3 North Carolina, SE USA
High Willhays 95 C5 ▲ SW England, United Kingdom
High Wycombe 95 F3 SE England, United Kingdom
Higüero, Punta 51 *headland* W Puerto Rico
Hiiumaa 83 D6 *island* W Estonia
Hikurangi 139 D2 North Island, New Zealand
Hildesheim 101 C4 N Germany
Hill Bank 55 B1 N Belize
Hillegom 84 C4 W Netherlands
Hillsborough 89 E2 E Northern Ireland, United Kingdom
Hilo 51 D3 Hawaii, USA, C Pacific Ocean
Hilversum 84 D4 C Netherlands
Himalayas 127 E2 ⛰ S Asia
Himeji 133 E6 SW Japan
Hims 123 B2 C Syria
Hinchinbrook Island 137 G2 *island* Queensland, NE Australia
Hinds 139 C6 SW New Zealand
Hindu Kush 125 F4 ⛰ Afghanistan/Pakistan
Hinesville 39 G5 Georgia, SE USA
Hinnøya 83 C2 *island* C Norway
Hinthada 131 A3 SW Burma (Myanmar)
Hirfanlı Barajı 121 C3 ⊡ C Turkey
Hirosaki 133 F3 C Japan
Hiroshima 133 D7 SW Japan
Hirson 97 E2 N France
Hisiu 141 B3 SW Papua New Guinea
Hispaniola 57 F4 *island* Dominion Republic/Haiti
Hitachi 133 G5 S Japan
Hitra 83 B4 *island* S Norway
Hjälmaren 83 C6 ◎ C Sweden
Hjørring 83 B6 N Denmark
Hkakabo Razi 131 A1 ▲ Burma (Myanmar)/China
Hlukhiv 109 E3 NE Ukraine
Hlybokaye 109 C2 N Belarus
Hoang Lien Son 131 C2 ⛰ N Vietnam
Hobart 137 G7 *state capital* Tasmania, SE Australia
Hobbs 44 E3 New Mexico, SW USA
Hobro 83 B6 N Denmark
Ho Chi Minh 131 C4 S Vietnam
Hocking River 40 F7 ≈ Ohio, N USA
Hodeida 123 B6 W Yemen
Hódmezővásárhely 105 E8 SE Hungary
Hodna, Chott El 112 D4 *salt lake* N Algeria
Hodonín 105 D6 SE Czech Republic
Hoeryong 133 C3 NE North Korea
Hof 101 D5 SE Germany
Hofu 133 D7 SW Japan
Hohenems 101 C7 W Austria
Hohe Tauern 101 D8 ⛰ W Austria
Hohhot 129 F3 N China
Hokianga Harbour 139 C2 *inlet* SE Tasman Sea
Hokitika 139 B6 South Island, New Zealand
Hokkaido 133 F1 *island* NE Japan
Holbrook 44 C2 Arizona, SW USA
Holden 47 D5 Utah, W USA
Holguín 57 D3 SE Cuba
Holin Gol 129 G2 N China
Hollabrunn 101 F6 NE Austria
Holland *see* Netherlands
Holly Springs 39 C4 Mississippi, S USA
Hollywood 39 G8 Florida, SE USA
Holman 33 G3 Victoria Island, Northwest Territories, N Canada
Holmsund 83 D4 N Sweden
Holon 123 G6 C Israel
Holstebro 83 B6 W Denmark
Holt 95 H1 E England, United Kingdom
Holycross 89 D5 S Ireland
Holyhead 93 A4 NW Wales, United Kingdom
Holy Island 93 D1 *island* NE England, United Kingdom
Holyoke 37 E4 Massachusetts, NE USA
Hombori 72 D3 S Mali
Homyel' 109 D3 SE Belarus
Hondo 44 G5 Texas, SW USA
Hondo 55 B1 ≈ Central America
Honduras 55 C3 ◆ *republic* Central America
Honduras, Gulf of 55 C2 *gulf* W Caribbean Sea
Hønefoss 83 B5 S Norway
Honey Lake 49 B6 ◎ California, W USA
Hong Kong 129 H6 S China
Honiara 141 E3 ● C Solomon Islands
Honiton 95 C5 SW England, United Kingdom
Honjo 133 F4 C Japan
Honolulu 51 B1 *state capital* O'ahu, Hawaii, USA
Honshu 133 G5 *island* SW Japan
Hoogeveen 84 E3 NE Netherlands
Hoogezand-Sappemeer 84 F2 NE Netherlands
Hoorn 84 D3 NW Netherlands
Hoover Dam 47 C7 *dam* Arizona/Nevada, W USA
Hopa 121 G2 NE Turkey
Hope 33 D4 British Columbia, SW Canada
Hope 50 E3 Alaska, USA
Hopedale 35 F2 Newfoundland and Labrador, NE Canada
Hopkinsville 39 D3 Kentucky, S USA
Horasan 121 G3 NE Turkey
Horki 109 D2 E Belarus
Horley 95 F4 SE England, United Kingdom
Horlivka 109 G5 E Ukraine
Hormuz, Strait of 123 E4 *strait* Iran/Oman
Horn, Cape 65 B9 *cape* S Chile
Horncastle 93 F5 E England, United Kingdom
Hornsea 93 F4 E England, United Kingdom
Horoshiri-dake 133 G2 ▲ Hokkaidō, N Japan
Horseleap 89 D4 C Ireland
Horsham 137 F6 Victoria, SE Australia
Horsham 95 F4 SE England, United Kingdom
Horst 84 E5 SE Netherlands
Horten 83 B5 S Norway
Horyn' 109 C4 ≈ NW Ukraine
Hosingen 84 E8 NE Luxembourg
Hotan 129 B3 NW China
Hotazel 76 C6 N South Africa
Hoting 83 C4 C Sweden
Hot Springs 39 B4 Arkansas, C USA
Houayxay 131 B2 N Laos
Houghton 40 C2 Michigan, N USA
Houghton Lake 40 D4 Michigan, N USA
Houilles 97 C6 N France
Houlton 37 G1 Maine, NE USA
Houma 39 C6 Louisiana, S USA
Houston 44 H4 Texas, SW USA
Hovd 129 C2 W Mongolia
Hove 95 F5 SE England, United Kingdom
Hoverla, Hora 109 B5 ▲ W Ukraine
Hövsgöl Nuur 129 D1 ◎ N Mongolia
Howar, Wadi 75 B2 ≈ Chad/Sudan
Howth 89 E4 E Ireland
Hoy 91 E1 *island* N Scotland, United Kingdom
Hoyerswerda 101 E4 E Germany
Hradec Králové 105 C5 N Czech Republic
Hranice 105 D6 E Czech Republic
Hrodna 109 B2 W Belarus
Huaihua 129 F5 S China
Huajuapan 53 F5 SE Mexico
Hualapai Peak 44 A2 ▲ Arizona, SW USA
Huambo 76 B4 C Angola
Huancayo 63 B5 C Peru
Huangshi 129 G4 C China
Huánuco 63 B5 C Peru
Huanuni 65 A2 W Bolivia
Huaraz 63 B5 W Peru
Huatabampo 53 C3 NW Mexico
Hubli 127 D6 SW India
Huch'ang 133 B4 N North Korea
Hucknall 93 D5 C England, United Kingdom
Huddersfield 93 D4 N England, United Kingdom
Hudiksvall 83 D4 C Sweden
Hudson Bay 35 B2 *bay* NE Canada
Hudson River 37 E4 ≈ New Jersey/New York, NE USA
Hudson Strait 33 J4 *strait* Northwest Territories/Québec, NE Canada
Hue 131 C3 C Vietnam
Huehuetenango 55 A3 W Guatemala
Huelva 99 B5 SW Spain
Huesca 99 F2 NE Spain
Huéscar 99 E5 S Spain
Hughenden 137 G3 Queensland, NE Australia
Hugo 43 D9 Oklahoma, C USA
Huich'on 133 B4 C North Korea
Huíla Plateau 76 B4 *plateau* S Angola
Huixtla 53 H6 SE Mexico
Hull 35 D5 Québec, SE Canada
Hull 93 E4 ≈ N England, United Kingdom
Hulst 84 C6 SW Netherlands
Hulun Buir 129 G1 NE China
Hulun Nur 129 F2 ◎ NE China
Humacao 51 E Puerto Rico
Humaitá 63 D4 N Brazil
Humber 93 F4 *estuary* E England, United Kingdom
Humboldt River 47 B5 ≈ Nevada, W USA
Humphreys Peak 44 A2 ▲ Arizona, SW USA
Humpolec 105 C6 C Czech Republic
Hunedoara 109 B6 SW Romania
Hünfeld 101 C5 C Germany
Hungary 105 D8 ◆ *republic* C Europe
Hunstanton 95 G1 E England, United Kingdom
Hunter Island 137 F7 *island* Tasmania, SE Australia
Huntingdon 95 F2 E England, United Kingdom
Huntington 39 F2 West Virginia, NE USA
Huntington Beach 49 C9 California, W USA
Huntly 139 D3 North Island, New Zealand
Huntly 91 E3 NE Scotland, United Kingdom
Huntsville 39 E4 Alabama, S USA
Huntsville 44 H4 Texas, SW USA
Huon Gulf 141 B2 *gulf* E Papua New Guinea
Hurghada 70 J3 E Egypt
Huron 43 C3 South Dakota, N USA
Huron, Lake 40 E3 ◎ Canada/USA
Hurunui 139 C6 ≈ South Island, New Zealand
Húsavík 83 A1 NE Iceland
Husum 101 B2 N Germany
Hutchinson 43 C6 Kansas, C USA
Huy 84 D7 E Belgium
Hvannadalshnúkur 83 B1 ⛛ S Iceland
Hvar 107 B3 *island* S Croatia
Hwange 76 D5 W Zimbabwe
Hyargas Nuur 129 D2 ◎ NW Mongolia
Hyderabad 127 E5 C India
Hyderabad 127 B3 SE Pakistan
Hyères 97 E7 SE France
Hyères, Îles d' 97 E7 *island group* S France
Hyesan 133 B4 NE North Korea
Hythe 95 H4 SE England, United Kingdom
Hyvinkää 83 E5 S Finland

I

Ialomița 109 C7 ≈ SE Romania
Iași 109 C6 NE Romania
Ibadan 72 E5 SW Nigeria
Ibar 107 D2 ≈ C Serbia
Ibarra 63 B3 N Ecuador
Iberian Peninsula 78 *physical region* Portugal/Spain
Ibérico, Sistema 99 E2 ⛰ NE Spain
Ibiza 99 G4 *island* Balearic Islands, Spain
Ica 63 B6 SW Peru
İçel *see* Mersin
Iceland 83 A1 ◆ *republic* N Atlantic Ocean
Iceland Plateau 143 B6 *undersea feature* S Greenland Sea
Idabel 43 E9 Oklahoma, C USA
Idaho 49 D3 ◐ *state* NW USA
Idaho Falls 47 D3 Idaho, NW USA
Idfu 70 J3 SE Egypt
Idîni 72 A2 W Mauritania
Idlib 123 B2 NW Syria
Idre 83 C4 C Sweden
Ieper 84 A6 W Belgium
Iferouâne 72 F2 N Niger
Ifôghas, Adrar des 72 E2 ⛰ NE Mali
Igarka 118 E3 N Russian Federation
Iglesias 103 A6 Sardinia, Italy
Igloolik 33 I3 Nunavut, N Canada
Igoumenitsa 107 D5 W Greece
Iguaçu, Rio 63 F8 ≈ Argentina/Brazil
Iguala 53 F5 S Mexico
Iguazu Falls 65 D4 *waterfall* Brazil/Argentina
Iguidi, 'Erg 70 C3 *desert* Algeria/Mauritania
Ihosy 76 G5 S Madagascar
Iisalmi 83 E4 C Finland
IJssel 84 E4 ≈ Netherlands
IJsselmeer 84 D3 ◎ N Netherlands
IJsselmuiden 84 E3 E Netherlands
Ijzer 84 A6 ≈ W Belgium
Ikaahuk *see* Sachs Harbour
Ikaluktutiak *see* Cambridge Bay
Ikaría 107 F6 *island* Dodecanese, Greece
Ikela 76 C2 C Dem. Rep. Congo
Iki 133 C7 *island* SW Japan
Ilagan 131 F3 Luzon, N Philippines
Iława 105 E2 N Poland
Ilebo 76 C2 W Dem. Rep. Congo
Île-de-France 97 D3 *region* N France
Ilford 95 G3 SE England, United Kingdom
Ilfracombe 95 B4 SW England, United Kingdom
Ílhavo 99 B3 N Portugal
Iliamna Lake 50 D2 ◎ Alaska, USA
Iligan 131 F5 S Philippines
Ilkeston 93 E5 C England, United Kingdom
Ilkley 93 D4 N England, United Kingdom
Illapel 65 A5 C Chile
Illichivs'k 109 E6 SW Ukraine
Illinois 40 B7 ◐ *state* C USA
Illinois River 40 B6 ≈ Illinois, N USA
Iloilo 131 F4 Panay Island, C Philippines
Ilorin 72 E4 W Nigeria
Ilovlya 111 B7 SW Russian Federation
Imatra 83 F4 SE Finland
Imisli 121 I2 C Azerbaijan
Imola 103 C3 N Italy
Imperatriz 63 G4 NE Brazil
Imperia 103 A3 NW Italy
Imphal 127 H3 NE India
Inagh 89 B5 W Ireland
Inarajan 51 SE Guam
Inarijärvi 83 E1 ◎ N Finland
Inawashiro-ko 133 F5 ◎ Honshu, C Japan
İncesu 121 D4 Turkey
Incheon 133 B5 NW South Korea
Independence 43 E6 Missouri, C USA
Independence Mountains 47 B4 ⛰ Nevada, W USA
India 127 D4 ◆ *republic* S Asia
Indiana 37 B5 Pennsylvania, NE USA
Indiana 40 C6 ◐ *state* N USA
Indianapolis 40 D7 *state capital* Indiana, N USA
Indian Church 55 B1 N Belize
Indian Ocean 15 *ocean*
Indianola 43 E5 Iowa, C USA
Indigirka 118 G2 ≈ NE Russian Federation
Indonesia 131 C7 ◆ *republic* SE Asia
Indore 127 D4 C India
Indus 127 B3 ≈ S Asia
Indus, Mouths of the 127 B3 *delta* S Pakistan
İnebolu 121 D2 N Turkey
Infiernillo, Presa del 53 E5 ⊡ S Mexico
Ingleborough 93 C4 ▲ N England, United Kingdom
Ingolstadt 101 C6 S Germany
Inhambane 76 E6 SE Mozambique
Inishannon 89 C7 S Ireland
Inishbofin 89 A4 *island* W Ireland
Inishcrone 89 C3 N Ireland
Inishkea North 89 A3 *island* NW Ireland
Inishkea South 89 A3 *island* NW Ireland
Inishmore 89 B4 *island* W Ireland
Inishshark 89 A4 *island* W Ireland
Inishtrahull 89 D1 *island* NW Ireland
Inishturk 89 A3 *island* W Ireland
Inn 101 D7 ≈ C Europe
Inner Hebrides 91 B5 *island group* W Scotland, United Kingdom
Inner Sound 91 C3 *strait* NW Scotland, United Kingdom
Innisfail 137 G2 Queensland, NE Australia
Innsbruck 101 C7 W Austria
Inowrocław 105 D3 C Poland
I-n-Sakane, 'Erg 72 D2 *desert* N Mali
I-n-Salah 70 D3 C Algeria
Inta 111 E3 NW Russian Federation
Interlaken 101 B8 SW Switzerland
International Falls 43 E1 Minnesota, N USA
Inukjuak 35 D2 Québec, NE Canada
Inuvik 33 F4 Northwest Territories, NW Canada
Inver 89 C2 N Ireland
Inveraray 91 C5 W Scotland, United Kingdom
Inverbervie 91 F4 NE Scotland, United Kingdom
Invercargill 139 B8 Sw New Zealand
Invergordon 91 D3 N Scotland, United Kingdom
Inverness 91 D3 N Scotland, United Kingdom
Inverurie 91 F3 NE Scotland, United Kingdom
Investigator Strait 137 E6 *strait* South Australia
Inyangani 76 E5 ▲ NE Zimbabwe
Ioánnina 107 D5 W Greece
Iola 43 E7 Kansas, C USA
Iona 91 B5 *island* W Scotland, United Kingdom
Iónia Nisiá *see* Ionian Islands
Ionian Islands 107 D5 *island group* W Greece
Ionian Sea 112 G3 *sea* C Mediterranean Sea
Íos 107 F6 *island* Cyclades, Greece
Iowa 43 E5 ◐ *state* C USA
Iowa City 43 F5 Iowa, C USA
Iowa Falls 43 E4 Iowa, C USA
Iowa River 40 A5 ≈ Iowa, C USA
Ipel' 105 E7 ≈ Hungary/Slovakia
Ipoh 131 B5 W Malaysia
Ippy 72 H5 C Central African Republic
Ipswich 137 H5 Queensland, E Australia
Ipswich 95 H2 E England, United Kingdom
Iqaluit 33 J3 *province capital* Baffin Island, Nunavut, NE Canada
Iquique 65 A3 N Chile
Iquitos 63 C4 N Peru
Irákleio 107 F7 Crete, Greece
Iran 123 E2 ◆ *republic* SW Asia
Iranian Plateau 123 E3 *plateau* N Iran
Irapuato 53 E4 C Mexico
Iraq 123 B2 ◆ *republic* SW Asia
Irbid 123 A2 N Jordan
Ireland 89 C4 ◆ *republic* NW Europe
Irian Jaya *see* Papua
Iringa 75 D7 C Tanzania
Iriomote-jima 133 A8 *island* Sakishima-shoto, SW Japan
Iriona 55 D2 NE Honduras
Irish Sea 87 C6 *sea* C British Isles
Irkutsk 118 F5 S Russian Federation
Iroise 97 A2 *sea* NW France
Iron Mountain 40 C3 Michigan, N USA
Ironwood 40 B2 Michigan, N USA
Irrawaddy 131 A2 ≈ W Burma (Myanmar)
Irrawaddy, Mouths of the 131 A3 *delta* SW Burma (Myanmar)
Irtysh 118 D4 ≈ C Asia
Irún 99 E1 N Spain
Iruña *see* Pamplona
Irvine 91 D6 W Scotland, United Kingdom
Irvinestown 89 D2 W Northern Ireland, United Kingdom
Isabela, Isla 63 A7 *island* Galapagos Islands, Ecuador
Isabella, Cordillera 55 D4 ⛰ NW Nicaragua
Isachsen 33 G2 Ellef Ringnes Island, Nunavut, N Canada
Ísafjördhur 83 A1 NW Iceland
Isbister 91 A6 NE Scotland, United Kingdom
Ise 133 F6 SW Japan
Isère 97 E5 ≈ E France
Isernia 103 D5 C Italy
Ise-wan 133 F6 *bay* S Japan
Isfahan 123 D2 C Iran
Ishigaki-jima 133 A8 *island* Sakishima-shoto, SW Japan
Ishikari-wan 133 F2 *bay* Hokkaidō, NE Japan
Ishim 118 C4 C Russian Federation
Ishim 118 D4 ≈ Kazakhstan/Russian Federation
Ishinomaki 133 G4 C Japan
Ishkoshim 125 G4 S Tajikistan
Isiro 76 D1 NE Dem. Rep. Congo
İskenderun 121 E5 S Turkey
Iskur 107 E3 ≈ NW Bulgaria
Iskur, Yazovir 107 E3 ⊡ W Bulgaria
Isla Cristina 99 B5 SW Spain
Islamabad 127 D1 ● NE Pakistan
Islay 91 B6 *island* SW Scotland, United Kingdom
Isle 97 C5 ≈ W France
Isle of Man 93 B3 *UK* ◇ NW Europe
Isle of Wight 95 E5 *island* , United Kingdom
Isles of Scilly 95 A3 *island group* SW England, United Kingdom
Ismoili Somoní, Qullai 125 G3 ▲ NE Tajikistan
Isna 70 J3 SE Egypt
Isoka 76 E3 NE Zambia
İsparta 120 B4 SW Turkey
İspir 121 F2 NE Turkey
Israel 123 G6 ◆ *republic* SW Asia
Issoire 97 D5 C France
Issyk-Kul', Ozero 125 H2 ◎ E Kyrgyzstan
Istanbul 120 B2 NW Turkey
Istra 107 A1 *cultural region* NW Croatia
Itabuna 63 H6 E Brazil
Itagüí 63 B2 W Colombia
Itaipú Dam 65 C4 *dam* Brazil/Paraguay
Itaipú, Represa de 63 F7 ⊡ Brazil/Paraguay
Itaituba 63 F4 NE Brazil
Italy 103 C4 ◆ *republic* S Europe
Ithaca 37 D4 New York, NE USA
Itoigawa 133 F5 C Japan
Iturup, Ostrov 118 I5 *island* Kurile Islands, SE Russian Federation
Itzehoe 101 C2 N Germany
Ivalo 83 E2 N Finland
Ivanhoe 137 F5 New South Wales, SE Australia
Ivano-Frankivs'k 109 B5 W Ukraine
Ivanovo 111 B5 W Russian Federation
Ivoire, Côte d' *see* Ivory Coast
Ivory Coast 72 C5 ◆ *republic* W Africa
Ivujivik 35 D1 Québec, NE Canada
Iwaki 133 G5 N Japan
Iwakuni 133 D7 SW Japan
Iwanai 133 F2 NE Japan
Iwate 133 G3 N Japan
Ixtapa 53 E5 S Mexico
Ixtepec 53 G5 SE Mexico
Iyo-nada 133 D7 *sea* S Japan
Izabal, Lago de 55 B3 ◎ E Guatemala
Izad Khvast 123 D3 C Iran
Izegem 84 B6 W Belgium
Izhevsk 111 D6 NW Russian Federation
Izmayil 109 D7 SW Ukraine
İzmir 120 A4 W Turkey
İzmit 120 B2 NW Turkey
İznik Gölü 120 B2 ◎ NW Turkey
Izu-hanto 133 G6 *peninsula* Honshu, S Japan
Izu-shoto 133 G6 *island group* S Japan

J

Jabal ash Shifa 123 A3 *desert* NW Saudi Arabia
Jabalpur 127 E4 C India
Jaca 99 F2 NE Spain
Jacaltenango 55 A3 W Guatemala
Jackman 37 F2 Maine, NE USA
Jackpot 47 C4 Nevada, W USA
Jackson 43 G7 Missouri, C USA
Jackson 39 D3 Tennessee, S USA
Jackson 39 C5 *state capital* Mississippi, S USA
Jacksonville 39 G6 Florida, SE USA
Jacksonville 40 B6 Illinois, N USA
Jacksonville 39 H4 North Carolina, SE USA
Jacksonville 44 H3 Texas, SW USA
Jacmel 57 F4 S Haiti
Jacobabad 127 C3 SE Pakistan
Jaén 99 D5 S Spain
Jaffna 127 E7 N Sri Lanka
Jagdalpur 127 E5 C India
Jagdaqi 129 G1 N China
Jaipur 127 D3 N India
Jaisalmer 127 C3 NW India
Jakarta 131 C7 ● Java, C Indonesia
Jakobstad 83 E4 W Finland
Jalalabad 125 G5 E Afghanistan
Jalandhar 127 D2 N India
Jalapa 55 D3 NW Nicaragua
Jalpa 53 E4 C Mexico
Jalu 70 H3 NE Libya
Jamaame 75 E5 S Somalia
Jamaica 57 C5 ◆ *commonwealth republic* W West Indies
Jamaica Channel 57 E4 *channel* Haiti/Jamaica

◐ Administrative region ◆ Country ● Country capital ◇ Dependent territory ○ Dependent territory capital ⛰ Mountain range ▲ Mountain ⛛ Volcano ≈ River ◎ Lake ⊡ Reservoir

Jambi *131 C7* Sumatra, W Indonesia
James Bay *35 C3 bay* Ontario/Québec, E Canada
James River *43 C4* ≈ North Dakota/South Dakota, N USA
James River *39 H2* ≈ Virginia, NE USA
Jamestown *37 B4* New York, NE USA
Jamestown *43 C2* North Dakota, N USA
Jammu *127 D2* NW India
Jammu and Kashmir *127 D2 disputed region* India/Pakistan
Jamnagar *127 C4* W India
Jamshedpur *127 F4* NE India
Jamuna *127 G4* ≈ C Bangladesh
Janesville *40 B5* Wisconsin, N USA
Jan Mayen *143 C6 Norwegian* ◇ N Atlantic Ocean
Jánoshalma *105 E8* S Hungary
Japan *133 G4* ◆ *monarchy* E Asia
Japan, Sea of *133 D5 sea* NW Pacific Ocean
Japiim *63 C5* W Brazil
Japurá, Rio *63 C3* ≈ Brazil/Colombia
Jaqué *55 I7* SE Panama
Jardines de la Reina, Archipiélago de los *57 C3 island group* C Cuba
Jarocin *105 D4* C Poland
Jarosław *105 G5* SE Poland
Jarqo'rg'on *125 F4* S Uzbekistan
Jarvis Island *135 US* ◇ C Pacific Ocean
Jasło *105 F5* SE Poland
Jastrzębie-Zdrój *105 D5* S Poland
Jatai *63 F6* C Brazil
Jaunpur *127 F3* N India
Java *131 C8 island* C Indonesia
Javalambre *99 E3* ▲ E Spain
Java Sea *131 D7 sea* W Indonesia
Jawhar *75 F5* S Somalia
Jaya, Puncak *131 H7* ▲ Papua, E Indonesia
Jayapura *131 I7* E Indonesia
Jaz Murian, Hamun-e *123 F3* ◎ SE Iran
Jebba *72 E4* W Nigeria
Jedburgh *91 F6* SE Scotland, United Kingdom
Jedda *123 B5* W Saudi Arabia
Jędrzejów *105 E5* C Poland
Jefferson City *43 F6 state capital* Missouri, C USA
Jefferson, Mount *47 B6* ▲ Nevada, W USA
Jeju-do *133 B8 island* S South Korea
Jeju Strait *133 B7 strait* S South Korea
Jelenia Góra *105 C4* SW Poland
Jelgava *83 E6* C Latvia
Jemappes *84 B7* S Belgium
Jember *131 D8* C Indonesia
Jena *101 C5* C Germany
Jengish Chokusu *129 B2* ▲ China/Kyrgyzstan (see also Pobedy, Pic)
Jenin *123 H6* N West Bank
Jérémie *57 E4* SW Haiti
Jerez de la Frontera *99 C6* SW Spain
Jerez de los Caballeros *99 C5* W Spain
Jericho *123 H6* E West Bank
Jerid, Chott el *70 E2 salt lake* SW Tunisia
Jersey *95 G6 UK* ◇ Channel Islands, NW Europe
Jerusalem *123 H6* ● NE Israel
Jesenice *101 E8* NW Slovenia
Jessore *127 G4* W Bangladesh
Jesús María *65 B5* C Argentina
Jhansi *127 E3* N India
Jharkhand *127 F3 state* NE India
Jhelum *127 D2* NE Pakistan
Jiamusi *129 H2* NE China
Jiangmen *129 F6* S China
Jiaxing *129 G4* SE China
Jiayi *129 H5* C Taiwan
Jiddah *see* Jedda
Jihlava *105 C6* S Czech Republic
Jilib *75 E5* S Somalia
Jilin *129 H2* NE China
Jilong *129 H5* N Taiwan
Jima *75 D4* C Ethiopia
Jiménez *53 D3* N Mexico
Jinan *129 G3* E China
Jin-do *133 B7 island* SW South Korea
Jingdezhen *129 G5* S China
Jinghong *129 D6* SW China
Jinhua *129 G4* SE China
Jining *129 G4* E China
Jining *see* Ulan Qab
Jinja *75 C5* S Uganda
Jinotega *55 D4* NW Nicaragua
Jinotepe *55 D5* SW Nicaragua
Jinzhong *129 F3* C China
Jinzhou *129 G3* NE China
Jiu *109 B7* ≈ S Romania
Jiujiang *129 G4* S China
Jixi *129 H2* NE China
Jizan *123 B6* SW Saudi Arabia
Jizzax *125 F3* C Uzbekistan
João Pessoa *63 I5* E Brazil
Jodhpur *127 C3* NW India
Joensuu *83 F4* SE Finland
Joetsu *133 F5* C Japan
Johannesburg *76 C6* NE South Africa
Johannesburg *49 D8* California, W USA
John Day *49 C3* Oregon, NW USA
John Day River *49 C3* ≈ Oregon, NW USA
John o'Groats *91 E2* N Scotland, United Kingdom
Johnson *43 B7* Kansas, C USA
Johnston Atoll *27 US* ◇ C Pacific Ocean
Johnstown *89 D5* SE Ireland
Johor Bahru *131 C6* W Malaysia
Joinville *63 G8* S Brazil
Jokkmokk *83 D3* N Sweden
Joliet *40 C5* Illinois, N USA
Jonava *83 E7* C Lithuania
Jonesboro *39 C3* Arkansas, C USA
Jönköping *83 C6* S Sweden
Jonquière *35 E4* Québec, SE Canada
Joplin *43 E7* Missouri, C USA
Jordan *125 G3* E Uzbekistan
Jordan *123 A3* ◆ *monarchy* SW Asia
Jorhat *127 H3* NE India
Jos *72 F4* C Nigeria
Jos Plateau *72 F4 plateau* C Nigeria
Jotunheimen *83 B5* ▲▲ S Norway
Joure *84 E2* N Netherlands
Joutseno *83 F5* SE Finland
Juan Aldama *53 D3* C Mexico
Juan de Fuca, Strait of *49 A1 strait* Canada/USA
Juazeiro *63 H5* E Brazil
Juazeiro do Norte *63 H5* E Brazil
Juba *75 C4* ● S South Sudan
Juba *75 E5* ≈ Ethiopia/Somalia
Júcar *99 E4* ≈ C Spain
Juchitán *53 G5* SE Mexico
Judenburg *101 E8* C Austria
Juigalpa *55 D5* S Nicaragua
Juiz de Fora *63 G7* SE Brazil
Juliaca *63 C6* SE Peru
Jumilla *99 E4* SE Spain
Junction *44 G4* Texas, SW USA
Junction City *43 D6* Kansas, C USA
Juneau *50 F4 state capital* Alaska, USA
Junín *65 B5* E Argentina
Jur *75 B3* ≈ N South Sudan
Jura *101 A8* ▲▲ France/Switzerland
Jura *91 B5 island* SW Scotland, United Kingdom
Jura, Sound of *91 C5 strait* W Scotland, United Kingdom
Jūrmala *83 E6* C Latvia
Juruá, Rio *63 C4* ≈ Brazil/Peru
Juruena, Rio *63 E5* ≈ W Brazil
Jutiapa *55 B3* S Guatemala
Juticalpa *55 D3* C Honduras
Jutland *83 B7 peninsula* W Denmark
Jyväskylä *83 E4* C Finland

K

K2 *127 D1* ▲ China/Pakistan
Kaamanen *83 E1* N Finland
Kaaresuvanto *83 D2* N Finland
Kabale *75 C5* SW Uganda
Kabinda *76 D3* SE Dem. Rep. Congo
Kābol *see* Kabul
Kabompo *76 D4* ≈ W Zambia
Kabul *125 F5* ● E Afghanistan
Kabwe *76 D4* C Zambia
Kachchh, Gulf of *127 B4 gulf* W India
Kachchh, Rann of *127 C4 salt marsh* India/Pakistan
Kadavu *141 J5 island* S Fiji
Kadavu Passage *141 J5 channel* S Fiji
Kadugli *75 C3* S Sudan
Kaduna *72 F4* C Nigeria
Kadzhi-Say *125 H2* NE Kyrgyzstan
Kaédi *72 B3* S Mauritania
Kaesŏng *133 B5* S North Korea
Kafue *76 D4* SE Zambia
Kafue *76 D4* ≈ C Zambia
Kaga Bandoro *72 G5* C Central African Republic
Kâgheṭ *72 C1 physical region* N Mauritania
Kagoshima *133 D8* SW Japan
Kahmard, Darya-ye *125 F4* ≈ NE Afghanistan
Kaho'olawe *51 C2 island* Hawaiian Islands, Hawaii, USA
Kahramanmaraş *121 E4* S Turkey
Kahuku *51 B1* O'ahu, Hawaii, USA
Kaiapoi *139 C6* South Island, New Zealand
Kaifeng *129 F4* C China
Kai, Kepulauan *131 G7 island group* SE Indonesia
Kaikohe *139 C1* North Island, New Zealand
Kaikoura *139 C5* South Island, New Zealand
Kailua *51 C2* Maui, Hawaii, USA
Kainji Reservoir *72 E4* ⊠ W Nigeria
Kaipara Harbour *139 C2 harbour* North Island, New Zealand
Kairouan *70 F1* E Tunisia
Kaiserslautern *101 B6* SW Germany
Kaitaia *139 C1* N New Zealand
Kaiwi Channel *51 C2 channel* Hawaii, USA
Kajaani *83 F3* C Finland
Kaka *125 D4* S Turkmenistan
Kake *50 F4* Kupreanof Island, Alaska, USA
Kakhovs'ke Vodoskhovyshche *109 E5* ⊠ SE Ukraine
Kakinada *127 E5* E India
Kaktovik *50 F1* Alaska, USA
Ka Lae *51 D3 headland* Hawaii, USA
Kalahari Desert *76 C6 desert* Southern Africa
Kalamariá *107 E4* N Greece
Kalamás *107 D5* ≈ W Greece
Kalámata *107 E6* S Greece
Kalamazoo *40 D5* Michigan, N USA
Kalaoa *51 D3* Hawaii, USA
Kalat *127 B2* SW Pakistan
Kalaupapa *51 C2* Moloka'i, Hawaii, USA
Kalbarri *137 A5* Western Australia
Kalecik *121 C3* N Turkey
Kalemie *76 D2* SE Dem. Rep. Congo
Kalgoorlie *137 C5* Western Australia
Kalima *76 D2* E Dem. Rep. Congo
Kalimantan *131 D6 geopolitcal region* Borneo, C Indonesia
Kaliningrad *83 E7* W Russian Federation
Kaliningrad *83 F7 province and enclave* W Russian Federation
Kalispell *47 C1* Montana, NW USA
Kalisz *105 D4* C Poland
Kalix *83 E3* N Sweden
Kalixälven *83 E3* ≈ N Sweden
Kalkarindji *137 D2* Northern Territory, N Australia
Kallavesi *83 F4* ◎ SE Finland
Kalloní *107 F5* Lesbos, E Greece
Kalmar *83 C6* S Sweden
Kalmthout *84 C5* N Belgium
Kaluga *111 A5* W Russian Federation
Kalyan *127 C5* W India
Kálymnos *107 F6 island* SE Greece
Kama *111 D5* ≈ NW Russian Federation
Kamchatka *118 I3 peninsula* E Russian Federation
Kamensk-Shakhtinskiy *111 A7* SW Russian Federation
Kamina *76 D3* S Dem. Rep. Congo
Kamloops *33 F7* British Columbia, SW Canada
Kampala *75 C5* ● S Uganda
Kampong Cham *131 C4* C Cambodia
Kâmpóng Saôm *131 C4* SW Cambodia (see also Sihanoukville)
Kampuchea *see* Cambodia
Kam"yanets'-Podil's'kyy *109 C5* W Ukraine
Kamyshin *111 B7* SW Russian Federation
Kanab *47 C6* Utah, W USA
Kananga *76 C2* S Dem. Rep. Congo
Kanash *111 C6* W Russian Federation
Kanazawa *133 F5* SW Japan
Kanchipuram *127 E6* SE India
Kandahar *125 E6* S Afghanistan
Kandalaksha *111 B2* NW Russian Federation
Kandangan *131 E7* C Indonesia
Kandi *72 E4* N Benin
Kandy *127 E8* C Sri Lanka
Kāne'ohe *51 B1* O'ahu, Hawaii, USA
Kangaroo Island *137 E6 island* South Australia
Kanggye *133 B4* N North Korea
Kanivs'ke Vodoskhovyshche *109 D4* ⊠ C Ukraine
Kankaanpää *83 E4* SW Finland
Kankakee *40 C6* Illinois, N USA
Kankan *72 B4* E Guinea
Kannur *127 D7* SW India (see also Cannanore)
Kano *72 F4* N Nigeria
Kanpur *127 E3* N India
Kansas *43 C6* ⬖ *state* C USA
Kansas City *43 E6* Kansas, C USA
Kansas City *43 E6* Missouri, C USA
Kansas River *43 D6* ≈ Kansas, C USA
Kansk *118 E5* S Russian Federation
Kantemirovka *111 A7* W Russian Federation
Kanto Plain *133 G5 plain* Honshu, C Japan
Kanye *76 D6* SE Botswana
Kaolack *72 A3* W Senegal
Kapelle *84 C5* SW Netherlands
Kapellen *84 C6* N Belgium
Kapoeta *75 C4* SW South Sudan
Kaposvár *105 D8* SW Hungary
Kappeln *101 C2* N Germany
Kapuas, Sungai *131 D6* ≈ Borneo, C Indonesia
Kapuskasing *35 C4* Ontario, S Canada
Kara-Balta *125 H2* N Kyrgyzstan
Karabük *121 C2* NW Turkey
Karachi *127 B3* SE Pakistan
Karagandy *118 C5* C Kazakhstan
Karaginskiy, Ostrov *118 I3 island* E Russian Federation
Karakol *125 H2* NE Kyrgyzstan
Karakoram Range *127 D1* ▲▲ C Asia
Karaman *121 C4* S Turkey
Karamay *129 C2* NW China
Karamea Bight *139 C5 gulf* South Island, New Zealand
Kara-Say *125 I2* NE Kyrgyzstan
Karasburg *76 C6* S Namibia
Kara Sea *118 D2 sea* Arctic Ocean
Kara Strait *111 E2 strait* N Russian Federation
Karatau *118 C6* S Kazakhstan
Karatau, Khrebet *125 F2* ▲▲ S Kazakhstan
Karbala' *123 C2* S Iraq
Kardítsa *107 D5* C Greece
Kargı *121 D2* N Turkey
Kariba *76 D4* N Zimbabwe
Kariba, Lake *76 D4* ⊠ Zambia/Zimbabwe
Karibib *76 B5* C Namibia
Karigasniemi *83 E1* N Finland
Karimata, Selat *131 C6 strait* W Indonesia
Karimnagar *127 E5* C India
Karin *75 F3* N Somalia
Karkar Island *141 B2 island* N Papua New Guinea
Karkinits'ka Zatoka *109 E6 gulf* S Ukraine
Karleby *see* Kokkola
Karlovac *107 B1* C Croatia
Karlovy Vary *105 A5* W Czech Republic
Karlskrona *83 C7* S Sweden
Karlsruhe *101 B6* SW Germany
Karlstad *83 C5* C Sweden
Karnal *127 D2* N India
Karnataka *127 D6 state* W India
Kárpathos *107 G7* SE Greece
Kárpathos *107 G7 island* SE Greece
Karpenísi *107 D5* C Greece
Kars *121 G2* NE Turkey
Karskoye More *see* Kara Sea
Karst *101 E8 physical region* Croatia/Slovenia
Karyés *107 E4* N Greece
Kaş *120 B5* SW Turkey
Kasai *76 C3* ≈ Angola/Dem. Rep. Congo
Kasaji *76 C3* S Dem. Rep. Congo
Kasama *76 E3* N Zambia
Kasese *75 C5* SW Uganda
Kashan *123 D2* C Iran
Kashi *129 A3* NW China
Kaskaskia River *40 B7* ≈ Illinois, N USA
Kasongo *76 D2* E Dem. Rep. Congo
Kasongo-Lunda *76 B3* SW Dem. Rep. Congo
Kásos *107 F7 island* S Greece
Kaspiysk *118 B9* SW Russian Federation
Kassala *75 D2* E Sudan
Kassel *101 C4* C Germany
Kastamonu *121 D2* N Turkey
Kastsyukovichy *109 E2* E Belarus
Kasulu *75 C6* W Tanzania
Kasumiga-ura *133 G5* ◎ Honshu, S Japan
Katahdin, Mount *37 G1* ▲ Maine, NE USA
Katalla *50 E3* Alaska, USA
Katanning *137 B6* Western Australia
Katchall Island *127 H6 island* Nicobar Islands, SE India
Kateríni *107 E4* N Greece
Katherine *137 D1* Northern Territory, N Australia
Kathmandu *127 F3* ● C Nepal
Katikati *139 D3* North Island, New Zealand
Katima Mulilo *76 D4* NE Namibia
Katiola *72 C5* C Ivory Coast
Katowice *105 E5* S Poland
Katsina *72 F4* N Nigeria
Kattaqo'rg'on *125 E3* C Uzbekistan
Kattegat *83 B7 strait* N Europe
Kaua'i *51 B1 island* Hawaiian Islands, Hawaii, USA
Kaua'i Channel *51 B1 channel* Hawaii, USA
Kaufbeuren *101 C7* S Germany
Kaulakahi Channel *51 A1 channel* Hawaii, USA
Kaunakakai *51 C2* Moloka'i, Hawaii, USA
Kaunas *83 E7* C Lithuania
Kauno Marios *105 G1* ⊠ S Lithuania
Kavála *107 E4* NE Greece
Kavali *127 E6* E India
Kavaratti *127 C7* Laccadive Islands, SW India
Kavarna *107 G2* NE Bulgaria
Kavieng *141 C1* NE Papua New Guinea
Kavir, Dasht-e *123 E2 salt pan* N Iran
Kawagoe *133 G5* S Japan
Kawasaki *133 G5* S Japan
Kawerau *139 E3* North Island, New Zealand
Kaya *72 D4* C Burkina
Kayan, Sungai *131 E6* ≈ Borneo, C Indonesia
Kayenta *44 C1* Arizona, SW USA
Kayes *72 B3* W Mali
Kayseri *121 D4* C Turkey
Kazach'ye *118 G3* NE Russian Federation
Kazakhstan *118 B5* ◆ *republic* C Asia
Kazakh Uplands *118 C5 uplands* C Kazakhstan
Kazan' *111 C6* W Russian Federation
Kazanlŭk *107 F3* C Bulgaria
Kazbek *121 G1* ▲ N Georgia
Kazerun *123 D3* S Iran
Keady *89 E3* S Northern Ireland, United Kingdom
Kea, Mauna *51 D3* ▲ Hawaii, USA
Kearney *43 C5* Nebraska, C USA
Keban Barajı *121 E3* ⊠ Turkey
Kebkabiya *75 A2* W Sudan
Kebnekaise *83 C2* ▲ N Sweden
Kecskemét *105 E8* C Hungary
Kediri *131 D8* Java, C Indonesia
Keetmanshoop *76 C6* S Namibia
Kefallonía *107 D5 island* Ionian Islands, Greece
Kehl *101 B6* SW Germany
Keïta *72 E3* C Niger
Keitele *83 E4* ◎ C Finland
Keith *137 F6* South Australia
Keith *91 E3* NE Scotland, United Kingdom
Kekaha *51 A1* Kaua'i, Hawaii, USA
Këk-Art *125 H3* SW Kyrgyzstan
Kékes *105 E7* ▲ N Hungary
Kells *89 D5* S Ireland
Kells *89 E4* E Ireland
Kélo *72 G4* SW Chad
Kelowna *33 F7* British Columbia, SW Canada
Kelso *91 F6* SE Scotland, United Kingdom
Kelso *49 B3* Washington, NW USA
Keluang *131 C6* W Malaysia
Kem' *111 B3* NW Russian Federation
Kemah *121 F3* E Turkey
Kemerovo *118 E5* C Russian Federation
Kemi *83 E3* NW Finland
Kemijärvi *83 E2* N Finland
Kemijoki *83 E3* ≈ NW Finland
Kemin *125 H2* N Kyrgyzstan
Kemmerer *47 D4* Wyoming, C USA
Kemmuna *112 B6 island* C Malta
Kempele *83 E3* C Finland
Kemp Land *142 D4 physical region* Antarctica
Kempten *101 C7* S Germany
Kendal *93 C3* NW England, United Kingdom
Kendari *131 F7* Celebes, C Indonesia
Kenema *72 B5* SE Sierra Leone
Kengtung *131 B2* E Burma (Myanmar)
Kenilworth *93 D6* C England, United Kingdom
Kénitra *70 C1* NW Morocco
Kenmare *89 B6* S Ireland
Kennebec River *37 G2* ≈ Maine, NE USA
Kennett *43 G7* Missouri, C USA
Kennewick *49 C3* Washington, NW USA
Kenora *35 A4* Ontario, S Canada
Kenosha *40 C5* Wisconsin, N USA
Kentau *118 C6* S Kazakhstan
Kentucky *39 E2* ⬖ *state* C USA
Kentucky Lake *39 C3* ⊠ Kentucky/Tennessee, S USA
Kenya *75 D5* ◆ *republic* E Africa
Keokuk *43 F5* Iowa, C USA
Kępno *105 D4* C Poland
Kerala *127 D7 state* S India
Kerch *109 G6* SE Ukraine
Kerch Strait *109 G7 strait* Black Sea/Sea of Azov
Kerema *141 B2* S Papua New Guinea
Kerguelen *15 island* C French Southern and Antarctic Territories
Kerí *107 D6* W Greece
Kerikeri *139 D1* North Island, New Zealand
Kerkenah, Îles de *112 E4 island group* E Tunisia
Kerkrade *84 E6* SE Netherlands
Kerkyra *see* Corfu
Kermadec Islands *135 island group* NE New Zealand
Kerman *123 E3* C Iran
Kermānshāh *123 C2* W Iran
Kerrville *44 G4* Texas, SW USA
Kerry Head *89 A5 headland* SW Ireland
Kerulen *129 F2* ≈ China/Mongolia
Keryrenia *see* Girne
Kesennuma *133 G4* C Japan
Keswick *93 C3* NW England, United Kingdom
Keszthely *105 D8* SW Hungary
Ketchikan *50 F4* Revillagigedo Island, Alaska, USA
Kettering *95 F2* C England, United Kingdom
Kettering *40 E7* Ohio, N USA
Kettle Falls *49 C1* Washington, NW USA
Keuruu *83 E4* C Finland
Kewanee *40 B6* Illinois, N USA
Keweenaw Peninsula *40 C2 peninsula* Michigan, N USA
Key Largo *39 G9* Key Largo, Florida, SE USA
Keynsham *95 D4* SW England, United Kingdom
Key West *39 G9* Florida Keys, Florida, SE USA
Khabarovsk *118 H5* SE Russian Federation
Khairpur *127 C3* SE Pakistan
Khambhat, Gulf of *127 C4 gulf* W India
Khandwa *127 D4* C India
Khanka, Lake *118 H5* ◎ China/Russian Federation
Khanthabouli *131 C3* S Laos
Khanty-Mansiysk *118 D4* C Russian Federation
Khao Laem Reservoir *131 A3* ⊠ W Thailand
Kharagpur *127 G4* NE India
Kharkiv *109 F4* NE Ukraine
Khartoum *75 C2* ● C Sudan
Khartoum North *75 C2* C Sudan
Khasavyurt *111 B9* SW Russian Federation
Khash, Dasht-e *125 D6 desert* SW Afghanistan
Khashm el Girba *75 D2* E Sudan
Khaskovo *107 F3* S Bulgaria
Khatanga *143 E3* N Russian Federation
Khaydarkan *125 G3* SW Kyrgyzstan
Kherson *109 E6* S Ukraine
Kheta *118 E3* ≈ N Russian Federation
Khmel'nyts'kyy *109 C5* W Ukraine
Khon Kaen *131 B3* E Thailand
Khor *118 H5* SE Russian Federation
Khorugh *125 G4* S Tajikistan
Khost *125 F5* E Afghanistan
Khouribga *70 C2* C Morocco
Khŭjand *125 F3* N Tajikistan
Khulm *125 F4* N Afghanistan
Khulna *127 G4* SW Bangladesh
Khust *109 B5* W Ukraine
Khvoy *123 C1* NW Iran
Khyber Pass *127 C1 pass* Afghanistan/Pakistan
Kia *141 E2* N Solomon Islands
Kibangou *76 B2* SW Congo
Kibombo *76 D2* E Dem. Rep. Congo
Kidderminster *93 D6* C England, United Kingdom
Kidlington *95 E3* C England, United Kingdom
Kiel *101 C2* N Germany
Kielce *105 E4* C Poland
Kielder Water *93 C2* ◎ N England, United Kingdom
Kieler Bucht *101 C2 bay* N Germany
Kiev *109 D4* ● N Ukraine
Kiev Reservoir *109 D4* ⊠ N Ukraine
Kiffa *72 B3* S Mauritania
Kigali *75 C6* ● C Rwanda
Kigoma *75 B6* W Tanzania
Kihei *51 C2* Maui, Hawaii, USA
Kii-suido *133 E7 strait* S Japan
Kikinda *107 D1* N Serbia
Kikwit *76 C2* W Dem. Rep. Congo
Kilauea *51 B1* Kaua'i, Hawaii, USA
Kilauea Caldera *51 D3 crater* Hawaii, USA
Kilbaha *89 B5* W Ireland
Kilbeggan *89 D4* C Ireland
Kilchu *133 C4* NE North Korea
Kilcogy *89 D3* N Ireland
Kilcolgan *89 C4* W Ireland
Kilcormac *89 D4* C Ireland
Kildare *89 E4* E Ireland
Kildorrery *89 C6* S Ireland
Kilimanjaro *75 D6* ⩕ NE Tanzania
Kilis *121 E5* S Turkey
Kilkee *89 B5* W Ireland
Kilkeel *89 F3* S Northern Ireland, United Kingdom
Kilkelly *89 C3* NW Ireland
Kilkenny *89 D5* S Ireland
Kilkinlea *89 B6* SW Ireland
Kilkís *107 E4* N Greece
Killagan *89 E1* N Northern Ireland, United Kingdom
Killala *89 B3* NW Ireland
Killala Bay *89 B3 inlet* NW Ireland
Killarney *89 B6* SW Ireland
Killeany *89 B4* W Ireland
Killeen *89 E3* S Northern Ireland, United Kingdom
Killeen *44 G4* Texas, SW USA
Killimer *89 B5* W Ireland
Killimor *89 C4* W Ireland
Killorglin *89 B6* SW Ireland
Killybegs *89 C2* NW Ireland
Killyleagh *89 F3* E Northern Ireland, United Kingdom
Kilmaine *89 B4* NW Ireland
Kilmarnock *91 D6* W Scotland, United Kingdom
Kilmurvy *89 B4* W Ireland
Kilrea *89 E2* N Northern Ireland, United Kingdom
Kilrush *89 B5* W Ireland
Kilwa Kivinje *75 D7* SE Tanzania
Kimbe *141 C2* E Papua New Guinea
Kimberley *76 D6* C South Africa
Kimberley Plateau *137 C2 plateau* Western Australia
Kimch'aek *133 C4* E North Korea
Kinabalu, Gunung *131 E5* ▲ East Malaysia
Kinbrace *91 D2* N Scotland, United Kingdom
Kincaslough *89 C1* N Ireland
Kinder Scout *93 D4* ▲ C England, United Kingdom
Kindersley *33 G7* Saskatchewan, S Canada
Kindia *72 B4* SW Guinea
Kindu *76 D2* C Dem. Rep. Congo
Kineshma *111 B5* W Russian Federatior
King City *49 B7* California, W USA
King Island *137 F7 island* Tasmania, SE Australia
Kingman *44 A2* Arizona, SW USA
Kingman Reef *135 US* ◇ C Pacific Oce
King's Lynn *95 G1* E England, United Kingdom
King Sound *137 C2 sound* Western Australia
Kingsport *39 F3* Tennessee, S USA
Kingston *57 D5* ● E Jamaica
Kingston *35 D6* Ontario, SE Canada
Kingston *37 E4* New York, NE USA
Kingston upon Hull *93 F4* E England, United Kingdom
Kingstown *57 K6* ● SW Saint Vincent and the Grenadines
Kingsville *44 G5* Texas, SW USA
King William Island *33 H3 island* Nunavut, N Canada
Kinnegad *89 D4* C Ireland
Kinrooi *84 E6* NE Belgium
Kinross *91 E5* ⬖ *cultural region* C Scotland, United Kingdom
Kinsale *89 C7* SW Ireland
Kinsalebeg *89 D6* S Ireland
Kinshasa *76 B2* ● W Dem. Rep. Congo
Kintyre *91 C6 peninsula* W Scotland, United Kingdom
Kintyre, Mull of *91 C6 headland* W Scotland, United Kingdom
Kinvara *89 C4* W Ireland
Kinyeti *75 C4* ▲ S South Sudan
Kipili *75 C7* W Tanzania
Kippure *89 E4* ▲ E Ireland
Kipushi *76 D3* SE Dem. Rep. Congo
Kirakira *141 F3* SE Solomon Islands
Kirghiz Range *125 G2* ▲▲ Kazakhstan/Kyrgyzstan
Kiribati *141 J1* ◆ *republic* C Pacific Ocean
Kırıkhan *121 E5* S Turkey
Kırıkkale *121 D3* C Turkey
Kirinyaga *75 D5* ⩕ C Kenya
Kirishi *111 A4* NW Russian Federation
Kiritimati *135 atoll* E Kiribati
Kiriwina Islands *141 C2 island group* S Papua New Guinea
Kirkby *93 C4* NW England, United Kingdom
Kirkby Stephen *93 D3* NW England, United Kingdom
Kirkcaldy *91 E5* E Scotland, United Kingdom
Kirkcudbright *91 D7* S Scotland, United Kingdom
Kirkenes *83 E1* N Norway
Kirkland Lake *35 C5* Ontario, S Canada

⬖ Administrative region ◆ Country ● Country capital ◇ Dependent territory ○ Dependent territory capital ▲▲ Mountain range ▲ Mountain ⩕ Volcano ≈ River ◎ Lake ⊠ Reservoir

rklareli 120 A2 NW Turkey
rkpatrick, Mount 142 C5 ▲ Antarctica
rksville 43 F5 Missouri, C USA
rkūk 123 C2 N Iraq
rkwall 91 E1 NE Scotland, United Kingdom
rkwood 43 G6 Missouri, C USA
rov 111 C5 W Russian Federation
rovo-Chepetsk 111 C5 NW Russian Federation
rovohrad 109 E5 C Ukraine
rriemuir 91 E4 E Scotland, United Kingdom
runa 83 D2 N Sweden
sangani 76 D1 NE Dem. Rep. Congo
skörei-víztároló 105 E7 E Hungary
skunfélegyháza 105 E8 C Hungary
slovodsk 111 A8 SW Russian Federation
smaayo 75 E5 S Somalia
ssidougou 72 B4 S Guinea
ssimmee, Lake 39 G7 Florida, SE USA
sumu 75 D5 W Kenya
svárda 105 F7 E Hungary
ta 72 B4 W Mali
takyushu 133 C7 SW Japan
tami 133 G1 NE Japan
tchener 35 C6 Ontario, S Canada
timat 33 E6 British Columbia, SW Canada
tinen 83 E2 N Finland
tob 125 F3 S Uzbekistan
twe 76 D4 C Zambia
tzbüheler Alpen 101 D7 W Austria
unga 141 A2 SW Papua New Guinea
valina 50 E1 Alaska, USA
valo 83 E3 ridge C Finland
vu, Lake 76 D2 Dem. Rep. Congo/Rwanda
wai Island 141 A3 island SW Papua New Guinea
zıl Irmak 121 D2 C Turkey
ladno 105 B5 NW Czech Republic
lagenfurt 101 E8 S Austria
laipėda 83 E7 NW Lithuania
lamath Falls 49 B4 Oregon, NW USA
lamath Mountains 49 B5 California/Oregon, W USA
lang 131 B6 W Malaysia
larälven 83 C5 Norway/Sweden
latovy 105 A6 W Czech Republic
lazienaveen 84 F3 NE Netherlands
lintsy 111 A5 W Russian Federation
lobuck 105 E4 S Poland
losters 101 C8 SE Switzerland
luczbork 105 D4 S Poland
lyuchevka 125 G2 NW Kyrgyzstan
lyuchevskaya Sopka, Vulkan 118 H3 E Russian Federation
naresborough 93 D3 N England, United Kingdom
nock 89 C3 NW Ireland
nocktopher 89 D6 SE Ireland
nokke-Heist 84 B5 NW Belgium
nowle 93 D6 C England, United Kingdom
noxville 39 F3 Tennessee, S USA
nud Rasmussen Land 33 I1 physical region N Greenland
obe 133 E6 SW Japan
øbenhavn see Copenhagen
obenni 72 B3 S Mauritania
oblenz 101 B5 W Germany
obryn 109 B3 SW Belarus
obuleti 121 G2 W Georgia
očevje 101 E9 S Slovenia
och Bihar 127 G3 NE India
ochi 133 E7 SW Japan
ochi 127 D7 SW India (see also Cochin)
odiak 50 D3 Kodiak Island, Alaska, USA
odiak Island 50 D3 island Alaska, USA
ofu 133 F5 S Japan
ogon 125 E3 C Uzbekistan
ogum-do 133 B7 island S South Korea
ohima 127 H3 E India
ohtla-Järve 83 F5 NE Estonia
oidu 72 B4 E Sierra Leone
okkola 83 E4 W Finland
oko 72 E4 W Nigeria
okomo 40 D6 Indiana, N USA
okrines 50 E2 Alaska, USA
okshaal-Tau 125 H3 China/Kyrgyzstan
okshetau 118 C5 N Kazakhstan
oksijde 84 A6 W Belgium
oksoak 35 D2 Québec, E Canada
okstad 76 D7 E South Africa
ola Peninsula 111 C3 peninsula NW Russian Federation
olari 83 E4 NW Finland
olárovo 105 D7 SW Slovakia
olda 72 A3 S Senegal
olding 83 B7 C Denmark
olguyev, Ostrov 111 C2 island NW Russian Federation
olhapur 127 D5 SW India
olín 105 B5 C Czech Republic
olka 83 E6 NW Latvia
olkata 127 G4 NE India
ollam 127 D7 SW India (see also Quilon)
öln see Cologne
oło 105 D3 C Poland
ołobrzeg 105 C2 NW Poland
olokani 72 C3 W Mali
olomna 111 B5 W Russian Federation
olpa 107 B1 Croatia/Slovenia
olpino 111 A4 NW Russian Federation
ol'skiy Poluostrov see Kola Peninsula
olwezi 76 D3 S Dem. Rep. Congo
Kolyma 118 H2 NE Russian Federation
Kolyma Range 118 H3 E Russian Federation
Komatsu 133 F5 SW Japan
Komoé 72 C4 E Ivory Coast
Komotiní 107 F4 NE Greece
Komsomolets, Ostrov 118 E1 island N Russian Federation
Komsomol'sk-na-Amure 118 H5 SE Russian Federation
Kondopoga 111 B4 NW Russian Federation
Konduz 125 F4 NE Afghanistan
Koné 141 G6 W New Caledonia
Köneürgenç 125 D2 N Turkmenistan
Kong Frederik VIII Land 143 B5 physical region NE Greenland
Kongolo 76 D2 E Dem. Rep. Congo
Kongor 75 C4 E South Sudan
Kongsberg 83 B5 S Norway
Konin 105 D3 C Poland
Kónitsa 107 D4 W Greece
Konosha 111 B4 NW Russian Federation
Konotop 109 E3 NE Ukraine
Konstanz 101 B7 S Germany
Konya 121 C4 C Turkey
Kopaonik 107 D3 S Serbia
Koper 101 E9 SW Slovenia
Köpetdag Gershi 125 C3 Iran/Turkmenistan
Koppeh Dagh 123 E1 Iran/Turkmenistan
Korat Plateau 131 B3 plateau E Thailand
Korçë 107 D4 SE Albania
Korčula 107 B3 island S Croatia
Korea Bay 129 G3 bay China/North Korea
Korea Strait 133 C7 channel Japan/South Korea
Korhogo 72 C4 N Ivory Coast
Kórinthos see Corinth
Koriyama 133 G4 C Japan
Korla 129 C2 NW China
Körmend 105 C8 W Hungary
Koro 141 J5 island C Fiji
Koróni 107 E6 S Greece
Koro Sea 141 J5 sea C Fiji
Korosten' 109 D4 NW Ukraine
Koro Toro 72 H3 N Chad
Kortrijk 84 B6 W Belgium
Koryak Range 118 I2 NE Russian Federation
Koryazhma 111 C4 NW Russian Federation
Kos 107 G6 island Dodecanese, Greece
Ko-saki 133 C7 headland Tsushima, SW Japan
Kościan 105 C3 C Poland
Kościerzyna 105 D2 NW Poland
Kosciuszko, Mount 137 G6 ▲ New South Wales, SE Australia
Koshikijima-retto 133 C8 island group SW Japan
Košice 105 F6 E Slovakia
Koson 125 E3 S Uzbekistan
Kosong 133 B5 SE North Korea
Kosovo 107 D3 ◆ republic SE Europe
Kossou, Lac de 72 C5 C Ivory Coast
Kostanay 118 C4 N Kazakhstan
Kostroma 111 B5 NW Russian Federation
Kostyantynivka 109 G5 SE Ukraine
Koszalin 105 C2 NW Poland
Kota 127 D3 N India
Kota Bharu 131 B5 W Malaysia
Kota Kinabalu 131 D5 N Malaysia
Kotel'nyy, Ostrov 118 F2 island N Russian Federation
Kotka 83 F5 S Finland
Kotlas 111 C4 NW Russian Federation
Kotovs'k 109 D5 SW Ukraine
Kotto 72 I5 Central African Republic/Dem. Rep. Congo
Kotuy 118 F3 N Russian Federation
Koudougou 72 D4 C Burkina
Koulamoutou 76 B2 C Gabon
Koulikoro 72 C4 SW Mali
Koumac 141 G6 W New Caledonia
Koumra 72 H4 S Chad
Kourou 63 F2 N French Guiana
Kousséri 72 G4 NE Cameroon
Koutiala 72 C4 S Mali
Kouvola 83 F5 S Finland
Kovel' 109 B4 NW Ukraine
Kozáni 107 D4 N Greece
Kozara 107 B2 NW Bosnia and Herzegovina
Kozhikode 127 D7 SW India (see also Calicut)
Kozloduy 107 E2 NW Bulgaria
Kozu-shima 133 F6 island E Japan
Kpalimé 72 D5 SW Togo
Kragujevac 107 D2 C Serbia
Kra, Isthmus of 131 B5 isthmus Malaysia/Thailand
Kraków 105 E5 S Poland
Kralendijk 57 G7 ○ E Bonaire
Kraljevo 107 D2 C Serbia
Kramators'k 109 G5 SE Ukraine
Kramfors 83 D4 C Sweden
Kranj 101 E8 NW Slovenia
Krasnoarmeysk 111 B7 W Russian Federation
Krasnodar 111 A8 SW Russian Federation
Krasnokamensk 118 G5 S Russian Federation
Krasnokamsk 111 D5 W Russian Federation
Krasnoyarsk 118 E5 S Russian Federation
Krasnystaw 105 G4 SE Poland
Krasnyy Kut 111 C7 W Russian Federation
Krasnyy Luch 109 G5 E Ukraine
Krefeld 101 A4 W Germany
Kremenchuk 109 E5 NE Ukraine
Kremenchuk Reservoir 109 D5 C Ukraine
Kreminna 109 G4 E Ukraine
Kremmling 47 E5 Colorado, C USA
Krishna 127 E5 C India
Krishnagiri 127 D6 SE India
Kristiansand 83 B6 S Norway
Kristianstad 83 C7 S Sweden
Kristiansund 83 B4 S Norway
Kriti see Crete
Kritikó Pélagos see Crete, Sea of
Krk 107 B1 island NW Croatia
Kronach 101 C5 E Germany
Kroonstad 76 D6 C South Africa
Kropotkin 111 A8 SW Russian Federation
Krosno 105 F5 SE Poland
Krosno Odrzańskie 105 B3 W Poland
Krško 101 F8 E Slovenia
Krung Thep, Ao 131 B4 bay S Thailand
Kruševac 107 D2 C Serbia
Kryms'ki Hory 109 F7 S Ukraine
Kryvyy Rih 109 E5 SE Ukraine
Ksar-el-Kebir 70 C1 NW Morocco
Kuala Lumpur 131 B6 ● W Malaysia
Kuala Terengganu 131 C5 W Malaysia
Kuantan 131 C6 W Malaysia
Kuban' 109 G6 SW Russian Federation
Kuching 131 D6 E Malaysia
Kuchnay Darwashan 125 E6 S Afghanistan
Kudus 131 D8 C Indonesia
Kugaaruk 33 H3 Nunavut, N Canada
Kugluktuk 33 G4 Nunavut, NW Canada
Kuhmo 83 F3 E Finland
Kuito 76 B4 C Angola
Kuji 133 G3 C Japan
Kula Kangri 127 G2 ▲ Bhutan/China
Kŭlob 125 F4 SW Tajikistan
Kulu 121 C3 W Turkey
Kulunda 118 D5 S Russian Federation
Kulunda Steppe 118 D5 grassland Kazakhstan/Russian Federation
Kuma 111 B8 SW Russian Federation
Kumamoto 133 D7 SW Japan
Kumanovo 107 D3 N Macedonia
Kumasi 72 D5 C Ghana
Kumba 72 F5 W Cameroon
Kumertau 111 D7 W Russian Federation
Kumo 72 F4 E Nigeria
Kumon Range 131 B1 N Burma (Myanmar)
Kunda 83 F5 NE Estonia
Kunene 76 B4 Angola/Namibia
Kungsbacka 83 B6 S Sweden
Kungur 111 D5 NW Russian Federation
Kunlun Mountains 129 B3 NW China
Kunming 129 E5 SW China
Kununurra 137 D2 Western Australia
Kuopio 83 F4 C Finland
Kupang 131 F8 C Indonesia
Kupiano 141 C3 S Papua New Guinea
Kup"yans'k 109 G4 E Ukraine
Kura 121 H2 SW Asia
Kurashiki 133 E6 SW Japan
Kurdistan 121 H4 cultural region SW Asia
Kŭrdzhali 107 F3 S Bulgaria
Kure 133 D7 SW Japan
Kure Dağları 121 D2 N Turkey
Kurile Islands 118 I4 island group SE Russian Federation
Kurile Trench 15 undersea feature NW Pacific Ocean
Kuril'sk 118 I5 Kurile Islands, SE Russian Federation
Kuril'skiye Ostrova see Kurile Islands
Kurnool 127 D6 S India
Kursk 111 A6 W Russian Federation
Kuruktag 129 C3 NW China
Kurume 133 D7 SW Japan
Kushiro 133 G2 NE Japan
Kuskokwim Mountains 50 D2 Alaska, USA
Kütahya 120 B3 W Turkey
Kutaisi 121 G1 W Georgia
Kutno 105 E3 C Poland
Kuujjuaq 35 E2 Québec, E Canada
Kuusamo 83 F3 E Finland
Kuwait 123 D3 ● E Kuwait
Kuwait 123 C3 ◆ monarchy SW Asia
Kuybyshev Reservoir 111 B6 W Russian Federation
Kuytun 129 C2 NW China
Kuznetsk 111 B6 W Russian Federation
Kvaløya 83 D1 island N Norway
Kvarnbergsvattnet 83 B3 N Sweden
Kvarner 107 B2 gulf W Croatia
Kwangju 133 B7 SW South Korea
Kwango 76 B3 Angola/Dem. Rep. Congo
Kwekwe 76 D5 C Zimbabwe
Kwidzyn 105 D2 N Poland
Kwigillingok 50 D2 Alaska, USA
Kwilu 76 C3 W Dem. Rep. Congo
Kyabé 72 H4 S Chad
Kyaikkami 131 B3 S Burma (Myanmar)
Kyakhta 118 F5 S Russian Federation
Kyjov 105 D6 SE Czech Republic
Kyklades see Cyclades
Kyle of Lochalsh 91 C4 N Scotland, United Kingdom
Kými 107 E5 C Greece
Kyoga, Lake 75 C5 C Uganda
Kyoto 133 E6 SW Japan
Kyrgyzstan 125 G2 ◆ republic C Asia
Kythira 107 E6 island S Greece
Kythnos 107 E6 island Cyclades, Greece
Kythrea see Değirmenlik
Kyushu 133 A7 island SW Japan
Kyustendil 107 E3 W Bulgaria
Kyyiv see Kiev
Kyzyl 118 E5 C Russian Federation
Kyzyl Kum 125 E2 desert Kazakhstan/Uzbekistan
Kyzylorda 118 C5 S Kazakhstan
Kyzyl-Suu 125 I2 NE Kyrgyzstan

L

La Algaba 99 C5 SW Spain
Laarne 84 B6 NW Belgium
Laâyoune 70 A3 ● NW Western Sahara
Labasa 141 J5 N Fiji
la Baule-Escoublac 97 B3 NW France
Labé 72 B4 NW Guinea
Laborec 105 F6 E Slovakia
Labrador 35 F2 cultural region Newfoundland and Labrador, SW Canada
Labrador City 35 F3 Newfoundland and Labrador, E Canada
Labrador Sea 35 F2 sea NW Atlantic Ocean
La Carolina 99 D5 S Spain
Laccadive Islands 127 C7 island group SW India
La Ceiba 55 D2 N Honduras
La Chaux-de-Fonds 101 A8 W Switzerland
Lachlan River 137 G5 New South Wales, SE Australia
la Ciotat 97 E7 SE France
La Concepción 55 F7 W Panama
Laconia 37 F3 New Hampshire, NE USA
La Coruña see A Coruña
La Crosse 40 B4 Wisconsin, N USA
La Cruz 55 D5 NW Costa Rica
Ladoga, Lake 111 A4 NW Russian Federation
Ladysmith 40 B3 Wisconsin, N USA
Lae 141 B2 W Papua New Guinea
Læsø 83 B6 island N Denmark
La Esperanza 55 C3 SW Honduras
Lafayette 40 C6 Indiana, N USA
Lafayette 39 B6 Louisiana, S USA
La Fé 56 A3 W Cuba
Lafia 72 F4 C Nigeria
la Flèche 97 C3 NW France
Lagdo, Lac de 72 F4 N Cameroon
Laghouat 70 D2 N Algeria
Lagos 72 E5 SW Nigeria
Lagos 99 A5 S Portugal
Lagos de Moreno 53 E4 SW Mexico
Lagouira 70 A4 SW Western Sahara
La Grande 49 C3 Oregon, NW USA
La Grange 39 E5 Georgia, SE USA
Lagunas 65 A3 N Chile
Lagunillas 65 B3 SE Bolivia
La Habana see Havana
Lahat 131 C7 Sumatra, W Indonesia
Laholm 83 C6 S Sweden
Lahore 127 D2 NE Pakistan
Lahr 101 B7 S Germany
Lahti 83 E5 S Finland
Laï 72 G4 S Chad
Lairg 91 D2 N Scotland, United Kingdom
La Junta 47 G6 Colorado, C USA
Lake Charles 39 B6 Louisiana, S USA
Lake District 93 C3 physical region NW England, United Kingdom
Lake Havasu City 44 A2 Arizona, SW USA
Lake Jackson 44 H5 Texas, SW USA
Lake King 137 B5 Western Australia
Lakeland 39 G7 Florida, SE USA
Lakeside 49 D9 California, W USA
Lakeview 49 C5 Oregon, NW USA
Lakewood 47 F5 Colorado, C USA
Lakonikós Kólpos 107 E6 gulf S Greece
Lakselv 83 E1 N Norway
Lakshadweep see Laccadive Islands
La Libertad 55 B2 N Guatemala
La Ligua 65 A5 C Chile
Lalín 99 B2 NW Spain
Lalitpur 127 F3 C Nepal
La Louvière 84 C7 S Belgium
la Maddalena 103 B5 Sardinia, Italy
Lamar 47 G6 Colorado, C USA
La Marmora, Punta 103 A6 ▲ Sardinia, Italy
Lambaréné 76 A2 W Gabon
Lambert Glacier 142 D4 glacier Antarctica
Lamego 99 B3 N Portugal
Lamesa 44 F3 Texas, SW USA
Lamezia Terme 103 F7 SE Italy
Lamía 107 E5 C Greece
Lamiti 141 J5 C Fiji
Lamlam, Mount 51 ▲ SW Guam
Lammermuir Hills 91 E6 SE Scotland, United Kingdom
Lamoni 43 E5 Iowa, C USA
Lampeter 93 B6 SW Wales, United Kingdom
Lamy 44 D2 New Mexico, SW USA
Lāna'i 51 C2 island Hawaii, USA
Lāna'i City 51 C2 Hawaii, USA
Lanark 91 D6 S Scotland, United Kingdom
Lanbi Kyun 131 A4 island Mergui Archipelago, S Burma (Myanmar)
Lancaster 93 C3 NW England, United Kingdom
Lancaster 49 C8 California, W USA
Lancaster 37 D5 Pennsylvania, NE USA
Lancaster Sound 33 H2 sound Nunavut, N Canada
Landen 84 D7 C Belgium
Lander 47 E6 Wyoming, C USA
Landerneau 97 A2 NW France
Landes 97 B5 cultural region SW France Europe
Land's End 95 A6 headland SW England, United Kingdom
Landshut 101 D7 SE Germany
Langar 125 E3 C Uzbekistan
Langholm 91 E7 S Scotland, United Kingdom
Langres 97 E3 N France
Langsa 131 B5 Sumatra, W Indonesia
Languedoc 97 D6 cultural region S France
Länkäran 121 J3 S Azerbaijan
Lansing 40 D5 state capital Michigan, N USA
Lanta, Ko 131 B5 island S Thailand
Lanzhou 129 E4 C China
Laojunmiao 129 D3 N China
Laon 97 E2 N France
La Orchila, Isla 57 I7 island N Venezuela
Laos 131 C3 ◆ republic SE Asia
La Palma 55 I6 SE Panama
La Paz 65 A2 ● W Bolivia
La Paz 53 C4 NW Mexico
La Paz, Bahía de 53 B3 bay W Mexico
La Pérouse Strait 133 F1 strait Japan/Russian Federation
Lapithos see Lapta
Lapland 83 D2 cultural region N Europe
La Plata 65 C5 E Argentina
La Pola 99 C1 N Spain
Lappeenranta 83 F5 SE Finland
Lapta 112 C6 NW Cyprus
Laptev Sea 118 F2 sea Arctic Ocean
Lapua 83 E4 W Finland
Łapy 105 G3 NE Poland
La Quiaca 65 B3 N Argentina
L'Aquila 103 D5 C Italy
Laramie 47 F4 Wyoming, C USA
Laramie Mountains 47 F4 Wyoming, C USA
Laredo 99 D1 N Spain
Laredo 44 G6 Texas, SW USA
Largo 39 F7 Florida, SE USA
Largo, Cayo 57 B3 island W Cuba
Largs 91 D6 W Scotland, United Kingdom
La Rioja 65 B4 NW Argentina
La Rioja 99 E2 cultural region N Spain
Lárisa 107 E5 C Greece
Lark 95 G2 E England, United Kingdom
Larkana 127 B3 SE Pakistan
Larnaca 112 D6 SE Cyprus
Lárnaka see Larnaca
Larne 89 F2 E Northern Ireland, United Kingdom
la Rochelle 97 B4 W France
la Roche-sur-Yon 97 B4 NW France
La Roda 99 E4 C Spain
La Romana 57 G4 E Dominican Republic
Las Cabezas de San Juan 99 C5 SW Spain
Las Cruces 44 D3 New Mexico, SW USA
La Serena 65 A5 C Chile
La Seu d'Urgell 99 G2 NE Spain
la Seyne-sur-Mer 97 E7 SE France
Lashio 131 B2 E Burma (Myanmar)
Lashkar Gah 125 E6 S Afghanistan
La Sila 103 E7 SW Italy
La Sirena 55 E4 E Nicaragua
Lask 105 E4 C Poland
Las Lomitas 65 C4 N Argentina
La Solana 99 D4 C Spain
La Spezia 103 B3 NW Italy
Las Tablas 55 G7 S Panama
Las Tunas 57 D3 E Cuba
Las Vegas 47 B7 Nevada, W USA
Lata 141 G3 Solomon Islands
Latacunga 63 B3 C Ecuador
la Teste 97 B5 SW France
Latina 103 C5 C Italy
La Tortuga, Isla 57 I7 island N Venezuela
La Tuque 35 E5 Québec, SE Canada
Latvia 83 E6 ◆ republic NE Europe
Lau Group 141 K5 island group E Fiji
Launceston 137 G7 Tasmania, SE Australia
Launceston 95 B5 SW England, United Kingdom
La Unión 55 D3 C Honduras
La Unión 99 F5 SE Spain
Laurel 37 D6 Delaware, NE USA
Laurel 39 C5 Mississippi, S USA
Laurel 47 E3 Montana, NW USA
Laurentian Mountains 35 E4 plateau Newfoundland and Labrador/Québec, Canada
Lauria 103 E6 S Italy
Laurinburg 39 G4 North Carolina, SE USA
Lausanne 101 A8 SW Switzerland
Laut, Pulau 131 E7 island C Indonesia
Laval 35 E5 Québec, SE Canada
Laval 97 C3 NW France
Lavanggu 141 F3 S Solomon Islands
La Vega 57 F4 C Dominican Republic
La Vila Joiosa see Villajoyosa
Lawrence 37 F4 Massachusetts, NE USA
Lawrenceburg 39 D3 Tennessee, S USA
Lawton 43 C8 Oklahoma, C USA
Layla 123 C5 C Saudi Arabia
Laytonville 49 B6 California, N USA
Laytown 89 E4 E Ireland
Lazarev Sea 142 B2 sea Antarctica
Lázaro Cárdenas 53 E5 SW Mexico
Leamington 35 C6 Ontario, S Canada
Leap 89 B7 S Ireland
Lebak 131 F5 Mindanao, S Philippines
Lebanon 43 F7 Missouri, C USA
Lebanon 37 F3 New Hampshire, NE USA
Lebanon 49 B3 Oregon, NW USA
Lebanon 123 A2 ◆ republic SW Asia
Lebap 125 D2 NE Turkmenistan
Lębork 105 D1 N Poland
Lebrija 99 C6 SW Spain
Lebu 65 A6 C Chile
le Cannet 97 F6 SE France
Lecce 103 F6 SE Italy
Lechainá 107 D5 S Greece
Leduc 33 G6 Alberta, SW Canada
Leech Lake 43 E2 Minnesota, N USA
Leeds 93 D4 N England, United Kingdom
Leek 84 E2 NE Netherlands
Leek 93 D5 C England, United Kingdom
Leer 101 B3 NW Germany
Leeuwarden 84 E2 N Netherlands
Leeward Islands 57 K4 island group E West Indies
Lefkáda 107 D5 island Ionian Islands, W Greece
Lefká Óri 107 E7 Crete, Greece
Legazpi City 131 F4 N Philippines
Legnica 105 C4 SW Poland
le Havre 97 C2 N France
Leicester 93 E5 C England, United Kingdom
Leiden 84 C4 W Netherlands
Leie 84 B6 Belgium/France
Leighton Buzzard 95 F3 E England, United Kingdom
Leinster 89 D5 cultural region E Ireland
Leinster, Mount 89 E5 ▲ SE Ireland
Leipzig 101 D4 E Germany
Leiria 99 A4 C Portugal
Leirvik 83 A5 S Norway
Leixlip 89 E4 E Ireland
Lek 84 D4 SW Netherlands
Leksand 83 C5 C Sweden
Lelystad 84 D3 C Netherlands
le Mans 97 C3 NW France
Lemesós see Limassol
Lemhi Range 47 C3 Idaho, NW USA
Lena 118 G3 NE Russian Federation
Leningradskaya 142 D6 SW Russian Federation
Lenti 105 C8 SW Hungary
Leoben 101 E7 C Austria
Leominster 93 C6 W England, United Kingdom
León 53 E4 C Mexico
León 55 D4 NW Nicaragua
León 99 C2 NW Spain
Leone 51 W American Samoa
Leonídio 107 E6 S Greece
Lepe 99 B5 S Spain
le Portel 97 D1 N France
le Puy 97 D5 C France
Léré 72 G4 SW Chad
Lérida see Lleida
Lerma 99 D2 N Spain
Leros 107 G6 island Dodecanese, Greece
Lerwick 91 B6 NE Scotland, United Kingdom
Lesbos 107 F5 island E Greece
Leshan 129 E5 C China
les Herbiers 97 B4 NW France
Leskovac 107 D3 SE Serbia
Lesotho 76 D6 ◆ monarchy S Africa
les Sables-d'Olonne 97 B4 NW France
Lesser Antilles 57 I5 island group E West Indies
Lesser Caucasus 121 G2 SW Asia
Lesser Sunda Islands 131 F8 island group C Indonesia
Leszno 105 C4 C Poland
Letchworth 95 F3 E England, United Kingdom
Lethbridge 33 G7 Alberta, SW Canada
Leti, Kepulauan 131 G8 island group E Indonesia
Letsôk-aw Kyun 131 A4 island Mergui Archipelago, S Burma (Myanmar)
Letterkenny 89 D2 NW Ireland
Leuven 84 C6 C Belgium
Leuze-en-Hainaut 84 B7 SW Belgium
Levanger 83 B4 C Norway
Levelland 44 F3 Texas, SW USA
Leverkusen 101 A5 W Germany
Levice 105 D7 SW Slovakia
Levin 139 D4 North Island, New Zealand
Lewes 95 G4 SE England, United Kingdom
Lewes 37 D6 Delaware, NE USA
Lewis, Butt of 91 B2 headland NW Scotland, United Kingdom
Lewis, Isle of 91 B2 island NW Scotland, United Kingdom
Lewis Range 47 C1 Montana, NW USA
Lewiston 47 B2 Idaho, NW USA
Lewiston 37 F3 Maine, NE USA
Lewistown 47 D2 Montana, NW USA
Lexington 39 E2 Kentucky, S USA
Lexington 43 C5 Nebraska, C USA
Leyland 93 C4 NW England, United Kingdom
Leyte 131 F4 island C Philippines
Leżajsk 105 F5 SE Poland
Lhasa 129 C4 W China
Lhazê 129 B4 China
L'Hospitalet de Llobregat 99 G2 NE Spain
Liancourt Rocks 133 C5 island group South Korea/Japan
Lianyungang 129 G4 E China
Liaoyuan 129 G2 NE China
Libby 47 C1 Montana, NW USA
Liberal 43 B7 Kansas, C USA
Liberec 105 B5 N Czech Republic
Liberia 55 D5 NW Costa Rica
Liberia 72 B5 ◆ republic W Africa
Libourne 97 C5 SW France
Libreville 76 A2 ● NW Gabon
Libya 70 F3 ◆ islamic state N Africa
Libyan Desert 70 H4 desert N Africa

Lichfield *93 D5* C England, United Kingdom
Lichtensfeld *101 C5* SE Germany
Lichtenvoorde *84 F4* E Netherlands
Lichuan *129 F4* C China
Lida *109 C2* W Belarus
Lidköping *83 C6* S Sweden
Lidzbark Warmiński *105 E2* N Poland
Liechtenstein *101 C8* ◆ *monarchy* C Europe
Liège *84 D7* E Belgium
Lienz *101 D8* W Austria
Liepāja *83 E6* W Latvia
Liezen *101 E7* C Austria
Liffey *89 E5* E Ireland
Lifford *89 D2* NW Ireland
Lifou *141 G6* *island* Îles Loyauté, E New Caledonia
Ligger Bay *95 A5* *bay* SW England, United Kingdom
Lighthouse Reef *55 C1* *reef* E Belize
Ligure, Appennino *103 B2* NW Italy
Ligurian Sea *103 A3* *sea* N Mediterranean Sea
Lihir Group *141 D1* *island group* NE Papua New Guinea
Lihue *51 B1* Kaua'i, Hawaii, USA
Likasi *76 D3* SE Dem. Rep. Congo
Liknes *83 A6* S Norway
Lille *97 D1* N France
Lillehammer *83 B5* S Norway
Lillestrøm *83 B5* S Norway
Lilongwe *76 E4* ● W Malawi
Lima *63 B5* ● W Peru
Limanowa *105 E5* S Poland
Limassol *112 C6* SW Cyprus
Limavady *89 E1* NW Northern Ireland, United Kingdom
Limerick *89 C5* SW Ireland
Límnos *107 F4* *island* E Greece
Limoges *97 C4* C France
Limón *55 F6* E Costa Rica
Limón *55 D2* NE Honduras
Limon *47 F5* Colorado, C USA
Limousin *97 C5* *cultural region* C France Europe
Limoux *97 D7* S France
Limpopo *76 E5* S Africa
Linares *65 A6* C Chile
Linares *53 E3* NE Mexico
Linares *99 D5* S Spain
Lincoln *93 E5* E England, United Kingdom
Lincoln *37 G2* Maine, NE USA
Lincoln *43 D5* *state capital* Nebraska, C USA
Lincoln Edge *93 E4* *ridge* E England, United Kingdom
Lincoln Sea *143 B4* *sea* Arctic Ocean
Linden *63 E2* E Guyana
Lindi *75 E7* SE Tanzania
Líndos *107 G6* Rhodes, Dodecanese, Greece
Line Islands *135* *island group* E Kiribati
Lingen *101 B3* NW Germany
Lingga, Kepulauan *131 C6* *island group* W Indonesia
Linköping *83 C6* S Sweden
Linnhe, Loch *91 C5* *inlet* W Scotland, United Kingdom
Linton *43 C2* North Dakota, N USA
Linz *101 E7* N Austria
Lion, Gulf of *97 D7* *gulf* S France
Lipari *103 D7* *island* Aeolian Islands, Italy
Lipetsk *111 B6* W Russian Federation
Lira *75 C5* N Uganda
Lisala *76 C1* N Dem. Rep. Congo
Lisboa *see* Lisbon
Lisbon *99 A4* ● W Portugal
Lisburn *89 E2* E Northern Ireland, United Kingdom
Lisdoonvarna *89 B5* W Ireland
Lisieux *97 C2* N France
Liski *111 A6* W Russian Federation
Lisnaskea *89 D3* W Northern Ireland, United Kingdom
Lisse *84 C4* W Netherlands
Listowel *89 B5* SW Ireland
Litang *129 D5* C China
Lithgow *137 G6* New South Wales, SE Australia
Lithuania *83 E7* ◆ *republic* NE Europe
Little Alföld *105 D7* *plain* Hungary/Slovakia
Little Andaman *127 H5* *island* Andaman Islands, SE India
Little Barrier Island *139 D2* *island* N New Zealand
Little Cayman *57 C4* *island* E Cayman Islands
Little Colorado River *47 D7* Arizona, SW USA
Little Falls *43 E3* Minnesota, N USA
Littlefield *44 F3* Texas, SW USA
Littlehampton *95 F5* SE England, United Kingdom
Little Inagua *57 E3* *island* S Bahamas
Little Minch, The *91 B3* *strait* NW Scotland, United Kingdom
Little Missouri River *43 A3* NW USA
Little Nicobar *127 H6* *island* Nicobar Islands, SE India
Little Ouse *95 G2* E England, United Kingdom
Little Rock *39 B4* *state capital* Arkansas, C USA
Little Saint Bernard Pass *97 F5* *pass* France/Italy
Little Sandy Desert *137 B4* *desert* Western Australia
Littleton *47 F5* Colorado, C USA
Littleton *37 F3* New Hampshire, NE USA
Liuzhou *129 F5* S China
Liverpool *35 F5* Nova Scotia, SE Canada
Liverpool *93 C4* NW England, United Kingdom
Liverpool Bay *93 E1* *bay* England/Wales, United Kingdom
Livingston *91 E5* C Scotland, United Kingdom
Livingston *47 D3* Montana, NW USA
Livingston *44 H4* Texas, SW USA
Livingstone *76 D4* S Zambia
Livingstone Mountains *139 A7* South Island, New Zealand
Livingston, Lake *44 H4* Texas, SW USA
Livojoki *83 E3* C Finland
Livonia *40 E5* Michigan, N USA
Livorno *103 B3* C Italy
Lizard Point *95 A6* *headland* SW England, United Kingdom
Ljubljana *101 E8* ● C Slovenia
Ljungby *83 C6* S Sweden
Ljusdal *83 C4* C Sweden
Ljusnan *83 C4* C Sweden
Llandeilo *93 B7* S Wales, United Kingdom
Llandovery *93 B6* S Wales, United Kingdom
Llandrindod Wells *93 C6* E Wales, United Kingdom
Llandudno *93 B4* N Wales, United Kingdom
Llanes *99 D1* N Spain
Llanos *63 C2* *physical region* Colombia/Venezuela
Llanwrtyd Wells *93 B6* C Wales, United Kingdom
Lleida *99 F2* NE Spain
Lleyn Peninsula *93 A5* *peninsula* NW Wales, United Kingdom
Llucmajor *99 H4* Majorca, Spain
Lobatse *76 D6* SE Botswana
Löbau *101 E4* E Germany
Lobito *76 B4* W Angola
Locarno *101 B8* S Switzerland
Lochboisdale *91 A4* NW Scotland, United Kingdom
Lochdon *91 C5* W Scotland, United Kingdom
Lochem *84 E4* E Netherlands
Lochgilphead *91 C5* W Scotland, United Kingdom
Lochinver *91 C2* N Scotland, United Kingdom
Lochmaddy *91 B3* NW Scotland, United Kingdom
Lochnagar *91 E4* ▲ C Scotland, United Kingdom
Lochy, Loch *91 C4* N Scotland, United Kingdom
Lockerbie *91 E7* S Scotland, United Kingdom
Lockport *37 C3* New York, NE USA
Lodja *76 C2* C Dem. Rep. Congo
Lodwar *75 D5* NW Kenya
Lodz *105 E4* C Poland
Lofoten *83 C2* *island group* C Norway
Logan *47 D4* Utah, W USA
Logan, Mount *33 E5* ▲ Yukon Territory, W Canada
Logansport *40 D6* Indiana, N USA
Logroño *99 E2* N Spain
Loibl Pass *101 E8* *pass* Austria/Slovenia
Loire *97 C3* C France
Loja *63 B4* S Ecuador
Lokitaung *75 D4* NW Kenya
Lokoja *72 E5* C Nigeria
Lola, Mount *49 B6* ▲ California, W USA
Lolland *83 B7* *island* S Denmark
Lom *107 E2* NW Bulgaria
Lomami *76 D2* C Dem. Rep. Congo
Lomas de Zamora *65 C5* E Argentina
Lombardia *see* Lombardy
Lombardy *103 C2* *cultural region* N Italy
Lombok, Pulau *131 E8* *island* Nusa Tenggara, C Indonesia
Lomé *72 D5* ● S Togo
Lomela *76 C2* C Dem. Rep. Congo
Lommel *84 D6* N Belgium
Lomond, Loch *91 D5* C Scotland, United Kingdom
Lomonosov Ridge *143 C4* *undersea feature* Arctic Ocean
Lompoc *49 C8* California, W USA
Łomża *105 F2* NE Poland
Loncoche *65 A6* C Chile
London *95 G4* ● SE England, United Kingdom
London *35 C6* Ontario, S Canada
London *39 F3* Kentucky, S USA
Londonderry *89 D2* NW Northern Ireland, United Kingdom
Londonderry, Cape *137 C1* *cape* Western Australia
Londrina *63 F7* S Brazil
Lone Pine *49 C7* California, W USA
Long Bay *39 H4* *bay* North Carolina/South Carolina, E USA
Long Beach *49 C9* California, W USA
Long Eaton *93 E5* C England, United Kingdom
Longford *89 D4* C Ireland
Long Island *57 E2* *island* C Bahamas
Long Island *37 E5* *island* New York, NE USA
Long Island Sound *37 F5* *sound* NE USA
Longlac *35 B4* Ontario, S Canada
Longmont *47 F5* Colorado, C USA
Longreach *137 G3* Queensland, E Australia
Long Strait *118 H1* *strait* NE Russian Federation
Longview *44 H3* Texas, SW USA
Longview *49 B3* Washington, NW USA
Longyan *129 G5* SE China
Longyearbyen *143 C5* ○ W Svalbard
Lons-le-Saunier *97 E4* E France
Loop Head *89 A5* *promontory* W Ireland
Lop Nur *129 C3* *seasonal lake* NW China
Loppersum *84 F2* NE Netherlands
Lorca *99 E5* S Spain
Lorengau *141 B1* Manus Island, N Papua New Guinea
Loreto *53 B3* W Mexico
Lorient *97 B3* NW France
Lorn, Firth of *91 B5* *inlet* W Scotland, United Kingdom
Lörrach *101 B7* S Germany
Lorraine *97 F2* *cultural region* NE France Europe
Los Alamos *44 D2* New Mexico, SW USA
Los Amates *55 B3* E Guatemala
Los Ángeles *65 A6* C Chile
Los Angeles *49 C8* California, W USA
Lošinj *107 A2* *island* W Croatia
Los Mochis *53 C3* C Mexico
Los Roques, Islas *57 H7* *island group* N Venezuela
Lossiemouth *91 E3* NE Scotland, United Kingdom
Los Testigos, Islas *57 J7* *island* NE Venezuela
Lot *97 C5* *cultural region* C France Europe
Lot *97 C6* S France
Lotagipi Swamp *75 D4* *wetland* Kenya/Sudan
Louangphabang *131 B3* N Laos
Loudéac *97 B2* NW France
Loudi *129 F5* S China
Louga *72 A3* NW Senegal
Loughborough *93 E5* C England, United Kingdom
Loughrea *89 C4* W Ireland
Louisburgh *89 B3* NW Ireland
Louisiade Archipelago *141 D3* *island group* SE Papua New Guinea
Louisiana *39 A5* ◐ *state* S USA
Louisville *39 E2* Kentucky, S USA
Louisville Ridge *14* *undersea feature* S Pacific Ocean
Loup River *43 C5* Nebraska, C USA
Lourdes *97 C6* S France
Louth *89 E3* NE Ireland
Louth *93 F4* E England, United Kingdom
Loutrá *107 E4* N Greece
Louvain-la Neuve *84 C7* C Belgium
Louviers *97 D2* N France
Loveland *47 F5* Colorado, C USA
Lovelock *47 A5* Nevada, W USA
Lovosice *105 B5* NW Czech Republic
Lóvua *76 C3* NE Angola
Lowell *47 C2* Idaho, NW USA
Lowell *37 F4* Massachusetts, NE USA
Lower California *53 B3* *peninsula* NW Mexico
Lower Hutt *139 D5* North Island, New Zealand
Lower Lough Erne *89 D2* SW Northern Ireland, United Kingdom
Lower Red Lake *43 E2* Minnesota, N USA
Lower Tunguska *118 E4* N Russian Federation
Lowestoft *95 H2* E England, United Kingdom
Loyauté, Îles *141 G6* *island group* S New Caledonia
Lualaba *76 D2* SE Dem. Rep. Congo
Luanda *76 B3* ● NW Angola
Luangwa *76 E4* Mozambique/Zambia
Luanshya *76 D4* C Zambia
Luarca *99 C1* N Spain
Lubaczów *105 G5* SE Poland
Lubań *105 B4* SW Poland
Lubango *76 B4* SW Angola
Lubao *76 D2* C Dem. Rep. Congo
Lübben *101 E4* E Germany
Lübbenau *101 E4* E Germany
Lubbock *44 F3* Texas, SW USA
Lübeck *101 C2* N Germany
Lubelska, Wyżyna *105 F4* *plateau* SE Poland
Lubin *105 C4* SW Poland
Lublin *105 F4* E Poland
Lubliniec *105 D5* S Poland
Lubny *109 E4* NE Ukraine
Lubsko *105 B4* W Poland
Lubumbashi *76 D3* SE Dem. Rep. Congo
Lucan *89 E4* E Ireland
Lucano, Appennino *103 E6* S Italy
Lucapa *76 C3* NE Angola
Lucca *103 C3* C Italy
Luce Bay *91 C7* *inlet* SW Scotland, United Kingdom
Lucena *131 F4* Luzon, N Philippines
Lucena *99 D5* S Spain
Lučenec *105 E7* C Slovakia
Lucknow *127 E3* N India
Luda Kamchiya *107 F3* E Bulgaria
Lüderitz *76 B6* SW Namibia
Ludhiana *127 D2* N India
Ludington *40 D4* Michigan, N USA
Ludlow *93 C6* W England, United Kingdom
Ludvika *83 C5* C Sweden
Ludwigsburg *101 B6* SW Germany
Ludwigsfelde *101 D4* NE Germany
Ludwigshafen *101 B6* W Germany
Ludwigslust *101 C3* N Germany
Ludza *83 F6* E Latvia
Luena *76 C3* E Angola
Lufira *76 D3* SE Dem. Rep. Congo
Lufkin *44 H4* Texas, SW USA
Luga *111 A4* NW Russian Federation
Lugano *101 B8* S Switzerland
Luganville *141 G4* C Vanuatu
Lugenda, Rio *76 F4* N Mozambique
Lugnaquillia Mountain *89 E5* ▲ E Ireland
Lugo *99 B1* NW Spain
Lugoj *109 A6* W Romania
Luhans'k *109 G5* E Ukraine
Lukenie *76 C2* C Dem. Rep. Congo
Łuków *105 F4* E Poland
Lukuga *76 D3* SE Dem. Rep. Congo
Luleå *83 D3* N Sweden
Luleälven *83 D3* N Sweden
Lulimba *76 D2* E Dem. Rep. Congo
Lulonga *76 C1* NW Dem. Rep. Congo
Luma *51* E American Samoa
Lumberton *39 H4* North Carolina, SE USA
Lumbo *76 F4* NE Mozambique
Lumi *141 A1* NW Papua New Guinea
Lumsden *139 B7* South Island, New Zealand
Lund *83 C7* S Sweden
Lundy *95 B4* *island* SW England, United Kingdom
Lüneburg *101 C3* N Germany
Lungué-Bungo *76 C4* Angola/Zambia
Luninyets *109 C3* SW Belarus
Lunteren *84 D4* C Netherlands
Luoyang *129 F4* C China
Lurgan *89 E2* S Northern Ireland, United Kingdom
Lúrio *76 F4* NE Mozambique
Lúrio, Rio *76 F4* NE Mozambique
Lusaka *76 D4* ● SE Zambia
Lut, Dasht-e *123 F3* *desert* E Iran
Luti *141 E2* NW Solomon Islands
Luton *95 F3* E England, United Kingdom
Łutselk'e *33 G5* Northwest Territories, W Canada
Luts'k *109 C4* NW Ukraine
Lutzow-Holm Bay *142 D3* *bay* Antarctica
Luuq *75 E4* SW Somalia
Luwego *75 D7* S Tanzania
Luxembourg *84 E9* ● S Luxembourg
Luxembourg *84 E8* ◆ *monarchy* NW Europe
Luxor *70 J3* E Egypt
Luza *111 C4* NW Russian Federation
Luzern *101 B8* C Switzerland
Luzon *131 F3* *island* N Philippines
Luzon Strait *131 F3* *strait* Philippines/Taiwan
L'viv *109 B4* W Ukraine
Lycksele *83 D3* N Sweden
Lyepyel' *109 D2* N Belarus
Lyme Bay *95 C5* *bay* S England, United Kingdom
Lyme Regis *95 D5* S England, United Kingdom
Lymington *95 E5* S England, United Kingdom
Lynchburg *39 G2* Virginia, NE USA
Lynn *37 F4* Massachusetts, NE USA
Lynn Lake *33 H6* Manitoba, C Canada
Lynton *95 C4* SW England, United Kingdom
Lyon *97 E5* E France
Lysychans'k *109 G4* E Ukraine
Lytham St Anne's *93 C4* NW England, United Kingdom
Lyttelton *139 C6* South Island, New Zealand

M

Maamturk Mountains *89 B4* W Ireland
Maaseik *84 E6* NE Belgium
Maastricht *84 E6* SE Netherlands
Mablethorpe *93 F4* E England, United Kingdom
Macao *129 G6* S China
Macapá *63 F3* N Brazil
Macclesfield *93 D5* C England, United Kingdom
Macdonnell Ranges *137 D3* Northern Territory, C Australia
Macduff *91 F3* NE Scotland, United Kingdom
Macedonia *107 D4* ◆ *republic* SE Europe
Maceió *63 I5* E Brazil
Macgillycuddy's Reeks *89 B6* SW Ireland
Machala *63 A4* SW Ecuador
Machanga *76 E5* E Mozambique
Machilipatnam *127 E5* E India
Machynlleth *93 B6* C Wales, United Kingdom
Mackay *137 G3* Queensland, NE Australia
Mackay, Lake *137 D3* *salt lake* Northern Territory/Western Australia
Mackenzie *33 F4* Northwest Territories, NW Canada
Mackenzie Bay *142 E4* *bay* Antarctica
Mackenzie Mountains *33 E4* Northwest Territories, NW Canada
Macleod, Lake *137 A4* Western Australia
Macomb *40 B6* Illinois, N USA
Macomer *103 A6* Sardinia, Italy
Mâcon *97 E4* C France
Macon *39 F5* Georgia, SE USA
Macon *43 F6* Missouri, C USA
Macroom *89 B6* SW Ireland
Macuspana *53 H5* SE Mexico
Ma'daba *123 A2* NW Jordan
Madagascar *76 G5* ◆ *republic* W Indian Ocean
Madang *141 B2* N Papua New Guinea
Made *84 C5* S Netherlands
Madeira, Rio *63 E4* Bolivia/Brazil
Madeleine, Îles de la *35 F4* *island group* Québec, E Canada
Madeline *49 C5* California, W USA
Madera *49 C7* California, W USA
Madhya Pradesh *127 E4* *state* C India
Madison *43 D4* South Dakota, N USA
Madison *40 B4* *state capital* Wisconsin, N USA
Madisonville *39 D2* Kentucky, S USA
Madiun *131 D8* C Indonesia
Madras *see* Chennai
Madre de Dios, Río *65 A1* Bolivia/Peru
Madre del Sur, Sierra *53 F5* S Mexico
Madre, Laguna *53 F3* *lagoon* NE Mexico
Madre, Laguna *44 H6* *lagoon* Texas, SW USA
Madre Occidental, Sierra *53 C3* C Mexico
Madre Oriental, Sierra *53 E4* C Mexico
Madrid *99 D3* ● C Spain
Madrid *99 D3* *cultural region* C Spain
Madurai *127 D7* S India
Madura, Pulau *131 E8* *island* C Indonesia
Maebashi *133 G5* S Japan
Mae Nam Nan *131 B3* NW Thailand
Maéwo *141 G4* *island* C Vanuatu
Mafia *75 E7* *island* E Tanzania
Magadan *118 H3* E Russian Federation
Magarida *141 C3* SW Papua New Guinea
Magdalena *65 B1* N Bolivia
Magdalena *53 B2* NW Mexico
Magdalena, Isla *53 B4* *island* W Mexico
Magdalena, Río *63 B3* C Colombia
Magdeburg *101 D4* C Germany
Magee, Island *89 F2* *island* E Northern Ireland, United Kingdom
Magelang *131 C8* C Indonesia
Magellan, Strait of *65 B9* *strait* Argentina/Chile
Magerøya *83 D1* *island* N Norway
Maggiore, Lake *103 B1* Italy/Switzerland
Maghera *89 E2* C Northern Ireland, United Kingdom
Maglie *103 F6* SE Italy
Magna *47 D5* Utah, W USA
Magnitogorsk *118 C4* C Russian Federation
Magnolia *39 B4* Arkansas, C USA
Magta' Lahjar *72 B3* SW Mauritania
Magtymguly *125 C3* W Turkmenistan
Mahajanga *76 G4* NW Madagascar
Mahakam, Sungai *131 E6* Borneo, C Indonesia
Mahalapye *76 D5* SE Botswana
Mahanadi *127 F4* E India
Maharashtra *127 D5* *state* W India
Mahbubnagar *127 D5* C India
Mahia Peninsula *139 E4* *peninsula* North Island, New Zealand
Mahilyow *109 D2* E Belarus
Mahmud-e Raqi *125 F5* NE Afghanistan
Maidan Shahr *125 F5* NW Afghanistan
Maidenhead *95 F3* S England, United Kingdom
Maidens, The *89 F2* *island group* E Northern Ireland, United Kingdom
Maidstone *95 G4* SE England, United Kingdom
Maiduguri *72 G4* NE Nigeria
Maimanah *125 E4* NW Afghanistan
Main *101 C5* C Germany
Mai-Ndombe, Lac *76 C2* W Dem. Rep. Congo
Maine *97 C2* *cultural region* NW France
Maine *37 F2* ◐ *state* NE USA
Maine, Gulf of *37 G3* *gulf* NE USA
Mainland *91 E1* *island* N Scotland, United Kingdom
Mainland *91 A6* *island* NE Scotland, United Kingdom
Mainz *101 B5* SW Germany
Maitri *142 C3* *Indian research station* Antarctica
Maizhokunggar *129 C4* W China
Majorca *99 H4* *island* E Spain
Makarov Basin *143 C4* *undersea feature* Arctic Ocean
Makassar *131 E7* Celebes, C Indonesia
Makassar Straits *131 E7* *strait* C Indonesia
Makay *76 G5* SW Madagascar
Makeni *72 B4* C Sierra Leone
Makhachkala *111 B9* SW Russian Federation
Makiyivka *109 G5* E Ukraine
Makkah *see* Mecca
Makkovik *35 G2* Newfoundland and Labrador, NE Canada
Makó *105 F8* SE Hungary
Makoua *76 B2* C Congo
Makran Coast *123 F4* *coastal region* SE Iran
Makrany *109 B3* SW Belarus
Makurdi *72 F5* C Nigeria
Malabo *72 F6* ● Isla de Bioco, NW Equatorial Guinea
Malacca, Strait of *131 B6* *strait* Indonesia/Malaysia
Malacky *105 C7* W Slovakia
Maladzyechna *109 C2* C Belarus
Málaga *99 D6* S Spain
Malahide *89 E4* E Ireland
Malaita *141 F3* *island* N Solomon Islands
Malakal *75 C3* N South Sudan
Malang *131 D8* Java, C Indonesia
Malanje *76 B3* NW Angola
Mälaren *83 D5* C Sweden
Malatya *121 E4* SE Turkey
Malawi *76 E4* ◆ *republic* S Africa
Malay Peninsula *131 B5* *peninsula* Malaysia/Thailand
Malaysia *131 C5* ◆ *monarchy* SE Asia
Malbork *105 E2* N Poland
Malchin *101 D2* N Germany
Malden *43 G7* Missouri, C USA
Malden Island *135* *atoll* E Kiribati
Maldives *127 C9* ◆ *republic* N Indian Ocean
Male *127 C8* ● C Maldives
Malekula *141 G5* *island* W Vanuatu
Malheur Lake *49 C4* Oregon, NW USA
Malheur River *49 C4* Oregon, NW USA
Mali *72 D3* ◆ *republic* W Africa
Mali Kyun *131 A4* *island* Mergui Archipelago, S Burma (Myanmar)
Malin *89 D1* NW Ireland
Malindi *75 E6* SE Kenya
Malin Head *89 D1* *headland* NW Ireland
Mallaig *91 C4* N Scotland, United Kingdom
Mallawi *70 I3* C Egypt
Mallorca *see* Majorca
Mallow *89 C6* SW Ireland
Malmberget *83 D2* N Sweden
Malmédy *84 E7* E Belgium
Malmö *83 C7* S Sweden
Malone *37 E2* New York, NE USA
Małopolska, Wyżyna *105 F5* *plateau* S Poland
Malozemel'skaya Tundra *111 D3* *physical region* NW Russian Federation
Malta *47 E1* Montana, NW USA
Malta *112 A6* ◆ *republic* C Mediterranean Sea
Malta Channel *103 D9* *strait* Italy/Malta
Malton *93 E4* N England, United Kingdom
Maluku *see* Moluccas
Malung *83 C5* C Sweden
Malvern Hills *93 C6* *hill range* W England, United Kingdom
Mamberamo, Sungai *131 I7* Papua, E Indonesia
Mamonovo *83 D7* W Russian Federation
Mamoré, Rio *65 B1* Bolivia/Brazil
Mamou *72 B4* W Guinea
Mamoudzou *76 G4* ○ C Mayotte
Mamuno *76 C5* W Botswana
Manacor *99 H4* Spain
Manado *131 F6* Celebes, C Indonesia
Managua *55 D5* ● W Nicaragua
Managua, Lake *55 D4* W Nicaragua
Manakara *76 G5* SE Madagascar
Manama *123 D4* ● N Bahrain
Mananjary *76 G5* SE Madagascar
Manapouri, Lake *139 A7* South Island, New Zealand
Manas, Gora *125 F2* ▲ Kyrgyzstan/Uzbekistan
Manau *141 C2* S Papua New Guinea
Manaus *63 E4* NW Brazil
Manavgat *121 C5* SW Turkey
Manbij *123 B1* N Syria
Manchester *93 D4* NW England, United Kingdom
Manchester *37 F3* New Hampshire, NE USA
Mandalay *131 A2* C Burma (Myanmar)
Mandan *43 B2* North Dakota, N USA
Mand, Rud-e *123 D3* S Iran
Mandurah *137 B5* Western Australia
Manduria *103 F6* SE Italy
Mandya *127 D6* C India
Manfredonia *103 E5* SE Italy
Mangai *76 C2* W Dem. Rep. Congo
Mangalmé *72 H4* SE Chad
Mangalore *127 D6* W India
Mangerton Mountain *89 B6* ▲ SW Ireland
Mangoky *76 F5* W Madagascar
Manhattan *43 D6* Kansas, C USA
Manicouagan, Réservoir *35 E4* Québec, E Canada
Manihiki *135* *atoll* N Cook Islands
Manila *131 F4* ● N Philippines
Manisa *120 A3* W Turkey
Manistee River *40 D4* Michigan, N USA
Manitoba *33 H6* ◐ *province* S Canada
Manitoba, Lake *33 H6* Manitoba, S Canada
Manitoulin Island *35 C5* *island* Ontario, S Canada
Manizales *63 B2* W Colombia
Manjimup *137 B6* Western Australia
Mankato *43 E3* Minnesota, N USA
Manlleu *99 G2* NE Spain
Manmad *127 D4* W India
Mannar *127 E7* NW Sri Lanka
Mannar, Gulf of *127 D8* *gulf* India/Sri Lanka
Mannheim *101 B6* SW Germany
Manokwari *131 H6* E Indonesia
Manono *76 D3* SE Dem. Rep. Congo
Manorhamilton *89 C3* NW Ireland
Manosque *97 E6* SE France
Mansa *76 D3* N Zambia
Mansel Island *33 I4* *island* Nunavut, NE Canada
Mansfield *93 E5* C England, United Kingdom
Mansfield *40 E6* Ohio, N USA
Mansfield *37 C4* Pennsylvania, NE USA
Mantova *103 C2* NW Italy
Manua Islands *51* *island group* E American Samoa
Manurewa *139 D2* North Island, New Zealand
Manus Island *141 B1* *island* N Papua New Guinea
Manzanares *99 D4* C Spain
Manzanillo *57 D3* E Cuba
Manzanillo *53 D5* SW Mexico
Manzhouli *129 F1* N China
Mao *72 G3* W Chad
Maó *99 H3* Minorca, E Spain
Maoke, Pegunungan *131 I7* Papua, E Indonesia

◐ Administrative region ◆ Country ● Country capital ◇ Dependent territory ○ Dependent territory capital Mountain range ▲ Mountain Volcano River Lake Reservoir

Maoming 129 F6 S China
Maputo 76 E6 ● S Mozambique
Maraa 141 A6 W French Polynesia
Marabá 63 G4 NE Brazil
Maracaibo 63 C1 NW Venezuela
Maracaibo, Lake 63 B2 inlet NW Venezuela
Maradah 70 G3 N Libya
Maradi 72 F3 S Niger
Maragheh 123 C1 NW Iran
Marajó, Baía de 63 G3 bay N Brazil
Marajó, Ilha de 63 F3 island N Brazil
Maranhão 63 G4 state E Brazil
Marañón, Río 63 B4 ≈ N Peru
Marathon 35 B4 Ontario, S Canada
Marathon 44 E4 Texas, SW USA
Maraza 121 I2 E Azerbaijan
Marbella 99 D6 S Spain
Marble Bar 137 B3 Western Australia
Marburg an der Lahn 101 B5 W Germany
March 95 G2 E England, United Kingdom
Marche 97 D4 cultural region C France
Marche-en-Famenne 84 D8 SE Belgium
Mar Chiquita, Laguna 65 B5 ◎ C Argentina
Marcy, Mount 37 E3 ▲ New York, NE USA
Mardan 127 C1 N Pakistan
Mar del Plata 65 C6 E Argentina
Mardin 121 F4 SE Turkey
Maré 141 G6 island Îles Loyauté, E New Caledonia
Mareeba 137 G2 Queensland, NE Australia
Maree, Loch 91 C3 ◎ N Scotland, United Kingdom
Marfa 44 E4 Texas, SW USA
Margarita, Isla de 63 D1 island N Venezuela
Margate 95 H4 SE England, United Kingdom
Margherita, Lake 75 D4 ◎ SW Ethiopia
Margow, Dasht-e 125 D6 desert SW Afghanistan
Mari 141 A3 SW Papua New Guinea
María Cleofas, Isla 53 C5 island C Mexico
Maria Island 137 G7 island Tasmania, SE Australia
María Madre, Isla 53 C4 island C Mexico
María Magdalena, Isla 53 C4 island C Mexico
Mariana Islands 15 island group Guam/ Northern Mariana Islands
Mariana Trench 15 undersea feature W Pacific Ocean
Mariánské Lázně 105 A5 W Czech Republic
Maribor 101 F8 NE Slovenia
Maridi 75 B4 S South Sudan
Marie Byrd Land 142 B5 physical region Antarctica
Marie-Galante 57 K5 island SE Guadeloupe
Mariental 76 C6 SW Namibia
Mariestad 83 C6 S Sweden
Marietta 39 E4 Georgia, SE USA
Marietta 40 F7 Ohio, N USA
Marília 63 F7 S Brazil
Marín 99 B2 NW Spain
Maringá 63 F7 S Brazil
Marion 40 B8 Illinois, N USA
Marion 43 F4 Iowa, C USA
Marion 40 E6 Ohio, N USA
Mariscal Estigarribia 65 C3 NW Paraguay
Maritsa 107 F3 ≈ SW Europe
Mariupol' 109 G5 SE Ukraine
Marka 75 F5 S Somalia
Market Harborough 93 E6 C England, United Kingdom
Markham, Mount 142 C5 ▲ Antarctica
Markounda 72 H5 NW Central African Republic
Marktredwitz 101 D5 E Germany
Marmande 97 C5 SW France
Marmara, Sea of 120 A2 sea NW Turkey
Marmaris 120 A5 SW Turkey
Marne 97 E2 cultural region N France Europe
Marne 97 E3 ≈ N France
Maro 72 H4 S Chad
Maroantsetra 76 G4 NE Madagascar
Maromokotro 76 G4 ▲ N Madagascar
Maroni 63 F2 ≈ French Guiana/Surinam
Maroua 72 G4 N Cameroon
Marquesas Islands 135 island group N French Polynesia
Marquette 40 C2 Michigan, N USA
Marrakech 70 C2 W Morocco
Marrawah 137 F7 Tasmania, SE Australia
Marree 137 E5 South Australia
Marsa al Burayqah 70 G3 N Libya
Marsabit 75 D5 N Kenya
Marsala 103 C8 Sicily, Italy
Marsberg 101 B4 W Germany
Marseille 97 E7 SE France
Marshall 43 D3 Minnesota, N USA
Marshall 44 I3 Texas, SW USA
Marshall Islands 135 ◆ republic W Pacific Ocean
Marsh Harbour 57 D1 Great Abaco, W Bahamas
Martigues 97 E6 SE France
Martin 105 E6 N Slovakia
Martinique 57 K5 French ◇ E West Indies
Martinique Passage 57 K5 channel Dominica/Martinique
Marton 139 D4 North Island, New Zealand
Martos 99 D5 S Spain
Mary 125 D4 S Turkmenistan
Maryborough 137 H4 Queensland, E Australia
Maryland 39 I2 ◐ state NE USA
Maryville 43 E5 Missouri, C USA
Maryville 39 F3 Tennessee, S USA
Masai Steppe 75 D6 grassland NW Tanzania
Masaka 75 C5 SW Uganda
Masan 133 C6 S South Korea
Masasi 75 D7 SE Tanzania
Masaya 55 D5 W Nicaragua
Maseru 76 D6 ● W Lesotho
Mashhad 123 F1 NE Iran
Masindi 75 C5 W Uganda
Masira, Gulf of 123 F5 bay E Oman
Mask, Lough 89 B4 ◎ W Ireland
Mason 44 G4 Texas, SW USA
Mason City 43 E4 Iowa, C USA
Masqat see Muscat
Massa 103 B3 C Italy
Massachusetts 37 F4 ◐ state NE USA
Massawa see Mits'iwa
Massena 37 D2 New York, NE USA
Massenya 72 G4 SW Chad
Massif Central 97 D5 plateau C France
Masterton 139 D5 North Island, New Zealand
Masuda 133 D7 SW Japan
Masvingo 76 E5 SE Zimbabwe
Matadi 76 B3 W Dem. Rep. Congo
Matagalpa 55 D4 C Nicaragua
Matale 127 E8 C Sri Lanka
Matamata 139 D3 North Island, New Zealand
Matamoros 53 F3 NE Mexico
Matane 35 F4 Québec, SE Canada
Matanzas 57 B2 NW Cuba
Matara 127 E8 S Sri Lanka
Mataram 131 E8 C Indonesia
Mataró 99 G2 E Spain
Matātula, Cape 51 headland W American Samoa
Mataura 139 B8 South Island, New Zealand
Mataura 139 B7 ≈ South Island, New Zealand
Matautu 141 B5 C Samoa
Matā'utu 141 K4 ○ N Wallis and Futuna
Mataveri 141 C6 Easter Island, Chile
Matera 103 E6 S Italy
Matías Romero 53 G5 SE Mexico
Matlock 93 D5 C England, United Kingdom
Mato Grosso 63 E6 state W Brazil
Mato Grosso do Sul 63 E7 state S Brazil
Matosinhos 99 B3 NW Portugal
Matsue 133 D6 SW Japan
Matsumoto 133 F5 S Japan
Matsuyama 133 D7 Shikoku, SW Japan
Matterhorn 101 B9 ▲ Italy/Switzerland
Matthew Town 57 E3 S Bahamas
Maturín 63 D1 NE Venezuela
Mau 127 E3 N India
Maui 51 D2 island Hawaii, USA
Maun 76 C5 C Botswana
Mauna Loa 51 D3 ⛰ Hawaii, USA
Mauritania 72 A2 ◆ republic W Africa
Mauritius 66 ◆ republic W Indian Ocean
Mawlamyine 131 B3 S Burma (Myanmar)
Mawson 142 E4 Australian research station Antarctica
Maya 55 B2 ≈ E Russian Federation
Mayaguana 57 F3 island SE Bahamas
Mayaguana Passage 57 E3 passage SE Bahamas
Mayagüez 57 H4 W Puerto Rico
Maybole 91 D6 W Scotland, United Kingdom
Maych'ew 75 D3 N Ethiopia
Maydan Shahr 125 F5 E Afghanistan
Mayfield 139 C6 South Island, New Zealand
May, Isle of 91 F5 island E Scotland, United Kingdom
Maykop 111 A8 SW Russian Federation
Maymyo 131 A2 C Burma (Myanmar)
Mayor Island 139 D3 island NE New Zealand
Mayotte 76 G4 French ◇ E Africa
Mazabuka 76 D4 S Zambia
Mazar-e Sharif 125 F4 N Afghanistan
Mazatlán 53 D4 C Mexico
Mazury 105 F2 physical region NE Poland
Mazyr 109 D3 SE Belarus
Mbabane 76 E6 ● NW Swaziland
Mbala 76 E3 NE Zambia
Mbale 75 C5 E Uganda
Mbandaka 76 C2 NW Dem. Rep. Congo
M'Banza Congo 76 B3 NW Angola
Mbanza-Ngungu 76 B2 W Dem. Rep. Congo
Mbarara 75 C5 SW Uganda
Mbé 72 G5 N Cameroon
Mbeya 75 C7 SW Tanzania
Mbuji-Mayi 76 C3 S Dem. Rep. Congo
McAlester 43 D8 Oklahoma, C USA
McAllen 44 G6 Texas, SW USA
McCamey 44 F4 Texas, SW USA
McCammon 47 D4 Idaho, NW USA
McComb 39 C6 Mississippi, S USA
McCook 43 B5 Nebraska, C USA
McDermitt 47 B4 Nevada, W USA
McKinley, Mount 50 D2 ▲ Alaska, USA
McKinley Park 50 E2 Alaska, USA
McLaughlin 43 B3 South Dakota, N USA
M'Clintock Channel 33 G3 channel Nunavut, N Canada
McMinnville 49 B3 Oregon, NW USA
McMurdo 142 C6 US research station Antarctica
McNary 44 D4 Texas, SW USA
McPherson 43 D6 Kansas, C USA
Mdantsane 76 D7 SE South Africa
Mead, Lake 47 C7 ⊠ Arizona/Nevada, W USA
Meadville 37 B4 Pennsylvania, NE USA
Mecca 123 B5 W Saudi Arabia
Mechelen 84 C6 C Belgium
Mecklenburger Bucht 101 C2 bay N Germany
Mecsek 105 D8 ⛰ SW Hungary
Medan 131 B6 E Indonesia
Medellín 63 B2 NW Colombia
Médenine 70 F2 SE Tunisia
Medford 49 B4 Oregon, NW USA
Mediaş 109 B6 C Romania
Medicine Hat 33 G7 Alberta, SW Canada
Medina 123 B4 W Saudi Arabia
Medinaceli 99 E3 N Spain
Medina del Campo 99 D3 N Spain
Mediterranean Sea 112 D4 sea Africa/Asia/Europe
Médoc 97 B5 cultural region SW France
Medvezh'yegorsk 111 B3 NW Russian Federation
Medway 95 G4 ≈ SE England, United Kingdom
Meekatharra 137 B4 Western Australia
Meerssen 84 E6 SE Netherlands
Meerut 127 D2 N India
Mehtar Lām 125 G5 E Afghanistan
Mejillones 65 A3 N Chile
Mek'ele 75 D2 N Ethiopia
Meknès 70 C1 N Morocco
Mekong 131 C4 ≈ SE Asia
Mekong, Mouths of the 131 C5 delta S Vietnam
Melaka 131 B6 SW Malaysia
Melanesia 141 G3 island group W Pacific Ocean
Melbourne 39 G7 Florida, SE USA
Melbourne 137 F6 state capital Victoria, SE Australia
Melghir, Chott 70 E2 salt lake E Algeria
Melilla 69 D1 S Spain
Melita 33 H7 Manitoba, S Canada
Melitopol' 109 F6 SE Ukraine
Melle 84 B6 NW Belgium
Melleray, Mount 89 D6 ▲ S Ireland
Mellerud 83 C6 S Sweden
Mellieha 112 B6 E Malta
Mellizo Sur, Cerro 65 A8 ▲ S Chile
Melo 65 D5 NE Uruguay
Melsungen 101 C5 C Germany
Melton Mowbray 93 E5 C England, United Kingdom
Melun 97 D3 N France
Melville Island 137 D1 island Northern Territory, N Australia
Melville Island 33 G2 island Parry Islands, Northwest Territories, NW Canada
Melville, Lake 35 G3 ◎ Newfoundland and Labrador, E Canada
Melville Peninsula 33 H3 peninsula Nunavut, NE Canada
Memmingen 101 C7 S Germany
Memphis 39 C3 Tennessee, S USA
Menai Bridge 93 B5 NW Wales, United Kingdom
Ménaka 72 E3 E Mali
Menaldum 84 D2 N Netherlands
Mende 97 D6 S France
Mendeleyev Ridge 143 C3 undersea feature Arctic Ocean
Mendi 141 B2 W Papua New Guinea
Mendip Hills 95 D4 hill range S England, United Kingdom
Mendocino, Cape 49 A5 headland California, W USA
Mendoza 65 A5 W Argentina
Menemen 120 A3 W Turkey
Menengiyn Tal 129 F2 plain E Mongolia
Menongue 76 B4 C Angola
Menorca see Minorca
Mentawai, Kepulauan 131 B7 island group W Indonesia
Meppel 84 E3 NE Netherlands
Merano 103 C1 N Italy
Mercedes 65 C4 NE Argentina
Mercedes 44 G6 Texas, SW USA
Meredith, Lake 44 E2 ⊠ Texas, SW USA
Mérida 53 H4 SE Mexico
Mérida 99 C4 W Spain
Mérida 63 C2 W Venezuela
Meridian 39 D5 Mississippi, S USA
Mérignac 97 B5 SW France
Merizo 51 SW Guam
Merowe 75 C2 desert W Sudan
Merredin 137 B5 Western Australia
Merrick 91 D7 ▲ S Scotland, United Kingdom
Merrimack River 37 F4 ≈ Massachusetts/New Hampshire, NE USA
Mersey 93 C4 ≈ NW England, UK
Mersin 121 D5 S Turkey
Merthyr Tydfil 93 C7 S Wales, United Kingdom
Merton 95 F4 SE England, United Kingdom
Meru 75 D5 C Kenya
Merzifon 121 D2 N Turkey
Merzig 101 A6 SW Germany
Mesa 44 B3 Arizona, SW USA
Messalo, Rio 76 F4 ≈ NE Mozambique
Messina 103 D8 Sicily, Italy
Messina see Musina
Messina, Strait of 103 E8 strait SW Italy
Mestia 121 G1 N Georgia
Mestre 103 D2 NE Italy
Metairie 39 C6 Louisiana, S USA
Metán 65 B4 N Argentina
Metapán 55 B3 NW El Salvador
Meta, Río 63 C2 ≈ Colombia/Venezuela
Métsovo 107 D4 C Greece
Metz 97 F2 NE France
Meulaboh 131 A6 Sumatra, W Indonesia
Meuse 97 E2 ≈ W Europe
Mexborough 93 E4 N England, United Kingdom
Mexicali 53 A1 NW Mexico
Mexico 43 F6 Missouri, C USA
Mexico 53 D3 ◆ federal republic N Central America
Mexico City 53 E5 ● C Mexico
Mexico, Gulf of 28 G3 gulf W Atlantic Ocean
Mezen' 111 C3 ≈ NW Russian Federation
Mezőtúr 105 F8 E Hungary
Mġarr 112 A6 N Malta
Miahuatlán 53 G6 SE Mexico
Miami 39 G9 Florida, SE USA
Miami 43 E7 Oklahoma, C USA
Miami Beach 39 G8 Florida, SE USA
Mianyang 129 E4 C China
Miastko 105 C2 N Poland
Michalovce 105 F6 E Slovakia
Michigan 40 D4 ◐ state N USA
Michigan, Lake 40 C4 ◎ N USA
Michurinsk 111 B6 W Russian Federation
Micronesia 135 ◆ federation W Pacific Ocean
Mid-Atlantic Ridge 14 undersea feature Atlantic Ocean
Middelburg 84 B5 SW Netherlands
Middelharnis 84 C5 SW Netherlands
Middelkerke 84 A6 W Belgium
Middle Andaman 127 H5 island SE India
Middle Atlas 70 C2 ⛰ N Morocco
Middlesboro 39 F3 Kentucky, S USA
Middlesbrough 93 E3 N England, United Kingdom
Middletown 37 D6 Delaware, NE USA
Middletown 37 E5 New Jersey, NE USA
Middletown 37 E4 New York, NE USA
Middlewich 93 C5 W England, United Kingdom
Mid-Indian Ridge 15 undersea feature C Indian Ocean
Midland 35 D5 Ontario, S Canada
Midland 40 E4 Michigan, N USA
Midland 43 B4 South Dakota, N USA
Midland 44 F3 Texas, SW USA
Midleton 89 C6 SW Ireland
Mid-Pacific Mountains 15 undersea feature NW Pacific Ocean
Midway Islands 27 US ◇ C Pacific Ocean
Miechów 105 E5 S Poland
Międzyrzec Podlaski 105 G3 E Poland
Międzyrzecz 105 C3 W Poland
Mielec 105 F5 SE Poland
Miercurea-Ciuc 109 C6 C Romania
Mieres del Camín 99 C1 NW Spain
Mī'ēso 75 E3 C Ethiopia
Miguel Asua 53 D3 C Mexico
Mijdrecht 84 D4 C Netherlands
Mikhaylovka 111 B7 SW Russian Federation
Mikun' 111 D4 NW Russian Federation
Mikura-jima 133 G6 island E Japan
Milan 103 B2 N Italy
Milano see Milan
Milas 120 A4 SW Turkey
Mildenhall 95 G2 E England, United Kingdom
Mildura 137 F5 Victoria, SE Australia
Miles 137 G4 Queensland, E Australia
Miles City 47 F2 Montana, NW USA
Milford Haven 93 A7 SW Wales, United Kingdom
Milford Haven 93 A7 inlet SW Wales, United Kingdom
Milford Sound 139 A7 South Island, New Zealand
Mil'kovo 118 I3 E Russian Federation
Milk River 33 G7 Alberta, SW Canada
Milk River 47 E1 ≈ Montana, NW USA
Milk, Wadi el 75 B2 ≈ C Sudan
Milledgeville 39 F5 Georgia, SE USA
Mille Lacs Lake 43 E2 ◎ Minnesota, N USA
Millennium Island 135 atoll Line Islands, E Kiribati
Millerovo 111 A7 SW Russian Federation
Millford 89 D1 NW Ireland
Millville 37 D6 New Jersey, NE USA
Mílos 107 F6 island Cyclades, Greece
Milton 139 B8 South Island, New Zealand
Milton Keynes 95 F3 SE England, United Kingdom
Milwaukee 40 C4 Wisconsin, N USA
Minas Gerais 63 H7 state E Brazil
Minatitlán 53 G5 E Mexico
Minbu 131 A2 W Burma (Myanmar)
Minch, The 91 C2 strait NW Scotland, United Kingdom
Mindanao 131 G5 island S Philippines
Mindelheim 101 C7 S Germany
Minden 101 B4 NW Germany
Mindoro 131 F4 island N Philippines
Mindoro Strait 131 E4 strait W Philippines
Minehead 95 C4 SW England, United Kingdom
Mineral Wells 44 G3 Texas, SW USA
Mingäçevir 121 I2 C Azerbaijan
Mingaora 127 C1 N Pakistan
Mingulay 91 A4 island NW Scotland, United Kingdom
Minho 99 B2 ≈ Portugal/Spain
Minicoy Island 127 C7 island SW India
Minna 72 E4 C Nigeria
Minneapolis 43 E3 Minnesota, N USA
Minnesota 43 D3 ◐ state N USA
Miño 99 B2 ≈ Portugal/Spain
Minorca 99 H3 island Balearic Islands, Spain
Minot 43 B1 North Dakota, N USA
Minsk 109 C2 ● C Belarus
Minskaya Wzvyshsha 109 C2 ⛰ C Belarus
Minto, Lac 35 D2 ◎ Québec, C Canada
Miraflores 53 C4 W Mexico
Miranda de Ebro 99 E2 N Spain
Miri 131 D5 E Malaysia
Mirim Lagoon 65 D5 lagoon Brazil/Uruguay
Mirjaveh 123 F3 SE Iran
Mirny 142 D5 Russian research station Antarctica
Mirnyy 118 F4 NE Russian Federation
Mirpur Khas 127 C3 SE Pakistan
Mirtoan Sea 107 E6 sea S Greece
Miskitos, Cayos 55 F3 island group NE Nicaragua
Miskolc 105 F7 NE Hungary
Misool, Pulau 131 G7 island Maluku, E Indonesia
Misratah 70 F2 NW Libya
Mission 43 B4 South Dakota, N USA
Mississippi 39 C5 ◐ state SE USA
Mississippi Delta 39 C7 delta Louisiana, S USA
Mississippi River 39 C4 ≈ C USA
Missoula 47 C2 Montana, NW USA
Missouri 43 E6 ◐ state C USA
Missouri River 43 C4 ≈ C USA
Mistassini, Lac 35 D4 ◎ Québec, SE Canada
Mistelbach an der Zaya 101 F6 NE Austria
Misti, Volcán 63 C6 ☼ S Peru
Mitchell 137 G4 Queensland, E Australia
Mitchell 49 C3 Oregon, NW USA
Mitchell 43 C4 South Dakota, N USA
Mitchell, Mount 39 F3 ▲ North Carolina, SE USA
Mitchell River 137 F2 ≈ Queensland, NE Australia
Mito 133 G5 S Japan
Mitrovicë 107 D3 N Kosovo
Mits'iwa 75 D2 E Eritrea
Mitspe Ramon 123 G7 S Israel
Mitú 63 C3 SE Colombia
Mitumba Range 76 D3 ⛰ E Dem. Rep. Congo
Miyako 133 G3 C Japan
Miyako-jima 133 G6 island SW Japan
Miyakonojo 133 D8 SW Japan
Miyazaki 133 D8 SW Japan
Mizen Head 89 A7 headland SW Ireland
Mjøsa 83 B5 ◎ S Norway
Mława 105 E3 C Poland
Mljet 107 C3 island S Croatia
Moab 47 D6 Utah, W USA
Moa Island 137 F1 island Queensland, NE Australia
Moala 141 J5 island S Fiji
Moanda 76 B2 SE Gabon
Moate 89 D4 C Ireland
Moba 76 D3 E Dem. Rep. Congo
Mobaye 72 H5 S Central African Republic
Moberly 43 F6 Missouri, C USA
Mobile 39 D6 Alabama, S USA
Mochudi 76 D6 SE Botswana
Mocímboa da Praia 76 F3 N Mozambique
Môco 76 B4 ▲ W Angola
Mocuba 76 F4 NE Mozambique
Modena 103 C3 N Italy
Modesto 49 B7 California, W USA
Modica 103 D8 Sicily, Italy
Modimolle 76 D6 NE South Africa
Moe 137 F6 Victoria, SE Australia
Moffat 91 E6 S Scotland, United Kingdom
Mogadishu 75 F5 ● S Somalia
Mogilno 105 D3 C Poland
Mogollon Rim 44 B2 cliff Arizona, SW USA
Mohammedia 70 C1 NW Morocco
Mohawk River 37 D4 ≈ New York, NE USA
Mohoro 75 D7 E Tanzania
Moi 83 A6 S Norway
Mo i Rana 83 C3 C Norway
Mõisaküla 83 E6 S Estonia
Moissac 97 C6 S France
Mojácar 99 E5 S Spain
Mojave 49 C8 California, W USA
Mojave Desert 49 D8 plain California, W USA
Mokpo 133 B7 SW South Korea
Mol 84 D6 N Belgium
Mold 93 C5 NE Wales, United Kingdom
Moldavia see Moldova
Molde 83 B4 S Norway
Moldo-Too, Khrebet 125 H2 ⛰ C Kyrgyzstan
Moldova 109 ◆ republic SE Europe
Molfetta 103 E6 SE Italy
Mölndal 83 B6 S Sweden
Molodezhnaya 142 E3 Russian research station Antarctica
Moloka'i 51 C1 island Hawaii, USA
Molopo 76 C6 seasonal river Botswana/ South Africa
Moluccas 131 G7 island group E Indonesia
Molucca Sea 131 F6 sea E Indonesia
Mombacho, Volcán 55 D5 ☼ SW Nicaragua
Mombasa 75 E6 SE Kenya
Møn 83 B7 island SE Denmark
Monach Islands 91 A3 island group NW Scotland, United Kingdom
Monaco 97 F6 ● S Monaco
Monaco 97 F6 ◆ monarchy W Europe
Monadhliath Mountains 91 D4 ⛰ N Scotland, United Kingdom
Monaghan 89 E3 N Ireland
Monahans 44 E4 Texas, SW USA
Mona, Isla 57 H4 island W Puerto Rico
Mona Passage 57 H4 channel Dominican Republic/Puerto Rico
Monbetsu 133 G1 NE Japan
Moncalieri 103 A2 NW Italy
Monchegorsk 111 B2 NW Russian Federation
Monclova 53 E3 NE Mexico
Moncton 35 F5 New Brunswick, SE Canada
Mondovì 103 A3 NW Italy
Moneygall 89 D5 C Ireland
Moneymore 89 E2 C Northern Ireland, United Kingdom
Monfalcone 103 D2 NE Italy
Monforte de Lemos 99 B2 NW Spain
Mongo 72 H4 C Chad
Mongolia 129 D2 ◆ republic E Asia
Mongu 76 C4 W Zambia
Monkey Bay 76 E4 SE Malawi
Monkey River Town 55 C2 SE Belize
Monmouth 93 C7 SE Wales, United Kingdom
Mono Lake 49 C7 ◎ California, W USA
Monóvar 99 F5 E Spain
Monroe 39 B5 Louisiana, S USA
Monrovia 72 B5 ● W Liberia
Mons 84 C7 S Belgium
Monselice 103 C2 NE Italy
Montana 107 E2 NW Bulgaria
Montana 47 D2 ◐ state NW USA
Montargis 97 D3 C France
Montauban 97 C6 S France
Montbéliard 97 F3 E France
Mont Cenis, Col du 97 F5 pass E France
Mont-de-Marsan 97 B6 SW France
Monteagudo 65 B3 S Bolivia
Monte Caseros 65 C5 NE Argentina
Monte Cristi 57 F4 NW Dominican Republic
Montego Bay 57 D4 W Jamaica
Montélimar 97 E6 E France
Montemorelos 53 E3 NE Mexico
Montenegro 107 C3 ◆ republic SW Europe
Monte Patria 65 A5 N Chile
Monterey 49 B7 California, W USA
Monterey Bay 49 B7 bay California, W USA
Montería 63 B2 NW Colombia
Montero 65 B2 C Bolivia
Monterrey 53 E3 NE Mexico
Montes Claros 63 G6 SE Brazil
Montevideo 65 C6 ● S Uruguay
Montevideo 43 D3 Minnesota, N USA
Montgenèvre, Col de 97 F5 pass France/Italy
Montgomery 93 C6 E Wales, United Kingdom
Montgomery 39 E5 state capital Alabama, S USA
Monthey 101 A8 SW Switzerland
Monticello 37 D4 New York, NE USA
Monticello 47 E6 Utah, W USA
Montluçon 97 D4 C France
Montoro 99 D5 S Spain
Montpelier 47 D4 Idaho, NW USA
Montpelier 37 E3 state capital Vermont, NE USA
Montpellier 97 D6 S France
Montréal 35 E5 Québec, SE Canada
Montrose 91 F4 E Scotland, United Kingdom
Montrose 47 E6 Colorado, C USA
Montserrat 57 J5 UK ◇ E West Indies
Monywa 131 A2 C Burma (Myanmar)
Monza 103 B2 N Italy
Monze 76 D4 S Zambia
Monzón 99 F2 NE Spain
Moonie 137 G4 Queensland, E Australia
Moora 137 B5 Western Australia
Moore 43 D8 Oklahoma, C USA
Moorea 141 A5 island Îles du Vent, W French Polynesia
Moore, Lake 137 B5 ◎ Western Australia
Moorhead 43 D2 Minnesota, N USA
Moose 47 D3 Wyoming, C USA
Moose 35 C4 ≈ Ontario, S Canada
Moosehead Lake 37 F1 ◎ Maine, NE USA
Moosonee 35 C4 Ontario, SE Canada
Mopti 72 C3 C Mali
Mora 83 C5 C Sweden
Morales 55 B3 E Guatemala
Morar, Loch 91 C4 ◎ N Scotland, United Kingdom
Moratalla 99 E5 SE Spain
Morava 105 D6 ≈ C Europe
Moravia 105 D6 cultural region E Czech Republic
Moray Firth 91 D3 inlet N Scotland, United Kingdom
Moreau River 43 B3 ≈ South Dakota, N USA
Morecambe 93 C3 NW England, United Kingdom
Morecambe Bay 93 C3 inlet NW England, United Kingdom
Moree 137 G5 New South Wales, SE Australia
Morelia 53 E5 S Mexico
Morena, Sierra 99 C5 ⛰ S Spain
Mórfou see Güzelyurt
Morgan City 39 B6 Louisiana, S USA
Morghab, Darya-ye 125 E4 ≈ Afghanistan/Turkmenistan
Moriarty 44 D2 New Mexico, SW USA
Morioka 133 G3 C Japan
Morlaix 97 A2 NW France
Morocco 70 B2 ◆ monarchy N Africa

Morogoro 75 D6 E Tanzania
Moro Gulf 131 F5 gulf S Philippines
Morón 57 D3 C Cuba
Mörön 129 D1 N Mongolia
Morondava 76 G5 W Madagascar
Moroni 76 F4 ● Grande Comore, NW Comoros
Morotai, Pulau 131 G6 island Moluccas, E Indonesia
Morpeth 93 D2 N England, United Kingdom
Morrinsville 139 D3 North Island, New Zealand
Morris 43 D3 Minnesota, N USA
Morris Jesup, Kap 143 C4 headland N Greenland
Morvan 97 E4 physical region C France
Moscow 111 B5 ● W Russian Federation
Moscow 47 B2 Idaho, NW USA
Mosel 97 F2 ≋ W Europe
Moselle 97 F3 ≋ W Europe
Mosgiel 139 B7 South Island, New Zealand
Moshi 75 D6 NE Tanzania
Mosjøen 83 C3 C Norway
Moskva 125 F4 SW Tajikistan
Moskva see Moscow
Mosonmagyaróvár 105 D7 NW Hungary
Mosquito Coast 55 E4 coastal region E Nicaragua
Mosquito Gulf 55 G6 gulf N Panama
Moss 83 B5 S Norway
Mosselbaai 76 C7 SW South Africa
Mossendjo 76 B2 SW Congo
Mossoró 63 I4 NE Brazil
Most 105 B5 NW Czech Republic
Mosta 112 B6 C Malta
Mostaganem 70 D1 NW Algeria
Mostar 107 C2 S Bosnia and Herzegovina
Mosul 123 C2 N Iraq
Mota del Cuervo 99 E4 C Spain
Motagua, Río 55 B3 ≋ Guatemala/Honduras
Motherwell 91 D6 C Scotland, United Kingdom
Motril 99 D6 S Spain
Motueka 139 C5 South Island, New Zealand
Motul 53 H4 SE Mexico
Motu Nui 141 C6 island Easter Island, Chile
Mouila 76 A2 C Gabon
Mould Bay 33 G2 Prince Patrick Island, Northwest Territories, N Canada
Moulins 97 D4 C France
Moundou 72 G4 SW Chad
Mountain Home 39 B3 Arkansas, C USA
Mountain Home 47 B4 Idaho, NW USA
Mountbellew Bridge 89 C4 C Ireland
Mount Desert Island 37 G3 island Maine, NE USA
Mount Gambier 137 F6 South Australia
Mount Hagen 141 B2 C Papua New Guinea
Mount Isa 137 F3 Queensland, C Australia
Mount Magnet 137 B4 Western Australia
Mount Pleasant 43 F5 Iowa, C USA
Mount Pleasant 40 D4 Michigan, N USA
Mount's Bay 95 A6 inlet SW England, United Kingdom
Mount Vernon 40 B7 Illinois, N USA
Mount Vernon 49 B1 Washington, NW USA
Mourne Mountains 89 E3 ▲▲ SE Northern Ireland, United Kingdom
Mouscron 84 B7 W Belgium
Moussoro 72 G3 W Chad
Moycullen 89 B4 W Ireland
Mo'ynoq 125 D1 NW Uzbekistan
Moyynkum, Peski 125 G1 desert S Kazakhstan
Mozambique 76 E5 ◆ republic S Africa
Mozambique Channel 76 F5 strait W Indian Ocean
Mpama 76 B2 ≋ C Congo
Mragowo 105 F2 NE Poland
Mtwara 75 E7 SE Tanzania
Muar 131 B6 W Malaysia
Muck 91 B4 island W Scotland, United Kingdom
Muckle Roe 91 A6 island NE Scotland, United Kingdom
Mucojo 76 F4 N Mozambique
Mudanjiang 129 H2 NE China
Muddy Gap 47 E4 Wyoming, C USA
Mufulira 76 D4 C Zambia
Muğla 120 A4 SW Turkey
Muine Bheag 89 E5 SE Ireland
Mukacheve 109 B5 W Ukraine
Mula 99 E5 SE Spain
Muleshoe 44 E2 Texas, SW USA
Mulhacén 99 D5 ▲ S Spain
Mulhouse 97 F3 NE France
Mullaghmore 89 C2 N Ireland
Mullan 89 D3 W Northern Ireland, United Kingdom
Mullaranny 89 B3 NW Ireland
Muller, Pegunungan 131 D6 ▲▲ Borneo, C Indonesia
Müllheim 101 B7 SW Germany
Mullingar 89 D4 C Ireland
Mull, Isle of 91 B5 island W Scotland, United Kingdom
Mulongo 76 D3 SE Dem. Rep. Congo
Multan 127 C2 E Pakistan
Multinational Station 142 A3 multinational research station Antarctica
Mumbai 127 C5 W India
Münchberg 101 D5 E Germany
München see Munich
Muncie 40 D6 Indiana, N USA
Munda 141 E2 NW Solomon Islands
Mungbere 76 D1 NE Dem. Rep. Congo
Munich 101 D7 SE Germany
Munster 101 B4 NW Germany
Munster 89 B6 cultural region S Ireland
Muonio 83 E2 N Finland
Muonionjoki 83 D2 ≋ Finland/Sweden
Muqdisho see Mogadishu
Mur 101 F8 ≋ C Europe
Muradiye 121 H3 E Turkey
Murchison River 137 B4 ≋ Western Australia
Murcia 99 F5 SE Spain
Murcia 99 E5 cultural region SE Spain
Mureş 109 A6 ≋ Hungary/Romania
Murfreesboro 39 E3 Tennessee, S USA
Murgap 125 D4 S Turkmenistan
Murgap 83 D4 ≋ Afghanistan/Turkmenistan
Murghob 125 H3 SE Tajikistan
Murgon 137 H4 Queensland, E Australia
Müritz 101 D3 ◎ NE Germany
Murmansk 111 C2 NW Russian Federation
Murmashi 111 B2 NW Russian Federation
Murom 111 B5 W Russian Federation
Muroran 133 F2 NE Japan
Muros 99 A1 NW Spain
Murray, Lake 141 A2 ◎ SW Papua New Guinea
Murray River 137 F5 ≋ SE Australia
Murrumbidgee River 137 F6 ≋ New South Wales, SE Australia
Murska Sobota 101 F8 NE Slovenia
Murupara 139 E3 North Island, New Zealand
Mururoa 135 atoll Îles Tuamotu, SE French Polynesia
Murwara 127 E4 N India
Murwillumbah 137 H5 New South Wales, SE Australia
Murzuq, Idhan 70 F4 desert SW Libya
Mürzzuschlag 101 F7 E Austria
Muş 121 G3 E Turkey
Musa, Jabal 70 I3 ▲ NE Egypt
Musala 107 E3 ▲ W Bulgaria
Muscat 123 F4 ● NE Oman
Muscatine 43 F5 Iowa, C USA
Musgrave Ranges 137 D4 ▲▲ South Australia
Musina 76 D5 NE South Africa
Muskegon 40 D4 Michigan, N USA
Muskegon River 40 D4 ≋ Michigan, N USA
Muskogee 43 E8 Oklahoma, C USA
Musoma 75 C5 N Tanzania
Musselshell River 47 E2 ≋ Montana, NW USA
Musters, Lago 65 A7 ◎ S Argentina
Muswellbrook 137 G5 New South Wales, SE Australia
Mut 121 C5 S Turkey
Mutare 76 E5 E Zimbabwe
Muy Muy 55 D4 C Nicaragua
Mwali 76 F4 island S Comoros
Mwanza 75 C6 NW Tanzania
Mweelrea 89 A4 ▲ W Ireland
Mweka 76 C2 C Dem. Rep. Congo
Mwene-Ditu 76 C3 S Dem. Rep. Congo
Mweru, Lake 76 D3 ◎ Dem. Rep. Congo/Zambia
Myadzyel 109 C2 N Belarus
Myanmar see Burma
Myeik 131 B4 S Burma (Myanmar)
Myingyan 131 A2 C Burma (Myanmar)
Myitkyina 131 B1 N Burma (Myanmar)
Mykolayiv 109 E6 S Ukraine
Mykonos 107 F6 island Cyclades, Greece
Mýrina 107 F4 Límnos, Greece
Myrtle Beach 39 H4 South Carolina, SE USA
Myślibórz 105 B3 NW Poland
Mysore 127 D6 W India
My Tho 131 C4 S Vietnam
Mytilíni 107 F5 Lesbos, Greece
Mzuzu 76 E3 N Malawi

N

Nā'ālehu 51 D3 Hawaii, USA
Naas 89 E4 C Ireland
Naberezhnyye Chelny 111 D6 W Russian Federation
Nacala 76 F4 NE Mozambique
Nacogdoches 44 I3 Texas, SW USA
Nadi 141 J5 Viti Levu, W Fiji
Nadur 112 A6 N Malta
Nadvoitsy 111 B3 NW Russian Federation
Nadym 118 D3 N Russian Federation
Náfpaktos 107 D5 C Greece
Náfplio 107 E6 S Greece
Naga 131 F4 N Philippines
Nagano 133 F5 S Japan
Nagaoka 133 F5 C Japan
Nagasaki 133 C8 SW Japan
Nagato 133 D7 Honshu, SW Japan
Nagercoil 127 D7 SE India
Nagles Mountains 89 C6 ▲▲ S Ireland
Nagorno-Karabakh 121 H2 former autonomous region SW Azerbaijan
Nagoya 133 F6 SW Japan
Nagpur 127 E4 C India
Nagqu 129 C4 W China
Nagykálló 105 F7 E Hungary
Nagykanizsa 105 C8 SW Hungary
Nagykőrös 105 E8 C Hungary
Naha 133 A8 Okinawa, SW Japan
Nahariya 123 H5 N Israel
Nahuel Huapí, Lago 65 A7 ◎ W Argentina
Nain 35 F2 Newfoundland and Labrador, NE Canada
Nairn 91 D3 N Scotland, United Kingdom
Nairobi 75 D5 ● S Kenya
Najin 133 C3 NE North Korea
Najran 123 C6 S Saudi Arabia
Nakamura 133 E7 Shikoku, SW Japan
Nakatsugawa 133 F6 SW Japan
Nakhodka 118 H6 SE Russian Federation
Nakhon Ratchasima 131 B3 E Thailand
Nakhon Sawan 131 B3 W Thailand
Nakhon Si Thammarat 131 B5 SW Thailand
Nakuru 75 D5 SW Kenya
Nal'chik 111 A8 SW Russian Federation
Nalut 70 F2 NW Libya
Namangan 125 G3 E Uzbekistan
Nam Co 129 C4 ◎ W China
Nam Dinh 131 C2 N Vietnam
Namhae-do 133 B7 island S South Korea
Namib Desert 76 B5 desert W Namibia
Namibe 76 B4 SW Angola
Namibia 76 B5 ◆ republic S Africa
Nam Ou 131 B2 ≋ N Laos
Nampa 47 B3 Idaho, NW USA
Namp'o 133 A5 SW North Korea
Nampula 76 F4 NE Mozambique
Namsan-ni 133 A4 NW North Korea
Namsos 83 C3 C Norway
Namur 84 D7 SE Belgium
Namwon 133 B6 S South Korea
Nanaimo 33 E7 Vancouver Island, British Columbia, SW Canada
Nanchang 129 F5 S China
Nancy 97 F3 NE France
Nandaime 55 D5 SW Nicaragua
Nanded 127 D5 C India
Nandyal 127 E6 E India
Nangnim-sanmaek 133 B4 ▲▲ C North Korea
Nanjing 129 G4 E China
Nanning 129 F6 S China
Nanping 129 G5 SE China
Nansen Basin 143 D4 undersea feature Arctic Ocean
Nansen Cordillera 143 C4 undersea feature Arctic Ocean
Nanterre 97 D2 N France
Nantes 97 B3 NW France
Nantucket Island 37 G4 island Massachusetts, NE USA
Nantwich 93 C5 W England, United Kingdom
Nanumaga 141 I2 atoll NW Tuvalu
Nanumea Atoll 141 I2 atoll NW Tuvalu
Nanyang 129 F4 C China
Napa 49 B6 California, W USA
Napier 139 E4 North Island, New Zealand
Naples 103 D6 S Italy
Naples 39 G8 Florida, SE USA
Napoli see Naples
Napo, Río 63 B3 ≋ Ecuador/Peru
Naracoorte 137 F6 South Australia
Nara Visa 44 E2 New Mexico, SW USA
Narbonne 97 D7 S France
Nares Strait 33 H1 strait Canada/Greenland
Narew 105 F3 ≋ E Poland
Narowlya 109 D3 SE Belarus
Närpes 83 D4 W Finland
Närpiö see Närpes
Narrabri 137 G5 New South Wales, SE Australia
Narrogin 137 B5 Western Australia
Narva 83 F5 NE Estonia
Narvik 83 D2 C Norway
Nar'yan-Mar 111 D3 NW Russian Federation
Naryn 125 H2 C Kyrgyzstan
Nashik 127 D5 W India
Nashua 37 F4 New Hampshire, NE USA
Nashville 39 D3 state capital Tennessee, S USA
Näsijärvi 83 E4 ◎ SW Finland
Nassau 57 D2 ● New Providence, N Bahamas
Nasser, Lake 70 J4 ◎ Egypt/Sudan
Nata 76 D5 NE Botswana
Natal 63 I4 E Brazil
Natchez 39 B5 Mississippi, S USA
Natchitoches 39 B5 Louisiana, S USA
Natitingou 72 D4 NW Benin
Natuna, Kepulauan 131 C6 island group W Indonesia
Nauru 141 G1 ◆ republic W Pacific Ocean
Navan 89 E4 E Ireland
Navapolatsk 109 D1 N Belarus
Navarra 99 E2 cultural region N Spain
Navassa Island 57 D4 US ◇ C West Indies
Navoiy 125 E3 C Uzbekistan
Navojoa 53 C3 NW Mexico
Navolato 53 C3 C Mexico
Nawabshah 127 B3 S Pakistan
Naxcivan 121 H3 SW Azerbaijan
Náxos 107 F6 island Cyclades, Greece
Nayoro 133 F2 NE Japan
Nay Pyi Taw 130 A3 ● C Burma (Myanmar)
Nazareth 123 H5 N Israel
Nazca Ridge 14 undersea feature E Pacific Ocean
Naze 133 B7 SW Japan
Nazilli 120 A4 SW Turkey
Nazret 75 D3 C Ethiopia
N'Dalatando 76 B3 NW Angola
Ndélé 72 H4 N Central African Republic
Ndendé 76 A2 S Gabon
Ndindi 76 A2 S Gabon
Ndjamena 72 G4 ● W Chad
Ndola 76 D4 C Zambia
Neagh, Lough 89 E2 ◎ E Northern Ireland, United Kingdom
Neápoli 107 D4 N Greece
Neápoli 107 E6 S Greece
Near Islands 50 A1 island group Aleutian Islands, Alaska, USA
Neath 93 B7 S Wales, United Kingdom
Nebaj 55 A3 W Guatemala
Neblina, Pico da 63 C3 ▲ NW Brazil
Nebraska 43 B5 ⬖ state C USA
Nebraska City 43 D5 Nebraska, C USA
Neches River 44 I4 ≋ Texas, SW USA
Neckar 101 B6 ≋ SW Germany
Necochea 65 C6 E Argentina
Neder Rijn 84 D4 ≋ C Netherlands
Nederweert 84 E6 SE Netherlands
Neede 84 F4 E Netherlands
Needles 49 E8 California, W USA
Neerpelt 84 D6 NE Belgium
Neftekamsk 111 D6 W Russian Federation
Negele 75 E4 C Ethiopia
Negev 123 G6 desert S Israel
Negombo 127 E8 SW Sri Lanka
Negotin 107 D2 E Serbia
Negra, Punta 63 A4 point NW Peru
Negro, Río 65 B6 ≋ E Argentina
Negro, Rio 63 D3 ≋ N South America
Negros 131 F5 island C Philippines
Neijiang 129 E5 C China
Nellore 127 E6 E India
Nelson 139 C5 South Island, New Zealand
Nelson 33 H6 ≋ Manitoba, C Canada
Néma 72 C3 SE Mauritania
Neman 83 E7 ≋ NE Europe
Nemours 97 D3 N France
Nemuro 133 H1 NE Japan
Nenagh 89 C5 C Ireland
Nendö 141 G3 island Santa Cruz Islands, E Solomon Islands
Nene 95 G2 ≋ E England, United Kingdom
Nepal 127 E3 ◆ monarchy S Asia
Nepean 35 D5 Ontario, SE Canada
Nephin 89 B3 ▲ W Ireland
Neretva 107 C2 ≋ Bosnia and Herzegovina/Croatia
Neris 109 C2 ≋ Belarus/Lithuania
Nerva 99 C5 SW Spain
Neryungri 118 G4 NE Russian Federation
Neskaupstadhur 83 B1 E Iceland
Ness, Loch 91 D4 ◎ N Scotland, United Kingdom
Néstos 107 E4 ≋ Bulgaria/Greece
Netanya 123 G6 C Israel
Netherlands 84 D3 ◆ monarchy NW Europe
Nettilling Lake 33 I3 ◎ Baffin Island, Nunavut, N Canada
Neubrandenburg 101 D3 NE Germany
Neuchâtel 101 A8 W Switzerland
Neuchâtel, Lac de 101 A8 ◎ W Switzerland
Neufchâteau 84 D8 SE Belgium
Neumünster 101 C2 N Germany
Neunkirchen 101 A6 SW Germany
Neuquén 65 A6 SE Argentina
Neuruppin 101 D3 NE Germany
Neusiedler See 101 F7 ◎ Austria/Hungary
Neustadt an der Weinstrasse 101 A6 SW Germany
Neustrelitz 101 D3 NE Germany
Neu-Ulm 101 C7 S Germany
Neuwied 101 B5 W Germany
Nevada 47 B5 ⬖ state W USA
Nevers 97 D4 C France
Nevinnomyssk 111 A8 SW Russian Federation
Nevşehir 121 D4 C Turkey
Newala 75 D7 SE Tanzania
New Albany 40 D7 Indiana, N USA
New Amsterdam 63 E2 E Guyana
Newark 37 E5 New Jersey, NE USA
Newark-on-Trent 93 E5 C England, United Kingdom
New Bedford 37 F4 Massachusetts, NE USA
New Bern 39 H3 North Carolina, SE USA
New Braunfels 44 G4 Texas, SW USA
Newbridge 89 C4 W Ireland
Newbridge on Wye 93 B6 C Wales, United Kingdom
New Britain 141 C2 island E Papua New Guinea
New Brunswick 35 F5 ⬖ province SE Canada
Newbury 95 E4 S England, United Kingdom
New Caledonia 141 D5 French ◇ SW Pacific Ocean
Newcastle 137 G5 New South Wales, SE Australia
Newcastle 89 F3 SE Northern Ireland, United Kingdom
New Castle 37 B5 Pennsylvania, NE USA
Newcastle 47 F3 Wyoming, C USA
Newcastle-under-Lyme 93 D5 C England, United Kingdom
Newcastle upon Tyne 93 D2 NE England, United Kingdom
Newcastle West 89 B5 SW Ireland
New Delhi 127 D3 ● N India
New England 37 F3 ⬖ cultural region NE USA
New Forest 95 E5 physical region S England, United Kingdom
Newfoundland 35 G4 island Newfoundland and Labrador, SE Canada
Newfoundland and Labrador 35 G3 ⬖ province E Canada
New Georgia 141 E2 island New Georgia Islands, NW Solomon Islands
New Georgia Islands 141 D3 island group NW Solomon Islands
New Glasgow 35 G5 Nova Scotia, SE Canada
New Guinea 141 A2 island Indonesia/Papua New Guinea
New Hampshire 37 E2 ⬖ state NE USA
New Hanover 141 C1 island NE Papua New Guinea
Newhaven 95 G5 SE England, United Kingdom
New Haven 37 E5 Connecticut, NE USA
New Iberia 39 B6 Louisiana, S USA
New Ireland 141 C1 island NE Papua New Guinea
New Jersey 37 E5 ⬖ state NE USA
Newman 137 B3 Western Australia
Newmarket 95 G2 E England, United Kingdom
Newmarket on Fergus 89 C5 W Ireland
New Mexico 44 D2 ⬖ state SW USA
New Orleans 39 C6 Louisiana, S USA
New Plymouth 139 D4 North Island, New Zealand
Newport 95 E5 S England, United Kingdom
Newport 93 C7 SE Wales, United Kingdom
Newport 39 E1 Kentucky, S USA
Newport 37 F4 Rhode Island, NE USA
Newport 37 E2 Vermont, NE USA
Newport News 39 I2 Virginia, NE USA
Newport Pagnell 95 F3 SE England, United Kingdom
New Providence 57 D1 island N Bahamas
Newquay 95 A5 SW England, United Kingdom
New Ross 89 E6 SE Ireland
Newry 89 E3 SE Northern Ireland, United Kingdom
New Siberian Islands 118 F2 island group N Russian Federation
New South Wales 137 F5 ⬖ state SE Australia
Newton 43 E5 Iowa, C USA
Newton 43 D7 Kansas, C USA
Newton Abbot 95 C5 SW England, United Kingdom
Newton Stewart 91 D7 S Scotland, United Kingdom
Newtown 89 C6 S Ireland
Newtownabbey 89 E2 E Northern Ireland, United Kingdom
Newtown St Boswells 91 E6 S Scotland, United Kingdom
Newtownstewart 89 D2 W Northern Ireland, United Kingdom
New Ulm 43 E3 Minnesota, N USA
New York 37 E5 New York, NE USA
New York 37 C4 ⬖ state NE USA
New Zealand 139 A5 ◆ commonwealth republic SW Pacific Ocean
Neyveli 127 E7 SE India
Ngangze Co 129 B4 ◎ W China
Ngaoundéré 72 G5 N Cameroon
Ngazidja 76 G4 island NW Comoros
Ngerulmud 134 ● N Palau
N'Giva 76 B4 S Angola
Ngo 76 B2 SE Congo
Ngoko 72 G6 ≋ Cameroon/Congo
Ngourti 72 G3 E Niger
Nguigmi 72 G3 SE Niger
Nguru 72 F4 NE Nigeria
Nha Trang 131 D4 S Vietnam
Nhulunbuy 137 E1 Northern Territory, N Australia
Niagara Falls 35 D6 Ontario, S Canada
Niagara Falls 37 B3 New York, NE USA
Niagara Falls 37 B3 waterfall Canada/USA
Niamey 72 E3 ● SW Niger
Niangay, Lac 72 D3 ◎ E Mali
Nia-Nia 76 D1 NE Dem. Rep. Congo
Nias, Pulau 131 A6 island W Indonesia
Nicaragua 55 D4 ◆ republic Central America
Nicaragua, Lake 55 E5 ◎ S Nicaragua
Nice 97 F6 SE France
Nicholls Town 57 D1 NW Bahamas
Nicobar Islands 127 H6 island group SE India
Nicosia 112 C6 ● C Cyprus
Nicoya 55 D6 W Costa Rica
Nicoya, Golfo de 55 E6 gulf W Costa Rica
Nicoya, Península de 55 D6 peninsula NW Costa Rica
Nida 83 E7 SW Lithuania
Nidzica 105 E2 NE Poland
Nieuw-Bergen 84 E5 SE Netherlands
Nieuwegein 84 D4 C Netherlands
Nieuw Nickerie 63 E2 NW Surinam
Niğde 121 D4 C Turkey
Niger 72 E3 ◆ republic W Africa
Niger 72 E4 ≋ W Africa
Niger Delta 66 delta S Nigeria
Nigeria 72 E4 ◆ federal republic W Africa
Niger, Mouths of the 72 E5 delta S Nigeria
Niigata 133 F4 C Japan
Niihama 133 E7 Shikoku, SW Japan
Ni'ihau 51 A1 island Hawaii, USA
Nii-jima 133 G6 island E Japan
Nijkerk 84 D4 C Netherlands
Nijlen 84 C6 N Belgium
Nijmegen 84 E4 SE Netherlands
Nikel' 111 B2 NW Russian Federation
Nikiniki 131 F8 S Indonesia
Nikopol' 109 F5 SE Ukraine
Nikšić 107 C3 SW Montenegro
Nile 70 I3 ≋ N Africa
Nile Delta 70 I2 delta N Egypt
Nîmes 97 E6 S France
Nine Degree Channel 127 C7 channel India/Maldives
Ninetyeast Ridge 15 undersea feature E Indian Ocean
Ningbo 129 G4 SE China
Ningo Group 141 A1 island group N Papua New Guinea
Niobrara River 43 C4 ≋ Nebraska/Wyoming, C USA
Nioro 72 B3 W Mali
Niort 97 C4 W France
Nipigon 35 B4 Ontario, S Canada
Nipigon, Lake 35 B4 ◎ Ontario, S Canada
Niš 107 D2 SE Serbia
Nisko 105 F5 SE Poland
Nísyros 107 G6 island Dodecanese, Greece
Nith 91 D6 ≋ S Scotland, United Kingdom
Nitra 105 D7 SW Slovakia
Nitra 105 D7 ≋ W Slovakia
Niue 135 Self-governing ◇ S Pacific Ocean
Niulakita 141 J3 atoll S Tuvalu
Niutao 141 J2 atoll NW Tuvalu
Nivernais 97 D4 cultural region C France
Nizamabad 127 D5 C India
Nizhnekamsk 111 C6 W Russian Federation
Nizhnevartovsk 118 D4 C Russian Federation
Nizhniy Novgorod 111 B5 W Russian Federation
Nizhniy Odes 111 D4 NW Russian Federation
Nizhyn 109 E4 NE Ukraine
Njombe 75 D7 S Tanzania
Nkayi 76 B2 S Congo
Nkongsamba 72 F5 W Cameroon
Nmai Hka 131 B1 ≋ N Burma (Myanmar)
Nobeoka 133 D8 SW Japan
Noboribetsu 133 F2 NE Japan
Nogales 53 B2 NW Mexico
Nogales 44 B4 Arizona, SW USA
Nokia 83 E4 W Finland
Nokou 72 G3 W Chad
Nola 72 G5 SW Central African Republic
Nolinsk 111 C5 NW Russian Federation
Nome 143 B1 Alaska, USA
Noord-Beveland 84 B5 island SW Netherlands
Noordwijk aan Zee 84 C4 W Netherlands
Nora 83 C5 C Sweden
Norak 125 F3 W Tajikistan
Norddeutsches Tiefland 105 A2 plain N Germany
Norden 101 B3 NW Germany
Norderstedt 101 C3 N Germany
Nordfriesische Inseln see North Frisian Islands
Nordhausen 101 C4 C Germany
Nordhorn 101 A3 NW Germany
Nordkapp see North Cape
Nore 89 D5 ≋ S Ireland
Norfolk 43 D5 Nebraska, C USA
Norfolk 39 I2 Virginia, NE USA
Norfolk Island 135 Australian ◇ SW Pacific Ocean
Norias 44 H6 Texas, SW USA
Noril'sk 118 E3 N Russian Federation
Norman 43 D8 Oklahoma, C USA
Normandie see Normandy
Normandy 97 C2 cultural region N France
Normanton 137 F2 Queensland, NE Australia
Norrköping 83 C6 S Sweden
Norrtälje 83 D5 C Sweden
Norseman 137 C5 Western Australia
Norsup 141 G5 Malekula, C Vanuatu
Northallerton 93 D3 N England, United Kingdom
Northam 137 B5 Western Australia
North America 28 continent
North American Basin 14 undersea feature W Sargasso Sea
Northampton 95 F2 C England, United Kingdom
North Andaman 127 H4 island Andaman Islands, SE India
North Bay 35 D5 Ontario, S Canada
North Berwick 91 E5 SE Scotland, United Kingdom
North Canadian River 44 G2 ≋ Oklahoma, C USA
North Cape 139 C1 headland North Island, New Zealand
North Cape 83 E1 headland N Norway
North Carolina 39 F3 ⬖ state SE USA
North Channel 40 E3 lake channel Canada/USA
North Channel 91 B6 strait Northern Ireland/Scotland, United Kingdom
North Charleston 39 G5 South Carolina, SE USA
North Dakota 43 B2 ⬖ state N USA
Northeim 101 C4 C Germany
Northern Cook Islands 135 island group N Cook Islands
Northern Dvina 111 C4 ≋ NW Russian Federation
Northern Ireland 87 C5 ⬖ national region United Kingdom
Northern Mariana Islands 135 US ◇ W Pacific Ocean
Northern Sporades 107 E5 island group E Greece
Northern Territory 137 D2 ⬖ territory N Australia
North Esk 91 E4 ≋ E Scotland, United Kingdom
North European Plain 78 plain N Europe
Northfield 43 E3 Minnesota, N USA
North Foreland 95 H3 headland SE England, United Kingdom

⬖ Administrative region ◆ Country ● Country capital ◇ Dependent territory ○ Dependent territory capital ▲▲ Mountain range ▲ Mountain ※ Volcano ≋ River ◎ Lake ⊠ Reservoir

North Frisian Islands 101 B2 *island group* N Germany
North Geomagnetic Pole 143 A4 *pole* Arctic Ocean
North Island 139 B2 *island* N New Zealand
North Korea 133 C4 ◆ *republic* E Asia
Northland 139 C1 *cultural region* North Island, New Zealand
North Las Vegas 47 B7 Nevada, W USA
North Little Rock 39 C4 Arkansas, C USA
North Platte 43 B5 Nebraska, C USA
North Platte River 43 B5 ≈ C USA
North Pole 143 C4 *pole* Arctic Ocean
North Ronaldsay 91 F1 *island* NE Scotland, United Kingdom
North Saskatchewan 33 G6 ≈ Alberta/Saskatchewan, S Canada
North Sea 78 *sea* NW Europe
North Siberian Lowland 118 E3 *lowlands* N Russian Federation
North Sound 89 B4 *sound* W Ireland
North Sound, The 91 E1 *sound* N Scotland, United Kingdom
North Taranaki Bight 139 C3 *gulf* North Island, New Zealand
North Tyne 93 D2 ≈ N England, United Kingdom
North Uist 91 A3 *island* NW Scotland, United Kingdom
North West Highlands 91 C3 ▲▲ N Scotland, United Kingdom
Northwest Pacific Basin 15 *undersea feature* NW Pacific Ocean
Northwest Territories 33 F4 ◐ *territory* NW Canada
Northwich 93 C5 C England, United Kingdom
Northwind Plain 143 B2 *undersea feature* Arctic Ocean
North York Moors 93 E3 *moorland* N England, United Kingdom
Norton Sound 50 D1 *inlet* Alaska, USA
Norway 83 A4 ◆ *monarchy* N Europe
Norwegian Sea 83 A4 *sea* NE Atlantic Ocean
Norwich 95 H2 E England, United Kingdom
Noshiro 133 F3 C Japan
Nosop 76 C6 ≈ E Namibia
Noteć 105 D3 ≈ NW Poland
Nottingham 93 E5 C England, United Kingdom
Nouâdhibou 72 A2 W Mauritania
Nouakchott 72 A2 ● SW Mauritania
Nouméa 141 G6 ○ S New Caledonia
Nova Gorica 101 E8 W Slovenia
Nova Iguaçu 63 G7 SE Brazil
Novara 103 B2 NW Italy
Nova Scotia 37 H2 ◐ *province* SE Canada
Novaya Sibir', Ostrov 118 G2 *island* NE Russian Federation
Novaya Zemlya 111 E1 *island group* N Russian Federation
Novi Sad 107 D1 N Serbia
Novoazovs'k 109 G5 E Ukraine
Novocheboksarsk 111 C6 W Russian Federation
Novocherkassk 111 A7 SW Russian Federation
Novodvinsk 111 C3 NW Russian Federation
Novokuznetsk 118 E5 S Russian Federation
Novolazarevskaya 142 C3 *Russian research station* Antarctica
Novo mesto 101 E9 SE Slovenia
Novomoskovsk 111 B6 W Russian Federation
Novomoskovs'k 109 F5 E Ukraine
Novorossiysk 111 A8 SW Russian Federation
Novoshakhtinsk 111 A7 SW Russian Federation
Novosibirsk 118 D5 C Russian Federation
Novotroitsk 111 D7 W Russian Federation
Novyy Buh 109 E5 S Ukraine
Nowogard 105 C2 NW Poland
Nowy Dwór Mazowiecki 105 E3 C Poland
Nowy Sącz 105 F6 S Poland
Nowy Tomyśl 105 C3 C Poland
Noyon 97 D2 N France
Ntomba, Lac 76 B2 ◎ NW Dem. Rep. Congo
Nubian Desert 75 C1 *desert* NE Sudan
Nueces River 44 G5 ≈ Texas, SW USA
Nueva Gerona 57 B3 NW Cuba
Nueva Guinea 55 E5 SE Nicaragua
Nueva Ocotepeque 55 B3 W Honduras
Nueva Rosita 53 E2 NE Mexico
Nuevitas 57 D3 E Cuba
Nuevo Casas Grandes 53 C2 N Mexico
Nuevo, Golfo 65 B7 *gulf* S Argentina
Nuevo Laredo 53 E2 NE Mexico
Nui Atoll 141 I2 *atoll* W Tuvalu
Nuku'alofa 135 ● Tongatapu, S Tonga
Nukufetau Atoll 141 I2 *atoll* C Tuvalu
Nukulaelae Atoll 141 J3 *atoll* E Tuvalu
Nukumanu Islands 141 E1 *island group* NE Papua New Guinea
Nukus 125 D2 W Uzbekistan
Nullarbor Plain 137 D5 *plateau* South Australia/Western Australia
Nunavut 33 H4 ◐ *territory* N Canada
Nuneaton 93 D6 C England, United Kingdom
Nunivak Island 50 C2 *island* Alaska, USA
Nunspeet 84 E4 E Netherlands
Nuoro 103 A6 Sardinia, Italy
Nuremberg 101 C6 S Germany
Nurmes 83 F4 E Finland
Nürnberg *see* Nuremberg
Nurota 125 E3 C Uzbekistan
Nusaybin 121 G4 SE Turkey
Nyagan' 118 D3 N Russian Federation
Nyainqentanglha Shan 129 C4 ▲▲ W China
Nyala 75 B3 W Sudan
Nyamtumbo 75 D7 S Tanzania
Nyandoma 111 B4 NW Russian Federation
Nyantakara 75 C6 NW Tanzania
Nyasa, Lake 76 E4 ◎ Malawi/Mozambique/Tanzania/Zambia
Nyeri 75 D5 C Kenya
Nyíregyháza 105 F7 NE Hungary
Nykøbing 83 B7 SE Denmark
Nyköping 83 D6 S Sweden
Nylstroom *see* Modimolle
Nyngan 137 G5 New South Wales, SE Australia
Nyurba 118 F4 NE Russian Federation
Nzega 75 C6 C Tanzania
Nzérékoré 72 B5 SE Guinea
N'Zeto 76 B3 NW Angola

O

Oahe, Lake 43 C3 ⊡ North Dakota/South Dakota, N USA
Oa'hu 51 B1 *island* Hawai'ian Islands, Hawaii, USA
Oakham 93 E5 C England, United Kingdom
Oak Harbor 49 B2 Washington, NW USA
Oakland 49 B7 California, W USA
Oakley 43 B6 Kansas, C USA
Oamaru 139 B7 South Island, New Zealand
Oa, Mull of 91 B6 *headland* W Scotland, United Kingdom
Oaxaca 53 F5 SE Mexico
Ob' 118 D3 ≈ C Russian Federation
Oban 91 C5 W Scotland, United Kingdom
Ob', Gulf of 118 D3 *gulf* N Russian Federation
Obihiro 133 G2 NE Japan
Obo 72 I5 E Central African Republic
Obock 75 E3 E Djibouti
Oborniki 105 C3 W Poland
Ocala 39 F7 Florida, SE USA
Ocaña 99 D3 C Spain
O Carballiño 99 B2 NW Spain
Occidental, Cordillera 65 A2 ▲▲ Bolivia/Chile
Ocean Falls 33 E6 British Columbia, SW Canada
Oceanside 49 D9 California, W USA
Ochamchire 121 G1 W Georgia
Ochil Hills 91 E5 ▲▲ C Scotland, United Kingdom
Ocotal 55 D4 NW Nicaragua
Ocozocuautla 53 G5 SE Mexico
October Revolution Island 118 F2 *island* N Russian Federation
Ocú 55 G7 S Panama
Odate 133 G3 C Japan
Ödemiş 120 A4 SW Turkey
Odense 83 B7 C Denmark
Oder 101 E3 ≈ C Europe
Oderhaff 105 B2 *bay* Germany/Poland
Odesa 109 E6 SW Ukraine
Odessa 44 F4 Texas, SW USA
Odienné 72 C4 NW Ivory Coast
Odoorn 84 F2 NE Netherlands
Odra *see* Oder
Of 121 F2 NE Turkey
Ofanto 103 E6 ≈ S Italy
Offenbach 101 B5 W Germany
Offenburg 101 B7 SW Germany
Ofu 51 *island* E American Samoa
Ogaden 75 F4 *plateau* Ethiopia/Somalia
Ogaki 133 F6 SW Japan
Ogallala 43 B5 Nebraska, C USA
Ogbomosho 72 E5 W Nigeria
Ogden 47 D5 Utah, W USA
Ogdensburg 37 D2 New York, NE USA
Ohio 40 E6 ◐ *state* N USA
Ohio River 40 F7 ≈ N USA
Ohrid, Lake 107 D4 ◎ Albania/Macedonia
Ohura 139 D3 North Island, New Zealand
Oil City 37 B4 Pennsylvania, NE USA
Oirschot 84 D5 S Netherlands
Oise 97 D2 ≈ N France
Oita 133 D7 Kyushu, SW Japan
Ojinaga 53 D2 N Mexico
Ojos del Salado, Cerro 65 A4 ▲ W Argentina
Okaihau 139 C1 North Island, New Zealand
Okanogan River 49 C1 ≈ Washington, NW USA
Okara 127 D2 E Pakistan
Okavango 76 C5 ≈ S Africa
Okavango Delta 76 C5 *wetland* N Botswana
Okayama 133 E6 SW Japan
Okazaki 133 F6 C Japan
Okeechobee, Lake 39 F8 ◎ Florida, SE USA
Okefenokee Swamp 39 F6 *wetland* Georgia, SE USA
Okehampton 95 C5 SW England, United Kingdom
Okhotsk 118 H3 E Russian Federation
Okhotsk, Sea of 118 H4 *sea* NW Pacific Ocean
Okhtyrka 109 F4 NE Ukraine
Okinawa 133 A8 SW Japan
Okinawa-shoto 133 A8 *island group* SW Japan
Oki-shoto 133 D6 *island group* SW Japan
Oklahoma 43 C8 ◐ *state* C USA
Oklahoma City 43 D8 *state capital* Oklahoma, C USA
Okmulgee 43 D8 Oklahoma, C USA
Oko, Wadi 75 D1 ≈ NE Sudan
Oktyabr'skiy 111 D6 SW Russian Federation
Okushiri-to 133 F2 *island* NE Japan
Öland 83 D7 *island* S Sweden
Olavarría 65 C6 E Argentina
Oława 105 D4 SW Poland
Olbia 103 B5 Sardinia, Italy
Oldebroek 84 E3 E Netherlands
Oldenburg 101 B3 NW Germany
Oldenburg 101 C2 N Germany
Oldenzaal 84 F4 E Netherlands
Oldham 93 D4 NW England, United Kingdom
Old Head of Kinsale 89 C7 *headland* SW Ireland
Olëkma 118 G4 ≈ C Russian Federation
Olëkminsk 118 G4 NE Russian Federation
Oleksandriya 109 E5 C Ukraine
Olenegorsk 111 B2 NW Russian Federation
Olenek 118 F3 NE Russian Federation
Olenëk 118 F3 ≈ NE Russian Federation
Oléron, Île d' 97 B4 *island* W France
Olevs'k 109 C4 N Ukraine
Ölgiy 129 C1 W Mongolia
Olhão 99 B5 S Portugal
Olifa 76 B4 NW Namibia
Oliva 99 F4 E Spain
Olivet 97 D3 C France
Olmaliq 125 F3 E Uzbekistan
Olomouc 105 D6 E Czech Republic
Olonets 111 B4 NW Russian Federation
Olosega 51 *island* E American Samoa
Olovyannaya 118 G5 S Russian Federation
Olpe 101 B5 W Germany
Olsztyn 105 E2 N Poland
Olt 109 B7 ≈ S Romania
Olvera 99 C6 SW Spain
Olympia 49 B2 *state capital* Washington, NW USA
Olympic Mountains 49 A2 ▲▲ Washington, NW USA
Olympus, Mount 107 D4 ▲ N Greece
Omagh 89 D2 W Northern Ireland, United Kingdom
Omaha 43 D5 Nebraska, C USA
Oman 123 E6 ◆ *monarchy* SW Asia
Oman, Gulf of 123 F4 *gulf* N Arabian Sea
Omboué 76 A2 W Gabon
Omdurman 75 C2 C Sudan
Ometepe, Isla de 55 D5 *island* S Nicaragua
Ommen 84 E3 E Netherlands
Omsk 118 D5 C Russian Federation
Omuta 133 D7 SW Japan
Onda 99 F3 E Spain
Öndörhaan 129 F2 E Mongolia
Onega 111 B3 NW Russian Federation
Onega 111 B4 ≈ NW Russian Federation
Onega, Lake 111 B4 ◎ NW Russian Federation
Oneida Lake 37 D3 ◎ New York, NE USA
O'Neill 43 C4 Nebraska, C USA
Oneonta 37 D4 New York, NE USA
Onex 101 A8 SW Switzerland
Ongjin 133 A5 SW North Korea
Ongole 127 E6 E India
Onitsha 72 F5 S Nigeria
Onon Gol 129 F2 ≈ N Mongolia
Onslow 137 A3 Western Australia
Onslow Bay 39 H4 *bay* North Carolina, E USA
Ontario 35 B4 ◐ *province* S Canada
Ontario, Lake 37 C3 ◎ Canada/USA
Ontinyent 99 F4 E Spain
Ontong Java Atoll 141 E2 *atoll* N Solomon Islands
Oostakker 84 B6 NW Belgium
Oostburg 84 B5 SW Netherlands
Oostende *see* Ostend
Oosterbeek 84 E4 SE Netherlands
Oosterhout 84 D5 S Netherlands
Opava 105 D5 E Czech Republic
Opelika 39 E5 Alabama, S USA
Opelousas 39 B6 Louisiana, S USA
Opmeer 84 D3 NW Netherlands
Opochka 111 A4 W Russian Federation
Opole 105 D5 S Poland
Oporto 99 B3 NW Portugal
Opotiki 139 E3 North Island, New Zealand
Oqtosh 125 E3 C Uzbekistan
Oradea 109 B6 NW Romania
Oran 70 D1 NW Algeria
Orange 137 G5 New South Wales, SE Australia
Orange 97 E6 SE France
Orangeburg 39 G4 South Carolina, SE USA
Orange River 76 C6 ≈ S Africa
Orange Walk 55 C1 N Belize
Oranienburg 101 D3 NE Germany
Oranjemund 76 B6 SW Namibia
Oranjestad 57 G7 ○ W Aruba
Oranmore 89 C4 W Ireland
Orbetello 103 C4 C Italy
Orcadas 142 A2 *Argentinian research station* South Orkney Islands, Antarctica
Orchard Homes 47 C2 Montana, NW USA
Ord River 137 D2 ≈ N Australia Oceania
Ordu 121 E2 N Turkey
Örebro 83 C5 C Sweden
Oregon 49 B4 ◐ *state* NW USA
Oregon City 49 B3 Oregon, NW USA
Orël 111 A6 W Russian Federation
Orem 47 D5 Utah, W USA
Ore Mountains 101 D5 ▲▲ Czech Republic/Germany
Orenburg 111 D7 W Russian Federation
Orense *see* Ourense
Orford Ness 95 H2 *cape* E England, United Kingdom
Organ Peak 44 D3 ▲ New Mexico, SW USA
Oriental, Cordillera 65 B3 ▲▲ Bolivia/Peru
Orihuela 99 F5 E Spain
Orikhiv 109 F5 SE Ukraine
Orin 47 F4 Wyoming, C USA
Orinoco, Río 63 D2 ≈ Colombia/Venezuela
Oriomo 141 A3 SW Papua New Guinea
Orissa 127 F5 *state* NE India
Oristano 103 A6 Sardinia, Italy
Orkney Islands 91 D1 *island group* N Scotland, United Kingdom
Orlando 39 G7 Florida, SE USA
Orléanais 97 D3 *cultural region* C France
Orléans 97 D3 C France
Orleans 37 G4 Massachusetts, NE USA
Ormskirk 93 C4 NW England, United Kingdom
Örnsköldsvik 83 D4 C Sweden
Orohena, Mont 141 B6 ⩓ Tahiti, W French Polynesia
Oromocto 35 F5 New Brunswick, SE Canada
Orsha 109 D2 NE Belarus
Orsk 111 D7 W Russian Federation
Orthez 97 B6 SW France
Ortona 103 D5 C Italy
Oruro 65 A2 W Bolivia
Orwell 95 H2 ≈ E England, United Kingdom
Osaka 133 F6 SW Japan
Osa, Península de 55 E7 *peninsula* S Costa Rica
Osborne 43 C6 Kansas, C USA
Osh 125 G3 SW Kyrgyzstan
Oshakati 76 B5 N Namibia
Oshawa 35 D6 Ontario, SE Canada
Oshikango 76 B4 N Namibia
O-shima 133 G6 *island* S Japan
Oshkosh 40 C4 Wisconsin, N USA
Osijek 107 C1 E Croatia
Oskaloosa 43 F5 Iowa, C USA
Oskarshamn 83 C6 S Sweden
Oslo 83 B5 ● S Norway
Osmaniye 121 E5 S Turkey
Osnabrück 101 B4 NW Germany
Osorno 65 A7 C Chile
Oss 84 D5 S Netherlands
Ossa, Serra d' 99 B4 ▲▲ SE Portugal
Ossora 118 I3 E Russian Federation
Ostend 84 A6 NW Belgium
Östersund 83 C4 C Sweden
Ostfriesische Inseln *see* East Frisian Islands
Ostiglia 103 C2 N Italy
Ostrava 105 D5 E Czech Republic
Ostróda 105 E2 NE Poland
Ostrołęka 105 F3 C Poland
Ostrov 111 A4 W Russian Federation
Ostrowiec Świętokrzyski 105 F4 C Poland
Ostrów Mazowiecka 105 F3 NE Poland
Ostrów Wielkopolski 105 D4 C Poland
Osumi-shoto 133 A7 *island group* SW Japan
Osumit, Lumi i 107 D4 ≈ SE Albania
Osuna 99 C5 SW Spain
Oswego 37 D3 New York, NE USA
Oswestry 93 C5 W England, United Kingdom
Otago Peninsula 139 B7 *peninsula* South Island, New Zealand
Otaki 139 D5 North Island, New Zealand
Otaru 133 F2 NE Japan
Otavi 76 B5 N Namibia
Otira 139 C6 South Island, New Zealand
Otjiwarongo 76 B5 N Namibia
Otley 93 D4 N England, United Kingdom
Otorohanga 139 D3 North Island, New Zealand
Otranto 112 G3 SE Italy
Otranto, Strait of 103 F7 *strait* Albania/Italy
Otrokovice 105 D6 E Czech Republic
Ōtsu 133 E6 Honshu, SW Japan
Ottawa 35 D5 ● Ontario, SE Canada
Ottawa 40 B5 Illinois, N USA
Ottawa 43 E6 Kansas, C USA
Ottawa Islands 35 C2 *island group* Nunavut, C Canada
Otterburn 93 D2 N England, United Kingdom
Ottignies 84 C7 C Belgium
Ottumwa 43 F5 Iowa, C USA
Ouachita Mountains 39 A3 ▲▲ Arkansas/Oklahoma, C USA
Ouachita River 39 B5 ≈ Arkansas/Louisiana, C USA
Ouagadougou 72 D4 ● C Burkina
Ouahigouya 72 D3 NW Burkina
Oualâta 72 C3 SE Mauritania
Ouanda Djallé 72 I4 NE Central African Republic
Ouarâne 72 B2 *desert* C Mauritania
Ouargla 70 E2 NE Algeria
Ouarzazate 70 C2 S Morocco
Oubangui 72 H5 ≈ C Africa
Ouessant, Île d' 97 A2 *island* NW France
Ouésso 76 B1 NW Congo
Oughterard 89 B4 W Ireland
Oujda 70 D1 NE Morocco
Oujeft 72 B2 C Mauritania
Oulu 83 E3 C Finland
Oulujärvi 83 E3 ◎ C Finland
Oulujoki 83 E3 ≈ C Finland
Ounasjoki 83 E2 ≈ N Finland
Ounianga Kébir 72 H2 N Chad
Oupeye 84 D7 E Belgium
Our 84 E8 ≈ NW Europe
Ourense 99 B2 NW Spain
Ourique 99 B5 S Portugal
Ourthe 84 E8 ≈ E Belgium
Ou-sanmyaku 133 G3 ▲▲ Honshū, C Japan
Ouse 93 E4 ≈ N England, United Kingdom
Outer Hebrides 91 A3 *island group* NW Scotland, United Kingdom
Outes 99 B1 NW Spain
Out Skerries 91 B6 *island group* NE Scotland, United Kingdom
Ouvéa 141 G6 *island* Îles Loyauté, NE New Caledonia
Ouyen 137 F6 Victoria, SE Australia
Ovalle 65 A5 N Chile
Ovar 99 B3 N Portugal
Overflakkee 84 B5 *island* SW Netherlands
Overijse 84 C7 C Belgium
Oviedo 99 C1 NW Spain
Owando 76 B2 C Congo
Owase 133 F6 SW Japan
Owatonna 43 E4 Minnesota, N USA
Owen, Mount 139 C5 ▲ South Island, New Zealand
Owensboro 39 D2 Kentucky, S USA
Owens Lake 49 D7 *salt flat* California, W USA
Owen Stanley Range 141 B3 ▲▲ S Papua New Guinea
Owerri 72 F5 S Nigeria
Owyhee River 49 D4 ≈ Idaho/Oregon, NW USA
Oxford 139 C6 South Island, New Zealand
Oxford 95 E3 S England, United Kingdom
Oxford Canal 95 E2 *canal* S England, United Kingdom
Oxkutzcab 53 H4 SE Mexico
Oxnard 49 C8 California, W USA
Oyama 133 G5 Honshu, S Japan
Oyem 76 A1 N Gabon
Oykel 91 D3 ≈ N Scotland, United Kingdom
Oyo 76 B2 C Congo
Oyo 72 E5 W Nigeria
Ozark 39 E6 Alabama, S USA
Ozark Plateau 43 E7 *plain* Arkansas/Missouri, C USA
Ozarks, Lake of the 43 F6 ⊡ Missouri, C USA
Ózd 105 E7 NE Hungary
Ozieri 103 A5 Sardinia, Italy

P

Pabbay 91 A3 *island* NW Scotland, United Kingdom
Pabna 127 G3 W Bangladesh
Pachuca 53 F5 C Mexico
Pacific Ocean 14 *ocean*
Padang 131 B6 Sumatra, W Indonesia
Paderborn 101 B4 NW Germany
Padova *see* Padua
Padre Island 44 H6 *island* Texas, SW USA
Padua 103 C2 NE Italy
Paducah 39 D2 Kentucky, S USA
Paektu-san 133 B3 ▲ China/North Korea
Paeroa 139 D3 North Island, New Zealand
Páfos 112 C6 W Cyprus
Pag 107 B2 *island* C Croatia
Page 44 B1 Arizona, SW USA
Pago Pago 135 ○ W American Samoa
Pāhala 51 D3 Hawaii, USA
Pahiatua 139 D4 North Island, New Zealand
Pāhoa 51 D3 Hawaii, USA
Paignton 95 C5 SW England, United Kingdom
Paihia 139 D1 North Island, New Zealand
Päijänne 83 E4 ◎ S Finland
Pailolo Channel 51 C2 *channel* Hawaii, USA
Paine, Cerro 65 A9 ▲ S Chile
Painted Desert 47 D7 *desert* Arizona, SW USA
Paisley 91 D6 W Scotland, United Kingdom
País Valenciano 99 F3 *cultural region* NE Spain
País Vasco *see* Basque Country, The
Pakistan 127 B2 ◆ *republic* S Asia
Pakokku 131 A2 C Burma (Myanmar)
Pakruojis 83 E7 N Lithuania
Paks 105 E8 S Hungary
Pakwach 75 C5 NW Uganda
Pakxe 131 C3 S Laos
Palafrugell 99 H2 NE Spain
Palagruža 107 B3 *island* SW Croatia
Palamós 99 H2 NE Spain
Palanpur 127 C4 W India
Palapye 76 D5 SE Botswana
Palatka 39 G6 Florida, SE USA
Palau 131 H6 ◆ *republic* W Pacific Ocean
Palawan 131 E5 *island* W Philippines
Palawan Passage 131 E4 *passage* W Philippines
Palembang 131 C7 W Indonesia
Palencia 99 D2 NW Spain
Palermo 103 C7 Sicily, Italy
Palestine 44 H3 Texas, SW USA
Pali 127 C3 N India
Palikir 135 ● Pohnpei, E Micronesia
Palk Strait 127 E7 *strait* India/Sri Lanka
Palliser, Cape 139 D5 *headland* North Island, New Zealand
Palma 99 H4 Balearic Islands, E Spain
Palma del Río 99 C5 S Spain
Palmar Sur 55 F6 SE Costa Rica
Palma Soriano 57 E4 E Cuba
Palmer 37 F4 Massachusetts, NE USA
Palmer 142 A4 *US research station* Antarctica
Palmer Land 142 B4 *physical region* Antarctica
Palmerston North 139 D4 North Island, New Zealand
Palmi 103 E8 SW Italy
Palm Springs 49 D9 California, W USA
Palmyra Atoll 135 US ◇ C Pacific Ocean
Palo Alto 49 B7 California, W USA
Palu 131 E6 Celebes, C Indonesia
Pamiers 97 C7 S France
Pamir 125 G4 ≈ Afghanistan/Tajikistan
Pamirs 125 G4 ▲▲ C Asia
Pamlico Sound 39 I3 *sound* North Carolina, SE USA
Pampa 44 F2 Texas, SW USA
Pampas 65 B6 *plain* C Argentina
Pamplona 99 E2 N Spain
Panaji 127 C6 W India
Panama 55 G7 ◆ *republic* Central America
Panama Canal 55 G6 *shipping canal* E Panama
Panama City 55 H6 ● C Panama
Panama City 39 E6 Florida, SE USA
Panama, Gulf of 55 H7 *gulf* S Panama
Panama, Isthmus of 55 H6 *isthmus* E Panama
Panay Island 131 E4 *island* C Philippines
Pančevo 107 D2 N Serbia
Panevėžys 83 E7 C Lithuania
Pangkalpinang 131 C7 W Indonesia
Panguitch 47 C6 Utah, W USA
Pantanal 63 E6 *swamp* SW Brazil
Pantelleria 103 B8 Sicily, Italy
Pantelleria, Isola di 112 F4 *island* SW Italy
Pánuco 53 F4 E Mexico
Paola 112 B6 E Malta
Papagayo, Golfo de 55 D5 *gulf* NW Costa Rica
Papakura 139 D2 North Island, New Zealand
Papantla 53 F4 E Mexico
Papa Stour 91 A6 *island* NE Scotland, United Kingdom
Papa Westray 91 E1 *island* NE Scotland, United Kingdom
Papeete 141 A5 ○ W French Polynesia
Papillion 43 D5 Nebraska, C USA
Papua 131 I7 *province* E Indonesia
Papua, Gulf of 141 B3 *gulf* S Papua New Guinea
Papua New Guinea 141 B2 ◆ *commonwealth republic* NW Melanesia
Papuk 107 C1 ▲▲ NE Croatia
Pará 63 F4 *state* NE Brazil
Paracel Islands 131 C3 *Disputed* ◇ SE Asia
Paraguay 65 B3 ◆ *republic* C South America
Paraguay 65 C3 ≈ C South America
Paraíba 63 I5 *state* E Brazil
Parakou 72 E4 C Benin
Paramaribo 63 F2 ● N Surinam
Paramushir, Ostrov 118 I4 *island* SE Russian Federation
Paraná 65 C5 E Argentina
Paraná 63 F8 *state* S Brazil
Paraná 65 C5 ≈ C South America
Paraparaumu 139 D5 North Island, New Zealand
Parchim 101 D3 N Germany
Parczew 105 G4 E Poland
Pardubice 105 C5 C Czech Republic
Parecis, Chapada dos 65 B1 ▲▲ W Brazil
Parepare 131 E7 Celebes, C Indonesia
Paria, Gulf of 57 J7 *gulf* Trinidad and Tobago/Venezuela
Paris 97 D2 ● N France
Paris 44 H2 Texas, SW USA
Parkersburg 39 F1 West Virginia, NE USA
Parkes 137 G5 New South Wales, SE Australia
Parma 103 C3 N Italy
Parnaíba 63 H4 E Brazil
Pärnu 83 E6 SW Estonia
Páros 107 F6 *island* SE Greece
Parral 65 A6 C Chile
Parramatta 137 G6 New South Wales, SE Australia
Parras 53 E3 NE Mexico
Parrett 95 D4 ≈ SW England, United Kingdom
Parsons 43 E7 Kansas, C USA
Partney 93 F5 E England, United Kingdom
Partry 89 B3 NW Ireland
Partry Mountains 89 B4 ▲▲ W Ireland
Pasadena 49 C8 California, W USA
Pasadena 44 H4 Texas, SW USA
Pasco 49 C3 Washington, NW USA
Pasewalk 101 E3 NE Germany
Pasinler 121 G3 NE Turkey
Pasłęk 105 E2 NE Poland

◐ Administrative region ◆ Country ● Country capital ◇ Dependent territory ○ Dependent territory capital ▲▲ Mountain range ▲ Mountain ⩓ Volcano ≈ River ◎ Lake ⊡ Reservoir

Pasni *127 A3* SW Pakistan
Paso de Indios *65 A7* S Argentina
Passau *101 D6* SE Germany
Passo Fundo *63 F8* S Brazil
Pasto *63 B3* SW Colombia
Patagonia *65 B7 semi arid region* Argentina/Chile
Patea *139 D4* North Island, New Zealand
Paterson *37 E5* New Jersey, NE USA
Pathein *131 A3* SW Burma (Myanmar)
Pátmos *107 F6 island* Dodecanese, Greece
Patna *127 F3* N India
Patnos *121 G3* E Turkey
Patos, Lagoa dos *63 F9 lagoon* S Brazil
Pátra *107 D5* S Greece
Patrickswell *89 C5* SW Ireland
Patuca, Río *55 E3* ≈ E Honduras
Pau *97 B6* SW France
Paulatuk *33 F3* Northwest Territories, NW Canada
Pavia *103 B2* N Italy
Pavlodar *118 D5* NE Kazakhstan
Pavlohrad *109 F5* E Ukraine
Pawn *131 B3* ≈ C Burma (Myanmar)
Paxoí *107 D5 island* Ionian Islands, Greece
Paysandú *65 C5* W Uruguay
Pazar *121 F2* NE Turkey
Pazardzhik *107 E3* C Bulgaria
Peach Springs *44 A2* Arizona, SW USA
Peak District *93 D5 physical region* C England, United Kingdom
Pearl City *51 B1* O'ahu, Hawaii, USA
Pearl Harbor *51 B2 inlet* O'ahu, Hawaii, USA, C Pacific Ocean
Pearl Islands *55 H6 island group* SE Panama
Pearl Lagoon *55 F4 lagoon* E Nicaragua
Pearl River *39 C6* ≈ Louisiana/ Mississippi, S USA
Pearsall *44 G5* Texas, SW USA
Peawanuk *35 C3* Ontario, C Canada
Pechora *111 D4* NW Russian Federation
Pechora *111 D3* ≈ NW Russian Federation
Pechora Sea *111 D2 sea* NW Russian Federation
Pecos *44 E4* Texas, SW USA
Pecos River *44 F4* ≈ New Mexico/ Texas, SW USA
Pécs *105 D9* SW Hungary
Pedro Juan Caballero *65 C3* E Paraguay
Peebles *91 E6* SE Scotland, United Kingdom
Peel *93 A3* W Isle of Man
Peer *84 D6* NE Belgium
Pegasus Bay *139 C6 bay* South Island, New Zealand
Pehuajó *65 B6* E Argentina
Peine *101 C4* C Germany
Peipus, Lake *83 E5* ◎ Estonia/ Russian Federation
Peiraías *see* Piraeus
Pejë *107 D3* W Kosovo
Pekalongan *131 D7* Java, C Indonesia
Pekanbaru *131 B6* Sumatra, W Indonesia
Pekin *40 B6* Illinois, N USA
Peking *see* Beijing
Pelagie *103 C9 island group* SW Italy
Pelly Bay *see* Kugaaruk
Peloponnese *107 D6 peninsula* S Greece
Pematangsiantar *131 A6* Sumatra, W Indonesia
Pemba *76 F4* NE Mozambique
Pemba *75 E6 island* E Tanzania
Pembroke *35 D5* Ontario, SE Canada
Pembroke *93 A7* SW Wales, United Kingdom
Pembroke Dock *93 A7* SW Wales, United Kingdom
Penas, Golfo de *65 A8 gulf* S Chile
Pendleton *49 C3* Oregon, NW USA
Pend Oreille, Lake *47 B1* ◎ Idaho, NW USA
Peniche *99 A4* W Portugal
Penn Hills *37 B5* Pennsylvania, NE USA
Pennine Alps *101 A8* ⛰ Italy/Switzerland
Pennines *93 D3* ⛰ N England, United Kingdom
Pennsylvania *37 C5* ◐ *state* NE USA
Penobscot River *37 G2* ≈ Maine, NE USA
Penong *137 E5* South Australia
Penonomé *55 G6* C Panama
Penrhyn *135 atoll* N Cook Islands
Penrith *93 C2* NW England, United Kingdom
Pensacola *39 D6* Florida, SE USA
Pentecost *141 H4 island* C Vanuatu
Pentland Firth *91 E1 strait* N Scotland, United Kingdom
Pentland Hills *91 E6 hill range* S Scotland, United Kingdom
Pen y Fan *93 B7* ▲ SE Wales, United Kingdom
Pen-y-ghent *93 D3* ▲ N England, United Kingdom
Penza *111 B6* W Russian Federation
Penzance *95 A6* SW England, United Kingdom
Peoria *40 B6* Illinois, N USA
Perchtoldsdorf *101 F7* NE Austria
Percival Lakes *137 C3 lakes* Western Australia
Perdido, Monte *99 F2* ▲ NE Spain
Pergamino *65 C5* E Argentina
Périgueux *97 C5* SW France
Perito Moreno *65 A8* S Argentina
Perleberg *101 D3* N Germany
Perm' *111 D5* NW Russian Federation
Pernambuco *63 H5 state* E Brazil
Pernik *107 E3* W Bulgaria
Perote *53 F5* E Mexico
Perpignan *97 D7* S France
Perryton *44 F1* Texas, SW USA
Perryville *43 G7* Missouri, C USA
Persian Gulf *123 D3 gulf* SW Asia
Perth *91 E5* C Scotland, United Kingdom
Perth *137 B5 state capital* Western Australia
Peru *65 A2* ◆ *republic* W South America
Peru Basin *14 undersea feature* E Pacific Ocean
Peru-Chile Trench *14 undersea feature* E Pacific Ocean
Perugia *103 C4* C Italy
Péruwelz *84 B7* SW Belgium
Pervomays'k *109 E5* S Ukraine
Pervyy Kuril'skiy Proliv *118 I4 strait* E Russian Federation
Pesaro *103 D3* C Italy
Pescara *103 D5* C Italy
Peshawar *127 C1* N Pakistan
Pessac *97 B5* SW France
Petah Tikva *123 H6* C Israel
Pétange *84 E9* SW Luxembourg
Petén Itzá, Lago *55 B2* ◎ N Guatemala
Peterborough *137 E5* South Australia
Peterborough *35 D6* Ontario, SE Canada
Peterborough *95 F2* E England, United Kingdom
Peterhead *91 F3* NE Scotland, United Kingdom
Peter I Island *142 A4 Norwegian* ◇ Antarctica
Peterlee *93 E3* N England, United Kingdom
Petersburg *39 H2* Virginia, NE USA
Petersfield *95 F4* S England, United Kingdom
Peto *53 H4* SE Mexico
Petrich *107 E4* SW Bulgaria
Petrodvorets *111 A4* NW Russian Federation
Petropavlovsk *118 C4* N Kazakhstan
Petropavlovsk-Kamchatskiy *118 I3* E Russian Federation
Petrozavodsk *111 B4* NW Russian Federation
Pevek *118 H2* NE Russian Federation
Pezinok *105 D7* W Slovakia
Pforzheim *101 B6* SW Germany
Pfungstadt *101 B6* W Germany
Phangan, Ko *131 B4 island* SW Thailand
Phenix City *39 E5* Alabama, S USA
Phetchaburi *131 B4* SW Thailand
Philadelphia *37 D5* Pennsylvania, NE USA
Philippines *131 D4* ◆ *republic* SE Asia
Philippine Sea *131 F3 sea* W Pacific Ocean
Philippine Trench *15 undersea feature* W Philippine Sea
Phitsanulok *131 B3* C Thailand
Phnom Penh *131 C4* ● S Cambodia
Phoenix *44 B3 state capital* Arizona, SW USA
Phoenix Islands *135 island group* C Kiribati
Phra Thong, Ko *131 A5 island* SW Thailand
Phuket *131 B5* SW Thailand
Phuket, Ko *131 A5 island* SW Thailand
Piacenza *103 B2* N Italy
Piatra-Neamț *109 C6* NE Romania
Piauí *63 G5 state* E Brazil
Picardie *see* Picardy
Picardy *97 D2 cultural region* N France Europe
Pichilemu *65 A5* C Chile
Pickering *93 E3* N England, United Kingdom
Picos *63 H4* E Brazil
Picton *139 D5* South Island, New Zealand
Piedmont *103 A2 cultural region* NW Italy
Piedmont *39 G3 escarpment* E USA
Piedras Negras *53 E2* NE Mexico
Pielavesi *83 E4* C Finland
Pielinen *83 F4* ◎ E Finland
Piemonte *see* Piedmont
Pierre *43 C3 state capital* South Dakota, N USA
Piešťany *105 D6* W Slovakia
Pietarsaari *see* Jakobstad
Pietermaritzburg *76 D6* E South Africa
Pietersburg *see* Polokwane
Pigs, Bay of *57 C3 bay* SE Cuba
Pijijiapán *53 H6* SE Mexico
Pikes Peak *47 E6* ▲ Colorado, C USA
Pikeville *39 F2* Kentucky, S USA
Piła *105 C3* C Poland
Pilar *65 C4* S Paraguay
Pilcomayo, Rio *65 C3* ≈ C South America
Pillsbury Sound *51 strait* C Virgin Islands (USA) North America Caribbean Sea Atlantic Ocean
Pinar del Río *57 B2* W Cuba
Pindus Mountains *107 D5* ⛰ C Greece
Pine Bluff *39 B4* Arkansas, C USA
Pine Creek *137 D1* Northern Territory, N Australia
Pinega *111 C4* ≈ NW Russian Federation
Pineiós *107 E4* ≈ C Greece
Pineland *44 I4* Texas, SW USA
Pingdingshan *129 F4* C China
Ping, Mae Nam *131 B3* ≈ W Thailand
Pinotepa Nacional *53 F6* SE Mexico
Pins, Île des *141 G6 island* E New Caledonia
Pinsk *109 C3* SW Belarus
Piombino *103 B4* C Italy
Piotrków Trybunalski *105 E4* C Poland
Piraeus *107 E5* C Greece
Pirata, Monte *51* ▲ E Puerto Rico
Piripiri *63 H4* E Brazil
Pirna *101 E5* E Germany
Pisa *103 B3* C Italy
Pisco *63 B6* SW Peru
Písek *105 B6* S Czech Republic
Pishan *129 B3* NW China
Pistoia *103 C3* C Italy
Pisz *105 F2* NE Poland
Pita *72 B4* NW Guinea
Pitcairn Islands *135 UK* ◇ C Pacific Ocean
Piteå *83 D3* N Sweden
Pitești *109 B7* S Romania
Pitlochry *91 D4* C Scotland, United Kingdom
Pit River *49 B5* ≈ California, W USA
Pittsburg *43 E7* Kansas, C USA
Pittsburgh *37 B5* Pennsylvania, NE USA
Pittsfield *37 E4* Massachusetts, NE USA
Piura *63 A4* NW Peru
Pivdennyy Buh *109 E5* ≈ S Ukraine
Placetas *57 C3* C Cuba
Plainview *44 F2* Texas, SW USA
Plano *44 H3* Texas, SW USA
Plasencia *99 C3* W Spain
Plate, River *65 C5 estuary* Argentina/Uruguay
Platinum *50 D2* Alaska, USA
Platte River *43 D5* ≈ Nebraska, C USA
Plattsburgh *37 E2* New York, NE USA
Plauen *101 D5* E Germany
Plei Ku *131 C4* C Vietnam
Plenty, Bay of *139 E3 bay* North Island, New Zealand
Plérin *97 B2* NW France
Plesetsk *111 C4* NW Russian Federation
Pleszew *105 D4* C Poland
Pleven *107 E2* N Bulgaria
Płock *105 E3* C Poland
Plöcken Pass *101 D8 pass* SW Austria
Ploiești *109 C7* SE Romania
Płońsk *105 E3* C Poland
Plovdiv *107 F3* C Bulgaria
Plymouth *57 J5* Trinidad and Tobago
Plymouth *95 B5* SW England, United Kingdom
Plynlimon *93 B6* ▲ C Wales, United Kingdom
Plzeň *105 A5* W Czech Republic
Po *103 C3* ≈ N Italy
Pobedy, Pik *129 B2* ▲ China/ Kyrgyzstan (see also Jengish Chokusu)
Pocahontas *39 C3* Arkansas, C USA
Pocatello *47 C4* Idaho, NW USA
Pochinok *111 A5* W Russian Federation
Pocking *101 D7* SE Germany
Pocklington Reef *141 E3 reef* SE Papua New Guinea
Poděbrady *105 B5* C Czech Republic
Podgorica *107 C3* ● S Montenegro
Podil's'ka Vysochyna *109 C5* ⛰ SW Ukraine
Podol'sk *111 A5* W Russian Federation
Pohang *133 C6* E South Korea
Poinsett, Cape *142 E5 cape* Antarctica
Pointe-à-Pitre *57 J5* C Guadeloupe
Pointe-Noire *76 A2* S Congo
Point Lay *50 E1* Alaska, USA
Poitiers *97 C4* W France
Poitou *97 B4 cultural region* W France
Pokhara *127 F3* C Nepal
Poland *105 D4* ◆ *republic* C Europe
Polatlı *121 C3* C Turkey
Polatsk *109 D1* N Belarus
Pólis *112 C6* W Cyprus
Pollença *99 H3* Majorca, Spain
Polokwane *76 D6* NE South Africa
Poltava *109 F4* NE Ukraine
Polyarnyy *111 C2* NW Russian Federation
Polynesia *135 island group* C Pacific Ocean
Pomerania *105 C2 cultural region* Germany/Poland
Pomeranian Bay *101 E2 bay* Germany/Poland
Pomio *141 C2* E Papua New Guinea
Pomorskiy Proliv *111 D3 strait* NW Russian Federation
Pompano Beach *39 G8* Florida, SE USA
Ponca City *43 D7* Oklahoma, C USA
Ponce *57 H4* C Puerto Rico
Pondicherry *127 E6* SE India
Pond Inlet *143 A4* Baffin Island, Nunavut, NE Canada
Ponferrada *99 C2* NW Spain
Poniatowa *105 F4* E Poland
Ponta Grossa *63 F8* S Brazil
Pontarlier *97 F4* E France
Ponteareas *99 B2* NW Spain
Ponte da Barca *99 B2* N Portugal
Pontevedra *99 B2* NW Spain
Pontiac *40 E5* Michigan, N USA
Pontianak *131 D6* C Indonesia
Pontivy *97 B3* NW France
Pontoise *97 D2* N France
Pontypool *93 C7* SE Wales, United Kingdom
Pontypridd *93 C7* S Wales, United Kingdom
Ponziane Island *103 C6 island* C Italy
Poole *95 E5* S England, United Kingdom
Poole Bay *95 E5 bay* S England, United Kingdom
Popayán *63 B3* SW Colombia
Poperinge *84 A6* W Belgium
Poplar Bluff *43 G7* Missouri, C USA
Popocatépetl *53 F5* ✷ S Mexico
Popondetta *141 C3* S Papua New Guinea
Poprad *105 E6* E Slovakia
Poprád *105 E6* ≈ Poland/Slovakia
Porbandar *127 C4* W India
Pordenone *103 D2* NE Italy
Pori *83 E5* SW Finland
Porirua *139 D5* C New Zealand
Porkhov *111 A4* W Russian Federation
Póros *107 D5* Kefallonía, Greece
Porsangenfijorden *83 E1 fjord* N Norway
Porsgrunn *83 B5* S Norway
Portadown *89 E2* S Northern Ireland, United Kingdom
Portaferry *89 F3* E Northern Ireland, United Kingdom
Portalegre *99 B4* E Portugal
Port Alexander *50 F4* Baranof Island, Alaska, USA
Port Alfred *76 D7* S South Africa
Port Angeles *49 B2* Washington, NW USA
Port Arthur *44 I4* Texas, SW USA
Port Askaig *91 B6* W Scotland, United Kingdom
Port Augusta *137 E5* South Australia
Port-au-Prince *57* ● C Haiti
Port Blair *127 H5* Andaman Islands, SE India
Port Charlotte *39 F8* Florida, SE USA
Port Douglas *137 G2* Queensland, NE Australia
Port Elizabeth *76 D7* S South Africa
Port Ellen *91 B6* W Scotland, United Kingdom
Port Erin *93 A4* SW Isle of Man
Porterville *49 C8* California, W USA
Port-Gentil *76 A2* W Gabon
Port Harcourt *72 E5* S Nigeria
Port Hardy *33 E7* Vancouver Island, British Columbia, SW Canada
Port Harrison *see* Inukjuak
Port Hedland *137 B3* Western Australia
Port Huron *40 E4* Michigan, N USA
Portimão *99 B5* S Portugal
Port Isaac Bay *95 A5 bay* SW England, United Kingdom
Portishead *95 D4* SW England, United Kingdom
Portland *137 F6* Victoria, SE Australia
Portland *37 F3* Maine, NE USA
Portland *49 B3* Oregon, NW USA
Portland *44 H5* Texas, SW USA
Portland Bill *95 D5 headland* S England, United Kingdom
Portland, Isle of *95 D5 island* SW England, United Kingdom
Port Laoise *89 D5* C Ireland
Port Lavaca *44 H5* Texas, SW USA
Port Lincoln *137 E6* South Australia
Port Louis *67* ● NW Mauritius
Port Macquarie *137 H5* New South Wales, SE Australia
Port Moresby *141 B3* ● New Guinea, SW Papua New Guinea
Porto *see* Oporto
Porto Alegre *63 F8* S Brazil
Portobelo *55 H6* N Panama
Port O'Connor *44 H5* Texas, SW USA
Portoferraio *103 B4* C Italy
Port of Ness *91 B2* NW Scotland, United Kingdom
Port-of-Spain *57 K7* ● C Trinidad and Tobago
Portogruaro *103 D2* NE Italy
Porto-Novo *72 E5* ● S Benin
Porto Torres *103 A5* Sardinia, Italy
Porto Velho *63 D5* W Brazil
Portoviejo *63 A4* W Ecuador
Port Pirie *137 E5* South Australia
Portree *91 B3* N Scotland, United Kingdom
Portrush *89 E1* N Northern Ireland, United Kingdom
Port Said *70 I2* N Egypt
Portskerra *91 D2* N Scotland, United Kingdom
Portsmouth *95 F5* S England, United Kingdom
Portsmouth *37 F3* New Hampshire, NE USA
Portsmouth *40 E7* Ohio, N USA
Portsmouth *39 I2* Virginia, NE USA
Port Sudan *75 D1* NE Sudan
Portugal *99 A3* ◆ *republic* SW Europe
Port-Vila *141 H5* ● Éfaté, C Vanuatu
Porvenir *65 A1* NW Bolivia
Porvenir *65 B9* S Chile
Porvoo *83 E5* S Finland
Posadas *65 C4* NE Argentina
Post *44 F3* Texas, SW USA
Posterholt *84 E6* SE Netherlands
Postojna *101 E9* SW Slovenia
Potenza *103 E6* S Italy
Poti *121 G1* W Georgia
Potiskum *72 F4* NE Nigeria
Potomac River *39 H1* ≈ NE USA
Potosí *65 B3* S Bolivia
Potsdam *101 D3* NE Germany
Potsdam *37 D2* New York, NE USA
Pottsville *37 D5* Pennsylvania, NE USA
Pouébo *141 G6* C New Caledonia
Poulton-le-Fylde *93 C4* NW England, United Kingdom
Po Valley *103 C3 valley* N Italy
Považská Bystrica *105 D6* W Slovakia
Poverty Bay *139 E4 inlet* North Island, New Zealand
Póvoa de Varzim *99 B2* NW Portugal
Powder River *47 F3* ≈ Montana/ Wyoming, NW USA
Powell *47 E3* Wyoming, C USA
Powell, Lake *47 D6* ◎ Utah, W USA
Poza Rica *53 F4* E Mexico
Poznań *105 C3* C Poland
Pozoblanco *99 D5* S Spain
Pozzallo *103 D9* Sicily, Italy
Prachatice *105 B6* S Czech Republic
Prague *105* ● NW Czech Republic
Praha *see* Prague
Praia *67* ● Santiago, S Cape Verde
Prairie du Chien *40 B4* Wisconsin, N USA
Prato *103 C3* C Italy
Pratt *43 C7* Kansas, C USA
Prattville *39 E5* Alabama, S USA
Pravia *99 C1* N Spain
Prenzlau *101 D3* NE Germany
Přerov *105 D6* E Czech Republic
Prescott *44 B2* Arizona, SW USA
Preseli, Mynydd *93 A6* ⛰ SW Wales, United Kingdom
Presidio *44 E5* Texas, SW USA
Prešov *105 F6* E Slovakia
Prespa, Lake *107 D4* ◎ SE Europe
Presque Isle *37 G1* Maine, NE USA
Prestatyn *93 C4* N Wales, United Kingdom
Preston *93 C4* NW England, United Kingdom
Prestwick *91 D6* W Scotland, United Kingdom
Pretoria *76 D6* ● NE South Africa (see also Tshwane)
Préveza *107 D5* W Greece
Pribilof Islands *50 B2 island group* Alaska, USA
Price *47 D5* Utah, W USA
Prichard *39 D6* Alabama, S USA
Prilep *107 D4* S Macedonia
Prince Albert *33 G6* Saskatchewan, S Canada
Prince Edward Island *35 G5* ◐ *province* SE Canada
Prince George *33 F6* British Columbia, SW Canada
Prince of Wales Island *137 F1 island* Queensland, E Australia
Prince of Wales Island *33 H3 island* Queen Elizabeth Islands, Nunavut, NW Canada
Prince Patrick Island *33 F2 island* Parry Islands, Northwest Territories, NW Canada
Prince Rupert *33 E6* British Columbia, SW Canada
Princess Charlotte Bay *137 G1 bay* Queensland, NE Australia
Princess Elizabeth Land *142 D4 physical region* Antarctica
Príncipe *72 E6 island* N Sao Tome and Principe
Prinzapolka *55 E4* NE Nicaragua
Pripet *109 C3* ≈ Belarus/Ukraine
Pripet Marshes *109 C3 forested and swampy region* Belarus/Ukraine
Prishtinë *107 D3* ● C Kosovo
Privas *97 E5* E France
Prizren *107 D3* S Kosovo
Probolinggo *131 D8* C Indonesia
Progreso *53 H4* SE Mexico
Prokhladnyy *111 B8* SW Russian Federation
Promyshlennyy *111 E3* NW Russian Federation
Prostějov *105 D6* E Czech Republic
Provence *97 E6 cultural region* SE France
Providence *37 F4 state capital* Rhode Island, NE USA
Provideniya *143 C1* NE Russian Federation
Provo *47 D5* Utah, W USA
Prudhoe Bay *50 F1* Alaska, USA
Pruszków *105 E3* C Poland
Prut *109 D6* ≈ E Europe
Prydz Bay *142 E4 bay* Antarctica
Pryluky *109 E4* NE Ukraine
Przemyśl *105 G5* C Poland
Psará *107 F5 island* E Greece
Psël *109 F4* ≈ Russian Federation/Ukraine
Pskov *111 A4* W Russian Federation
Ptsich *109 D3* ≈ SE Belarus
Ptuj *101 F8* NE Slovenia
Pucallpa *63 B5* C Peru
Puck *105 D1* N Poland
Pudasjärvi *83 E3* C Finland
Puebla *53 F5* S Mexico
Pueblo *47 F6* Colorado, C USA
Puerto Acosta *65 A2* W Bolivia
Puerto Aisén *65 A7* S Chile
Puerto Ángel *53 G6* SE Mexico
Puerto Ayacucho *63 D2* SW Venezuela
Puerto Baquerizo Moreno *63 B7* Galapagos Islands, Ecuador
Puerto Barrios *55 C2* E Guatemala
Puerto Cabezas *55 E3* NE Nicaragua
Puerto Cortés *55 C2* NW Honduras
Puerto Deseado *65 B8* SE Argentina
Puerto Escondido *53 F6* SE Mexico
Puerto Lempira *55 E3* E Honduras
Puertollano *99 D4* C Spain
Puerto Maldonado *63 C5* E Peru
Puerto Montt *65 A7* C Chile
Puerto Natales *65 A9* S Chile
Puerto Obaldía *55 I6* NE Panama
Puerto Plata *57 G4* N Dominican Republic
Puerto Princesa *131 E4* Palawan, W Philippines
Puerto Rico *51 US* ◇ C West Indies
Puerto San Julián *65 B8* SE Argentina
Puerto Suárez *65 C2* E Bolivia
Puerto Vallarta *53 D5* SW Mexico
Puerto Varas *65 A7* C Chile
Puerto Viejo *55 E5* NE Costa Rica
Puget Sound *49 B2 sound* Washington, NW USA
Pukaki, Lake *139 B6* ◎ SW New Zealand
Pukatikei, Maunga *141 D6* ✷ Easter Island, Chile
Pukch'ong *133 B4* E North Korea
Pukekohe *139 D3* North Island, New Zealand
Pula *107 A2* NW Croatia
Pulaski *39 G2* Virginia, NE USA
Puławy *105 F4* E Poland
Pul-e Khumri *125 F4* NE Afghanistan
Pullman *49 D2* Washington, NW USA
Pułtusk *105 F3* C Poland
Pune *127 C5* W India
Punjab *127 D2 cultural region* India/Pakistan
Puno *63 C6* SE Peru
Punta Alta *65 B6* E Argentina
Punta Arenas *65 A9* S Chile
Punta, Cerro de *51* ▲ C Puerto Rico
Punta Gorda *55 B2* SE Belize
Punta Gorda *55 E5* SE Nicaragua
Puntarenas *55 E6* W Costa Rica
Puntland *75 F3 cultural region* NE Somalia
Pupuya, Nevado *65 A2* ▲ W Bolivia
Puri *127 F5* E India
Purmerend *84 D3* C Netherlands
Purus, Rio *63 D4* ≈ Brazil/Peru
Püspökladány *105 F7* E Hungary
Putney *37 E3* Vermont, NE USA
Putorana Mountains *118 E3* ⛰ N Russian Federation
Putrajaya *131 B6* ● Peninsular Malaysia
Puttalam *127 E7* W Sri Lanka
Puttgarden *101 C2* N Germany
Putumayo, Río *63 C4* ≈ NW South America
Pu'u 'Ula'ula *51 C2* ▲ Maui, Hawaii, USA
Pu'uwai *51 A1* Ni'ihau, Hawaii, USA
Pwllheli *93 B5* NW Wales, United Kingdom
Pyatigorsk *111 A8* SW Russian Federation
Pyay *131 A3* C Burma (Myanmar)
Pyongyang *133 A5* ● SW North Korea
Pyramid Lake *47 A5* ◎ Nevada, W USA
Pyrenees *99 F2* ⛰ SW Europe
Pyrgos *107 D6* S Greece
Pyrzyce *105 B3* NW Poland

Q

Qaidam Pendi *129 D3 basin* C China
Qal'aikhum *125 G3* S Tajikistan
Qalat *125 F6* S Afghanistan
Qal'eh-ye Now *125 E4* NW Afghanistan
Qamanittuaq *see* Baker Lake
Qamdo *129 D4* China
Qarokul *125 G3* E Tajikistan
Qarshi *125 E3* S Uzbekistan
Qasr al Farafirah *70 I3* W Egypt
Qatar *123 D4* ◆ *monarchy* SW Asia
Qattara Depression *70 I3 desert* NW Egypt
Qausuittuq *see* Resolute
Qazimämmäd *121 J2* SE Azerbaijan
Qazvin *123 D2* N Iran
Qilian Shan *129 D3* ⛰ N China
Qina *70 J3* E Egypt
Qingdao *129 G3* E China
Qinghai Hu *129 D3* ◎ C China
Qinhuangdao *129 G3* E China
Qinzhou *129 F6* S China
Qiqihar *129 G2* NE China
Qira *129 B3* NW China
Qitai *129 C2* NW China
Qizilrabot *125 H4* SE Tajikistan
Qom *123 D2* N Iran
Qo'ng'irot *125 D2* NW Uzbekistan
Qo'qon *125 G3* E Uzbekistan
Quang Ngai *131 D3* C Vietnam
Quanzhou *129 G5* SE China
Quanzhou *129 F5* S China
Qu'Appelle *33 H7* ≈ Saskatchewan, S Canada
Quarles, Pegunungan *131 E7* ⛰ Sulawesi, C Indonesia
Quartu Sant' Elena *103 A6* Sardegna, Italy
Quba *121 I2* N Azerbaijan
Québec *35 D3 province capital* Québec, SE Canada
Québec *35 E5* ◐ *province* SE Canada
Queen Charlotte Islands *33 D6 island group* British Columbia, SW Canada
Queen Charlotte Sound *33 D6 sea area* British Columbia, W Canada
Queen Elizabeth Islands *33 G2 island group* Nunavut, N Canada
Queensland *137 F3* ◐ *state* N Australia
Queenstown *139 B7* South Island, New Zealand
Queenstown *76 D7* S South Africa
Quelimane *76 E5* NE Mozambique
Quemado *44 C2* New Mexico, SW USA
Quepos *55 E6* S Costa Rica
Querétaro *53 E4* C Mexico
Quesada *55 E6* N Costa Rica
Quetta *127 B2* SW Pakistan
Quezaltenango *55 A3* W Guatemala
Quilon *127 D7* SW India (see also Kollam)
Quilty *89 B5* W Ireland
Quimper *97 A2* NW France
Quimperlé *97 A3* NW France
Quinault *49 B2* Washington, NW USA
Quincy *40 A6* Illinois, N USA
Quito *63 B3* ● N Ecuador

◐ Administrative region ◆ Country ● Country capital ◇ Dependent territory ○ Dependent territory capital ⛰ Mountain range ▲ Mountain ✷ Volcano ≈ River ◎ Lake ▣ Reservoir

Qurghonteppa 125 F4 SW Tajikistan
Quy Nhon 131 D4 C Vietnam

R

Raahe 83 E3 W Finland
Raalte 84 E3 E Netherlands
Raamsdonksveer 84 D5 S Netherlands
Raasay 91 B3 *island* NW Scotland, United Kingdom
Rába 105 C8 ≈ Austria/Hungary
Rabat 70 C1 ● NW Morocco
Rabat 112 A5 W Malta
Rabaul 141 D1 E Papua New Guinea
Rabinal 55 B3 C Guatemala
Rabka 105 E6 S Poland
Rabyanah Ramlat 70 G4 *desert* SE Libya
Race, Cape 35 H4 *cape* Newfoundland, E Canada
Rach Gia 131 C4 S Vietnam
Racine 40 C5 Wisconsin, N USA
Rádeyilikóé *see* Fort Good Hope
Radom 105 F4 C Poland
Radomsko 105 E4 C Poland
Radzyń Podlaski 105 F4 E Poland
Raetihi 139 D4 North Island, New Zealand
Rafaela 65 B5 E Argentina
Raga 75 B4 W South Sudan
Ragged Island Range 57 D3 *island group* S Bahamas
Ragusa 103 D8 Sicily, Italy
Rahimyar Khan 127 C3 SE Pakistan
Raichur 127 D5 C India
Rainier, Mount 49 B2 🌋 Washington, NW USA
Rainy Lake 43 E1 ◎ Canada/USA
Raipur 127 E4 C India
Rajahmundry 127 E5 E India
Rajang, Batang 131 D6 ≈ East Malaysia
Rajapalaiyam 127 D7 SE India
Rajasthan 127 C3 *state* NW India
Rajkot 127 C4 W India
Rajshahi 127 G3 W Bangladesh
Rakaia 139 C6 ≈ South Island, New Zealand
Raleigh 39 H3 *state capital* North Carolina, SE USA
Râmnicu Vâlcea 109 B7 C Romania
Ramree Island 131 A3 *island* W Burma (Myanmar)
Ramsey 93 B3 NE Isle of Man
Ramsgate 95 H4 SE England, United Kingdom
Rancagua 65 A5 C Chile
Ranchi 127 F4 N India
Randers 83 B6 C Denmark
Rangiora 139 C6 South Island, New Zealand
Rangitikei 139 D4 ≈ North Island, New Zealand
Rangoon 131 A3 S Burma (Myanmar)
Rangpur 127 G3 N Bangladesh
Rankin Inlet 33 H4 Nunavut, C Canada
Rannoch Moor 91 D4 *heathland* C Scotland, United Kingdom
Rapid City 43 A3 South Dakota, N USA
Rāpina 83 F6 SE Estonia
Rarotonga 135 *island* S Cook Islands
Rasht 123 D1 NW Iran
Ratän 83 C4 C Sweden
Rathfriland 89 E3 SE Northern Ireland, United Kingdom
Rathkeale 89 C5 SW Ireland
Rathlin Island 89 E1 *island* N Northern Ireland, United Kingdom
Ráth Luirc 89 C6 S Ireland
Rathmelton 89 D1 N Ireland
Rathmore 89 B6 SW Ireland
Rathmullan 89 D1 N Ireland
Rathnew 89 E5 E Ireland
Rat Islands 50 A1 *island group* Aleutian Islands, Alaska, USA
Ratlam 127 D4 C India
Ratnapura 127 E8 S Sri Lanka
Raton 44 E1 New Mexico, SW USA
Rättvik 83 C5 C Sweden
Raufarhöfn 83 B1 NE Iceland
Raukumara Range 139 E3 ⛰ North Island, New Zealand
Raurkela 127 F4 E India
Rauma 83 D5 SW Finland
Ravenglass 93 B3 NW England, United Kingdom
Ravenna 103 C3 N Italy
Ravi 127 C2 ≈ India/Pakistan
Rawalpindi 127 D1 NE Pakistan
Rawa Mazowiecka 105 E4 C Poland
Rawicz 105 C4 C Poland
Rawlinna 137 C5 Western Australia
Rawlins 47 E4 Wyoming, C USA
Rawson 65 B7 SE Argentina
Rayong 131 B4 S Thailand
Razazah, Buhayrat ar 123 B2 ◎ C Iraq
Razgrad 107 F2 N Bulgaria
Razim, Lacul 109 D7 *lagoon* NW Black Sea
Reading 95 F4 S England, United Kingdom
Reading 37 D5 Pennsylvania, NE USA
Real, Cordillera 58 ⛰ C Ecuador
Realicó 65 B5 C Argentina
Rebecca, Lake 137 C5 ◎ Western Australia
Rebun-to 133 F1 *island* NE Japan
Recife 63 I5 E Brazil
Recklinghausen 101 A4 W Germany
Recogne 84 D8 SE Belgium
Reconquista 65 C4 C Argentina
Red Bluff 49 B5 California, W USA
Redcar 93 E2 N England, United Kingdom
Red Deer 33 G7 Alberta, SW Canada
Redding 49 B5 California, W USA
Redditch 93 D6 W England, United Kingdom
Redhill 95 F4 SE England, United Kingdom
Redon 97 B3 NW France
Red River 43 D1 ≈ Canada/USA
Red River 131 B2 ≈ China/Vietnam
Red River 44 G2 ≈ S USA
Red River 39 B6 ≈ Louisiana, S USA
Redruth 95 A6 SW England, United Kingdom
Red Sea 123 A4 *sea* Africa/Asia
Red Wing 43 F3 Minnesota, N USA
Reefton 139 C5 South Island, New Zealand
Ree, Lough 89 D4 ◎ C Ireland
Reese River 47 B5 ≈ Nevada, W USA
Refahiye 121 F3 C Turkey
Regensburg 101 D6 SE Germany
Regenstauf 101 D6 SE Germany
Regestan 125 E6 *desert region* S Afghanistan
Reggane 70 D3 C Algeria
Reggio di Calabria 103 E8 SW Italy
Reggio nell'Emilia 103 C3 N Italy
Regina 33 H7 *province capital* Saskatchewan, S Canada
Rehoboth 76 B5 C Namibia
Rehovot 123 G6 C Israel
Reid 137 D5 Western Australia
Ré, Île de 97 B4 *island* W France
Reims 97 E2 N France
Reindeer Lake 33 H5 ◎ Manitoba/Saskatchewan, C Canada
Reinga, Cape 139 C1 *headland* North Island, New Zealand
Reinosa 99 D1 N Spain
Reliance 33 G5 Northwest Territories, C Canada
Rendsburg 101 C2 N Germany
Rengat 131 B6 Sumatra, W Indonesia
Rennell 141 E3 *island* S Solomon Islands
Rennes 97 B3 NW France
Reno 47 A5 Nevada, W USA
Republican River 47 G5 ≈ Kansas/Nebraska, C USA
Repulse Bay 33 I3 Northwest Territories, N Canada
Resistencia 65 C4 NE Argentina
Reşiţa 109 A7 W Romania
Resolute 33 H2 Cornwallis Island, Nunavut, N Canada
Resolution Island 35 E1 *island* Nunavut, NE Canada
Réthymno 107 F7 SE Greece
Réunion 76 H6 *French* ◇ W Indian Ocean
Reus 99 G3 E Spain
Reutlingen 101 B7 S Germany
Reuver 84 E6 SE Netherlands
Revillagigedo, Islas 53 B5 *island group* W Mexico
Rexburg 47 D3 Idaho, NW USA
Reyes 65 A2 NW Bolivia
Rey, Isla del 55 H6 *island* Archipiélago de las Perlas, SE Panama
Reykjavík 83 A1 ● W Iceland
Reynosa 53 F3 C Mexico
Rezé 97 B3 NW France
Rhein *see* Rhine
Rheine 101 B4 NW Germany
Rheinisches Schiefergebirge 101 A5 ⛰ W Germany
Rhine 84 E4 ≈ W Europe
Rhinelander 40 B3 Wisconsin, N USA
Rho 103 B2 N Italy
Rhode Island 37 F5 ◈ *state* NE USA
Rhodes 107 G6 *island* Dodecanese, Greece
Rhodope Mountains 107 E3 ⛰ Bulgaria/Greece
Rhône 97 E6 ≈ France/Switzerland
Rhossili 93 B7 S Wales, United Kingdom
Rhum 91 B4 *island* W Scotland, United Kingdom
Ribble 93 C4 ≈ NW England, United Kingdom
Ribeira 99 A2 NW Spain
Ribeirão Preto 63 G7 S Brazil
Riberalta 65 B1 N Bolivia
Rice Lake 40 A3 Wisconsin, N USA
Richard Toll 72 A3 N Senegal
Richfield 47 D6 Utah, W USA
Richland 49 C3 Washington, NW USA
Richmond 139 C5 South Island, New Zealand
Richmond 93 D3 N England, United Kingdom
Richmond 39 E2 Kentucky, S USA
Richmond 39 H2 *state capital* Virginia, NE USA
Richmond Range 139 C5 ⛰ South Island, New Zealand
Ricobayo, Embalse de 99 B2 ⊡ NW Spain
Ridder 118 D5 E Kazakhstan
Ridgecrest 49 D8 California, W USA
Ridsdale 93 D2 N England, United Kingdom
Ried im Innkreis 101 D7 NW Austria
Riemst 84 D7 NE Belgium
Riesa 101 D4 E Germany
Riga 83 E6 ● C Latvia
Riga, Gulf of 83 E6 *gulf* Estonia/Latvia
Riggins 47 B3 Idaho, NW USA
Riihimäki 83 E5 S Finland
Rijeka 107 B1 NW Croatia
Rijn *see* Rhine
Rijssen 84 E4 E Netherlands
Rimah, Wadi ar 123 C4 *dry watercourse* C Saudi Arabia
Rimini 103 D3 N Italy
Rimouski 35 E4 Québec, SE Canada
Ringebu 83 B4 S Norway
Ringkøbing Fjord 83 A7 *fjord* W Denmark
Ringvassøya 83 C1 *island* N Norway
Ringwood 95 E5 S England, United Kingdom
Rio Branco 63 D5 W Brazil
Río Bravo 53 F3 C Mexico
Río Cuarto 65 B5 C Argentina
Rio de Janeiro 63 H7 SE Brazil
Río Gallegos 65 B9 S Argentina
Río Grande 65 B9 S Argentina
Rio Grande 63 F9 S Brazil
Río Grande 53 D4 C Mexico
Rio Grande 47 F7 ≈ Texas, SW USA
Rio Grande do Norte 63 I4 *state* E Brazil
Rio Grande do Sul 63 F8 *state* S Brazil
Ríohacha 63 C1 N Colombia
Río Lagartos 53 I4 SE Mexico
Riom 97 D5 C France
Río Verde 53 E4 C Mexico
Ripoll 99 G2 NE Spain
Ripon 93 D3 N England, United Kingdom
Rishiri-to 133 F1 *island* NE Japan
Ritidian Point 51 *headland* N Guam
Rivas 55 D5 SW Nicaragua
Rivera 65 C5 NE Uruguay
River Falls 40 A3 Wisconsin, N USA
Riverside 49 D9 California, W USA
Riverstown 89 C6 S Ireland
Riverton 139 A8 South Island, New Zealand
Riverton 47 E4 Wyoming, C USA
Riviera 44 G6 Texas, SW USA
Rivière-du-Loup 35 E5 Québec, SE Canada
Rivne 109 C4 NW Ukraine
Rivoli 103 A2 NW Italy
Riyadh 123 C4 ● C Saudi Arabia
Rize 121 F2 NE Turkey
Rkiz 72 A3 W Mauritania
Road Town 57 I4 ○ C British Virgin Islands
Roag, Loch 91 A2 *inlet* NW Scotland, United Kingdom
Roanne 97 E4 E France
Roanoke 39 G2 Virginia, NE USA
Roanoke River 39 H3 ≈ North Carolina/Virginia, SE USA
Roatán 55 D2 N Honduras
Robin Hood's Bay 93 E3 N England, United Kingdom
Robson, Mount 33 F6 ▲ British Columbia, SW Canada
Robstown 44 H5 Texas, SW USA
Roca Partida, Isla 53 B5 *island* W Mexico
Rocas, Atol das 63 I4 *island* E Brazil
Rochdale 93 D4 NW England, United Kingdom
Rochefort 84 D8 SE Belgium
Rochefort 97 B4 W France
Rochester 43 F4 Minnesota, N USA
Rochester 37 F3 New Hampshire, NE USA
Rochester 37 C3 New York, NE USA
Rockford 40 B5 Illinois, N USA
Rockhampton 137 H4 Queensland, E Australia
Rock Hill 39 G4 South Carolina, SE USA
Rock Island 40 B5 Illinois, N USA
Rock Sound 57 E2 Eleuthera Island, C Bahamas
Rock Springs 47 E4 Wyoming, C USA
Rocky Mount 39 H3 North Carolina, SE USA
Rocky Mountains 28 ⛰ Canada/USA
Roden 84 E2 NE Netherlands
Rodez 97 D6 S France
Rodos *see* Rhodes
Roermond 84 E6 SE Netherlands
Roeselare 84 B6 W Belgium
Rogers 39 B3 Arkansas, C USA
Roi Et 131 C3 E Thailand
Rokiškis 83 F7 NE Lithuania
Rokycany 105 B5 W Czech Republic
Rolla 43 F6 Missouri, C USA
Roma 137 G4 Queensland, E Australia
Roma *see* Rome
Roman 109 C6 NE Romania
Romania 109 B6 ◆ *republic* SE Europe
Rome 103 C5 ● C Italy
Rome 39 E4 Georgia, SE USA
Romford 95 G3 SE England, United Kingdom
Romney Marsh 95 G4 *physical region* SE England, United Kingdom
Romny 109 E4 NE Ukraine
Rømø 83 A7 *island* SW Denmark
Romsey 95 E4 S England, United Kingdom
Ronda 99 C6 S Spain
Rondônia 63 D5 *state* W Brazil
Rondonópolis 63 F6 W Brazil
Ronne 83 C7 E Denmark
Ronne Ice Shelf 142 B4 *ice shelf* Antarctica
Roosendaal 84 C5 S Netherlands
Roosevelt Island 142 C6 *island* Antarctica
Roraima 63 D3 *state* N Brazil
Roraima, Mount 63 D2 ▲ N South America
Roros 83 B4 S Norway
Rosa, Lake 57 E3 ◎ S Bahamas
Rosalia, Punta 141 C5 *headland* Easter Island, Chile
Rosario 65 C5 C Argentina
Rosario 65 C3 C Paraguay
Rosarito 53 A1 NW Mexico
Roscommon 89 C4 C Ireland
Roscommon 40 D4 Michigan, N USA
Roscrea 89 D5 C Ireland
Roseau 57 K5 ● SW Dominica
Roseburg 49 B4 Oregon, NW USA
Rosenberg 44 H4 Texas, SW USA
Rosengarten 101 C3 N Germany
Rosenheim 101 D7 S Germany
Roslavl' 111 A5 W Russian Federation
Rosmalen 84 D5 S Netherlands
Ross 139 B6 SW New Zealand
Rossano 103 E7 SW Italy
Ross Carbery 89 B7 S Ireland
Ross Ice Shelf 142 C5 *ice shelf* Antarctica
Rosslare 89 E6 SE Ireland
Rosslare Harbour 89 E6 SE Ireland
Rosso 72 A3 SW Mauritania
Ross-on-Wye 93 C6 W England, United Kingdom
Rossosh' 111 A7 W Russian Federation
Ross Sea 142 C6 *sea* Antarctica
Rostock 101 D2 NE Germany
Rostov-na-Donu 111 A7 SW Russian Federation
Roswell 44 E3 New Mexico, SW USA
Rother 95 F4 ≈ S England, United Kingdom
Rothera 142 A4 *UK research station* Antarctica
Rotherham 93 E4 N England, United Kingdom
Rothesay 91 C6 W Scotland, United Kingdom
Rotorua 139 D3 North Island, New Zealand
Rotorua, Lake 139 D3 ◎ NE New Zealand
Rotterdam 84 C4 SW Netherlands
Rottweil 101 B7 S Germany
Rotuma 141 I4 *island* NW Fiji
Roubaix 97 D1 N France
Rouen 97 D2 N France
Round Rock 44 G4 Texas, SW USA
Roundstone 89 B4 W Ireland
Roundwood 89 E5 E Ireland
Rousay 91 E1 *island* N Scotland, United Kingdom
Roussillon 97 D7 *cultural region* S France
Rouyn-Noranda 35 D5 Québec, SE Canada
Rovaniemi 83 E3 N Finland
Rovigo 103 C3 NE Italy
Rovuma, Rio 76 F4 ≈ Mozambique/Tanzania
Roxas City 131 F4 C Philippines
Royale, Isle 40 C1 *island* Michigan, N USA
Royal Leamington Spa 93 D6 C England, United Kingdom
Royal Tunbridge Wells 95 G4 SE England, United Kingdom
Royan 97 B4 W France
Royston 95 G3 E England, United Kingdom
Rožňava 105 E6 E Slovakia
Ruapehu, Mount 139 D4 🌋 North Island, New Zealand
Ruapuke Island 139 B8 *island* SW New Zealand
Ruatoria 139 E3 North Island, New Zealand
Ruawai 139 D2 North Island, New Zealand
Rubizhne 109 G4 E Ukraine
Ruby Mountains 47 B5 ⛰ Nevada, W USA
Rudnyy 118 C4 N Kazakhstan
Rufiji 75 D7 ≈ E Tanzania
Rufino 65 B5 C Argentina
Rugby 93 E6 C England, United Kingdom
Rugeley 93 D5 C England, United Kingdom
Rügen 101 D2 *cape* NE Germany
Ruhr Valley 101 A4 *industrial region* W Germany
Rukwa, Lake 75 C7 ◎ SE Tanzania
Rumbek 75 B4 C South Sudan
Rum Cay 57 E2 *island* C Bahamas
Rumia 105 D1 N Poland
Runanga 139 C5 South Island, New Zealand
Runcorn 93 C4 C England, United Kingdom
Rundu 76 C5 NE Namibia
Ruoqiang 129 C3 NW China
Rupel 84 C6 ≈ N Belgium
Rupert, Rivière de 35 D4 ≈ Québec, C Canada
Ruse 107 F2 N Bulgaria
Rushden 95 F2 C England, United Kingdom
Rushmore, Mount 43 A4 ▲ South Dakota, N USA
Russellville 39 B3 Arkansas, C USA
Russian Federation 118 D4 ◆ *republic* Asia/Europe
Rustavi 121 H2 SE Georgia
Ruston 39 B5 Louisiana, S USA
Rutland 37 E3 Vermont, NE USA
Rutland Water 93 E5 ◎ C England, United Kingdom
Rutog 129 A4 W China
Ruvuma 75 D7 ≈ Mozambique/Tanzania
Ruwenzori 75 B5 ⛰ Dem. Rep. Congo/Uganda
Ružomberok 105 E6 N Slovakia
Rwanda 75 B6 ◆ *republic* C Africa
Ryazan' 111 B6 W Russian Federation
Rybinsk 111 B5 W Russian Federation
Rybnik 105 D5 S Poland
Rye 95 G4 SE England, United Kingdom
Rye 93 E3 ≈ N England, United Kingdom
Ryki 105 F4 E Poland
Rypin 105 E3 C Poland
Rysy 105 E6 ▲ S Poland
Ryukyu Islands 133 A7 *island group* SW Japan
Rzeszów 105 F5 SE Poland
Rzhev 111 A5 W Russian Federation

S

Saale 101 D4 ≈ C Germany
Saalfeld 101 C5 C Germany
Saarbrücken 101 A6 SW Germany
Saaremaa 83 D6 *island* W Estonia
Saariselkä 83 E2 N Finland
Šabac 107 D2 W Serbia
Sabadell 99 G2 E Spain
Sabah 131 E5 *cultural region* Borneo, E Malaysia Asia
Sab'atayn, Ramlat as 123 C7 *desert* C Yemen
Sabaya 65 A3 S Bolivia
Saberi, Hamun-e 123 F3 ◎ Afghanistan/Iran
Sabha 70 F3 C Libya
Sabinas 53 E2 NE Mexico
Sabinas Hidalgo 53 E3 NE Mexico
Sabine Lake 39 A6 ◎ Louisiana/Texas, S USA
Sabine River 44 I4 ≈ Louisiana/Texas, SW USA
Sable, Cape 39 G9 *headland* Florida, SE USA
Sable, Île de 141 E5 *island* NW New Caledonia
Sable Island 35 G5 *island* Nova Scotia, SE Canada
Sabzevar 123 E1 NE Iran
Sachsen *see* Saxony
Sachs Harbour 33 F3 Banks Island, Northwest Territories, N Canada
Sacramento 49 B6 *state capital* California, W USA
Sacramento Mountains 44 D3 ⛰ New Mexico, SW USA
Sacramento River 49 B6 ≈ California, W USA
Sacramento Valley 49 B6 *valley* California, W USA
Sa'dah 123 C6 NW Yemen
Sado 133 F4 *island* C Japan
Säffle 83 C5 C Sweden
Safford 44 C3 Arizona, SW USA
Saffron Walden 95 G3 SE England, United Kingdom
Safi 70 B2 W Morocco
Safid Kuh, Selseleh-ye 125 D5 ⛰ W Afghanistan
Saga 133 D7 Kyūshū, SW Japan
Sagaing 131 A2 C Burma (Myanmar)
Sagami-nada 133 G6 *inlet* SW Japan
Saganaga Lake 43 F1 ◎ Minnesota, N USA
Sagar 127 E4 C India
Saginaw 40 E4 Michigan, N USA
Saginaw Bay 40 E4 *lake bay* Michigan, N USA
Sagua la Grande 57 C2 C Cuba
Sagunt *see* Sagunto
Sagunto 99 F4 E Spain
Sahara 72 D2 *desert* Libya/Algeria
Saharan Atlas 70 D2 ⛰ Algeria/Morocco
Sahel 72 E3 *physical region* C Africa
Sahiwal 127 D2 E Pakistan
Saidpur 127 F3 NW Bangladesh
Saimaa 83 F4 ◎ SE Finland
St Albans 95 F3 E England, United Kingdom
Saint Albans 39 F2 West Virginia, NE USA
St Aldhelm's Head 95 E5 *headland* S England, United Kingdom
St Andrews 91 E5 E Scotland, United Kingdom
St Anne 95 H5 Alderney, Channel Islands
St. Anthony 35 G3 Newfoundland, SE Canada
Saint Augustine 39 G6 Florida, SE USA
St Austell 95 B5 SW England, United Kingdom
St Austell Bay 95 B6 *bay* SW England, United Kingdom
St-Barthélemy 57 J4 *island* N Guadeloupe
St Bees Head 93 B3 *headland* NW England, United Kingdom
St-Brieuc 97 B2 NW France
St. Catharines 35 D6 Ontario, S Canada
St Catherine's Point 95 E5 *headland* S England, United Kingdom
St-Chamond 97 E5 E France
Saint Clair, Lake 37 A4 ◎ Canada/USA
St-Claude 97 E4 E France
Saint Cloud 43 E3 Minnesota, N USA
St. Croix 51 *island* S Virgin Islands (USA)
Saint Croix River 40 A3 ≈ Minnesota/Wisconsin, N USA
St David's 93 A7 SW Wales, United Kingdom
St-Dié 97 F3 NE France
St-Egrève 97 E5 E France
Saintes 97 B4 W France
St-Étienne 97 E5 E France
St-Flour 97 D5 C France
St-Gaudens 97 C6 S France
Saint George 137 G4 Queensland, E Australia
Saint George 47 C6 Utah, W USA
St. George's 57 K7 ● SW Grenada
St-Georges 35 E5 Québec, SE Canada
St George's Channel 89 F6 *channel* Ireland/Wales, United Kingdom
Saint Helena 26 *UK* ◇ C Atlantic Ocean
St. Helena Bay 76 B7 *bay* SW South Africa
St Helens 93 C4 NW England, United Kingdom
Saint Helens, Mount 49 B2 🌋 Washington, NW USA
St Helier 95 H6 ○ S Jersey, Channel Islands
Saint Ignace 40 D3 Michigan, N USA
St Ives 95 A6 E England, United Kingdom
St Ives 95 B3 SW England, United Kingdom
St-Jean, Lac 35 E4 ◎ Québec, SE Canada
St. John 35 F5 New Brunswick, SE Canada
St John 95 H6 N Jersey
St. John 51 *island* Virgin Islands (USA)
Saint John River 37 G1 ≈ Canada/USA
St John's 57 J4 ● Antigua, Antigua and Barbuda
St. John's 35 H4 Newfoundland, E Canada
Saint Johns 44 C2 Arizona, SW USA
St John's Point 89 C2 *headland* N Ireland
Saint Joseph 43 E6 Missouri, C USA
Saint Kitts and Nevis 57 I5 ◆ *commonwealth republic* E West Indies
St. Lawrence, Gulf of 35 F4 *gulf* NW Atlantic Ocean
Saint Lawrence Island 50 C1 *island* Alaska, USA
Saint Lawrence River 37 D2 ≈ Canada/USA
St. Lawrence Seaway 35 F4 *seaway* Canada/USA North America Gulf of St.Lawrence N Atlantic Ocean
St-Lô 97 C2 N France
St-Louis 97 F3 NE France
Saint Louis 72 A3 NW Senegal
Saint Louis 43 G6 Missouri, C USA
St Lucia 57 J6 ◆ *commonwealth republic* SE West Indies
St. Lucia Channel 57 K6 *channel* Martinique/Saint Lucia North America Atlantic Ocean
St Magnus Bay 91 A6 *bay* N Scotland, United Kingdom
St-Malo 97 B2 NW France
St-Malo, Golfe de 97 B2 *gulf* NW France
St Margaret's Hope 91 E1 NE Scotland, United Kingdom
St-Martin 57 J4 *island* N Guadeloupe
St Mary 95 H6 Jersey, Channel Islands
St. Matthias Group 141 C1 *island group* NE Papua New Guinea
St. Moritz 101 C8 SE Switzerland
St-Nazaire 97 B3 NW France
St Neots 95 F2 E England, United Kingdom
St-Omer 97 D1 N France
Saint Paul 43 E3 *state capital* Minnesota, N USA
St Peter Port 95 G6 ○ C Guernsey, Channel Islands
Saint Petersburg 111 A4 NW Russian Federation
Saint Petersburg 39 F7 Florida, SE USA
St-Pierre and Miquelon 35 G4 *French* ◇ NE North America
St-Quentin 97 D2 N France
St. Thomas 51 *island* Virgin Islands (USA)
Saint Vincent 57 J6 *island* N Saint Vincent and the Grenadines
Saint Vincent and the Grenadines 57 I6 ◆ *commonwealth republic* SE West Indies
Saint Vincent Passage 57 K6 *passage* Saint Lucia/Saint Vincent and the Grenadines
Sajama, Nevado 65 A2 ▲ W Bolivia
Sajószentpéter 105 F7 NE Hungary
Sakakawea, Lake 43 B2 ⊡ North Dakota, N USA
Sakata 133 F4 C Japan
Sakhalin 118 I4 *island* SE Russian Federation
Saki 121 I2 NW Azerbaijan
Sakishima-shoto 133 A8 *island group* SW Japan
Sala 83 C5 C Sweden
Sala Consilina 103 E6 S Italy
Salado, Río 65 B4 ≈ E Argentina
Salado, Río 65 B5 ≈ C Argentina
Salalah 123 E6 SW Oman
Salamá 55 B3 C Guatemala
Salamanca 65 A5 C Chile
Salamanca 99 C3 NW Spain
Salang Tunnel 125 F4 *tunnel* C Afghanistan Asia
Salantai 83 E7 NW Lithuania
Salavat 111 D6 W Russian Federation
Šalčininkai 83 F7 SE Lithuania
Salcombe 95 C6 SW England, United Kingdom
Sale 137 G6 Victoria, SE Australia
Salé 70 C1 NW Morocco
Salekhard 118 D3 N Russian Federation
Salelologa 141 A5 C Samoa
Salem 127 D7 SE India
Salem 49 B3 *state capital* Oregon, NW USA
Salerno 103 D6 S Italy
Salerno, Gulf of 103 D6 *gulf* S Italy
Salford 93 D4 NW England, United Kingdom
Salihorsk 109 C3 S Belarus
Salina 43 D6 Kansas, C USA
Salina 47 D6 Utah, W USA
Salina Cruz 53 G6 SE Mexico
Salinas 49 B7 California, W USA
Salisbury 95 E4 S England, United Kingdom
Salisbury Plain 95 E4 *plain* S England, United Kingdom

◈ Administrative region ◆ Country ● Country capital ◇ Dependent territory ○ Dependent territory capital ⛰ Mountain range ▲ Mountain 🌋 Volcano ≈ River ◎ Lake ⊡ Reservoir

Salliq *see* Coral Harbour
Salmon *47 C3* Idaho, NW USA
Salmon River *47 B3* ≈ Idaho, NW USA
Salmon River Mountains *47 B3* ⛰ Idaho, NW USA
Salo *83 E5* SW Finland
Salon-de-Provence *97 E6* SE France
Salonica *107 E4* N Greece
Sal'sk *111 A8* SW Russian Federation
Salta *65 B4* NW Argentina
Saltash *95 B5* SW England, United Kingdom
Saltillo *53 E3* NE Mexico
Salt Lake City *47 D5 state capital* Utah, W USA
Salto *65 C5* N Uruguay
Salton Sea *49 D9* ◎ California, W USA
Salvador *63 H6* E Brazil
Salween *131 B2* ≈ SE Asia
Salyan *127 E3* W Nepal
Salzburg *101 D7* N Austria
Salzgitter *101 C4* C Germany
Salzwedel *101 C3* N Germany
Samalayuca *53 C2* N Mexico
Samar *131 F4 island* C Philippines
Samara *111 C6* W Russian Federation
Samarinda *131 E6* C Indonesia
Samarqand *125 F3* C Uzbekistan
Sambalpur *127 F4* E India
Sambava *76 H4* NE Madagascar
Sambir *109 B4* NW Ukraine
Sambre *97 E1* ≈ Belgium/France
Samfya *76 D3* N Zambia
Samoa *141 B4* ◆ *monarchy* W Polynesia
Sámos *107 F5 island* Dodecanese, SE Greece
Samothraki *107 F4 island* NE Greece
Sampit *131 D7* C Indonesia
Sam Rayburn Reservoir *44 I4* ⊡ Texas, SW USA
Samsun *121 E2* N Turkey
Samtredia *121 G1* W Georgia
Samui, Ko *131 B5 island* SW Thailand
San *72 C3* C Mali
San *105 G5* ≈ SE Poland
Sana *123 C6* ● W Yemen
Sana *107 B2* ≈ NW Bosnia and Herzegovina
San'a' *see* Sana
Sanae *142 B3 South African research station* Antarctica
Sanaga *72 G5* ≈ C Cameroon
Sanandaj *123 C2* W Iran
San Andrés, Isla de *55 F4 island* NW Colombia
San Andrés Tuxtla *53 G5* E Mexico
San Angelo *44 F4* Texas, SW USA
San Antonio *55 B2* S Belize
San Antonio *65 A5* C Chile
San Antonio *44 G5* Texas, SW USA
San Antonio Oeste *65 B7* E Argentina
Sanaw *123 D6* NE Yemen
San Benedicto, Isla *53 B5 island* W Mexico
San Benito *55 B2* N Guatemala
San Bernardino *49 D8* California, W USA
San Blas *53 C3* C Mexico
San Blas, Cape *39 D7 headland* Florida, SE USA
San Blas, Cordillera de *55 H6* ⛰ NE Panama
San Carlos *55 E5* S Nicaragua
San Carlos *44 C3* Arizona, SW USA
San Carlos de Bariloche *65 A7* SW Argentina
San Clemente Island *49 C9 island* Channel Islands, California, W USA
San Cristóbal *63 C2* W Venezuela
San Cristobal *141 F3 island* SE Solomon Islands
San Cristóbal de Las Casas *53 H5* SE Mexico
San Cristóbal, Isla *63 B7 island* Galapagos Islands, Ecuador
Sancti Spíritus *57 C3* C Cuba
Sancy, Puy de *97 D5* ▲ C France
Sandakan *131 E5* E Malaysia
Sandanski *107 E3* SW Bulgaria
Sanday *91 E1 island* NE Scotland, United Kingdom
Sandbach *93 D5* W England, United Kingdom
Sanders *44 C2* Arizona, SW USA
Sand Hills *43 B4* ⛰ Nebraska, C USA
San Diego *49 D9* California, W USA
Sandnes *83 A5* S Norway
Sandomierz *105 F5* C Poland
Sandown *95 E5* S England, United Kingdom
Sandpoint *47 B1* Idaho, NW USA
Sandray *91 A4 island* NW Scotland, United Kingdom
Sand Springs *43 D7* Oklahoma, C USA
Sandusky *40 E5* Ohio, N USA
Sandvika *83 B5* S Norway
Sandviken *83 D5* C Sweden
Sandy City *47 D5* Utah, W USA
Sandy Lake *35 A3* ◎ Ontario, C Canada
San Esteban *55 D3* C Honduras
San Fernando *99 C6* S Spain
San Fernando *57 K7* Trinidad, Trinidad and Tobago
San Fernando del Valle de Catamarca *65 B4* NW Argentina
San Francisco *49 B7* California, W USA
San Francisco del Oro *53 D3* N Mexico
San Francisco de Macorís *57 G4* C Dominican Republic
Sangan, Kuh-e *125 E5* ⛰ C Afghanistan
San Ġiljan *112 B6* N Malta
Sangir, Kepulauan *131 F6 island group* N Indonesia
Sangli *127 D5* W India
Sangmélima *72 G6* S Cameroon
Sangre de Cristo Mountains *44 E1* ⛰ Colorado/New Mexico, C USA
San Ignacio *55 B2* W Belize
San Ignacio *65 B2* N Bolivia
San Ignacio *53 B3* W Mexico
San Joaquin Valley *49 C7 valley* California, W USA
San Jorge, Gulf of *65 B8 gulf* S Argentina
San José *55 E6* ● C Costa Rica
San José *65 C2* E Bolivia
San José *55 A4* S Guatemala
San Jose *49 B7* California, W USA
San José del Guaviare *63 C3* S Colombia
San Juan *65 A5* W Argentina
San Juan *51* ○ NE Puerto Rico
San Juan Bautista *65 C4* S Paraguay
San Juan del Norte *55 E5* SE Nicaragua
San Juanito, Isla *53 C4 island* C Mexico
San Juan Mountains *47 E6* ⛰ Colorado, C USA
San Juan, Río *55 E5* ≈ Costa Rica/Nicaragua
San Juan River *47 E6* ≈ Colorado/Utah, W USA
Sankt Gallen *101 B7* NE Switzerland
Sankt-Peterburg *see* Saint Petersburg
Sankt Pölten *101 E7* N Austria
Sankuru *76 C2* ≈ C Dem. Rep. Congo
Şanlıurfa *121 F4* S Turkey
San Lorenzo *65 B3* S Bolivia
Sanlúcar de Barrameda *99 C6* S Spain
San Lucas Cape *53 C4 headland* W Mexico
San Luis *65 B5* C Argentina
San Luis *55 B2* NE Guatemala
San Luis *53 A1* NW Mexico
San Luis Obispo *49 B8* California, W USA
San Luis Potosí *53 E4* C Mexico
San Marcos *55 A3* W Guatemala
San Marcos *44 G4* Texas, SW USA
San Marino *103 D3* ● C San Marino
San Marino *103 D3* ◆ *republic* S Europe
San Martín *142 A4* C Argentina
San Matías *65 C2* E Bolivia
San Matías, Gulf of *65 B7 gulf* E Argentina
Sanmenxia *129 F4* C China
San Miguel *55 B4* SE El Salvador
San Miguel *53 D2* N Mexico
San Miguel de Tucumán *65 B4* N Argentina
San Miguelito *55 E5* S Nicaragua
San Miguelito *55 H6* C Panama
San Miguel, Río *65 B2* ≈ E Bolivia
Sanok *105 F6* SE Poland
San Pablo *65 B3* S Bolivia
San Pedro *55 C1* NE Belize
San-Pédro *72 C5* S Ivory Coast
San Pedro *53 D3* NE Mexico
San Pedro de la Cueva *53 C2* NW Mexico
San Pedro Mártir, Sierra *53 A2* ⛰ NW Mexico
San Pedro Sula *55 C3* NW Honduras
San Rafael *65 A5* W Argentina
San Rafael Mountains *49 C8* ⛰ California, W USA
San Ramón de la Nueva Orán *65 B3* N Argentina
San Remo *103 A3* NW Italy
San Salvador *55 B4* ● SW El Salvador
San Salvador *57 E2 island* E Bahamas
San Salvador de Jujuy *65 B3* N Argentina
Sansanné-Mango *72 D4* N Togo
San Sebastián *99 E1* N Spain (see also Donostia)
Sansepolcro *103 C4* C Italy
San Severo *103 E5* SE Italy
Santa Ana *65 B2* N Bolivia
Santa Ana *55 B4* NW El Salvador
Santa Ana *49 D9* California, W USA
Santa Barbara *53 D3* N Mexico
Santa Barbara *49 C8* California, W USA
Santa Catalina *55 G6* W Panama
Santa Catalina de Armada *99 B1* NW Spain
Santa Catalina Island *49 C9 island* Channel Islands, California, W USA
Santa Catarina *63 F8 state* S Brazil
Santa Clara *57 C3* C Cuba
Santa Cruz *65 B2* C Bolivia
Santa Cruz *49 B7* California, W USA
Santa Cruz del Quiché *55 A3* W Guatemala
Santa Cruz, Isla *63 B7 island* Galapagos Islands, Ecuador
Santa Cruz Islands *141 G3 island group* E Solomon Islands
Santa Cruz, Río *65 A8* ≈ S Argentina
Santa Elena *55 B2* W Belize
Santa Fe *65 C5* C Argentina
Santa Fe *44 D2 state capital* New Mexico, SW USA
Santa Genoveva *53 B4* ▲ W Mexico
Santa Isabel *141 E2 island* N Solomon Islands
Santa Lucia Range *49 B8* ⛰ California, W USA
Santa Margarita, Isla *53 B4 island* W Mexico
Santa Maria *63 F8* S Brazil
Santa Maria *49 C8* California, W USA
Santa Maria *141 G4 island* N Vanuatu
Santa María, Isla *63 A7 island* Galapagos Islands, Ecuador
Santa Marta *63 B1* N Colombia
Santander *99 D1* N Spain
Santarém *63 F4* N Brazil
Santarém *99 A4* W Portugal
Santa Rosa *65 B6* C Argentina
Santa Rosa *49 B6* California, W USA
Santa Rosa *44 E2* New Mexico, SW USA
Santa Rosa de Copán *55 B3* W Honduras
Santa Rosa Island *49 B9 island* California, W USA
Sant Carles de la Ràpita *99 F3* NE Spain
Santiago *65 A5* ● C Chile
Santiago *57 G4* N Dominican Republic
Santiago *55 G7* S Panama
Santiago *99 B1* NW Spain
Santiago de Cuba *57 E4* E Cuba
Santiago del Estero *65 B4* C Argentina
Sant Joan d'Alacant *99 F5* E Spain
Santo Domingo *57 G4* ● SE Dominican Republic
Santorini *107 F6 island* Cyclades, SE Greece
Santos *63 G7* S Brazil
Santo Tomé *65 C4* NE Argentina
San Valentín, Cerro *65 A8* ▲ S Chile
San Vicente *55 C4* C El Salvador
São Francisco, Rio *63 G6* ≈ E Brazil
Sao Hill *75 D7* S Tanzania
São João da Madeira *99 B3* N Portugal
São Luís *63 G4* NE Brazil
São Manuel, Rio *63 E5* ≈ C Brazil
Saona, Isla *57 G4 island* SE Dominican Republic
Saône *97 E5* ≈ E France
São Paulo *63 G7* S Brazil
São Paulo *63 F7 state* S Brazil
São Roque, Cabo de *63 I4 headland* E Brazil
São Tomé *72 E6* ● S Sao Tome and Principe
São Tomé *72 F6 island* S Sao Tome and Principe
Sao Tome and Principe *72 E6* ◆ *republic* E Atlantic Ocean
São Vicente, Cabo de *99 A5 cape* S Portugal
Sapele *72 E5* S Nigeria
Sa Pobla *99 H4* Majorca, Spain
Sappir *123 H7* S Israel
Sapporo *133 F2* NE Japan
Sapri *103 E6* S Italy
Sapulpa *43 D8* Oklahoma, C USA
Saqqez *123 C2* NW Iran
Sarahs *125 D4* S Turkmenistan
Sarajevo *107 C2* ● SE Bosnia and Herzegovina
Saraktash *111 D7* W Russian Federation
Saran' *118 C5* C Kazakhstan
Sarandë *107 D4* S Albania
Saransk *111 B6* W Russian Federation
Sarasota *39 F8* Florida, SE USA
Saratoga Springs *37 E3* New York, NE USA
Saratov *111 B7* W Russian Federation
Sarawak *131 D6 cultural region* Borneo, S Malaysia
Sardegna *see* Sardinia
Sardinia *103 B6 island* W Italy
Sargodha *127 C2* NE Pakistan
Sarh *72 H4* S Chad
Sari *123 D1* N Iran
Saría *107 G7 island* SE Greece
Sarıkamış *121 G3* NE Turkey
Sarikol Range *125 H3* ⛰ China/Tajikistan
Sariwon *133 A5* SW North Korea
Sark *95 H6 island* SE Guernsey
Şarkışla *121 E3* C Turkey
Sarmiento *65 B7* S Argentina
Sarnia *35 C6* Ontario, S Canada
Sarny *109 C4* NW Ukraine
Sarpsborg *83 B5* S Norway
Sartène *97 G6* Corsica, France
Sarthe *97 C3 cultural region* N France Europe
Sárti *107 E4* N Greece
Sarygamyş Köli *125 C2 salt lake* Kazakhstan/Uzbekistan
Sary-Tash *125 G3* SW Kyrgyzstan
Sasalaguan, Mount *51* ▲ S Guam
Sasebo *133 C7* SW Japan
Saskatchewan *33 G5* ◐ *province* SW Canada
Saskatchewan *33 H6* ≈ Manitoba/Saskatchewan, C Canada
Saskatoon *33 G7* Saskatchewan, S Canada
Sasovo *111 B6* W Russian Federation
Sassandra *72 C5* S Ivory Coast
Sassandra *72 C5* ≈ S Ivory Coast
Sassari *103 A5* Sardinia, Italy
Sassenheim *84 C4* W Netherlands
Sassnitz *101 D2* NE Germany
Sátoraljaújhely *105 F7* NE Hungary
Satpura Range *127 D4* ⛰ C India
Satsuma-Sendai *133 D8* SW Japan
Satsunan-shoto *133 A7 island group* SW Japan
Sattanen *83 E2* NE Finland
Satu Mare *109 B5* NW Romania
Saudi Arabia *123 C5* ◆ *monarchy* SW Asia
Saulkrasti *83 E6* C Latvia
Sault Sainte Marie *40 D2* Michigan, N USA
Sault Ste. Marie *35 C5* Ontario, S Canada
Saumur *97 C3* NW France
Saurimo *76 C3* NE Angola
Savá *55 D2* N Honduras
Savai'i *141 A4 island* NW Samoa
Savannah *39 G5* Georgia, SE USA
Savannah River *39 G5* ≈ Georgia/South Carolina, SE USA
Save *107 D2* ≈ SE Europe
Save, Rio *76 E5* ≈ Mozambique/Zimbabwe
Saverne *97 F3* NE France
Savigliano *103 A2* NW Italy
Savinskiy *111 C4* NW Russian Federation
Savissivik *143 A4* N Greenland
Savoie *97 E5 cultural region* E France Europe
Savona *103 B3* NW Italy
Savu Sea *131 F8 sea* S Indonesia
Sawel Mountain *89 E2* ▲ C Northern Ireland, United Kingdom
Sawhaj *70 I3* C Egypt
Sawqirah *123 E6* S Oman
Saxony *101 D4 cultural region* E Germany
Saýat *125 E3* E Turkmenistan
Sayaxché *55 B2* N Guatemala
Sayhut *123 D6* E Yemen
Saynshand *129 F2* SE Mongolia
Sayre *37 D4* Pennsylvania, NE USA
Say'un *123 D6* C Yemen
Scafell Pike *93 C3* ▲ NW England, United Kingdom
Scandinavia *78 geophysical region* NW Europe
Scapa Flow *91 E1 sea basin* N Scotland, United Kingdom
Scarborough *57 K7* N Trinidad and Tobago
Scarborough *93 F3* N England, United Kingdom
Scarp *91 A2 island* NW Scotland, United Kingdom
Schaerbeek *84 C6* C Belgium
Schaffhausen *101 B7* N Switzerland
Schagen *84 C3* NW Netherlands
Scheessel *101 C3* NW Germany
Schefferville *35 E3* Québec, E Canada
Scheldt *84 C6* ≈ W Europe
Schell Creek Range *47 C5* ⛰ Nevada, W USA
Schenectady *37 E4* New York, NE USA
Schertz *44 G5* Texas, SW USA
Schiermonnikoog *84 E1 island* Waddeneilanden, N Netherlands
Schijndel *84 D5* S Netherlands
Schiltigheim *97 F3* NE France
Schleswig *101 C2* N Germany
Schleswig-Holstein *101 C2 state* N Germany
Schönebeck *101 D4* C Germany
Schoten *84 C6* N Belgium
Schouwen *84 B5 island* SW Netherlands
Schwäbische Alb *101 B7* ⛰ S Germany
Schwandorf *101 D6* SE Germany
Schwarzwald *see* Black Forest
Schwaz *101 D7* W Austria
Schweinfurt *101 C5* SE Germany
Schwerin *101 C3* N Germany
Schwyz *101 B8* C Switzerland
Scioto River *40 E7* ≈ Ohio, N USA
Scotch Corner *93 D3* N England, United Kingdom
Scotia Sea *142 A2 sea* SW Atlantic Ocean
Scotland *91 C4* ◐ *national region* , United Kingdom
Scott Base *142 C6 NZ research station* Antarctica
Scottsbluff *43 A5* Nebraska, C USA
Scottsboro *39 E4* Alabama, S USA
Scottsdale *44 B3* Arizona, SW USA
Scousburgh *91 A7* NE Scotland, United Kingdom
Scranton *37 D4* Pennsylvania, NE USA
Scunthorpe *93 E4* E England, United Kingdom
Scutari, Lake *107 C3* ◎ Albania/Montenegro
Seaford *95 G5* SE England, United Kingdom
Searcy *39 B3* Arkansas, C USA
Seascale *93 B3* NW England, United Kingdom
Seattle *49 B2* Washington, NW USA
Sébaco *55 D4* W Nicaragua
Sebastían Vizcaíno, Bahía *53 A2 bay* NW Mexico
Secunderabad *127 E5* C India
Sedan *97 E2* N France
Seddon *139 D5* C New Zealand
Seddonville *139 C5* South Island, New Zealand
Sédhiou *72 A4* SW Senegal
Sedona *44 B2* Arizona, SW USA
Seesen *101 C4* C Germany
Segezha *111 B3* NW Russian Federation
Ségou *72 C3* C Mali
Segovia *99 D3* C Spain
Séguédine *72 G2* NE Niger
Seguin *44 G5* Texas, SW USA
Segura *99 E5* ≈ S Spain
Seinäjoki *83 E4* W Finland
Seine *97 D2* ≈ N France
Seine, Baie de la *97 C2 bay* N France
Sejong City *133 B6* ● (administrative) South Korea
Sekondi-Takoradi *72 D5* S Ghana
Selby *93 E4* N England, United Kingdom
Selenga *129 E2* ≈ Mongolia/Russian Federation
Sélestat *97 F3* NE France
Selfoss *83 A1* SW Iceland
Sélibabi *72 B3* S Mauritania
Selkirk *91 E6* SE Scotland, United Kingdom
Selma *49 C7* California, W USA
Semarang *131 D8* Java, C Indonesia
Sembé *76 B1* NW Congo
Semey *118 D5* E Kazakhstan
Seminole *44 E3* Texas, SW USA
Seminole, Lake *39 E6* ⊡ Florida/Georgia, SE USA
Semnān *123 E2* N Iran
Semois *84 D8* ≈ SE Belgium
Senachwine Lake *40 B6* ◎ Illinois, N USA
Sendai *133 G4* C Japan
Sendai-wan *133 G4 bay* E Japan
Senec *105 D7* W Slovakia
Senegal *72 A3* ◆ *republic* W Africa
Senegal *72 A3* ≈ W Africa
Seney Marsh *40 D2 wetland* Michigan, N USA
Senftenberg *101 E4* E Germany
Sênggê Zangbo *129 B4* ≈ W China
Senica *105 D6* W Slovakia
Senja *83 C1 island* N Norway
Senkaku-shoto *133 A8 island group* SW Japan
Senlis *97 D2* N France
Sennar *75 C3* C Sudan
Sens *97 D3* C France
Seoul *133 B6* ● NW South Korea
Sepik *141 A2* ≈ Indonesia/Papua New Guinea
Sept-Îles *35 F4* Québec, SE Canada
Serahs *125 D4* S Turkmenistan
Seraing *84 D7* E Belgium
Seram, Pulau *131 G7 island* Maluku, E Indonesia
Serang *131 C7* Java, C Indonesia
Serasan, Selat *131 D6 strait* Indonesia/Malaysia
Serbia *107 C3* ◆ *federal republic* SE Europe
Serdar *125 C3* W Turkmenistan
Seremban *131 B6* SW Malaysia
Serengeti Plain *75 C6 plain* N Tanzania
Serenje *76 D4* E Zambia
Serhetabat *125 D4* S Turkmenistan
Sérifos *107 E6 island* Cyclades, Greece
Serov *118 C4* C Russian Federation
Serowe *76 D5* SE Botswana
Serpukhov *111 A5* W Russian Federation
Sesto San Giovanni *103 B2* N Italy
Sète *97 D6* S France
Setesdal *83 B5 valley* S Norway
Sétif *70 E1* N Algeria
Setté Cama *76 A2* SW Gabon
Settle *93 D3* N England, United Kingdom
Setúbal *99 A4* W Portugal
Setúbal, Baía de *99 A5 bay* W Portugal
Seul, Lac *35 A4* ◎ Ontario, S Canada
Sevan *121 H2* C Armenia
Sevan, Lake *121 H2* ◎ E Armenia
Sevastopol' *109 F7* S Ukraine
Sevenoaks *95 G4* SE England, United Kingdom
Severn *35 B3* ≈ Ontario, S Canada
Severn *93 C5* ≈ England/Wales, United Kingdom
Severnaya Zemlya *118 E2 island group* N Russian Federation
Severnyy *111 E3* NW Russian Federation
Severodvinsk *111 C3* NW Russian Federation
Severomorsk *111 C2* NW Russian Federation
Sevier Lake *47 C6* ◎ Utah, W USA
Sevilla *see* Seville
Seville *99 B5* SW Spain
Seychelles *66* ◆ *republic* W Indian Ocean
Seydhisfjördhur *83 B1* E Iceland
Seýdi *125 E3* E Turkmenistan
Seymour *44 G3* Texas, SW USA
Sfântu Gheorghe *109 C6* C Romania
Sfax *70 F2* E Tunisia
's-Gravenhage *see* Hague, the
's-Gravenzande *84 C4* W Netherlands
Sgurr Na Lapaich *91 C3* ▲ NW Scotland, United Kingdom
Shache *129 A3* NW China
Shackleton Ice Shelf *142 E5 ice shelf* Antarctica
Shaftesbury *95 D4* S England, United Kingdom
Shahany, Ozero *109 D6* ◎ SW Ukraine
Shahrak *125 E5* C Afghanistan
Shahr-e Kord *123 D2* C Iran
Shahrud *123 E1* N Iran
Shalkar *118 B5* W Kazakhstan
Shamrock *44 F2* Texas, SW USA
Shanghai *129 G4* E China
Shangrao *129 G5* S China
Shannon *89 C5* W Ireland
Shannon *89 B5* ≈ W Ireland
Shannon Erne Waterway *89 D3 canal* N Ireland
Shannon, Mouth of the *89 A5 estuary* W Ireland
Shan Plateau *131 B2 plateau* E Burma (Myanmar)
Shantou *129 G5* S China
Shaoguan *129 F5* S China
Shapinsay *91 E1 island* NE Scotland, United Kingdom
Shar *118 D5* E Kazakhstan
Sharjah *123 E4* NE United Arab Emirates
Shark Bay *137 A4 bay* Western Australia
Sharon *37 B4* Pennsylvania, NE USA
Shashe *76 D5* ≈ Botswana/Zimbabwe
Shasta Lake *49 B5* ⊡ California, W USA
Shawnee *43 D8* Oklahoma, C USA
Shchëkino *111 A6* W Russian Federation
Shchors *109 E3* N Ukraine
Shchuchinsk *118 C5* N Kazakhstan
Shchuchyn *109 B2* W Belarus
Shebekino *111 A6* W Russian Federation
Shebeli *75 E4* ≈ Ethiopia/Somalia
Sheboygan *40 C4* Wisconsin, N USA
Shebshi Mountains *72 F4* ⛰ E Nigeria
Sheelin, Lough *89 D3* ◎ C Ireland
Sheerness *95 G4* SE England, United Kingdom
Sheffield *93 D4* N England, United Kingdom
Shelby *47 D1* Montana, NW USA
Sheldon *43 D4* Iowa, C USA
Shelekhov Gulf *118 H3 gulf* E Russian Federation
Shendi *75 C2* NE Sudan
Shenyang *129 G2* NE China
Shepherd Islands *141 H5 island group* C Vanuatu
Shepparton *137 F6* Victoria, SE Australia
Shepton Mallet *95 D4* SW England, United Kingdom
Sherbrooke *35 E5* Québec, SE Canada
Shereik *75 C1* N Sudan
Sheridan *47 E3* Wyoming, C USA
Sherman *44 H3* Texas, SW USA
's-Hertogenbosch *84 D5* S Netherlands
Shetland Islands *91 A7 island group* NE Scotland, United Kingdom
Shevchenko *see* Aktau
Shiant Islands *91 B3 island group* NW Scotland, United Kingdom
Shibetsu *133 G1* NE Japan
Shibirghan *125 E4* N Afghanistan
Shibushi-wan *133 D8 bay* SW Japan
Shihezi *129 C2* NW China
Shijiazhuang *129 F3* E China
Shikarpur *127 C3* S Pakistan
Shikoku *133 E7 island* SW Japan
Shilabo *75 F4* E Ethiopia
Shildon *93 D2* N England, United Kingdom
Shiliguri *127 G3* NE India
Shilka *118 G5* ≈ S Russian Federation
Shillelagh *89 E5* E Ireland
Shillong *127 G3* NE India
Shimbiris *75 F3* ▲ N Somalia
Shimoga *127 D6* W India
Shimonoseki *133 D7* Honshu, SW Japan
Shinano-gawa *133 F5* ≈ Honshū, C Japan
Shindand *125 D5* W Afghanistan
Shingū *133 F7* Honshu, SW Japan
Shinjō *133 G4* Honshu, C Japan
Shin, Loch *91 D2* ◎ N Scotland, United Kingdom
Shinyanga *75 C6* NW Tanzania
Shiprock *44 C1* New Mexico, SW USA
Shiraz *123 D3* S Iran
Shivpuri *127 D3* C India
Shizugawa *133 G4* NE Japan
Shizuoka *133 F6* Honshu, S Japan
Shkodër *107 D3* NW Albania
Shoreham-by-Sea *95 F5* SE England, United Kingdom
Shoshoni *47 E4* Wyoming, C USA
Shostka *109 E3* NE Ukraine
Show Low *44 C2* Arizona, SW USA
Shreveport *39 A5* Louisiana, S USA
Shrewsbury *93 C5* W England, United Kingdom
Shu *118 C6* SE Kazakhstan
Shumagin Islands *50 C3 island group* Alaska, USA
Shumen *107 F2* NE Bulgaria
Shuqrah *123 C7* SW Yemen
Shymkent *118 B6* S Kazakhstan
Sialum *141 B2* C Papua New Guinea
Šiauliai *83 E7* N Lithuania
Sibay *111 D7* W Russian Federation
Siberia *118 E4 physical region* NE Russian Federation
Siberut, Pulau *131 A6 island* Kepulauan Mentawai, W Indonesia
Sibi *127 B2* SW Pakistan
Sibiti *76 B2* S Congo
Sibiu *109 B6* C Romania
Sibolga *131 B6* Sumatra, W Indonesia
Sibu *131 D6* E Malaysia
Sibut *72 H5* S Central African Republic
Sibuyan Sea *131 F4 sea* W Pacific Ocean
Sichon *131 B5* SW Thailand
Sichuan Pendi *129 E4 basin* C China
Sicilia *see* Sicily
Sicily *103 C8 island* S Italy
Sicily, Strait of *103 B8 strait* C Mediterranean Sea
Siderno *103 E8* SW Italy
Sidi Barrâni *70 H2* NW Egypt
Sidi Bel Abbès *70 D1* NW Algeria
Sidlaw Hills *91 E5* ⛰ E Scotland, United Kingdom
Sidley, Mount *142 B5* ▲ Antarctica
Sidmouth *95 C5* SW England, United Kingdom
Sidney *47 F2* Montana, NW USA
Sidney *43 A5* Nebraska, C USA
Sidney *40 E6* Ohio, N USA
Siedlce *105 F3* C Poland
Siegen *101 B5* W Germany
Siemiatycze *105 G3* NE Poland
Siena *103 C4* C Italy
Sieradz *105 D4* C Poland
Sierpc *105 E3* C Poland
Sierra Leone *72 A5* ◆ *republic* W Africa
Sierra Madre *55 A3* ⛰ Guatemala/Mexico
Sierra Morena *112 B4* ⛰ SW Spain Europe
Sierra Nevada *99 D6* ⛰ S Spain
Sierra Nevada *49 B6* ⛰ W USA
Sierra Vieja *44 E4* ⛰ Texas, SW USA
Sierra Vista *44 C4* Arizona, SW USA
Sífnos *107 E6 island* Cyclades, Greece
Sigli *131 A5* Sumatra, W Indonesia
Siglufjördhur *83 B1* N Iceland
Signal Peak *44 A3* ▲ Arizona, SW USA
Signy *142 A3 UK research station* South Orkney Islands, Antarctica
Siguatepeque *55 C3* W Honduras
Siguiri *72 B4* NE Guinea
Sihanoukville *131 C4* SW Cambodia (see also Kâmpóng Saôm)
Siilinjärvi *83 F4* C Finland
Siirt *121 G4* SE Turkey
Sikasso *72 C4* S Mali
Sikeston *43 G7* Missouri, C USA
Siklós *105 D9* SW Hungary
Silchar *127 H3* NE India

◐ Administrative region ◆ Country ● Country capital ◇ Dependent territory ○ Dependent territory capital ⛰ Mountain range ▲ Mountain ⛰ Volcano ≈ River ◎ Lake ⊡ Reservoir

Silesia 105 D4 *physical region* SW Poland
Silicon Valley 49 B7 ⬖ *industrial region* California, SW USA North America
Silifke 121 D5 S Turkey
Siling Co 129 C4 ◎ W China
Silisili 141 A4 ▲ C Samoa
Silistra 107 F2 NE Bulgaria
Šilutė 83 E7 W Lithuania
Silvan 121 F4 SE Turkey
Silverek 121 F4 SE Turkey
Simav 120 B3 W Turkey
Simav Çayı 120 A3 ≈ NW Turkey
Simcoe, Lake 37 B2 ◎ Ontario, S Canada
Simeto 103 D8 ≈ Sicilia, Italy, C Mediterranean Sea
Simeulue, Pulau 131 A6 *island* NW Indonesia
Simferopol' 109 F7 S Ukraine
Simpelveld 84 E6 SE Netherlands
Simplon Pass 101 B8 *pass* S Switzerland
Simpson Desert 137 E4 *desert* Northern Territory/South Australia
Sinai 70 J2 *physical region* NE Egypt
Sincelejo 63 B2 NW Colombia
Sinclair, Lake 39 E4 ⊠ Georgia, SE USA
Sind 127 B3 *cultural region* SE Pakistan
Sindelfingen 101 B6 SW Germany
Sines 99 A5 S Portugal
Singapore 131 C6 ● S Singapore
Singapore 131 C6 ◆ *republic* SE Asia
Singen 101 B7 S Germany
Singida 75 D6 C Tanzania
Singkawang 131 D6 C Indonesia
Siniscola 103 B5 Sardinia, Italy
Sinmi-do 133 A5 *island* NW North Korea
Sinoie, Lacul 109 D7 *lagoon* SE Romania
Sinop 121 D2 N Turkey
Sinp'o 133 B4 E North Korea
Sinsheim 101 B6 SW Germany
Sint-Michielsgestel 84 D5 S Netherlands
Sint-Niklaas 84 C6 N Belgium
Sint-Pieters-Leeuw 84 B7 C Belgium
Sintra 99 A4 W Portugal
Sinuiju 133 A4 W North Korea
Sinujiif 75 F3 NE Somalia
Sion 101 A8 SW Switzerland
Sion Mills 89 D2 W Northern Ireland, United Kingdom
Sioux City 43 D4 Iowa, C USA
Sioux Falls 43 D4 South Dakota, N USA
Siping 129 G2 NE China
Siple, Mount 142 A5 ▲ Siple Island, Antarctica
Siquirres 55 F6 E Costa Rica
Siracusa *see* Syracuse
Sir Edward Pellew Group 137 E2 *island group* Northern Territory, NE Australia
Siret 109 C6 ≈ Romania/Ukraine
Sirikit Reservoir 131 B3 ◎ N Thailand
Sirjan 123 E3 S Iran
Şırnak 121 G4 SE Turkey
Sirte, Gulf of 70 G2 *gulf* N Libya
Sisimiut 143 A5 S Greenland
Sitges 99 G3 NE Spain
Sittard 84 E6 SE Netherlands
Sittoung 131 A3 ≈ S Burma (Myanmar)
Sittwe 131 A2 W Burma (Myanmar)
Siuna 55 E3 NE Nicaragua
Sivas 121 E3 C Turkey
Sivers'kyy Donets' 109 F4 ≈ Russian Federation/Ukraine
Siwah 70 H3 NW Egypt
Six-Fours-les-Plages 97 E7 SE France
Siyäzän 121 J2 NE Azerbaijan
Skagerrak 83 B6 *channel* N Europe
Skagit River 49 B1 ≈ Washington, NW USA
Skalka 83 D2 ◎ N Sweden
Skegness 93 F5 E England, United Kingdom
Skellefteå 83 D3 N Sweden
Skellefteälven 83 D3 ≈ N Sweden
Skerries 89 E4 E Ireland
Ski 83 B5 S Norway
Skiddaw 93 C2 ▲ NW England, United Kingdom
Skikda 70 E1 NE Algeria
Skipton 93 D3 N England, United Kingdom
Skopje 107 D3 ● N FYR Macedonia
Skovorodino 118 G5 SE Russian Federation
Skriveri 83 E6 S Latvia
Skudnesfjorden 83 A5 *fjord* S Norway
Skull 89 B7 SW Ireland
Skye, Isle of 91 B3 *island* NW Scotland, United Kingdom
Skýros 107 F5 *island* Northern Sporádes, E Greece
Slagelse 83 B7 E Denmark
Slane 89 E4 E Ireland
Slaney 89 E5 ≈ SE Ireland
Slatina 109 B7 S Romania
Slavonski Brod 107 C1 NE Croatia
Sławno 105 C2 NW Poland
Sleaford 93 E5 E England, United Kingdom
Sleat, Sound of 91 C4 *strait* NW Scotland, United Kingdom
Sliema 112 B6 N Malta
Slieve Gamph 89 C3 ▲▲ N Ireland
Slieve League 89 C2 ▲▲ Donegal, N Ireland Europe
Slieve Mish Mountains 89 B6 ▲▲ SW Ireland
Slievenamon 89 D6 ▲ S Ireland
Sligo 89 C3 NW Ireland
Sligo Bay 89 C2 *inlet* NW Ireland
Sliven 107 F3 C Bulgaria
Slough 95 F3 S England, United Kingdom
Slovakia 105 E6 ◆ *republic* C Europe
Slovenia 101 E8 ◆ *republic* SE Europe
Slovenské rudohorie 105 E6 ▲▲ C Slovakia
Slov"yans'k 109 G4 E Ukraine
Słubice 105 B3 W Poland
Sluch 109 C4 ≈ NW Ukraine
Słupsk 105 D1 N Poland
Slutsk 109 C3 S Belarus
Slyne Head 89 A4 *headland* W Ireland
Smallwood Reservoir 35 F3 ◎ Newfoundland, S Canada
Smara 70 B3 N Western Sahara
Smederevo 107 D2 N Serbia
Smederevska Palanka 107 E2 C Serbia
Smoky Hill River 47 H5 ≈ Kansas, C USA
Smøla 83 B4 *island* W Norway
Smolensk 111 A5 W Russian Federation
Snaefell 93 B3 ▲ C Isle of Man
Snake River 49 C2 ≈ NW USA
Snake River Plain 47 C4 *plain* Idaho, NW USA
Sneek 84 E2 N Netherlands
Sneem 89 B6 SW Ireland
Sněžka 105 C5 ▲ N Czech Republic/Poland
Snina 105 F6 E Slovakia
Snowdon 93 B5 ▲ NW Wales, United Kingdom
Snowdonia 93 B5 ▲▲ NW Wales, United Kingdom
Snowdrift *see* Lutselk'e
Snyder 44 F3 Texas, SW USA
Sobradinho, Represa de 63 G5 ⊠ E Brazil
Sochi 111 A8 SW Russian Federation
Society Islands 135 *island group* W French Polynesia
Socorro 44 D2 New Mexico, SW USA
Socorro, Isla 53 B5 *island* W Mexico
Socotra 123 D7 *island* SE Yemen
Socuéllamos 99 E4 C Spain
Sodankylä 83 E2 N Finland
Söderhamn 83 D5 C Sweden
Södertälje 83 D5 C Sweden
Sodiri 75 B2 C Sudan
Sofia 107 E3 ● W Bulgaria
Sofiya *see* Sofia
Sogamoso 63 C2 C Colombia
Sognefjorden 83 A5 *fjord* NE North Sea
Sokcho 133 B5 N South Korea
Söke 120 A4 SW Turkey
Sokhumi 121 F1 NW Georgia
Sokodé 72 D4 C Togo
Sokol 111 B4 NW Russian Federation
Sokolov 105 A5 W Czech Republic
Sokone 72 A3 W Senegal
Sokoto 72 E4 NW Nigeria
Sokoto 72 E4 ≈ NW Nigeria
Solapur 127 D5 W India
Sol, Costa del 99 D6 *coastal region* S Spain
Solec Kujawski 105 D3 C Poland
Solihull 93 D6 C England, United Kingdom
Solikamsk 111 D5 NW Russian Federation
Sol'-Iletsk 111 D7 W Russian Federation
Solingen 101 A4 W Germany
Sollentuna 83 D5 C Sweden
Solomon Islands 141 F2 ◆ *commonwealth republic* W Pacific Ocean
Solomon Sea 141 C2 *sea* W Pacific Ocean
Soltau 101 C3 NW Germany
Sol'tsy 111 A4 W Russian Federation
Solway Firth 93 B2 *inlet* England/ Scotland, United Kingdom
Solwezi 76 D4 NW Zambia
Soma 133 G4 C Japan
Somalia 75 F4 ◆ *republic* E Africa
Somaliland 75 F3 *cultural region* E Africa
Somali Plain 15 *undersea feature* W Indian Ocean
Sombrero 57 J4 *island* N Anguilla
Someren 84 E5 SE Netherlands
Somerset 39 E3 Kentucky, S USA
Somerset Island 33 H2 *island* Queen Elizabeth Islands, Nunavut, NW Canada
Somerton 44 A3 Arizona, SW USA
Somme 97 D1 ≈ N France
Somotillo 55 D4 NW Nicaragua
Somoto 55 D4 NW Nicaragua
Songea 75 D7 S Tanzania
Songkhla 131 B5 SW Thailand
Sonora 44 F4 Texas, SW USA
Sonoran Desert 49 D9 *desert* Mexico/ USA
Sonsonate 55 B4 W El Salvador
Sopot 105 D2 N Poland
Sopron 105 C7 NW Hungary
Sorgues 97 E6 SE France
Sorgun 121 D3 C Turkey
Soria 99 E2 N Spain
Sorong 131 G6 E Indonesia
Sørøya 83 D1 *island* N Norway
Sortavala 111 A3 NW Russian Federation
Sosnovyy Bor 111 A4 W Russian Federation
Sotkamo 83 F3 C Finland
Sŏul *see* Seoul
Soúrpi 107 E5 C Greece
Sousse 70 F1 NE Tunisia
South Africa 76 C7 ◆ *republic* S Africa
South America 65 *continent*
Southampton 95 E4 S England, United Kingdom
Southampton Island 33 I4 *island* Nunavut, NE Canada
South Andaman 127 H5 *island* SE India
South Australia 137 D4 ⬖ *state* S Australia
South Bend 40 D5 Indiana, N USA
South Bruny Island 137 G7 *island* Tasmania, SE Australia
South Carolina 39 F4 ⬖ *state* SE USA
South China Sea 131 E3 *sea* SE Asia
South Dakota 43 B3 ⬖ *state* N USA
South Downs 95 F4 *hill range* SE England, United Kingdom
Southeast Indian Ridge 15 *undersea feature* Indian Ocean/Pacific Ocean
South East Point 137 F7 *headland* Victoria, S Australia
Southend-on-Sea 95 G3 E England, United Kingdom
Southern Alps 139 B6 ▲▲ South Island, New Zealand
Southern Cook Islands 135 *island group* S Cook Islands
Southern Cross 137 B5 Western Australia
Southern Indian Lake 33 H5 ◎ Manitoba, C Canada
Southern Ocean 14 *ocean* Atlantic Ocean/Indian Ocean/Pacific Ocean
Southern Uplands 91 D6 ▲▲ S Scotland, United Kingdom
South Esk 91 E4 ≈ E Scotland, United Kingdom
South Foreland 95 H4 *headland* SE England, United Kingdom
South Geomagnetic Pole 142 C5 *pole* Antarctica
South Georgia 142 A2 *island* South Georgia and the South Sandwich Islands, SW Atlantic Ocean
South Goulburn Island 137 E1 *island* Northern Territory, N Australia
South Indian Basin 15 *undersea feature* Indian Ocean/Pacific Ocean
South Island 139 C6 *island* S New Zealand
South Korea 133 A6 ◆ *republic* E Asia
South Lake Tahoe 49 C6 California, W USA
South Molton 95 C4 SW England, United Kingdom
South Orkney Islands 142 A3 *island group* Antarctica
South Platte River 47 G5 ≈ Colorado/ Nebraska, C USA
South Pole 142 C5 *pole* Antarctica
Southport 93 C4 NW England, United Kingdom
South Ronaldsay 91 E1 *island* NE Scotland, United Kingdom
South Sandwich Islands 142 A2 *island group* SE South Georgia and the South Sandwich Islands
South Sandwich Trench 142 B2 *undersea feature* SW Atlantic Ocean
South Shetland Islands 142 A3 *island group* Antarctica
South Shields 93 E2 NE England, United Kingdom
South Sioux City 43 D4 Nebraska, C USA
South Sound 89 B5 *sound* W Ireland
South Sudan 75 B4 ◆ *republic* N Africa
South Taranaki Bight 139 C4 *bight* SE Tasman Sea
South Tyne 93 C2 ≈ N England, United Kingdom
South Uist 91 A3 *island* NW Scotland, United Kingdom
South West Cape 139 A8 *headland* SW New Zealand
Southwest Indian Ridge 15 *undersea feature* SW Indian Ocean
Southwest Pacific Basin 14 *undersea feature* SE Pacific Ocean
Southwold 95 H2 E England, United Kingdom
Soweto 76 D6 NE South Africa
Spain 99 C3 ◆ *monarchy* SW Europe
Spalding 93 F5 E England, United Kingdom
Spanish Town 57 D4 C Jamaica
Sparks 47 A5 Nevada, W USA
Spartanburg 39 F4 South Carolina, SE USA
Spárti 107 E6 S Greece
Spearfish 43 A3 South Dakota, N USA
Spencer 43 E4 Iowa, C USA
Spencer Gulf 137 E6 *gulf* South Australia
Spennymoor 93 D2 N England, United Kingdom
Spey 91 E3 ≈ NE Scotland, United Kingdom
Spijkenisse 84 C4 SW Netherlands
Spin Buldak 125 E6 S Afghanistan
Spitsbergen 143 C5 *island* NW Svalbard
Split 107 B2 S Croatia
Spokane 49 D2 Washington, NW USA
Spratly Islands 131 D4 *disputed* ◇ SE Asia
Spree 101 E4 ≈ E Germany
Spring City 47 D5 Utah, W USA
Springer 44 E1 New Mexico, SW USA
Springfield 47 G6 Colorado, C USA
Springfield 37 E4 Massachusetts, NE USA
Springfield 43 E7 Missouri, C USA
Springfield 40 E6 Ohio, N USA
Springfield 49 B4 Oregon, NW USA
Springfield 40 B6 *state capital* Illinois, N USA
Spring Hill 39 F7 Florida, SE USA
Springs Junction 139 C5 South Island, New Zealand
Springsure 137 G4 Queensland, E Australia
Springville 47 D5 Utah, W USA
Spruce Knob 39 G2 ▲ West Virginia, NE USA
Spurn Head 93 F4 *headland* E England, United Kingdom
Sri Aman 131 D6 E Malaysia
Sri Jayawardanapura Kotte 127 E8 ● (legislative) W Sri Lanka
Srikakulam 127 F5 E India
Sri Lanka 127 D8 ◆ *republic* S Asia
Srinagar 127 D1 N India
Stabroek 84 C5 N Belgium
Stack Skerry 91 D1 *island* N Scotland, United Kingdom
Stade 101 C3 NW Germany
Stadskanaal 84 F2 NE Netherlands
Stafford 93 D5 C England, United Kingdom
Staines 95 F4 SE England, United Kingdom
Staithes 93 E3 N England, United Kingdom
Stakhanov 109 G4 E Ukraine
Stalowa Wola 105 F5 SE Poland
Stamford 93 E5 E England, United Kingdom
Stamford 37 E5 Connecticut, NE USA
Stanhope 93 D3 N England, United Kingdom
Stanley 65 C9 ○ E Falkland Islands
Stanley 93 D2 N England, United Kingdom
Stanthorpe 137 H5 Queensland, E Australia
Staphorst 84 E3 E Netherlands
Starachowice 105 F4 C Poland
Stara Zagora 107 F3 C Bulgaria
Starbuck Island 135 *island* E Kiribati
Stargard Szczeciński 105 B2 NW Poland
Starkville 39 D4 Mississippi, S USA
Starobil's'k 109 G4 E Ukraine
Starogard Gdański 105 D2 N Poland
Starominskaya 111 A7 SW Russian Federation
Start Bay 95 C6 *bay* SW England, United Kingdom
Start Point 95 C6 *headland* SW England, United Kingdom
Staryy Oskol 111 A6 W Russian Federation
State College 37 C5 Pennsylvania, NE USA
Statesboro 39 G5 Georgia, SE USA
Staunton 39 G2 Virginia, NE USA
Stavanger 83 A5 S Norway
Stavropol' 111 A8 SW Russian Federation
Steamboat Springs 47 E5 Colorado, C USA
Steenwijk 84 E3 N Netherlands
Steinkjer 83 C4 C Norway
Stendal 101 D3 C Germany
Stephenville 44 G3 Texas, SW USA
Steps Point 51 *headland* W American Samoa
Sterling 47 G5 Colorado, C USA
Sterling 40 B5 Illinois, N USA
Sterlitamak 111 D6 W Russian Federation
Steubenville 40 F6 Ohio, N USA
Stevenage 95 F3 E England, United Kingdom
Stevens Point 40 B3 Wisconsin, N USA
Stewart Island 139 A8 *island* S New Zealand
Steyr 101 E7 N Austria
Stickford 93 F5 E England, United Kingdom
Stillwater 43 D7 Oklahoma, C USA
Stirling 91 D5 C Scotland, United Kingdom
Stjørdalshalsen 83 B4 C Norway
Stockach 101 B7 S Germany
Stockdale 44 G5 Texas, SW USA
Stockholm 83 D5 ● C Sweden
Stockport 93 D4 NW England, United Kingdom
Stockton 49 B7 California, W USA
Stockton-on-Tees 93 E3 N England, United Kingdom
Stockton Plateau 44 E4 *plain* Texas, SW USA
Stoke-on-Trent 93 D5 C England, United Kingdom
Stone 93 D5 C England, United Kingdom
Stonehaven 91 F4 NE Scotland, United Kingdom
Støren 83 B4 S Norway
Stornoway 91 B2 NW Scotland, United Kingdom
Storsjön 83 C4 ◎ C Sweden
Storuman 83 D3 N Sweden
Storuman 83 C3 ◎ N Sweden
Stour 95 D4 ≈ E England, United Kingdom
Stour 95 H3 ≈ S England, United Kingdom
Stourport-on-Severn 93 D6 W England, United Kingdom
Stowmarket 95 G2 E England, United Kingdom
Strabane 89 D2 W Northern Ireland, United Kingdom
Stradbally 89 D5 C Ireland
Strakonice 105 B6 S Czech Republic
Stralsund 101 D2 NE Germany
Strangford Lough 89 F3 *inlet* E Northern Ireland, United Kingdom
Stranraer 91 C7 S Scotland, United Kingdom
Strasbourg 97 F3 NE France
Stratford 139 D4 North Island, New Zealand
Stratford 44 F1 Texas, SW USA
Stratford-upon-Avon 93 D6 C England, United Kingdom
Strathy Point 91 D2 *headland* N Scotland, United Kingdom
Straubing 101 D6 SE Germany
Strehaia 109 B7 SW Romania
Strelka 118 E4 C Russian Federation
Strickland 141 A2 ≈ SW Papua New Guinea
Stromboli 103 D7 ⋏ Isola Stromboli, SW Italy
Stromeferry 91 C3 N Scotland, United Kingdom
Stromness 91 E1 N Scotland, United Kingdom
Strömstad 83 B6 S Sweden
Strömsund 83 C4 C Sweden
Stronsay 91 E1 *island* NE Scotland, United Kingdom
Stroud 95 D3 C England, United Kingdom
Strymónas 107 E4 ≈ Bulgaria/Greece
Stryy 109 B5 NW Ukraine
Studholme 139 B7 South Island, New Zealand
Sturgis 43 A3 South Dakota, N USA
Stuttgart 101 B6 SW Germany
Stykkishólmur 83 A1 W Iceland
Styr 109 C4 ≈ Belarus/Ukraine
Suakin 75 D1 NE Sudan
Subotica 107 D1 N Serbia
Suceava 109 C5 NE Romania
Suck 89 C4 ≈ C Ireland
Suckling, Mount 141 C3 ▲ S Papua New Guinea
Sucre 65 B3 ● S Bolivia
Sudan 75 B2 ◆ *republic* N Africa
Sudbury 35 C5 Ontario, S Canada
Sudbury 95 G2 E England, United Kingdom
Sudd 75 B4 *swamp region* C South Sudan
Sudeten 105 C5 ▲▲ Czech Republic/Poland
Sue 75 B4 ≈ S South Sudan
Sueca 99 F4 E Spain
Suez 70 I2 NE Egypt
Suez Canal 70 I2 *canal* NE Egypt
Suez, Gulf of 112 J6 *gulf* NE Egypt
Suğla Gölü 121 C5 ◎ SW Turkey
Suhar 123 E4 N Oman
Sühbaatar 129 E1 N Mongolia
Suhl 101 C5 C Germany
Suir 89 D6 ≈ S Ireland
Sujawal 127 B3 SE Pakistan
Sukabumi 131 C8 C Indonesia
Sukagawa 133 G5 C Japan
Sukhona 111 C4 ≈ NW Russian Federation
Sukkur 127 C3 SE Pakistan
Sukumo 133 E7 Shikoku, SW Japan
Sulaiman Range 127 C2 ▲▲ C Pakistan
Sula, Kepulauan 131 F7 *island group* C Indonesia
Sulawesi *see* Celebes
Sule Skerry 91 D1 *island* N Scotland, United Kingdom
Sullana 63 A4 NW Peru
Sulphur Springs 44 H3 Texas, SW USA
Sulu Archipelago 131 F5 *island group* SW Philippines
Sulu Sea 131 E5 *sea* SW Philippines
Sulyukta 125 F3 SW Kyrgyzstan
Sumatra 131 B6 *island* W Indonesia
Sumba, Pulau 131 E8 *island* Nusa Tenggara, C Indonesia
Sumba, Selat 131 E8 *strait* Nusa Tenggara, S Indonesia
Sumbawanga 75 C7 W Tanzania
Sumbe 76 B3 W Angola
Sumburgh 91 A7 NE Scotland, United Kingdom
Sumburgh Head 91 A7 *headland* NE Scotland, United Kingdom
Sumeih 75 B3 S Sudan
Summer Isles 91 C3 *island group* NW Scotland, United Kingdom
Summer Lake 49 C4 ◎ Oregon, NW USA
Sumqayit 121 J2 E Azerbaijan
Sumy 109 F4 NE Ukraine
Sunch'on 133 B7 S South Korea
Sunda, Selat 131 C7 *strait* Jawa/ Sumatera, SW Indonesia
Sunderland 93 E2 NE England, United Kingdom
Sundsvall 83 D4 C Sweden
Sungaipenuh 131 B7 Sumatra, W Indonesia
Sunnyvale 49 B7 California, W USA
Suntar 118 F4 NE Russian Federation
Sunyani 72 D5 W Ghana
Suomussalmi 83 F3 E Finland
Suoyarvi 111 B3 NW Russian Federation
Superior 40 A2 Wisconsin, N USA
Superior, Lake 40 C1 ◎ Canada/USA
Sur 123 F5 NE Oman
Surabaya 131 D8 C Indonesia
Surakarta 131 D8 S Indonesia
Šurany 105 D7 SW Slovakia
Surat 127 C4 W India
Sur, Cabo 141 C6 *cape* Easter Island, Chile
Sûre 84 E8 ≈ W Europe
Surendranagar 127 C4 W India
Surfers Paradise 137 H5 Queensland, E Australia
Surgut 118 D4 C Russian Federation
Surinam 63 E2 ◆ *republic* N South America
Surkhob 125 G3 ≈ C Tajikistan
Surt 70 G2 N Libya
Surtsey 83 A2 *island* S Iceland
Suruga-wan 133 G6 *bay* SE Japan
Susa 103 A2 NE Italy
Susanville 49 C5 California, W USA
Susitna 50 E2 Alaska, USA
Susquehanna River 37 C5 ≈ New York/Pennsylvania, NE USA
Susteren 84 E6 SE Netherlands
Susuman 118 H3 E Russian Federation
Sutlej 127 C2 ≈ India/Pakistan
Sutton 95 F4 SE England, United Kingdom
Sutton Coldfield 93 D6 C England, United Kingdom
Suva 141 J5 ● Viti Levu, W Fiji
Suwałki 105 G2 NE Poland
Suwon 133 B6 NW South Korea
Svalbard 143 C5 *Norwegian* ◇ Arctic Ocean
Svartisen 83 C3 *glacier* C Norway
Sveg 83 C4 C Sweden
Svenstavik 83 C4 C Sweden
Svetlograd 111 A8 SW Russian Federation
Svobodnyy 118 H5 SE Russian Federation
Svyataya Anna Trough 143 D4 *undersea feature* N Kara Sea
Svyetlahorsk 109 D3 SE Belarus
Swakopmund 76 B5 W Namibia
Swale 93 D3 ≈ N England, United Kingdom
Swalinbar 89 D3 N Ireland
Swanage 95 E5 S England, United Kingdom
Swan Islands 55 E1 *island group* NE Honduras
Swansea 93 B7 S Wales, United Kingdom
Swansea Bay 93 B7 *bay* S Wales, United Kingdom
Swarzędz 105 D3 W Poland
Swaziland 76 E6 ◆ *monarchy* S Africa
Sweden 83 C4 ◆ *monarchy* N Europe
Sweetwater 44 F3 Texas, SW USA
Sweetwater River 47 E4 ≈ Wyoming, C USA
Świdnica 105 C5 SW Poland
Świdwin 105 C2 NW Poland
Świebodzice 105 C4 SW Poland
Świebodzin 105 C3 W Poland
Świecie 105 D2 C Poland
Swilly, Lough 89 D1 *inlet* N Ireland
Swindon 95 E3 S England, United Kingdom
Swinford 89 C3 NW Ireland
Świnoujście 105 B2 NW Poland
Switzerland 101 A8 ◆ *federal republic* C Europe
Swords 89 E4 E Ireland
Sydney 35 G5 Cape Breton Island, Nova Scotia, SE Canada
Sydney 137 G6 *state capital* New South Wales, SE Australia
Syeverodonets'k 109 G4 E Ukraine
Syktyvkar 111 D4 NW Russian Federation
Sylhet 127 G3 NE Bangladesh
Syowa 142 D3 *Japanese research station* Antarctica
Syracuse 103 D8 Sicily, Italy
Syracuse 37 D3 New York, NE USA
Syr Darya 118 B5 ≈ C Asia
Syria 123 B2 ◆ *republic* SW Asia
Syrian Desert 123 B2 *desert* SW Asia
Sýros 107 F6 *island* Cyclades, Greece
Syvash, Zatoka 109 F6 *inlet* S Ukraine
Syzran' 111 C6 W Russian Federation
Szamotuły 105 C3 W Poland
Szczecin 105 B2 NW Poland
Szczecinek 105 C2 NW Poland
Szczeciński, Zalew 105 B2 *bay* Germany/Poland
Szczytno 105 F2 NE Poland
Szeged 105 E8 SE Hungary
Székesfehérvár 105 D8 W Hungary
Szekszárd 105 D8 S Hungary
Szolnok 105 E8 C Hungary
Szombathely 105 C8 W Hungary
Szprotawa 105 C4 W Poland

T

Table Rock Lake 43 E7 ⊠ Arkansas/ Missouri, C USA
Table Top 44 B3 ▲ Arizona, SW USA
Tábor 105 B6 S Czech Republic
Tabora 75 C6 W Tanzania
Tabriz 123 C1 NW Iran
Tabuaeran 135 *atoll* E Kiribati
Tabubil 141 A2 SW Papua New Guinea
Tabūk 123 A3 NW Saudi Arabia
Tabwemasana, Mount 141 F4 ▲ W Vanuatu
Täby 83 D5 C Sweden
Tacaná, Volcán 55 A3 ⋏ Guatemala/Mexico
Tachov 105 A5 W Czech Republic
Tacloban 131 F4 Leyte, C Philippines
Tacna 63 C6 SE Peru
Tacoma 49 B2 Washington, NW USA
Tacuarembó 65 C5 C Uruguay
Tademait, Plateau du 70 D3 *plateau* C Algeria
Tadine 141 G6 E New Caledonia
Taebaek-sanmaek 133 B5 ▲▲ E South Korea
Taedong-gang 133 B4 ≈ C North Korea
Taff 93 C7 ≈ SE Wales, United Kingdom
Taganrog 111 A7 SW Russian Federation
Taganrog, Gulf of 109 G5 *gulf* Russian Federation/Ukraine
Taghmon 89 E6 SE Ireland
Taguatinga 63 G5 C Brazil
Tagula Island 141 D3 *island* SE Papua New Guinea
Tagus 99 B4 ≈ Portugal/Spain
Tahat 70 E4 ▲ SE Algeria
Tahiti 141 B6 *island* W French Polynesia
Tahlequah 43 E8 Oklahoma, C USA

Tahoe, Lake 49 B6 California/Nevada, W USA
Tahoua 72 E3 W Niger
Taiarapu, Presqu'île de 141 B6 *peninsula* W French Polynesia
Taibei 129 H5 ● N Taiwan (see also Taipei)
Taieri 139 B7 South Island, New Zealand
Taihape 139 D4 C New Zealand
Tailem Bend 137 F6 South Australia
Tain 91 D3 N Scotland, United Kingdom
Tainan 129 H5 S Taiwan
Taipei 129 H5 ● N Taiwan (see also Taibei)
Taiping 131 B5 Peninsular Malaysia
Taiwan 131 F2 ◆ *republic* E Asia
Taiwan 129 H6 *island* Taiwan
Taiwan Strait 129 G5 *strait* China/Taiwan
Taiyuan 129 F3 C China
Taizhong 129 H5 C Taiwan
Ta'izz 123 C7 SW Yemen
Tajikistan 125 F3 ◆ *republic* C Asia
Takamatsu 133 E7 Shikoku, SW Japan
Takaoka 133 F5 Honshu, SW Japan
Takapuna 139 D2 North Island, New Zealand
Takikawa 133 G2 NE Japan
Takla Makan Desert 129 B3 *desert* NW China
Takuu Islands 141 E2 *island group* NE Papua New Guinea
Talamanca, Cordillera de 55 F6 S Costa Rica
Talara 63 A4 NW Peru
Talas 125 G2 NW Kyrgyzstan
Talaud, Kepulauan 131 G6 *island group* E Indonesia
Talavera de la Reina 99 D3 C Spain
Talca 65 A6 C Chile
Talcahuano 65 A6 C Chile
Taldykorgan 118 D6 SE Kazakhstan
Tallahassee 39 E6 *state capital* Florida, SE USA
Tallinn 83 E5 ● NW Estonia
Tallow 89 C6 S Ireland
Tallulah 39 C5 Louisiana, S USA
Talnakh 118 E3 N Russian Federation
Taloga 43 C8 Oklahoma, C USA
Taloqan 125 F4 NE Afghanistan
Taltal 65 A4 N Chile
Talvik 83 D1 N Norway
Tamabo, Banjaran 131 E6 East Malaysia
Tamale 72 D4 C Ghana
Tamanrasset 70 E4 S Algeria
Tamar 95 B5 SW England, United Kingdom
Tamazunchale 53 F4 C Mexico
Tambacounda 72 B3 SE Senegal
Tambea 141 E3 C Solomon Islands
Tambov 111 B6 W Russian Federation
Tambura 75 B4 SW South Sudan
Tâmchekkeṭ 72 B3 S Mauritania
Tamiahua, Laguna de 53 F4 *lagoon* E Mexico
Tamil Nadu 127 E7 *cultural region* SE India Asia
Tampa 39 F7 Florida, SE USA
Tampa Bay 39 F8 *bay* Florida, SE USA
Tampere 83 E5 W Finland
Tampico 53 F4 C Mexico
Tamuning 51 NW Guam
Tamworth 137 G5 New South Wales, SE Australia
Tamworth 93 D5 C England, United Kingdom
Tana 75 E5 SE Kenya
Tanabe 133 E7 Honshu, SW Japan
Tana Bru 83 E1 N Norway
Tana, Lake 75 D3 NW Ethiopia
Tanami Desert 137 D2 *desert* Northern Territory, N Australia
Tandil 65 C6 E Argentina
Tane Range 131 B3 W Thailand
Tanga 75 D6 E Tanzania
Tanganyika, Lake 75 B6 E Africa
Tangaroa, Maunga 141 C6 Easter Island, Chile
Tanggula Shan 129 C4 W China
Tangier 70 C1 NW Morocco
Tangra Yumco 129 B4 W China
Tangshan 129 G3 E China
Tanimbar, Kepulauan 131 G8 *island group* Maluku, E Indonesia
Tanna 141 H5 *island* S Vanuatu
Tan-Tan 70 B2 SW Morocco
Tanzania 75 C6 ◆ *republic* E Africa
Taos 44 D1 New Mexico, SW USA
Taoudenni 72 C1 N Mali
Tapachula 53 H6 SE Mexico
Tapajós, Rio 63 E4 NW Brazil
Tarabulus *see* Tripoli
Taranaki, Mount 139 C4 North Island, New Zealand
Tarancón 99 E3 C Spain
Taransay 91 A3 *island* NW Scotland, United Kingdom
Taranto 103 F6 SE Italy
Taranto, Gulf of 103 E7 *gulf* S Italy
Tarare 97 E5 E France
Tarascon 97 E6 SE France
Taravao 141 B6 W French Polynesia
Taraz 118 C6 S Kazakhstan
Tarazona 99 E2 NE Spain
Tarbat Ness 91 D3 *headland* N Scotland, United Kingdom
Tarbert 91 C6 W Scotland, United Kingdom
Tarbert 91 B3 NW Scotland, United Kingdom
Tarbes 97 C6 S France
Tarcoola 137 E5 South Australia
Taree 137 H5 New South Wales, SE Australia
Târgoviște 109 C7 S Romania
Târgu Jiu 109 B7 W Romania
Târgu Mureș 109 B6 C Romania
Tarija 65 B3 S Bolivia
Tarim 123 D6 C Yemen
Tarim Basin 129 B3 *basin* NW China
Tarim He 129 B3 NW China
Tarn 97 D6 S France
Tarnobrzeg 105 F5 SE Poland
Tarnów 105 F5 S Poland
Taron 141 D2 NE Papua New Guinea
Tarragona 99 G3 E Spain
Tàrrega 99 G2 NE Spain
Tarsus 121 D5 S Turkey
Tartu 83 E6 SE Estonia
Tartus 123 A2 W Syria
Tarvisio 103 D2 NE Italy
Tashkent 125 F2 ● E Uzbekistan
Tash-Kumyr 125 G2 W Kyrgyzstan
Tasikmalaya 131 C8 Java, C Indonesia
Tasman Bay 139 C5 *inlet* South Island, New Zealand
Tasmania 137 F7 ◐ *state* SE Australia
Tasman Sea 134 *sea* SW Pacific Ocean
Tassili-n-Ajjer 70 E4 *plateau* E Algeria
Tatabánya 105 D7 NW Hungary
Tathlith 123 C5 S Saudi Arabia
Tatra Mountains 105 E6 Poland/Slovakia
Tatum 44 E3 New Mexico, SW USA
Tatvan 121 G4 SE Turkey
Ta'ū 51 *island* E American Samoa
Taumarunui 139 D3 North Island, New Zealand
Taunggyi 131 A2 C Burma (Myanmar)
Taunton 95 C4 SW England, United Kingdom
Taupo 139 D3 N New Zealand
Taupo, Lake 139 D3 North Island, New Zealand
Tauranga 139 D3 North Island, New Zealand
Taurus Mountains 121 C5 S Turkey
Tautira 141 B6 W French Polynesia
Tavas 120 B4 SW Turkey
Taveuni 141 J5 *island* N Fiji
Tavira 99 B5 S Portugal
Tavy 95 B5 SW England, United Kingdom
Taw 95 C5 SW England, United Kingdom
Tawakoni, Lake 44 H3 Texas, SW USA
Tawau 131 E5 E Malaysia
Taxco 53 F5 S Mexico
Taxiatosh 125 D2 W Uzbekistan
Taxtako'pir 125 D2 NW Uzbekistan
Tay 91 D4 C Scotland, United Kingdom
Tay, Firth of 91 E5 *inlet* E Scotland, United Kingdom
Tay, Loch 91 D5 C Scotland, United Kingdom
Taylor 44 H4 Texas, SW USA
Tayma 123 B3 NW Saudi Arabia
Taymyr, Ozero 118 F3 N Russian Federation
Taymyr, Poluostrov 118 E2 *peninsula* N Russian Federation
Taz 118 E3 N Russian Federation
Tbilisi 121 H2 ● SE Georgia
Tczew 105 D2 N Poland
Teahupoo 141 B6 W French Polynesia
Te Anau 139 A7 South Island, New Zealand
Te Anau, Lake 139 A7 South Island, New Zealand
Teapa 53 G5 SE Mexico
Tecomán 53 D5 SW Mexico
Tecpan 53 E5 S Mexico
Tees 93 D2 N England, United Kingdom
Tefé 63 D4 N Brazil
Tegal 131 D7 Java, C Indonesia
Tegelen 84 E5 SE Netherlands
Tegucigalpa 55 C3 ● SW Honduras
Tehran 123 D2 ● N Iran
Tehuacán 53 F5 S Mexico
Tehuantepec 53 G5 SE Mexico
Tehuantepec, Gulf of 53 G6 *gulf* S Mexico
Tehuantepec, Isthmus of 53 F5 *isthmus* SE Mexico
Teifi 93 B6 SW Wales, United Kingdom
Teignmouth 95 C5 SW England, United Kingdom
Tejen 125 D3 S Turkmenistan
Te Kao 139 C1 North Island, New Zealand
Tekax 53 H4 SE Mexico
Tekeli 118 D6 SE Kazakhstan
Tekirdağ 120 A2 NW Turkey
Tekong, Pulau 131 C6 *island* E Singapore
Te Kuiti 139 D3 North Island, New Zealand
Tela 55 C2 NW Honduras
Tel Aviv-Yafo 123 G6 C Israel
Telford 93 C5 W England, United Kingdom
Tembagapura 131 H7 E Indonesia
Teme 93 C6 England/Wales, United Kingdom
Temirtau 118 C5 C Kazakhstan
Tempe 44 B3 Arizona, SW USA
Tempio Pausania 103 A5 Sardinia, Italy
Temple 44 H4 Texas, SW USA
Templemore 89 D5 C Ireland
Temuco 65 A6 C Chile
Temuka 139 C7 SW New Zealand
Tenby 93 A7 SW Wales, United Kingdom
Ten Degree Channel 127 H5 *strait* Andaman and Nicobar Islands, India, E Indian Ocean
Ténenkou 72 C3 C Mali
Ténéré 72 F2 *physical region* C Niger
Tengger Shamo 129 E3 *desert* N China
Tengréla 72 C4 N Ivory Coast
Tenkodogo 72 D4 S Burkina
Tennant Creek 137 E3 Northern Territory, C Australia
Tennessee 39 D3 ◐ *state* SE USA
Tennessee River 39 D4 S USA
Tepic 53 D4 C Mexico
Teplice 105 B5 NW Czech Republic
Tequila 53 D4 SW Mexico
Teraina 135 *atoll* Line Islands, E Kiribati
Teramo 103 D4 C Italy
Tercan 121 F3 NE Turkey
Teresina 63 H4 NE Brazil
Terevaka, Maunga 141 C5 Easter Island, Chile
Términos, Laguna de 53 G5 *lagoon* SE Mexico
Termiz 125 F4 S Uzbekistan
Termoli 103 E5 C Italy
Terneuzen 84 B5 SW Netherlands
Terni 103 C4 C Italy
Ternopil' 109 C4 W Ukraine
Terracina 103 D5 C Italy
Terrassa 99 G2 E Spain
Terre Adélie 142 D6 *physical region* Antarctica
Terre Haute 40 C7 Indiana, N USA
Terrell 44 H3 Texas, SW USA
Terschelling 84 D1 *island* Waddeneilanden, N Netherlands
Teruel 99 F3 E Spain
Tervuren 84 C6 C Belgium
Teseney 75 D2 W Eritrea
Tessalit 72 D2 NE Mali
Tessaoua 72 F3 S Niger
Tessenderlo 84 D6 NE Belgium
Test 95 E4 S England, United Kingdom
Tete 76 E4 NW Mozambique
Teterow 101 D2 NE Germany
Tétouan 70 C1 N Morocco
Tevere *see* Tiber
Teviot 91 E6 SE Scotland, United Kingdom
Te Waewae Bay 139 A8 *bay* South Island, New Zealand
Texana, Lake 44 H5 Texas, SW USA
Texarkana 39 A4 Arkansas, C USA
Texarkana 44 I3 Texas, SW USA
Texas 44 F4 ◐ *state* S USA
Texas City 44 I5 Texas, SW USA
Texel 84 C2 *island* Waddeneilanden, NW Netherlands
Texoma, Lake 44 H2 Oklahoma/Texas, C USA
Teziutlán 53 F5 S Mexico
Thailand 131 B3 ◆ *monarchy* SE Asia
Thailand, Gulf of 131 B4 *gulf* SE Asia
Thai Nguyen 131 C2 N Vietnam
Thakhèk 131 C3 C Laos
Thamarīt 123 E6 SW Oman
Thame 95 F3 C England, United Kingdom
Thames 139 D3 N New Zealand
Thames 95 F3 S England, United Kingdom
Thandwe 131 A3 W Burma (Myanmar)
Thar Desert 127 C3 *desert* India/Pakistan
Tharthar, Buhayrat ath 123 B2 C Iraq
Thásos 107 F4 Thásos, E Greece
Thásos 107 F4 *island* E Greece
Thatcham 95 E4 S England, United Kingdom
Thaton 131 B3 S Burma (Myanmar)
Thayetmyo 131 A3 C Burma (Myanmar)
The Dalles 49 B3 Oregon, NW USA
The Mumbles 93 B7 S Wales, United Kingdom
The Pas 33 H6 Manitoba, C Canada
Thermaic Gulf 107 E4 *gulf* N Greece
Thermopolis 47 E3 Wyoming, C USA
Thessaloniki *see* Salonica
Thetford 95 G2 E England, United Kingdom
The Valley 57 J4 ○ E Anguilla
The Village 43 D8 Oklahoma, C USA
The Woodlands 44 H4 Texas, SW USA
Thief River Falls 43 D2 Minnesota, N USA
Thiers 97 D5 C France
Thiès 72 A3 W Senegal
Thimphu 127 G3 ● W Bhutan
Thio 141 G6 C New Caledonia
Thionville 97 F2 NE France
Thirsk 93 D3 N England, United Kingdom
Thiruvananthapuram 127 D7 SW India (see also Trivandrum)
Tholen 84 C5 *island* SW Netherlands
Thomasville 39 F6 Georgia, SE USA
Thompson 33 H6 Manitoba, C Canada
Thonon-les-Bains 97 F4 E France
Thoreau 44 C2 New Mexico, SW USA
Thorlákshöfn 83 A1 SW Iceland
Thornbury 95 D3 SW England, United Kingdom
Thornhill 91 D6 S Scotland, United Kingdom
Thouars 97 C4 W France
Thracian Sea 107 F4 *sea* Greece/Turkey
Three Gorges Dam 129 F4 *dam* C China
Three Kings Islands 139 B1 *island group* N New Zealand
Thrissur 127 D7 SW India (see also Trichur)
Thuin 84 C7 S Belgium
Thun 101 B8 W Switzerland
Thunder Bay 35 B4 Ontario, S Canada
Thuner See 101 A8 C Switzerland
Thung Song 131 B5 SW Thailand
Thurles 89 D5 S Ireland
Thurso 91 E2 N Scotland, United Kingdom
Tianjin 129 G3 E China
Tianshui 129 E4 C China
Tiarei 141 B6 W French Polynesia
Ti'avea 141 B5 SE Samoa
Tiber 103 C4 C Italy
Tiberias, Lake 123 H5 N Israel
Tibesti 72 G2 N Africa
Tibet 129 B4 *cultural region* W China
Tibet, Plateau of 129 B4 *plateau* W China
Tiburón, Isla 53 B2 *island* NW Mexico
Tîchît 72 B2 C Mauritania
Ticul 53 H4 SE Mexico
Tidjikja 72 B2 C Mauritania
Tienen 84 D7 C Belgium
Tien Shan 125 H2 C Asia
Tierp 83 D5 C Sweden
Tierra del Fuego 65 B9 *island* Argentina/Chile
Tifton 39 F6 Georgia, SE USA
Tighina 109 D6 E Moldova
Tigris 123 C3 Iraq/Turkey
Tiguentourine 70 E3 E Algeria
Tijuana 53 A1 NW Mexico
Tikhoretsk 111 A8 SW Russian Federation
Tikhvin 111 B4 NW Russian Federation
Tikirarjuaq *see* Whale Cove
Tiksi 118 G3 NE Russian Federation
Tilburg 84 D5 S Netherlands
Tillabéri 72 D3 W Niger
Tílos 107 G6 *island* Dodecanese, Greece
Timan Ridge 111 D3 *ridge* NW Russian Federation
Timanskiy Kryazh *see* Timan Ridge
Timaru 139 C7 South Island, New Zealand
Timbedgha 72 C3 SE Mauritania
Timbuktu 72 D3 N Mali
Timișoara 109 A6 W Romania
Timmins 35 C4 Ontario, S Canada
Timor 131 F8 *island* C Indonesia
Timor Sea 131 G8 *sea* E Indian Ocean
Timrå 83 D4 C Sweden
Tindouf 70 B3 W Algeria
Tineo 99 C1 N Spain
Tínos 107 F6 *island* Cyclades, SE Greece
Tipitapa 55 D4 W Nicaragua
Tipperary 89 C5 S Ireland
Tip Top Mountain 35 B4 ▲ Ontario, S Canada
Tirana 107 D4 ● C Albania
Tiranë *see* Tirana
Tiraspol 109 D6 E Moldova
Tiree 91 B5 *island* W Scotland, United Kingdom
Tirol 101 C8 *cultural region* Austria/Italy
Tiruchchirappalli 127 E7 SE India
Tisa 107 D1 SE Europe
Tiszakécske 105 E8 C Hungary
Titicaca, Lake 63 C6 Bolivia/Peru
Titule 76 D1 N Dem. Rep. Congo
Tiverton 95 C5 SW England, United Kingdom
Tivoli 103 C5 C Italy
Tizimín 53 I4 SE Mexico
Tizi Ouzou 70 E1 N Algeria
Tiznit 70 B2 SW Morocco
Tlaquepaque 53 E5 C Mexico
Tlaxcala 53 F5 C Mexico
Tlemcen 70 D1 NW Algeria
Toamasina 76 G5 E Madagascar
Toba, Danau 131 A6 Sumatra, W Indonesia
Tobago 57 K7 *island* NE Trinidad and Tobago
Toba Kakar Range 127 B2 NW Pakistan
Tobermory 91 B4 W Scotland, United Kingdom
Tobol 118 C4 Kazakhstan/Russian Federation
Tobol'sk 118 D4 C Russian Federation
Tobruk 70 H2 NE Libya
Tocantins 63 G5 *state* C Brazil
Tocantins, Rio 63 G4 N Brazil
Tocoa 55 D2 N Honduras
Tocopilla 65 A3 N Chile
Todi 103 C4 C Italy
Todos os Santos, Baía de 63 I6 *bay* E Brazil
Togo 72 D4 ◆ *republic* W Africa
Tokanui 139 B8 South Island, New Zealand
Tokar 75 D2 NE Sudan
Tokat 121 E3 N Turkey
Tokelau 135 NZ ◇ W Polynesia
Tokmak 125 H2 N Kyrgyzstan
Tokoroa 139 D3 North Island, New Zealand
Tokounou 72 B4 C Guinea
Tokushima 133 E7 Shikoku, SW Japan
Tokyo 133 F5 ● Honshu, S Japan
Toledo 99 D4 C Spain
Toledo 40 E5 Ohio, N USA
Toledo Bend Reservoir 44 I3 Louisiana/Texas, SW USA
Toliara 76 F6 SW Madagascar
Tolmin 101 E8 W Slovenia
Tolna 105 D8 S Hungary
Tolosa 99 E1 N Spain
Toluca 53 F5 S Mexico
Tol'yatti 111 C6 W Russian Federation
Tomah 40 B4 Wisconsin, N USA
Tomakomai 133 G2 NE Japan
Tomar 99 B4 W Portugal
Tomaszów Lubelski 105 G5 E Poland
Tomaszów Mazowiecki 105 E4 C Poland
Tombigbee River 39 D5 Alabama/Mississippi, S USA
Tombstone 44 C4 Arizona, SW USA
Tombua 76 B4 SW Angola
Tomelloso 99 E4 C Spain
Tomini, Gulf of 131 F6 *bay* Celebes, C Indonesia
Tomintoul 91 E4 N Scotland, United Kingdom
Tommot 118 G4 NE Russian Federation
Tomsk 118 D5 C Russian Federation
Tomür Feng 129 B2 ▲ China/Kyrgyzstan
Tonawanda 37 B3 New York, NE USA
Tonga 141 K6 ◆ *monarchy* SW Pacific Ocean
Tongatapu 141 K6 *island* Tongatapu Group, S Tonga
Tonga Trench 14 *undersea feature* S Pacific Ocean
Tongchuan 129 F4 C China
Tongeren 84 D7 NE Belgium
Tongking, Gulf of 131 C3 *gulf* China/Vietnam
Tongliao 129 G2 N China
Tongtian He 129 C4 C China
Tongue 91 D2 N Scotland, United Kingdom
Tongue River 47 E3 Montana, NW USA
Tonj 75 B4 C South Sudan
Tônlé Sap 131 C4 W Cambodia
Tonopah 47 B6 Nevada, W USA
Tonosí 55 G7 S Panama
Tooele 47 D5 Utah, W USA
Toormore 89 B7 S Ireland
Toowoomba 137 H4 Queensland, E Australia
Topeka 43 D6 *state capital* Kansas, C USA
Topoľčany 105 D6 W Slovakia
Tor Bay 95 C5 *bay* SW England, United Kingdom
Torez 109 G5 SE Ukraine
Torgau 101 D4 E Germany
Torhout 84 B6 W Belgium
Torino *see* Turin
Toriu 141 C2 E Papua New Guinea
Torneträsk 83 D2 N Sweden
Tornio 83 E3 NW Finland
Tornionjoki 83 E2 Finland/Sweden
Toro 99 C2 N Spain
Toronto 35 D6 *province capital* Ontario, S Canada
Toros Dağları *see* Taurus Mountains
Torquay 95 C5 SW England, United Kingdom
Torrance 49 C9 California, W USA
Torre, Alto da 99 A3 ▲ C Portugal
Torre del Greco 103 D6 S Italy
Torrejón de Ardoz 99 D3 C Spain
Torrelavega 99 D1 N Spain
Torrens, Lake 137 E5 *salt lake* South Australia
Torrent 99 F4 E Spain
Torreón 53 D3 NE Mexico
Torres Islands 141 G4 *island group* N Vanuatu
Torres Strait 141 A3 *strait* Australia/Papua New Guinea
Torres Vedras 99 A4 C Portugal
Torridge 95 B5 SW England, United Kingdom
Torridon, Loch 91 C3 *inlet* NW Scotland, United Kingdom
Torrington 47 F4 Wyoming, C USA
To'rtko'l 125 D2 W Uzbekistan
Tortosa 99 F3 E Spain
Toruń 105 D3 C Poland
Tory Island 89 C1 *island* NW Ireland
Tory Sound 89 C1 *sound* N Ireland
Torzhok 111 A5 W Russian Federation
Tosa-wan 133 E7 *bay* SW Japan
Toscana *see* Tuscany
Toscano, Arcipelago 103 B4 *island group* C Italy
Toshkent *see* Tashkent
Totana 99 E5 SE Spain
Tottori 133 E6 SW Japan
Touâjîl 72 B2 N Mauritania
Toubkal, Jbel 70 B2 ▲ W Morocco
Touggourt 70 E2 NE Algeria
Toukoto 72 B3 W Mali
Toul 97 E3 NE France
Toulon 97 E7 SE France
Toulouse 97 C6 S France
Touraine 97 C3 *cultural region* C France
Tourcoing 97 D1 N France
Tournai 84 B7 SW Belgium
Tours 97 C3 C France
Tovarkovskiy 111 B6 W Russian Federation
Towcester 95 E2 C England, United Kingdom
Townsville 137 G3 Queensland, NE Australia
Towraghoudi 125 D4 NW Afghanistan
Towson 39 H1 Maryland, NE USA
Towuti, Danau 131 F7 Celebes, C Indonesia
Toyama 133 F5 SW Japan
Toyama-wan 133 F5 *bay* W Japan
Toyota 133 F6 SW Japan
Tozeur 70 E2 W Tunisia
Trabzon 121 F2 NE Turkey
Traiskirchen 101 F7 NE Austria
Tralee 89 B6 SW Ireland
Tralee Bay 89 A6 *bay* SW Ireland
Transantarctic Mountains 142 C5 Antarctica
Transnistria 109 D5 *cultural region* NE Moldova
Transylvania 109 B6 *cultural region* NW Romania
Transylvanian Alps 109 B7 C Romania
Trapani 103 C7 Sicily, Italy
Traralgon 137 G6 Victoria, SE Australia
Trasimeno, Lago 103 C4 C Italy
Traverse City 40 D3 Michigan, N USA
Travis, Lake 44 G4 Texas, SW USA
Trbovlje 101 E8 C Slovenia
Třebíč 105 C6 C Czech Republic
Trebišov 105 F6 E Slovakia
Trélazé 97 C3 NW France
Trelew 65 B7 SE Argentina
Tremelo 84 C6 C Belgium
Trenčín 105 D6 W Slovakia
Trenque Lauquen 65 B6 E Argentina
Trent 93 E4 C England, United Kingdom
Trento 103 C2 N Italy
Trenton 37 D5 *state capital* New Jersey, NE USA
Tres Arroyos 65 C6 E Argentina
Tres Marías, Islas 53 C5 *island group* C Mexico
Treviso 103 D2 NE Italy
Trevose Head 95 A5 *headland* SW England, United Kingdom
Trichur 127 D7 SW India (see also Thrissur)
Trier 101 A6 SW Germany
Trieste 103 D2 NE Italy
Trikala 107 D5 C Greece
Trim 89 E4 E Ireland
Trincomalee 127 E7 NE Sri Lanka
Trinidad 65 B2 N Bolivia
Trinidad 65 C5 S Uruguay
Trinidad 47 F6 Colorado, C USA
Trinidad 57 K7 *island* C Trinidad and Tobago
Trinidad and Tobago 57 K7 ◆ *republic* SE West Indies
Trinity River 44 H4 Texas, SW USA
Tripoli 70 F2 ● NW Libya
Trípoli 107 E6 S Greece
Tripoli 123 A2 N Lebanon
Tripolitania 70 F3 *cultural region* NW Libya
Tristan da Cunha 26 *St. Helena* ◇ SE Atlantic Ocean
Trivandrum 127 D7 SW India (see also Thiruvananthapuram)
Trnava 105 D7 W Slovakia
Troglav 107 B2 ▲ Bosnia and Herzegovina/Croatia
Trois-Rivières 35 E5 Québec, SE Canada
Trollhättan 83 C6 S Sweden
Tromsø 83 D1 N Norway
Trondheim 83 B4 S Norway
Trondheimsfjorden 83 B4 *fjord* S Norway
Troódos 112 C6 C Cyprus
Troon 91 D6 W Scotland, United Kingdom
Trowbridge 95 D4 S England, United Kingdom
Troy 39 E5 Alabama, S USA
Troy 37 E4 New York, NE USA
Troyes 97 E3 N France
Trujillo 55 D2 NE Honduras
Trujillo 63 B5 NW Peru
Trujillo 99 C4 W Spain
Truro 35 G5 Nova Scotia, SE Canada
Truro 95 A6 SW England, United Kingdom
Trzcianka 105 C3 C Poland
Trzebnica 105 C4 SW Poland
Tsalka 121 H2 S Georgia
Tsarevo 107 G3 E Bulgaria
Tsetserleg 129 E2 C Mongolia
Tshela 76 B2 W Dem. Rep. Congo
Tshikapa 76 C3 SW Dem. Rep. Congo
Tshuapa 76 C2 C Dem. Rep. Congo
Tshwane 76 D6 ● NE South Africa (see also Pretoria)
Tsu 133 F6 SW Japan
Tsugaru-kaikyo 133 F3 *strait* N Japan
Tsumeb 76 C5 N Namibia
Tsuruga 133 E6 SW Japan
Tsuruoka 133 F4 C Japan
Tsushima 133 C7 *island group* SW Japan
Tuam 89 C4 W Ireland
Tuamotu Islands 135 *island group* N French Polynesia
Tuapi 55 E3 NE Nicaragua
Tuapse 111 A8 SW Russian Federation
Tuba City 44 B1 Arizona, SW USA
Tubbergen 84 F3 E Netherlands
Tubize 84 C7 C Belgium
Tubmanburg 72 B5 NW Liberia
Tucson 44 B3 Arizona, SW USA
Tucumcari 44 E2 New Mexico, SW USA
Tucuruí, Represa de 63 G4 NE Brazil
Tudela 99 E2 N Spain
Tufi 141 C3 S Papua New Guinea
Tuguegarao 131 F3 N Philippines
Tuktoyaktuk 33 F3 Northwest Territories, NW Canada
Tula 111 A6 W Russian Federation
Tulancingo 53 F5 C Mexico
Tulare Lake Bed 49 B8 *salt flat* California, W USA
Tulcán 63 B3 N Ecuador
Tulcea 109 D7 E Romania
Tulia 44 F2 Texas, SW USA
Tullamore 89 D4 C Ireland
Tulle 97 D5 C France
Tulln 101 F7 NE Austria
Tullow 89 E5 SE Ireland
Tully 137 G2 Queensland, NE Australia
Tulsa 43 D7 Oklahoma, C USA
Tulsk 89 C3 C Ireland
Tuluá 63 B3 W Colombia

◐ Administrative region ◆ Country ● Country capital ◇ Dependent territory ○ Dependent territory capital Mountain range ▲ Mountain Volcano River Lake Reservoir

ulun 118 E5 S Russian Federation
ulun Islands 141 D2 *island group* NE Papua New Guinea
umbes 63 A4 NW Peru
umen 133 B3 ≈ E Asia
umkur 127 D6 W India
ummel 91 D4 ≈ C Scotland, United Kingdom
unduru 75 D7 S Tanzania
ungsten 33 F5 Northwest Territories, W Canada
unis 70 F1 ● NE Tunisia
unis, Golfe de 112 E4 *gulf* NE Tunisia
unisia 70 E2 ◆ *republic* N Africa
unja 63 C2 C Colombia
uong Duong 131 C3 N Vietnam
upelo 39 D4 Mississippi, S USA
upiza 65 B3 S Bolivia
urangi 139 D4 North Island, New Zealand
uran Lowland 125 D2 *plain* C Asia
urayf 123 B2 NW Saudi Arabia
urbat 127 A3 SW Pakistan
urda 109 B6 NW Romania
urín 103 A2 El Salvador
urin 103 A2 NW Italy
urkana, Lake 75 D5 ◎ N Kenya
urkey 121 C3 ◆ *republic* SW Asia
urkish Republic of Northern Cyprus 112 D6 ◇ *disputed territory* Cyprus
urkistan 118 C6 S Kazakhstan
ürkmenabat 125 E3 E Turkmenistan
ürkmen Aylagy 125 B3 *lake gulf* W Turkmenistan
ürkmenbaşy 125 B2 W Turkmenistan
urkmenistan 125 B3 ◆ *republic* C Asia
urks and Caicos Islands 57 F3 *UK* ◇ N West Indies
urku 83 E5 SW Finland
urlock 49 B7 California, W USA
urnagain, Cape 139 D5 *headland* North Island, New Zealand
urnhout 84 D6 N Belgium
urnov 105 B5 N Czech Republic
urpan 129 C2 NW China
urriff 91 F3 NE Scotland, United Kingdom
uscaloosa 39 D5 Alabama, S USA
uscany 103 C4 *cultural region* C Italy Europe
uticorin 127 D7 SE India
utuila 51 *island* W American Samoa
uvalu 141 H2 ◆ *commonwealth republic* SW Pacific Ocean
uwayq, Jabal 123 C5 ▲▲ C Saudi Arabia
uxpan 53 E5 C Mexico
uxpan 53 D4 C Mexico
uxpán 53 F4 E Mexico
uxtepec 53 G5 S Mexico
uxtla 53 H5 SE Mexico
uy Hoa 131 D4 S Vietnam
uzla 107 C2 NE Bosnia and Herzegovina
uz, Lake 121 C3 ◎ C Turkey
ver' 111 A5 W Russian Federation
weed 91 E6 ≈ England/Scotland, United Kingdom
weedmouth 93 D1 N England, United Kingdom
win Falls 47 C4 Idaho, NW USA
ychy 105 E5 S Poland
yler 44 H3 Texas, SW USA
ympáki 107 F7 Crete, Greece
ynda 118 G5 SE Russian Federation
yne 91 F7 ≈ N England, United Kingdom
ynemouth 93 D2 NE England, United Kingdom
yrrhenian Sea 103 B6 *sea* N Mediterranean Sea
yumen' 118 C4 C Russian Federation
yup 125 I2 NE Kyrgyzstan
ywi 93 B6 ≈ S Wales, United Kingdom
ywyn 93 B6 W Wales, United Kingdom
ziá 107 F6 *island* Cyclades, SE Greece

U

bangi *see* Oubangui
be 133 D7 SW Japan
beda 99 D5 S Spain
beraba 63 G7 SE Brazil
berlândia 63 F7 SE Brazil
bon Ratchathani 131 C3 E Thailand
brique 99 C6 SW Spain
cayali, Río 63 B4 ≈ C Peru
chiura-wan 133 F2 *bay* NW Pacific Ocean
chquduq 125 E2 N Uzbekistan
ckfield 95 G4 SE England, United Kingdom
çtagan Gumy 125 C2 *desert* NW Turkmenistan
daipur 127 D3 N India
ddevalla 83 B6 S Sweden
dine 103 D2 NE Italy
don Thani 131 B3 N Thailand
dupi 127 D6 SW India
ele 76 C1 ≈ NE Dem. Rep. Congo
elzen 101 C3 N Germany
fa 111 D6 W Russian Federation
ganda 75 C5 ◆ *republic* E Africa
ig 91 B3 N Scotland, United Kingdom
íge 76 B3 NW Angola
inta Mountains 47 D5 ▲▲ Utah, W USA
itenhage 76 D7 S South Africa
ithoorn 84 D4 C Netherlands
khta 111 D4 NW Russian Federation
kiah 49 B6 California, W USA
kmergė 83 E7 C Lithuania
kraine 109 C4 ◆ *republic* SE Europe
laanbaatar *see* Ulan Bator
Ulaangom 129 D1 NW Mongolia
Ulan Bator 129 E2 ● C Mongolia
Ulanhad 129 G2 N China (see also Chifeng)
Ulanhot 129 G2 N China
Ulan Qab 129 F3 N China
Ulan-Ude 118 F5 S Russian Federation
Ulft 84 E4 E Netherlands
Ullapool 91 C3 N Scotland, United Kingdom
Ullswater 93 C3 ◎ NW England, United Kingdom
Ulm 101 C7 S Germany
Ulsan 133 C6 SE South Korea
Ulsta 91 B6 NE Scotland, United Kingdom
Ulster 89 D2 *cultural region* N Ireland
Ulungur Hu 129 C2 ◎ NW China
Uluru 137 D4 *rocky outcrop* Northern Territory, C Australia
Ulverston 93 C4 NW England, United Kingdom
Ul'yanovsk 111 C6 W Russian Federation
Umán 53 H4 SE Mexico
Uman' 109 D5 C Ukraine
Umbro-Marchigiano, Appennino 103 D4 ▲▲ C Italy
Umeå 83 D4 N Sweden
Umeälven 83 D3 ≈ N Sweden
Umiat 50 E1 Alaska, USA
Umm Buru 75 A2 W Sudan
Umm Ruwaba 75 C3 C Sudan
Umnak Island 50 B2 *island* Aleutian Islands, Alaska, USA
Umtata 76 D7 SE South Africa
Una 107 B1 ≈ Bosnia and Herzegovina/Croatia
Unac 107 B2 ≈ W Bosnia and Herzegovina
Unalaska Island 50 B3 *island* Aleutian Islands, Alaska, USA
Uncía 65 B2 C Bolivia
Uncompahgre Peak 47 E6 ▲ Colorado, C USA
Ungava Bay 35 E2 *bay* Québec, E Canada
Ungava Peninsula 35 D1 *peninsula* Québec, SE Canada
Üngüz Angyrsyndaky Garagum 125 C3 *desert* N Turkmenistan
Unimak Island 50 B3 *island* Aleutian Islands, Alaska, USA
Union City 39 D3 Tennessee, S USA
Uniontown 37 B5 Pennsylvania, NE USA
United Arab Emirates 123 E4 ◆ *federation* SW Asia
United Kingdom 87 D5 ◆ *monarchy* NW Europe
United States of America 29 ◆ *federal republic* North America
Unst 91 B5 *island* NE Scotland, United Kingdom
Ünye 121 E2 W Turkey
Upala 55 E5 NW Costa Rica
Upemba, Lac 76 D3 ◎ SE Dem. Rep. Congo
Upolu 141 B5 *island* SE Samoa
Upper Darby 37 D5 Pennsylvania, NE USA
Upper Klamath Lake 49 B4 ◎ Oregon, NW USA
Upper Lough Erne 89 D3 ◎ Ireland/United Kingdom
Upper Red Lake 43 E2 ◎ Minnesota, N USA
Uppsala 83 D5 C Sweden
Uqsuqtuuq *see* Gjoa Haven
Ural 118 B4 ≈ Kazakhstan/Russian Federation (see also Zhayyk)
Ural Mountains 118 C3 ▲▲ Kazakhstan/Russian Federation
Ural'sk 118 B4 NW Kazakhstan
Ural'skiye Gory *see* Ural Mountains
Urbandale 43 E5 Iowa, C USA
Ure 93 D3 ≈ N England, United Kingdom
Uren' 111 C5 W Russian Federation
Urganch 125 D2 W Uzbekistan
Urgut 125 F3 C Uzbekistan
Urlingford 89 D5 SE Ireland
Urmia, Lake 123 C1 ◎ NW Iran
Uroteppa 125 F3 NW Tajikistan
Uruapan 53 E5 SW Mexico
Uruguay 65 C5 ◆ *republic* E South America
Uruguay 65 C5 ≈ E South America
Ürümqi 129 C2 NW China
Urup, Ostrov 118 I4 *island* Kurile Islands, Russian Federation
Uruzgan 125 F5 C Afghanistan
Usa 111 E3 ≈ NW Russian Federation
Uşak 120 B3 W Turkey
Ushuaia 65 B9 S Argentina
Usinsk 111 D3 NW Russian Federation
Usk 93 B6 ≈ SE Wales, United Kingdom
Usol'ye-Sibirskoye 118 F5 C Russian Federation
Ussel 97 D5 C France
Ussuriysk 118 H6 SE Russian Federation
Ustica 103 C7 Sicily, Italy
Ust'-Ilimsk 118 F4 C Russian Federation
Ústí nad Labem 105 B5 NW Czech Republic
Ustka 105 C1 N Poland
Ust'-Kamchatsk 118 I3 E Russian Federation
Ust'-Kamenogorsk 118 D5 E Kazakhstan
Ust'-Kut 118 F5 C Russian Federation
Ustyurt Plateau 125 C1 *plateau* Kazakhstan/Uzbekistan
Usulután 55 C4 SE El Salvador
Usumacinta, Río 55 A2 ≈ Guatemala/Mexico
Utah 47 C5 ◈ *state* W USA
Utah Lake 47 C5 ◎ Utah, W USA
Utica 37 D3 New York, NE USA
Utrecht 84 D4 C Netherlands
Utsunomiya 133 G5 S Japan
Uttaranchal 127 E2 *state* N India
Uttar Pradesh 127 E3 *state* N India
Uttoxeter 93 D5 C England, United Kingdom
Utupua 141 G3 *island* E Solomon Islands
Uulu 83 E6 SW Estonia
Uvalde 44 G5 Texas, SW USA
Uvs Nuur 129 D1 ◎ Mongolia/Russian Federation
'Uwaynāt, Jabal al 75 B1 ▲ Libya/Sudan
Uyo 72 F5 S Nigeria
Uyuni 65 B3 W Bolivia
Uzbekistan 125 D2 ◆ *republic* C Asia
Uzhhorod 109 B5 W Ukraine

V

Vaal 76 D6 ≈ C South Africa
Vaals 84 E7 SE Netherlands
Vaasa 83 D4 W Finland
Vaassen 84 E4 E Netherlands
Vác 105 E7 N Hungary
Vadodara 127 C4 W India
Vaduz 101 C8 ● W Liechtenstein
Váh 105 D6 ≈ W Slovakia
Vaitogi 51 W American Samoa
Vaitupu 141 J2 *atoll* C Tuvalu
Valdai Hills 111 A5 *hill range* W Russian Federation
Valday 111 A4 W Russian Federation
Valdecañas, Embalse de 99 C4 ⊠ W Spain
Valdepeñas 99 D4 C Spain
Valdés, Península 65 B7 *peninsula* SE Argentina
Valdez 50 E3 Alaska, USA
Valdivia 65 A6 C Chile
Val-d'Or 35 D5 Québec, SE Canada
Valdosta 39 F6 Georgia, SE USA
Valence 97 E5 E France
Valencia 99 F4 E Spain
Valencia 63 D1 N Venezuela
Valencia, Gulf of 99 F4 *gulf* E Spain
Valencia Island 89 A6 *island* SW Ireland
Valenciennes 97 E1 N France
Valentine 43 B4 Nebraska, C USA
Valjevo 107 D2 W Serbia
Valkenswaard 84 D5 S Netherlands
Valladolid 53 I4 SE Mexico
Valladolid 99 D2 NW Spain
Vall d'Uxó 99 F4 E Spain
Vallejo 49 B6 California, W USA
Vallenar 65 A4 N Chile
Valletta 112 B6 ● E Malta
Valley City 43 C2 North Dakota, N USA
Válljohka 83 E1 N Norway
Valls 99 G3 NE Spain
Valparaíso 65 A5 C Chile
Valparaiso 40 C5 Indiana, N USA
Valverde del Camino 99 C5 SW Spain
Van 121 G3 E Turkey
Vanadzor 121 H2 N Armenia
Van Buren 37 G1 Maine, NE USA
Vanceboro 37 H2 Maine, NE USA
Vancouver 33 F7 British Columbia, SW Canada
Vancouver 49 B3 Washington, NW USA
Vancouver Island 33 E7 *island* British Columbia, SW Canada
Van Diemen Gulf 137 D1 *gulf* Northern Territory, N Australia
Vänern 83 C6 ◎ S Sweden
Vangaindrano 76 G6 SE Madagascar
Van Gölü *see* Van, Lake
Van Horn 44 E4 Texas, SW USA
Vanikolo 141 G3 *island* Santa Cruz Islands, E Solomon Islands
Vanimo 141 A1 NW Papua New Guinea
Van, Lake 121 G4 *salt lake* E Turkey
Vannes 97 B3 NW France
Vantaa 83 E5 S Finland
Vanua Lava 141 G4 *island* Banks Islands, N Vanuatu
Vanua Levu 141 J5 *island* N Fiji
Vanuatu 141 E4 ◆ *republic* SW Pacific Ocean
Van Wert 40 D6 Ohio, N USA
Vao 141 G6 S New Caledonia
Varanasi 127 F3 N India
Varangerfjorden 83 F1 *fjord* N Norway
Varangerhalvøya 83 E1 *peninsula* N Norway
Varaždin 107 B1 N Croatia
Varberg 83 B6 S Sweden
Vardar 107 E4 ≈ FYR Macedonia/Greece
Varde 83 B7 W Denmark
Varese 103 B2 N Italy
Vârful Moldoveanu 109 B6 ▲ C Romania
Varkaus 83 F4 C Finland
Varna 107 G2 E Bulgaria
Varnenski Zaliv 120 A1 *bay* E Bulgaria
Vasa *see* Vaasa
Vasilikí 107 D5 Lefkáda, Ionian Islands, W Greece
Vaslui 109 D6 C Romania
Västerås 83 C5 C Sweden
Vatican City 103 C5 ◆ *papal state* S Europe
Vatnajökull 83 A1 *glacier* SE Iceland
Vättern 83 C6 ◎ S Sweden
Vaughn 44 D2 New Mexico, SW USA
Vaupés, Río 63 C3 ≈ Brazil/Colombia
Vavuniya 127 E7 N Sri Lanka
Vawkavysk 109 B3 W Belarus
Växjö 83 C6 S Sweden
Vaygach, Ostrov 111 E2 *island* NW Russian Federation
Veendam 84 F2 NE Netherlands
Veenendaal 84 D4 C Netherlands
Vega 83 C3 *island* C Norway
Veisiejai 83 E7 S Lithuania
Vejer de la Frontera 99 C6 SW Spain
Veldhoven 84 D5 S Netherlands
Velebit 107 B2 ▲▲ C Croatia
Velenje 101 E8 N Slovenia
Velika Morava 107 D2 ≈ C Serbia
Velikiye Luki 111 A5 W Russian Federation
Velikiy Novgorod 111 A4 W Russian Federation
Veliko Turnovo 107 F3 N Bulgaria
Vel'ký Krtíš 105 E7 C Slovakia
Vella Lavella 141 D2 *island* New Georgia Islands, NW Solomon Islands
Vellore 127 E6 SE India
Velsen-Noord 84 C3 W Netherlands
Vel'sk 111 C4 NW Russian Federation
Vendôme 97 C3 C France
Venezia *see* Venice
Venezuela 63 C2 ◆ *republic* N South America
Venezuela, Gulf of 63 C1 *gulf* NW Venezuela
Venice 103 D2 NE Italy
Venice 39 C7 Louisiana, S USA
Venice, Gulf of 103 D3 *gulf* N Adriatic Sea
Venlo 84 E5 SE Netherlands
Venta 83 E6 ≈ Latvia/Lithuania
Vent, Îles du 141 A6 *island group* Archipel de la Société, W French Polynesia
Ventimiglia 103 A3 NW Italy
Ventspils 83 E6 NW Latvia
Vera 65 C4 C Argentina
Veracruz 53 F5 E Mexico
Vercelli 103 B2 NW Italy
Verdalsøra 83 C4 C Norway
Verde, Costa 99 D1 *coastal region* N Spain
Verden 101 B3 NW Germany
Verkhoyanskiy Khrebet 118 G3 ▲▲ NE Russian Federation
Vermillion 43 D4 South Dakota, N USA
Vermont 37 E3 ◈ *state* NE USA
Vernal 47 D5 Utah, W USA
Vernon 44 G2 Texas, SW USA
Verona 103 C2 NE Italy
Versailles 97 D2 N France
Verviers 84 E7 E Belgium
Vesdre 84 E7 ≈ E Belgium
Vesoul 97 F3 E France
Vesterålen 83 C2 *island* NW Norway
Vestfjorden 83 C2 *fjord* C Norway
Vestmannaeyjar 83 A2 S Iceland
Vesuvius 103 D6 ⩓ S Italy
Veszprém 105 D8 W Hungary
Veurne 84 A6 W Belgium
Viacha 65 A2 W Bolivia
Viana do Castelo 99 B2 NW Portugal
Vianen 84 D4 C Netherlands
Viareggio 103 B3 C Italy
Viborg 83 B6 NW Denmark
Vic 99 G2 NE Spain
Vicenza 103 C2 NE Italy
Vichy 97 D4 C France
Vicksburg 39 C5 Mississippi, S USA
Victoria 67 ● SW Seychelles
Victoria 33 E7 *province capital* Vancouver Island, British Columbia, SW Canada
Victoria 112 A6 NW Malta
Victoria 44 H5 Texas, SW USA
Victoria 137 F6 ◈ *state* SE Australia
Victoria Falls 76 C5 *waterfall* Zambia/Zimbabwe
Victoria Island 33 G3 *island* Northwest Territories/Nunavut, NW Canada
Victoria, Lake 75 C5 ◎ Kenya/Tanzania/Uganda
Victoria Land 142 D6 *physical region* Antarctica
Victoria, Mount 141 I5 ▲ Viti Levu, W Fiji
Victoria River 137 D2 ≈ Western Australia
Victorville 49 D8 California, W USA
Vidalia 39 F5 Georgia, SE USA
Vidin 107 E2 NW Bulgaria
Viedma 65 B7 E Argentina
Vienna 101 F7 ● NE Austria
Vienne 97 E5 E France
Vienne 97 C4 ≈ W France
Vientiane 131 B3 ● C Laos
Vieques 51 E Puerto Rico
Vieques, Isla de 51 *island* E Puerto Rico
Vierzon 97 D3 C France
Vietnam 131 C4 ◆ *republic* SE Asia
Vieux Fort 57 K6 S Saint Lucia
Vigo 99 B2 NW Spain
Vijayawada 127 E5 SE India
Vila do Conde 99 B2 NW Portugal
Vilafranca del Penedès 99 G2 NE Spain
Viļaka 83 F6 NE Latvia
Vilalba 99 B1 NW Spain
Vila Nova de Gaia 99 B3 NW Portugal
Vila Real 99 B3 N Portugal
Vilhelmina 83 C3 N Sweden
Viliya 109 C2 ≈ W Belarus
Villa Acuña 53 E2 NE Mexico
Villa Bella 65 B1 N Bolivia
Villacarrillo 99 E5 S Spain
Villach 101 E8 S Austria
Villacidro 103 A6 Sardinia, Italy
Villafranca de los Barros 99 C4 W Spain
Villahermosa 53 H5 SE Mexico
Villajoyosa 99 F4 E Spain
Villa María 65 B5 C Argentina
Villa Martín 65 A3 SW Bolivia
Villanueva 53 E4 C Mexico
Villanueva de la Serena 99 C4 W Spain
Villanueva de los Infantes 99 E4 C Spain
Villarrica 65 C4 SE Paraguay
Villavicencio 63 C2 C Colombia
Villaviciosa 99 C1 N Spain
Villazón 65 B3 S Bolivia
Villena 99 F4 E Spain
Villeurbanne 97 E5 E France
Villingen-Schwenningen 101 B7 S Germany
Vilnius 83 F7 ● SE Lithuania
Vilvoorde 84 C6 C Belgium
Vilyuy 118 G4 ≈ NE Russian Federation
Viña del Mar 65 A5 C Chile
Vinaròs 99 F3 E Spain
Vincennes 40 C7 Indiana, N USA
Vindhya Range 127 D4 ▲▲ N India
Vineland 37 D5 New Jersey, NE USA
Vinh 131 C3 N Vietnam
Vinita 43 E7 Oklahoma, C USA
Vinnytsya 109 D5 C Ukraine
Vinson Massif 142 A4 ▲ Antarctica
Viranşehir 121 F4 SE Turkey
Virginia 89 D3 N Ireland
Virginia 43 E2 Minnesota, N USA
Virginia 39 H2 ◈ *state* NE USA
Virginia Beach 39 I2 Virginia, NE USA
Virgin Islands (USA) 51 *US* ◇ E West Indies
Virgin Passage 51 *passage* Puerto Rico/Virgin Islands (USA)
Virovitica 107 C1 NE Croatia
Virton 84 D9 SE Belgium
Vis 107 B3 *island* S Croatia
Visakhapatnam 127 F5 SE India
Visalia 49 C7 California, W USA
Visby 83 D6 SE Sweden
Viscount Melville Sound 33 G2 *sound* Northwest Territories, N Canada
Visé 84 E7 E Belgium
Viseu 99 B3 N Portugal
Vistula 105 E2 ≈ C Poland
Vistula Lagoon 105 E1 *lagoon* Poland/Russian Federation
Viterbo 103 C4 C Italy
Vitiaz Strait 141 B2 *strait* NE Papua New Guinea
Viti Levu 141 I5 *island* W Fiji
Vitim 118 G5 ≈ C Russian Federation
Vitória 63 H7 SE Brazil
Vitória da Conquista 63 H6 E Brazil
Vitoria-Gasteiz 99 E2 N Spain
Vitré 97 B3 NW France
Vitsyebsk 109 D2 NE Belarus
Vittoria 103 D8 Sicily, Italy
Vizianagaram 127 F5 E India
Vlaardingen 84 C4 SW Netherlands
Vladikavkaz 111 B9 SW Russian Federation
Vladimir 111 B5 W Russian Federation
Vladivostok 118 H6 SE Russian Federation
Vlagtwedde 84 F2 NE Netherlands
Vlieland 84 C2 *island* Waddeneilanden, N Netherlands
Vlijmen 84 D5 S Netherlands
Vlissingen 84 B5 SW Netherlands
Vlorë 107 C4 SW Albania
Vöcklabruck 101 E7 NW Austria
Vohimena, Tanjona 76 F6 *headland* S Madagascar
Voiron 97 E5 E France
Vojvodina 107 D1 *cultural region* N Serbia
Volga 111 B7 ≈ NW Russian Federation
Volga Uplands 111 B6 ▲▲ W Russian Federation
Volgodonsk 111 A7 SW Russian Federation
Volgograd 111 B7 SW Russian Federation
Volkhov 111 A4 NW Russian Federation
Volnovakha 109 G5 SE Ukraine
Volodymyr-Volyns'kyy 109 B4 NW Ukraine
Vologda 111 B4 W Russian Federation
Vólos 107 E5 C Greece
Vol'sk 111 C6 W Russian Federation
Volta 72 D5 ≈ SE Ghana
Volta, Lake 72 D5 ⊠ SE Ghana
Volturno 103 D5 ≈ S Italy
Volzhskiy 111 B7 SW Russian Federation
Voorst 84 E4 E Netherlands
Vorderrhein 101 B8 ≈ SE Switzerland
Vorkuta 111 E3 NW Russian Federation
Voronezh 111 A6 W Russian Federation
Võrtsjärv 83 E6 ◎ SE Estonia
Võru 83 F6 SE Estonia
Vosges 97 F3 ▲▲ NE France
Vostok 142 D5 *Russian research station* Antarctica
Vranov nad Topľou 105 F6 E Slovakia
Vratsa 107 E3 NW Bulgaria
Vrbas 107 C1 NW Serbia
Vrbas 107 C2 ≈ N Bosnia and Herzegovina
Vršac 107 D1 NE Serbia
Vsetín 105 D6 E Czech Republic
Vukovar 107 C1 E Croatia
Vulcano, Isola 103 D7 *island* Aeolian Islands, Italy
Vung Tau 131 C4 S Vietnam
Vunisea 141 J5 SE Fiji
Vyatka 111 C5 ≈ NW Russian Federation
Vyborg 111 A4 NW Russian Federation

Wa 72 D4 NW Ghana
Waal 84 D4 ≈ S Netherlands
Waala 141 F6 W New Caledonia
Wabash 40 D6 Indiana, N USA
Wabash River 40 D6 ≈ N USA
Waco 44 H4 Texas, SW USA
Waddan 70 G3 NW Libya
Waddeneilanden *see* West Frisian Islands
Waddenzee 84 D2 *sea* SE North Sea
Waddington, Mount 33 E7 ▲ British Columbia, SW Canada
Wadebridge 95 B5 SW England, United Kingdom
Wadi Halfa 75 C1 N Sudan
Wad Medani 75 C2 C Sudan
Waflia 131 G7 E Indonesia
Wagga Wagga 137 G6 New South Wales, SE Australia
Wagin 137 B5 Western Australia
Wah 127 C1 NE Pakistan
Wahai 131 G7 E Indonesia
Wahiawā 51 B1 O'ahu, Hawaii, USA
Wahibah Sands 123 E5 *desert* N Oman
Wahpeton 43 D2 North Dakota, N USA
Waiau 139 A8 ≈ South Island, New Zealand
Waigeo, Pulau 131 G6 *island* Maluku, E Indonesia
Waikaremoana, Lake 139 E3 ◎ North Island, New Zealand
Wailuku 51 C2 Maui, Hawaii, USA
Waimate 139 B7 South Island, New Zealand
Waimea 51 D2 Hawaii, USA
Waiouru 139 D4 North Island, New Zealand
Waipara 139 C6 South Island, New Zealand
Waipawa 139 D4 North Island, New Zealand
Waipukurau 139 D4 North Island, New Zealand
Wairau 139 C5 ≈ South Island, New Zealand
Wairoa 139 E4 North Island, New Zealand
Wairoa 139 D2 ≈ North Island, New Zealand
Waitaki 139 B7 ≈ South Island, New Zealand
Waitara 139 C4 North Island, New Zealand
Waiuku 139 D3 North Island, New Zealand
Wakasa-wan 133 E6 *bay* C Japan
Wakatipu, Lake 139 B7 ◎ South Island, New Zealand
Wakayama 133 E6 SW Japan
Wakefield 93 D4 N England, United Kingdom
Wakkanai 133 F1 NE Japan
Wałbrzych 105 C5 SW Poland
Walcourt 84 C8 S Belgium
Wałcz 105 C2 NW Poland
Wales 50 D1 Alaska, USA
Wales 93 B6 ◈ *national region* Wales, United Kingdom
Walgett 137 G5 New South Wales, SE Australia
Walker Lake 47 A6 ◎ Nevada, W USA
Wallace 47 B2 Idaho, NW USA
Wallachia 109 B7 *cultural region* S Romania
Wallasey 93 C4 NW England, United Kingdom
Walla Walla 49 C3 Washington, NW USA
Wallis and Futuna 141 I4 *French* ◇ C Pacific Ocean
Wallis, Îles 141 K4 *island group* N Wallis and Futuna
Walney, Isle of 93 C3 *island* NW England, United Kingdom
Walnut Ridge 39 C3 Arkansas, C USA
Walsall 93 D6 C England, United Kingdom
Walvis Bay 76 B5 NW Namibia
Wanaka 139 B7 South Island, New Zealand
Wanaka, Lake 139 A7 ◎ South Island, New Zealand
Wandel Sea 143 C5 *sea* Arctic Ocean
Wanganui 139 D4 North Island, New Zealand
Wangaratta 137 G6 Victoria, SE Australia
Wanlaweyn 75 F5 SW Somalia
Wanzhou 129 F4 C China
Warangal 127 E5 C India
Warburg 101 B4 W Germany
Ware 33 E6 British Columbia, W Canada
Waremme 84 D7 E Belgium
Waren 101 D3 NE Germany
Warkworth 139 D2 North Island, New Zealand
Warminster 95 D4 S England, United Kingdom
Warm Springs 47 B6 Nevada, W USA
Warnemünde 101 D2 NE Germany
Warner 43 E8 Oklahoma, C USA
Warnes 65 B2 C Bolivia
Warrego River 137 G5 *seasonal river* New South Wales/Queensland, E Australia
Warren 40 E5 Michigan, N USA
Warren 40 F6 Ohio, N USA
Warren 37 B4 Pennsylvania, NE USA
Warri 72 E5 S Nigeria
Warrington 93 C4 C England, United Kingdom
Warrnambool 137 F6 Victoria, SE Australia
Warsaw 105 F3 ● C Poland
Warszawa *see* Warsaw
Warta 105 D4 ≈ W Poland

◈ Administrative region ◆ Country ● Country capital ◇ Dependent territory ○ Dependent territory capital ▲▲ Mountain range ▲ Mountain ⩓ Volcano ≈ River ◎ Lake ⊠ Reservoir

Warwick 137 H5 Queensland, E Australia
Warwick 93 D6 C England, United Kingdom
Warwick 37 F4 Rhode Island, NE USA
Washington 93 D2 NE England, United Kingdom
Washington 40 C7 Indiana, N USA
Washington 49 B2 ◈ state NW USA
Washington DC 39 H1 ● District of Columbia, NE USA
Washington, Mount 37 F3 ▲ New Hampshire, NE USA
Wash, The 95 G1 inlet E England, United Kingdom
Waspam 55 E3 NE Nicaragua
Waterbury 37 E4 Connecticut, NE USA
Waterford 89 D6 S Ireland
Waterloo 43 F4 Iowa, C USA
Watersmeet 40 B2 Michigan, N USA
Watertown 37 D3 New York, NE USA
Watertown 43 D3 South Dakota, N USA
Waterville 89 A6 SW Ireland
Waterville 37 G2 Maine, NE USA
Watford 95 F3 E England, United Kingdom
Watford City 43 A2 North Dakota, N USA
Watrous 44 E2 New Mexico, SW USA
Watsa 76 D1 NE Dem. Rep. Congo
Watts Bar Lake 39 E3 ⊠ Tennessee, S USA
Wau 75 B4 C South Sudan
Waukegan 40 C5 Illinois, N USA
Waukesha 40 C4 Wisconsin, N USA
Wausau 40 B3 Wisconsin, N USA
Waveney 95 H2 ≈ E England, United Kingdom
Waverly 43 F4 Iowa, C USA
Wavre 84 C7 C Belgium
Wawa 35 C5 Ontario, S Canada
Wawa, Río 55 E3 ≈ NE Nicaragua
Waycross 39 F6 Georgia, SE USA
Wé 141 G6 E New Caledonia
Weald, The 95 G4 lowlands SE England, United Kingdom
Weam 141 A3 SW Papua New Guinea
Wear 93 D2 ≈ N England, United Kingdom
Webster City 43 E4 Iowa, C USA
Weddell Plain 142 B3 undersea feature SW Atlantic Ocean
Weddell Sea 142 B3 sea SW Atlantic Ocean
Weed 49 B5 California, W USA
Weener 101 B3 NW Germany
Weert 84 E6 SE Netherlands
Weesp 84 D4 C Netherlands
Węgorzewo 105 F2 NE Poland
Weimar 101 C5 C Germany
Weiser 47 B3 Idaho, NW USA
Weissenburg in Bayern 101 C6 SE Germany
Weiswampach 84 E8 N Luxembourg
Wejherowo 105 D1 NW Poland
Weldiya 75 E3 N Ethiopia
Welkom 76 D6 C South Africa
Welland 93 F5 ≈ C England, United Kingdom
Wellesley Islands 137 F2 island group Queensland, N Australia
Wellingborough 95 F2 C England, United Kingdom
Wellington 139 D5 ● North Island, New Zealand
Wellington 95 C4 SW England, United Kingdom
Wellington 43 D7 Kansas, C USA
Wellington 44 F2 Texas, SW USA
Wellington, Isla 65 A8 island S Chile
Wells 47 C5 Nevada, W USA
Wellsford 139 D2 North Island, New Zealand
Wells, Lake 137 C4 ◎ Western Australia
Wells-next-the-Sea 95 G1 E England, United Kingdom
Wels 101 E7 N Austria
Welshpool 93 C5 E Wales, United Kingdom
Wemmel 84 C6 C Belgium
Wenatchee 49 C2 Washington, NW USA
Wenchi 72 D5 W Ghana
Wenquan 129 C4 C China
Wenzhou 129 G5 SE China
Werkendam 84 D5 S Netherlands
Weser 101 B3 ≈ NW Germany
Wessel Islands 137 E1 island group Northern Territory, N Australia
West Antarctica 142 B5 physical region Antarctica
West Bank 123 H6 disputed region SW Asia
West Bend 40 C4 Wisconsin, N USA
West Bengal 127 F4 state NE India
West Bromwich 93 D6 C England, United Kingdom
West Burra 91 A6 island NE Scotland, United Kingdom
West Des Moines 43 E5 Iowa, C USA
Westerland 101 B2 N Germany
Western Australia 137 B3 ◈ state W Australia
Western Dvina 83 F6 ≈ W Europe
Western Ghats 127 C5 ▲▲ SW India
Western Sahara 70 A3 Disputed ◇ N Africa
Western Sayans 118 E5 ▲▲ S Russian Federation
Western Scheldt 84 B5 inlet S North Sea
West Falkland 65 B8 island W Falkland Islands
West Fargo 43 D2 North Dakota, N USA
West Frisian Islands 84 D1 island group N Netherlands
Westhope 43 B1 North Dakota, N USA
West Memphis 39 C3 Arkansas, C USA
Weston-super-Mare 95 D4 SW England, United Kingdom
West Palm Beach 39 G8 Florida, SE USA
Westport 89 B3 W Ireland
Westport 139 C5 South Island, New Zealand
Westray 91 E1 island NE Scotland, United Kingdom
West Siberian Plain 118 D4 plain C Russian Federation
West Virginia 39 F2 ◈ state NE USA
Wetar, Pulau 131 E8 island Kepulauan Damar, E Indonesia
Wetherby 93 D4 N England, United Kingdom
Wetzlar 101 B5 W Germany
Wevok 50 E1 Alaska, USA
Wewak 141 A1 NW Papua New Guinea
Wexford 89 E6 SE Ireland
Weyburn 33 H7 Saskatchewan, S Canada
Weymouth 95 D5 S England, United Kingdom
Wezep 84 E3 E Netherlands
Whakatane 139 E3 North Island, New Zealand
Whale Cove 33 H4 Nunavut, C Canada
Whalsay 91 B6 island NE Scotland, United Kingdom
Whangarei 139 D2 North Island, New Zealand
Wharfe 93 D3 ≈ N England, United Kingdom
Whataroa 139 B6 South Island, New Zealand
Wheatland 47 F4 Wyoming, C USA
Wheeler Peak 47 C5 ▲ Nevada, W USA
Wheeler Peak 44 D1 ▲ New Mexico, SW USA
Wheeling 39 G1 West Virginia, NE USA
Whernside 93 C3 ▲ N England, United Kingdom
Whitby 93 E3 N England, United Kingdom
Whitchurch 93 C5 W England, United Kingdom
Whitefish 47 C1 Montana, NW USA
Whitehaven 93 B3 NW England, United Kingdom
Whitehead 89 F2 E Northern Ireland, United Kingdom
Whitehorse 33 E5 territory capital Yukon Territory, W Canada
White Nile 75 C3 ≈ C South Sudan
White River 43 F8 ≈ Arkansas, SE USA
White River 47 E5 ≈ Colorado/Utah, C USA
White River 40 C7 ≈ Indiana, N USA
White River 43 B4 ≈ South Dakota, N USA
White Sea 111 B3 sea Arctic Ocean
Whites Town 89 E3 NE Ireland
White Sulphur Springs 47 D2 Montana, NW USA
White Volta 72 D4 ≈ Burkina/Ghana
Whitewater Baldy 44 C3 ▲ New Mexico, SW USA
Whithorn 91 D7 S Scotland, United Kingdom
Whitianga 139 D2 North Island, New Zealand
Whitley Bay 93 D2 NE England, United Kingdom
Whitney, Mount 49 C7 ▲ California, W USA
Whitstable 95 H4 SE England, United Kingdom
Whitsunday Group 137 H3 island group Queensland, E Australia
Whyalla 137 E5 South Australia
Wichita 43 D7 Kansas, C USA
Wichita Falls 44 G2 Texas, SW USA
Wick 91 E2 N Scotland, United Kingdom
Wickenburg 44 B2 Arizona, SW USA
Wicklow 89 E5 E Ireland
Wicklow Mountains 89 E5 ▲▲ E Ireland
Widnes 93 C4 NW England, United Kingdom
Wieliczka 105 E5 S Poland
Wieluń 105 D4 C Poland
Wien see Vienna
Wiener Neustadt 101 F7 E Austria
Wierden 84 E3 E Netherlands
Wiesbaden 101 B5 W Germany
Wigan 93 C4 NW England, United Kingdom
Wigston 93 E6 C England, United Kingdom
Wigton 93 C2 NW England, United Kingdom
Wigtown 91 D7 S Scotland, United Kingdom
Wigtown Bay 91 D7 bay SW Scotland, United Kingdom
Wijchen 84 E5 SE Netherlands
Wijk bij Duurstede 84 D4 C Netherlands
Wilcannia 137 F5 New South Wales, SE Australia
Wilhelm, Mount 141 A2 ▲ C Papua New Guinea
Wilhelmshaven 101 B3 NW Germany
Wilkes Barre 37 D5 Pennsylvania, NE USA
Wilkes Land 142 E5 physical region Antarctica
Willard 44 D2 New Mexico, SW USA
Willcox 44 C3 Arizona, SW USA
Willebroek 84 C6 C Belgium
Willemstad 57 H7 ○ SE Curaçao
Williamsport 37 C5 Pennsylvania, NE USA
Williston 43 A1 North Dakota, N USA
Willow Springs 43 F7 Missouri, C USA
Wilmington 37 D5 Delaware, NE USA
Wilmington 39 H4 North Carolina, SE USA
Wilmington 40 E7 Ohio, N USA
Wilmslow 93 D4 W England, United Kingdom
Wilrijk 84 C6 N Belgium
Wilton 37 F2 Maine, NE USA
Winchester 95 E4 S England, United Kingdom
Winchester 39 H1 Virginia, NE USA
Windermere 93 C3 ◎ NW England, United Kingdom
Windhoek 76 B5 ● C Namibia
Wind Mountain 44 D3 ▲ New Mexico, SW USA
Windorah 137 F4 Queensland, C Australia
Windsor 35 C6 Ontario, S Canada
Windsor 95 F3 S England, United Kingdom
Windsor 37 E4 Connecticut, NE USA
Windward Islands 57 K6 island group E West Indies
Windward Passage 57 E4 channel Cuba/Haiti
Winisk 35 C3 ≈ Ontario, S Canada
Winnebago, Lake 40 C4 ◎ Wisconsin, N USA
Winnemucca 47 B5 Nevada, W USA
Winnipeg 33 H7 province capital Manitoba, S Canada
Winnipeg, Lake 33 H6 ◎ Manitoba, C Canada
Winona 43 F3 Minnesota, N USA
Winschoten 84 F2 NE Netherlands
Winsen 101 C3 N Germany
Winslow 44 B2 Arizona, SW USA
Winston Salem 39 G3 North Carolina, SE USA
Winsum 84 D2 NE Netherlands
Winterswijk 84 F4 E Netherlands
Winterthur 101 B7 NE Switzerland
Winton 137 F3 Queensland, E Australia
Winton 139 B8 South Island, New Zealand
Wisbech 95 G2 E England, United Kingdom
Wisconsin 40 B3 ◈ state N USA
Wisconsin Dells 40 B4 Wisconsin, N USA
Wisconsin Rapids 40 B4 Wisconsin, N USA
Wisconsin River 40 B4 ≈ Wisconsin, N USA
Wisła see Vistula
Wismar 101 C2 N Germany
Witham 93 F5 ≈ E England, United Kingdom
Withernsea 93 F4 E England, United Kingdom
Witney 95 E3 S England, United Kingdom
Wittenberge 101 D3 N Germany
Wittlich 101 A5 SW Germany
Wittstock 101 D3 NE Germany
Witu Islands 141 C2 island group E Papua New Guinea
Władysławowo 105 D1 N Poland
Włocławek 105 E3 C Poland
Włodawa 105 G4 SE Poland
Wlotzkasbaken 76 B5 W Namibia
Wodonga 137 G6 Victoria, SE Australia
Wodzisław Śląski 105 D5 S Poland
Woking 95 F4 SE England, United Kingdom
Wokingham 95 F4 S England, United Kingdom
Wolds, The 93 F5 hill range E England, United Kingdom
Wolds, The 93 F4 hill range N England, United Kingdom
Wolf Point 47 F1 Montana, NW USA
Wolf River 40 C3 ≈ Wisconsin, N USA
Wolfsberg 101 E8 SE Austria
Wolfsburg 101 C4 N Germany
Wolgast 101 D2 NE Germany
Wollaston Lake 33 H5 Saskatchewan, C Canada
Wollongong 137 G6 New South Wales, SE Australia
Wolvega 84 E2 N Netherlands
Wolverhampton 93 D5 C England, United Kingdom
Wonju 133 B5 N South Korea
Wonsan 133 B5 SE North Korea
Woodburn 49 B3 Oregon, NW USA
Woodland 49 B6 California, W USA
Woodlark Island 141 C3 island SE Papua New Guinea
Woodruff 40 B3 Wisconsin, N USA
Woods, Lake of the 35 A4 ◎ Canada/USA
Woodville 139 D4 North Island, New Zealand
Woodward 43 C7 Oklahoma, C USA
Wooler 93 D1 N England, United Kingdom
Wootton Bassett 95 E3 S England, United Kingdom
Worcester 76 C7 SW South Africa
Worcester 93 D6 W England, United Kingdom
Worcester 37 F4 Massachusetts, NE USA
Workington 93 B2 NW England, United Kingdom
Worksop 93 E4 C England, United Kingdom
Worland 47 E3 Wyoming, C USA
Worms 101 B6 SW Germany
Worthing 95 F5 SE England, United Kingdom
Worthington 43 D4 Minnesota, N USA
Woudrichem 84 D5 S Netherlands
Wragby 93 F4 E England, United Kingdom
Wrangel Island 118 H1 island NE Russian Federation
Wrangel Plain 143 C3 undersea feature Arctic Ocean
Wrath, Cape 91 C2 headland N Scotland, United Kingdom
Wrexham 93 C5 NE Wales, United Kingdom
Wrocław 105 C4 SW Poland
Września 105 D3 C Poland
Wuday 'ah 123 C6 S Saudi Arabia
Wuhai 129 E3 N China
Wuhan 129 F4 C China
Wuhu 129 G4 E China
Wukari 72 F5 E Nigeria
Wuliang Shan 129 D5 ▲▲ SW China
Wuppertal 101 A4 W Germany
Würzburg 101 C6 SW Germany
Wuxi 129 G4 E China
Wye 93 C7 ≈ England/Wales, United Kingdom
Wyndham 137 D2 Western Australia
Wyoming 40 D5 Michigan, N USA
Wyoming 47 E3 ◈ state C USA
Wyre 93 C4 ≈ NW England, United Kingdom
Wyszków 105 F3 NE Poland

Xaafuun, Raas 75 G3 cape NE Somalia
Xaçmaz 121 I1 N Azerbaijan
Xai-Xai 76 E6 S Mozambique
Xalapa 53 F5 SE Mexico
Xankändi 121 I3 SW Azerbaijan
Xánthi 107 F4 NE Greece
Xàtiva 99 F4 E Spain
Xiamen 129 G5 SE China
Xi'an 129 F4 C China
Xianggang see Hong Kong
Xiangkhoang, Plateau de 131 B2 plateau N Laos
Xiangtan 129 F5 S China
Xiao Hinggan Ling 129 G1 ▲▲ NE China
Xichang 129 E5 C China
Xigazê 129 C4 W China
Xi Jiang 131 D2 ≈ S China
Xilinhot 129 F2 N China
Xingu, Rio 63 F5 ≈ C Brazil
Xingxingxia 129 D3 C China
Xining 129 E4 C China
Xinxiang 129 F4 C China
Xinyang 129 F4 C China
Xinzo de Limia 99 B2 NW Spain
Xiva 125 D2 W Uzbekistan
Xixón see Gijón
Xuddur 75 E4 SW Somalia
Xuwen 129 F6 S China
Xuzhou 129 G4 E China

Ya'an 129 E5 C China
Yabelo 75 D4 C Ethiopia
Yablis 55 E3 NE Nicaragua
Yablonovyy Khrebet 118 G5 ▲▲ S Russian Federation
Yabrai Shan 129 E3 ▲▲ NE China
Yafran 70 F2 NW Libya
Yahualica 53 E4 SW Mexico
Yakima 49 C2 Washington, NW USA
Yakima River 49 C2 ≈ Washington, NW USA
Yakutat 50 E3 Alaska, USA
Yakutsk 118 G4 NE Russian Federation
Yalong Jiang 129 D4 ≈ C China
Yalova 120 B2 NW Turkey
Yalta 109 F7 S Ukraine
Yalu 133 A4 ≈ China/North Korea
Yamagata 133 G4 C Japan
Yamaguchi 133 D7 SW Japan
Yamal, Poluostrov 118 D3 peninsula N Russian Federation
Yambio 75 B4 S South Sudan
Yambol 107 F3 E Bulgaria
Yamdena, Pulau 131 G8 island Kepulauan Tanimbar, E Indonesia
Yamoussoukro 72 C5 ● C Ivory Coast
Yamuna 127 E3 ≈ N India
Yana 118 G3 ≈ NE Russian Federation
Yanbu 'al Bahr 123 A4 W Saudi Arabia
Yandina 141 E3 Russell Islands, C Solomon Islands Oceania
Yangambi 76 D1 N Dem. Rep. Congo
Yangiyo'l 125 F2 E Uzbekistan
Yangon see Rangoon
Yangtze 129 F4 ≈ C China
Yangzhou 129 G4 E China
Yankton 43 D4 South Dakota, N USA
Yantai 129 G3 E China
Yaoundé 72 F5 ● S Cameroon
Yapen, Pulau 131 H7 island E Indonesia
Yaqui, Río 53 C2 ≈ NW Mexico
Yaransk 111 C5 NW Russian Federation
Yare 95 H2 ≈ E England, United Kingdom
Yarega 111 D4 NW Russian Federation
Yarmouth 35 F5 Nova Scotia, SE Canada
Yaroslavl' 111 B5 W Russian Federation
Yasawa Group 141 I5 island group NW Fiji
Yasyel'da 109 C3 ≈ SW Belarus
Yatsushiro 133 D8 SW Japan
Yavari, Rio 63 C4 ≈ Brazil/Peru
Yaviza 55 I6 SE Panama
Yazd 123 E3 C Iran
Yazoo City 39 C5 Mississippi, S USA
Yecheng 129 A3 NW China
Yefremov 111 A6 W Russian Federation
Yekaterinburg 118 C4 C Russian Federation
Yelets 111 A6 W Russian Federation
Yell 91 B6 island NE Scotland, United Kingdom
Yellowknife 33 G5 territory capital Northwest Territories, W Canada
Yellow River 129 G3 ≈ C China
Yellow Sea 129 G4 sea E Asia
Yellowstone National Park 47 D3 national park Wyoming, NW USA
Yellowstone River 47 E2 ≈ Montana/Wyoming, NW USA
Yell Sound 91 A6 strait N Scotland, United Kingdom
Yelwa 72 E4 W Nigeria
Yemen 123 C6 ◆ republic SW Asia
Yemva 111 D4 NW Russian Federation
Yenakiyeve 109 G5 E Ukraine
Yendi 72 D4 NE Ghana
Yengisar 129 A3 NW China
Yenierenköy 112 D6 NE Cyprus
Yenisey 118 E4 ≈ Mongolia/Russian Federation
Yeovil 95 D4 SW England, United Kingdom
Yeppoon 137 H4 Queensland, E Australia
Yerevan 121 H3 ● C Armenia
Yeu, Île d' 97 B4 island NW France
Yevlax 121 I2 C Azerbaijan
Yevpatoriya 109 F7 S Ukraine
Yeya 109 G5 ≈ SW Russian Federation
Yichang 129 F4 C China
Yigo 51 NE Guam
Yıldızeli 121 E3 N Turkey
Yinchuan 129 E3 N China
Yining 129 B2 NW China
Yogyakarta 131 C8 Java, C Indonesia
Yokohama 133 G6 S Japan
Yokote 133 G4 C Japan
Yola 72 G4 E Nigeria
Yona 51 E Guam
Yonago 133 E6 SW Japan
Yong'an 129 G5 SE China
Yonghung 133 B5 E North Korea
Yonkers 37 E5 New York, NE USA
Yonne 97 D3 ≈ C France
York 93 E3 N England, United Kingdom
York 43 D5 Nebraska, C USA
York 37 C5 Pennsylvania, NE USA
York, Cape 137 G1 headland Queensland, NE Australia
Yorkshire Dales 93 D3 physical region N England, United Kingdom
Yorkton 33 H7 Saskatchewan, S Canada
Yoro 55 C3 C Honduras
Yoshkar-Ola 111 C5 W Russian Federation
Youghal 89 D6 S Ireland
Youngstown 40 F6 Ohio, N USA
Yreka 49 B5 California, W USA
Ythan 91 F3 ≈ NE Scotland, United Kingdom
Yucatan Channel 53 I3 channel Cuba/Mexico
Yucatan Peninsula 53 H4 peninsula Guatemala/Mexico
Yueyang 129 G5 S China
Yukon River 50 D2 ≈ Canada/USA
Yukon Territory 33 E4 ◈ territory NW Canada
Yulin 129 F6 S China
Yuma 44 A3 Arizona, SW USA
Yushu 129 D4 C China
Yuty 65 C4 S Paraguay
Yuzhno-Sakhalinsk 118 I5 SE Russian Federation

Z

Zaanstad 84 D3 C Netherlands
Zabaykal'sk 118 G5 S Russian Federation
Zabid 123 B7 W Yemen
Ząbkowice Śląskie 105 C5 SW Poland
Zábřeh 105 C5 E Czech Republic
Zacapa 55 B3 E Guatemala
Zacatecas 53 E4 C Mexico
Zacatepec 53 F5 S Mexico
Zadar 107 B2 SW Croatia
Zadetkyi Kyun 131 A4 island Mergui Archipelago, S Burma (Myanmar)
Zafra 99 C4 W Spain
Zagreb 107 B1 ● N Croatia
Zagros Mountains 123 D3 ▲▲ W Iran
Zahedan 123 F3 SE Iran
Záhony 105 F6 NE Hungary
Zákynthos 107 D6 island W Greece
Zalaegerszeg 105 G2 W Hungary
Zalău 109 B6 NW Romania
Zalim 123 B5 W Saudi Arabia
Zambezi 76 C4 W Zambia
Zambezi 76 E4 ≈ S Africa
Zambia 76 D4 ◆ republic S Africa
Zamboanga 131 F5 S Philippines
Zambrów 105 F3 E Poland
Zamora 99 C2 NW Spain
Zamora de Hidalgo 53 E5 SW Mexico
Zamość 105 G5 E Poland
Zanda 129 A4 W China
Zanesville 40 F6 Ohio, N USA
Zanjan 123 D1 NW Iran
Zanzibar 75 D6 E Tanzania
Zanzibar 75 E6 island E Tanzania
Zaozhuang 129 G4 E China
Zapadna Morava 107 D2 ≈ C Serbia
Zapadnaya Dvina 111 A5 W Russian Federation
Zapala 65 A6 W Argentina
Zapolyarnyy 111 B2 NW Russian Federation
Zaporizhzhya 109 F5 SE Ukraine
Zaqatala 121 I1 NW Azerbaijan
Zara 121 E3 C Turkey
Zarafshon 125 E2 N Uzbekistan
Zaragoza 99 F2 NE Spain
Zaranj 125 D6 SW Afghanistan
Zarasai 83 F7 E Lithuania
Zárate 65 C5 E Argentina
Zarautz 99 E1 N Spain
Zarghun Shahr 125 F5 SE Afghanistan
Zaria 72 F4 C Nigeria
Żary 105 B4 W Poland
Zawiercie 105 E5 S Poland
Zawilah 70 F4 C Libya
Zaysan, Ozero 118 D6 ◎ E Kazakhstan
Zduńska Wola 105 E4 C Poland
Zealand 83 B7 island E Denmark
Zeebrugge 84 B5 NW Belgium
Zeewolde 84 D3 C Netherlands
Zeidskoye Vodokhranilishche 125 D4 ⊠ E Turkmenistan
Zeist 84 D4 C Netherlands
Zele 84 C6 NW Belgium
Zelenoborskiy 111 B2 NW Russian Federation
Zelenograd 111 B5 W Russian Federation
Zelenogradsk 83 D7 W Russian Federation
Zelzate 84 B6 NW Belgium
Zemst 84 C6 C Belgium
Zemun 107 D2 N Serbia
Zenica 107 C2 Federacija Bosna I Hercegovina, C Bosnia and Herzegovina
Zeravshan 125 F3 ≈ Tajikistan/Uzbekistan
Zermatt 101 B8 SW Switzerland
Zevenaar 84 E4 SE Netherlands
Zevenbergen 84 C5 S Netherlands
Zeya Reservoir 118 G4 ⊠ SE Russian Federation
Zgierz 105 E4 C Poland
Zgorzelec 105 B4 SW Poland
Zhanaozen 118 B5 W Kazakhstan
Zhangjiakou 129 F3 E China
Zhangzhou 129 G5 SE China
Zhanjiang 129 F6 S China
Zhaoqing 129 F6 S China
Zhayyk 118 B4 ≈ Kazakhstan (see also Ural)
Zheleznogorsk 111 A6 W Russian Federation
Zhengzhou 129 F4 C China
Zhezkazgan 118 C5 C Kazakhstan
Zhlobin 109 D3 SE Belarus
Zhodzina 109 D2 C Belarus
Zhongshan 142 D4 Chinese research station Antarctica
Zhosaly 118 B5 SW Kazakhstan
Zhovkva 109 B4 NW Ukraine
Zhovti Vody 109 E5 E Ukraine
Zhytomyr 109 D4 NW Ukraine
Zibo 129 G3 E China
Zielona Góra 105 C4 W Poland
Zierikzee 84 C5 SW Netherlands
Zigong 129 E5 C China
Ziguinchor 72 A4 SW Senegal
Žilina 105 D6 N Slovakia
Zimbabwe 76 E5 ◆ republic S Africa
Zimovniki 111 B7 SW Russian Federation
Zinder 72 F3 S Niger
Zittau 101 E5 E Germany
Zlín 105 D6 E Czech Republic
Złotów 105 D2 C Poland
Żnin 105 D3 C Poland
Znojmo 105 C6 SE Czech Republic
Zoetermeer 84 C4 W Netherlands
Zomba 76 E4 S Malawi
Zongo 76 C1 N Dem. Rep. Congo
Zonguldak 121 C2 NW Turkey
Zonhoven 84 D6 NE Belgium
Żory 105 D5 S Poland
Zouar 72 G2 N Chad
Zouérat 72 B1 N Mauritania
Zrenjanin 107 D1 N Serbia
Zug 101 B8 C Switzerland
Zugspitze 101 C7 ▲ S Germany
Zuid-Beveland 84 B5 island SW Netherlands
Zuider Zee see IJsselmeer
Zuidhorn 84 E2 NE Netherlands
Zuidlaren 84 F2 NE Netherlands
Zula 75 D2 E Eritrea
Zundert 84 C5 S Netherlands
Zunyi 129 E5 S China
Zürich 101 B7 N Switzerland
Zurich, Lake 101 B8 ◎ NE Switzerland
Zürichsee see Zurich, Lake
Zutphen 84 E4 E Netherlands
Zuwarah 70 F2 NW Libya
Zuyevka 111 D5 NW Russian Federation
Zvenyhorodka 109 E5 C Ukraine
Zvishavane 76 D5 S Zimbabwe
Zvolen 105 E6 C Slovakia
Zwedru 72 C5 E Liberia
Zwettl 101 E6 NE Austria
Zwevegem 84 B7 W Belgium
Zwickau 101 D5 E Germany
Zwolle 84 E3 E Netherlands
Zyryanovsk 118 D5 E Kazakhstan

◈ Administrative region ◆ Country ● Country capital ◇ Dependent territory ○ Dependent territory capital ▲▲ Mountain range ▲ Mountain Volcano ≈ River ◎ Lake ⊠ Reservoir

NORTH AMERICA

CANADA

UNITED STATES OF AMERICA

MEXICO

BELIZE

COSTA RICA

EL SALVADOR

GUATEMALA

HONDURAS

GRENADA

HAITI

JAMAICA

ST KITTS & NEVIS

ST LUCIA

ST VINCENT & THE GRENADINES

TRINIDAD & TOBAGO

SOUTH AMERICA

COLOMBIA

URUGUAY

CHILE

PARAGUAY

AFRICA

ALGERIA

EGYPT

LIBYA

MOROCCO

TUNISIA

LIBERIA

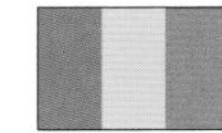
MALI

MAURITANIA

NIGER

NIGERIA

SENEGAL

SIERRA LEONE

TOGO

BURUNDI

DJIBOUTI

ERITREA

ETHIOPIA

KENYA

RWANDA

SOUTH SUDAN

SOMALIA

SOUTH AFRICA

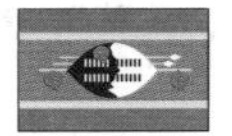
SWAZILAND

ZAMBIA

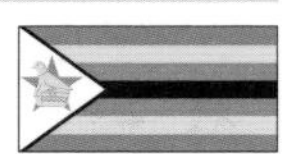
ZIMBABWE

EUROPE

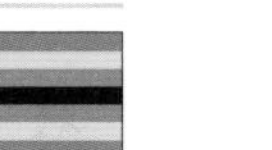

DENMARK

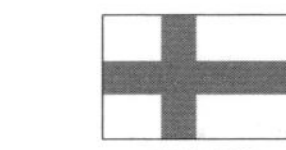
FINLAND

ICELAND

NORWAY

MONACO

ANDORRA

PORTUGAL

SPAIN

ITALY

SAN MARINO

VATICAN CITY

AUSTRIA

LIECHTENSTEIN

CROATIA

MACEDONIA

MONTENEGRO

SERBIA

KOSOVO (disputed)

BULGARIA

GREECE

MOLDOVA

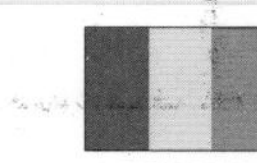
ROMANIA

ASIA

ARMENIA

AZERBAIJAN

GEORGIA

TURKEY

IRAQ

ISRAEL

JORDAN

LEBANON

IRAN

KAZAKHSTAN

KYRGYZSTAN

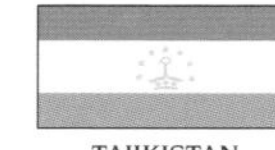
TAJIKISTAN

TURKMENISTAN

UZBEKISTAN

AFGHANISTAN

PAKISTAN

TAIWAN

JAPAN

BRUNEI

INDONESIA

EAST TIMOR

MALAYSIA

SINGAPORE

BURMA

AUSTRALASIA & OCEANIA

MAURITIUS

SEYCHELLES

AUSTRALIA

NEW ZEALAND

PAPUA NEW GUINEA

SOLOMON ISLANDS

MARSHALL ISLANDS

MICRONESIA